GCSE Science

Complete Revision and Practice

Contents

Section One — Humans as Organisms

Section Two — Maintenance of Life

Section Three — Environment

Section Four — Inheritance and Selection

Section Five — Metals

Section Six — Earth Materials

Section Seven — Patterns of Chemical Change

Contents

Section Eight — Structures and Bonding

Section Nine — Energy

Section Ten — Electricity

Section Eleven — Forces

Section Twelve — Waves and Radiation

The Periodic Table

You should be pretty familiar with the 35 elements shown shaded.

You don't really need to know anything about the others.

Each cell: Mass number, Symbol, Name, Atomic number.

Periods	Group I	Group II											Group III	Group IV	Group V	Group VI	Group VII	Group O
1								1 H Hydrogen 1										4 He Helium 2
2	7 Li Lithium 3	9 Be Beryllium 4											11 B Boron 5	12 C Carbon 6	14 N Nitrogen 7	16 O Oxygen 8	19 F Fluorine 9	20 Ne Neon 10
3	23 Na Sodium 11	24 Mg Magnesium 12											27 Al Aluminium 13	28 Si Silicon 14	31 P Phosphorus 15	32 S Sulphur 16	35.5 Cl Chlorine 17	40 Ar Argon 18
4	39 K Potassium 19	40 Ca Calcium 20	45 Sc Scandium 21	48 Ti Titanium 22	51 V Vanadium 23	52 Cr Chromium 24	55 Mn Manganese 25	56 Fe Iron 26	59 Co Cobalt 27	59 Ni Nickel 28	64 Cu Copper 29	65 Zn Zinc 30	70 Ga Gallium 31	73 Ge Germanium 32	75 As Arsenic 33	79 Se Selenium 34	80 Br Bromine 35	84 Kr Krypton 36
5	85.5 Rb Rubidium 37	88 Sr Strontium 38	89 Y Yttrium 39	91 Zr Zirconium 40	93 Nb Niobium 41	96 Mo Molybdenum 42	98 Tc Technetium 43	101 Ru Ruthenium 44	103 Rh Rhodium 45	106 Pd Palladium 46	108 Ag Silver 47	112 Cd Cadmium 48	115 In Indium 49	119 Sn Tin 50	122 Sb Antimony 51	128 Te Tellurium 52	127 I Iodine 53	131 Xe Xenon 54
6	133 Cs Caesium 55	137 Ba Barium 56	139 La Lanthanum 57	178.5 Hf Hafnium 72	181 Ta Tantalum 73	184 W Tungsten 74	186 Re Rhenium 75	190 Os Osmium 76	192 Ir Iridium 77	195 Pt Platinum 78	197 Au Gold 79	201 Hg Mercury 80	204 Tl Thallium 81	207 Pb Lead 82	209 Bi Bismuth 83	210 Po Polonium 84	210 At Astatine 85	222 Rn Radon 86
7	223 Fr Francium 87	226 Ra Radium 88	227 Ac Actinium 89															

Mass number → (top number); Atomic number → (bottom number)

The Lanthanides	140 Ce Cerium 58	141 Pr Praseodymium 59	144 Nd Neodymium 60	147 Pm Promethium 61	150 Sm Samarium 62	152 Eu Europium 63	157 Gd Gadolinium 64	159 Tb Terbium 65	162 Dy Dysprosium 66	165 Ho Holmium 67	167 Er Erbium 68	169 Tm Thulium 69	173 Yb Ytterbium 70	175 Lu Lutetium 71
The Actinides	232 Th Thorium 90	231 Pa Protactinium 91	238 U Uranium 92	237 Np Neptunium 93	242 Pu Plutonium 94	243 Am Americium 95	247 Cm Curium 96	247 Bk Berkelium 97	251 Cf Californium 98	254 Es Einsteinium 99	253 Fm Fermium 100	256 Md Mendelevium 101 (the old rogue)	254 No Nobelium 102	257 Lr Lawrencium 103

Common Ions You Really Should Know

1^+ ions	2^+ ions	3^+ ions	$4^+/4^-$	3^-	2^- ions	1^- ions
Li^+ (lithium)	Mg^{2+} (magnesium)	Al^{3+} (aluminium)	Very rare	Fairly rare	O^{2-} (oxide)	F^- (fluoride)
Na^+ (sodium)	Ca^{2+} (calcium)	Fe^{3+} (iron(III))			S^{2-} (sulphide)	Cl^- (chloride)
K^+ (potassium)	Ba^{2+} (barium)	Cr^{3+} (chromium(III))				Br^- (bromide)
Cu^+ (copper(I))	Cu^{2+} (copper(II))					I^- (iodide)
Ag^+ (silver)	Fe^{2+} (iron(II))	Note that copper and iron can both form _two_ different ions.				NO_3^- (nitrate)
H^+ (hydrogen)	Zn^{2+} (zinc)				SO_4^{2-} (sulphate)	OH^- (hydroxide)
NH_4^+ (ammonium)	Pb^{2+} (lead)				CO_3^{2-} (carbonate)	HCO_3^- (hydrogencarbonate)
These atoms lose _one_ electron to form 1^+ ions. (NH_4^+ isn't an atom)	These atoms lose _two_ electrons to form 2^+ ions	These atoms lose _three_ electrons to form 3^+ ions	Atoms find it very hard to gain or lose three or four electrons.		These atoms/molecules gain _two_ electrons to form 2^- ions	These atoms/molecules gain _one_ electron to form 1^- ions

Published by Coordination Group Publications Ltd

Editors:
Richard Parsons, Claire Thompson, Julie Schofield.

Contributors:
Tony Aldridge, Ruth Amos, Stuart Barker, Jennifer Bilbrough, Paul Burton, Rosemary Cartwright, Martin Chester, Chris Dennett, Philippa Falshaw, Jonathon Grange, Anna Guy, Dominic Hall, Gemma Hallam, Theo Haywood, Phillipa Hulme, Sharon Keeley, Munir Kawar, Diana Lazarewicz, Richard Man, John Maunder, John Myers, Claire Reed, Glenn Rogers, Alice Shepperson, Emma Singleton, Amber Storey, Phil Taylor, James Paul Wallis, Sharon Watson, Jim Wilson, Suzanne Worthington.

Illustrations by Sandy Gardner e-mail: illustrations@sandygardner.co.uk. With thanks to Jeff Cole for the proofreading.

ISBN 1 84146 380 9
Website: www.cgpbooks.co.uk
Printed by Elanders Hindson, Newcastle upon Tyne.
Clipart source: CorelDRAW

Cells

Plant cells and **animal cells** have their **differences**

You need to be able to draw these two cells with all the details for each.

Animal *cell*

FOUR THINGS THEY BOTH HAVE IN COMMON:

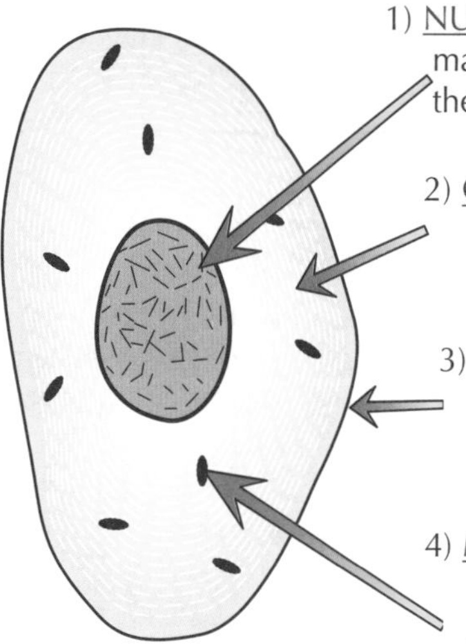

1) NUCLEUS contains genetic material that controls what the cell does.

2) CYTOPLASM contains enzymes that speed up biological reactions.

3) CELL MEMBRANE holds the cell together and controls what goes in and out.

4) MITOCHONDRIA turn glucose and oxygen into energy.

Plant *cell*

THREE EXTRAS THAT ONLY THE PLANT CELL HAS:

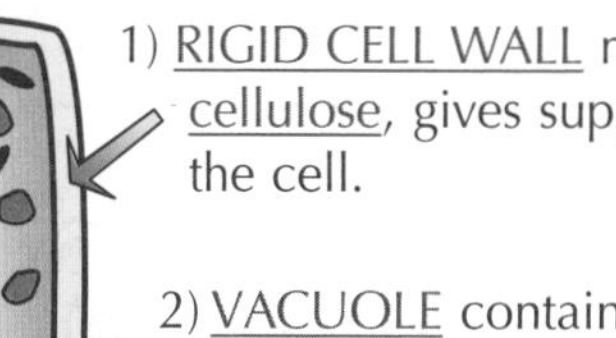

1) RIGID CELL WALL made of cellulose, gives support for the cell.

2) VACUOLE contains cell sap, a weak solution of sugar and salts.

3) CHLOROPLASTS containing chlorophyll for photosynthesis. Found in the green parts of plants.

Cells are ***specialised*** *for their* ***function***

Most cells are specialised for a specific job, and in the Exam you'll probably have to explain why the cell they've shown you is so good at its job. It's a lot easier if you've already learnt them.

1) ***Red blood cells*** *are designed to* ***carry oxygen***

1) Doughnut shaped to allow maximum oxygen absorption by the haemoglobin they contain. They are doughnut shaped rather than long to allow smooth passage through the capillaries.
2) They're unusual because they don't need a nucleus.

2) ***Sperm and egg cells*** *are specialised for* ***reproduction***

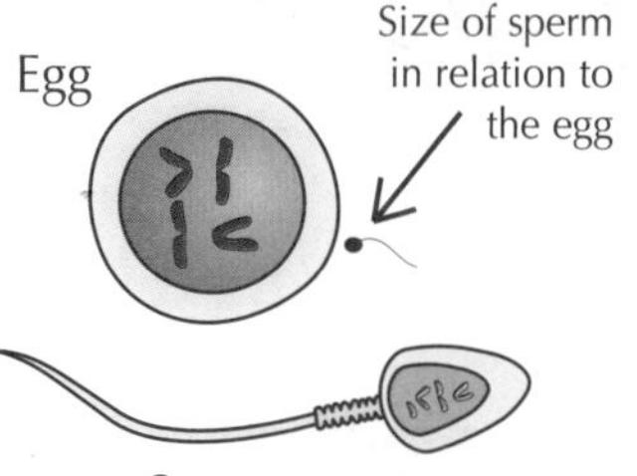

1) The egg cell has huge food reserves to provide nutrition for the developing embryo.
2) When a sperm fuses with the egg, the egg's membrane instantly changes to prevent any more sperm getting in.
3) A long tail gives the sperm the mobility needed for its long journey to find the egg.
4) The sperm also has a short life-span so only the fittest survive the race to the egg.

3) Other ***important examples***

There are three other important examples of specialised human cells: WHITE BLOOD CELLS, NEURONS and CELLS IN THE INTESTINES. Look them up and see how they're specialised. (P.12, 18 and 42).

Cells, Organs and the Digestive System

Levels of *organisation*

This can apply to plants as well as animals.

A group of SIMILAR CELLS is called a TISSUE.
A group of DIFFERENT TISSUES form an ORGAN.
A GROUP OF ORGANS working together form an ORGAN SYSTEM, or even A WHOLE ORGANISM.

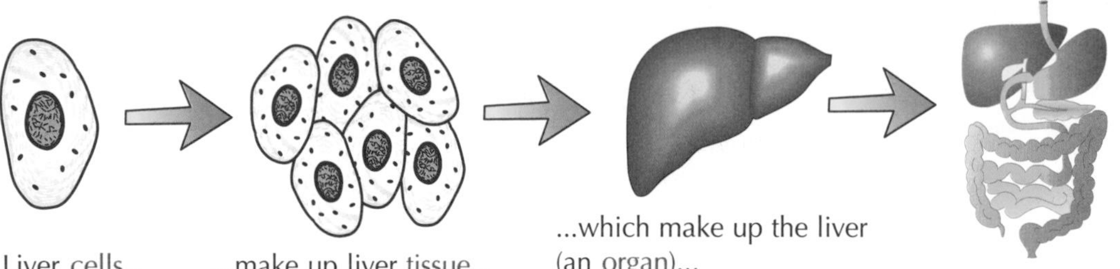

Liver cells... ...make up liver tissue... ...which make up the liver (an organ)... ...and the liver and other organs make the digestive system (an organ-system).

The *Eight* main parts of the *digestive system* to learn:

Tongue

Salivary glands

Produce an enzyme called amylase in the saliva to start the breakdown of starch.

Liver

Where bile is produced.

Gullet

Small intestine

1) Produces the protease, amylase and lipase enzymes.
2) This is also where the "food" is absorbed into the blood.
3) The inner surface is covered with villi to increase the surface area. It's also very long.

Large intestine

Where excess water is absorbed from the food.

Stomach

1) It pummels the food with its muscular walls.
2) It produces protease enzymes.
3) It produces hydrochloric acid for two reasons:
   a) To kill bacteria
   b) To give the right pH for the protease enzyme to work (pH 2 — acidic).

Pancreas

Produces the lot: amylase, lipase and the protease enzymes.

Rectum

Where the faeces (made up mainly of indigestible food) are stored before they leave through the anus.

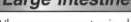

Digestive Enzymes

The human diet is made up of carbohydrates, proteins and fats — and we have three enzymes to break them down.

Enzymes break down big molecules into small ones

1) Starch, proteins and fats are BIG molecules which can't pass through cell walls into the blood.
2) Sugars, amino acids and fatty acids/glycerol are much smaller molecules which can pass easily into the blood.
3) Enzymes act as catalysts to break down the BIG molecules into the smaller ones.

1) Amylase converts starch into simple sugars

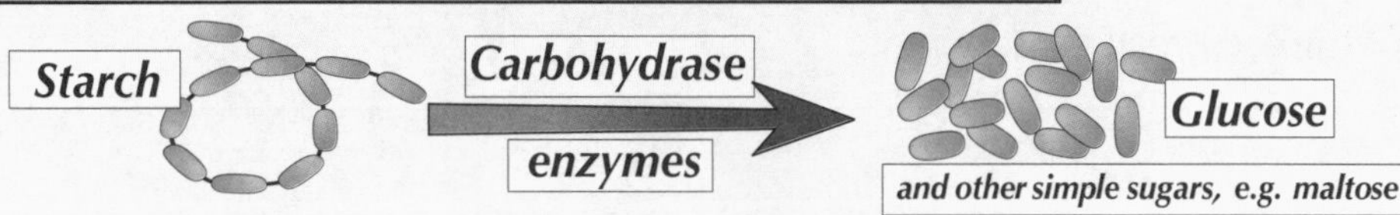

Amylase is produced in three places:

1) The SALIVARY GLANDS
2) The PANCREAS
3) The SMALL INTESTINE

2) Protease converts proteins into amino acids

Protease is produced in three places:

1) The STOMACH (where it's called *pepsin*)
2) The PANCREAS
3) The SMALL INTESTINE

3) Lipase converts fats into fatty acids and glycerol

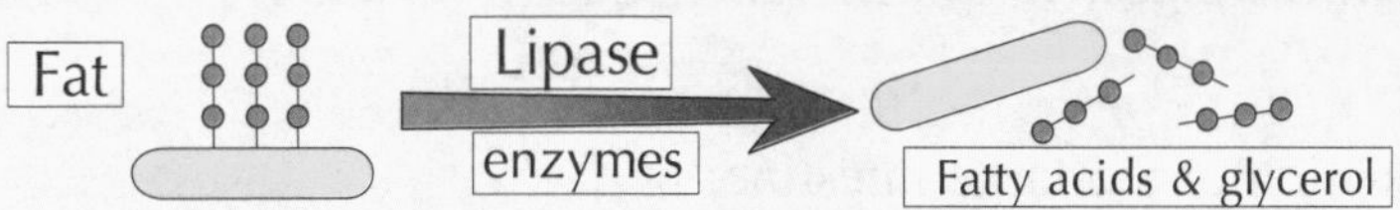

Lipase is produced in two places:

1) The PANCREAS
2) The SMALL INTESTINE

Bile neutralises the stomach acid and emulsifies fats

1) Bile is produced in the LIVER. It's stored in the gall bladder before it's released into the small intestine.
2) The hydrochloric acid in the stomach makes the pH too acidic for enzymes in the small intestine to work properly. Bile is alkaline — it neutralises the acid and make conditions alkaline. The enzymes in the small intestine work best in these alkaline conditions.
3) It emulsifies fats. In other words it breaks the fat into tiny droplets. This gives a much bigger surface area of fat for the enzyme lipase to work on.

Check you know it all

There are a lot of facts here, but it all counts — you're expected to know every bit of information in this mini-section. So, take a deep breath, read it and learn it, then close the book and write it all down.

Warm-Up and Exam Question

These warm-up questions should ease you gently in and make sure you've got the basics straight. If there's anything you've forgotten, check up on the facts before you do the exam question.

Warm-up Questions

1) State which part of a plant cell: (a) contains cell sap; (b) supports the cell; (c) carries out photosynthesis; (d) contains genetic material; (e) controls what goes in and out of the cell.
2) Give two ways in which the egg cell is specially adapted for reproduction.
3) Where is bile produced?
4) What increases the surface area of the inside of the small intestine?
5) From where do faeces leave the body?
6) What are the two purposes of hydrochloric acid in the stomach?
7) What does lipase break fat down into?

Exam Question

1 The diagram below shows part of the human digestive system.

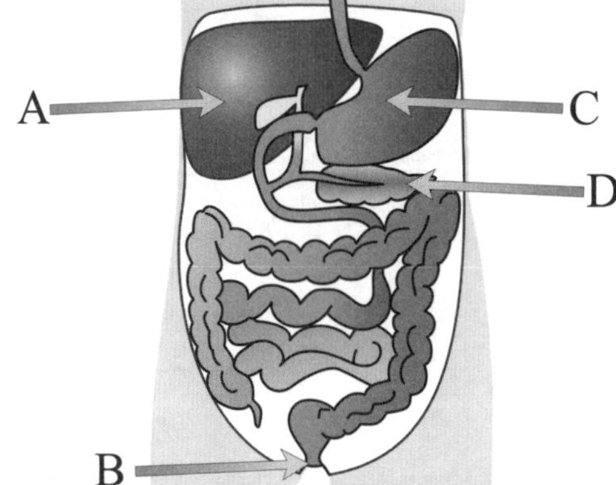

(a) Name each part of the digestive system labelled A, B, C and D.

(4 marks)

(b) Describe one function of the large intestine.

(1 mark)

(c) Describe two features of the small intestine that help it to absorb the products of digestion.

(2 marks)

(d) Complete the table below:

Food substance	Digestive Enzyme	Product(s) of digestion
Starch		
	Protease	
		Fatty acids and glycerol

(6 marks)

The Respiratory System

Cells need oxygen for respiration and they produce carbon dioxide as a waste product.
The job of breathing is to get oxygen into the body and remove the carbon dioxide.

The Thorax

Learn this diagram really well:

1) The thorax is the top part of your 'body' which is protected by the ribcage.
2) The lungs are like big pink sponges.
3) The trachea splits into two tubes called "bronchi" (each one is "a bronchus"), one going to each lung.
4) The bronchi split into progressively smaller tubes called bronchioles.
5) The bronchioles finally end at small bags called alveoli where the gas exchange takes place.
6) The diaphragm separates the thorax from the abdomen.

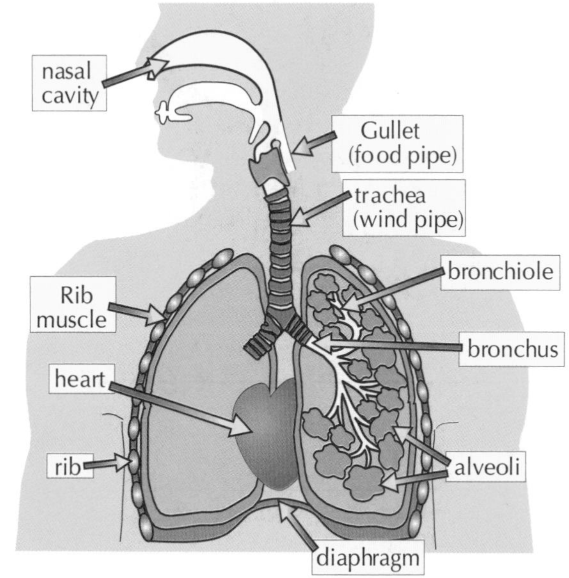

Ventilation

Moving air INTO and OUT OF the lungs is called VENTILATION.

Breathing in...

1) Rib muscles and diaphragm contract.
2) Thorax volume increases.
3) Air is drawn in due to decreased pressure.

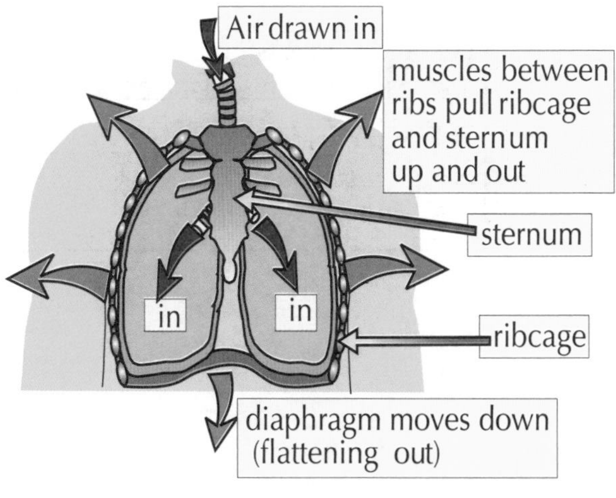

...and breathing out

1) Rib muscles and diaphragm relax.
2) Thorax volume decreases.
3) Air is forced out due to increased pressure.

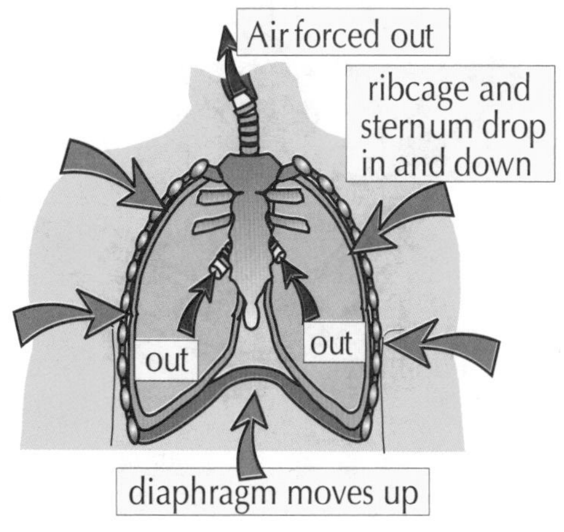

The Respiratory System

Alveoli

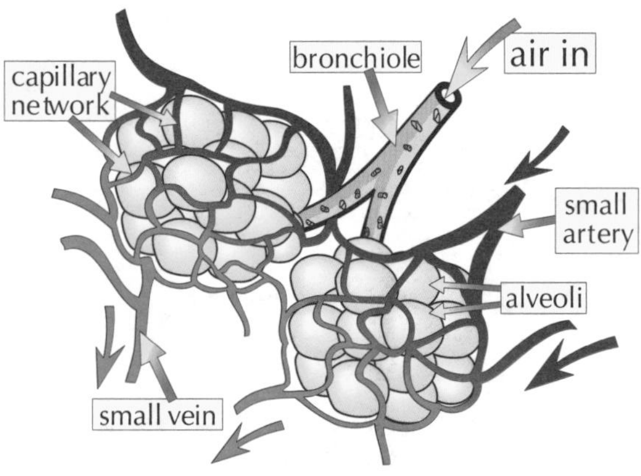

1) The job of the lungs is to transfer oxygen to the blood and to remove waste carbon dioxide from it.
2) To do this the lungs contain millions of alveoli where gas exchange takes place.
3) Oxygen combines with haemoglobin in the blood to form "oxyhaemoglobin". (Haemoglobin is the stuff that makes red blood cells red.)

The alveoli are an ideal exchange surface. They have:

1) A very large surface area (about $70m^2$ in total).
2) A moist lining for dissolving gases.
3) Very thin walls.
4) A copious blood supply.

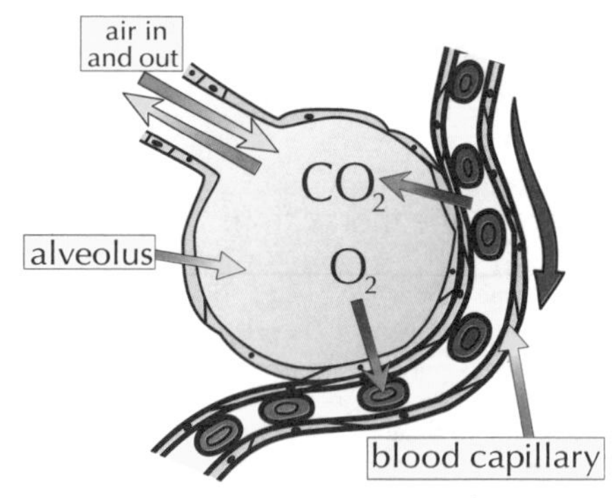

Gas exchange at the cells

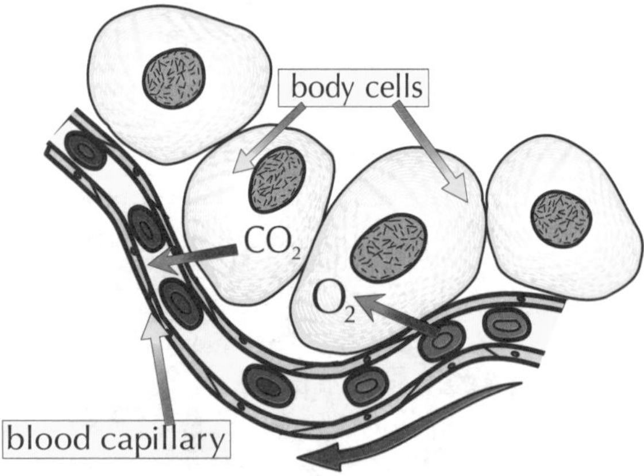

1) When the blood reaches the cells, oxygen is released from the oxyhaemoglobin in the red blood cells and diffuses into the body cells.
2) At the same time, carbon dioxide diffuses into the blood (plasma) to be carried back to the lungs.

Aerobic and Anaerobic Respiration

Respiration is NOT "breathing in and out"

1) Respiration is NOT breathing in and breathing out.
2) Respiration actually goes on in every cell in your body.
3) Respiration is the process of converting glucose (a sugar) to energy.
4) It takes place in plants too. All living things "respire". They convert "food" into energy.

RESPIRATION is the process of CONVERTING GLUCOSE TO ENERGY, which goes on in EVERY CELL

5) Energy released by respiration is used for four things:
   a) build larger molecules from smaller ones
   b) enable muscle contraction
   c) maintain a steady body temperature
   d) power active transport

Aerobic respiration needs plenty of oxygen

1) Aerobic respiration is what happens if there's plenty of oxygen available.
2) "Aerobic" just means "with oxygen" and it's the ideal way to convert glucose into energy.
3) Aerobic respiration inside cells happens in the mitochondria.

You need to learn the word equation:

$$\text{glucose} + \text{oxygen} \rightarrow \text{carbon dioxide} + \text{water} + \text{energy}$$

Anaerobic respiration doesn't use oxygen at all

1) Anaerobic respiration is what happens if there's no oxygen available. "Anaerobic" means "without oxygen".
2) It's the incomplete breakdown of glucose which is NOT the best way to convert glucose into energy because it produces lactic acid.
   You need to learn the word equation:

$$\text{glucose} \rightarrow \text{energy} + \text{lactic acid}$$

3) Anaerobic respiration does not produce nearly as much energy as aerobic respiration — but it's useful in emergencies.

Fitness and the oxygen debt

1) During vigorous exercise, your body can't supply enough oxygen to your muscles. They get fatigued and can stop contracting efficiently.
2) To get the energy they need, muscles start doing anaerobic respiration instead. This isn't great — the incomplete breakdown of glucose produces a build up of lactic acid in the muscles, which gets painful.
3) The advantage is that at least you can keep on using your muscles for a while longer.
4) After resorting to anaerobic respiration, when you stop you'll have an oxygen debt.
5) In other words you have to "repay" the oxygen which you didn't manage to get to your muscles in time, because your lungs, heart and blood couldn't keep up with the demand earlier on.
6) This means you have to keep breathing hard for a while after you stop to get oxygen into your muscles to oxidise the painful lactic acid to harmless CO_2 and water.

One big deep breath and learn it all

Learning these four sections well enough to write it all down from memory isn't so difficult.
You don't have to write it out word for word, just make sure you get the important points about each bit.

Warm-Up and Exam Questions

Take a deep breath and go through these warm-up questions one by one.
If you don't know the basic facts there's no way you'll cope with the exam questions.

Warm-up Questions

1) What muscles are involved in changing the volume of the thorax during breathing?
2) Give a definition of respiration.
3) Write the word equation for aerobic respiration.
4) What happens to pulse and breathing rate when carbon dioxide and lactic acid levels rise in the blood?

Exam Questions

1 The diagram on the right shows the breathing system of a human.

a) Name the structures A – E.

(5 marks)

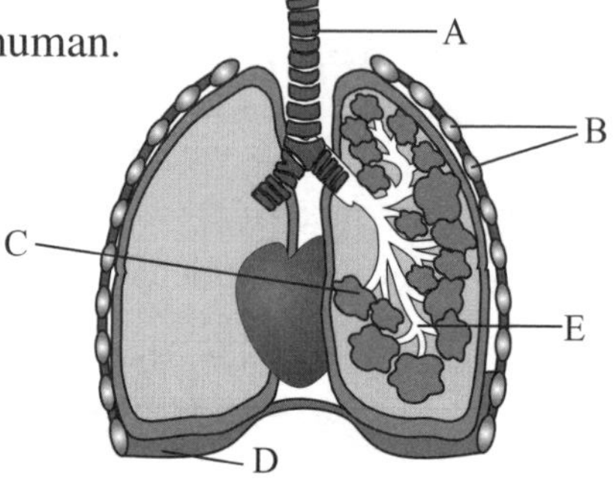

b) Which two gases are exchanged in the lungs?

(2 marks)

c) Describe the mechanism by which air is drawn into the lungs.

(4 marks)

d) List four ways in which the alveoli are specially adapted for gaseous exchange.

(4 marks)

2 Jason went jogging for 20 minutes. The table below shows the concentration of lactic acid in Jason's blood during this period of exercise:

Time from start (mins)	0	2	4	6	8	10	12	14	16	18	20
Concentration of lactic acid in the blood (mg/100cm^3)	3	12	27	39	39	36	29	23	19	17	16

a) Plot a graph of the data in the table. Draw in a smooth curve to join the points.

(4 marks)

b) Use your graph to find the time when the concentration of lactic acid in Jason's blood was 15mg/100cm^3.

(1 mark)

c) What happens to your muscles when the concentration of lactic acid rises in your blood?

(1 mark)

d) What is an oxygen debt?

(2 marks)

e) Write the word equation for anaerobic respiration in human muscle cells.

(1 mark)

The Circulatory System

The circulatory system's main function is to get food and oxygen to every cell in the body. The diagram shows the basic layout, but make sure you learn the five important points too.

It's a Double Circulatory System

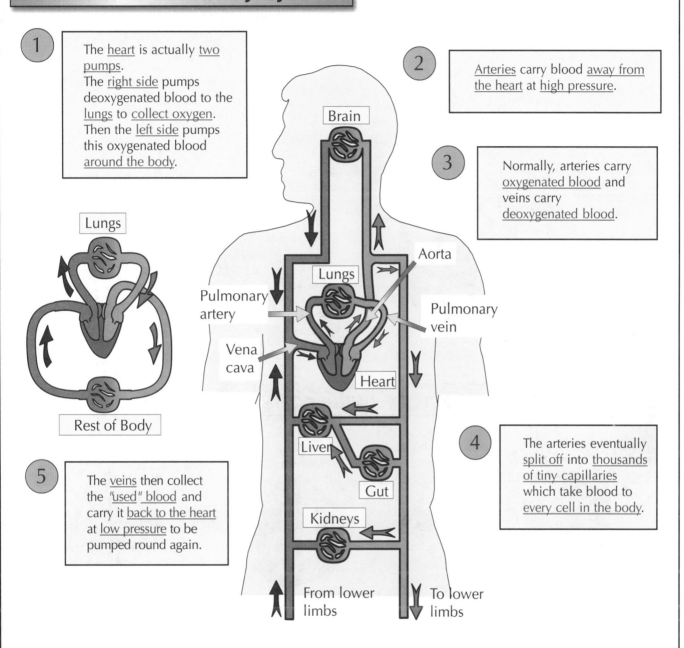

1. The heart is actually two pumps. The right side pumps deoxygenated blood to the lungs to collect oxygen. Then the left side pumps this oxygenated blood around the body.

2. Arteries carry blood away from the heart at high pressure.

3. Normally, arteries carry oxygenated blood and veins carry deoxygenated blood.

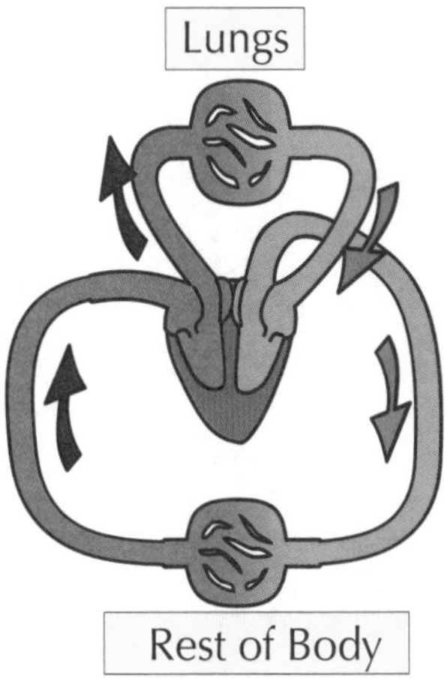

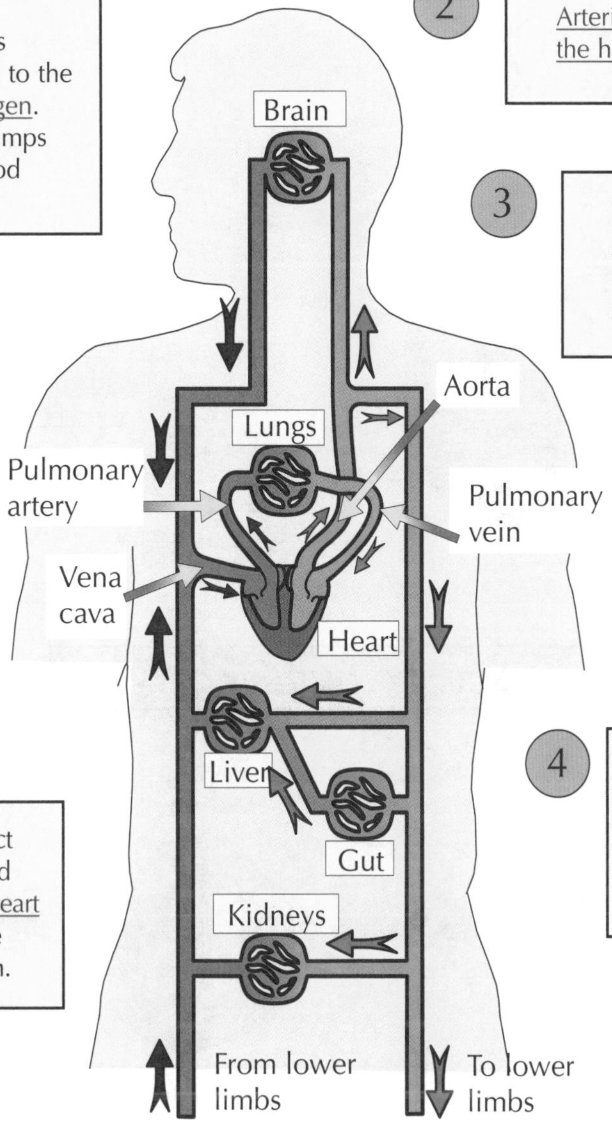

4. The arteries eventually split off into thousands of tiny capillaries which take blood to every cell in the body.

5. The veins then collect the "used" blood and carry it back to the heart at low pressure to be pumped round again.

Lungs
Rest of Body

Brain
Lungs
Aorta
Pulmonary artery
Pulmonary vein
Vena cava
Heart
Liver
Gut
Kidneys
From lower limbs
To lower limbs

Fish don't have a double circulation system, but all fast-moving creatures like mammals and birds do.

It's a pretty clever system, and it's difficult to understand how a single pump system could ever have "evolved" into a double one like this — because it has to be all or nothing for it to work. So to go straight from a single pump heart that pumps to the lungs and then on to the rest of the body, to the double pump system shown above is really quite a mutation.

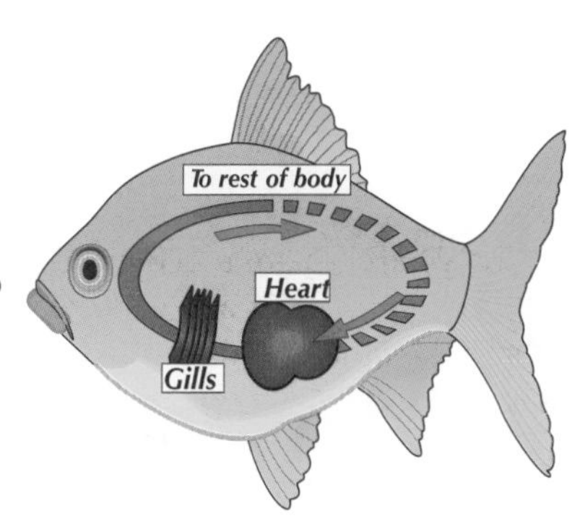

The Heart and Pumping Cycle

The heart is made almost entirely of muscle. And it's a double pump.
Visualise this diagram with its bigger side full of red, oxygenated blood, and its smaller side full of blue, deoxygenated blood, and learn that the left side is bigger.

Learn this *diagram* of the *heart* with all its *labels*

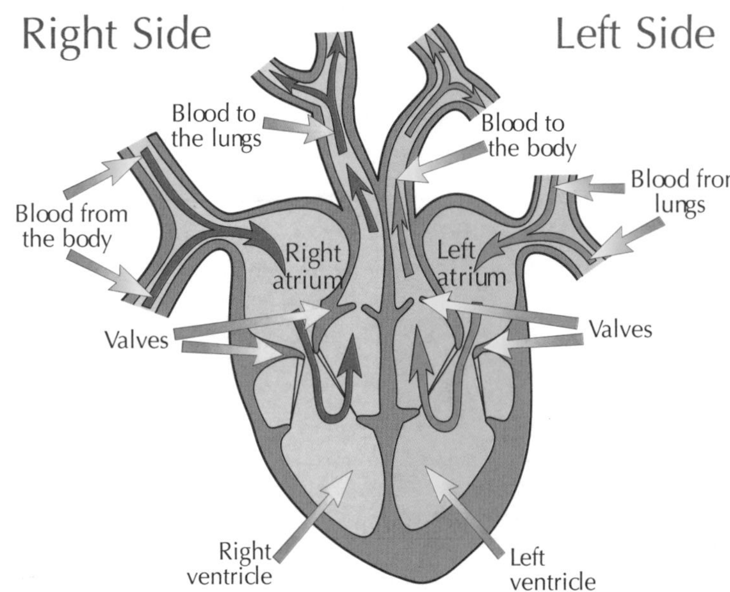

1) The right side of the heart receives deoxygenated blood from the body and pumps it only to the lungs, so it has thinner walls than the left side.
2) The left side receives oxygenated blood from the lungs and pumps it out round the whole body, so it has thicker, more muscular walls.
3) The ventricles are much bigger than the atria because they push blood round the body.
4) The valves are for preventing backflow of blood.

Learn the *three stages* of the *pumping cycle*

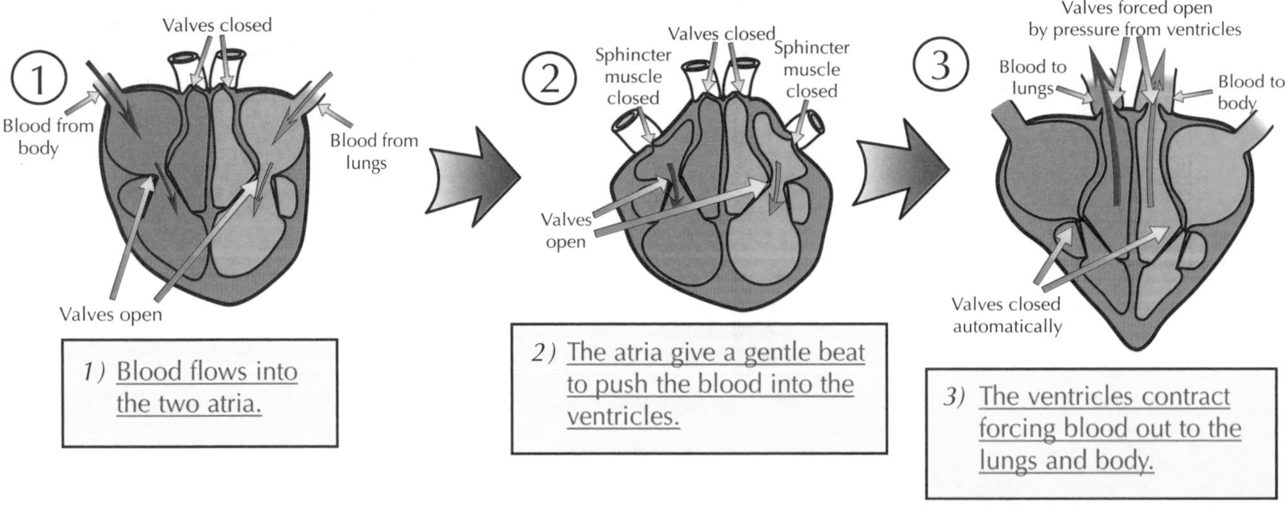

1) Blood flows into the two atria.

2) The atria give a gentle beat to push the blood into the ventricles.

3) The ventricles contract forcing blood out to the lungs and body.

4) The blood flows down the arteries, the atria fill again and the whole cycle starts over.

The ventricles are much more powerful, and when they beat, the valves between the atria and ventricles pop shut automatically to prevent backflow into the atria. Sphincters wouldn't be strong enough.

As soon as the ventricles relax, valves pop shut to prevent backflow of blood (back into the ventricles) as it is now under a fair bit of pressure in the arteries.

Arteries, Veins and Capillaries

There are three different types of blood vessel and you need to know all about them:

Arteries carry blood under *pressure*

1) Arteries carry oxygenated blood away from the heart.
2) It comes out of the heart at high pressure, so the artery walls have to be strong and elastic.
3) Note how thick the walls are compared to the size of the hole down the middle (the "lumen").

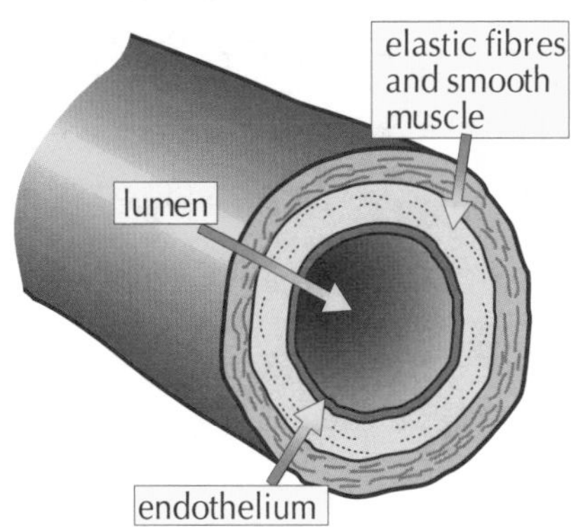

Capillaries are really *small*

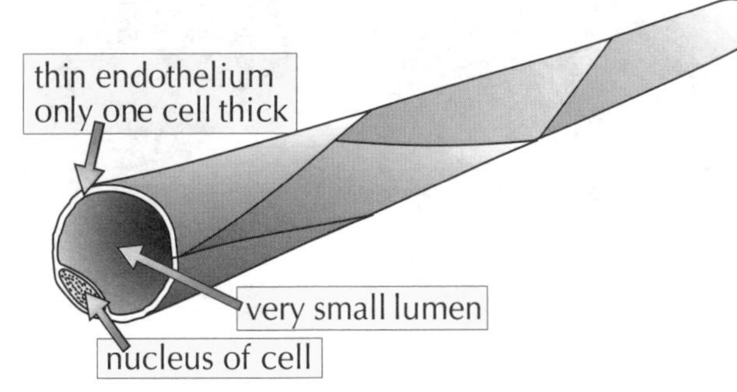

1) Capillaries deliver food and oxygen direct to the body tissues and take waste products away.
2) Their walls are usually only one cell thick to make it easy for stuff to pass in and out of them.
3) They are too small to see.

Veins take blood *back* to the heart

1) Veins carry deoxygenated blood back to the heart.
2) The blood is at lower pressure in the veins so the walls do not need to be so thick.
3) They have a bigger lumen than arteries to help blood flow.
4) They also have valves to help keep the blood flowing in the right direction.

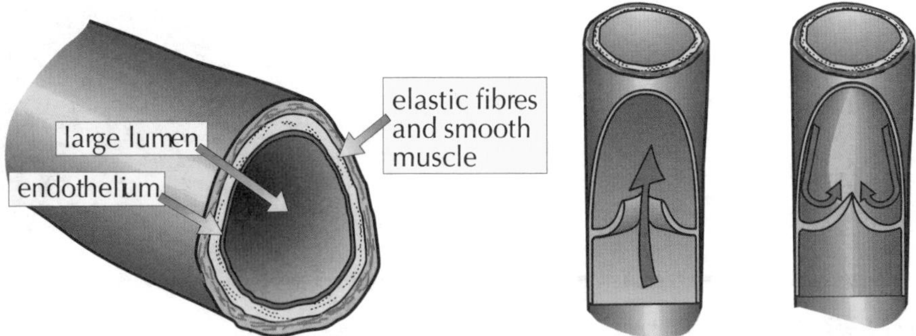

The Blood

Plasma

This is a pale straw-coloured liquid which carries just about everything:

1) Red and white blood cells and platelets.
2) Digested food products like glucose and amino acids.
3) Carbon dioxide from the organs to the lungs.
4) Urea from the liver to the kidneys.
5) Hormones.
6) Antibodies (including antitoxins) produced by the white blood cells.

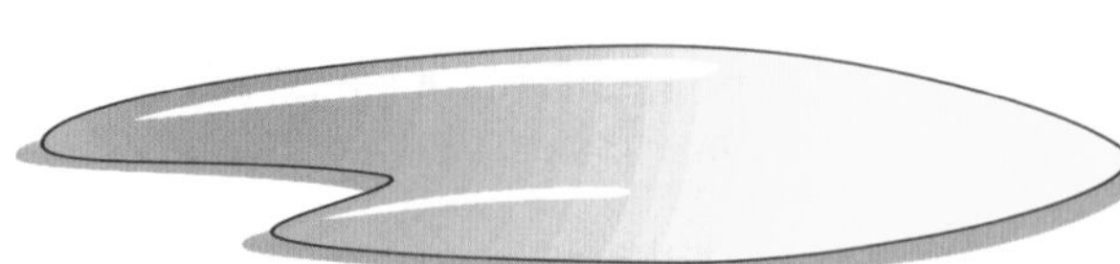

Red blood cells

1) Their job is to carry oxygen from the lungs to all the cells in the body.
2) They have a squashed disc shape to give maximum surface area for absorbing oxygen.
3) They contain haemoglobin which is very red, and which contains a lot of iron.
4) In the lungs, haemoglobin absorbs oxygen to become oxyhaemoglobin. In body tissues the reverse happens to release oxygen to the cells.
5) Red blood cells have no nucleus (they don't need one).

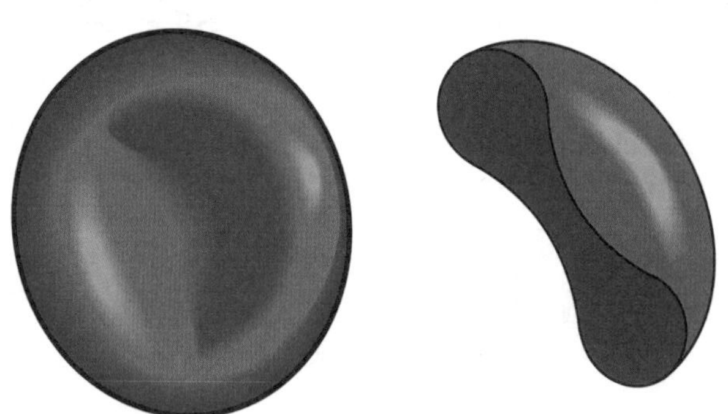

White blood cells

1) Their main role is defence against disease.
2) They have a big nucleus.
3) They envelop unwelcome microorganisms.
4) They produce antibodies to fight bacteria.
5) They produce antitoxins to neutralise the toxins produced by bacteria.

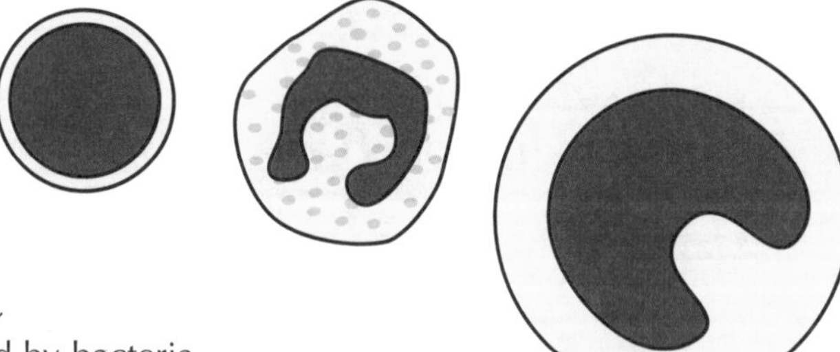

Platelets

1) These are small fragments of cells.
2) They have no nucleus.
3) They help the blood to clot at a wound.

Plasma carries everything

Learn the facts until you can write them down from memory. You should know it well enough to answer questions like "What is the function of blood plasma?" or "What do white blood cells do?"

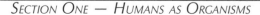

Warm-Up and Exam Questions

Warm-up Questions

1) What is a double circulatory system?
2) How thick is the wall of a capillary?
3) Which side of the heart receives deoxygenated blood?
4) What is the purpose of the valves in veins?
5) What is the purpose of red blood cells?
6) What is the name of the substance found in red blood cells that binds with oxygen?

Exam Questions

Exam questions are the best way to practise what you've learnt. After all, they're exactly what you'll have to do on the big day — so work through these very carefully.

1 The diagram on the right shows the structure of the human heart.

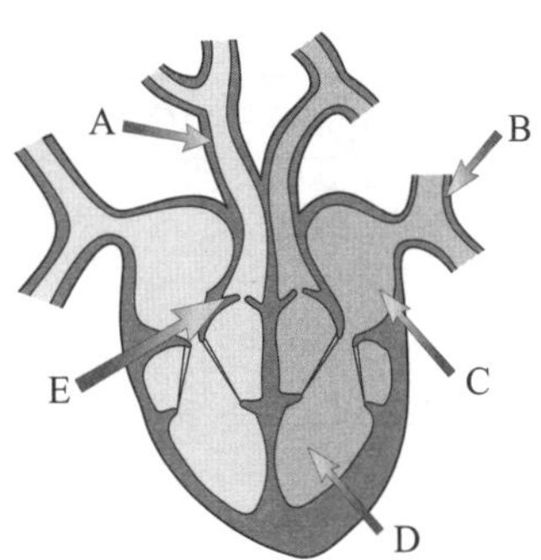

a) Name structures A — E.

(5 marks)

b) Complete the following table comparing an artery and a vein.

Vein	Artery
Carries blood .... heart	Carries blood .... heart
Carries blood at ...... pressure	Carries blood at .... pressure
Carries .... blood (except pulmonary vein)	Carries .... blood (except pulmonary artery)
Size of lumen is .... compared to thickness of walls	Size of lumen is .... compared to thickness of walls

(4 marks)

2 This question is about the blood.

a) Give one function of each of the following:
i) white blood cells ii) plasma iii) platelets

(3 marks)

b) Give two ways in which red blood cells are specially adapted to their job.

(2 marks)

Disease

Two types of microorganism: bacteria and viruses

Microorganisms can get inside you and make you feel ill. There are two main types:

Bacteria are very small living cells

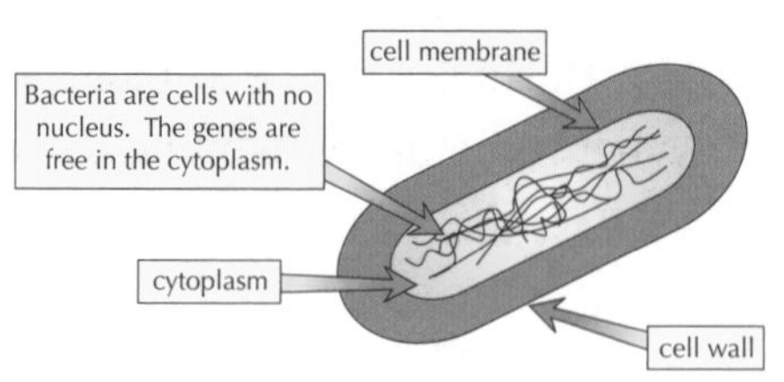

1) These are very small cells, (about 1/100th the size of your body cells), which reproduce rapidly inside your body.
2) They make you feel ill by doing two things:
    a) damaging your cells
    b) producing toxins.
3) Don't forget that some bacteria are useful if they're in the right place, like in your digestive system.

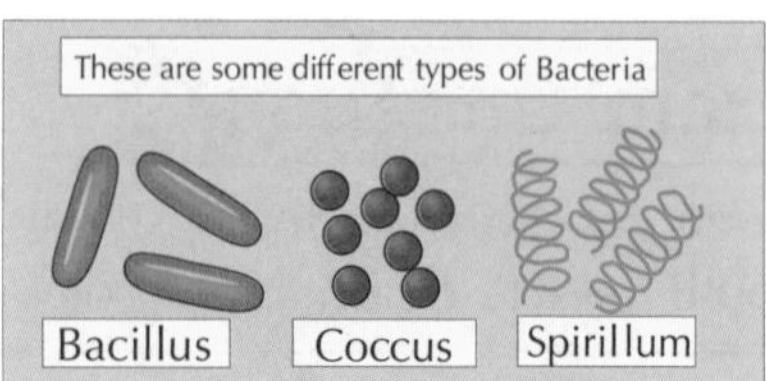

Viruses are not cells — they're much smaller

1) These are not cells. They are very very small, about 1/100th the size of a bacterium.
2) They are no more than a coat of protein around a DNA strand.
3) They make you feel ill by damaging your cells.
4) They replicate themselves by invading the nucleus of a living cell and using the DNA it contains to produce many copies of themselves.
5) The cell then bursts, releasing all the new viruses.
6) In this way viruses can reproduce very quickly.

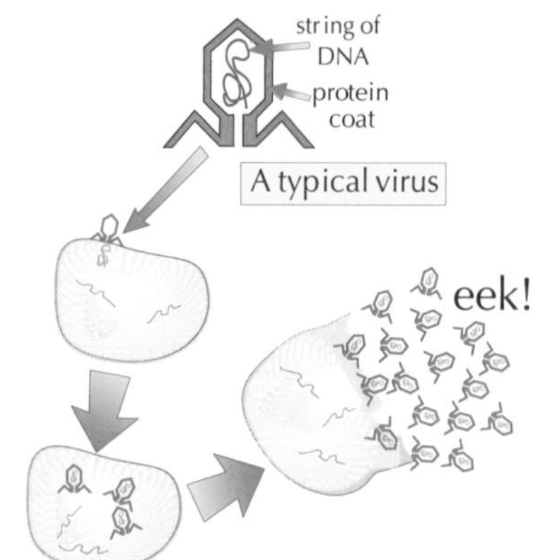

The body has three ways of defending itself

Diseases can be caused when microorganisms such as certain bacteria and viruses enter the body. Disease is more likely to occur if large numbers of microorganisms enter the body as a result of unhygienic conditions or contact with infected people. However we do have some defences.

1) The skin and eyes are barriers

Undamaged skin is a very effective barrier against microorganisms.
Eyes produce a chemical which kills bacteria on the surface of the eye.

2) The blood clots to seal cuts

As well as stopping your blood from gushing out and making a mess, the clotting also prevents any passing microorganisms from entering your body through your skin.

3) The breathing system produces sticky mucus

The whole respiratory tract (nasal passage, trachea and lungs) is lined with mucus and cilia which catch dust and bacteria before they reach the lungs.

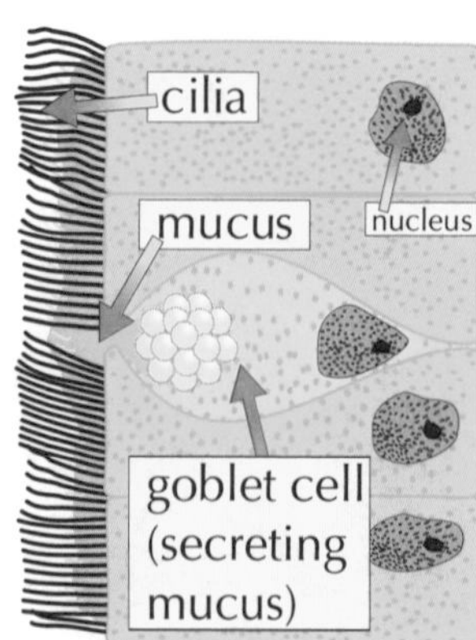

Disease

Once micro-organisms have entered our bodies they will reproduce rapidly unless they are destroyed. Your 'immune system' does just that and white blood cells are the most important part of it.

*Your **immune system**: white blood cells*

They travel around in your blood and crawl into every part of you, constantly patrolling for microorganisms. When they come across an invading microorganism they have three lines of attack:

*1) **Consuming** them*

White blood cells can engulf foreign cells and "ingest" (absorb) them.

*2) Producing **antibodies***

When your white blood cells come across a foreign cell they will start to produce chemicals called antibodies to kill the new invading cells. The antibodies are then produced rapidly and flow all round the body to kill all similar bacteria or viruses.

*3) Producing **antitoxins***

Antitoxins counter the effect of any poisons (toxins) produced by the invading bacteria.

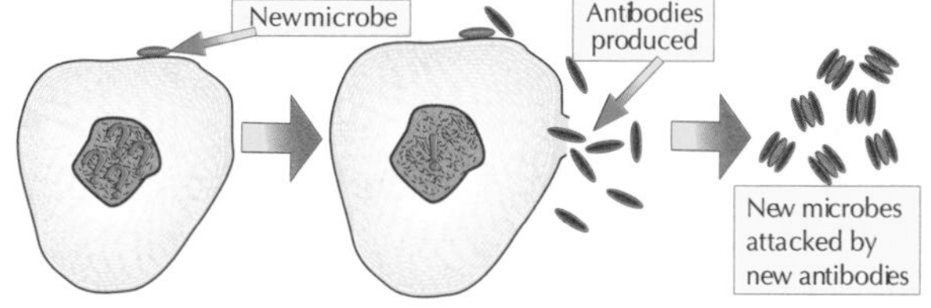

***Immunisation** — getting antibodies ready for attack*

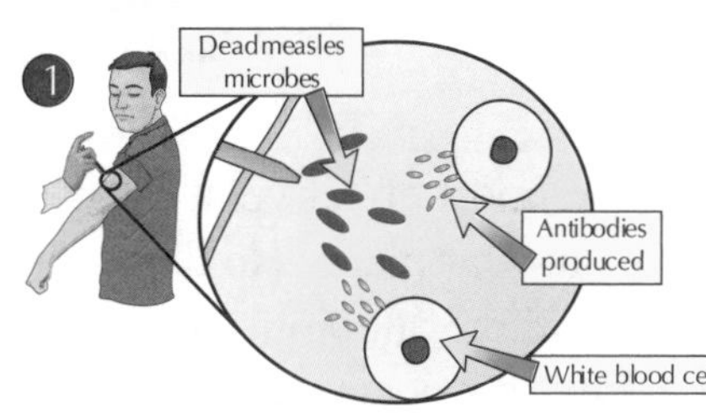

1) Once your white cells have produced antibodies to tackle a new strain of bacteria or virus you are said to have developed "natural immunity" to it.
2) This means if the same microorganisms attack again they'll be killed by the antibodies you already have for them, and you won't get ill.
3) The trouble is when a new microorganism appears, it takes your white blood cells a few days to produce the antibodies to deal with them and in that time you can get very ill.

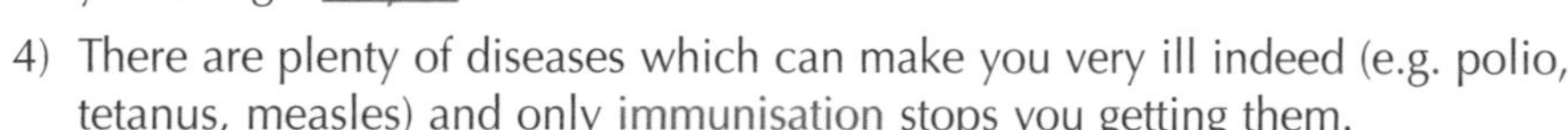

4) There are plenty of diseases which can make you very ill indeed (e.g. polio, tetanus, measles) and only immunisation stops you getting them.

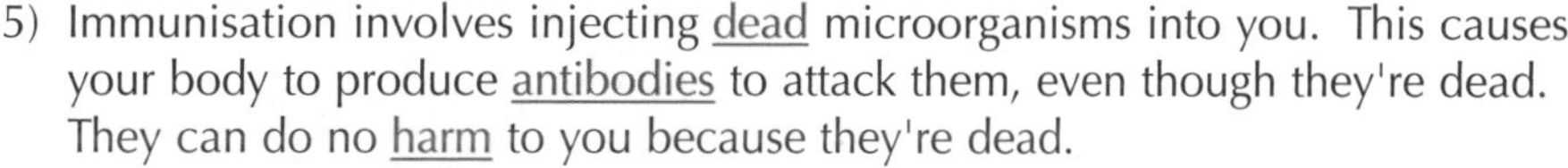

5) Immunisation involves injecting dead microorganisms into you. This causes your body to produce antibodies to attack them, even though they're dead. They can do no harm to you because they're dead.
6) If live microorganisms of the same type appeared after you are immune to them, they'd be killed immediately by the antibodies which you have already developed against them.

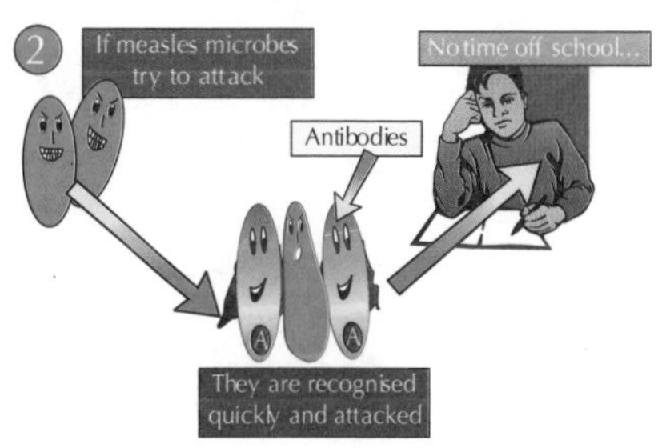

***Antibiotics** kill **bacteria** but **not** viruses*

1) Antibiotics are drugs that kill bacteria without killing your own body cells.
2) They are very useful for clearing up infections that your body is having trouble with.
3) However they don't kill viruses. Flu and colds are caused by viruses and basically, you're on your own.
4) There are no drugs to kill viruses and you just have to wait for your body to deal with them and suffer in the meantime.

Remember — antibiotics DO NOT kill viruses

Three sections to learn here — those numbered points are important. Do a mini-essay for each one to make sure you've got white blood cells and immunisation sorted out in your head.

Warm-Up and Exam Questions

Warm-up Questions

1) What is missing from bacteria, that is present in both animal and plant cells?
2) Which are classed as cells, bacteria or viruses?
3) Describe the structure of a virus.
4) Name 3 ways in which the body defends itself against the entry of microbes.
5) What are antibiotics?

Exam Questions

1 When microbes enter the body they may make us ill.

(a) What do microbes do to make you ill, after entering the body?

(2 marks)

(b) What is meant by 'natural immunity'?
Explain how you become naturally immune to a microbe.

(4 marks)

(c) Smoking can damage the cilia in the respiratory tract. Explain how this can make our bodies less able to defend against the entry of microbes that attack the respiratory system.

(3 marks)

2 Rageh carried out an experiment to see which of three antibiotics were most effective at killing a particular strain of bacteria. He grew a layer of bacteria on an agar plate. He then added paper discs that had been previously soaked in either one of the three antibiotics to the agar plate. He left the agar plate for 24 hours. The diagram below shows his results.

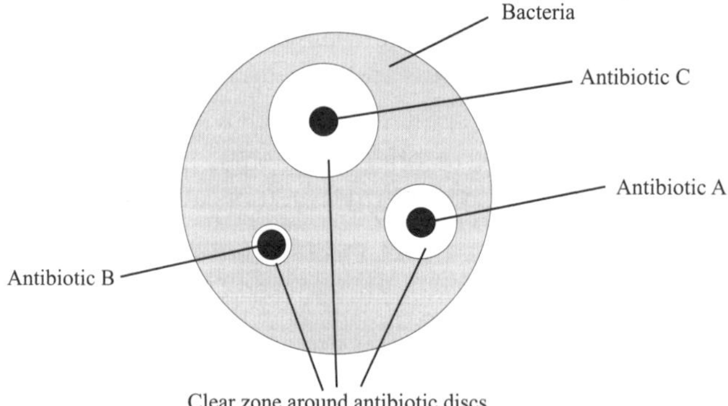

(a) Using Rageh's results, explain which antibiotic, A, B, or C, is the most effective at killing the bacteria.

(2 marks)

(b) What could Rageh do to make sure that his results were reliable?

(1 mark)

(c) Rageh wants to carry out a similar experiment to see which antibiotic is most effective at killing a particular virus. Give two reasons why this experiment could not be carried out using viruses instead of bacteria.

(2 marks)

Diffusion

Diffusion means spreading out

"Diffusion" is really simple. It's just the gradual net movement of particles from places where there are lots of them to places where there are fewer of them. That's all it is — it's just the natural tendency for stuff to spread out. You also have to learn the formal definition, which is this:

DIFFUSION is the NET MOVEMENT OF PARTICLES from a region of HIGH CONCENTRATION to an area of LOW CONCENTRATION

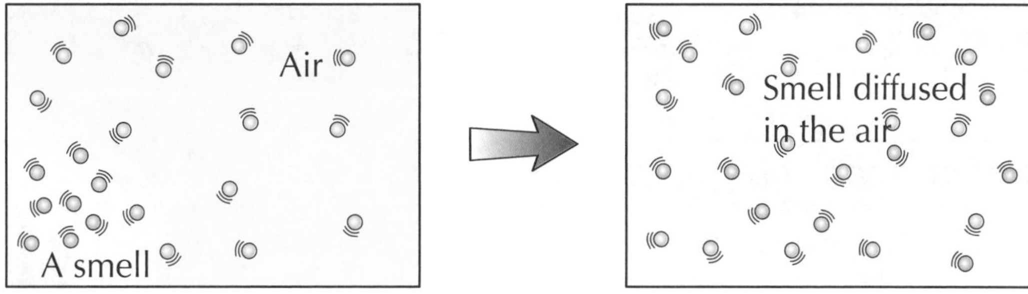

Diffusion through cell membranes is selective...

Cell membranes are quite clever because they hold everything inside the cell, but, they let substances in and out as well. Only very small molecules can diffuse through cell membranes though — things like glucose, water or ions.

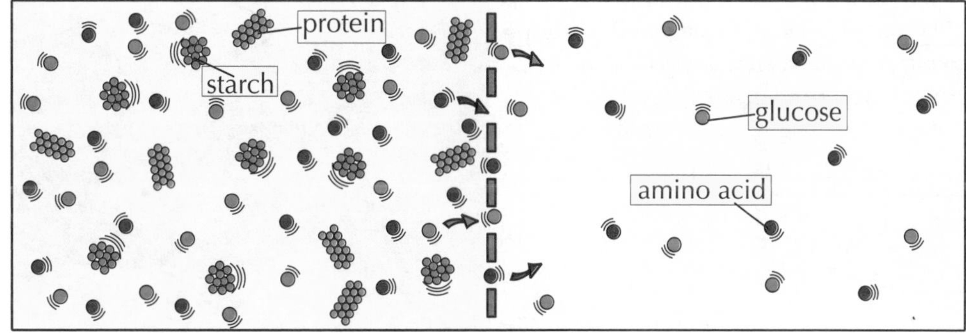

1) Notice that big molecules like starch or proteins can't diffuse through cell membranes — they could ask you exactly that in the Exam.
2) Just like with diffusion in air, particles flow through the cell membrane from where there's a high concentration (a lot of them) to where there's a low concentration (not so many of them).
3) The rate of diffusion is directly affected by the concentration gradient — "the GREATER the difference in concentration the FASTER the rate of diffusion".

Diffusion in the Digestive and Respiratory Systems

The *small molecules* can *diffuse* into the *blood*

Glucose, amino acids, fatty acids and glycerol molecules are small enough to diffuse into the blood.

When there's a high concentration of these molecules in the gut they will "diffuse" normally into the blood.

When there's a low concentration in the gut special cells are needed because the concentration gradient is the wrong way.

They then travel to where they're needed, and then diffuse out again. It's all clever stuff.

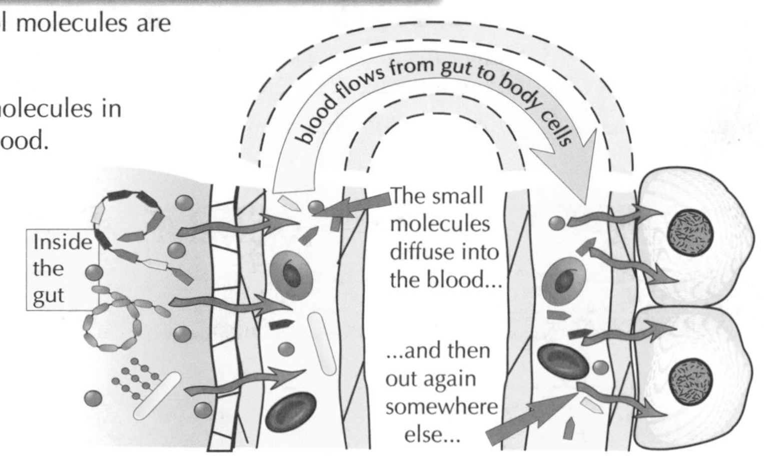

Villi provide a really *big surface area*

The inside of the small intestine is covered in millions and millions of these tiny little projections called villi.
They increase the surface area in a big way so that digested food is absorbed much more quickly into the blood.

Notice they have: 1) a single layer of cells
2) a very good blood supply to assist quick absorption.

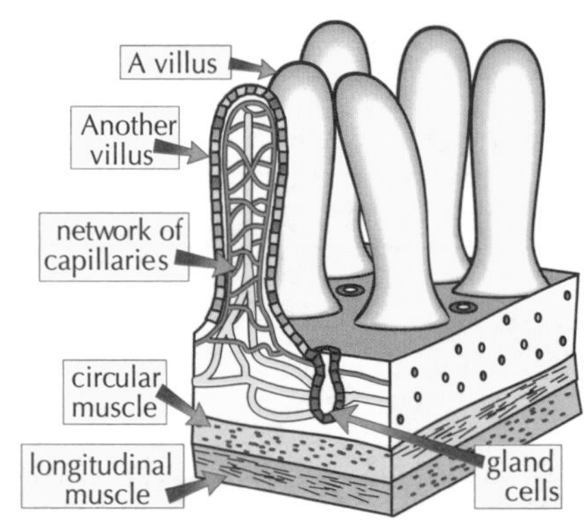

Gas exchange in the *lungs*

You've seen this before on page six, but I've put it here as well because it's about diffusion. Don't panic, it's just the same stuff.

The lungs contain millions and millions of little air sacs called ALVEOLI (see diagram opposite) which are specialised to maximise the diffusion of oxygen and CO_2.
The alveoli are an ideal exchange surface.
They have:

1) An enormous surface area (about $70m^2$ in total).
2) A moist lining for dissolving gases.
3) Very thin walls.
4) A copious blood supply.

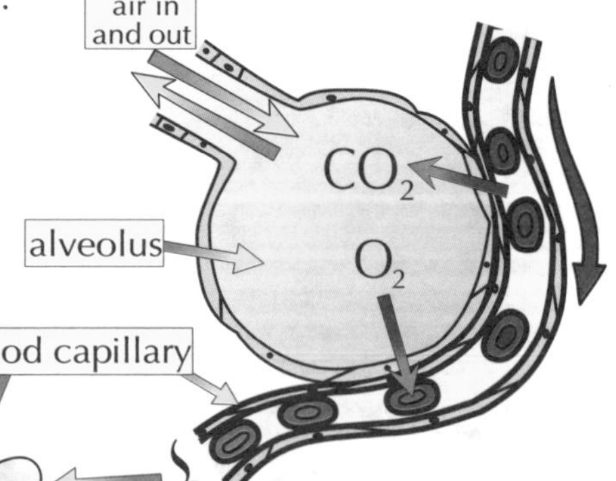

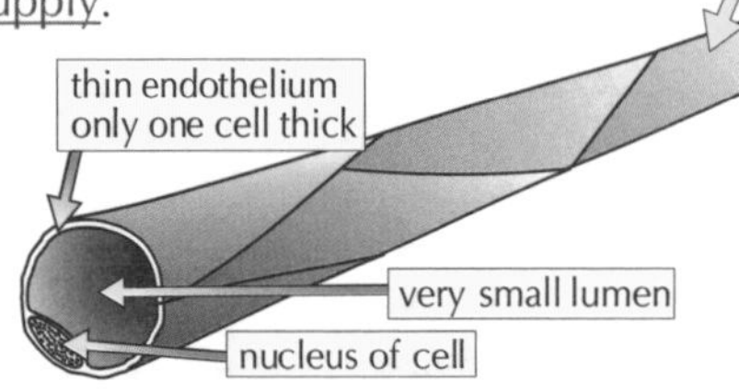

5) The blood capillaries aid the diffusion of gases as their walls are usually only one cell thick making it easy for stuff to pass in and out of them.
6) To give you an idea of the size of things here — the capillaries are normally too small to see.

This is a very easy page to learn...

You should understand and remember what goes on and why this all works so well.
A clear visual image in your head of these diagrams makes it a lot easier. Learn the diagrams, words and all.

Warm-Up and Exam Question

There's only one way to do well in the exam — learn the facts and then practise lots of exam questions to see what it'll be like on the big day. We couldn't have made that easier for you — so do it.

Warm-up Questions

1) Write a definition of diffusion.
2) What effect does it have on the rate of diffusion if the concentration gradient increases?
3) Why can't starch molecules diffuse out of cells?
4) Describe how villi are well-suited for aiding the diffusion of food molecules into the blood.

Exam Question

1 Diffusion occurs in both plants and animals.

a) Gases move in and out of leaves by diffusion.
Give a definition of diffusion.

....

....

(2 marks)

b) Name two places in the human body where diffusion occurs.
For each place, explain why diffusion is needed.

Place 1 ....

Why diffusion is needed ....

....

....

Place 2 ....

Why diffusion is needed ....

....

....

(4 marks)

Revision Summary for Section One

There's a lot to learn in Section One, but it's all fairly straightforward and factual.
Nothing too difficult to understand, just lots of facts and diagrams to learn.
Keep practising these questions till you can answer them all without hesitation.

1) Sketch a typical animal cell with labels, adding a brief description for each label.
2) Sketch three different animal cells and describe their specialised functions.
3) Give an animal example of this sequence: cells → tissues → organ → organ-system → organism.
4) Sketch the diagram on the right, adding the names for parts A to H.
5) Write down at least one detail for each of the labelled parts.
6) What *exactly* do enzymes do in the digestive system?
7) List the three main types of digestive enzyme, which foods they act on, and what they produce.
8) Where is bile produced and stored? What does it do?
9) Draw a diagram of the breathing system, showing all your breathing equipment.
10) What is 'ventilation'? Describe the stages of the process.
11) Where are alveoli found? How big are they and what are they for? Give four features of them.
12) What is 'respiration'? Give a proper definition.
13) What is 'aerobic respiration'? Give the word equation for it.
14) What is 'anaerobic respiration'? Give the word equation for what happens in our bodies.
15) Why can your muscles hurt during vigorous exercise? What is the oxygen debt?
16) Draw a diagram of the human circulatory system: heart, lungs, arteries, veins, etc.
17) Explain why it is called a *double* circulatory system, and describe the pressure and oxygen content of the blood in each bit. What are the big words for saying whether the blood is carrying oxygen or not?
18) Draw a full diagram of the heart with all the labels. Explain how the two halves differ.
19) How do ventricles and atria compare, and why are they different? What are the valves for?
20) Describe briefly with diagrams the three stages of the pumping cycle for the heart.
21) Sketch an artery, a capillary, and a vein, with labels, and explain the features of all three.
22) Sketch a red blood cell and a white blood cell and give details about each.
23) Sketch some blood plasma. List all the things that are carried in the plasma (around 10).
24) Sketch some platelets. What do they do?
25) How exactly do bacteria make you feel ill? Sketch a bacterium.
26) What do viruses do inside you to replicate? Illustrate with sketches.
27) Describe the body's three defences to keep microorganisms out.
28) What is meant by your 'immune system'? What is the most important part of it?
29) List the three ways that white blood cells deal with invading microorganisms.
30) Give full details of the process of immunisation. How does it work?
31) What are antibiotics? What will they work on and what will they not work on?
32) Give the strict definition of diffusion.
33) Why are cell membranes clever?
34) Give examples of substances that will and substances that won't diffuse through cell membranes.

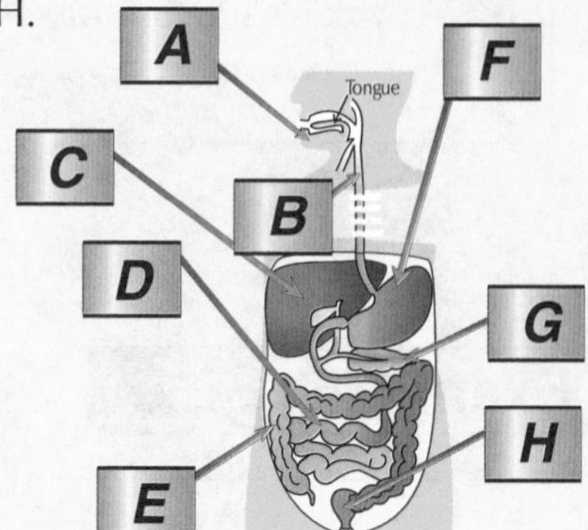

Plant Structure

Plant cells have:

As you saw on page 1, plant cells have the following features:

1) Nucleus
 controls what the cell does.

2) Cytoplasm
 where the chemical reactions happen.

3) Cell membrane
 holds the cell together and controls what goes in and out.

4) Rigid cell wall to give support.

5) Vacuole containing cell sap.

6) Green chloroplasts containing chlorophyll.

7) Mitochondria turn glucose and oxygen into energy.

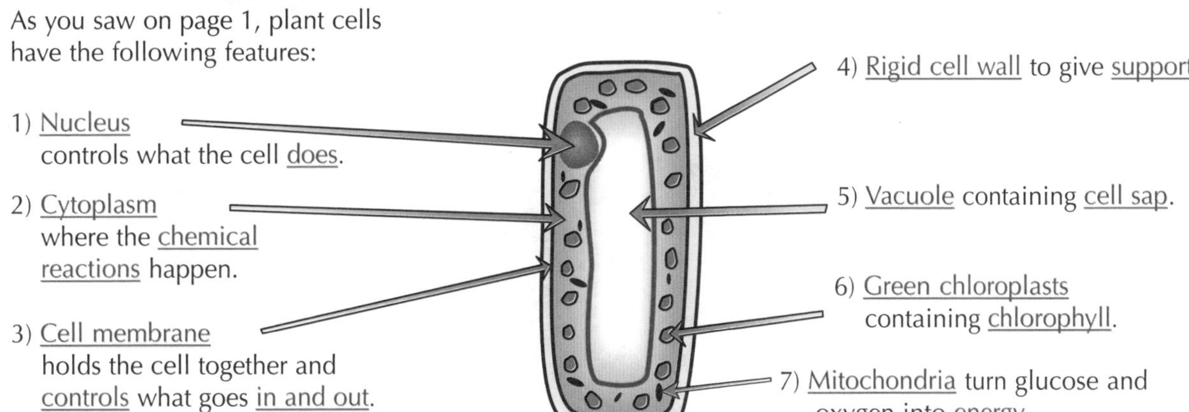

Specialised plant cells

Just like with animal cells, plants have cells that are particularly well-suited to doing certain jobs. This is an exam favourite, so learn all the numbered points well.

1) Palisade leaf cells are designed for photosynthesis

1) Packed with chloroplasts for photosynthesis.
2) Tall shape means a lot of surface area exposed down the side for absorbing CO_2 from the air in the leaf.
3) Tall shape also means a good chance of light hitting a chloroplast before it reaches the bottom of the cell.

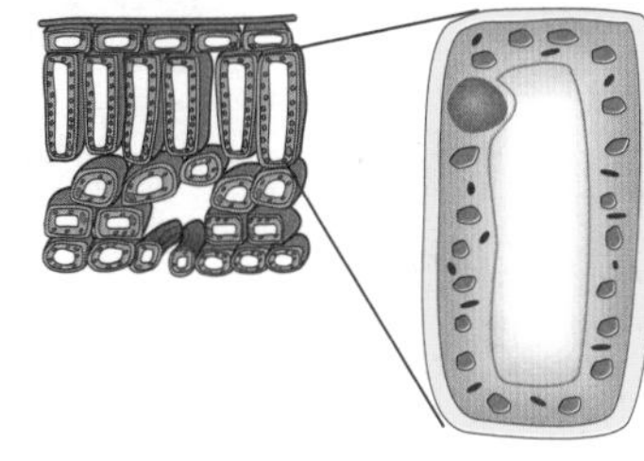

2) Guard cells are designed to open and close

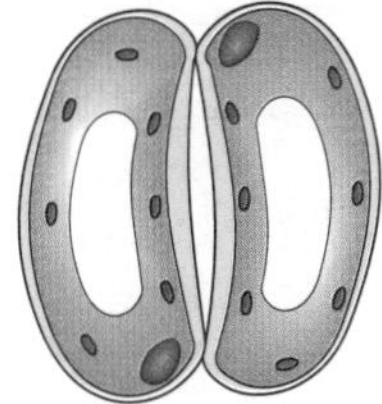

1) Special kidney shape which opens and closes the stomata (a single pore is a stoma) as the cells go turgid or flaccid.
2) Thin outer walls and thickened inner walls make this opening and closing function work properly.
3) They're also sensitive to light and close at night to conserve water.

3) Xylem cells are designed for water transport

1) Xylem tissue forms a xylem tube made up of dead cells joined end to end with no end walls between them.
2) The side walls are strong and stiff to give the plant support.
3) The xylem tubes carry water and minerals from the roots up to the leaves in the transpiration stream.

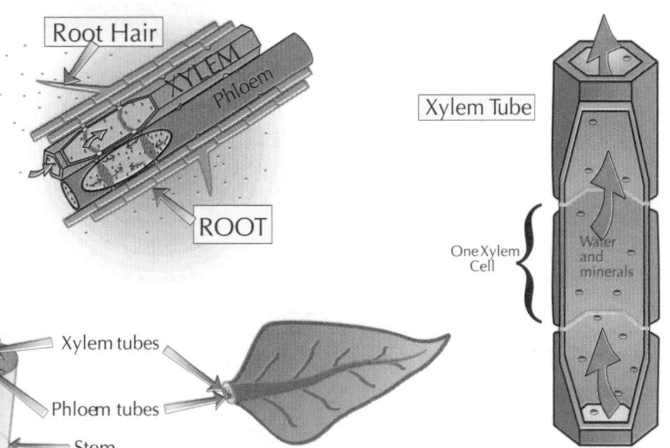

(There's more about the phloem and xylem tubes on page 33.)

Plant Structure

You have to know all these parts of the plant and what they do:

*The **five different bits** of a **plant** all do **different jobs***

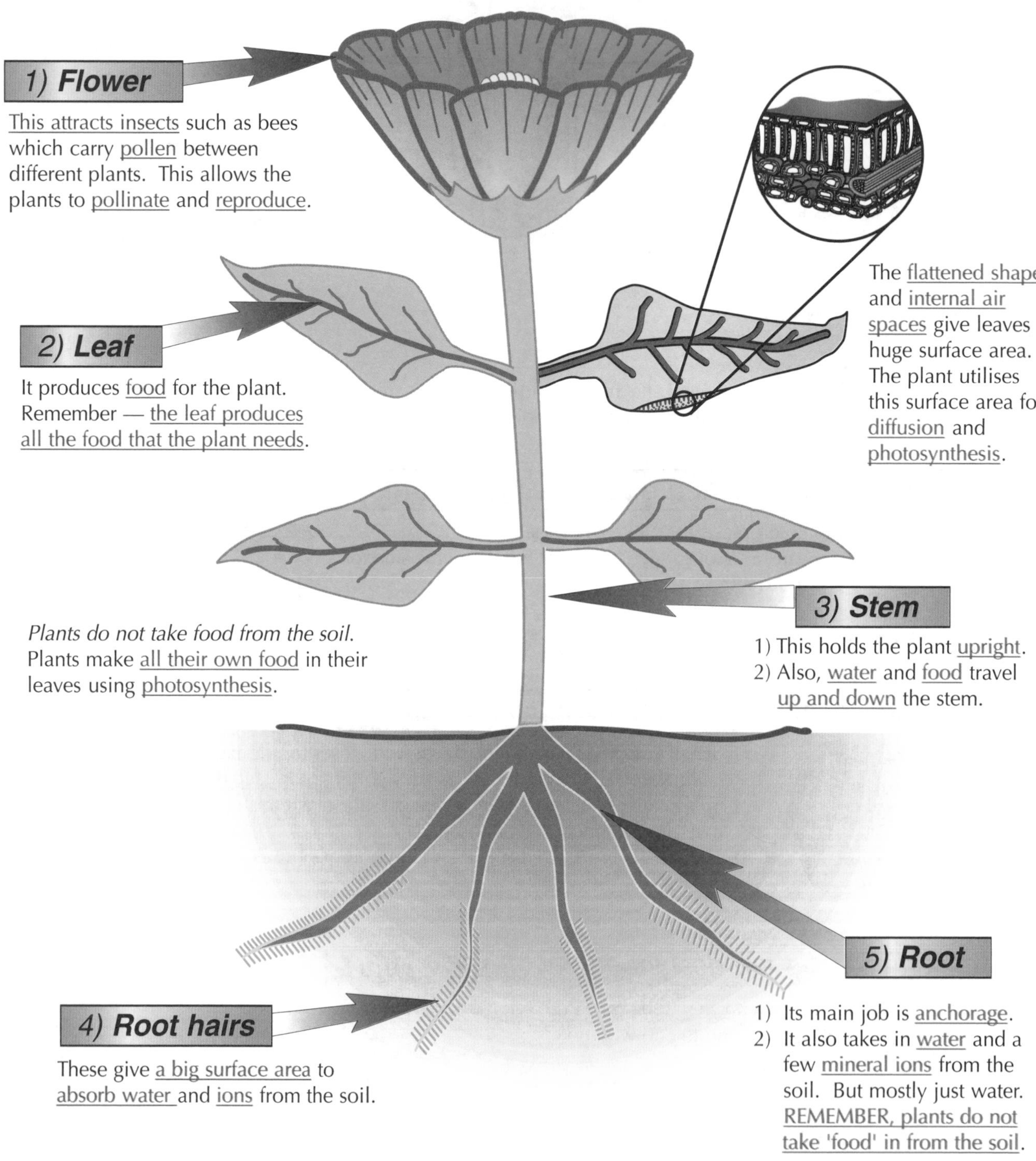

1) Flower
This attracts insects such as bees which carry pollen between different plants. This allows the plants to pollinate and reproduce.
2) Leaf
It produces food for the plant. Remember — the leaf produces all the food that the plant needs.
The flattened shape and internal air spaces give leaves a huge surface area. The plant utilises this surface area for diffusion and photosynthesis.
3) Stem
1) This holds the plant upright.
2) Also, water and food travel up and down the stem.
Plants do not take food from the soil. Plants make all their own food in their leaves using photosynthesis.
4) Root hairs
These give a big surface area to absorb water and ions from the soil.
5) Root
1) Its main job is anchorage.
2) It also takes in water and a few mineral ions from the soil. But mostly just water. REMEMBER, plants do not take 'food' in from the soil.

You definitely need to learn all that

Everything on this page is there to be learnt because it's very likely to come up in your Exams. This is pretty basic stuff, but it can still catch you out if you don't learn it properly. For example: "What is the main function of the root?". A lot of people might answer that with "Taking food in from the soil" — which is of course wrong. LEARN these facts. They all count. They're all worth marks in the Exam. Practise until you can sketch the diagram and write down all the details, without looking back.

Warm-Up and Exam Question

Warm-up Questions

1) Give two ways in which the palisade leaf cell is specially adapted to carry out photosynthesis.
2) By what process do plants make their own food?
3) What is the purpose of the flower?
4) What type of tubes carry water and minerals?

Exam Question

1 This diagram shows a plant cell:

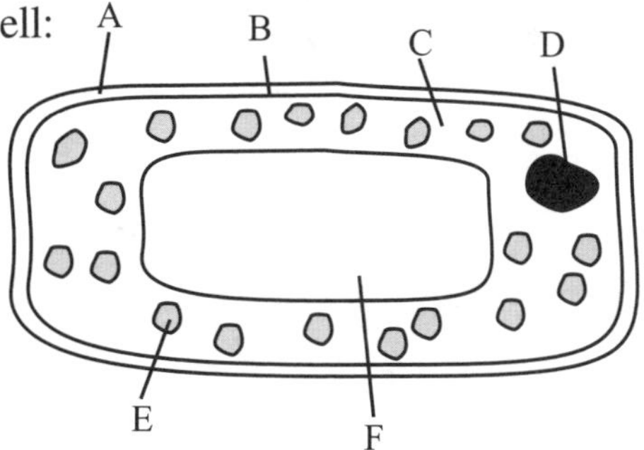

a) Name structures A – F in the diagram.

(6 marks)

b) Complete the following table showing the jobs of various structures found in cells. The first one has been done for you.

STRUCTURE	Mitochondrion	Cell membrane	Chloroplast	Cell wall	Nucleus
JOB	*To release energy from food*				

(4 marks)

c) Match the names in column 1 to the descriptions in column 2.

<u>Column 1</u>	<u>Column 2</u>
Organ	a group of similar cells
Organism	a group of organs working together
Tissue	a group of different tissues
Organ System	a living thing

(4 marks)

d) This diagram shows a pair of guard cells:

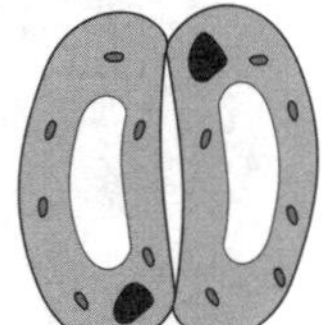

(i) What is the function of guard cells?

(1 mark)

(ii) Describe two features of the cell that make it specially adapted for its role and explain each adaptation.

(2 marks)

Plant Nutrition

Photosynthesis produces **glucose** from **sunlight**

1) Photosynthesis is the process that produces 'food' in plants. The 'food' it produces is glucose.
2) Photosynthesis takes place in the leaves of all green plants — this is what leaves are for.

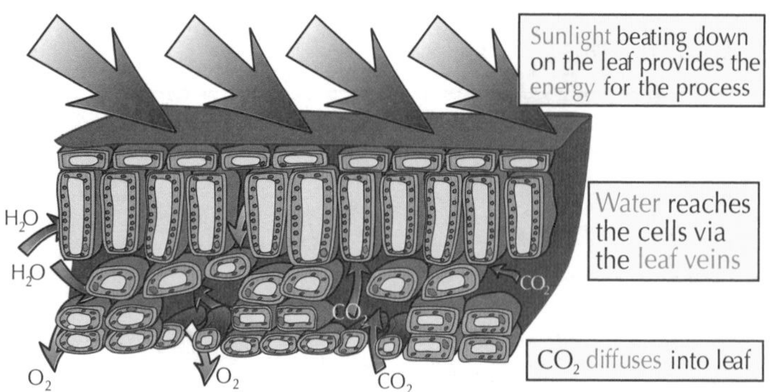

Three Features:

1) Leaves are thin and flat to provide a big surface area to catch lots of sunlight.
2) The palisade cells are near the top of the leaf and are packed with chloroplasts.
3) Guard cells control the movement of gases into and out of the leaf.

Learn the **equation** for **photosynthesis**:

$$\text{Carbon dioxide} + \text{water} \xrightarrow[\text{chlorophyll}]{\text{LIGHT ENERGY}} \text{glucose} + \text{oxygen}$$

Four things are **needed** for photosynthesis to happen:

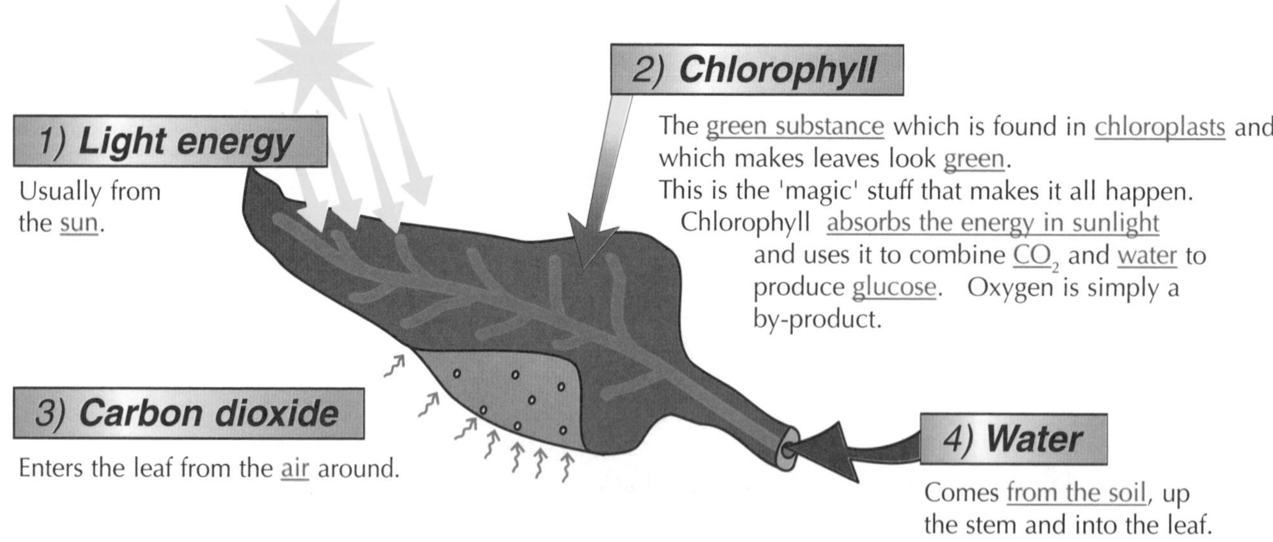

1) Light energy

Usually from the sun.

2) Chlorophyll

The green substance which is found in chloroplasts and which makes leaves look green.
This is the 'magic' stuff that makes it all happen.
Chlorophyll absorbs the energy in sunlight and uses it to combine CO_2 and water to produce glucose. Oxygen is simply a by-product.

3) Carbon dioxide

Enters the leaf from the air around.

4) Water

Comes from the soil, up the stem and into the leaf.

Plant Nutrition

The rate of photosynthesis is affected by three factors:

1) The amount of **light**

The chlorophyll uses light energy to perform photosynthesis. It can only do it as fast as the light energy is arriving. Chlorophyll actually only absorbs the red and blue ends of the visible light spectrum, but not the green light in the middle, which is reflected back. This is why the plant looks green.

2) The amount of **carbon dioxide**

CO_2 and water are the raw materials. Water is never really in short supply in a plant but only 0.03% of the air around is CO_2 so it's actually pretty scarce as far as plants are concerned.

3) The **temperature**

Chlorophyll is like an enzyme so it works best when it's warm but not too hot. The rate of photosynthesis depends on how 'happy' the chlorophyll enzyme is: the optimum temperature is WARM but not too hot.

Three important graphs for **rate of photosynthesis**

At any given time one or other of the above three factors will be the limiting factor which is keeping the photosynthesis down at the rate it is.

1) Not enough **light** slows down the rate of photosynthesis

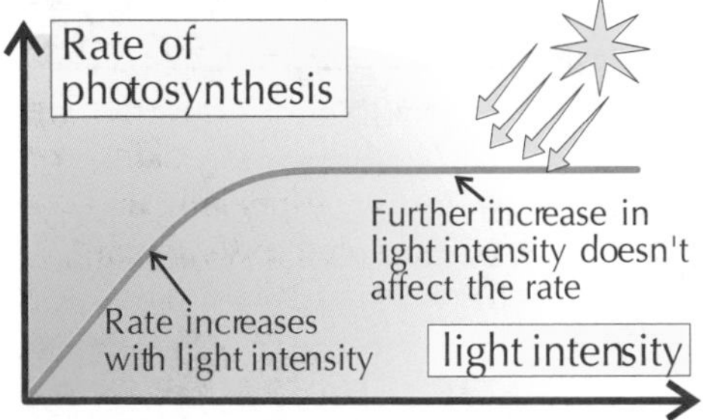

1) As the light level is raised, the rate of photosynthesis increases steadily but only up to a certain point.
2) Beyond that, it won't make any difference because then it'll be either the temperature or the CO_2 level which is the limiting factor.

2) Too little **carbon dioxide** also slows it down

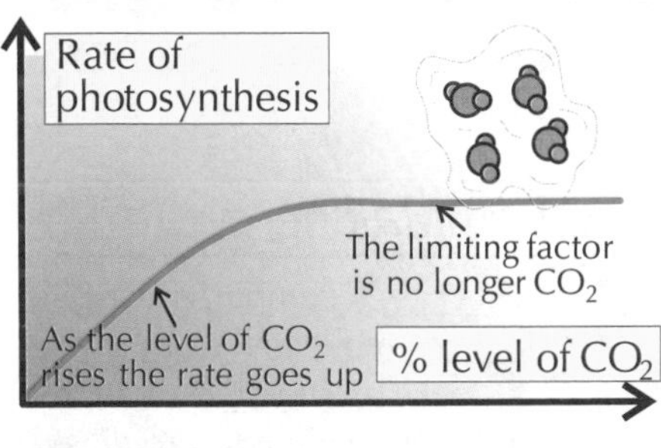

1) As with light intensity the amount of CO_2 will only increase the rate of photosynthesis up to a point. After this the graph flattens out showing that CO_2 is no longer the limiting factor.
2) As long as light and CO_2 are in plentiful supply then the factor limiting photosynthesis must be temperature.

3) The **temperature** has to be just right

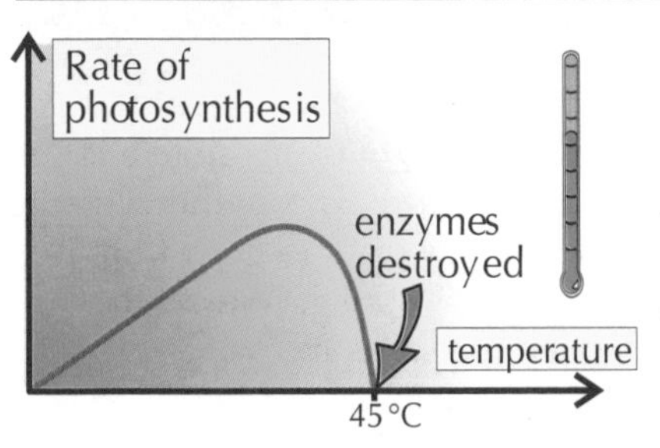

1) Note that you can't really have too much light or CO_2. The temperature however must not get too high or it denatures the chlorophyll enzymes. *(Denaturing an enzyme means changing it so that it can no longer do its job.)*
2) This happens at about 45°C (which is pretty hot for outdoors, though greenhouses can get that hot if you're not careful).
3) Usually, though, if the temperature is the limiting factor it's because it's too low, and things need warming up a bit.

Plant Nutrition

1) For *respiration*

1) Plants manufacture glucose in their leaves.
2) They then use some of the glucose initially for respiration.
3) This releases energy which enables them to convert the rest of the glucose into various other useful substances which they can use to build new cells and grow.
4) To produce some of these substances they also need to gather a few minerals from the soil.

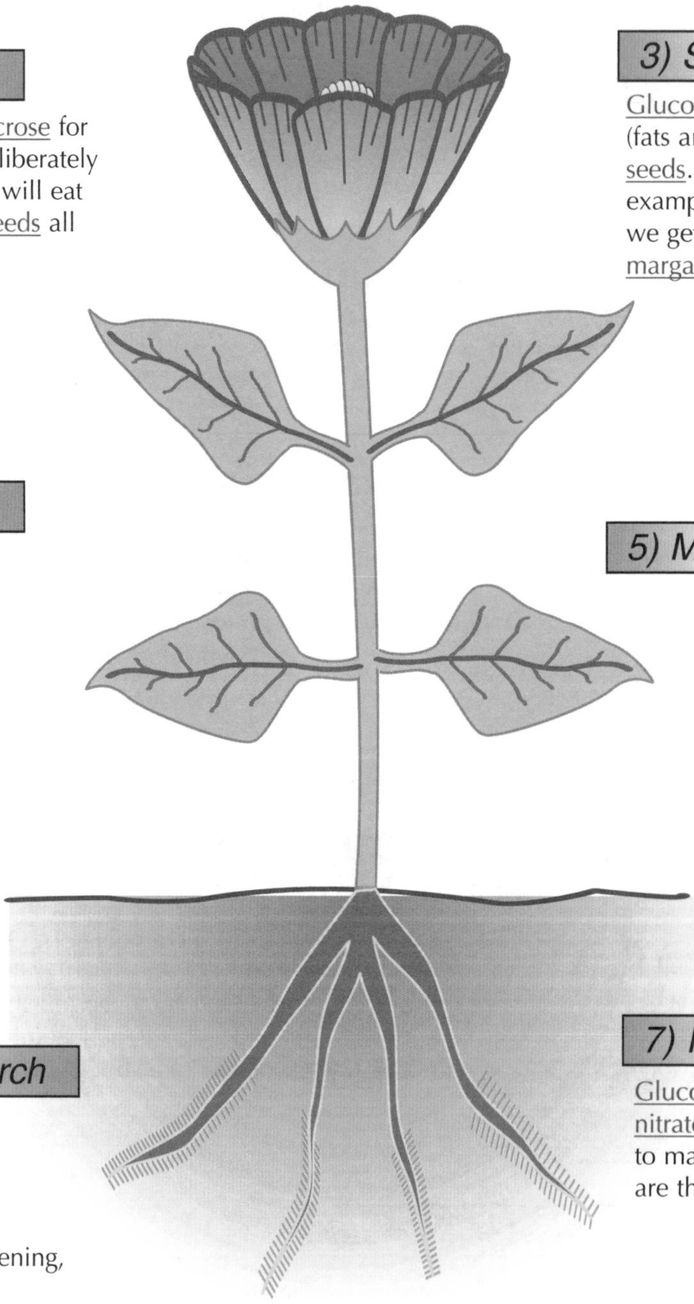

2) Making *fruits*

Glucose is turned into sucrose for storing in fruits. Fruits deliberately taste nice so that animals will eat them and so spread the seeds all over the place.

3) Stored in *seeds*

Glucose is turned into lipids (fats and oils) for storing in seeds. Sunflower seeds, for example, contain a lot of oil — we get cooking oil and margarine from them.

4) For *transport*

The energy from glucose is also needed to transport substances around the plant and for active uptake of minerals in the roots.

5) Making *cell walls*

Glucose is converted into cellulose for making cell walls, especially in a rapidly growing plant.

6) *Stored* as starch

Glucose is turned into starch and stored in roots, stems and leaves, ready for use when photosynthesis isn't happening, like in the winter.

7) Making *proteins*

Glucose is combined with nitrates (collected from the soil) to make amino acids, which are then made into proteins.

Potato and carrot plants store a lot of starch in their roots over the winter to enable a new plant to grow from it the following spring. We eat the swollen roots.

Glucose as starch is insoluble which makes it much better for storing, because it doesn't bloat the storage cells by osmosis like glucose would.

Plant Nutrition

For healthy growth plants need these three really important mineral ions which they can only obtain from the soil through their roots:

The **three** essential **minerals**

1) Nitrates

— for making amino acids and for the "synthesis" (making) of proteins.

2) Phosphates

— have an important role in reactions involved in photosynthesis and respiration.

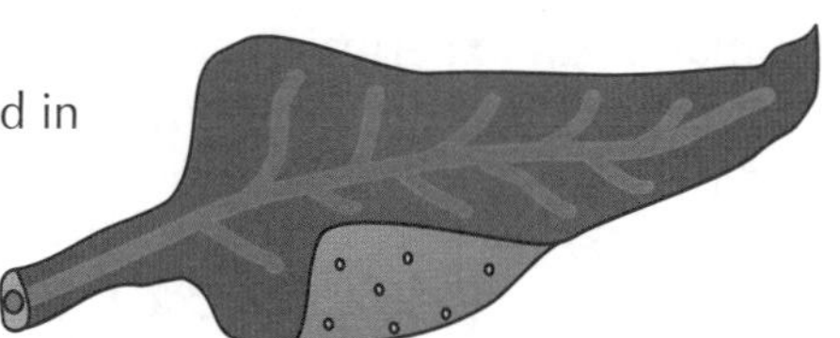

3) Potassium

— helps the enzymes involved in photosynthesis and respiration to work.

Lack of these nutrients causes **deficiency symptoms**:

1) Lack of **nitrates**

— Stunted growth and yellow older leaves.

2) Lack of **phosphates**

— Poor root growth and purple younger leaves.

3) Lack of **potassium**

— Yellow leaves with dead spots.

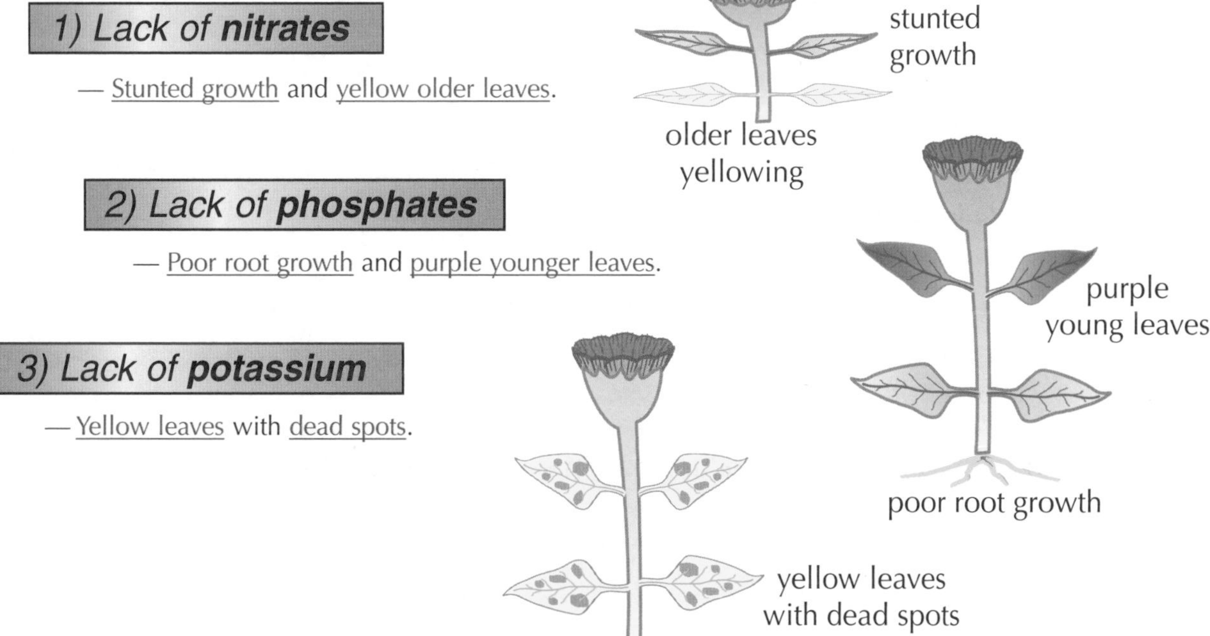

Remember the four things needed for photosynthesis

Plant nutrition is bound to be in the Exams. On the previous pages there are a few diagrams, the photosynthesis equation, and the four necessary conditions, then two pages on nutrients. Just keep learning them until you can cover the page and write everything down from memory. Only then will you really know it all.

Warm-Up and Exam Questions

Warm-up Questions

1) Write down the word equation for photosynthesis.
2) What do guard cells do?
3) What is the name of the green substance found in chloroplasts?
4) What happens to the rate of photosynthesis when the temperature gets too high (above 45°C)?
5) What is the storage carbohydrate of plants?
6) What are the symptoms of potassium deficiency in plants?

Exam Questions

1 Elodea is a pond plant. An experiment was set up, as in the diagram below, to investigate how light intensity affects the rate of photosynthesis.

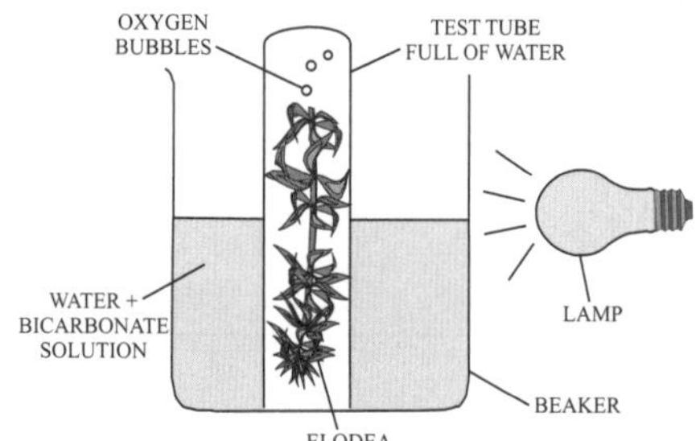

The number of bubbles released in 1 minute was recorded, with the lamp at different distances from the beaker. The results were recorded in the table below:

DISTANCE BETWEEN LAMP AND BEAKER (CM)	0	10	20	30	40	50
NO. OXYGEN BUBBLES PRODUCED IN 1 MINUTE	48	40	32	24	12	8

a) Draw a graph of these results.

(4 marks)

b) Suggest a reason for leaving the apparatus for 2 minutes before recording the bubbles each time the lamp was moved to a new distance.

(1 mark)

c) Why was the bicarbonate solution added to the water at the start of the experiment?

(1 mark)

d) What conclusion can you make about light intensity and photosynthesis from the results?

(1 mark)

e) Give two other factors, apart from light intensity, that affect the rate of photosynthesis.

(2 marks)

2 a) Match the correct mineral in list A to its use in plants, in list B.

A	B
POTASSIUM	Making amino acids
NITRATES	Involved in photosynthesis and respiration
PHOSPHATES	Involved in enzyme action

(3 marks)

b) What are the symptoms of nitrogen deficiency in plants?

(2 marks)

Transport Processes I

Remember — **Diffusion** is the **Spreading Out** of a substance

Diffusion is also covered on p17, but it's relevant here as well, so here is a reminder of the definition:

> DIFFUSION is the NET MOVEMENT OF PARTICLES from a region of HIGH CONCENTRATION to an area of LOW CONCENTRATION

Diffusion of **gases in leaves** is vital for **photosynthesis**

The simplest type of diffusion is where different gases diffuse through each other, like when a smell spreads out through the air in a room. Diffusion of gases also happens in leaves and it's very likely to be in the Exam.

So learn it now:

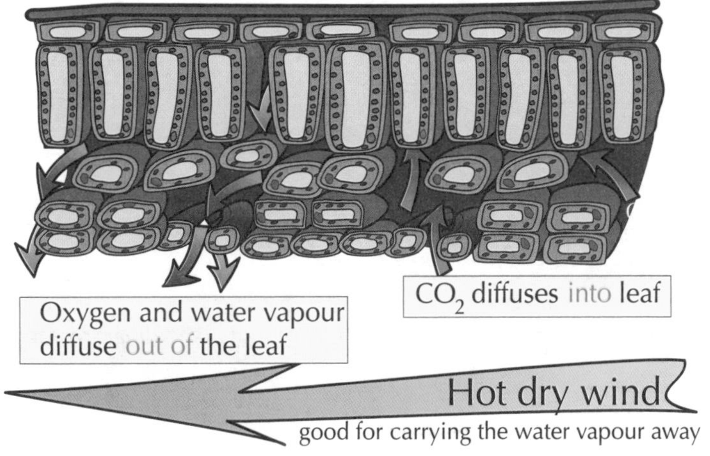
Oxygen and water vapour diffuse out of the leaf
CO_2 diffuses into leaf
Hot dry wind
good for carrying the water vapour away

1) For photosynthesis to happen, carbon dioxide gas has to get inside the leaves.
2) It does this by diffusion through the tiny little holes under the leaf called stomata.
3) At the same time water vapour and oxygen diffuse out through the same tiny little holes.
4) The water vapour escapes by diffusion because there's a lot of it inside the leaf and less of it in the air outside.
5) This diffusion causes transpiration and it goes quicker when the air around the leaf is kept dry — ie: transpiration is quickest in hot, dry, windy conditions.

Transport Processes I

Transpiration is the loss of water from the plant

1) It's caused by the evaporation of water from inside the leaves. Most of the action involves the stomata shown on the following page.
2) This creates a slight shortage of water in the leaf which draws more water up from the rest of the plant which in turn draws more up from the roots.
3) It has two beneficial effects: a) it transports minerals from the soil b) it cools the plant.

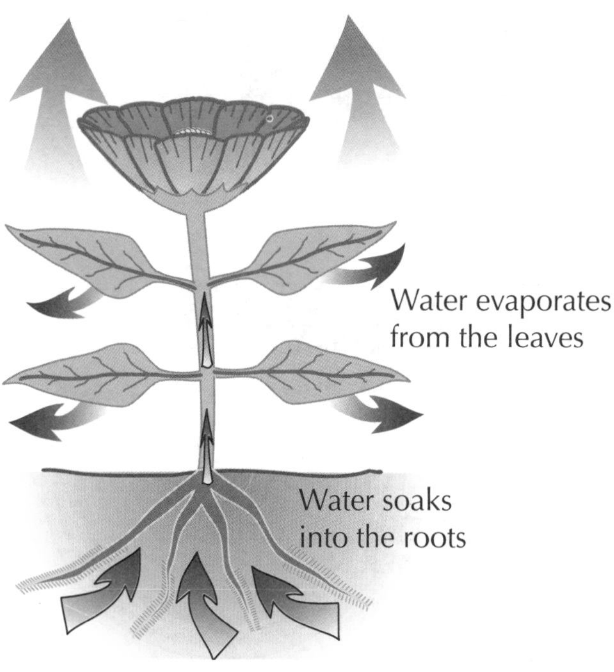

Four factors which affect it

The rate of transpiration is affected by four things:

1) Amount of light
2) Temperature
3) Amount of air movement
4) Humidity of the surrounding air

It's clear that the biggest rate of transpiration occurs in hot, dry, windy, conditions ie: perfect clothes-drying weather.

By contrast a cool, cloudy, humid day with no wind will produce minimum transpiration.

This constant stream of water has the advantage of transporting vital minerals from the soil into the roots and then all around the plant.

The uptake of water and minerals happens almost entirely at the root hairs (see diagrams on P. 31 & 35).

Leaves help to limit transpiration

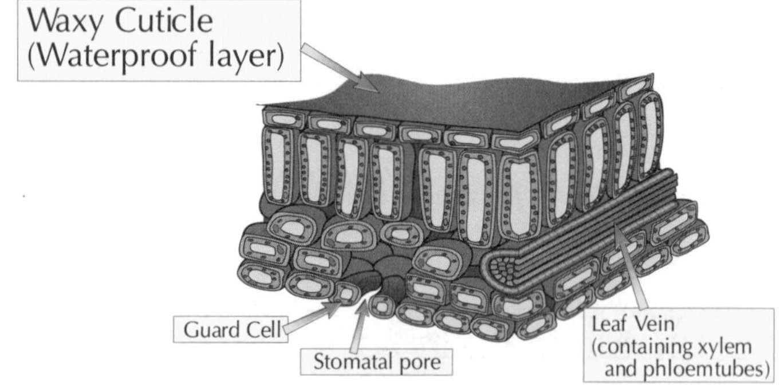

The leaves on most plants have a waxy top layer to limit transpiration.
As you'd expect, plants living in drier conditions have a thicker layer of wax.

Transport Processes I

Root hair cell

1) The cells on plant roots grow into long "hairs" which stick out into the soil.
2) This gives the root a big surface area for absorbing water and minerals from the soil.
3) Water is taken in almost entirely at the root hairs.
4) Minerals are also taken in at the root hairs.
5) However this uptake of minerals is against the concentration gradient, so it needs "active uptake" to make it happen. (See P.35.)

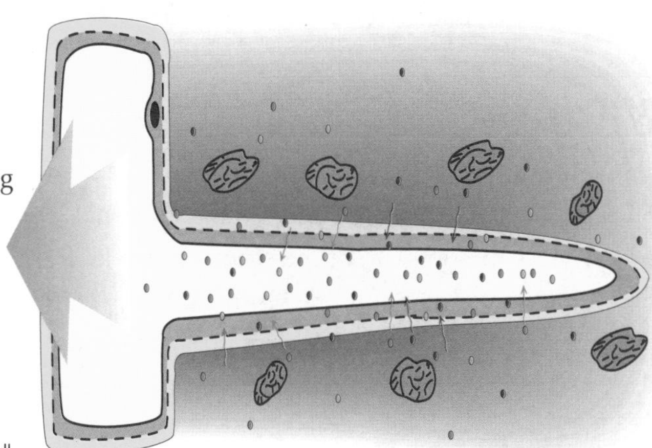

Turgor pressure supports plant tissues

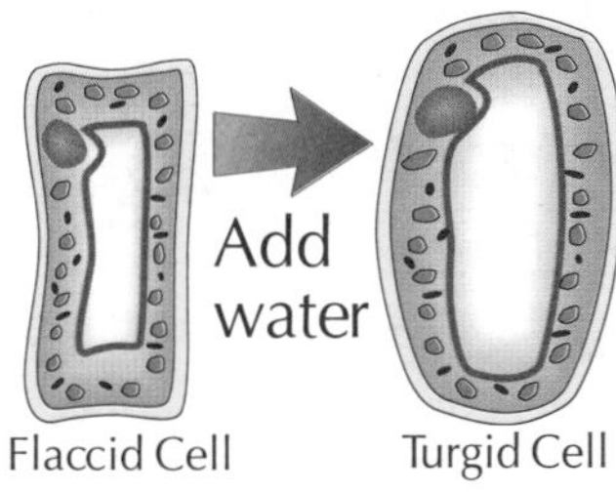

1) When a plant is well watered, all its cells will draw water into themselves by osmosis and become turgid.
2) The contents of the cell start to push against the cell wall, a bit like a balloon in a shoebox, and thereby give support to the plant tissues.
3) Leaves are entirely supported by this turgor pressure. We know this because if there's no water in the soil, a plant starts to wilt and the leaves droop. This is because the cells start to lose water and thus lose their turgor pressure.

Stomata are pores which open and close automatically

1) Stomata close automatically when supplies of water from the roots start to dry up.
2) The guard cells control this. When water is scarce, they become flaccid, and they change shape, which closes the stomatal pores.
3) This prevents any more water being lost, but also stops CO_2 getting in, so the photosynthesis stops as well. Limiting water loss is especially important in younger plants as water pressure is their main method of support.

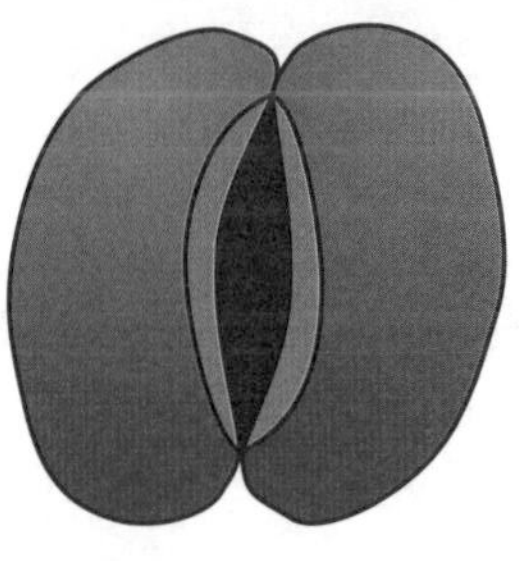

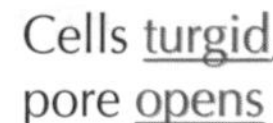
Cells turgid, pore opens

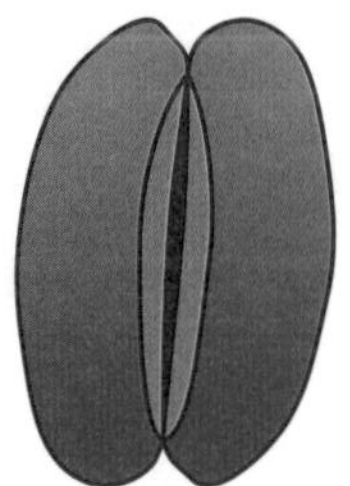
Cells flaccid, pore closes

Water is vital to plants — Learn how they get it and how they lose it

The main things to learn here are: why diffusion is needed for photosynthesis, what transpiration is (and what affects it), plus all the main points about root hairs, turgor pressure and stomata. Write a mini-essay for each topic to check you understand it all — and can remember all the details.

Warm-Up and Exam Question

There's no point in skimming through the section and glancing over the questions. Do the warm-up questions and go back over any bits you don't know. Then practise and practise the exam question.

Warm-up Questions

1) What is transpiration?
2) List four factors which affect transpiration.
3) What is the purpose of the stomata in a leaf?
4) What do we mean when we say a cell is "turgid"?

Exam Question

Imagine if you opened up your exam paper and all the answers were already written in for you. Hmm, well I'm afraid that's not going to happen — the only way you'll do well is through hard work now.

1 The diagram below shows how an experiment was set up to investigate water loss from leaves.

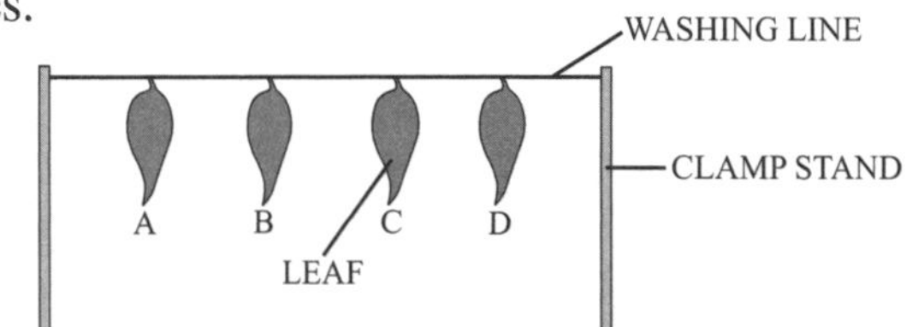

A — Both sides covered with petroleum jelly
B — Bottom surface of leaf covered in petroleum jelly
C — Top surface of leaf covered in petroleum jelly
D — No petroleum jelly

The mass of each leaf was recorded at the start of the experiment, and again 2 days later. The table below shows the results.

LEAF	MASS AT START (g)	MASS AT END (g)	% LOSS IN MASS
A	2.0	1.9	5
B	2.1	1.8	14
C	1.9	1.4	26
D	2.3	1.6	

(a) Work out the percentage loss in mass for leaf D.

(2 marks)

(b) Why is it important to calculate the percentage loss in mass for leaves, rather than just the actual loss in mass?

(1 mark)

(c) Explain the results for each of the leaves, A – D.

(4 marks)

(d) Give three environmental factors that would also affect the rate of transpiration.

(3 marks)

(e) Name the type of vessel that transports the water through the plant.

(1 mark)

Transport Processes II

Plants need to transport various things around inside themselves, and they have tubes for doing this.

Phloem and *xylem* vessels transport *different* things

1) Flowering plants have two separate sets of tubes for transporting stuff around the plant.
2) Both sets of tubes go to every part of the plant, but they are totally separate.
3) They usually run alongside each other.

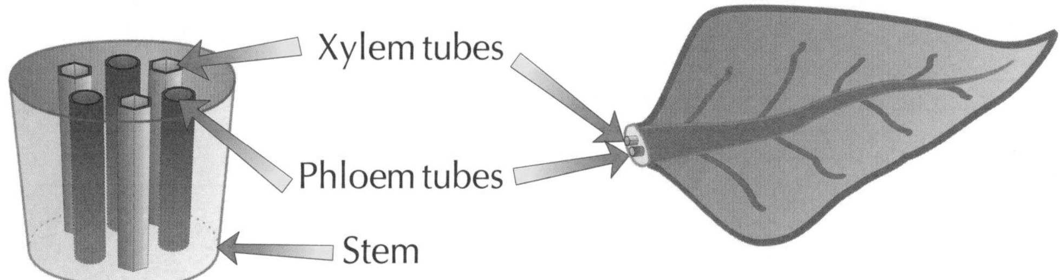

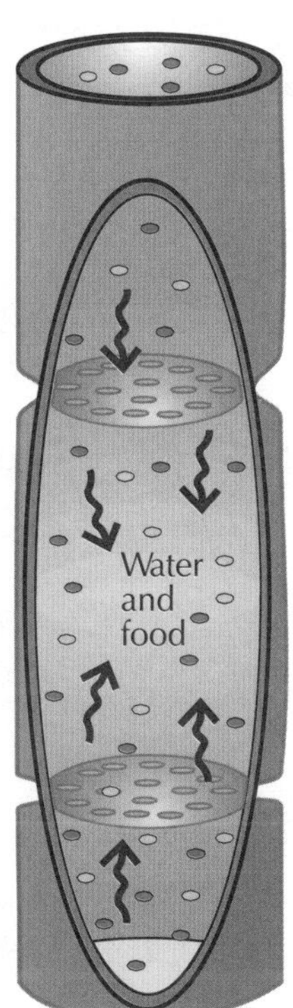

Phloem tubes transport *food:*

1) Made of living cells with perforated end-plates to allow stuff to flow through.
2) They transport food made in the leaves to all other parts of the plant, in both directions.
3) They carry sugars, fats, proteins etc. to growing regions in shoot tips and root tips and to/from storage organs in the roots.

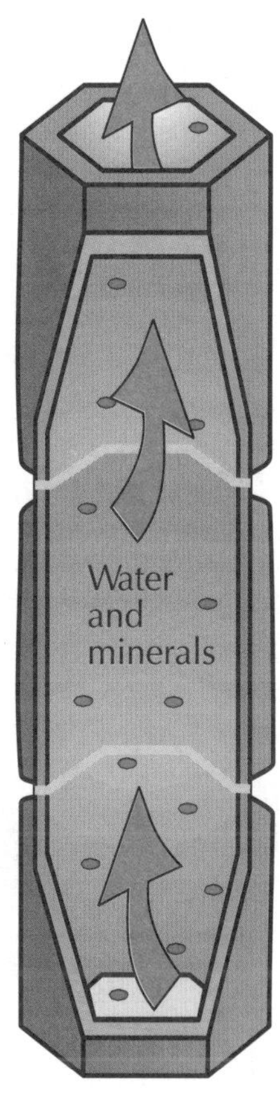

Xylem tubes take water *up:*

1) Made of dead cells joined end to end with no end walls between them.
2) The side walls are strong and stiff and contain lignin. This gives the plant support.
3) They carry water and minerals from the roots up to the leaves in the transpiration stream.

Phloem and *xylem* extend into the *roots*

1) The phloem carries substances down to the roots for growth or for storage and may later carry them back up again.
2) The xylem carries water and minerals, (which are taken in by the roots), up to the stem and into the leaves.

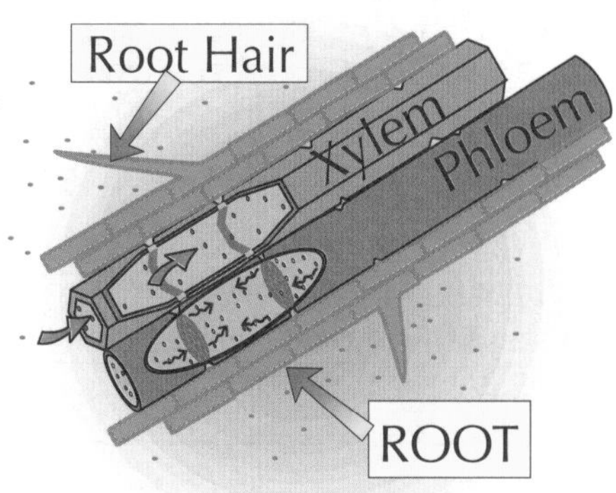

Transport Processes II

Osmosis is a special case of diffusion

OSMOSIS is the movement of water molecules across a partially permeable membrane from a region of HIGH WATER CONCENTRATION to a region of LOW WATER CONCENTRATION.

1) A partially permeable membrane is just one with really small holes in it. So small, in fact, that only water molecules can pass through them, and bigger molecules like glucose can't.
2) Visking tubing is a partially permeable membrane that you should learn the name of. It's also called dialysis tubing because it's used in kidney dialysis machines.
3) The water molecules actually pass both ways through the membrane in a two-way traffic.
4) But because there are more on one side than the other there's a steady net flow into the region with fewer water molecules, ie: into the stronger solution (of glucose).
5) This causes the glucose-rich region to fill up with water. The water acts like it's trying to dilute it, so as to "even up" the concentration either side of the membrane.

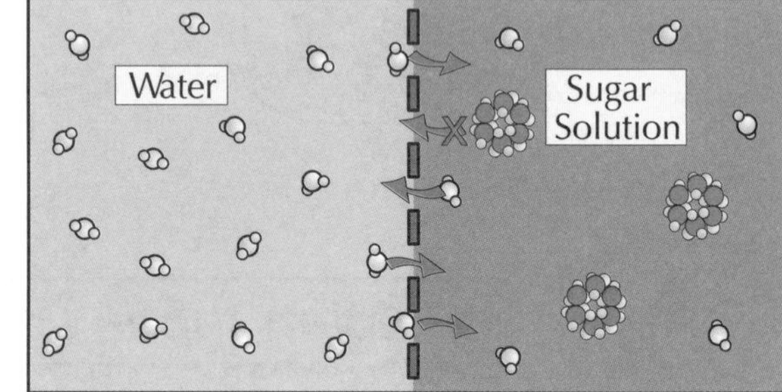

Net movement of water molecules

6) OSMOSIS makes plant cells swell up if they're surrounded by weak solution and they become TURGID. This is really useful for giving support to green plant tissue and for opening stomatal guard cells.
7) Animal cells don't have a cell wall and can easily burst if put into pure water because they take in so much water by osmosis.

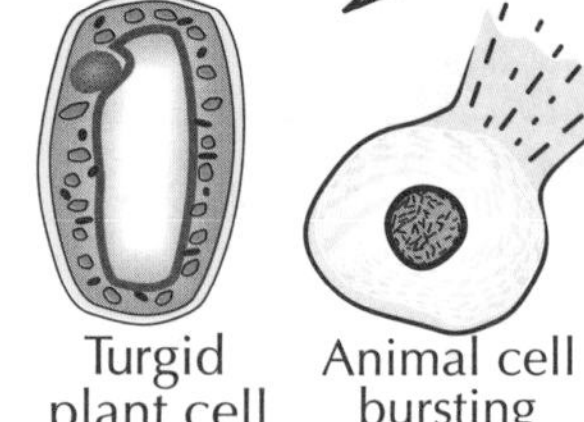

Turgid plant cell

Animal cell bursting

Two osmosis experiments — which often come up in exams

1) Potato Tubes

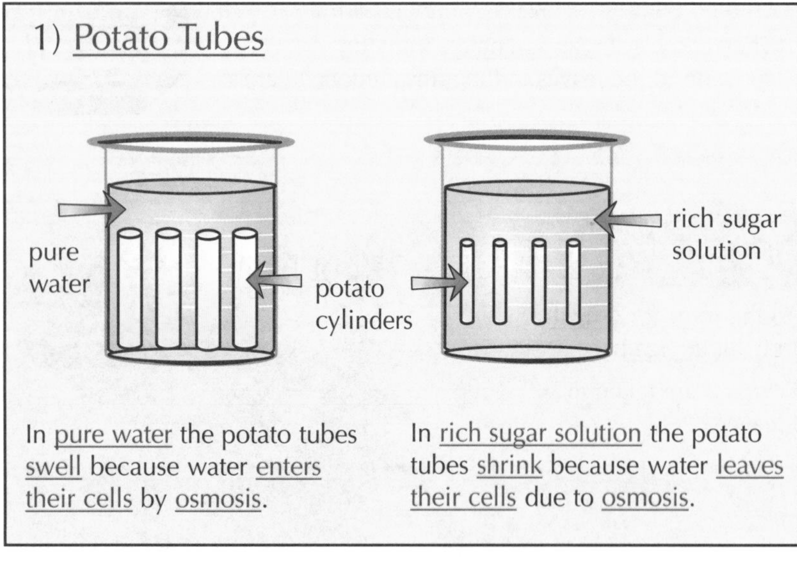

In pure water the potato tubes swell because water enters their cells by osmosis.

In rich sugar solution the potato tubes shrink because water leaves their cells due to osmosis.

2) Visking Tubing

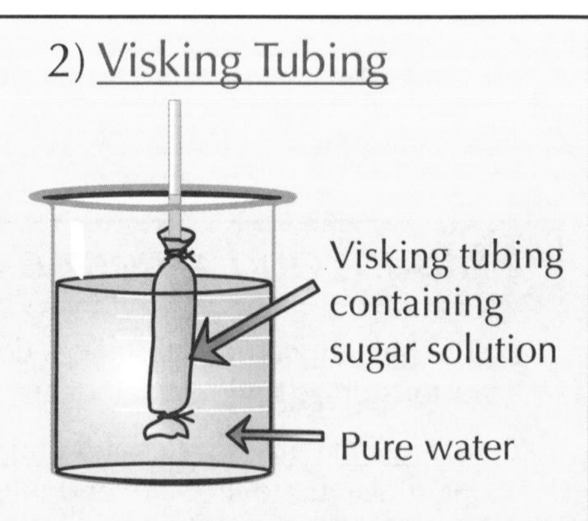

The water rises up the tube because water enters through the visking tubing by osmosis. The glucose molecules are too big to diffuse out into the water.

Transport Processes II

Sometimes substances need to be absorbed against the concentration gradient, i.e. from a lower to a higher concentration. This process is called ACTIVE UPTAKE.

Root hairs take in *minerals* using *active uptake*

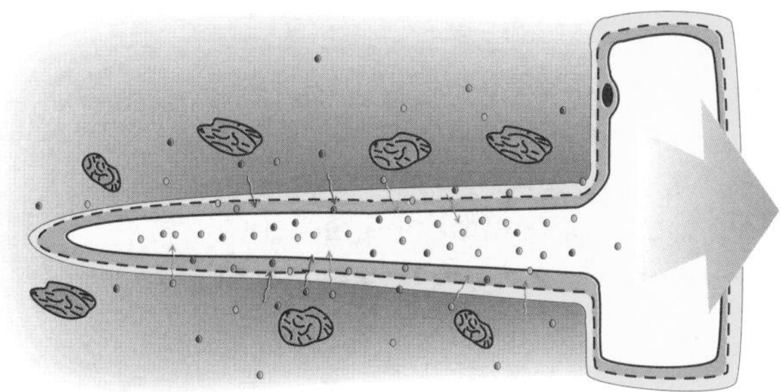

Root hair cell

1) The cells on plant roots grow into long "hairs" which stick out into the soil.
2) This gives the plant a big surface area for absorbing water and minerals from the soil.
3) The concentration of minerals is higher in the root hair cell than in the soil around it.
4) So normal diffusion doesn't explain how minerals are taken up into the root hair cell.
5) They should go the other way if they followed the rules of diffusion.
6) The answer is that a process called "active uptake" is responsible.
7) Active uptake allows the plant to absorb minerals against the concentration gradient. This is essential for its growth. But active uptake needs energy from respiration to make it work.

Exchange surfaces are adapted *for* effectiveness

Everything in plants and animals is specialised. This includes the cells, the tissues, organs, organ-systems and indeed whole organisms. Roots and leaves are specialised to exchange materials — learn them.

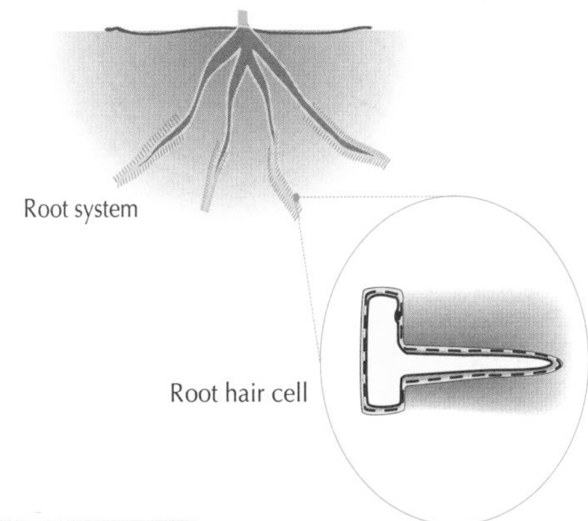

Roots

A large root network and the root hair cells help produce a large surface area at the bottom of the plant. This surface area is used to obtain water and minerals from the soil.

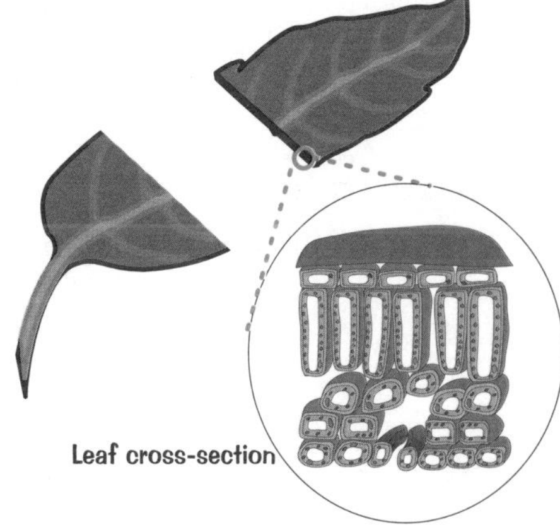

Leaves

A flattened shape and internal air spaces give leaves a huge surface area. You can see how the plant utilises this surface area for diffusion and photosynthesis on P.24 & 29.

Villi and *alveoli* in animals

Villi in the small intestine and alveoli in the lungs provide a large surface area, as discussed in Section One.

Make sure you know your phloem from your xylem

There are important differences between xylem and phloem tubes — make sure you learn all the details. Osmosis can be very confusing too. In normal diffusion, glucose molecules move, but with small enough holes they can't. That's when only water moves through the membrane, and then it's called osmosis. And don't forget about active uptake and how plants are adapted for it. Lots of details — you need to learn them all.

Warm-Up and Exam Question

You could skim through this page in a few minutes, but there's no point unless you check over any bits you don't know and make sure you understand everything. It's not quick but it's the only way.

Warm-up Questions

1) What do phloem tubes carry?
2) What type of tubes carry water and minerals?
3) What is meant by a 'partially permeable membrane'?
4) Give a definition of osmosis.
5) What process allows molecules to be taken up against their concentration gradient?

Exam Question

Exam questions don't vary that wildly — the basic format is usually the same.
So spend a bit of time learning how to answer this one.
The answers are in the back, so you can check where you lost marks and read up on that bit.

1 An experiment was set up as shown below. The level of the solution in the glass tube was then measured every minute. The results are shown in the graph below.

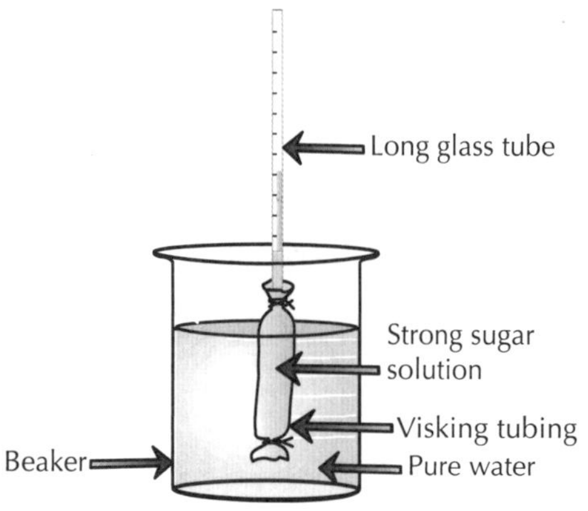

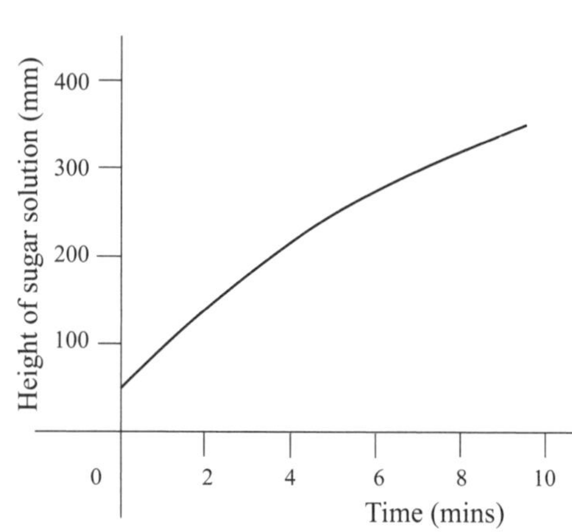

a) Why did the solution rise in the glass tube?

(2 marks)

b) What was the level of the solution at 5 minutes?

(1 mark)

c) How much longer did it take for the solution to reach its maximum height in the glass tube (350mm)?

(1 mark)

Plant Hormones

Auxins are plant *growth hormones*

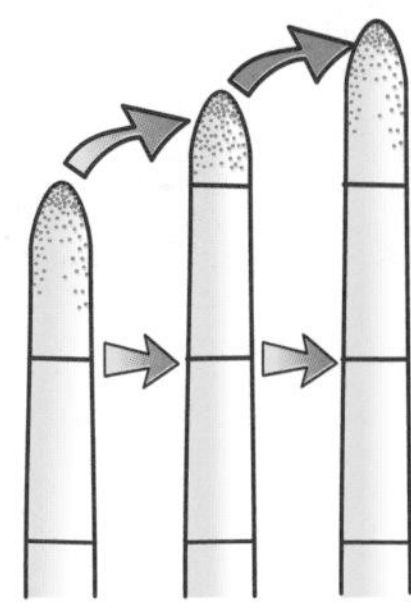

1) Auxins are hormones which control growth at the tips of shoots and roots.
2) Auxin is produced in the tips and diffuses backwards to stimulate the cell elongation process which occurs in the cells just behind the tips.
3) If the tip of a shoot is removed, no auxin will be available and the shoot may stop growing.

Auxins change the *direction* of root and shoot growth

You'll note below that extra auxin promotes growth in the shoot but actually inhibits growth in the root — but also note that this produces the desired result in both cases.

1) *Shoots* bend *towards the light*

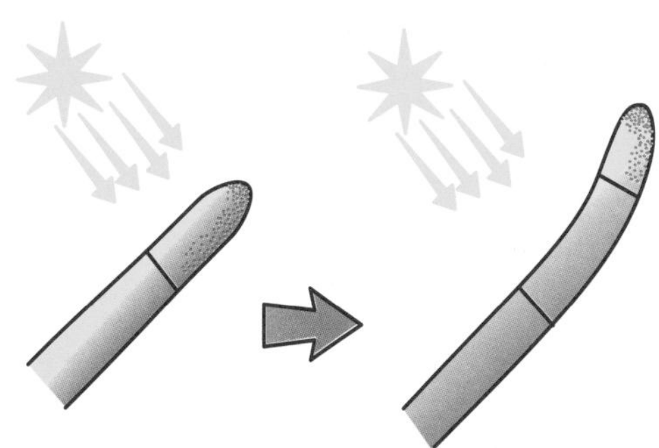

1) When a shoot tip is exposed to light, it provides more auxin on the side that is in the shade than the side which is in the light.
2) This causes the shoot to grow faster on the shaded side and it bends towards the light.

2) *Shoots* bend *away from gravity*

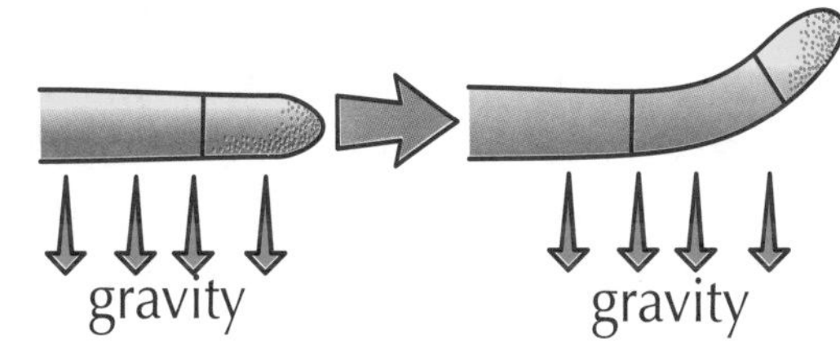

1) When a shoot finds itself growing sideways, gravity produces an unequal distribution of auxin in the tip, with more auxin on the lower side.
2) This causes the lower side to grow faster, thus bending the shoot upwards.

3) *Roots* bend *towards gravity*

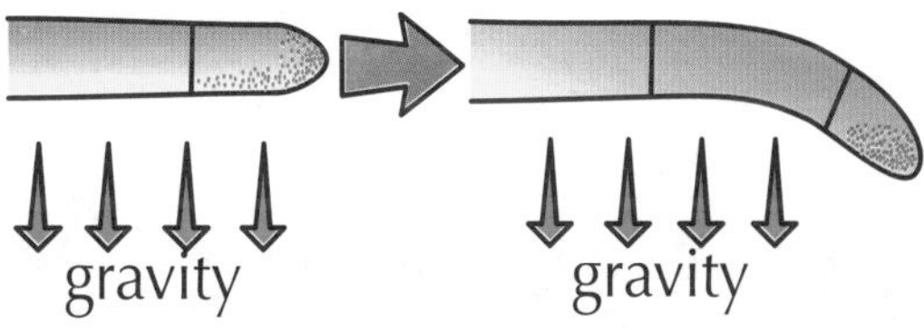

1) A root growing sideways will experience the same redistribution of auxin to the lower side.
2) But in a root the extra auxin actually inhibits growth, causing it to bend downwards instead.

4) *Roots* bend *towards moisture*

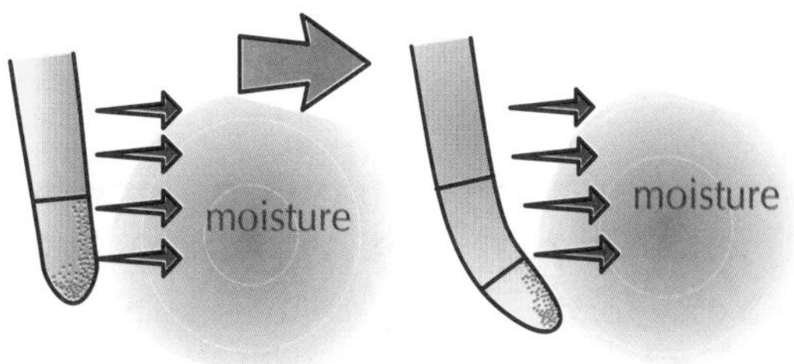

1) An uneven degree of moisture either side of a root will cause more auxin to appear on the side with more moisture.
2) This inhibits growth on that side, causing the root to grow in that direction, towards the moisture.

Plant Hormones

Plant hormones have a lot of uses in the food growing business.

1) Controlling the **ripening of fruit**

1) The ripening of fruits can be controlled either while they are still on the plant, or during transport to the shops.
2) This allows the fruit to be picked while it's still unripe (and therefore firmer and less easily damaged).
3) It can then be sprayed with ripening hormone and it will ripen on the way to the supermarket to be perfect just as it reaches the shelves.

2) Growing from **cuttings** with **rooting compound**

1) A cutting is part of a plant that has been cut off it, like the end of a branch with a few leaves on it.
2) Normally, if you stick cuttings in the soil they won't grow, but if you add rooting compound, which is a plant growth hormone, they will produce roots rapidly and start growing as new plants.
3) This enables growers to produce lots of clones (exact copies) of a really good plant very quickly.

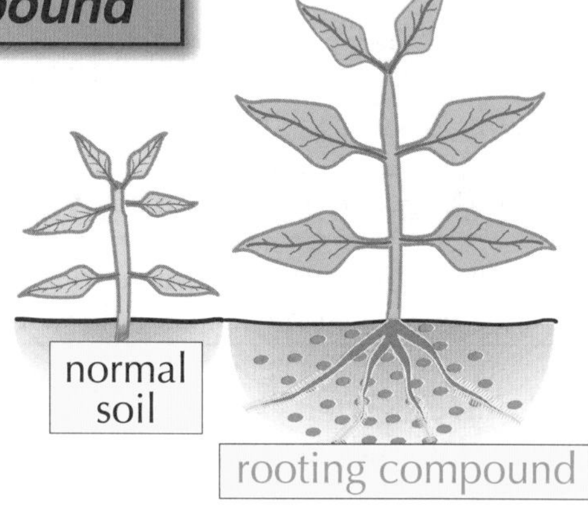

3) **Killing weeds**

1) Most weeds growing in fields of crops or in a lawn are broad-leaved, in contrast to grass which has very narrow leaves.
2) Selective weedkillers have been developed from plant growth hormones which only affects the broad-leaved plants.
3) They totally disrupt their normal growth patterns, which soon kills them, whilst leaving the grass untouched.

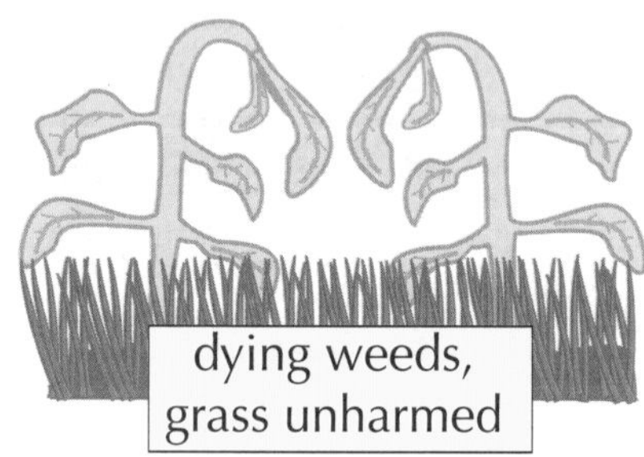

4) Producing **seedless fruit**

You can use hormones to produce seedless satsumas and seedless grapes which are more convenient for consumers than those 'natural' ones full of pips.

There's not too much to learn about plant hormones

An easy couple of pages — just three points on auxins, together with a diagram, and then four ways that shoots and roots change direction, with a diagram for each. Then four uses of plant hormones. You just have to learn it. Then close the book and write down the main points from memory. Then try again, and again...

Warm-Up and Exam Question

Warm-up Questions

1) What are auxins?
2) Explain how a shoot tip bends towards the light.
3) What are selective weedkillers made from?
4) Why is it an advantage to the fruit seller to pick fruit when they are still unripe?
5) Why is rooting compound so useful to commercial plant growers?

Exam Question

There's no better preparation for exam questions than doing... err... practice exam questions. Hang on, what's this I see...

1 (a) Complete the following table to indicate whether roots and shoots grow towards, or away from, light and gravity.

	LIGHT	GRAVITY
SHOOT		
ROOT		

(2 marks)

(b) What is the name of the plant growth hormone that brings about the above responses?

(1 mark)

(c) A clinostat can be used to investigate the effect of gravity on root and shoot growth. A class set up an experiment as in the diagram below.

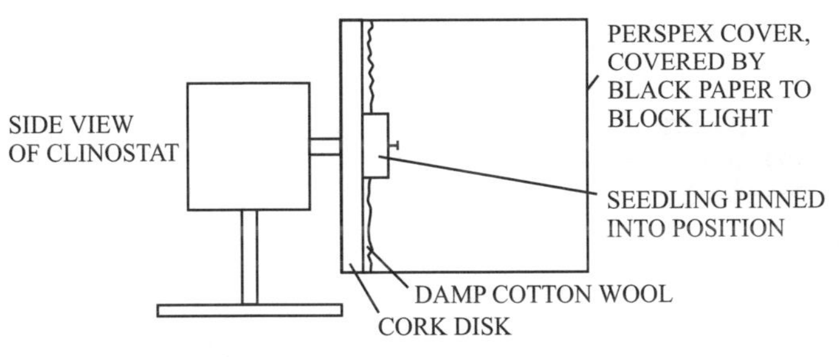

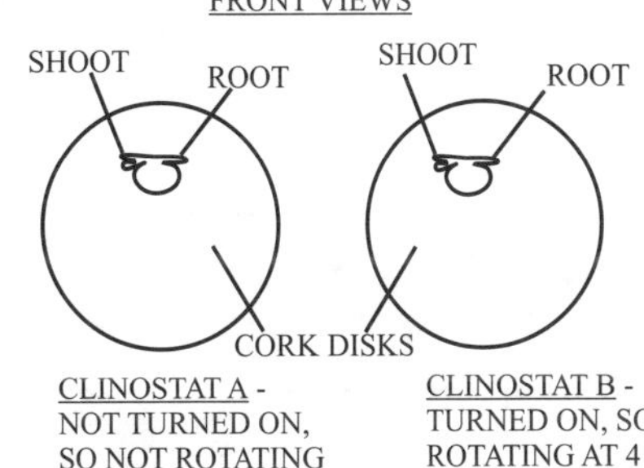

(i) Draw what you would expect the seedling in Clinostat B to look like after 3 days.

(2 marks)

(ii) Explain why you think it would look like this.

(2 marks)

(iii) How might the seedling in Clinostat A differ from that in B after 3 days?

(2 marks)

(d) Give two uses of plant hormones by man.

(2 marks)

The Nervous System

Learn the eye with all its labels:

1) The tough outer sclera has a transparent region at the front called the cornea.
2) The pupil is the hole in the middle of the iris, which the light goes through.
3) The size of the pupil is controlled by the muscular iris.
4) The lens is held in position by suspensory ligaments and ciliary muscles.
5) The retina is the light sensitive part and is covered in receptor cells. The cornea and lens produce an image on the retina.
6) Receptor cells send impulses to the brain along neurons in the optic nerve.

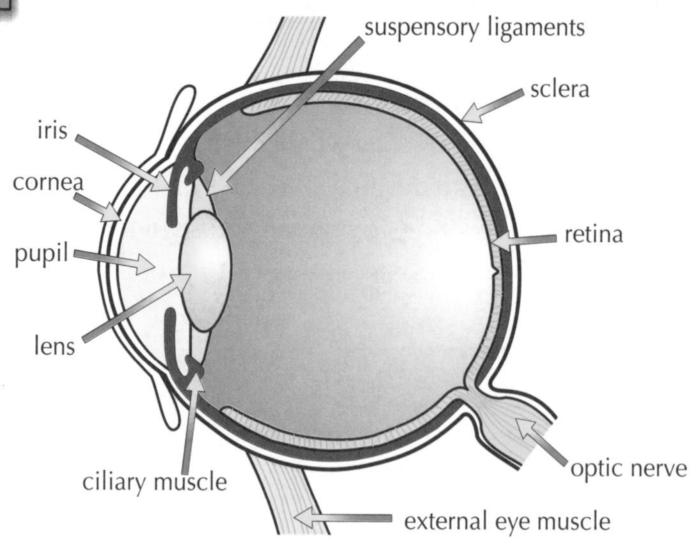

Adjusting for light and dark — the iris

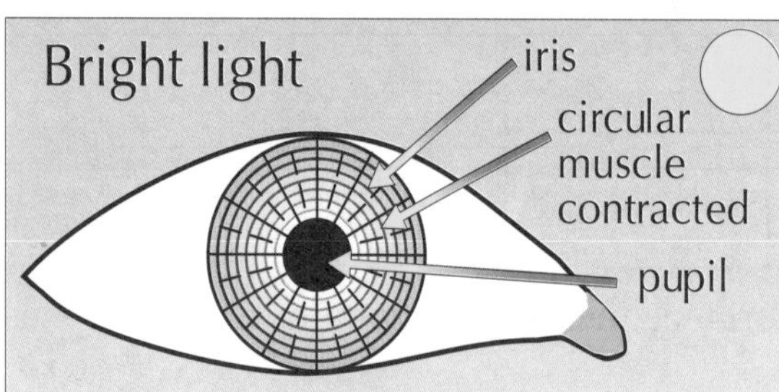

1) The circular muscles contract.
2) The iris closes up, the pupil gets smaller.
3) Less light gets into the eye.

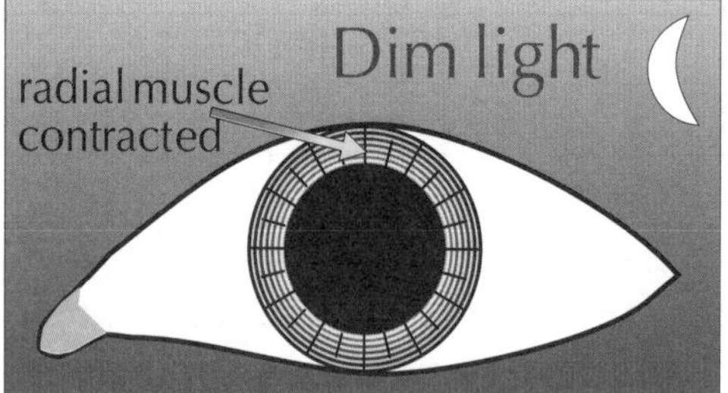

1) The radial muscles contract.
2) The iris opens out, the pupil gets bigger.
3) This lets more light into the eye.

Focusing on near and distant objects

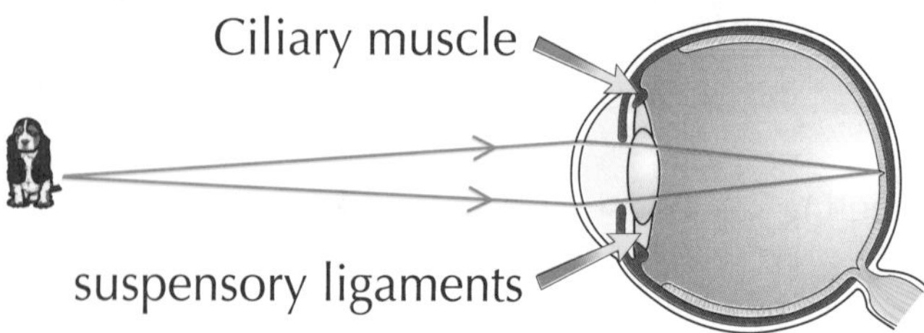

To look at DISTANT objects:

1) The ciliary muscles relax, which allows the suspensory ligaments to pull tight.
2) This makes the lens go thin.

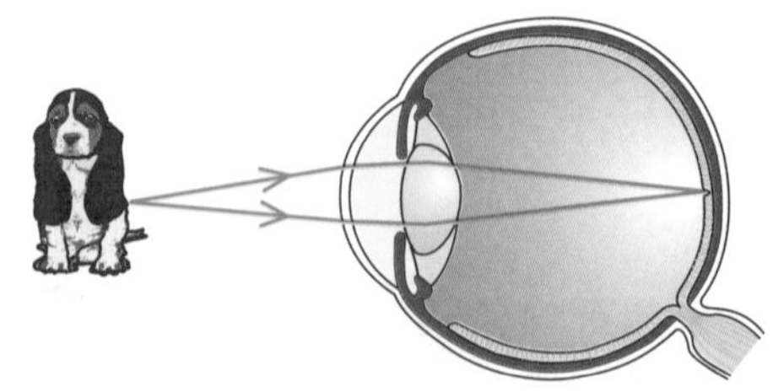

To look at NEAR objects:

1) The ciliary muscles contract which slackens the suspensory ligaments.
2) The lens becomes fat.

The Nervous System

Sense organs and receptors

The five sense organs are:

eyes   ears   nose   tongue   skin

These five different sense organs all contain different receptors.
Receptors are groups of cells which are sensitive to a stimulus such as light or heat.

SENSE ORGANS AND RECEPTORS

Don't get them mixed up:
The eye is a sense organ — it contains light-receptors.
The ear is a sense organ — it contains sound-receptors.

Receptors are cells which change energy (eg: light energy) into electrical impulses.

The Five Sense Organs and the stimuli that each one is sensitive to:

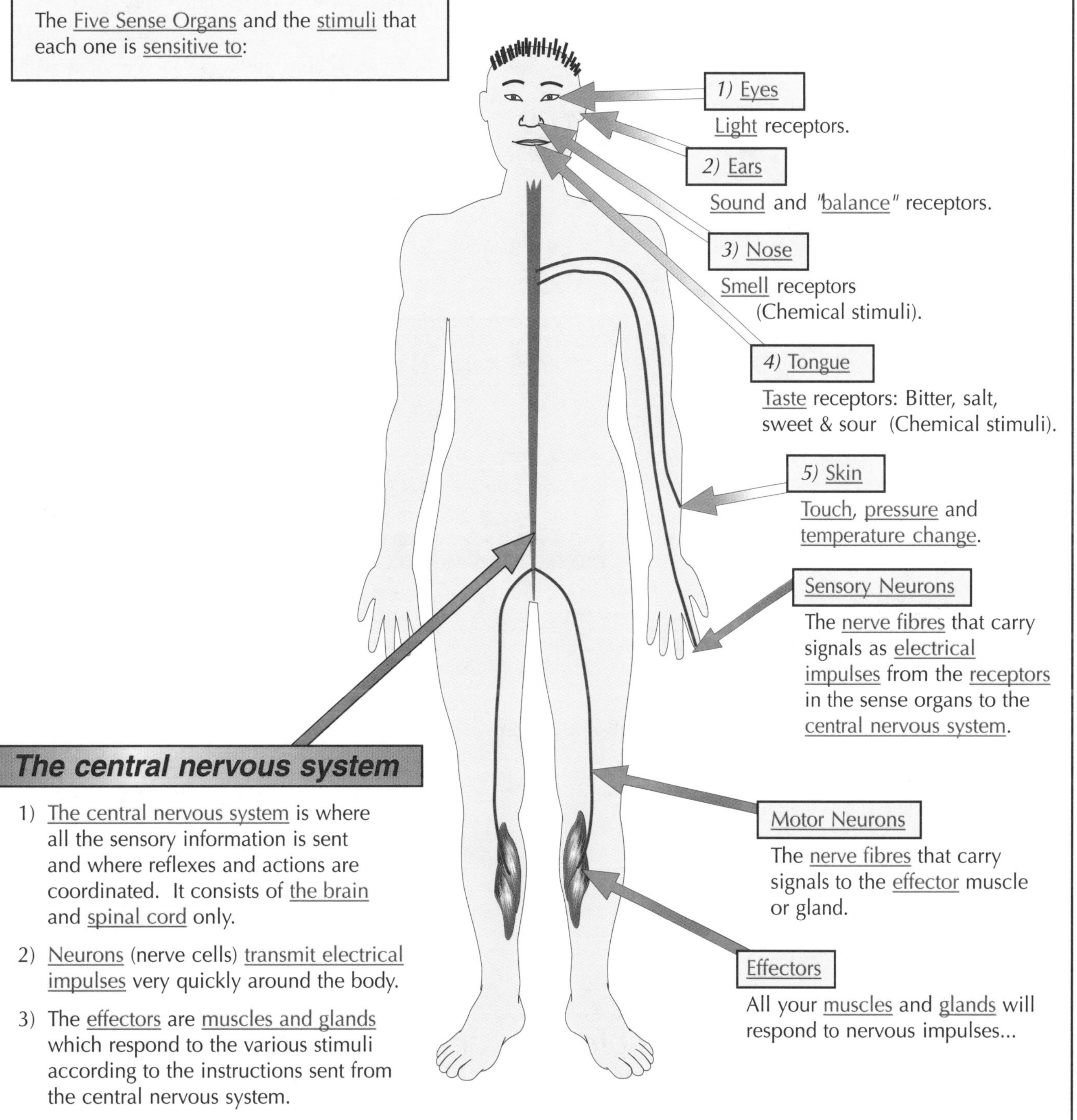

1) Eyes
Light receptors.
2) Ears
Sound and "balance" receptors.
3) Nose
Smell receptors (Chemical stimuli).
4) Tongue
Taste receptors: Bitter, salt, sweet & sour (Chemical stimuli).
5) Skin
Touch, pressure and temperature change.
Sensory Neurons
The nerve fibres that carry signals as electrical impulses from the receptors in the sense organs to the central nervous system.
Motor Neurons
The nerve fibres that carry signals to the effector muscle or gland.
Effectors
All your muscles and glands will respond to nervous impulses...

The central nervous system

1) The central nervous system is where all the sensory information is sent and where reflexes and actions are coordinated. It consists of the brain and spinal cord only.
2) Neurons (nerve cells) transmit electrical impulses very quickly around the body.
3) The effectors are muscles and glands which respond to the various stimuli according to the instructions sent from the central nervous system.

The Nervous System

The three types of neuron are all much the same

The THREE TYPES of NEURON are:

1) SENSORY neuron
2) MOTOR neuron
3) RELAY neuron (or CONNECTOR neuron).

(They're all *pretty much the same*, they're just *connected to different things*, that's all.)

The reflex arc allows very quick responses

A Typical Reflex Arc

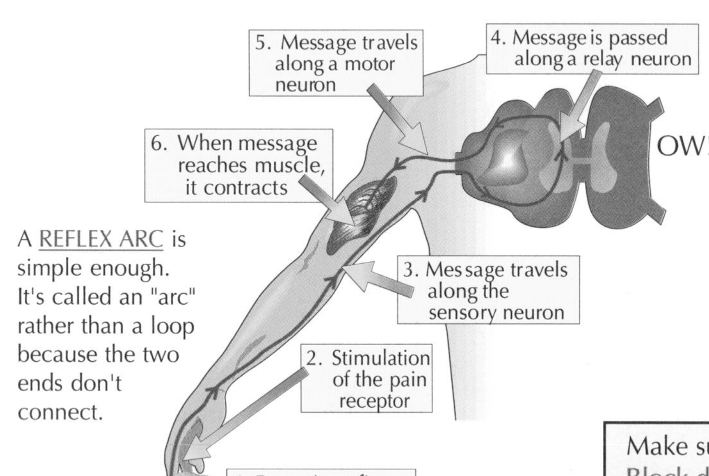
5. Message travels along a motor neuron
4. Message is passed along a relay neuron
OW!
6. When message reaches muscle, it contracts
3. Message travels along the sensory neuron
2. Stimulation of the pain receptor
1. Bee stings finger

A REFLEX ARC is simple enough. It's called an "arc" rather than a loop because the two ends don't connect.

1) The nervous system allows very quick responses because it uses electrical impulses.
2) Reflex actions are automatic (ie: done without thinking) so they are even quicker.
3) Reflex actions save your body from injury, eg: pulling your hand off a hot object for you.
4) A muscle responds by contracting, a gland responds by secreting.

Make sure you also learn the Block diagram of a Reflex Arc:

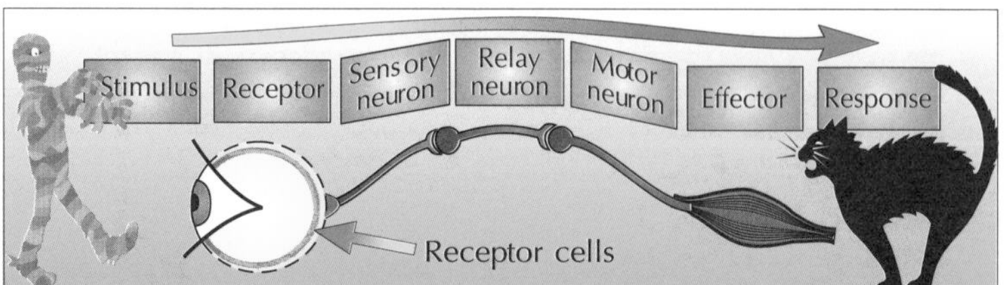
Stimulus
Receptor
Sensory neuron
Relay neuron
Motor neuron
Effector
Response
Receptor cells

Synapses use chemicals

1) The connection between two neurons is called a synapse.
2) The nerve signal is transferred by chemicals which diffuse across the gap.
3) These chemicals then set off a new electrical signal in the next neuron.

A Synapse

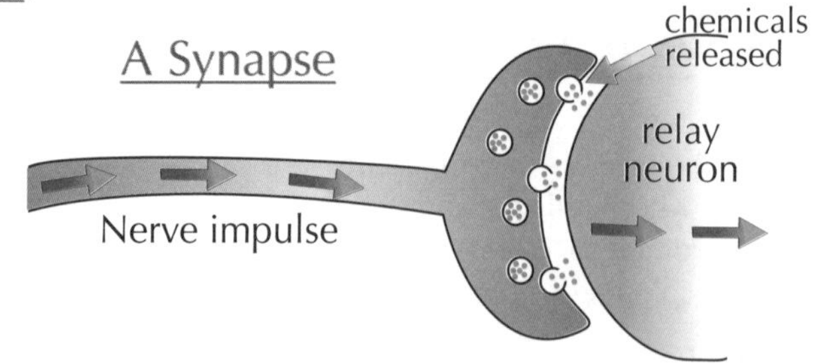
chemicals released
relay neuron
Nerve impulse

Nervous System = 5 sense organs + neurons + brain + spinal cord

All this stuff on the nervous system basically just boils down to a few diagrams and a few notes on each one. Start by learning the diagrams then keep working at it until you can draw the diagram and write out all the details without looking at the book.

Warm-Up and Exam Questions

Receptors and neurons and reflexes and... It's enough to set your head spinning. But you've got to get these basic facts clear in your head — these warm-up questions should show you how you're getting on.

Warm-up Questions

1) What do receptors do?
2) List the five sense organs.
3) Describe how the eye reacts to bright light.
4) List the three types of neuron.
5) What is a reflex action?

Exam Questions

1 The diagram opposite shows a reflex arc.

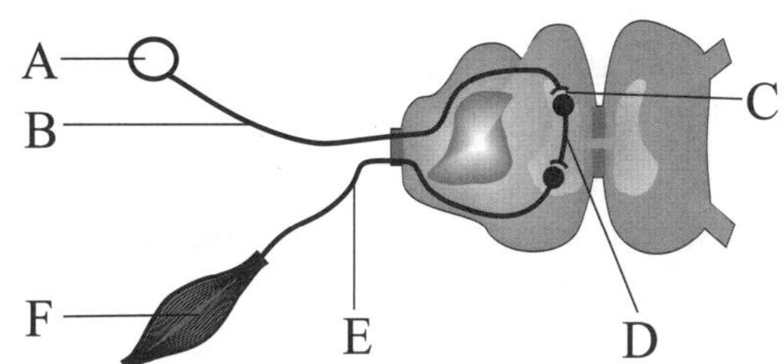

a) Name the parts A – F on the diagram.
(6 marks)

b) Explain the following terms:

Stimulus Receptor Effector
(3 marks)

c) Copy and complete the table on the right to show what type of receptors are found in each of the five sense organs. The first has been done for you.

Sense Organ	Receptor(s)
Eyes	Light
Ears	.... and ....
Nose	....
Tongue	....
Skin	.... and ....

(6 marks)

2 The diagram below shows the junction of two neurons.

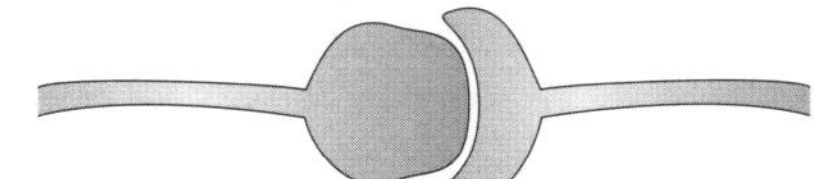

a) What is the name given to the junction of two neurons?
(1 mark)

b) Draw an arrow on the diagram to show the direction of the nerve impulses.
(1 mark)

c) Describe how the nerve impulses travel across this junction.
(2 marks)

d) Copy and complete the box diagram of a reflex arc below.

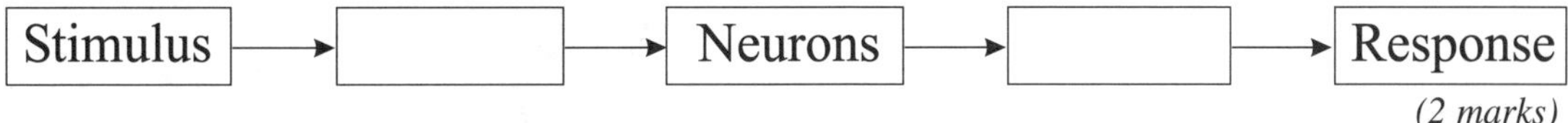

(2 marks)

e) Give one reason why reflex actions are important to the body.
(1 mark)

Homeostasis

Homeostasis covers all the functions of your body which try to maintain a "constant internal environment".

Learn the definition:

HOMEOSTASIS — the maintenance of a CONSTANT INTERNAL ENVIRONMENT

There are six different bodily levels that need to be controlled:

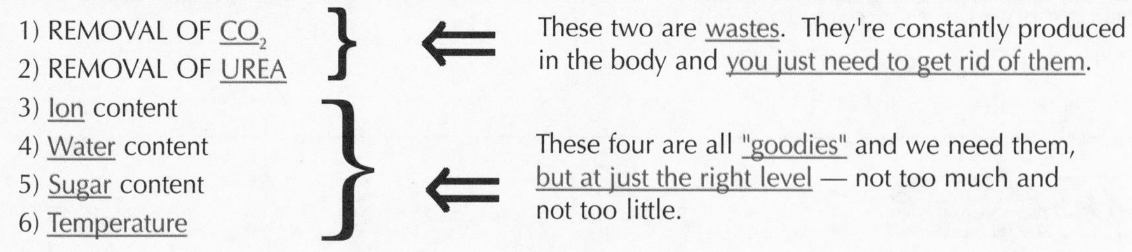

1) REMOVAL OF CO_2
2) REMOVAL OF UREA

⇐ These two are wastes. They're constantly produced in the body and you just need to get rid of them.

3) Ion content
4) Water content
5) Sugar content
6) Temperature

⇐ These four are all "goodies" and we need them, but at just the right level — not too much and not too little.

All your body's cells are bathed in tissue fluid, which is just blood plasma which has leaked out of the capillaries (on purpose).

To keep all your cells working properly, this fluid must be just right — in other words, the six things above must be kept at the right level — not too high, and not too low.

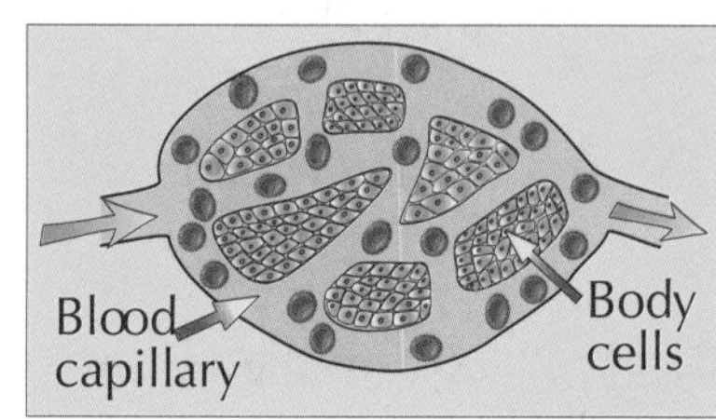

*Learn the **organs** involved in **homeostasis**:*

The Brain

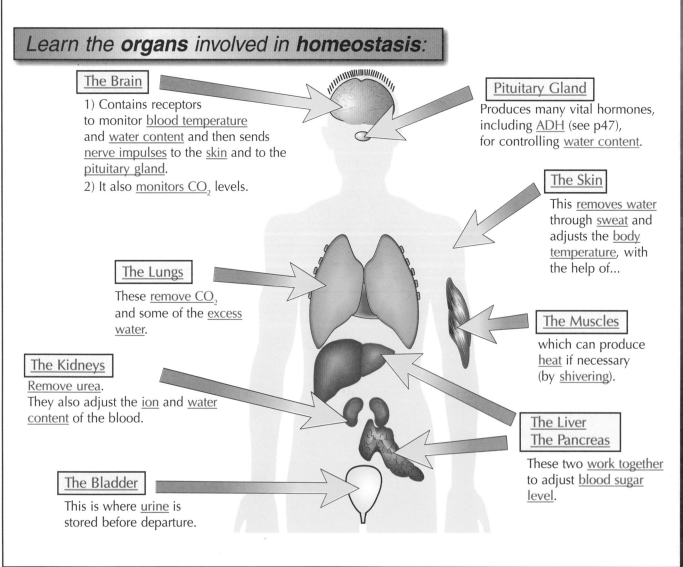

1) Contains receptors to monitor blood temperature and water content and then sends nerve impulses to the skin and to the pituitary gland.
2) It also monitors CO_2 levels.

Pituitary Gland

Produces many vital hormones, including ADH (see p47), for controlling water content.

The Skin

This removes water through sweat and adjusts the body temperature, with the help of...

The Lungs

These remove CO_2 and some of the excess water.

The Muscles

which can produce heat if necessary (by shivering).

The Kidneys

Remove urea.
They also adjust the ion and water content of the blood.

The Liver
The Pancreas

These two work together to adjust blood sugar level.

The Bladder

This is where urine is stored before departure.

Homeostasis

Controlling our **body temperature**

All enzymes work best at a certain temperature. The enzymes within the human body work best at about 37°C.

When you're too cold your body shivers (increasing your metabolism) to produce heat.

When you're too hot you produce sweat which cools you down. You then replenish this loss by eating or drinking.

1) There is a thermoregulatory centre in the brain which acts as your own personal thermostat.
2) It contains receptors that are sensitive to the blood temperature in the brain.
3) The thermoregulatory centre also receives impulses from the skin.
4) These impulses provide information about skin temperature.

The skin has **three tricks** for altering body **temperature**

1) The skin is very important for keeping the human body at 37°C.
2) The thermoregulatory centre senses changes and sends nervous impulses to the skin.
3) Sweating, blood supply and what the hairs are doing help control body temperature:

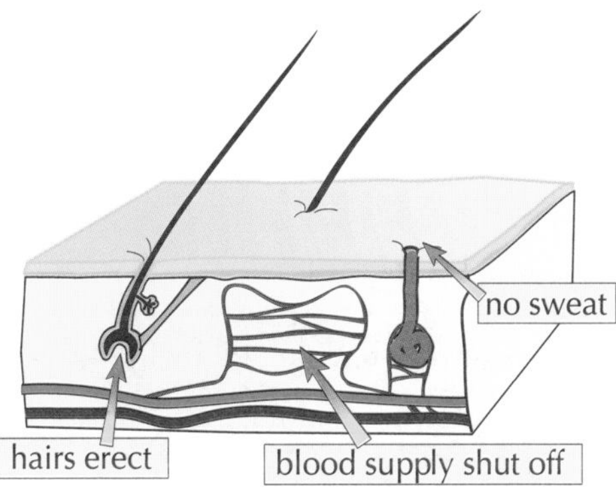

*When you're **too cold:***

1) Hairs stand on end to keep you warm.
2) No sweat is produced.
3) The blood supply to the skin closes off.

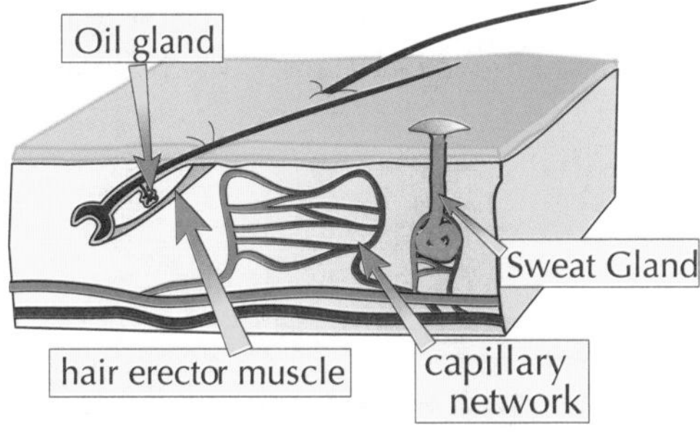

*When you're **too hot:***

1) Hairs lie flat.
2) Sweat is produced which evaporates to cool you down.
3) The blood supply to the skin opens up to release body heat.

Homeostasis

Kidneys basically act as filters to "clean the blood"

The kidneys perform three main roles:

1) *Removal of urea* from the blood.

2) *Adjustment of ions* in the blood.

3) *Adjustment of water content* of the blood.

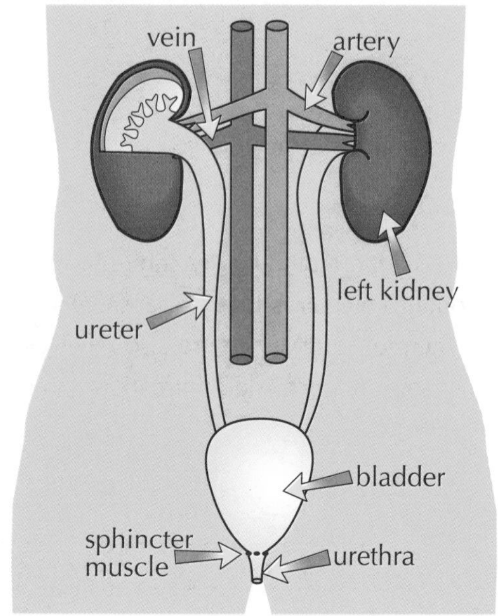

1) Removal of urea

1) Urea is produced in the liver.

2) Proteins can't be stored by the body so excess amino acids are broken down by the liver into fats and carbohydrates.

3) The waste product is urea which is passed into the blood to be filtered out by the kidneys. Urea is also lost partly in sweat. Urea is poisonous.

2) Adjustment of ion content

1) Ions, such as sodium ions, are taken into the body in food, and then absorbed into the blood.

2) Excess ions are removed by the kidneys. For example, a salty meal will contain far too much salt and the kidneys will remove the excess salt ions from the blood.

3) Some ions are also lost in sweat (which tastes salty, you'll have noticed).

4) But the important thing to remember is that the balance is always maintained by the kidneys.

3) Adjustment of water content

Water is taken in to the body as food and drink and is lost from the body in three ways:
1) in urine 2) in sweat 3) in breath

There's a need for the body to constantly balance the water coming in against the water going out. The amount lost in the breath is fairly constant, which means the water balance is between:

1) Liquids consumed

2) Amount sweated out

3) Amount dumped by the kidneys into the urine.

On a cold day, if you don't sweat, you'll produce more urine which will be pale and dilute.
On a hot day, you sweat a lot, your urine will be dark-coloured, concentrated and little of it.
The water lost when it is hot has to be taken in as food and drink to restore the balance.

Homeostasis

Three stages of **filtration** in the **kidneys**

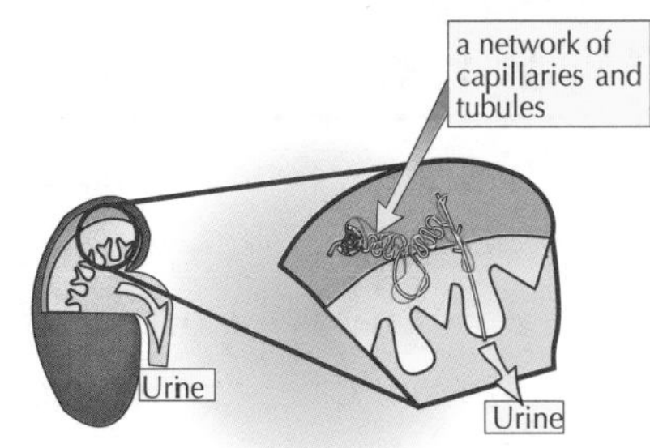
a network of capillaries and tubules
Urine
Urine

1) Ultrafiltration:

a) A high pressure is built up which squeezes water, urea, ions and glucose out of the blood and into the kidney tubule.
b) However, big molecules like proteins are not squeezed out. They stay in the blood.

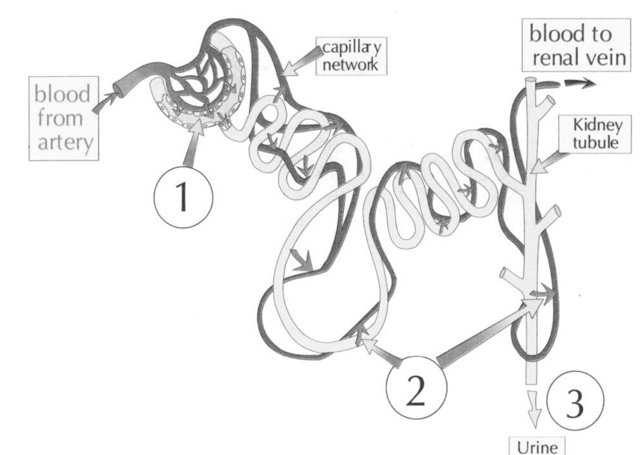
blood from artery
capillary network
blood to renal vein
Kidney tubule
1
2
3
Urine

2) Reabsorption:

Useful substances are reabsorbed:
a) All the sugar is reabsorbed. This involves the process of active uptake.
b) Sufficient ions are reabsorbed. Excess ions are not. Active uptake is needed.
c) Sufficient water is reabsorbed, according to the level of the hormone ADH (see below).

3) Release of wastes:

a) All urea and excess ions and water are not reabsorbed.
b) These continue out of the kidney, into the ureter and down to the bladder as urine.

ADH (Anti Diuretic Hormone)* — water regulation

The brain monitors the water content of the blood and instructs the pituitary gland to release ADH into the blood accordingly, as shown below:

Too little water in blood

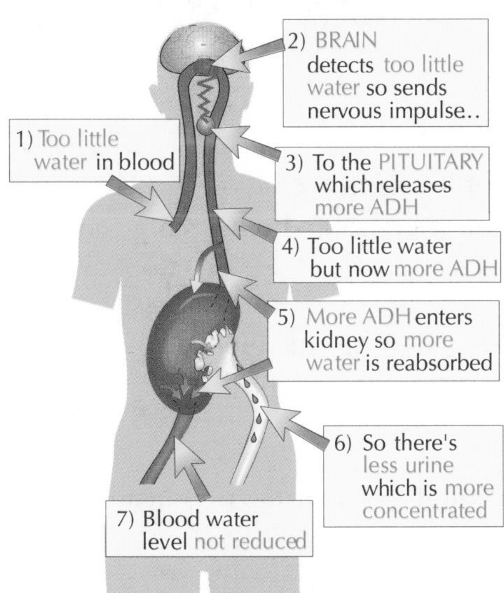
1) Too little water in blood
2) BRAIN detects too little water so sends nervous impulse..
3) To the PITUITARY which releases more ADH
4) Too little water but now more ADH
5) More ADH enters kidney so more water is reabsorbed
6) So there's less urine which is more concentrated
7) Blood water level not reduced

Too much water in blood

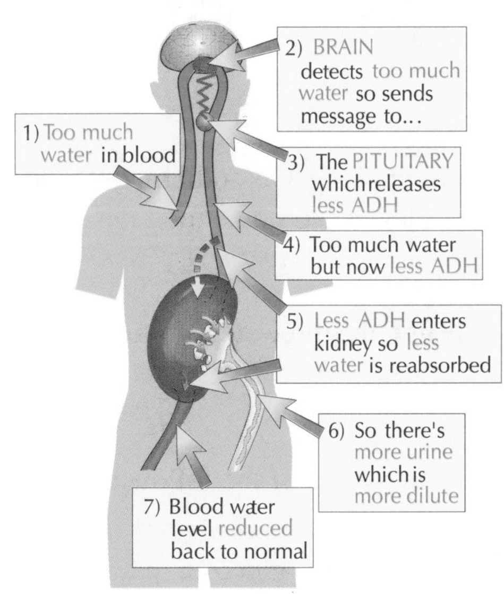
1) Too much water in blood
2) BRAIN detects too much water so sends message to...
3) The PITUITARY which releases less ADH
4) Too much water but now less ADH
5) Less ADH enters kidney so less water is reabsorbed
6) So there's more urine which is more dilute
7) Blood water level reduced back to normal

**Diuretic* just means, "causing an increase in the flow of urine" so *anti*-diuretic means acting to stop you urinating.

Homeostasis is what keeps everything as it should be

There's some tricky stuff in this section, that's for sure. ADH is pretty difficult to understand, but stick at it. Practise redrawing the diagrams with all the numbered notes on, and eventually it'll start to sink in.

Warm-Up and Exam Questions

Warm-up Questions

1) What is homeostasis?
2) Which organ removes CO_2 from the blood?
3) What is the other main waste product removed from the blood?
4) Which organ removes it?
5) Name the two organs that work together to control the level of sugar in the blood.
6) Which hormone is released in order to regulate the reabsorption of water into the blood from nephrons?

Exam Questions

1 It is important to control the level of water in the blood.
Paul is backpacking in the Australian outback and has run out of water.

a) A part of Paul's brain will detect that he is in danger of becoming dehydrated. Which gland will release a hormone to regulate the level of water in his blood?

(1 mark)

b) Explain how and where this regulation will be achieved.

(3 marks)

c) When Paul reaches his hostel and drinks a large quantity of water, how will his body now react to having excess water in the blood?

(3 marks)

d) Name two waste substances that are excreted in the urine along with excess water.

(2 marks)

2 Mineral ions, such as sodium, must be kept at the right levels in the blood.
Sodium levels would be too high if the person ate a lot of crisps and other salty foods.

a) Name the three steps involved in kidney nephrons 'filtering' the blood.

(3 marks)

b) Which three of the following substances will be found in the urine of a healthy person?

water; ions; glucose; proteins; urea

(3 marks)

Hormones and Drugs

Hormones are chemical messengers sent in the blood

1) Hormones are chemicals released directly into the blood.
2) They are carried in the blood to other parts of the body.
3) They are produced in various glands (endocrine glands) as shown on the diagram.
4) They travel all over the body but only affect particular cells in particular places.
5) They travel at "the speed of blood".
6) They have long-lasting effects.
7) They control things that need constant adjustment.

Learn this definition:
HORMONES are chemical messengers which travel in the blood to activate target cells.

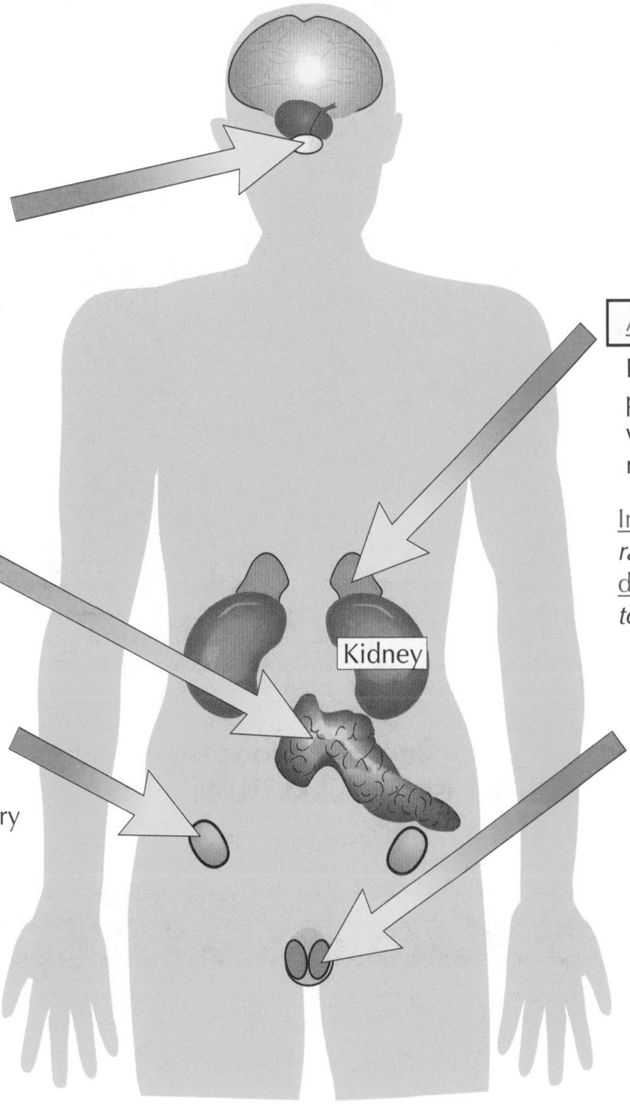

The Pituitary Gland

This produces many important hormones: LH, FSH and ADH. These tend to control other glands, as a rule.

Adrenal Gland

Produces adrenaline which prepares the body with the well known fight or flight reaction:

Increased *blood sugar, heart rate, breathing rate, and* diversion *of blood from skin to muscles.*

Pancreas

Produces insulin and glucagon for the control of blood sugar.

Kidney

Ovaries — females only

Produce oestrogen which promotes all female secondary sexual characteristics during puberty:
1) Extra hair in places.
2) Changes in body proportions.
3) Egg production.

Testes — males only

Produce testosterone which promotes all male secondary sexual characteristics at puberty:
1) Extra hair in places.
2) Changes in body proportions.
3) Sperm production.

Hormones and nerves do similar jobs, but there are important differences

Nerves:
1) Very fast message.
2) Act for a very short time.
3) Act on a very precise area.
4) Immediate reaction.

Hormones:
1) Slower message.
2) Act for a long time.
3) Act in a more general way.
4) Longer-term reaction.

Hormones and Drugs

Insulin and glucagon are hormones which control how much sugar there is in your blood. LEARN how:

Insulin and *glucagon* control *blood sugar* levels

1) Eating carbohydrate foods puts a lot of glucose into the blood from the gut.
2) Normal metabolism of cells removes glucose from the blood.
3) Vigorous exercise removes much more glucose from the blood.
4) Obviously, to keep the level of blood glucose controlled there has to be a way to add or remove glucose from the blood. This is achieved by two hormones: *insulin* and *glucagon* which are released by the pancreas.

Blood glucose level **too high** — insulin is **added**

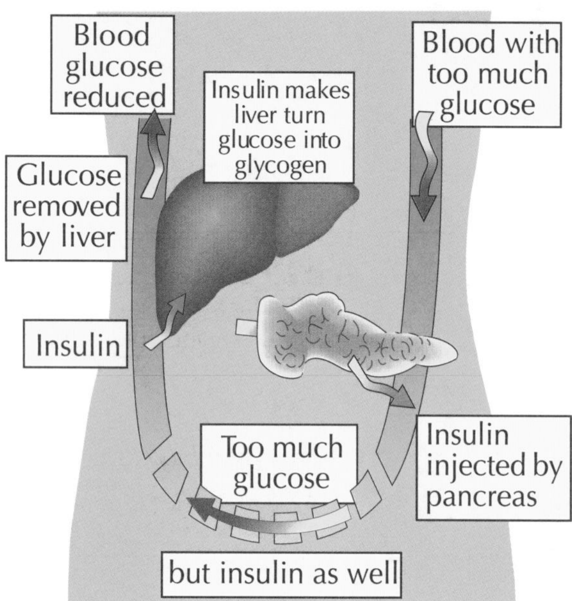

Blood glucose level **too low** — glucagon is **added**

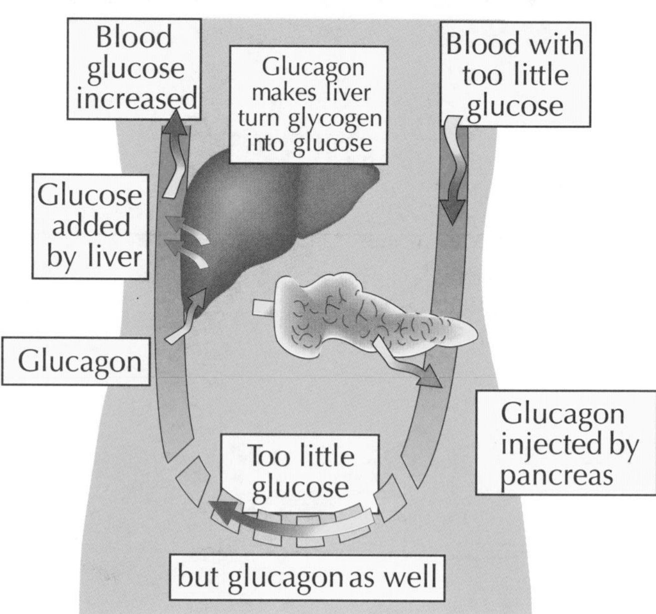

Remember, the addition of insulin reduces the blood sugar level and the addition of glucagon increases the blood sugar level.

Diabetes — the *pancreas* stops making *enough insulin*

1) Diabetes is a disease in which the pancreas doesn't produce enough insulin.

2) The result is that a person's blood sugar can rise to a level that can kill them.

3) The problem can be controlled in two ways:

   A) Avoiding foods rich in carbohydrate (which turns to glucose when digested).
   It can also be helpful to take exercise after eating carbohydrates... ie: trying to use up the extra glucose by doing physical activity, but this isn't usually very practical.

   B) Injecting insulin into the blood before meals (especially if high in carbohydrates).
   This will make the liver remove the glucose from the blood as soon as it enters it from the gut, when the (carbohydrate-rich) food is being digested. This stops the level of glucose in the blood from getting too high and is a very effective treatment.

Hormones and Drugs

Solvents

1) Solvents are found in a variety of "household" items e.g. glues, paints, etc.
2) They are dangerous and have many damaging effects on your body and personality.
3) They cause hallucinations and adversely affect personality and behaviour.
4) They cause damage to the lungs, brain, liver and kidney.

Alcohol

1) The main effect of alcohol is to reduce the activity of the nervous system. The positive aspect of this is that it makes us feel less inhibited — alcohol in moderation can help people to socialise and relax with each other.
2) However, if alcohol is allowed to take over, it can wreck your life. And it does wreck a lot of people's lives.
3) Once alcohol starts to take over someone's life there are many harmful effects:
   a) Alcohol is basically poisonous. Too much alcohol will cause severe damage to the liver and the brain leading to liver disease and a noticeable drop in brain function.
   b) Too much alcohol impairs judgement which can cause accidents, and it can also severely affect the person's work and home life.
   c) Serious dependency on alcohol (addiction) will eventually lead to loss of job, loss of income and the start of a severe downward spiral.

Smoking tobacco

Smoking is no good to anyone except the cigarette companies. Once someone has started smoking there's no easy way back. For many people, it's a one way trip. Smokers are generally no happier than non-smokers, even when they're smoking. What may start off as something "different" to do, rapidly becomes something they have to do, just to feel OK. But non-smokers feel just as good without spending £20 or more each week and damaging their health at the same time.

Most people start smoking to fit in — they have an image in their head of how they want to appear and smoking seems the perfect fashion accessory. People don't understand how addictive it is. It might look cool at 16, but won't necessarily seem so good aged 20 with a new group of friends who don't smoke. But by then it's too late because it's an addiction.

And by age 60 it'll have cost over £40,000 (enough to buy a Ferrari). That's quite an expensive fashion accessory.

The Physical Effects of Tobacco on Your Body

Tobacco smoke does this inside your body:

1) It coats the inside of your lungs with tar so they become extremely inefficient.
2) It covers the cilia in tar, preventing them from getting bacteria out of your lungs.
3) It causes disease of the heart and blood vessels, leading to heart attacks and strokes.
4) It causes lung cancer. A few years back, people didn't know this for sure but, out of every ten lung cancer patients, nine of them smoke. It's now widely accepted that there's a connection.
5) It causes severe loss of lung function leading to diseases like emphysema and bronchitis, in which the inside of the lungs is severely damaged. People with severe bronchitis can't manage even a brisk walk, because their lungs can't get enough oxygen into the blood. It eventually kills over 20,000 people in Britain every year.
6) Carbon monoxide in tobacco smoke stops haemoglobin carrying as much oxygen. In pregnant women this deprives the foetus of oxygen, leading to a small baby at birth. In short, "smoking chokes your baby".

Learn all the grim facts

The thing about smoking is that the effect of the nicotine is actually pretty negligible — other than to make you addicted to it. Anyway, it's the disease aspects they concentrate on most in the Exam. Learn the rest for a nice life.

Warm-Up and Exam Questions

Warm-up Questions

1) What are hormones?
2) When is insulin released?
3) What is diabetes?
4) Which gland produces adrenaline?

Exam Questions

1 a) Complete the following table, comparing nervous and hormonal responses, by putting a ring around the correct answer in each of the shaded boxes.

	Nerves	Hormones
Speed of message	fast/slow	fast/slow
How long the effect lasts	long/short	long/short
Precision of area affected	very precise/more general	very precise/more general

(3 marks)

b) On the right is a diagram showing some of the endocrine glands in the human body.

Name the glands labelled A — E.

(5 marks)

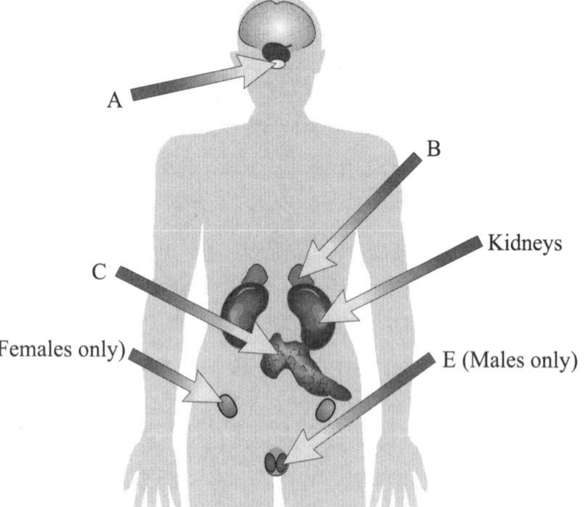

c) Which hormone is involved in the fight or flight reaction?

(1 mark)

d) Give three ways in which the hormone mentioned in c) prepares the body for danger.

(3 marks)

2 The graph below shows how John's blood sugar levels vary over a 24-hour period.

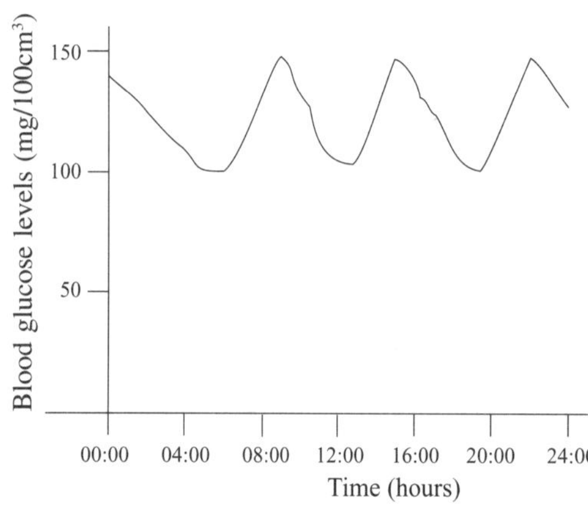

a) Give the times when John's blood sugar is at its highest.

(3 marks)

b) What is causing these peaks in John's blood sugar levels?

(1 mark)

c) After the peaks — what is causing the drop in blood sugar levels?

(2 marks)

d) From the graph, what evidence is there that there is a mechanism to prevent John's blood sugar level from dropping to a dangerous level?

(1 mark)

Revision Summary for Section Two

A quick way to learn this section is to make use of all the pictures — these are usually far easier to remember than lists of facts. Once you know the pictures it's fairly simple to tag on any extra details. You'll soon find that simply drawing the picture will help you recall the rest. So even if the question doesn't ask for a picture it's still worth doing a quick sketch.

Try all these questions — keep going till you can answer all of them.

1) Sketch a typical plant cell with all its labels and three specific plant cells with all their features.
2) Sketch a typical plant and label the five important parts. Explain exactly what each bit does.
3) What does photosynthesis do? Write down the word equation for photosynthesis.
4) Sketch a leaf and show the four things needed for photosynthesis.
5) What are the three variable quantities which affect the rate of photosynthesis?
6) Sketch a graph for each quantity in 5) and explain the shape. (Remember to label the axes.)
7) What seven things is the glucose produced by photosynthesis used for?
8) List the three main minerals needed for healthy plant growth and what they are needed for.
9) What are the deficiency symptoms for each of the three main minerals?
10) What is the definition of diffusion and why is it important for photosynthesis?
11) What is transpiration? What causes it? What benefits does it bring?
12) How do leaves help to limit transpiration? What does this mean for plants in drier climates?
13) What are the four factors which affect the rate of transpiration?
14) How are minerals absorbed by the roots?
15) What is turgor pressure? How does it come about and what use is it to plants?
16) Explain what stomata do and how they do it.
17) What are the two types of tubes in plants? Whereabouts are they found in plants?
18) List three features for both types of tube and sketch them both.
19) Give the full strict definition of osmosis. What does it do to plant and animal cells in water?
20) Give full details of the potato tubes experiment and the visking tubing experiment.
21) What is unusual about active uptake? How do roots use it?
22) Describe how roots and leaves are specialised for the exchange of materials.
23) What are auxins? Where are they produced?
24) Name the four ways that auxins affect roots and shoots. Give full details for all four.
25) List the four commercial uses of plant hormones. Why are ripening hormones useful?
26) Explain what rooting compound is used for. How do hormonal weed killers work?
27) Sketch a diagram of an eye and add labels. Add brief details to the labelled parts.
28) Using diagrams, show how the eye adjusts to light and dark.
29) Describe how the eye focuses on near and distant objects.
30) Draw a diagram showing the main parts of the nervous system.
31) List the five sense organs and say what kind of receptors each one has.
32) What are effectors? What two things make up the central nervous system?
33) Describe how a reflex arc works and why it's a good thing. Explain how a synapse works.
34) What is the proper definition of homeostasis? What are the six bodily levels involved?
35) Draw a diagram of the body showing the eight organs involved in homeostasis.
36) How does your skin help you to stay at a constant temperature?
37) What is the basic function of the kidneys? What *three* particular things do they deal with?
38) Draw and label a diagram showing where the three stages of filtration occur in the kidneys.
39) Draw diagrams to explain how ADH is involved in regulating the water content of the blood.
40) Draw a diagram of the body and label the five places where hormones are produced.
41) Give the proper definition of hormones. How are they different from nerves?
42) Explain what happens with insulin and glucagon when the blood sugar is too high and when it is too low.
43) What is diabetes? Describe the two ways that it can be controlled.
44) Explain the dangers of drinking alcohol. Explain why smoking is generally a bad idea.
45) List in detail all the major health problems that result from smoking.

Adaptation & Competition

Four factors affect the individual organisms

These four physical factors fluctuate throughout the day and year.
Organisms live, grow and reproduce in places where, and at times when, these conditions are suitable.

1) The TEMPERATURE — this is rarely ideal for any organism.
2) The availability of WATER — vital to all living organisms.
3) The amount of LIGHT available — very important to plants, but it also affects the visibility for animals.
4) OXYGEN and CARBON DIOXIDE — these affect respiration & photosynthesis.

The size of any **population** depends on **five factors**

1) The total amount of food or nutrients available.
2) The amount of competition there is (from other species) for the same food or nutrients.
3) The amount of light available (this applies only to plants really).
4) The number of predators (or grazers) who may eat the animal (or plant) in question.
5) Disease.

All these factors help to explain why the types of organisms vary from place to place and from time to time.
The dynamics of plant and animal populations are really quite similar:
Plants often compete with each other for space, and for water and nutrients from the soil.
Animals often compete with each other for space, food and water.

Generally organisms will **thrive** if:

1) There's plenty of the good things in life: food, water, space, shelter, light, etc.
2) They're better than the competition at getting it (better *adapted*).
3) They don't get eaten.
4) They don't get ill.

Populations of **prey** and **predators** go in **cycles**

In a community containing prey and predators (as most of them do of course):
1) The population of any species is usually limited by the amount of food available.
2) If the population of the prey increases, then so will the population of the predators.
3) However as the population of predators increases, the number of prey will decrease.

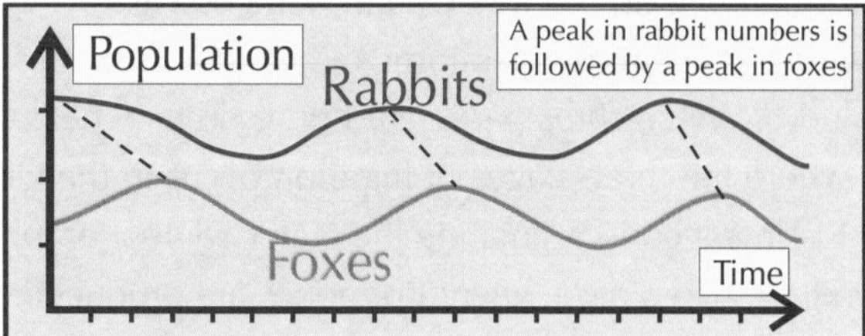

ie: More grass means more rabbits.
More rabbits means more foxes.
But more foxes means fewer rabbits.
Eventually less rabbits will mean fewer foxes again.
This up and down pattern continues...

Adaptation & Competition

If you learn the features that make these animals and plants well adapted, you'll be able to apply them to any other similar creatures they might give you in the Exam.

The **Polar Bear** — Designed for **Arctic** Conditions

The polar bear has all these features: (which many other Arctic creatures also have)

1) Large size and compact shape (i.e. rounded), including small ears, to keep the surface area to a minimum (compared to the body weight) — this all reduces heat loss.
2) A thick layer of blubber for insulation and also to survive hard times when food is scarce.
3) Thick hairy coat for keeping the body heat in.
4) Greasy fur which sheds water after swimming to prevent cooling due to evaporation.
5) White fur to match the surroundings for camouflage.
6) Strong swimmer to catch food in the water and strong runner to run down prey on land.
7) Big, wide feet (big surface area) to spread the weight on snow and ice.

The **Camel** — Designed for **Desert** Conditions

The camel has all these features (most of which are shared by other desert creatures):

1) It can store a lot of water easily — it can drink up to 20 gallons at once.
2) It loses very little water. There's little urine and very little sweating.
3) It can tolerate big changes in its own body temperature to remove the need for sweating.
4) Large, wide feet to spread load on soft sand.
5) All fat is stored in the hump, there is no layer of body fat. This helps it to lose body heat.
6) Large surface area. The shape of a camel is anything but compact, which gives it more surface area to lose body heat to its surroundings.
7) Its sandy colour gives good camouflage.

The **Cactus** is also Well Adapted for the **Desert**

1) It has no leaves — to reduce water loss.
2) It has a small surface area compared to its size *(1000 × less than normal plants)* which also reduces water loss.
3) It stores water in its thick stem.
4) Spines stop herbivores eating them.
5) Shallow but very extensive roots ensure water is absorbed quickly over a large area.

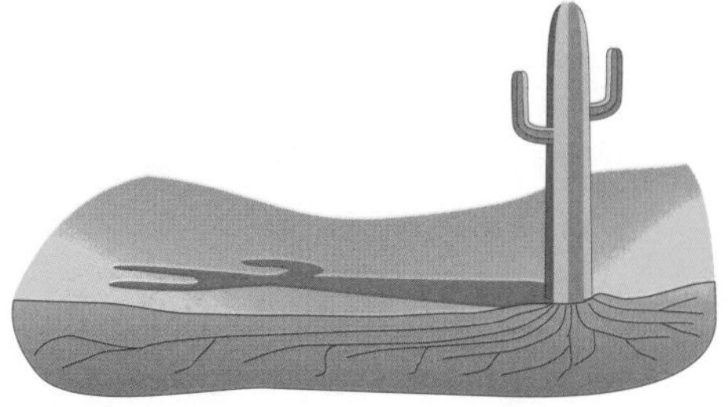

Remember — everything goes in cycles

Population sizes is a strange topic. It's mostly common sense, but it does get quite fiddly. Anyway, learn all the points on this page and you'll be OK in the exam.

Warm-Up and Exam Questions

By the time the big day comes you need to know all the facts in these warm-up questions and all the exam questions like the back of your hand. It's not a barrel of laughs, but it's the only way to get good marks.

Warm-up Questions

1) What environmental resources do organisms compete for?
2) Give five ways in which a camel is adapted for desert conditions.
3) Give five ways in which a polar bear is adapted for arctic conditions.

Exam Questions

1 Foxes feed on rabbits.
The graph on the right shows how the population size of these animals changes with time.

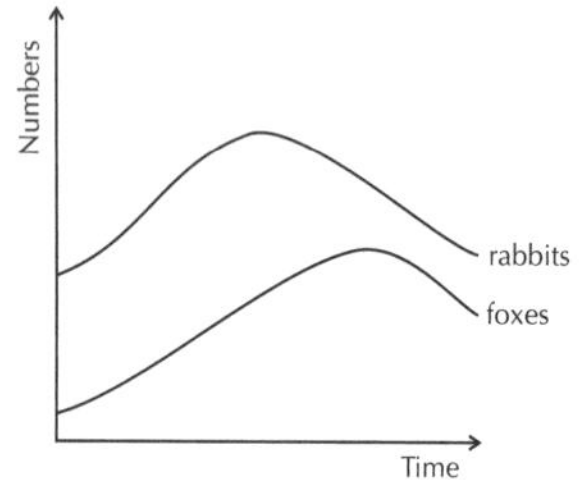

a) Give two factors that can affect the size of an animal population.

(2 marks)

b) Describe what would happen to the fox population if the number of rabbits increased.

(1 mark)

c) Rabbits feed on grass. Describe what would happen to the fox and grass populations if a disease killed all the rabbits.

(2 marks)

2 Different organisms have features that enable them to survive in different environments. The cactus, for example, is found in warm, desert areas.

a) List four adaptive features of cacti.

(4 marks)

b) For each of the features you have listed, explain how it helps in its survival in these conditions.

(4 marks)

Energy and Biomass

Each **trophic level** you go up, there are **fewer of them...**

In other words, each time you go up one trophic level (step in the food chain) the number of organisms goes down — a lot. It takes a lot of food from the level below to keep any one animal alive.
This gives us this number pyramid:

1 Fox
100 Rabbits
5,000 Dandelions

This is the basic idea, but there are cases where the pyramid is not a pyramid at all:

Number pyramids sometimes look **wrong**

This is a pyramid except for the top layer which is much bigger:

500 Fleas
1 Fox
100 Rabbits
5,000 Dandelions

This is a pyramid apart from the bottom layer which is much smaller than you'd expect:

1 Partridge
1000 Ladybirds
3,000 Aphids
1 Pear tree

Biomass pyramids are always **Pyramid-Shaped**

Even when number pyramids seem to look wrong like this, the pyramid of biomass will look right.
Biomass is just how much all the creatures at each level would "weigh" if you put them all together.
So the one pear tree would have a big biomass and the hundreds of fleas would have a very small biomass.

Biomass pyramids are always the right shape:

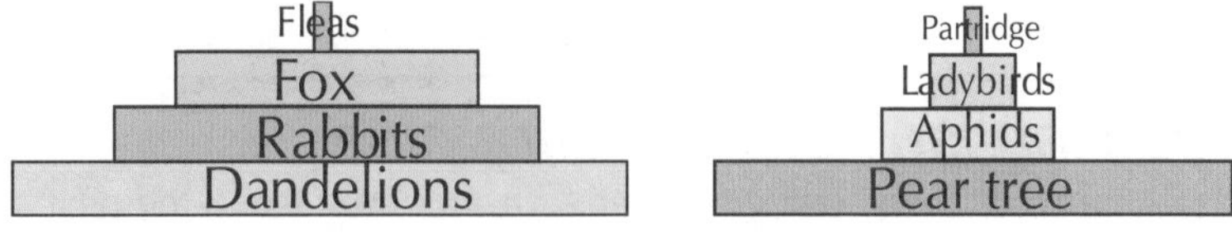

Energy and Biomass

All that Energy gets Used Up

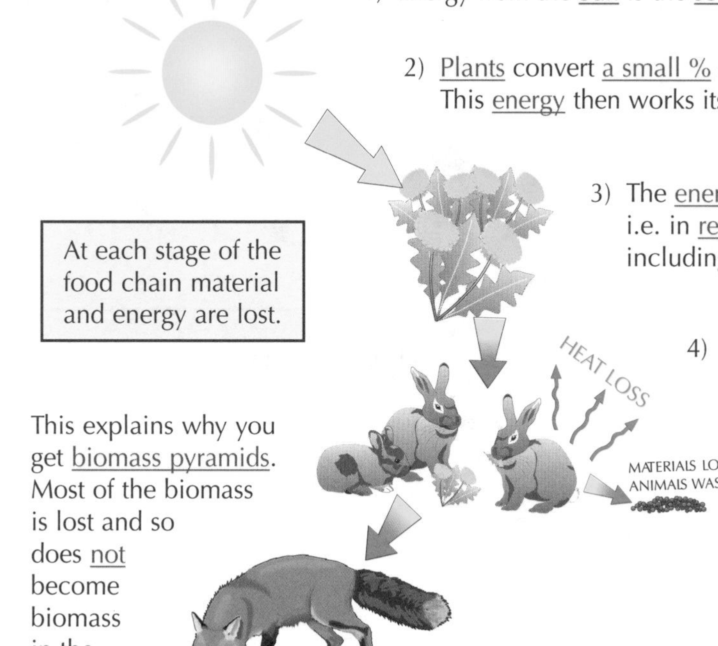

1) Energy from the Sun is the source of energy for all life on Earth.

2) Plants convert a small % of the light energy that falls on them into glucose. This energy then works its way through the food web.

3) The energy lost at each stage is used for staying alive, i.e. in respiration, which powers all life processes, including movement.

4) Most of this energy is eventually lost to the surroundings as heat. This is especially true for mammals and birds whose bodies must be kept at a constant temperature which is normally higher than their surroundings.

5) Material and energy is also lost from the food chain in the droppings — they burn when dried, proving they still have chemical energy in them.

At each stage of the food chain material and energy are lost.

This explains why you get biomass pyramids. Most of the biomass is lost and so does not become biomass in the next level up.

Three ways to improve the "efficiency" of food production

1) Reducing the number of stages in food chains

1) For a given area of land, you can produce a lot more food (for humans) by growing crops rather than by grazing animals. This is because you are reducing the number of stages in the food chain. Only 10% of the food beef cattle eat becomes useful meat for people to eat.
2) However, don't forget that just eating crops can quickly lead to malnutrition through lack of essential proteins and minerals, unless a varied enough diet is achieved. Also remember that some land is unsuitable for growing crops (like moorland or fellsides). In these places, animals like sheep and deer are often the best way to get food from the land.

2) Restricting the energy lost by farm animals

1) In many countries (including Britain), animals like pigs and chickens are often reared in strict conditions of limited movement and artificial warmth, in order to reduce their energy losses to a minimum.
2) In other words if you keep them still enough and hot enough they won't need feeding as much. It's as simple and as horrible as that.
3) But intensively reared animals like chickens and pigs, kept in a little shed all their life, still require land indirectly because they still need feeding, so land is needed to grow their "feed" on.

3) Using hormones to regulate ripening

This is covered in Section Two.

Efficient food production isn't always very nice

You've got to think of all this in terms of energy being transferred from one stage to the next: Sun to plants to animals to bigger animals and eventually to someone's dining table. And at each stage, loads of energy gets lost.

Warm-Up and Exam Question

It's easy to think you've learnt everything in the section until you try the warm-up questions.
Don't panic if there are bits you've forgotten. Just go back over that bit until it's firmly fixed in your brain.

Warm-up Questions

1) What happens to the number of organisms as you go up the trophic levels?
2) For this food chain, draw and label a pyramid of numbers.

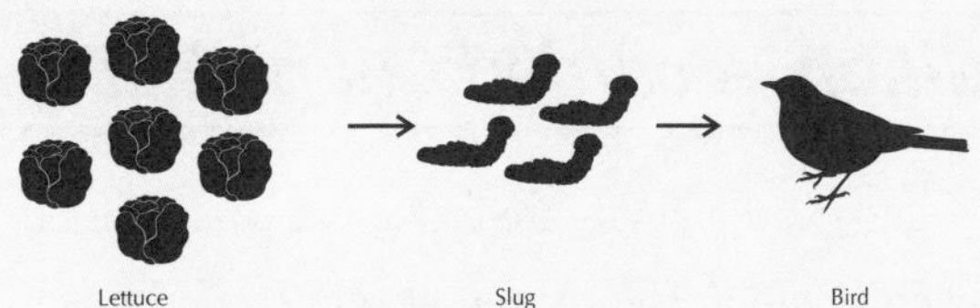

3) Energy is transferred along the food chain. In what ways can this energy be lost?

Exam Question

Take your time to go through this example and make sure you understand it all.
If any of the facts are baffling you it's not too late to take another peek over the section.

1 The ultimate source of energy for most life on Earth is the Sun.
Light energy is converted by plants into glucose. This then works its way along the food chain. However, the amount of energy transferred between each trophic level is very small.

a) Explain what is meant by a trophic level.

(1 mark)

b) Look at the food chain below. How many trophic levels are there?

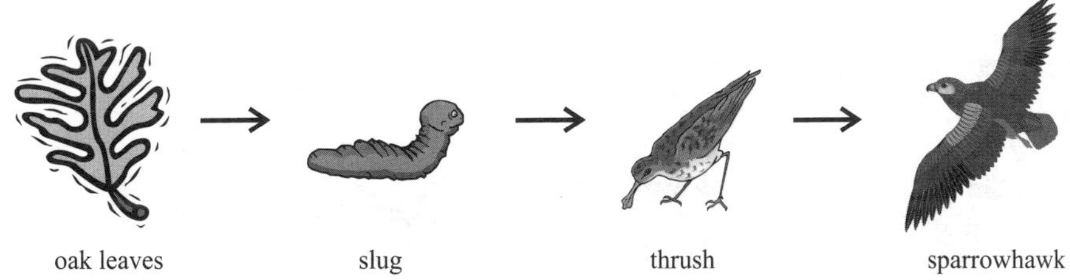

(1 mark)

c) It is possible to increase the amount of energy transferred between trophic levels on a particular area of land. This may be done in farming to improve the efficiency of food production. Give two ways that the efficiency of energy transfer can be improved.

(2 marks)

d) Suggest one benefit to farmers in reducing energy losses in their farm animals.

(1 mark)

Waste Material

1) Living things are made of materials they take from the world around them.
2) When they decompose, ashes are returned to ashes, and dust to dust, as it were.
3) In other words the elements they contain are returned to the soil where they came from originally.
4) These elements are then used by plants to grow and the whole cycle repeats over and over again.

Decomposition *is carried out by* ***bacteria*** *and* ***fungi***

1) All plant matter and dead animals are broken down (digested) by microbes.
2) This happens everywhere in nature, and also in compost heaps and sewage works.
3) All the important elements are thus recycled:
   Carbon, Hydrogen, Oxygen and Nitrogen.
4) The ideal conditions for creating compost are:
   a) WARMTH
   b) MOISTURE
   c) OXYGEN (AIR)
   d) MICROORGANISMS (i.e. bacteria and fungi)
   e) ORGANIC MATTER cut into small pieces.

   Make sure you learn them — all five.

The ***carbon cycle*** *shows how* ***carbon*** *is* ***recycled***

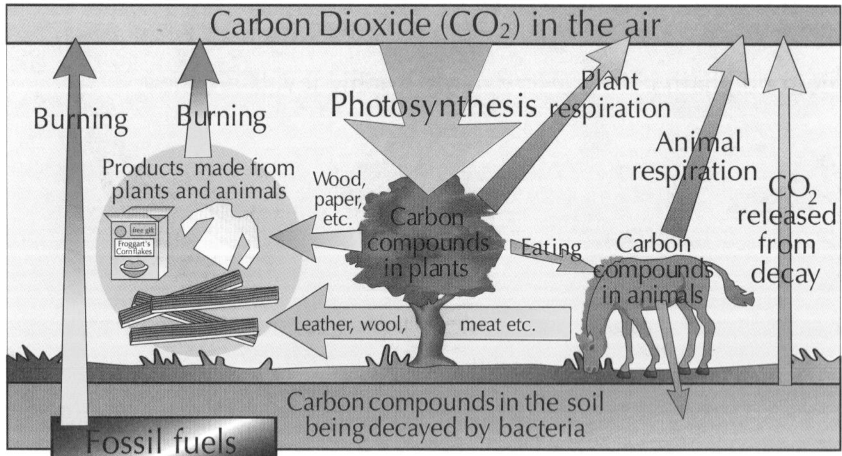

Learn these important points about the diagram:

1) There's only one arrow going down. The whole thing is "powered" by photosynthesis.
2) Both plant and animal respiration put CO_2 back into the atmosphere.
3) Plants convert the carbon in CO_2 from the air into fats, carbohydrates and proteins.
4) These can then go three ways: be eaten, decay or be turned into useful products by man.
5) Eating transfers some of the fats, proteins and carbohydrates to new fats, carbohydrates and proteins in the animal doing the eating.
6) Ultimately these plant and animal products either decay or are burned and CO_2 is released.

Waste Material

The **Nitrogen Cycle**

The constant cycling of nitrogen through the atmosphere, soil and living organisms is called the nitrogen cycle.

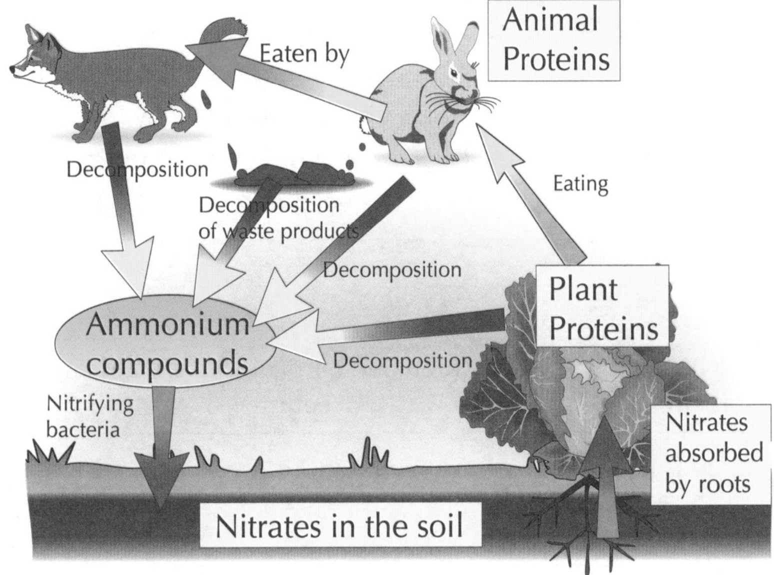

There are **five** simple stages to learn

1) Green plants absorb nitrogen in the form of nitrates from the soil. Nitrogen is an important element in making proteins for plants and animals.
2) Animals can't use nitrogen directly and so must therefore eat and digest plants to obtain it. Of course other animals then eat these animals to get their nitrogen.
3) Any organic waste, i.e. rotting plants or dead animals or animal poo, is broken down by microbes into ammonium compounds. By the time the microbes and other organisms that break down this decaying matter have finished, almost all the energy originally captured by the green plants has been recycled. Organisms such as the microbes, that do this decomposing job, are called detritus feeders. Detritus is simply the name given to all the decaying matter.
4) Nitrifying bacteria turn the ammonium compounds produced by the microbes into useful nitrates.
5) These nitrates can then once more be absorbed by the roots of green plants.

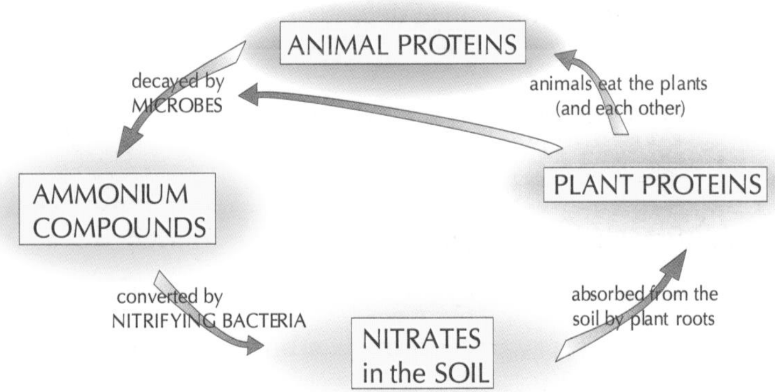

More cycles to learn

Learn the five ideal conditions for compost making. Sketch out the Carbon Cycle, making sure it contains all the labels. Practise drawing it out from memory. Then do the same for the Nitrogen Cycle.

Warm-Up and Exam Questions

Warm-up Questions

1) What happens to nearly all living matter when it dies?
2) Give three processes which return carbon dioxide to the environment.
3) In what chemical form is nitrogen absorbed by plants?
4) What are the sources of ammonium compounds in the nitrogen cycle?
5) Why do all living organisms need nitrogen?

Exam Questions

If you haven't learnt the carbon and nitrogen cycle diagrams, STOP RIGHT NOW. Very naughty. If you have, well done: you may proceed.

1 Bacteria play a very important role in the nitrogen cycle.

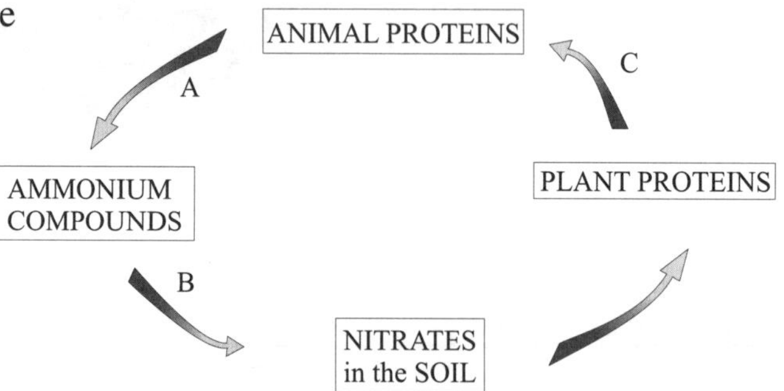

a) What do the plants make from the nitrates they absorb?

(1 mark)

b) What type of bacteria convert ammonium compounds into useful nitrates?

(1 mark)

c) What is occurring at stages A, B and C?

(3 marks)

d) What is meant by the term detritus?

(1 mark)

2 a) What is meant by the term decomposition?

(2 marks)

b) Name two types of organism that cause decay.

(2 marks)

c) What are the optimum conditions for decay to occur?

(3 marks)

3 The answers to the questions below can be taken from the following list.

photosynthesis respiration decay burning fungi nitrifying bacteria

a) Which of the above remove(s) carbon dioxide from the environment?

b) Which process(es) return(s) carbon dioxide back to the environment?

c) Which micro-organisms are involved in the nitrogen cycle?

d) Which micro-organisms are involved in the carbon cycle?

(6 marks)

Human Impact on the Environment

There are Too Many People

1) The population of the world is currently rising out of control — as the graph shows.
2) This is mostly due to modern medicine which has stopped widespread death from disease.
3) It's also due to modern farming methods which can now provide the food needed for so many hungry mouths.
4) The death rate is now much lower than the birth rate in many under-developed countries. In other words there are lots more babies born than people dying.
5) This creates big problems for those countries trying to cope with all those extra people.
6) Even providing basic health care and education (about contraception) is difficult, never mind finding them places to live, and food to eat.

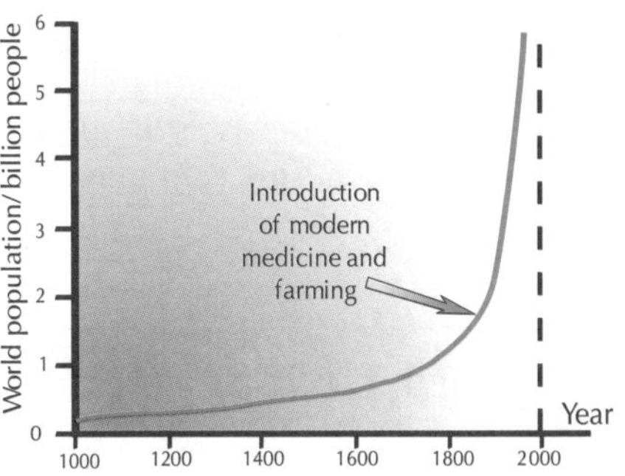

Increasing living standards adds even more pressure

The rapidly increasing population is not the only pressure on the environment. The increasing standard of living amongst more developed countries also demands more from the environment.
These two factors mean that:

1) Raw materials, including non-renewable energy resources, are rapidly being used up;
2) more and more waste is being produced;
3) unless waste is properly handled more pollution will be caused.

When the Earth's population was much smaller, the effects of human activity were usually small and local.

More people means less land for plants and animals

There are four main ways that humans reduce the amount of land available for other animals and plants.

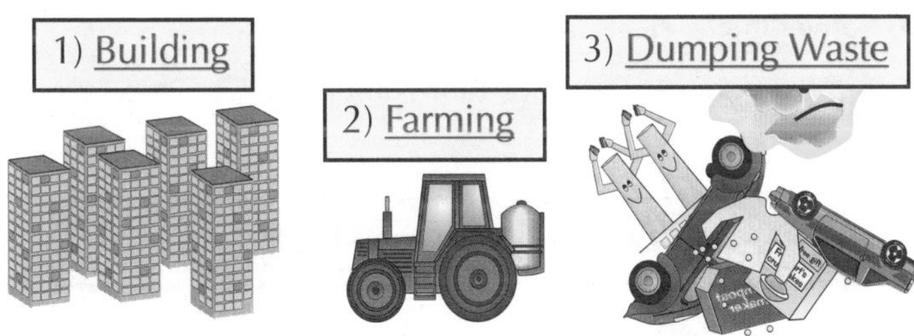

More people means more environmental damage

Human activity can pollute all three parts of the environment:

1) Water — with sewage, fertiliser and toxic chemicals;
2) Air — with smoke and gases such as sulphur dioxide;
3) Land — with toxic chemicals, such as pesticides and herbicides. These may then be washed from the land into water.

Human Impact on the Environment

Burning fossil fuels releases CO_2

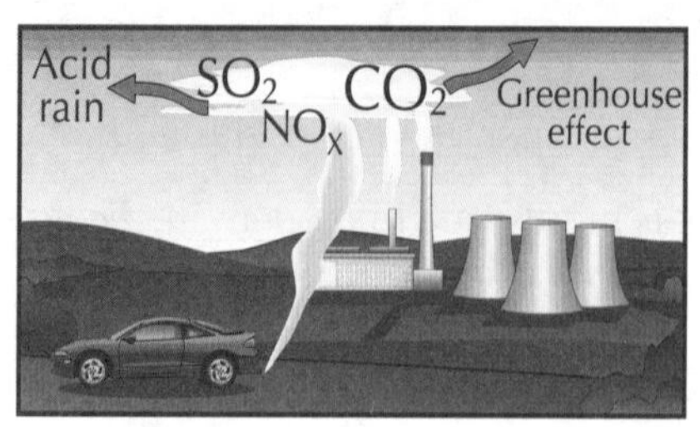

1) Fossil fuels are coal, oil and natural gas.
2) The main culprits who burn these are cars and power stations.
3) They release mostly carbon dioxide, which is adding to the Greenhouse Effect.
4) But they also release sulphur dioxide and oxides of nitrogen, which are causing acid rain.

Burning fossil fuels causes acid rain

1) When fossil fuels are burned they release mostly carbon dioxide which is increasing the Greenhouse Effect. They also release two other harmful gases:
   a) sulphur dioxide   b) various nitrogen oxides.
2) When these mix with clouds they form acids. This then falls as acid rain.
3) Cars and power stations are the main causes of acid rain.

Acid rain kills fish, trees and statues

1) Acid rain causes lakes to become acidic which has a severe effect on their ecosystems. The plants and animals in lakes just can't survive if the water is too acidic.
2) The way this happens is that the acid causes aluminium salts from soil to dissolve into the water. The resulting aluminium ions are poisonous to many fish and birds.
3) Acid rain kills trees.
4) Acid rain damages limestone buildings and ruins stone statues.

Acid rain is prevented by cleaning up emissions

1) Power stations now have Acid Gas Scrubbers to take the harmful gases out before they release their fumes into the atmosphere.
2) Cars are now being fitted with catalytic converters to clean up their exhaust gases.
3) The other way of reducing acid rain is simply to reduce our usage of fossil fuels.

Deforestation increases CO_2 and the greenhouse effect

Britain is almost completely deforested. Now many under-developed tropical countries are doing the same — for timber and to provide land for agriculture. Apart from the loss of millions of species, this also causes a major increase in the greenhouse gas, carbon dioxide (CO_2).

Deforestation increases CO_2 in the atmosphere in two ways:

1) The trees unsuitable for timber are burned, releasing CO_2 directly into the atmosphere. Microbes also release CO_2 by decaying the felled trees that remain.
2) Because living trees use CO_2 for photosynthesis, removing these trees means less CO_2 is removed from the atmosphere.

Human Impact on the Environment

Carbon dioxide and *methane trap heat* from the *sun*

1) The temperature of the Earth is a balance between the heat it gets from the sun and the heat it radiates back out into space.
2) The atmosphere acts like an insulating layer and keeps some of the heat in.
3) This is exactly what happens in a greenhouse or a conservatory. The sun shines into it and the glass keeps the heat in so it just gets hotter and hotter.
4) There are several different gases in the atmosphere which are very good at keeping the heat in. They are called "greenhouse gases". The main ones that people are concerned about are methane and carbon dioxide, because the levels of these are rising quite sharply.
5) The Greenhouse Effect is increasing, causing the Earth to warm up very slowly.

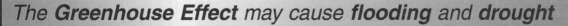

The *Greenhouse Effect* may cause *flooding* and *drought*

1) Changes in weather patterns and climate could cause problems of drought or flooding.
2) The melting of the polar ice-caps would raise sea-levels and could cause flooding to many low-lying coastal parts of the world including many major cities.

Modern *industrial life* is increasing the Greenhouse Effect

1) The level of CO_2 in the atmosphere used to be nicely balanced between the CO_2 released by respiration (of animals and plants) and the CO_2 absorbed by photosynthesis.
2) However, mankind has been burning massive amounts of fossil fuels in the last two hundred years or so.
3) We have also been cutting down trees all over the world to make space for living and farming (deforestation).
4) The level of CO_2 in the atmosphere has gone up by about 20%, and will continue to rise ever more steeply as long as we keep burning fossil fuels.

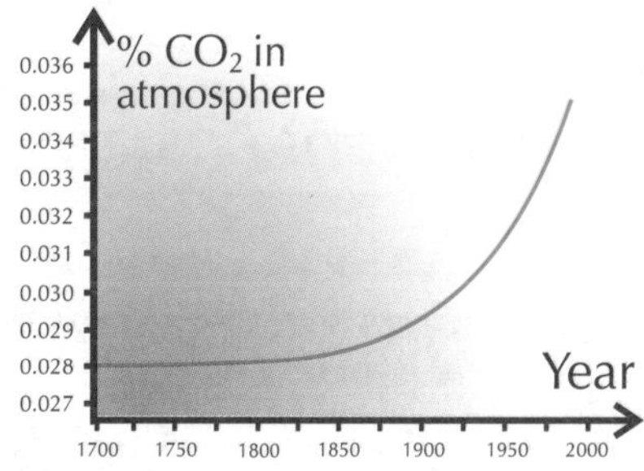

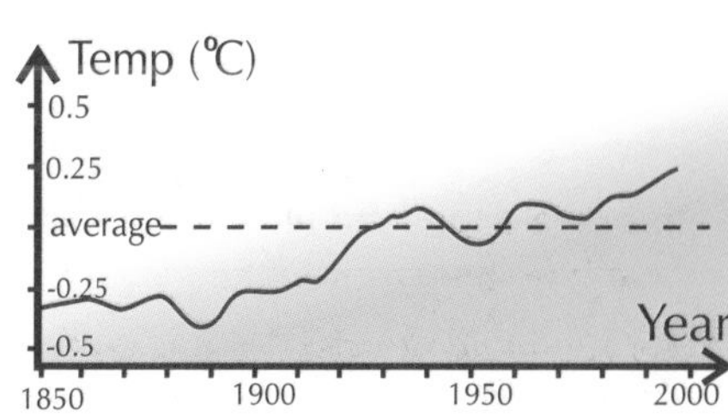

Methane is also a problem

1) Methane gas is also contributing to the Greenhouse Effect.
2) It's produced naturally from various sources, such as natural marshland.
3) However, the two sources of methane which are on the increase are:
   a) Rice growing
   b) Cattle rearing — it's the cows' flatulence that's the problem.

Human Impact on the Environment

Farming produces a lot of food

1) Farming is important to us because it allows us to produce a lot of food from less and less land.
2) These days it has become quite a high-tech industry. Food production is big business.
3) The great advantage of this is a huge variety of top quality foods, all year round, at cheap prices.
4) This is a far cry from Britain 50 years ago when food had to be rationed by the government because there simply wasn't enough for everyone. That's hard to imagine today... but try...

However, fertilisers damage lakes and rivers — Eutrophication

1) Fertilisers which contain nitrates are essential to modern farming.
2) Without them crops wouldn't grow nearly so well, and food yields would be well down.
3) This is because the crops take nitrates out of the soil and these nitrates need to be replaced.
4) The problems start if some of the rich fertiliser finds its way into rivers and streams.
5) This happens quite easily if too much fertiliser is applied, especially if it rains soon afterwards.
6) The result is eutrophication, which basically means "too much of a good thing".
(Raw sewage pumped into rivers also causes EUTROPHICATION by providing food for microorganisms.)

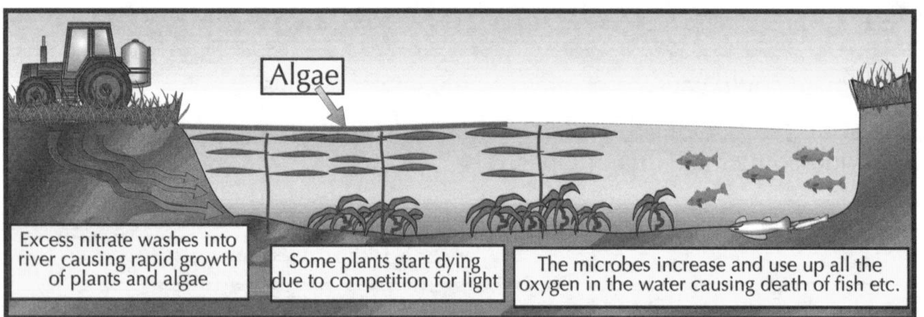
Algae
Excess nitrate washes into river causing rapid growth of plants and algae
Some plants start dying due to competition for light
The microbes increase and use up all the oxygen in the water causing death of fish etc.

As the picture shows, too many nitrates in the water cause a sequence of "mega-growth", "mega-death" and "mega-decay" involving most of the plant and animal life in the water.

7) Farmers need to take a lot more care when spreading artificial fertilisers.

Development has to be sustainable

'Sustainable development' is a big exam topic. Learn this definition:

SUSTAINABLE DEVELOPMENT meets the needs of today's population without harming the ability of future generations to meet their own needs.

1) Farming and burning fossil fuels are necessary for our standards of living and there's more demand on them as the population gets bigger.
2) There's only so much abuse the planet can take. Nowadays, developers can't easily build huge power stations or create big landfill sites without a fight. They have to take greater care to sustain the delicate balance on Earth — the gases in the atmosphere and disposal of waste are just two of the things they have to look at.
3) *Sustainable development* is environmentally friendly. Most development today must be able to continue into the future with as little damage as possible to the planet.
4) In the Exam, make sure you remember the details about the environmental problems that development causes. If you get an essay question, always include these details — as they demonstrate your 'scientific knowledge'.
5) You will also have to weigh up the advantages and disadvantages. That's all your essay needs to be — write about the advantages, then the disadvantages, then make a conclusion.

This is a very important area of science right now

We're in the middle of a population explosion, we're polluting the planet we live on, and it's all getting worse the more people there are. This is very important stuff. You will definitely get a question on it — it's really topical right now. Write a mini-essay summarising the current environmental problems to check you understand it all.

Warm-Up and Exam Questions

The greenhouse effect and atmospheric pollution — these are nice easy topics that you should know a bit about already. Anyway, time to test exactly what you do and don't know...

Warm-up Questions

1) What are the two main gases responsible for the greenhouse effect?
2) Give two consequences of the greenhouse effect.
3) Explain how acid rain results from the burning of fossil fuels.
4) What precautions can we take to prevent acid rain?
5) Other than the burning of fossil fuels, give two other causes of atmospheric pollution.

Exam Questions

1 Humans have reduced the amount of land available to plants and other animals.

a) State three ways in which humans have used this land.

(3 marks)

b) Large-scale deforestation is affecting CO_2 levels in the air.
Why is there a need for deforestation?

(2 marks)

c) Explain how large-scale deforestation is altering the levels of CO_2 in the atmosphere.

(5 marks)

2 Many trees, fish and statues are being destroyed by acid rain.

a) Circle the correct word(s) to complete the sentences below.

- When fossil fuels burn, they release mostly **sulphur dioxide/CO_2/nitrogen oxides**.
- When oxides of sulphur and nitrogen mix with clouds, they form **alkalis/acids/SO_2**.
- Acid causes aluminium salts from the soil to **melt/dissolve/fall** into the water.

(3 marks)

b) State three ways to prevent acid rain formation.

(3 marks)

3 a) Explain why a farmer would use fertilisers to ensure a high yield of crop.

(2 marks)

b) What is meant by eutrophication?

(1 mark)

c) Draw a flow-chart to show the effects of eutrophication in a river ecosystem.

(4 marks)

Revision Summary for Section Three

You need to practise writing down all you can remember on each topic, and then checking back to see what you missed. These questions give you a good idea of what you should know.
You need to practise and practise them — till they become easy.

1) Name the four factors that affect individual organisms on a daily basis.
2) What are the five basic things which determine the size of a population of a species?
3) Sketch a graph of prey and predator populations over time and explain the shapes.
4) List seven survival features of the polar bear and of the camel.
5) Describe how a cactus is adapted to living in very dry conditions.
6) What are number pyramids? Why do you generally get a pyramid of numbers?
7) Why do number pyramids sometimes go wrong, and which pyramids are always right?
8) Where does the energy in a food chain originate? Name three ways in which the energy is lost.
9) Explain how you might improve the efficiency of food production.
10) Which two types of organism are responsible for the decay of organic matter?
11) What are the five ideal conditions for making compost? Draw a compost maker.
12) What is the Carbon Cycle all to do with?
    Copy and fill in as much of it from memory as you can.

13) What is the Nitrogen Cycle all about? Draw as much of it from memory as you can.
14) Describe the five stages of the Nitrogen Cycle in as much detail as you can.
15) What is happening to the world's population? What is largely responsible for this trend?
16) What problems does a rapidly increasing population create for a country?
17) What are the four main ways humans reduce the land available for other animals and plants?
18) What effect does the ever-increasing number of people have on the environment?
19) Which gases cause acid rain? Where do these gases come from?
20) What are the three main harmful effects of acid rain? Explain exactly how fish are killed.
21) Give three ways that acid rain can be reduced.
22) How is deforestation linked to the Greenhouse Effect?
23) Which two gases are the biggest cause of the Greenhouse Effect?
24) Explain how the Greenhouse Effect happens. What dire consequences could there be?
25) What is causing the rise in levels of each the two problem gases? What is the solution?
26) What is the great bonus of modern farming methods? What are the drawbacks?
27) What happens when too much nitrate fertiliser is put onto fields? Give full details.
28) What is the big fancy name given to this problem? How can it be avoided?
29) What is the definition of 'sustainable development'? Why is it necessary?

Genetics

1) Young plants and animals obviously resemble their parents. In other words they show similar characteristics such as jagged leaves or perfect eyebrows.
2) However young animals and plants can also differ from their parents and each other.
3) These similarities and differences lead to variation within the same species.
4) The word "variation" sounds far more complicated. All it means is how animals or plants of the same species look or behave slightly different from each other. You know, a bit taller or a bit fatter or a bit more scary-to-look-at, etc.

There are two causes of variation: Genetic Variation and Environmental Variation. Read on, and learn...

1) Genetic variation

1) All animals are bound to be slightly different from each other because their genes are slightly different.
2) Genes are the code inside all your cells which determine how you turn out. We all end up with a slightly different set of genes.
3) The exceptions to that rule are identical twins, because their genes are exactly the same. But even identical twins are never completely identical — and that's because of the other factor:

2) Environmental variation is shown up by twins

If you're not sure what "environment" means, think of it as "upbringing" instead — it's pretty much the same thing — how and where you were "brought up".
Since we know the twins' genes are identical, any differences between them must be caused by slight differences in their environment throughout their lives.
Twins give us a fairly good idea of how important the two factors (genes and environment) are, compared to each other, at least for animals — plants always show much greater variation due to differences in their environment than animals do, as explained below.

3) Environmental variation in plants is much greater

Plants are strongly affected by:
1) Temperature
2) Sunlight
3) Moisture level
4) Soil composition

For example, plants may grow twice as big or twice as fast due to fairly modest changes in environment such as the amount of sunlight or rainfall they're getting, or how warm it is or what the soil is like.

A cat, on the other hand, born and bred in the North of Scotland, could be sent out to live in equatorial Africa and would show no significant changes — it would look the same.

Animal characteristics not affected at all by environment:

1) EYE COLOUR.
2) HAIR COLOUR in most animals (but not humans where vanity plays a big part).
3) INHERITED DISEASES like haemophilia, cystic fibrosis, etc.
4) BLOOD GROUP.

And that's about it — so learn those four in case they ask you.

4) Combinations of genetic and environmental variation

Everything else is determined by a mixture of genetic and environmental factors:
Body weight, height, skin colour, condition of teeth, academic or athletic prowess, etc. etc.

The tricky bit is working out just how significant environmental factors are for all these other features.

Genetics

Mendel's **pea plant** experiments

Gregor Mendel was an Austrian monk who trained in mathematics and natural history at the University of Vienna. On his garden plot at the monastery, Mendel noted how characteristics in plants were passed on from one generation to the next. The results of his research became the foundation of modern genetics.

The diagrams show two crosses for height in pea plants that Mendel carried out...

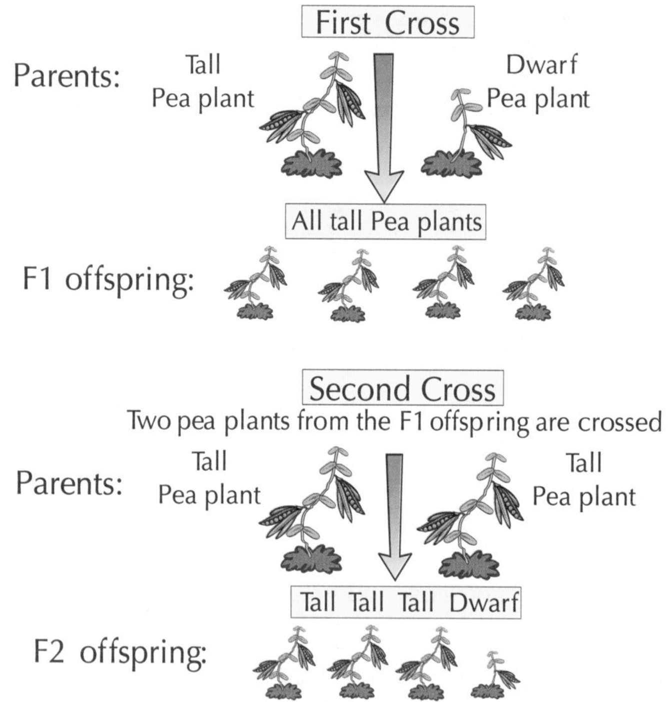

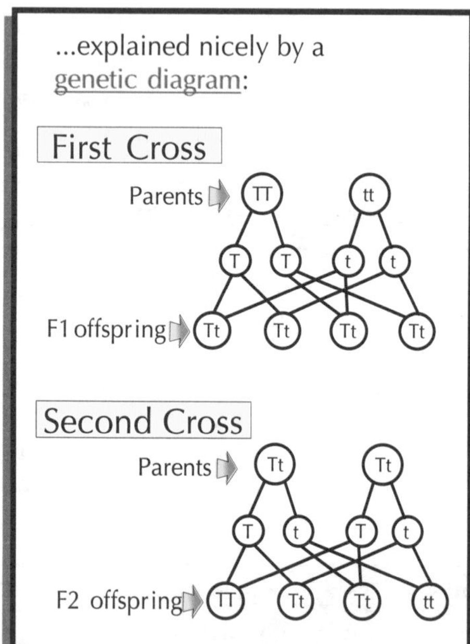

Mendel had shown that the height characteristic in pea plants was determined by "hereditary units" passed on from each parent. The ratios of tall and dwarf plants in the F1 and F2 offspring showed that the unit for tall plants, T, was dominant over the unit for dwarf plants, t.

Mendel's conclusions

Mendel reached these 3 important conclusions about heredity in plants:

1) Characteristics in plants are determined by "hereditary units".
2) Hereditary units are passed on from both parents, one unit from each parent.
3) Hereditary units can be dominant or recessive — if an individual has both the dominant and the recessive unit for a characteristic, the dominant characteristic will be expressed.

From the benefit of modern science we know that the "hereditary units" are of course genes. In Mendel's time this technology was not as advanced and the importance of his work was not to be realised until after his death.

Genetics

If you're going to get anywhere with this topic you definitely need to learn these confusing words and exactly what they mean. You have to make sure you know exactly what DNA is, what and where chromosomes are, and what and where a gene is. If you don't get that sorted out first, then anything else you read about them won't make a lot of sense to you.

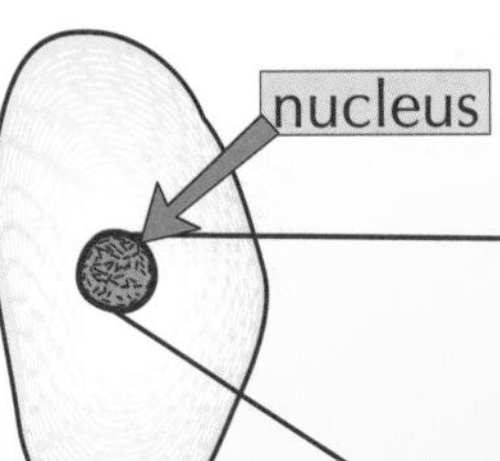

The human cell nucleus contains 23 pairs of chromosomes. They are all well known and numbered. We all have two No.19 chromosomes and two No.12s etc.

A single chromosome

A pair of chromosomes. (They're always in pairs, one from each parent.)

Short sections of a chromosome are called *GENES*. We know that certain sections of certain chromosomes do particular things, e.g. the hair colour gene.

DNA molecule

A gene, a short length of the chromosome...

...which is quite a long length of DNA.

The arms are held together in the centre

An allele is another name for a gene, so these sections of chromosome are also alleles. (When there are two different versions of the same gene you call them alleles instead of genes)

The DNA is coiled up to form the arms of the chromosome.

Homozygous — is an individual with two alleles the same for that particular gene, e.g. HH or hh.

Heterozygous — is an individual with two alleles different for that particular gene, e.g. Hh.

Meiosis — is the process of cell division which creates sperm or egg cells. Meiosis only happens in the ovaries or the testes.

Mitosis — is the process of cell division where one cell splits into two identical cells.

Gamete — is either a sperm cell or an egg cell. All gametes have half the number of chromosomes of a body cell.

Zygote — is the delightful name given to each newly-formed human life, just after the (equally delightfully-named) *gametes* fuse together at fertilisation.

You need to learn all those technical words

There are a lot of difficult terms here — but you really must learn them. Cover the page and scribble down all the diagrams and details. Keep going until you know it all.

Warm-Up and Exam Questions

Warm-up Questions

1) What are the two types of variation?
2) What are the four main environmental factors that affect how plants turn out?
3) Give four characteristics of animals that are not affected by environment.
4) What were Mendel's three important conclusions about heredity in plants?
5) What is a gene?
6) How many pairs of chromosomes are found in a human cell?

Exam Questions

1 The data below was collected from a pair of 18-year-old identical twins who had been separated at birth and brought up in different environments.

Feature	Eye colour	Height (cm)	Hair length	Blood group	Weight (kg)	Middle finger length (cm)
Danielle	Blue	170	Long	AB	75	8
Joanne	Blue	160	Short	AB	60	7.5

Using the above information state which features are determined purely by genetics and which are determined by both environment and genetics.

(3 marks)

2 Gregor Mendel was an Austrian monk who investigated how characteristics were passed on in plants. He reached three important conclusions:

(i) Characteristics in plants are determined by 'hereditary units'.

(ii) Hereditary units are passed on from both parents, one unit from each parent.

(iii) Hereditary units can be dominant or recessive — if an individual has both the dominant and recessive unit for a characteristic, the dominant characteristic will be expressed.

a) What is the proper biological term for these 'hereditary units'?

(1 mark)

b) Mendel crossed a true breeding smooth pea plant with a true breeding wrinkled pea plant.
The genetic diagram below shows this genetic cross.
B represents the allele for smooth peas. b represents the allele for wrinkled peas.

Parental characteristics	smooth peas	×	wrinkled peas
Parental alleles	BB	×	bb
Gametes	all (B)		all (b)
F_1 generation characteristics		all Bb	
F_1 generation alleles		all smooth peas	

If two pea plants from the F_1 generation above were then crossed, what would be the likely ratio of smooth pea plants to wrinkled pea plants? Show your working.

(3 marks)

Cell Division and Fertilisation

"Mitosis is when a cell reproduces itself ASEXUALLY by splitting to form two identical offspring that are called clones."

The really riveting part of the whole process is how the chromosomes split inside the cell.

DNA all spread out in long strings.

DNA forms into chromosomes. Remember, the double arms are already duplicates of each other.

Chromosomes line up along centre and then the cell fibres pull them apart.

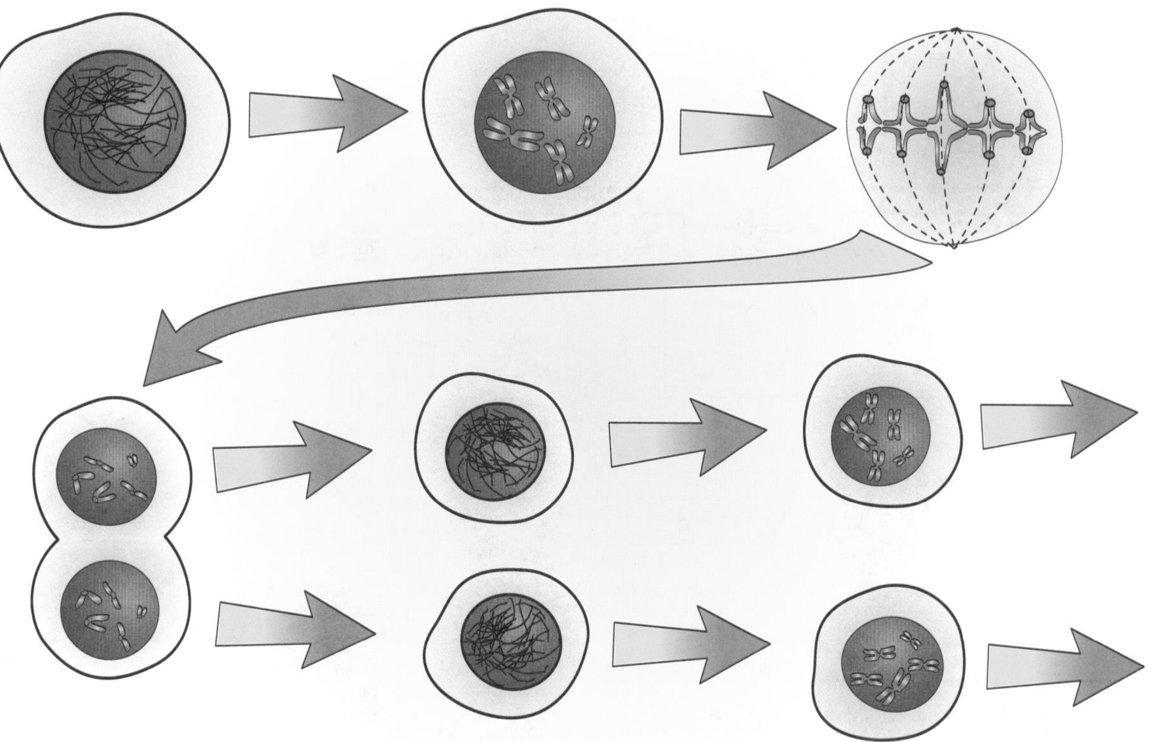

Membranes form around the two sets of chromosome threads. These become the nuclei of the two daughter cells.

The threads unwind into long strands of DNA and the whole process then starts over again.

(Note that the single chromosome threads have now duplicated themselves — see next page.)

Mitosis and asexual reproduction

Mitosis produces new cells identical to the original cell. This is how all plants and animals grow and produce replacement cells. Cells throughout our body divide and multiply by this process.
However some organisms also reproduce using this kind of cell division, bacteria being a good example.
This is known as asexual reproduction. Here is a definition of it, for you to learn:

In asexual reproduction there is only one parent, and the offspring therefore have exactly the same genes as the parent (ie: they're clones - see P.79 & 80).

This is because all the cells in both parent and offspring were produced by ordinary cell division, so they must all have identical genes in their cell nuclei. Asexual reproduction therefore produces no variation. Some plants reproduce asexually, e.g. potatoes, strawberries and daffodils (see P.80).

Cell Division and Fertilisation

Genes are chemical instructions

1) A gene is a length of DNA.
2) DNA is a long list of coded instructions on how to put the organism together and make it work.
3) Each separate gene is a separate chemical instruction to a particular type of cell.
4) Cells make proteins by stringing amino acids together in a particular order.
5) There are only about 20 different amino acids, but they make up thousands of different proteins.
6) Genes simply tell cells in what order to put the amino acids together.
7) That determines what proteins the cell produces, e.g. haemoglobin, or keratin, etc.
8) That in turn determines what type of cell it is, e.g. red blood cell, skin cell, etc.

DNA replicates itself to form chromosomes

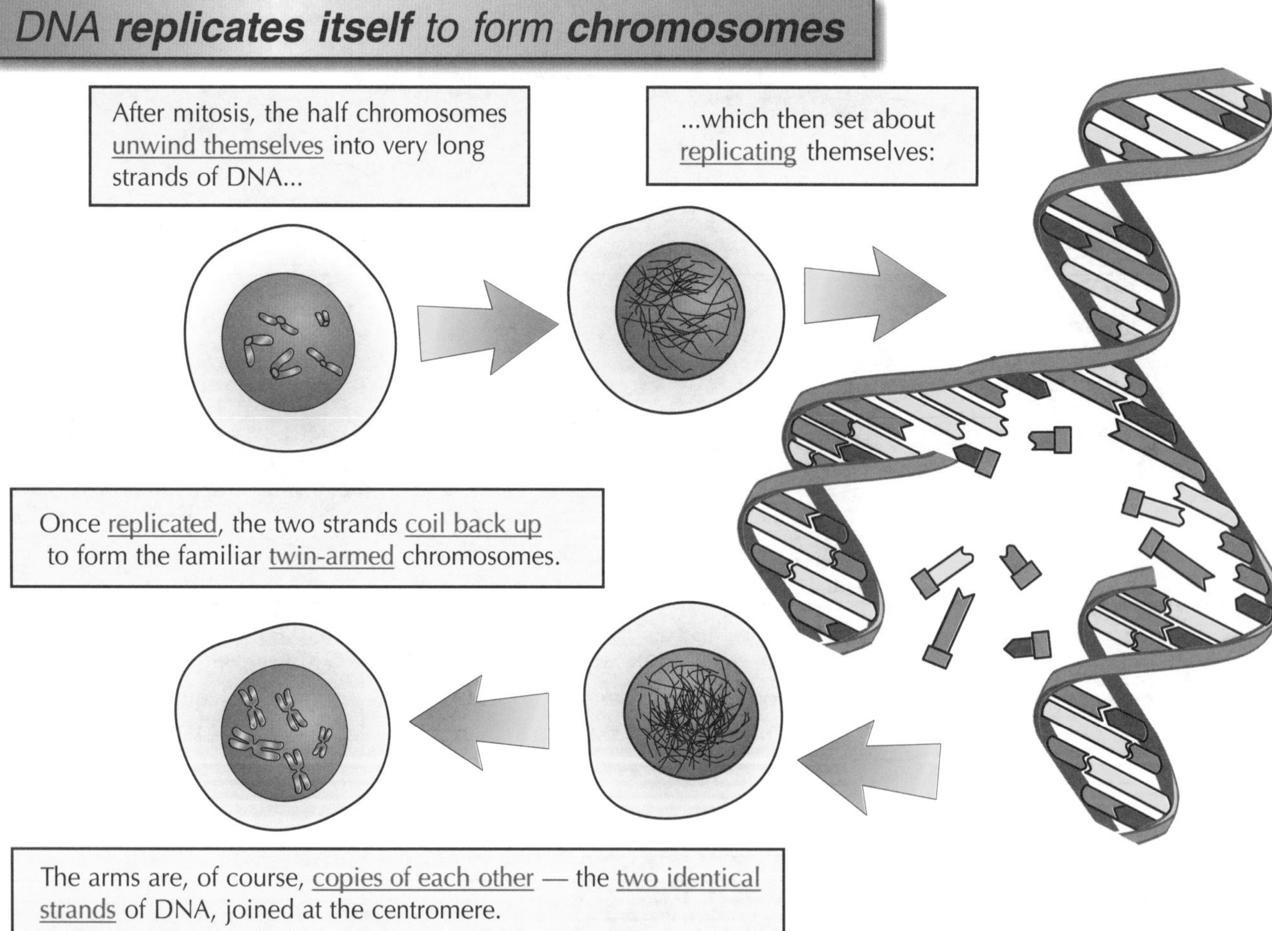

After mitosis, the half chromosomes unwind themselves into very long strands of DNA...
...which then set about replicating themselves:
Once replicated, the two strands coil back up to form the familiar twin-armed chromosomes.
The arms are, of course, copies of each other — the two identical strands of DNA, joined at the centromere.

Three bases — a code for a particular amino acid

1) The DNA double helix is made up of four different "bases" (shown in the diagram as different colours).
2) Three bases = a code for one particular amino acid.
3) The order of the bases controls the order that amino acids are put together to make a different protein.
4) As the DNA unwinds itself, new bases (floating about in the nucleus) join on only where they fit, and (as the diagram shows) this ensures the resulting two new DNA strands exactly match the original. It's all clever stuff.
5) By the way, DNA isn't fancy colours like this. It's just to make the page look interesting.

Cell Division and Fertilisation

Mitosis is where cells clone themselves. Meiosis is the other type of cell division. It only happens in the reproductive organs (ovaries and testes).

> Meiosis produces "cells which have half the proper number of chromosomes". Such cells are also known as "gametes".

These cells are "genetically different" from each other because the genes all get shuffled up during meiosis and each gamete only gets half of them, selected at random.
The diagrams below will make it a lot clearer — but you have to study them pretty hard.

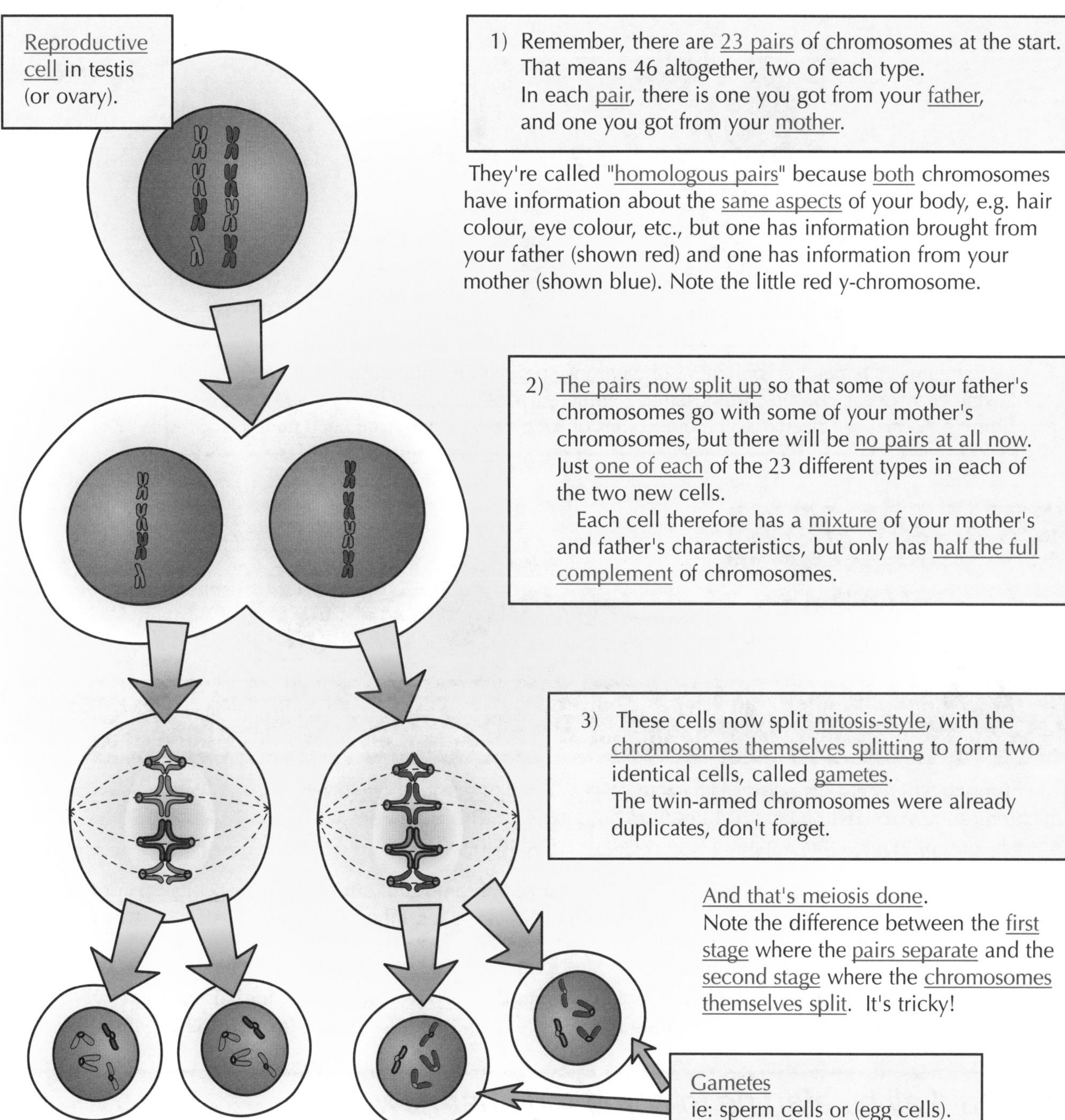

Reproductive cell in testis (or ovary).
1) Remember, there are 23 pairs of chromosomes at the start. That means 46 altogether, two of each type. In each pair, there is one you got from your father, and one you got from your mother.
They're called "homologous pairs" because both chromosomes have information about the same aspects of your body, e.g. hair colour, eye colour, etc., but one has information brought from your father (shown red) and one has information from your mother (shown blue). Note the little red y-chromosome.
2) The pairs now split up so that some of your father's chromosomes go with some of your mother's chromosomes, but there will be no pairs at all now. Just one of each of the 23 different types in each of the two new cells.
Each cell therefore has a mixture of your mother's and father's characteristics, but only has half the full complement of chromosomes.
3) These cells now split mitosis-style, with the chromosomes themselves splitting to form two identical cells, called gametes. The twin-armed chromosomes were already duplicates, don't forget.
And that's meiosis done. Note the difference between the first stage where the pairs separate and the second stage where the chromosomes themselves split. It's tricky!
Gametes
ie: sperm cells or (egg cells).

Cell Division and Fertilisation

There are 23 pairs of human chromosomes

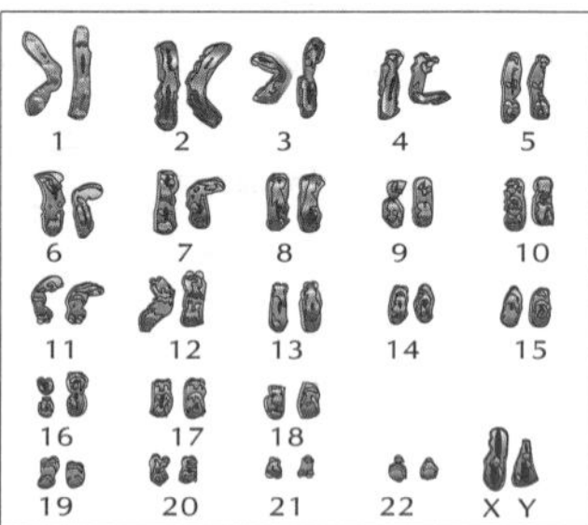

They are well known and numbered. In every cell nucleus we have two of each type. The diagram shows the 23 pairs of chromosomes from a human cell. One chromosome in each pair is inherited from each of our parents. Normal body cells have 46 chromosomes, in 23 homologous pairs.

Remember, "homologous" means that the two chromosomes in each pair are equivalent to each other. In other words, the number 19 chromosomes from both your parents pair off together, as do the number 17s, etc. What you don't get is the number 12 chromosome from one parent pairing off with, say, the number 5 chromosome from the other.

Reproductive cells undergo meiosis to produce gametes:

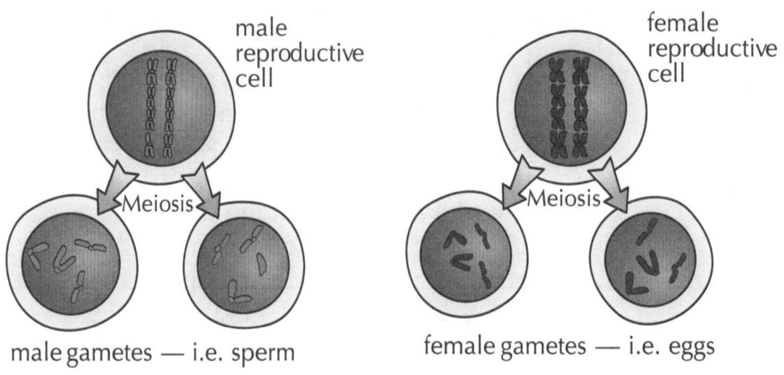

The gametes remember, only have one chromosome to describe each bit of you, one copy of each of the chromosomes numbered 1 to 23.
But a normal cell needs two chromosomes of each type — one from each parent, so...

Sexual reproduction

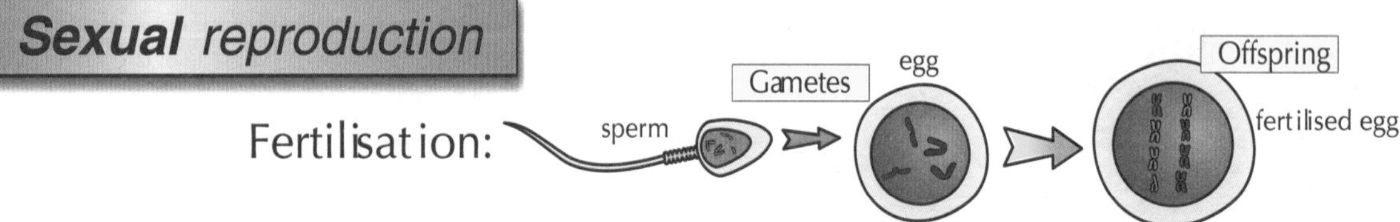

Sexual reproduction involves the fusion of male and female gametes (sex cells). Because there are two parents, the offspring contains a mixture of their parents genes.

The offspring will receive its outward characteristics as a mixture from the two sets of chromosomes, so it will inherit features from both parents. This is why sexual reproduction produces more variation than asexual reproduction.

When the gametes meet up during fertilisation, the 23 single chromosomes in one gamete will all pair off with their appropriate "partner chromosomes" from the other gamete to form the full 23 pairs again, No.4 with No.4, No.13 with No.13, etc. etc.

Don't forget, the two chromosomes in a pair both contain the same basic genes, e.g. for hair colour, etc. When single chromosomes meet up at fertilisation, they seek out their counterpart from the other gamete.

It should all be starting to come together now

You need to learn the definitions of mitosis and meiosis and the diagrams showing the sequence for each — along with the definitions of asexual and sexual reproduction. You also need to learn all the details about DNA, chromosomes and bases. There's a lot to learn, but at least it's quite interesting.

Warm-Up and Exam Questions

Warm-up Questions

1) What are the two types of cell division?
2) What is the purpose of meiosis?
3) What is fertilisation?

Exam Questions

1 Below are some diagrams showing the different stages of mitosis.

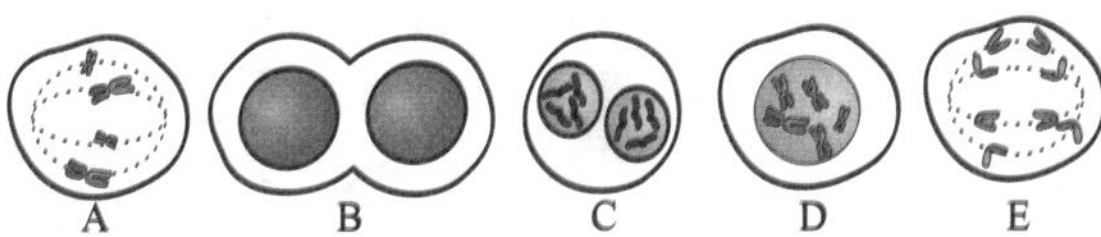

a) Write the letters of the diagrams in the correct boxes below, to show what order the stages take place in.

(5 marks)

b) What are the three main purposes of mitosis?

(3 marks)

c) Give two ways in which mitosis differs from meiosis.

(2 marks)

2 The diagram below shows a cell with four chromosomes.
The cell undergoes meiosis to produce four new cells represented by circles A – D.

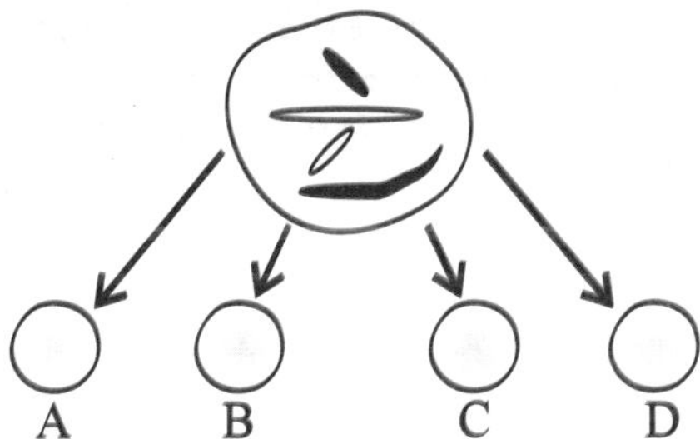

a) Complete the circles A – D to show the chromosomes at the end of meiosis.

(2 marks)

b) Why is meiosis important for sexual reproduction?

(2 marks)

c) In humans, mitosis occurs in all body cells. Where does meiosis occur?

(1 mark)

d) What is the name for the type of cells produced in meiosis?

(1 mark)

Breeding Plants and Animals

Selective breeding is very simple

Selective breeding is also called artificial selection, because humans artificially select the plants or animals that are going to breed and flourish, according to what characteristics we want from them.
This is the basic process involved in selective breeding:

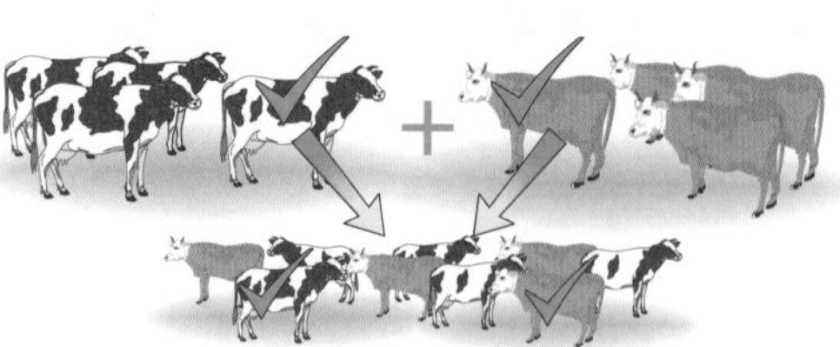

1) From your existing stock select the ones which have the best characteristics.
2) Breed them with each other.
3) Select the best of the offspring, and combine them with the best that you already have and breed again.
4) Continue this process over several generations to develop the desired traits.

Selective breeding is very useful in farming

Artificial Selection like this is used in most areas of modern farming, to great benefit:

1) Better beef

Selectively breeding beef cattle to get the best beef (taste, texture, appearance, etc.).

2) Better milk

Selectively breeding milking cows to increase milk yield and resistance to disease.

3) Better chickens

Selectively breeding chickens to improve egg size and number of eggs per hen.

4) Better wheat

Selectively breeding wheat to produce new varieties with better yields and better disease-resistance too.

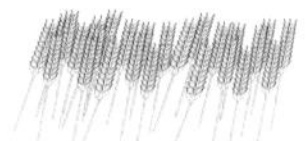

5) Better flowers

Selectively breeding flowers to produce bigger and better and more colourful ones.

The main drawback is a reduction in the gene pool

In farming, animals are selectively bred to develop the best features, which are basically:

A) Maximum Yield of meat, milk, grain etc.

B) Good Health and Disease Resistance.

1) But selective breeding reduces the number of alleles in a population because the farmer keeps breeding from the "best" animals or plants — the same ones all the time.
2) This can cause serious problems if a new disease appears, as all the plants or animals could be wiped out.
3) This is made more likely because all the stock are closely related to each other, so if one of them is going to be killed by a new disease, the others are also likely to succumb to it.

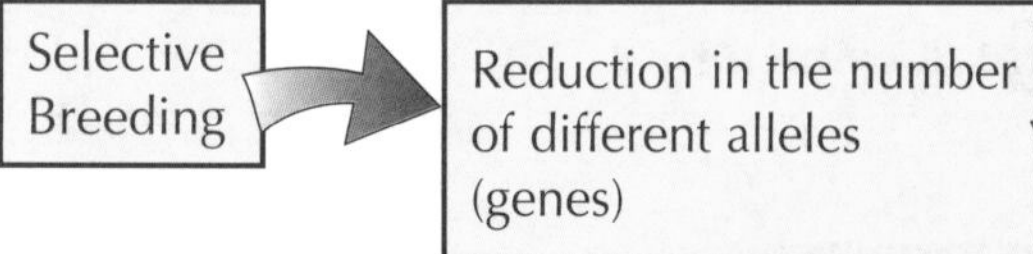

Less chance of any resistant alleles being present in the population

Nothing to selectively breed a new strain from

Breeding Plants and Animals

Learn this definition of clones: **CLONES are GENETICALLY IDENTICAL ORGANISMS**

Clones occur naturally in both plants and animals. Identical twins are clones of each other. These days clones are very much a part of the high-tech farming industry.

Embryo transplants in cows

Normally, farmers only breed from their best cows and bulls. However, such traditional methods would only allow the prize cow to produce one new offspring each year. These days the whole process has been transformed using embryo transplants:

1) Sperm are taken from the prize bull.
2) They're checked for genetic defects and which sex they are.
3) They can also be frozen and used at a later date.
4) Selected prize cows are given hormones to make them produce lots of eggs.
5) The cows are then artificially inseminated.
6) The embryos are taken from prize cows and checked for sex and genetic defects.
7) The embryos are developed and split (to form clones) before any cells become specialised.
8) These embryos are implanted into other cows, where they grow. They can also be frozen and used at a later date.

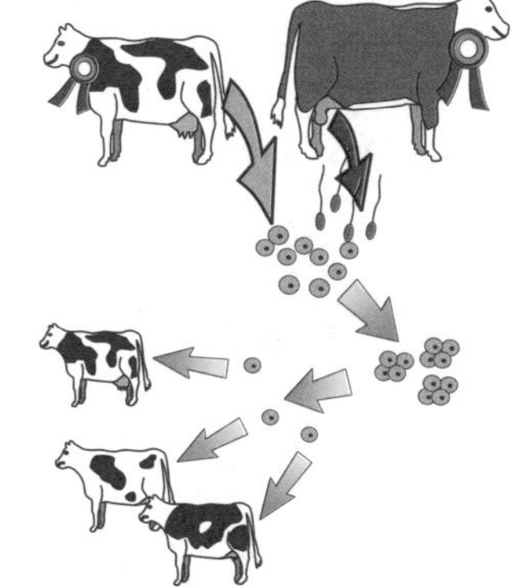

Advantages of embryo transplants — hundreds of ideal offspring

a) Hundreds of "ideal" offspring can be produced every year from the best bull and cow.
b) The original prize cow can keep producing prize eggs all year round.

Disadvantages — reduced gene pool

Only the usual drawback with clones — a reduced "gene pool" leading to vulnerability to new diseases.

Genetic engineering is great — in theory

This is a new science with exciting possibilities, but dangers too. The basic idea is to move sections of DNA (genes) from one organism to another so that it produces useful biological products.

We presently use bacteria to produce human insulin for diabetes sufferers and also to produce human growth hormone for children who aren't growing properly.

Genetic engineering involves these important stages:

1) The useful gene is "cut" from the DNA of say a human.
2) This is done using enzymes. Particular enzymes will cut out particular bits of DNA.
3) Enzymes are then used to cut the DNA of a bacterium and the human gene is then inserted.
4) Again this "splicing" of a new gene is controlled by certain specific enzymes.
5) The bacterium is now cultivated and soon there are millions of similar bacteria all producing, say human insulin.
6) This can be done on an industrial scale and the useful product can be separated out.
7) The same approach can also be used to transfer useful genes into animal embryos. Sheep for example can be developed which produce useful substances (i.e. drugs) in their milk. This is a very easy way to produce drugs.

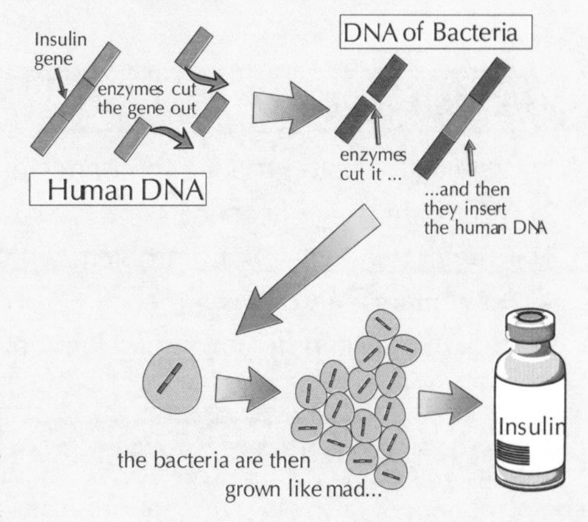

Breeding Plants and Animals

*Many plants produce **clones** — all by themselves*

This means they produce exact genetic copies of themselves without involving another plant.
Here are three common ones:

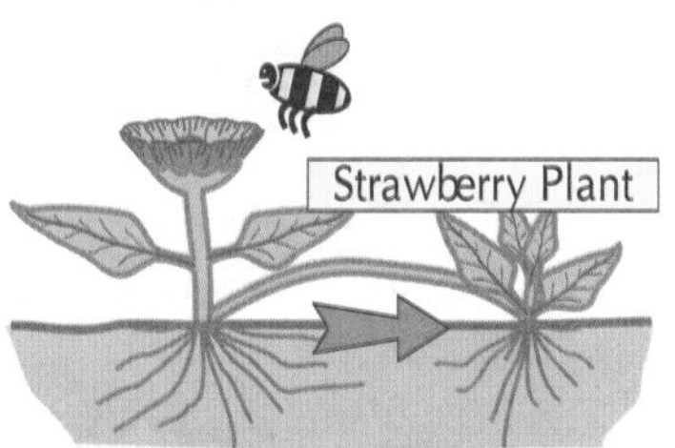

1) Strawberry plants producing *runners*.

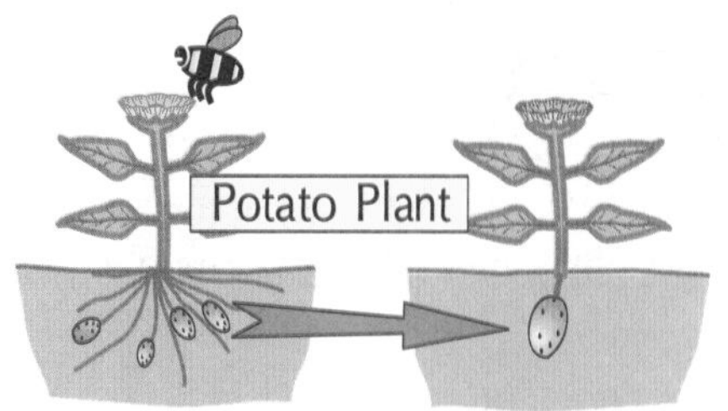

2) New potato plants growing from tubers of old plant.

3) Bulbs such as daffodils growing new bulbs off the side of them.

*Gardeners make **clones** from **cuttings***

1) Gardeners are familiar with taking cuttings from good parent plants, and then planting them to produce identical copies (clones) of the parent plant.
2) The cuttings are kept in a damp atmosphere until their roots develop.
3) These plants can be produced quickly and cheaply.
4) These days, this basic technique has been given the full high-tech treatment by commercial plant breeders:

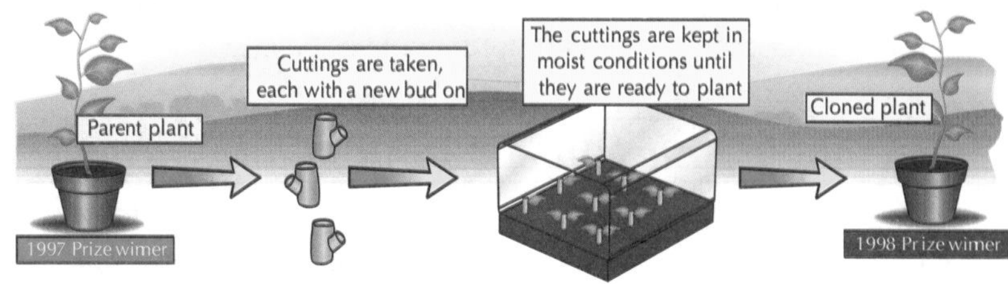

*The essentials of **commercial cloning**:*

Tissue culture

This is where, instead of starting with at least a stem and bud, they just put a few plant cells in a growth medium with hormones and it just grows into a new plant. Just like that.

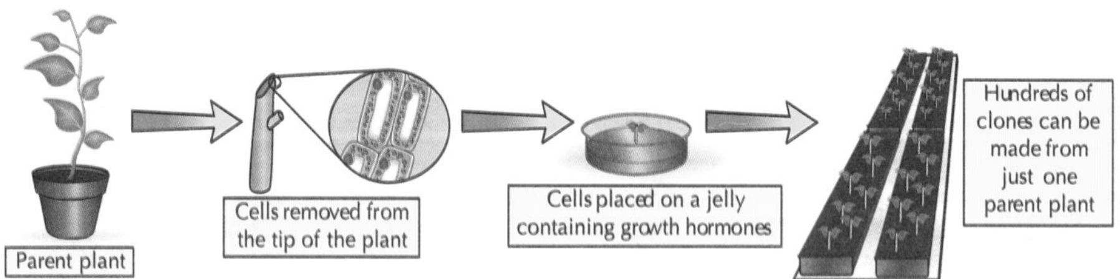

Advantages of tissue culture:

1) Very fast — can produce thousands of plantlets in a few weeks.
2) Very little space needed.
3) Can grow all year — no problem with weather or seasons.
4) New plants are disease-free.
5) New plants can be developed (very quickly) by splicing new genes into plantlets and seeing how they turn out.

Disadvantages of tissue culture:

Only the usual drawback with clones — a reduced "gene pool" leading to vulnerability to new diseases.

Breeding Plants and Animals

Science isn't just about cold hard facts any more. There's loads of stuff about whether or not the science is right or wrong. These moral questions are all part of "ethical issues", and come up all the time in exams. No matter what you believe, to get the marks for a question on this, you've got to learn what the different issues are:

Selective Breeding is seen by some people as Playing God

At the moment selective breeding is allowed in law — so that *should* make it OK.
Not everyone thinks so. Learn what the issues are and the examples given.

1) Some people think it's wrong to manipulate nature to force the evolution of animals for our benefit only.
2) For example, to produce cows that would die if we didn't milk them, because we've bred them to produce too much milk. Or to breed pigs with so much meat on them that they can't stand up. Some think it's cruel and wrong and others think it's just what we need to provide nutritious food at a cheap price.
3) At the moment there are no laws against selective breeding and most people see it as normal farming practice.

Cloning — medical breakthrough or a step too far?

1) The biggest issue in cloning at the moment is the cloning of human embryos.
2) Several groups of scientists want to clone human embryos to get replacement tissues and organs for people who need them.
3) A lot of people die at the moment because transplanted organs are rejected by their bodies.
   Using organs from embryos cloned from themselves would save their lives.
4) Some countries (including Britain and Japan) have banned human cloning because they think it is morally wrong. People argue that to create a life for spare parts and then kill it is wrong. Even though a lot of countries allow abortion of embryos at this stage of life.

Genetic engineering or "Designer Babies"?

There are loads of issues to do with genetic engineering. Learn these four:

1) A big problem for the future of human genetic engineering is the "designer baby" problem – parents might be able to choose the genes for their baby.
2) Changing the genetic make-up of any organisms may affect ecosystems in ways laboratory testing can't predict.
3) Large seed corporations can make sure they get money every year by selling plants that won't produce fertile seeds, or by producing plants that only respond to their fertilisers.
4) Genetic engineering may also mean that we can produce crops that grow in places they wouldn't before, saving lives in droughts and opening up freezing climates to farming.

Where will it all end — that's the question

Selective breeding is very simple. In the Exam you might be asked: "What is meant by selective breeding". That's when you write down the four points at the top of p78. Then they might ask you to "Suggest other ways that farmers in Sussex might use selective breeding to improve their yield". That's when you list some of the examples that you've learnt. This does get a bit tricky because the ethical issues are pretty controversial — but stick to learning both sides of the argument and you'll be just fine.

Warm-Up and Exam Questions

Warm-up Questions

1) What is selective breeding?
2) What is the main drawback of selective breeding?
3) What are clones?
4) What is genetic engineering?
5) Give three ethical issues arising from genetic engineering.

Exam Questions

1 The diagram on the right shows how human insulin is genetically engineered.

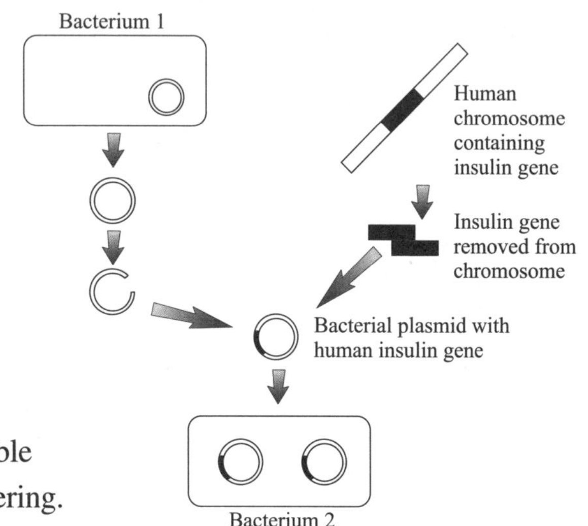

a) How is the insulin gene removed from the human DNA?

(1 mark)

b) The new bacterium containing the human insulin gene is later cloned.

(i) What is the definition of a clone?

(1 mark)

(ii) Suggest why bacteria are such suitable organisms for use in genetic engineering.

(2 marks)

c) Before human insulin could be genetically engineered, diabetics had to inject themselves with pig insulin. Give two advantages of genetically engineered insulin over pig insulin.

(2 marks)

2 The diagram below shows two ways that a plant breeder could breed plants.

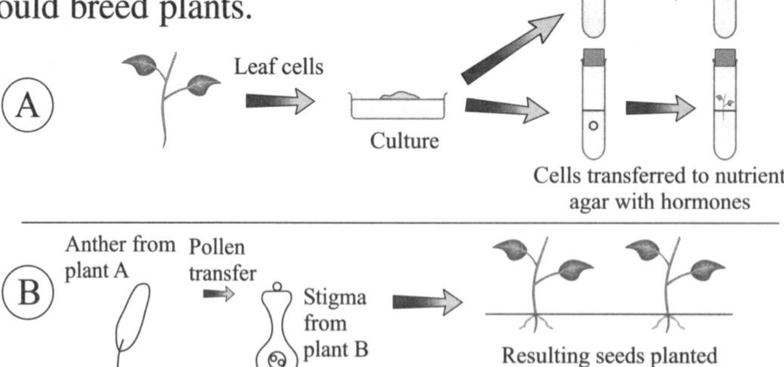

a) How do the offspring in process A compare genetically to their parents?

(1 mark)

b) Give three advantages to the breeder of using the tissue culture technique.

(3 marks)

c) What type of reproduction occurs in cross-pollination?

(1 mark)

d) Give one advantage of using cross-pollination to breed plants.

(1 mark)

Evolution

Fossils are the "remains" of plants and animals which lived millions of years ago.

There are **four ways** that **fossils** can be **formed**:

1) From the **hard parts** of animals

(Most fossils happen this way.)

Things like bones, teeth, shells, etc., which don't decay easily, can last a long time when buried. They're eventually replaced by minerals as they decay, forming a rock-like substance shaped like the original hard part. The surrounding sediments also turn to rock, but the fossil stays distinct inside the rock, and eventually someone digs it up.

2) From the **softer parts** of animals or plants — **petrification**

Sometimes fossils are formed from the softer parts which somehow haven't decayed. The soft material gradually becomes "petrified" (turns to stone) as it slowly decays and is replaced by minerals.
This is rare, since there are very few occasions when decay occurs so slowly.

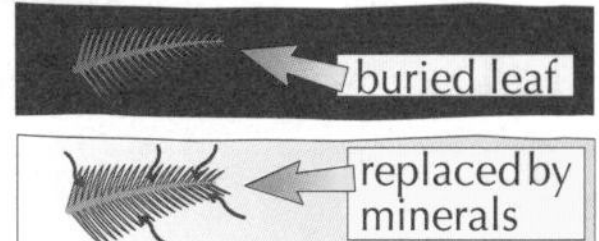

3) As **traces** of the animal or plant

When sediment turns into rock, everything in it is preserved. Even if geologists can't find animal or plant fossils, they can use footprints, burrows and the tracks of plant roots as evidence of what was there.

4) In places where **no decay** happens

The whole original plant or animal may survive for thousands of years:

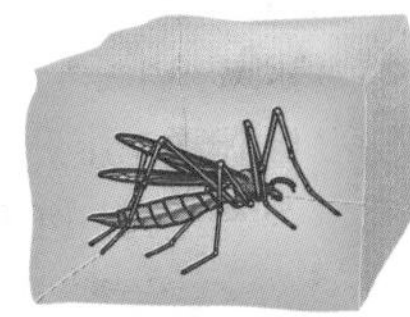

a) AMBER — no oxygen or moisture for the decay microorganisms. Insects are often found fully preserved in amber, which is a clear yellow "stone" made of fossilised resin that ran out of an ancient tree hundreds of millions of years ago, engulfing the insect.

b) GLACIERS — too cold for the decay microorganisms to work. Apparently a hairy mammoth was found fully preserved in a glacier somewhere several years ago.

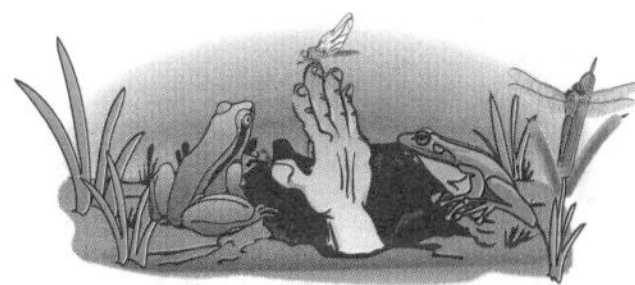

c) WATERLOGGED BOGS — too acidic for decay microorganisms. A 10,000 year old man was found in a bog a while back. He was a bit squashed but otherwise quite well preserved, although it was clear he had been murdered.

Evidence from **rock** and **soil strata**

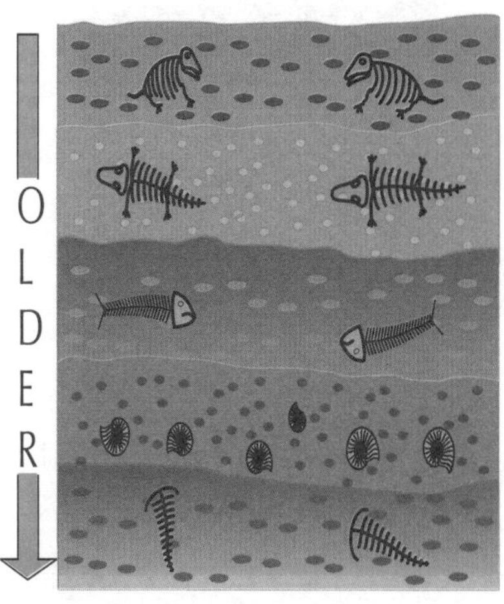

The fossils found in rock layers tell us two things:

1) What the creatures and plants looked like.
2) How long ago they existed, by the type of rock they're in.
Generally speaking, the deeper you find the fossil, the older it will be, though of course rocks get pushed upwards and eroded, so very old rocks can become exposed.

Fossils are usually dated by geologists who already know the age of the rock. The Grand Canyon in Arizona is about 1 mile deep. It was formed by a river slowly cutting down through layers of rock. The rocks at the bottom are about 1,000,000,000 years old, and the fossil record in the sides is pretty amazing.

Evolution

The Theory of Evolution — important stuff

1) This suggests that all the animals and plants on Earth gradually "evolved" over millions of years, rather than just suddenly popping into existence. Makes sense.
2) Life on Earth began as simple organisms living in water and gradually everything else evolved from there. And it only took about 3,000,000,000 years.

Fossils provide evidence for it

1) Fossils provide lots of evidence for evolution.
2) They show how today's species have changed and developed over millions of years.
3) There are quite a few "missing links" though because the fossil record is incomplete.
4) This is because very very few dead plants or animals actually turn into fossils.
5) Most just decay away completely.

Darwin's Finches Evolved to Suit Different Islands

1) When Darwin went to the Galapagos Islands, he saw that many of the islands had their own unique species of finch.
2) Each finch had a beak and body well adapted to the kind of food found on its particular island.
3) The finches were different species, but they all looked very similar.
4) Darwin realised that the finches had evolved from a common ancestor.
5) He proposed that originally a few seed-eating finches had flown to the islands from the mainland. Over millions of years the finches adapted to the foods available on each island — and evolved into separate species.

Seed Eater

Insect Eater

Extinction is the End of the Line

The dinosaurs and hairy mammoths became extinct and it's only fossils that tell us they ever existed at all.

There are three ways a species can become extinct:

1) The environment changes too quickly.
2) A new predator kills them all.
3) A disease kills them all.
4) They can't compete with another (new) species for food.

As the environment slowly changes, it will gradually favour certain new characteristics amongst the members of the species and over many generations those features will proliferate.

In this way, the species constantly adapts to its changing environment. But if the environment changes too fast the whole species may be wiped out, i.e. extinction.

Evolution

Darwin's theory of natural selection is ace

1) This theory is a major step towards a comprehensive explanation for all life on Earth.
2) However, it caused some trouble at the time, because for the first time ever, there was a highly plausible explanation for our own existence, without the need for a "Creator".
3) This was bad news for the religious authorities of the time, who tried to ridicule Darwin's ideas. But, as they say, "the truth will out".

Darwin made **four important observations**:

1) All organisms produce more offspring than could possibly survive.
2) But population numbers tend to remain fairly constant over long periods of time.
3) Organisms in a species show wide variation due to different genes.
4) Some of the variations are inherited and passed on to the next generation.

...and then made these **two deductions**:

1) Since most offspring don't survive, all organisms must have to struggle for survival. (Predation, disease and competition cause large numbers of individuals to die).
2) The ones who survive and reproduce will pass on their genes.

This is the famous "Survival of the fittest" statement. Organisms with slightly less survival-value will probably perish first, leaving the strongest and fittest to pass on their genes to the next generation.

Scary example: Bacteria adapt to beat antibiotics

The "survival of the fittest" affects bacteria just the same as other living things. The trouble is that we're giving them all the help they need to get more and more resistant to our bacterial weapons — antibiotics.

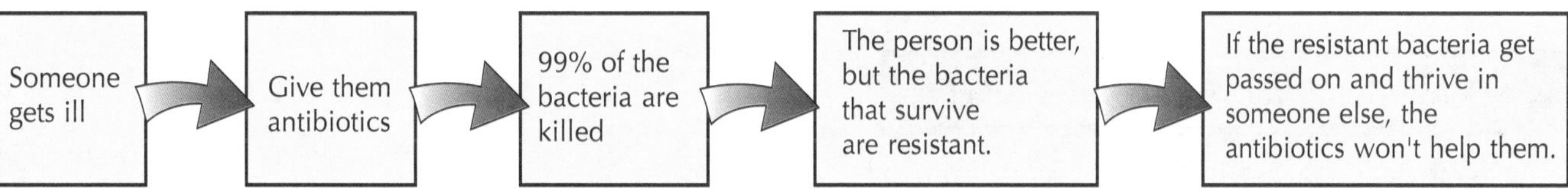
Someone gets ill
Give them antibiotics
99% of the bacteria are killed
The person is better, but the bacteria that survive are resistant.
If the resistant bacteria get passed on and thrive in someone else, the antibiotics won't help them.

Overuse of antibiotics is making things worse:

1) Nowadays people expect to get antibiotics for colds and throat infections and stuff.
2) The doctor gives them antibiotics in case it's a bacterial infection.
3) This produces resistant bacteria as shown above.
4) When a resistant bacteria arrives, we have to invent new antibiotics and then the process happens again.
5) Nowadays bacteria are getting resistant at such a rate the development of antibiotics can't keep up.

Lamarck's theory on evolution

Darwin's theory of evolution is fairly reliable. There was another theory which you need to know about by a man called LAMARCK. His theory was that:

Animals evolve features according to how much they use them

So giraffes, ever stretching to higher branches and straining their necks, passed on this fact to their offspring, who were then born with slightly longer necks. The theory isn't great and seems to be comprehensively disproved by experiments on mice who had their tails cut off for generation after generation and still grew tails just as long even though their forefathers never made any use of theirs.

Evolution

A mutation occurs when an organism develops with some strange new characteristic that no other member of the species has had before. For example if someone was born with blue hair it would be caused by a mutation. Some mutations are beneficial, but most are disastrous (e.g. blue hair).

Radiation and certain chemicals cause mutations

Mutations occur 'naturally', probably caused by "natural" background radiation (from the sun, and rocks etc.) or just the laws of chance that every now and then the DNA doesn't quite copy itself properly.
However the chance of mutation is increased by exposing yourself to:

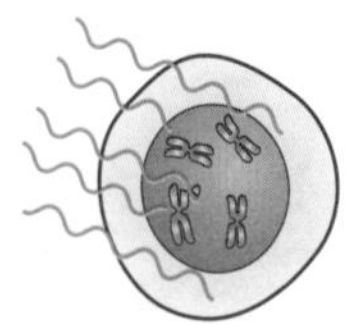

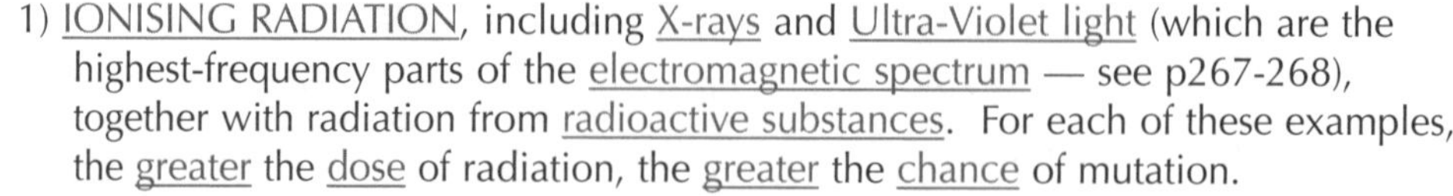

1) IONISING RADIATION, including X-rays and Ultra-Violet light (which are the highest-frequency parts of the electromagnetic spectrum — see p267-268), together with radiation from radioactive substances. For each of these examples, the greater the dose of radiation, the greater the chance of mutation.

2) CERTAIN CHEMICALS which are known to cause mutations. Such chemicals are called mutagens. If the mutations produce cancer then the chemicals are often called carcinogens. Cigarette smoke contains chemical mutagens (or carcinogens).

Mutations are caused by faults in the DNA

There are several ways that mutations happen, but in the end they're all down to faulty DNA.
Mutations usually happen when the DNA is replicating itself and something goes wrong.
Since genes and chromosomes are made of DNA, there are several different definitions of what a mutation is.

However this is the one you need to learn for the Exam:

> A MUTATION is a change in a gene, DNA or the number of chromosomes in a cell, which leads to genetic variation.

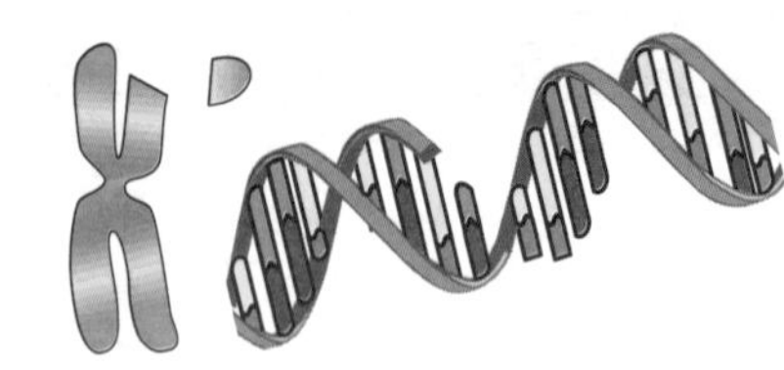

Most mutations are harmful

1) If a mutation occurs in reproductive cells, then the young may develop abnormally or die at an early stage of their development.
2) If a mutation occurs in body cells, the mutant cells may start to multiply in an uncontrolled way and invade other parts of the body. This is what we know as cancer.

Some mutations are beneficial, giving us "evolution"

1) Blue budgies appeared suddenly as a mutation amongst yellow budgies. This is a good example of a neutral effect. It didn't harm its chances of survival and so it flourished (and at one stage, every grandma in Britain had one).

2) Very occasionally, a mutation will give the organism a survival advantage over its relatives. This is natural selection and evolution at work. A good example is the mutation in a bacterium that makes it resistant to antibiotics, as discussed on page 85.

Mutations — sometimes good, sometimes bad

This is pretty interesting stuff — which makes it easier to learn, at least. Use the mini-essay method here. And make sure you learn every fact. Dinosaurs never did proper revision and look what happened to them. (Mind you they did last about 200 million years, which is about 199.9 million more than we have, so far...)

Warm-Up and Exam Questions

Warm-up Questions

1) What are fossils?
2) What does the 'Theory of Evolution' suggest?
3) What provides evidence for this 'Theory of Evolution'?
4) How did Darwin explain the different species of finches he found on the Galapagos Islands?
5) What does 'extinction' mean? Name three ways that species can become extinct.
6) Who proposed the 'Theory of Natural Selection'?
7) What are the three main reasons that organisms die young in the wild?
8) Give a definition of a mutation.
9) What is cancer?

Exam Questions

1 The diagram on the right shows the fossil record for various groups of vertebrates. The width of each band represents the amount of fossil remains found from each period.

Era	Period	Years Ago
Cenozoic	Quarternary	2M
	Tertiary	70M
Mesozoic	Cretaceous	135M
	Jurassic	180M
	Triassic	225M
Palaeozoic	Permian	270M
	Carboniferous	350M
	Devonian	400M
	Silurian	440M
	Ordovician	500M
	Cambrian	570M

a) During which era did reptiles probably evolve?
(1 mark)

b) During which period did the first amphibian probably evolve?
(1 mark)

c) During which period were fish probably most abundant?
(1 mark)

d) What are fossils?
(1 mark)

e) Give a suggestion for the evolutionary progression from fish to the other vertebrates.
(2 marks)

2 The peppered moth is a good example of the process of evolution. Before the Industrial Revolution, most peppered moths were light in colour. They were well camouflaged on the light, lichen-covered tree trunks. During the Industrial Revolution, however, the air became polluted and soot settled on the trees, meaning the light-coloured moths were easily seen. Any dark-coloured moths (which were also more resistant to pollution) tended to survive and grow in number. After the Clean Air Act in 1956, the amount of soot on the trees gradually decreased, and the number of light-coloured moths began to increase again.

a) What genetic process caused the black peppered moth in the first place?
(1 mark)

b) Name the process of evolution described in the passage above.
(1 mark)

c) Explain what happened to the two types of moth after the Clean Air Act in 1956.
(4 marks)

d) Charles Darwin put forward the 'Theory of Natural Selection' in his book 'The Origin of Species', published in 1859. Give three of Darwin's observations which led him to his theory.
(3 marks)

Genes and DNA

There are 23 matched pairs of chromosomes in every human body cell.
You'll notice the 23rd pair are labelled XY. They're the two chromosomes that decide whether you turn out male or female. They're called the X and Y chromosomes because they look like an X and a Y.

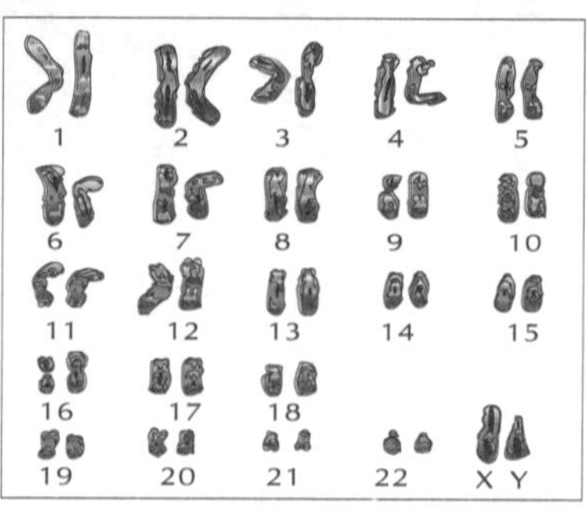

All MEN have an X and a Y chromosome: XY
The Y chromosome is DOMINANT and causes MALE characteristics.
All WOMEN have two X chromosomes: XX
The XX combination allows FEMALE characteristics to develop.

The diagram below shows the way the male XY chromosomes and female XX chromosomes split up to form the gametes (eggs or sperm), and then combine together at fertilisation.

The criss cross lines show all the possible ways the X and Y chromosomes could combine.

Remember, only one of these would actually happen for any offspring.
What the diagram shows us is the relative probability of each type of zygote (offspring) occurring.

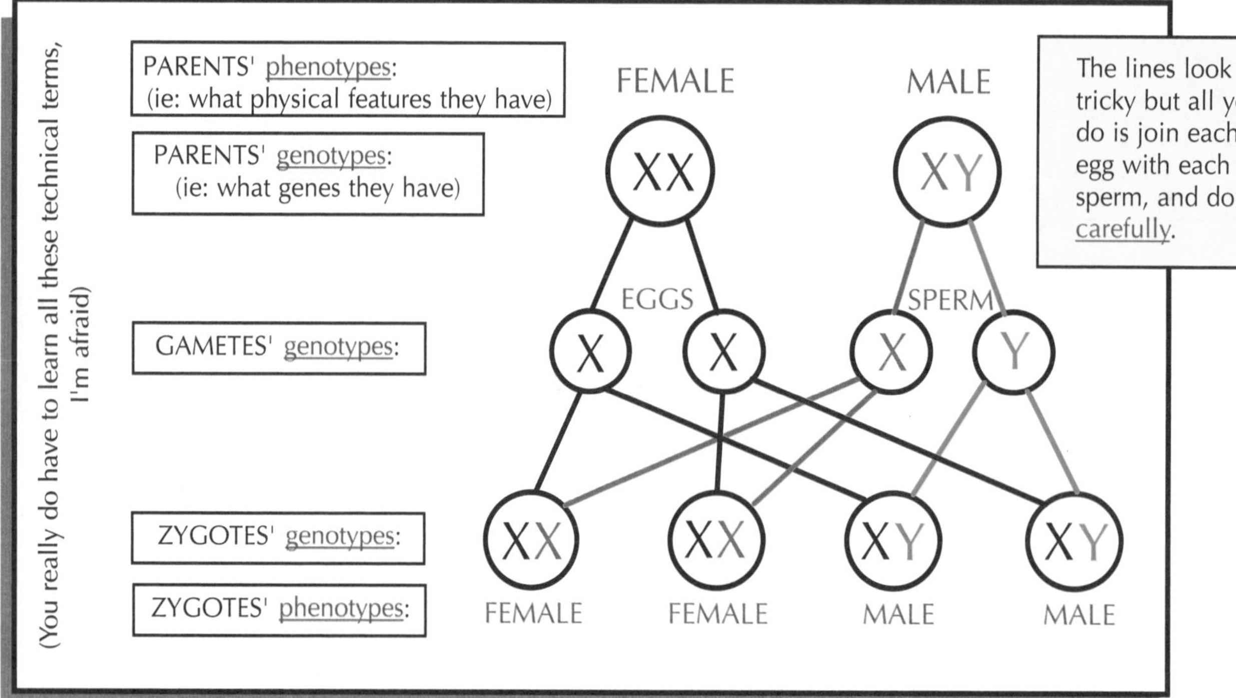

The other way of doing this is with a chequerboard type diagram. If you don't understand how it works, ask your teacher to explain it. The pairs of letters in the middle show the gene types of the possible offspring.

Both diagrams show that there'll be the same proportion of male and female offspring, because there are two XX results and two XY results.

Don't forget that this 50:50 ratio is only a probability.
If you had four kids they could all be boys.

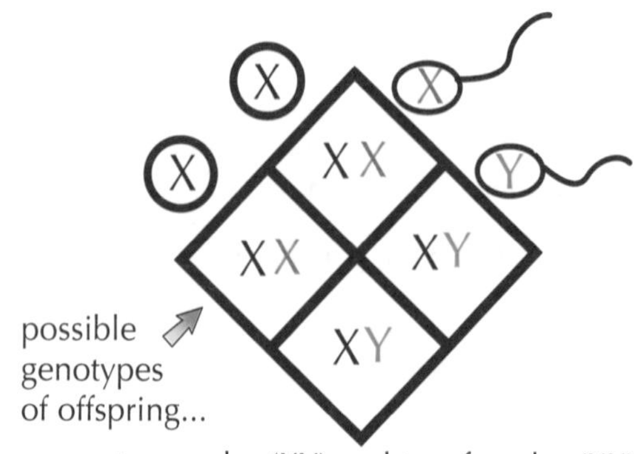

...two males (XY) and two females (XX).

At the end of the day it's just a 50:50 chance

Make sure you know all about X and Y chromosomes and who has what combination.
The diagrams are really important. Practise reproducing them until you can do it effortlessly.

Genes and DNA

Breeding **two plants** or **animals** who have **one gene different**

The best way to see what you get is with a diagram like either of these:

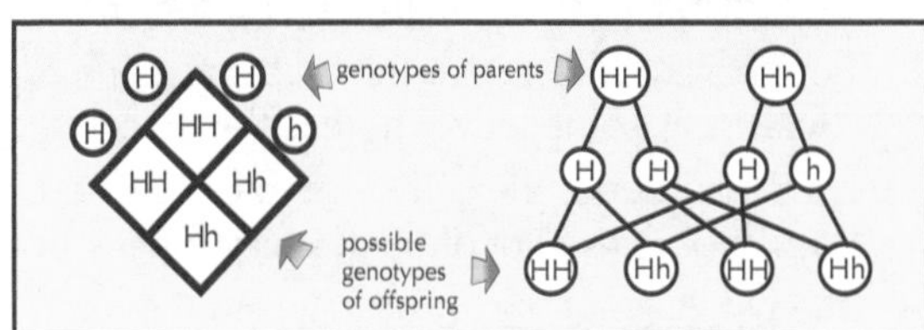

But first learn all these technical terms — it's difficult to follow what's going on if you don't:

1) Allele

2) Dominant and recessive

— self explanatory. A dominant allele dominates a recessive allele.

3) "Parental", "F1" and "F2" generations

— pretty obvious. The two originals that you cross are the parental generation, their kids are the F1 generation and the "grandchildren" are the F2 generation.

4) Homozygous and heterozygous

— "Homo-" means "same kind of things", "Hetero-" means "different kind of things".
They stick "-zygous" on the end to show we're talking about genes, (rather than any other aspect of Biology).
So...

"Homozygous recessive" is the descriptive 'shorthand' for this:	hh
"Homozygous dominant" is the 'shorthand' for:	HH
"Heterozygous" is the 'shorthand' for:	Hh

"A Homozygote" or "A Heterozygote" are how you refer to people with such genes.

Example — Hamsters

Let's take a thoroughbred crazy hamster, genotype hh, with a thoroughbred normal hamster, genotype HH, and cross breed them. You must learn this whole diagram thoroughly, till you can do it all yourself:

P1 Parents' *PHYSICAL TYPE*: Normal Crazy
P1 Parents' *GENE TYPE*:

Gametes' *GENE TYPE*:

F1 Zygotes' *GENE TYPE*:
F1 Zygotes' *PHYSICAL TYPE*: *They're all normal*

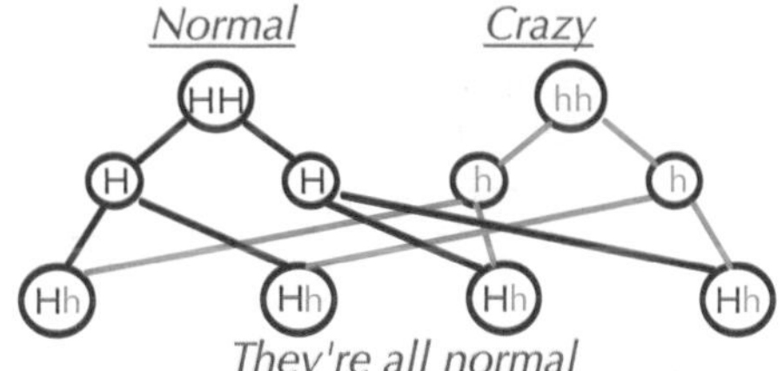

If two of these F1 generation now breed they will produce the F2 generation:

F1 Parents' *PHYSICAL TYPE*: Normal Normal
F1 Parents' *GENE TYPE*:

Gametes' *GENE TYPE*:

F2 Zygotes' *GENE TYPE*:
F2 Zygotes' *PHYSICAL TYPE*: Normal Normal Normal *CRAZY*

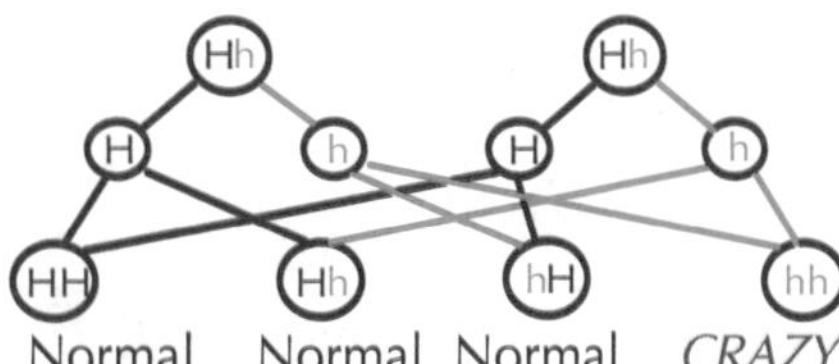

This gives a 3 : 1 ratio of Normal to Crazy Offspring in the F2 generation.

Remember that "results" like this are only probabilities.

It doesn't mean it will happen.

See how those fancy words start to roll off the tongue...

The diagram and all its fancy words need to be second nature to you. So practise writing it out from memory until you get it all right. Because when you can do one — you can do them all.

Genes and DNA

Cystic Fibrosis is caused by a recessive gene (allele)

1) Cystic Fibrosis is a genetic disease which affects about 1 in 1600 people in the UK.
2) Both parents must have the defective gene for the disorder to be passed on although both may be carriers. A carrier is somebody who has the defective gene without actually having the disorder.
3) It's a disorder of the cell membranes caused by a defective gene. The result of the defective gene is that the body produces a lot of thick sticky mucus in the lungs, which has to be removed by massage.
4) The blockage of the air passages in the lungs causes a lot of chest infections.
5) Physiotherapy and antibiotics clear them up but slowly the sufferer becomes more and more ill. There's still no cure or effective treatment for this condition.

The genetics behind cystic fibrosis is actually very straightforward. The gene which causes cystic fibrosis is a recessive gene, c, carried by about 1 person in 20.

The usual genetic inheritance diagram illustrates what goes on:

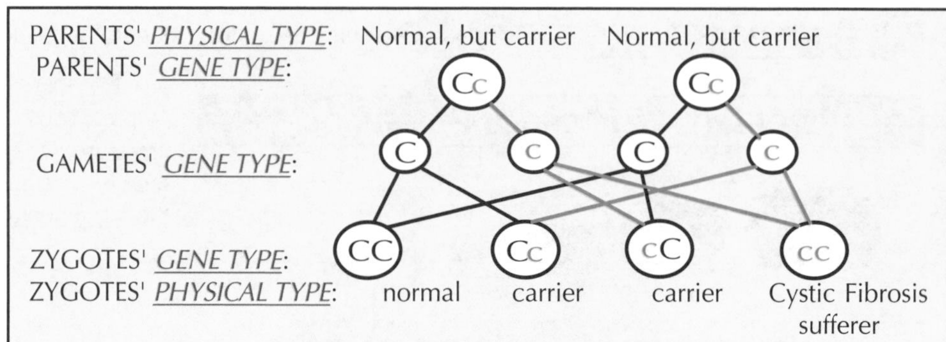

This diagram illustrates the 1 in 4 chance of a child having the disease, if both parents are carriers.

Sickle Cell Anaemia — caused by a recessive allele

normal cell sickle cell

1) This disease causes the red blood cells to be shaped like sickles instead of the normal round shape. They then get stuck in the capillaries which deprives body cells of oxygen.
2) Parents may be carriers without showing the symptoms, but both parents must have the defective gene for the disease to appear in any of their children.

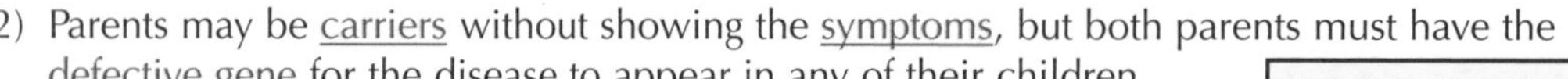

Normal, but carrier Normal, but carrier
Ss Ss
S s S s
SS Ss sS ss
normal carrier carrier Sickle cell sufferer

3) Yet even though sufferers may die before they can reproduce, the occurrence of sickle cell anaemia doesn't always die out as you'd expect it to, especially in Africa.
4) This is because carriers of the recessive allele which causes it are more immune to malaria. Hence, being a carrier increases their chance of survival in some parts of the world, even though some of their offspring are going to die young from sickle cell anaemia.
5) The genetics are identical to Cystic Fibrosis because both diseases are caused by a recessive allele. Hence if both parents are carriers there's a 1 in 4 chance each child will develop it:

Huntington's Chorea is caused by a dominant allele

1) This disorder of the nervous system, results in shaking, erratic body movements and severe mental eterioration.
2) The disorder can be inherited from one parent who has the disorder.
3) The "carrier" parent will of course be a sufferer too since the allele is dominant, but the symptoms do not appear until after the age of 40, by which time the allele has been passed on to children and even grandchildren. Hence the disease persists.
4) Unlike Cystic Fibrosis and Sickle Cell Anaemia, this disease is caused by a dominant allele.
5) This results in a 50% chance of each child inheriting the disease if just one parent is a carrier. These are seriously grim odds.

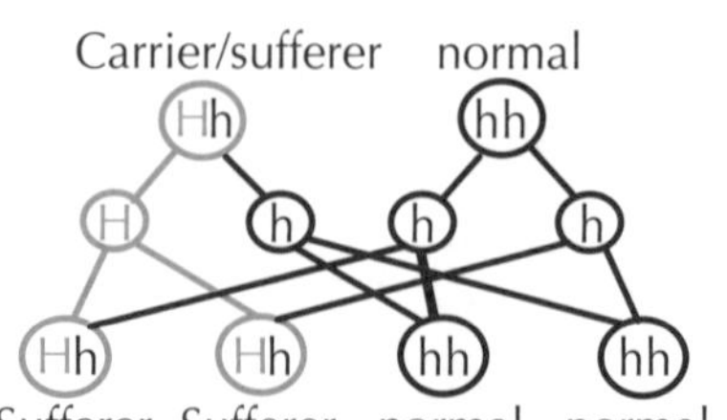

Learn the facts then see what you know

These diseases are all mentioned in the syllabus and questions on them are very likely. You need to learn all this very basic information on all three. Cover the page and scribble it all down.

Warm-Up and Exam Question

Take a deep breath and go through these warm-up questions one by one.
If you don't know these basic facts there's no way you'll cope with the exam questions.

Warm-up Questions

1) What is meant by the term 'phenotype'?
2) What is meant by a 'homozygous genotype'?
3) What are the symptoms of Huntington's Chorea?
4) What type of allele causes Cystic Fibrosis?
5) What is different about the type of allele that causes Huntington's Chorea compared to the alleles that cause Cystic Fibrosis and Sickle Cell Anaemia?

Exam Question

1 a) When a thoroughbred tall pea plant is crossed with a thoroughbred short pea plant, all the offspring are tall.

(i) Which is the recessive allele in the above cross?

(1 mark)

(ii) All the F_1 generation plants are tall. Explain how the combination of their genes is different from the parental tall pea plants.

(1 mark)

b) Cystic Fibrosis is a genetic disease, caused by a recessive allele, which affects about 1 in 1600 people in the UK.

(i) What are the physical symptoms of this defective gene?

(2 marks)

(ii) Complete the diagram below to show the likely genotypes of the children when the parents are both carriers.

Parental phenotypes	Normal (carrier)	×	Normal (carrier)
Parental genotypes	Ff	×	Ff
Gametes	(F) (f)	×	(F) (f)

	F	f

(4 marks)

(iii) Explain why the parents are said to be carriers of this disease.

(2 marks)

(iv) Which child or children from the above cross have cystic fibrosis?

(1 mark)

Hormones

1) The monthly release of an egg from a woman's ovaries and the build up and break down of a protective lining in the womb is called the menstrual cycle.
2) Hormones released by the pituitary gland and the ovaries control the different stages of the menstrual cycle.

There are **three main hormones** involved

1) FSH (Follicle Stimulating Hormone):

1) Produced by the pituitary gland.
2) Causes an egg to develop in one of the ovaries.
3) Stimulates the ovaries to produce oestrogen.

2) Oestrogen:

1) Produced in the ovaries.
2) Causes pituitary to produce LH.
3) Inhibits the further release of FSH.

3) LH (Luteinising Hormone):

1) Produced by the pituitary gland.
2) Stimulates the release of an egg at around the middle of the menstrual cycle.

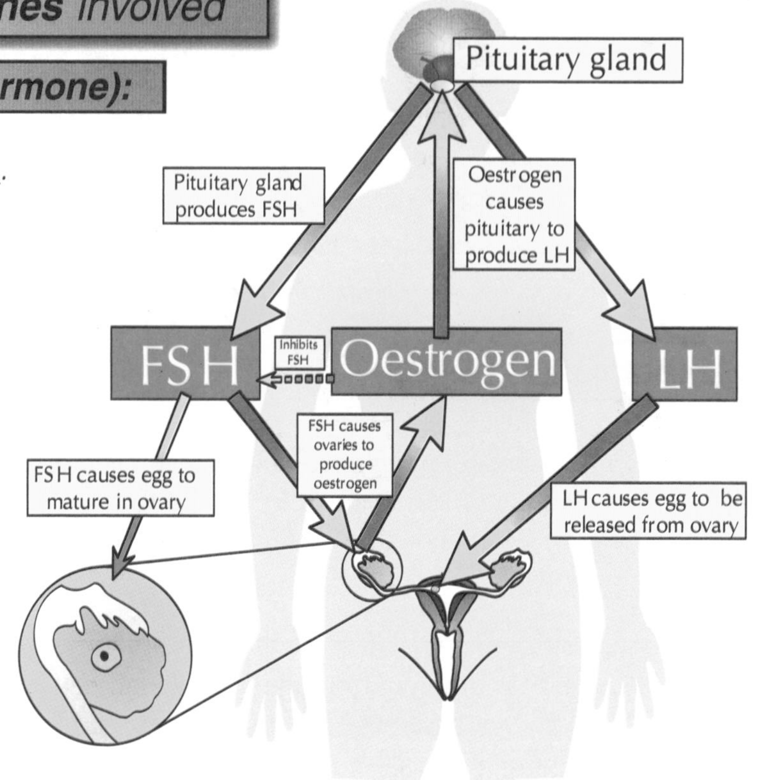

Pituitary gland
Pituitary gland produces FSH
Oestrogen causes pituitary to produce LH
FSH
Inhibits FSH
Oestrogen
LH
FSH causes ovaries to produce oestrogen
FSH causes egg to mature in ovary
LH causes egg to be released from ovary

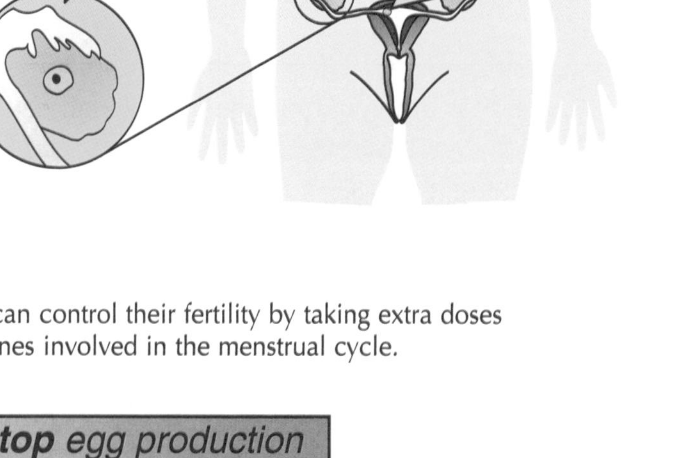

Oestrogen and FSH can both be used to artificially control fertility (see below).

The control of **fertility**

Women can control their fertility by taking extra doses of hormones involved in the menstrual cycle.

Oestrogen in **"the Pill"** is used to **stop** egg production

1) "The Pill", as it's known, is an oral contraceptive that contains oestrogen.
2) It may seem kind of strange but even though oestrogen stimulates the release of eggs, if oestrogen is taken every day to keep the level of it permanently high, it inhibits the production of FSH and after a while egg production stops and stays stopped.
3) They also have their drawbacks as the hormones can produce side-effects such as headaches and nausea. They are also not 100% effective at preventing pregnancy.

FSH is used to **stimulate** egg production in **fertility treatment**

1) A hormone called FSH can be taken by women (who have low level of FSH) to stimulate egg production in their ovaries.

2) In fact FSH (Follicle Stimulating Hormone) stimulates the ovaries to produce oestrogen which in turn stimulates the release of an egg.

3) But you do have to be careful with the dosage of these drugs or too many eggs can be released resulting in multiple births.

It's a complicated process

It's difficult to get a full understanding of how these three hormones all interact with each other to keep the monthly cycle going. Just learn what's on the page and you should be fine.

Warm-Up and Exam Question

The warm-up questions run quickly over the basic facts you'll need in the exam.
Unless you've learnt the facts first you'll find the exam question pretty difficult.

Warm-up Questions

1) Name a hormone that is produced in the ovaries.
2) Name two other hormones involved in the menstrual cycle that aren't produced in the ovaries.
3) What does oestrogen do in the menstrual cycle?

Exam Question

Exam questions are the best way to practise what you've learnt.
After all, they're exactly what you'll have to do on the big day — so get stuck in.

1 a) A woman's menstrual cycle is controlled by hormones such as Luteinising Hormone.

Name **two** other hormones which control the menstrual cycle.

....

....

(2 marks)

b) Name **two** places in the adult female body where these hormones are produced.

....

....

(2 marks)

c) Describe the part that Luteinising Hormone plays in controlling the menstrual cycle.

....

....

(1 mark)

d) A contraceptive pill can be taken regularly by women to stop them conceiving.

(i) Describe briefly how this pill works.

....

....

....

(3 marks)

(ii) Suggest one disadvantage of this method of contraception.

....

....

(1 mark)

Revision Summary for Section Four

All that business about genes and chromosomes — it's pretty serious stuff. It takes a real effort to get your head round it all. There are a lot of complicated words, for one thing. Anyway, use these questions to find out what you know — and what you don't. Then look back and learn the bits you didn't know. Then try the questions again, and again.

1) What are the two types of variation? Describe their relative importance for plants and animals.
2) Name the four factors affecting environmental variation in plants.
3) What causes the small differences between "identical" twins?
4) Draw a set of diagrams showing the relationship between: cell, nucleus, chromosomes, genes, DNA.
5) On page 71 there are 6 fancy words to do with genetics. List them all — with explanations.
6) Give a definition of mitosis. Draw a set of diagrams showing what happens in mitosis.
7) What is asexual reproduction? Give a proper definition for it. How does it involve mitosis?
8) Where does meiosis take place? What kind of cells does meiosis produce?
9) Draw out the sequence of diagrams showing what happens during meiosis.
10) How many pairs of chromosomes are there in a normal human cell nucleus?
11) What happens to the chromosome numbers during meiosis and then during fertilisation?
12) What is sexual reproduction? Give a proper definition for it.
13) Describe the basic procedure in selective breeding (of cows).
    Give three other examples of selective breeding.
14) What is meant by selective breeding?
15) Describe the advantages and disadvantages of selective breeding.
16) Give a good account of embryo transplants, and a good account of genetic engineering.
17) Describe the drawbacks and ethical problems concerning the use of genetic engineering.
18) Write down all you know on cloned plants.
19) Describe fully the four ways that fossils can form. Give examples of each type.
20) Describe three places where no decay occurs. Explain why there is no decay.
21) Explain how fossils found in rocks support the theory of evolution.
22) Give details about the theory of evolution. Give evidence for the theory.
23) Describe three ways that a species can become extinct.
24) What were Darwin's four observations and two deductions?
25) Describe two examples of how natural selection changes animals.
26) What are X and Y chromosomes to do with? Who has what combination?
27) Copy and complete the genetic inheritance diagram and the chequerboard diagram opposite to show how these genes are passed on.
28) Give brief explanations of the following words:
    a) Allele; b) Homozygous; c) Heterozygous.
29) Write down the fancy terms given to the following combinations of genes: a) HH; b) hh; c) Hh.
30) Starting with parental gene types HH and hh, draw a full genetic inheritance diagram to show the eventual gene types of the F1 and F2 generations.
31) Describe how radiation causes mutations. What else can cause mutations?
32) Name two things that increase the chance of a mutation occurring.
33) Describe the symptoms and treatment of Cystic Fibrosis. What causes this disease?
34) Give the cause and symptoms of Sickle Cell Anaemia. Why does it not die out?
35) Explain the grim odds for Huntington's Chorea.
36) List the three hormones involved in the menstrual cycle.
    Write down where they are produced and what they do.
37) Describe two examples of ways to manipulate fertility. What drawbacks are there to each method?

The Periodic Table

Today's Periodic Table lists Elements in order of Atomic Number

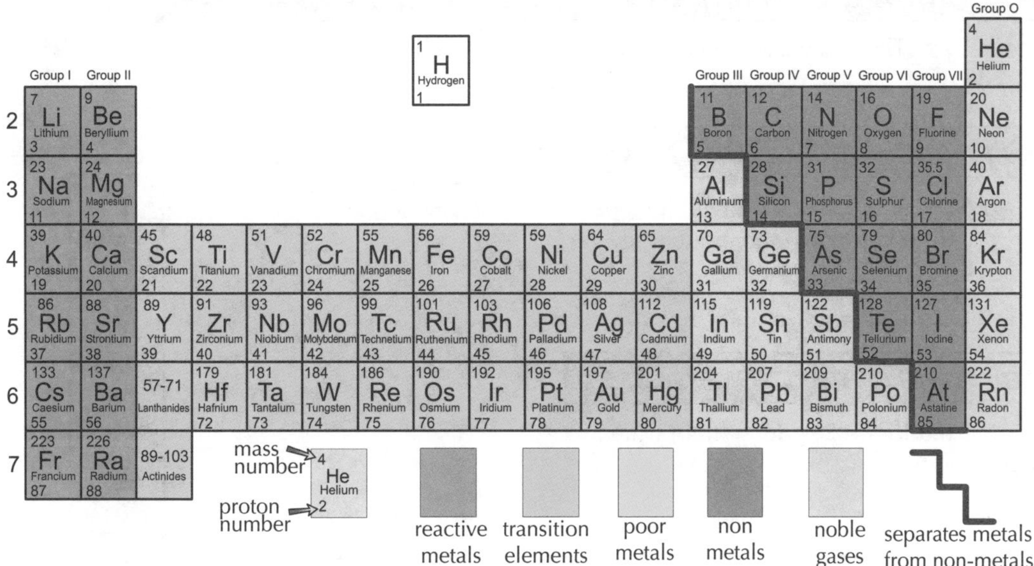

1) The Periodic Table shows the elements in order of proton number (or atomic number).
2) It's laid out so that elements with similar properties are in columns.
3) These vertical columns are called Groups and Roman Numerals are often used for them.
4) For example the Group II elements are Be, Mg, Ca, Sr, Ba and Ra.
   They're all metals which form 2+ ions and they have many other similar properties.
5) The rows are called periods. Each new period represents another full shell of electrons.
6) The elements in each Group all have the same number of electrons in their outer shell.
7) That's why they have similar properties. And that's why we arrange them in this way.

***Argon** doesn't quite follow the pattern*

1) Argon is in Group 0, Period 3. It has an atomic mass of 40.
2) Potassium, which comes next in the table, has an atomic mass of 39. If you trace your eye over the table, you'll spot that this is rather curious — generally, the elements get heavier.
3) The reason is that elements are arranged in order of atomic number, Z. It just happens that argon has a couple of extra neutrons which give it a greater mass than potassium, so its mass number is higher.

*More than **three-quarters** of the elements are **metals***

Three quarters is a big chunk.

Make sure you remember where the metals are — in the two left-hand columns and in the big central block.

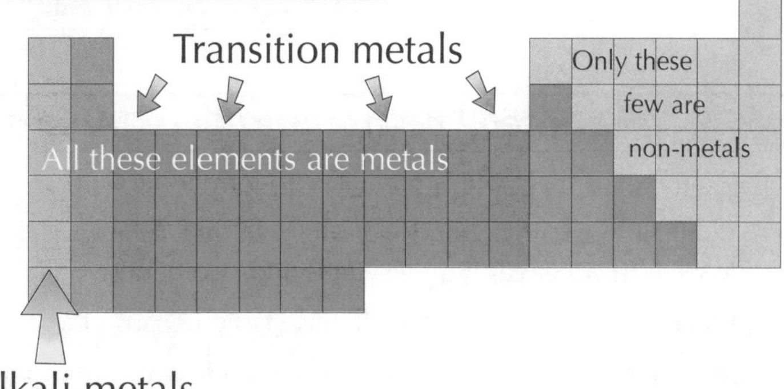

The Alkali Metals

They're called 'alkali metals' because their oxides and hydroxides dissolve in water to give an alkaline solution.

1) They are: **Lithium, Sodium, Potassium** and a couple more

Know those three names. They may also mention Rubidium and Caesium.

2) The alkali metals are very **reactive**

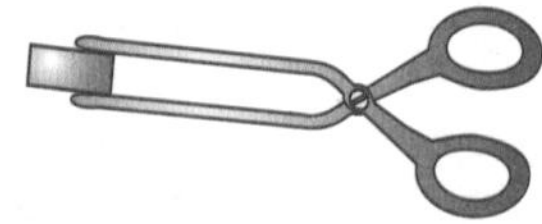

They have to be stored in oil and handled with forceps (they burn the skin). As you go down the group, they get more reactive.

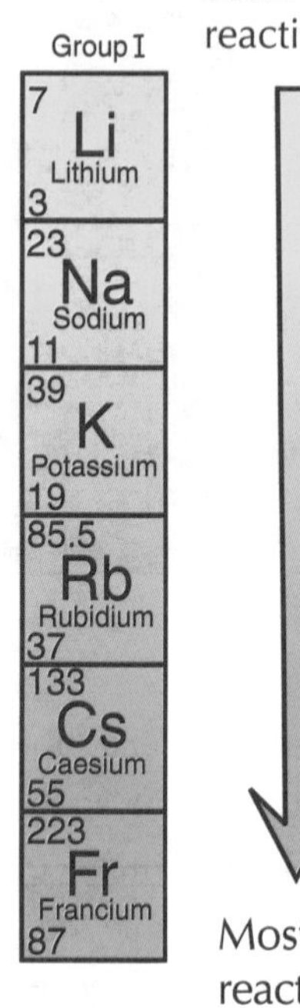

3) The alkali metals are **low density**

The first three (Li, Na and K) are less dense than water.
So they float on it.

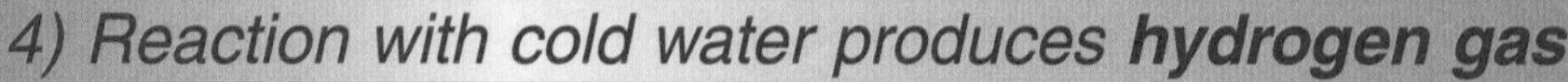

4) Reaction with cold water produces **hydrogen gas**

1) When lithium, sodium or potassium are put in water, they react very vigorously.
2) They move around the surface, fizzing furiously.
3) They produce hydrogen. Potassium gets hot enough to ignite it. A lighted splint will indicate hydrogen by producing the notorious "squeaky pop" as the H_2 ignites.
4) Sodium and potassium melt in the heat of the reaction.
5) They form a hydroxide in solution, ie: aqueous OH^- ions.

$$2Na_{(s)} + 2H_2O_{(l)} \rightarrow 2NaOH_{(aq)} + H_{2\,(g)}$$
$$2K_{(s)} + 2H_2O_{(l)} \rightarrow 2KOH_{(aq)} + H_{2\,(g)}$$

The solution becomes alkaline, which changes the colour of the universal indicator from green to purple.

5) Alkali metal **oxides** and **hydroxides** are **alkaline**

This means that they'll react with acids to form neutral salts, like this:

$$NaOH + HCl \rightarrow H_2O + NaCl \text{ (salt)}$$
$$Na_2O + 2HCl \rightarrow H_2O + 2NaCl \text{ (salt)}$$

6) All alkali metal **compounds** are **ionic** and **dissolve** easily

1) Alkali metals react with non-metals to form ionic compounds.
2) All alkali metal compounds are ionic, so they form crystals which dissolve in water easily to give colourless solutions.
3) Alkali metal compounds are all very stable because the alkali metals are so reactive.
4) Because they always form ionic compounds with giant ionic lattices the compounds all look pretty much the same, i.e. white crystals like the regular 'salt' we put on food.

Transition Metals

Transition metals are less reactive and so do not react (corrode) so quickly with oxygen and water.

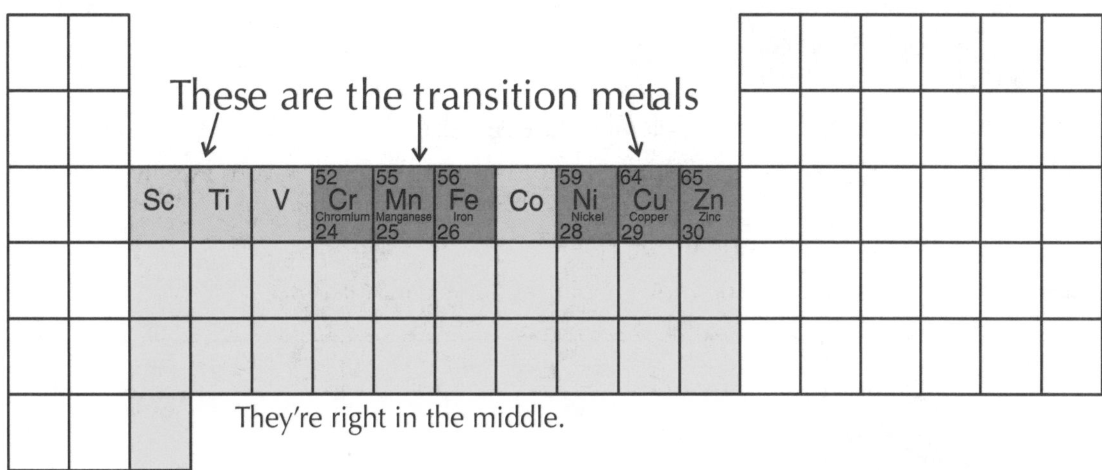

1) They are **Chromium, Manganese, Iron, Nickel, Copper, Zinc**

You need to know the ones shown in red fairly well. If they wanted to be mean in the Exam they could cheerfully mention one of the others like scandium, cobalt, titanium or vanadium. Don't let it hassle you. They'll just be testing how well you can "apply scientific knowledge to new information". In other words, just assume these "new" transition metals follow all the properties you've already learnt for the others — that's all it is.

2) **Transition metals** all have **high melting points** and **high densities**

They're typical metals. They have the properties you would expect of a proper metal:

1) Good conductors of heat and electricity (eg copper wire).
2) Very hard, tough and strong.
3) High melting points — iron melts at 1500°C, copper melts at 1100°C and zinc melts at 400°C. Mercury is the exception to this rule because it is liquid at room temperature.

3) **Transition metals** and their **compounds** make **good catalysts**

1) Iron is the catalyst used in the Haber process for making ammonia.
2) Manganese (IV) oxide is a good catalyst for the decomposition of hydrogen peroxide.
3) Nickel is useful as a catalyst for turning oils into fats (hydrogenation) for making margarine.

4) The **compounds** are very **colourful**

1) The compounds are colourful due to the transition metal ion which they contain.

   e.g. Potassium chromate (VI) is yellow.

   Potassium manganate (VII) is purple.

   Copper (II) sulphate is blue.

2) The colour of people's hair and also the colours in gemstones like blue sapphires and green emeralds are all due to transition metals. Weathered copper is a lovely green as well. If that's not enough for you, they're also used to make pottery glazes.

Lots of pretty colours — that's what we like to see

Three quarters of all elements are metals — that's quite a lot. And there's quite a bit to learn about alkali and transition metals. First try to remember the headings. Then learn the details under each.

Warm-Up and Exam Questions

These warm-up questions should ease you gently in and make sure you've got the basics straight. If there's anything you've forgotten, check up on the facts before you do the exam questions.

Warm-up Questions

1) Roughly what fraction of known elements are metals?
2) How does lithium react when dropped in cold water? Write the word equation for this reaction.
3) Name a metal which floats on water.
4) List two examples of transition metals being used as catalysts.

Exam Questions

Expect to get some kind of question about this stuff in the exam.

1 Potassium reacts violently when it is dropped into a beaker of cold water.

a) Write down the two products of this reaction.

potassium hydroxide + hydrogen.

(1 mark)

b) Write a balanced equation for the reaction.

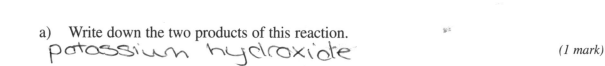

~~potassium +~~

$2K + 2H_2O \rightarrow 2KOH + H_2$

(1 mark)

c) Sodium reacts less violently than potassium when it is dropped into water. Explain why in terms of electron arrangement.

(3 marks)

There's a bit of overlap with section eight here, so you may want to have a look at that first.

2 This question is about the transition metals.

a) Would you expect the transition metals to be good conductors of electricity?

Yes, typical metals

(1 mark)

b) A catalyst is a substance that speeds up a chemical reaction without being used up in the reaction. Transition metals are used as catalysts in some industrial reactions. Which transition metal is used as a catalyst when hydrogenating vegetable oils to make margarine?

Nickel

(1 mark)

c) Manganese can form a manganate(VII) ion, MnO_4^-.
What colour is potassium manganate(VII), $KMnO_4$?

purple

(1 mark)

Reactivity Series of Metals

You must learn this *reactivity series*

You really should know which are the more reactive metals and which are the less reactive ones.

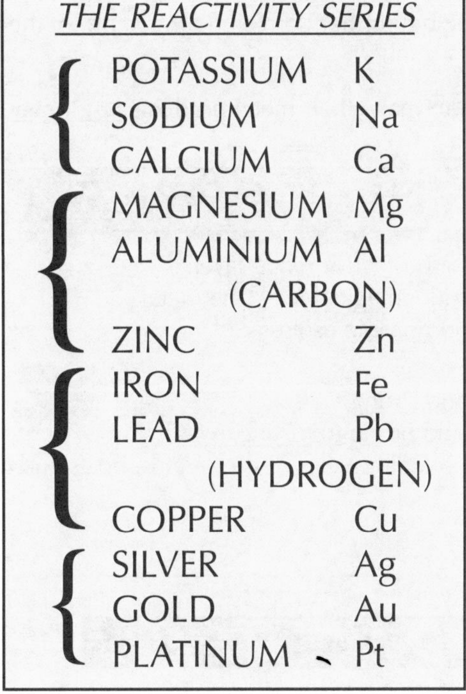

	THE REACTIVITY SERIES		
Very Reactive	POTASSIUM	K	Metals above carbon must be extracted from their ores by electrolysis.
	SODIUM	Na	
	CALCIUM	Ca	
Fairly Reactive	MAGNESIUM	Mg	
	ALUMINIUM	Al	
	(CARBON)		
	ZINC	Zn	Metals below carbon can be extracted from their ore using reduction with coke or charcoal.
Not very Reactive	IRON	Fe	
	LEAD	Pb	
	(HYDROGEN)		
	COPPER	Cu	Metals below hydrogen don't react with water or acid. They don't easily tarnish or corrode. Found in the ground in their pure metal form.
Not at all Reactive	SILVER	Ag	
	GOLD	Au	
	PLATINUM	Pt	

This reactivity series was determined by doing experiments to see how strongly metals react.
The three standard reactions to determine reactivity are with 1) air 2) water and 3) dilute acid.
These are important so make sure you know about all three in reasonable detail, as follows:

Reacting metals in *air*

1) Most metals will lose their bright surface over a period of time (they "tarnish").

2) The dull finish they get is due to a layer of oxide that forms when they react with oxygen in the air.

3) Heating them makes it easier to see how reactive they are, compared to each other.

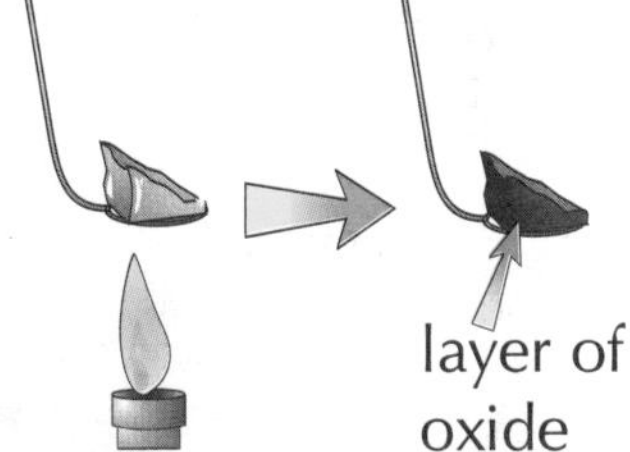

4) The equation is simple:

Metal + Oxygen → Metal Oxide

Reaction with Air

POTASSIUM SODIUM CALCIUM MAGNESIUM	Burn very easily with a bright flame
ALUMINIUM ZINC IRON LEAD COPPER	React slowly with air when heated
SILVER GOLD	No reaction

Examples: 1) $2Fe + O_2 \rightarrow 2FeO$ 2) $4Na + O_2 \rightarrow 2Na_2O$

Corrosion of Metals

Corrosion is **oxidation**

1) Reactive metals form oxides quite quickly when exposed to the air. This is corrosion.
2) Most metals form quite decent hard oxides that make a good protective layer.
3) A little helpful oxidation like this is a good thing but further corrosion turns more of the metal into its oxide, making it look horrid and go all crumbly.
4) Manufacturers prevent or slow down corrosion to make their metal products last longer.

Iron is made into **steel** which is **cheap** and **strong**

Unfortunately, iron is one metal that doesn't form a protective oxide layer. Instead, iron forms the most appalling red flaky oxide imaginable — the metal we use the most just had to be the one that turns to horrible useless rust.

IRON AND STEEL: ADVANTAGES: Cheap and strong.
DISADVANTAGES: Heavy, and prone to rusting away.
USED FOR: Bridges, buildings, cars, lorries, trains, boats and definitely NOT aeroplanes.

Bond **zinc** to it or add **chromium** to **prevent corrosion**

1) Bonding a layer of zinc metal onto the surface of steel stops it rusting. The zinc soon reacts with the air to form zinc oxide which gives a good protective layer. This is called *'sacrificial protection'* — any metal more reactive than iron can be used but it's mostly zinc or magnesium. Iron and steel treated in this way are used for: bridges, buildings and dustbins.
2) Mixing the steel with chromium makes an alloy called stainless steel. It doesn't oxidise so it's used for shiny cutlery and pans.

Aluminium is **light, strong** and **corrosion-resistant**

Strictly speaking you shouldn't say it's 'light', you should say it has 'low density'. Whatever. All I know is, it's a lot easier to lift and move around than iron or steel.

ADVANTAGES:
1) Lightweight. (*'low density'*)
2) It's easy to bend and shape.
3) It's also a good conductor of heat and electricity.
4) Doesn't corrode due to the protective layer of oxide which quickly covers it. This oxide is helpful corrosion — it forms a barrier to oxygen and water, stopping further corrosion.

DISADVANTAGES: Not as strong as steel and a bit more expensive.

USED FOR:
Ladders, aeroplanes, drink cans (tin-plated steel ones can rust if damaged), greenhouse frames and window frames, big power cables on pylons.

Its **alloys** are **stronger** and **harder**

1) Mixing aluminium with other metals makes it stronger, stiffer and harder.
2) A common aluminium alloy is made by adding magnesium.

Metals are a lot more interesting than most people ever realise

At last some chemistry which is useful in everyday life. Anyway, whether you're building your own rocket or not, you'll still have to learn it all for the Exam.

Warm-Up and Exam Question

The warm-up questions run quickly over the basic facts you'll need in the exam. The exam questions come later — but unless you've learnt the facts first you'll find the exams tougher than old boots.

Warm-up Questions

1) Which is more reactive, aluminium or lead?
2) Is magnesium more reactive than carbon?
3) What metal is used to make aeroplane bodies and wings?
4) Why is iron used to make bridges?

Exam Question

This exam question is exactly like you'll get in the real exam, so make sure you can do it. Don't be tempted to look the answers up in the back of the book — they won't be there in the real thing.

1 This table shows the reactivity series.

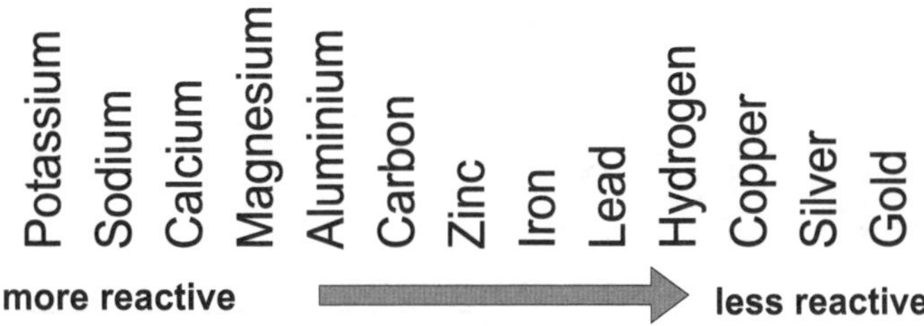

a) Which metals in the table are found in the ground in their pure state?

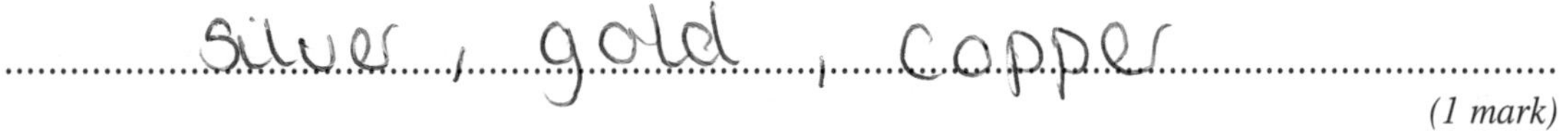

(1 mark)

b) Which metals can't be reduced by carbon, and must be extracted by electrolysis?

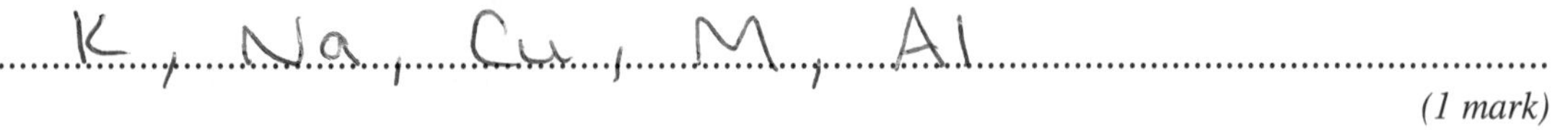

(1 mark)

c) Use the reactivity series to explain why silver won't react with water.

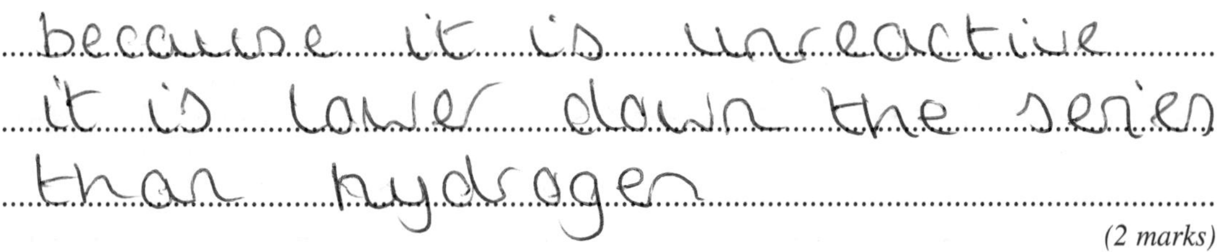

because it is unreactive
it is lower down the series
than hydrogen

(2 marks)

Metals Reacting with Water and Acid

*Reacting metals with **water***

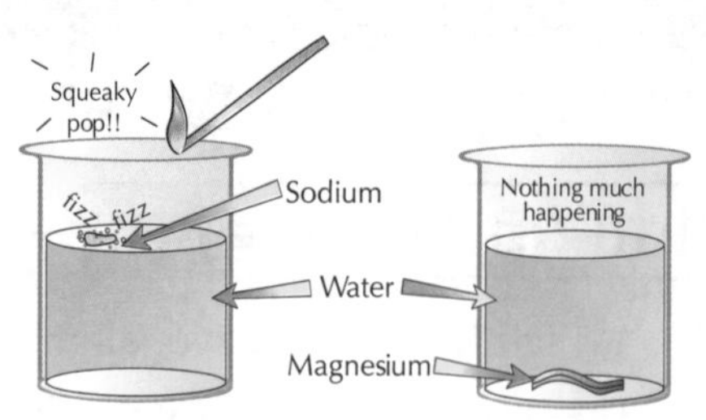

1) If a metal reacts with water it will always release hydrogen.
2) The more reactive metals react with cold water to form hydroxides:

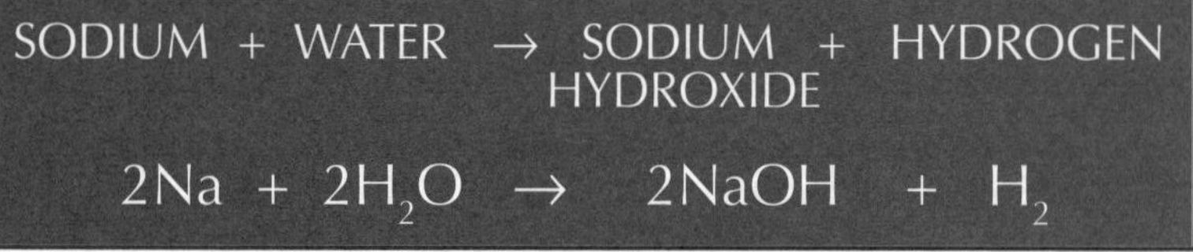

SODIUM + WATER → SODIUM HYDROXIDE + HYDROGEN

$$2Na + 2H_2O \rightarrow 2NaOH + H_2$$

3) The less reactive metals don't react quickly with water but will react with steam to form oxides:

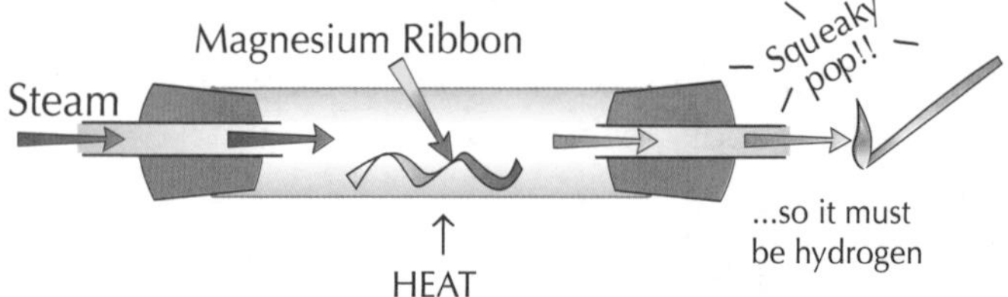

ZINC + WATER → ZINC OXIDE + HYDROGEN

$$Zn + H_2O \rightarrow ZnO + H_2$$

Reaction with Water

POTASSIUM SODIUM CALCIUM	React with cold water
MAGNESIUM ALUMINIUM ZINC	React with steam
IRON	Reacts reversibly with steam
LEAD COPPER SILVER GOLD	No reaction with water or steam

*Reacting metals with **dilute acid***

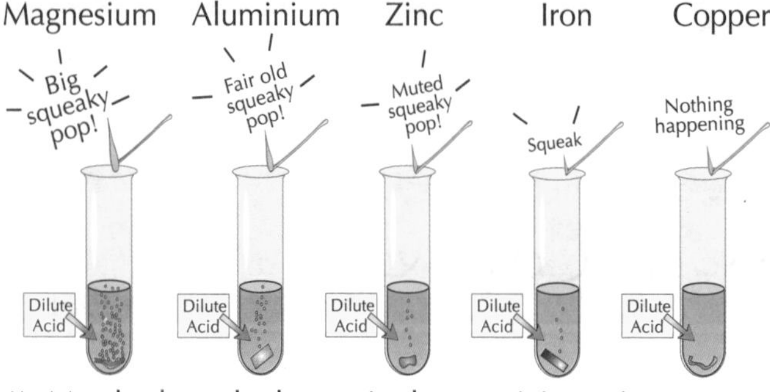

1) Metals above hydrogen in the reactivity series react with acids. Those below hydrogen won't.
2) The reaction becomes slower as you go down the series — as you'd expect.
3) The equation is simple:

METAL + ACID → SALT + HYDROGEN

$$Mg + 2HCl \rightarrow MgCl_2 + H_2$$

Reaction with Dilute Acid

POTASSIUM SODIUM CALCIUM	Violent reaction with dilute acids
MAGNESIUM ALUMINIUM ZINC IRON	React fairly well with dilute acids
LEAD COPPER SILVER GOLD	No reaction with dilute acids

*These reactions with water and acids are **"competition reactions"***

1) If the metal is more reactive than hydrogen it pushes the hydrogen out, hence the bubbles.
2) The metal replaces the hydrogen in the compound. Eg: in water, the metal "steals" the oxygen from the hydrogen to form a metal oxide. The hydrogen is then released as gas bubbles.
3) If the metal is less reactive than hydrogen, then it won't be able to displace it and nothing will happen.

Displacement Reactions

There's only one golden rule here:

A MORE reactive metal can displace a LESS reactive metal from a compound

1) This is such a simple idea, surely.
2) You know all about the reactivity series — some metals react more strongly than others.
3) So if you put a reactive metal like magnesium in a chemical solution you'd expect it to react.
4) If the chemical solution is a dissolved metal compound, then the reactive metal that you add will replace the less reactive metal in the compound.
5) The metal that's 'kicked out' will then appear as fresh metal somewhere in the solution.
6) But if the metal added is less reactive than the one in solution, then no reaction will take place.
7) Carbon and hydrogen (non-metals) will also displace less reactive metals from their oxides.

*The virtually world famous **iron nail in copper sulphate** demo*

A more reactive metal will displace a less reactive metal:

1) Put an iron nail in a solution of copper(II) sulphate and you'll see two things happen:
   a) The iron nail will become coated with copper.
   b) The blue solution will turn colourless.
2) This is because the iron is more reactive than the copper and displaces it from the solution.
3) This produces fresh copper metal on the nail and a colourless solution of iron sulphate.

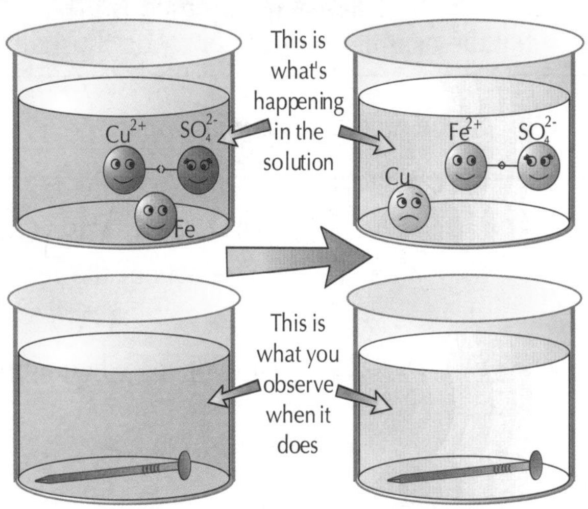

Cu^{2+}
SO_4^{2-}
Fe
This is what's happening in the solution
Fe^{2+}
SO_4^{2-}
Cu
This is what you observe when it does

You'll always see a deposit of metal and possibly a colour change:

The equation is very very easy:

$$\text{iron} + \text{copper sulphate} \rightarrow \text{iron sulphate} + \text{copper}$$
$$Fe + CuSO_4 \rightarrow FeSO_4 + Cu$$

*There are lots of different examples, **but they're all the same...***

Just remember the golden rule at the top of the page, and you can't go wrong.
The equations are always simple. The only tricky bit comes if the metals aren't both 2+ ions like in this one:

$$\text{zinc} + \text{silver nitrate} \rightarrow \text{zinc nitrate} + \text{silver}$$
$$Zn + 2AgNO_3 \rightarrow Zn(NO_3)_2 + 2Ag$$

But remember, if the metal added is less reactive, nothing will happen.
For example if you add iron to magnesium sulphate there'll be no reaction.

All this just to say "some metals react more than others"

I must say there are quite a lot of tricky details in these two pages. It's tempting to say that they can't possibly expect you to know them all. But then you look at the Exam questions and there they are, asking you precisely these kinds of tricky details. That's the way it goes — just got to learn it, that's all.

Warm-Up and Exam Questions

There's only one way to do well in the exam — learn the facts and then practise lots of exam questions to see what it'll be like on the big day. We couldn't have made it easier for you — so do it.

Warm-up Questions

1) Does calcium react with cold water?
2) Does aluminium react with cold water? Does it react with water at all?
3) What would happen if you put zinc in a test tube and poured dilute sulphuric acid on it?
4) What about if you did the same thing with magnesium?
5) Describe what happens when you put an iron nail in copper sulphate solution.
6) Explain your answer to 5).

Exam Questions

Take a look at these exam questions. They're not too hard but they should give you a good idea of what the examiners might ask. You'll usually get at least one metal reactions question in the exam.

1 Some metals react with water.

a) What are the products of the reaction between sodium and water? *(2 marks)*

b) What are the products of the reaction between aluminium and steam? *(2 marks)*

c) Describe what happens when aluminium is dropped into cold water. *(1 mark)*

2 This question is about the reaction of metals with acids.

a) What acid reacts with metals to produce sulphates? *(1 mark)*

b) 0.5g of magnesium is added to a test tube of dilute hydrochloric acid. Bubbles of a gas are produced.

i) State what gas is produced, and describe a test for this gas. *(2 marks)*

ii) Write a balanced equation for the reaction between hydrochloric acid and magnesium. *(2 marks)*

iii) 0.5g of zinc is added to a test tube of dilute hydrochloric acid. Bubbles of gas are produced more slowly than when magnesium is added. Explain why this is. *(1 mark)*

iv) Would you expect any bubbles of gas to be produced if 0.5g of copper was added to a test tube of dilute hydrochloric acid? Explain your answer. *(2 marks)*

Extracting Metals from Ores

Rocks, minerals and ores

1) A rock is a mixture of minerals.

2) A mineral is any solid element or compound found naturally in the Earth's crust.
Examples: Diamond (carbon), quartz (silicon dioxide), bauxite (Al_2O_3).

3) A metal ore is defined as a mineral or minerals which contain enough metal in them to make it worthwhile extracting the metal from it.

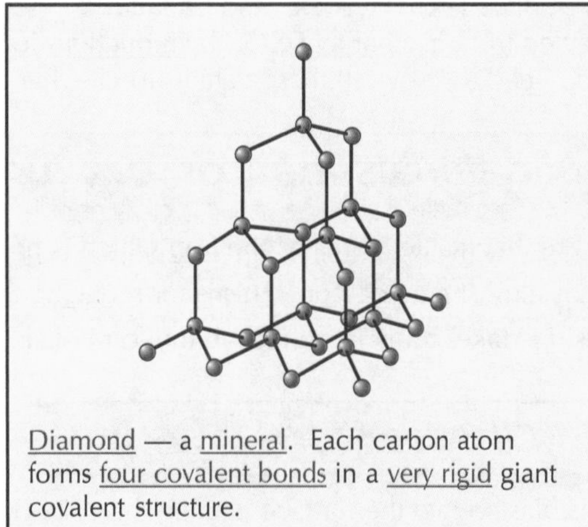

Diamond — a mineral. Each carbon atom forms four covalent bonds in a very rigid giant covalent structure.

Metals are **extracted** using **carbon** or **electrolysis**

1) Extracting a metal from its ore involves a chemical reaction to separate the metal out.
2) In many cases the metal is found as an oxide. There are three ores you need to know:

a) *Iron ore* is called *Haematite*, which is iron (III) oxide, formula Fe_2O_3.
b) *Aluminium ore* is called *Bauxite*, which is aluminium oxide, formula Al_2O_3.
c) *Copper ore* is called *Malachite*, which is copper (II) carbonate, formula $CuCO_3$.

3) The two common ways of extracting a metal from its ore are:
a) Chemical reduction using carbon or carbon monoxide (e.g. iron).
b) Electrolysis (breaking the ore down by passing an electric current through it).

4) Gold is one of the few metals found as a metal rather thanin a chemical compound (an ore). It can be found in its pure form in rivers etc.

5) This is because gold is so unreactive.

Gold Nuggets

More reactive metals are **harder to get**

1) The more reactive metals took longer to be discovered (e.g. aluminium, sodium).
2) The more reactive metals are also harder to extract from their mineral ores.
3) The above two facts are obviously related. It's obvious when you think about it.

Even primitive people could find gold easily enough just by scrabbling about in streams, and then melt it into ingots and jewellery and statues, but coming up with a fully operational electrolysis plant to extract sodium metal from rock salt, just by paddling about a bit... unlikely.

Extracting Iron — The Blast Furnace

Iron is a very common element in the Earth's crust, but good iron ores are only found in a few select places around the world, such as Australia and Canada.
Iron is extracted from haematite, Fe_2O_3, by reduction (ie: removal of oxygen) in a blast furnace.
You really do need to know all these details about what goes on in a blast furnace, including the equations.

The raw materials are *iron ore, coke* and *limestone*

1) The iron ore (haematite) contains the iron which is pretty important.
2) The coke is almost pure carbon. This is for reducing the iron oxide to iron metal.
3) The limestone takes away impurities in the form of slag.

Reducing the *iron ore* to *iron*:

1) Hot air is blasted into the furnace making the coke burn much faster than normal and the temperature rises to about 1500°C.
2) The coke burns and produces carbon dioxide:

$$C + O_2 \rightarrow CO_2$$

carbon + oxygen → carbon dioxide

3) The CO_2 then reacts with unburnt coke to form CO:

$$CO_2 + C \rightarrow 2CO$$

carbon dioxide + carbon → carbon monoxide

4) The carbon monoxide then REDUCES the iron ore to iron:

$$3CO + Fe_2O_3 \rightarrow 3CO_2 + 2Fe$$

carbon monoxide + iron (III) oxide → carbon dioxide + iron

The carbon monoxide itself combines with the oxygen in iron oxide to form carbon dioxide. This is OXIDATION.

5) The iron is of course molten at this temperature and it's also very dense so it runs straight to the bottom of the furnace where it's tapped off.

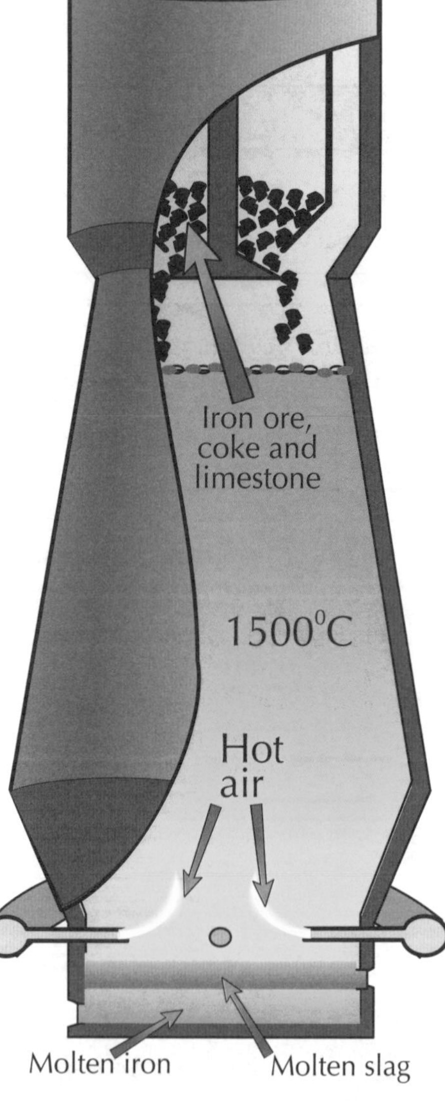

Removing the *impurities*:

1) The main impurity is sand, (silicon dioxide). This is still solid even at 1500°C and would tend to stay mixed in with the iron. The limestone removes it.
2) The limestone is decomposed by the heat into calcium oxide and CO_2.

$$CaCO_3 \rightarrow CaO + CO_2$$

3) The calcium oxide then reacts with the sand to form calcium silicate or slag which is molten and can be tapped off:

$$CaO + SiO_2 \rightarrow CaSiO_3 \quad \text{(molten slag)}$$

4) The cooled slag is solid, and is used for:
   1) Road building   2) Fertiliser

Remember — Reactivity dictates how metals are extracted

Two pages on metals and their ores. Every bit of it is important and could be tested in the Exam, including the equations. Use the mini-essay method to check you know a) why it's harder to extract the more reactive metals and b) how iron is extracted using the blast furnace.

Warm-Up and Exam Question

I know that you'll be champing at the bit to get into the exam question, but these basic warm-up questions are invaluable for getting the basic facts straight first.

Warm-up Questions

1) What is an ore?
2) What's the usual method for getting iron out of iron ore?
3) Bauxite is an ore of which metal?
4) Is gold found in the ground as an **ore** or as the **metal**?

Exam Question

You know the routine by now — work carefully through this exam question and make sure you understand it. If you're struggling, go back over the stuff in the last few pages and try again.

1 In a blast furnace, coke is burnt to reduce iron ore to iron.

a) What is the main element in coke?

(1 mark)

b) Coke burns to produce carbon dioxide.

i) Write a balanced equation for the burning of coke.

(2 marks)

ii) Carbon dioxide reacts with unburnt coke. Complete this equation to show this.

$\mathbf{CO_2 + C \rightarrow}$ ....

(1 mark)

c) Carbon monoxide (CO) reacts with iron(III) oxide (Fe_2O_3) to produce iron.

i) Write a balanced equation to show this.

(2 marks)

ii) What happens to the iron produced in this reaction?

(1 mark)

Extracting Aluminium — Electrolysis

A **molten state** is needed for **electrolysis**

1) Aluminium is more reactive than carbon so it has to be extracted from its ore by electrolysis.
2) The basic ore is bauxite, and after mining and purifying a white powder is left.
3) This is pure aluminium oxide, Al_2O_3, which has a very high melting point of over 2000°C.
4) For electrolysis to work a molten state is required, and heating to 2000°C would be expensive.

Cryolite is used to **lower the temperature** (and costs)

1) Instead, the aluminium oxide is dissolved in molten cryolite (a less common ore of aluminium).
2) This brings the melting point down to about 900°C, which makes it much cheaper and easier.
3) The electrodes are made of graphite (carbon).
4) The graphite anode (+ve) does need replacing quite often. It keeps reacting to form CO_2.

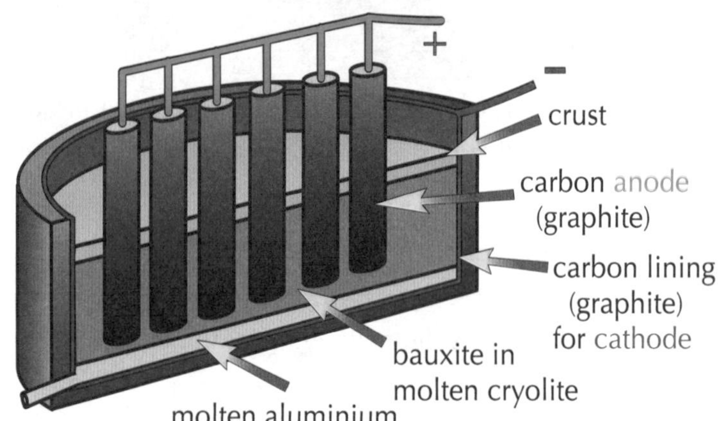

Electrolysis — turning **ions** into the **atoms** you want

This is the main object of the exercise:

1) Make the aluminium oxide molten to release the aluminium ions, Al^{3+} so they're free to move.
2) Stick electrodes in — so that the positive Al^{3+} ions will head straight for the negative electrode.
3) At the negative electrode they just can't help picking up some of the spare electrons, and 'zup' — they've turned into aluminium atoms and they sink to the bottom. Pretty clever.

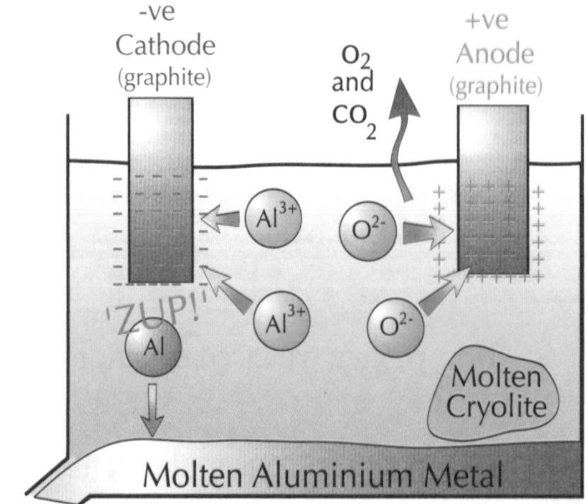

Overall, this is a REDOX reaction and you need to know the reactions at both electrodes:

At the Cathode (–ve):

$$Al^{3+} + 3e^- \rightarrow Al$$

(REDUCTION — a gain of electrons)

At the Anode (+ve):

$$2O^{2-} \rightarrow O_2 + 4e^-$$

(OXIDATION — a loss of electrons)

Purifying Copper — Electrolysis

1) Aluminium is a very reactive metal and has to be removed from its ore by electrolysis.
2) Copper is a very unreactive metal. Not only is it below carbon in the reactivity series, it's also below hydrogen, which means that copper doesn't even react with water.
3) So copper is obtained very easily from its ore by reduction with carbon.

Very pure *copper is needed for* ***electrical*** *conductors*

1) The copper produced by reduction isn't pure enough for use in electrical conductors.
2) The purer it is, the better it conducts. Electrolysis is used to obtain very pure copper.

The cathode starts as a thin piece of pure copper and more pure copper adds to it.

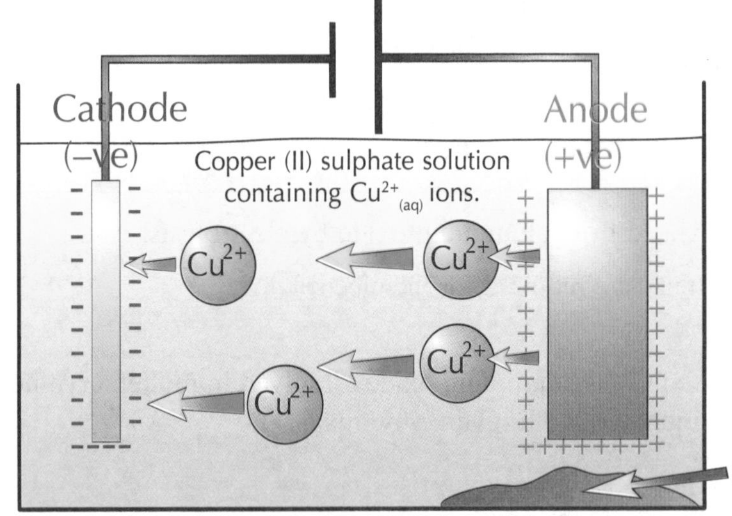

The anode is just a big lump of impure copper, which will dissolve.

The electrical supply acts by:
1) Pulling electrons off copper atoms at the anode causing them to go into solution as Cu^{2+} ions.
2) Then offering electrons at the cathode to nearby Cu^{2+} ions to turn them back into copper atoms.
3) The impurities are dropped at the anode as a sludge, whilst pure copper atoms bond to the cathode.
4) The electrolysis can go on for weeks and the cathode is often twenty times bigger at the end of it.

Pure copper is deposited on the pure cathode (–ve)

The reaction at the *CATHODE* is:

$$Cu^{2+}_{(aq)} + 2e^- \rightarrow Cu_{(s)}$$

This is an example of reduction.
The copper ions have been reduced to copper atoms by gaining electrons.

Copper dissolves from the impure anode (+ve)

The reaction at the *ANODE* is:

$$Cu_{(s)} \rightarrow Cu^{2+}_{(aq)} + 2e^-$$

Copper atoms have been oxidised into copper ions by losing electrons.
Overall, this is an example of a REDOX reaction. Reduction and oxidation can only occur simultaneously.

Electrolysis can take an... awfully... long... time...

Two pages on electrolysis, with several important points to learn for each. Initially you might find it easiest to cover the sections one at a time and try to recall the details in your head.
Ultimately though you should aim to repeat it all in one go with the whole page covered.

Warm-Up and Exam Questions

You must be getting used to the routine by now — the warm-up questions run over the basic facts, then the exam questions give you an idea how you'd cope on the day.

Warm-up Questions

1) Which is more reactive, aluminium or copper?
2) What is the name of the most common ore of aluminium?
3) Write down the reactions at the electrodes when aluminium is extracted using electrolysis.
4) Write down the reactions at the electrodes in the purification of copper by electrolysis.

Exam Questions

Exam questions are the best way to practise what you've learnt. After all, they're exactly what you'll have to do on the big day — so work through these questions very carefully.

1 Aluminium is separated from aluminium oxide by electrolysis.

a) Why is a molten state required for the electrolyte?

(2 marks)

b) The electrolyte used is aluminium oxide dissolved in molten cryolite, rather than just molten aluminium oxide. Explain why this is.

(2 marks)

c) What is the melting temperature of the electrolyte?

(1 mark)

d) i) Write down the ionic equation (without state symbols) showing what happens at the cathode.

(2 marks)

ii) Write down the ionic equation (without state symbols) showing what happens at the anode.

(2 marks)

iii) Explain why the graphite anode needs to be replaced frequently.

(2 marks)

2 Copper is purified by electrolysis.

a) What would you see happening to the pure copper electrode during electrolysis?

(1 mark)

b) What would you see happening to impurities from the lump of impure copper during electrolysis?

(1 mark)

c) Finish these ionic equations.

At the impure electrode: $\mathbf{Cu_{(s)} \rightarrow}$ .... $\mathbf{+ 2e^-}$

At the pure electrode: $\mathbf{Cu^{2+}_{(aq)} +}$ .... $\mathbf{\rightarrow Cu_{(s)}}$

(1 mark)

d) What is the copper sulphate solution for?

(2 marks)

Acids and Alkalis

The pH scale and universal indicator

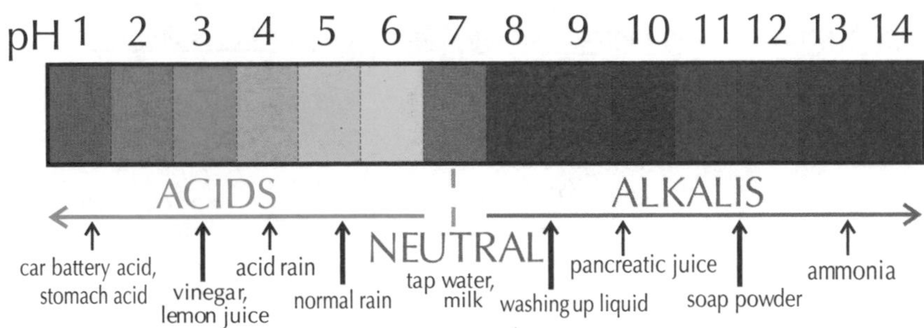

An indicator is just a dye that changes colour

The dye changes colour depending on whether it's in an acid or in an alkali.
Universal indicator is a very useful combination of dyes which give the colours shown above.

The pH scale goes from 1 to 14

1) The strongest acid has pH 1. The strongest alkali has pH 14.
2) If something is neutral it has pH 7 (eg: pure water).
3) Anything less than 7 is acid. Anything more than 7 is alkaline. (An alkali can also be called a base.)

Acids have H+ ions   Alkalis have OH- ions

The strict definitions of acids and alkalis are:

ACIDS are substances which form $H^+_{(aq)}$ *ions* when added to *water*.
ALKALIS are substances which form $OH^-_{(aq)}$ *ions* when added to *water*.

Neutralisation

This is the equation for any neutralisation reaction. Make sure you learn it:

acid + alkali hydroxide solution → neutral salt solution + water

Neutralisation can also be seen in terms of ions like this, so learn it too:

$$H^+_{(aq)} + OH^-_{(aq)} \rightarrow H_2O_{(l)}$$

(This is called an ionic equation.)

Three "real life" examples of neutralisation:

1) Indigestion is caused by too much hydrochloric acid in the stomach.
Indigestion tablets contain alkalis such as magnesium oxide, which neutralise the excess HCl.
2) Fields with acidic soils can be improved no end by adding lime (See P.116).
The lime added to fields is calcium hydroxide $Ca(OH)_2$ which is of course an alkali.
3) Lakes affected by acid rain can also be neutralised by adding lime. This saves the fish.

Acids and Alkalis

Acid + Metal → Salt + Hydrogen

This is written big because it's definitely worth remembering. Here's the typical experiment:

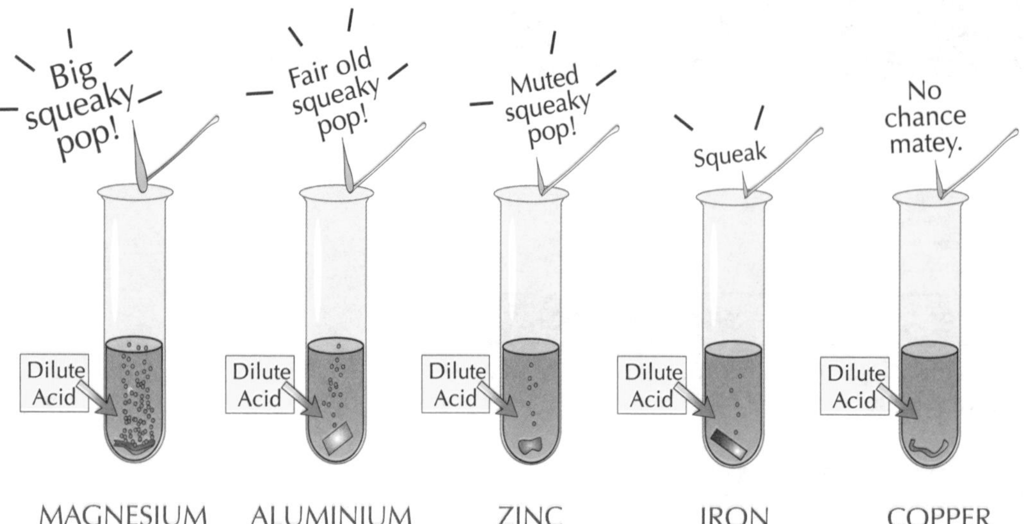

Copper is *less reactive* than *hydrogen* so it doesn't react with dilute acids at all.

1) The more reactive the metal, the faster it will go.
2) Copper does not react with dilute acids at all — because it's less reactive than hydrogen.
3) The speed of reaction is indicated by the rate at which the bubbles of hydrogen are given off.
4) The hydrogen is confirmed by the burning splint test giving the notorious 'squeaky pop'.
5) The type of salt produced depends on which metal is used, and which acid is used:

Hydrochloric acid *produces* ***chloride*** *salts:*

$2HCl + Mg \rightarrow MgCl_2 + H_2$ (Magnesium chloride)

$6HCl + 2Al \rightarrow 2AlCl_3 + 3H_2$ (Aluminium chloride)

$2HCl + Zn \rightarrow ZnCl_2 + H_2$ (Zinc chloride)

Sulphuric acid *produces* ***sulphate*** *salts:*

$H_2SO_4 + Mg \rightarrow MgSO_4 + H_2$ (Magnesium sulphate)

$3H_2SO_4 + 2Al \rightarrow Al_2(SO_4)_3 + 3H_2$ (Aluminium sulphate)

$H_2SO_4 + Zn \rightarrow ZnSO_4 + H_2$ (Zinc sulphate)

Nitric acid *produces* ***nitrate*** *salts when neutralised, but...*

Nitric acid reacts fine with alkalis, to produce nitrates. But it can play silly devils with metals and produce nitrogen oxides instead, so we'll ignore it here. Chemistry's a really messy subject sometimes.

Ammonia *produces* ***ammonium*** *salts*

Ammonia dissolves in water to make an alkaline solution.
This is neutralised with acids to make ammonium salts.

Acids and Alkalis

Metal **oxides** and metal **hydroxides** are **alkalis**

1) Metal oxides and metal hydroxides are generally alkalis.
2) Oxides and hydroxides of transition metals won't dissolve in water. They are called BASES.
3) Other metal oxides and metal hydroxides dissolve in water to produce alkaline solutions.
4) All metal oxides and hydroxides react with acids to form a salt and water:

Acid + Metal Oxide → Salt + Water

Acid + Metal Hydroxide → Salt + Water

(These are neutralisation reactions of course)

The **combination** of metal and acid decides the **salt**

This is pretty easy, so try and get the hang of it:

Hydrochloric acid	+	Copper oxide	→	Copper chloride	+	water
Hydrochloric acid	+	Sodium hydroxide	→	Sodium chloride	+	water
Sulphuric acid	+	Zinc oxide	→	Zinc sulphate	+	water
Sulphuric acid	+	Calcium hydroxide	→	Calcium sulphate	+	water
Nitric acid	+	Magnesium oxide	→	Magnesium nitrate	+	water
Nitric acid	+	Potassium hydroxide	→	Potassium nitrate	+	water

The symbol equations are all pretty much the same. Here are two of them:

$$H_2SO_4 + ZnO \rightarrow ZnSO_4 + H_2O$$
$$HNO_3 + KOH \rightarrow KNO_3 + H_2O$$

An **indicator** shows when the reaction is **finished**

The best way to tell that you've made a neutral salt and water is to use an indicator. Otherwise you'd have to keep dunking in a sad little piece of litmus paper to test it.

Universal indicator is the best to use and it doesn't affect the reaction at all. It'll go red when you add it to the acid. Then as you add the alkali to it, it'll change to orange, yellow then green when all that's left is the salt and water.

Neutralisation reactions always end up with salt and water

You've got to be a pretty serious career chemist to find this stuff interesting.
Normal people just have to grin and bear it. Oh, and learn it as well, of course
— don't forget the small matter of those little Exams you've got coming up...

Warm-Up and Exam Question

These warm-up questions should ease you gently in and make sure you've got the basics straight. If there's anything you've forgotten, check up on the facts before you do the exam question.

Warm-up Questions

1) What colour is universal indicator in strong acid?
2) Washing-up liquid has a pH of 8. Is this an acid or alkali?
3) Indigestion tablets contain magnesium oxide. Is this an acid or alkali?
4) What ions are always formed when an acid is added to water?
5) Acid + Hydroxide → Salt + What?
6) Acid + Metal → Salt + What?

Exam Question

1 This question is about acids, alkalis and pH.

a) Acids and alkalis ionise in aqueous solution.

(i) What ion is always present in an aqueous solution of acid?

(1 mark)

(ii) What ion is always present in an aqueous solution of alkali?

(1 mark)

(iii) A general neutralisation reaction can be represented by the following word equation:

acid + alkali → salt + water.

Complete the following general ionic equation for a neutralisation reaction.

.... + ... → H_2O

(2 marks)

b) Universal indicator was used to measure the pH of several different substances:

Substance **A**	Indicator went blue-green
Substance **B**	Indicator went orange
Substance **C**	Indicator went red
Substance **D**	Indicator went indigo

(i) Which substance is a weak acid?

(1 mark)

(ii) Which substance is ammonia?

(1 mark)

(iii) Substance C is naturally present in the body. Suggest what substance C might be.

(1 mark)

c) The soil in Fred's garden has a pH of 5.4. What ionic compound could he add to the soil to make it neutral?

(1 mark)

Revision Summary for Section Five

There's some serious Chemistry in this section. All I can say is, just keep trying to learn it. These questions will give you some idea of how well you're doing. For any you can't do, you'll find the answers somewhere in Section Five.

1) What proportion of the elements are metals? Why is argon an oddity?
2) Write down the twelve common metals in the order of the Reactivity Series.
3) Where do carbon and hydrogen fit in to the Reactivity Series and what is the significance of their positions?
4) Describe the reaction of all twelve metals when heated in air.
5) What is the word equation for a metal reacting with oxygen?
6) What is corrosion?
7) Describe the plus and minus points of iron (and steel), and give four uses for it.
8) Describe two methods used to stop iron and steel rusting.
9) Describe the plus and minus points of aluminium, and give four uses for it.
10) How can aluminium be made stronger and harder?
11) Describe the reaction of all twelve metals with water (or steam).
12) Describe the reaction of all twelve metals with dilute acid.
13) What type of reaction is this? Give two examples, with equations.
14) What is the 'golden rule' of metal displacement reactions?
15) What are the tell-tale signs that a metal displacement reaction has taken place?
16) A lead weight is put into a beaker containing zinc nitrate. What happens?
17) An iron beaker is filled with silver nitrate. What happens?
18) What are rocks, ores and minerals? Name a metal found as itself rather than an ore.
19) Give the chemical formulae of these three ores: iron ore, aluminium ore and copper ore.
20) What are the two methods for extracting metals from their ores?
21) What property of the metal decides which method is needed?
22) Draw a diagram of a blast furnace. What are the three raw materials used in it?
23) Write down the equations for how iron is obtained from its ore in the blast furnace.
24) How are the impurities removed from the iron? Give equations.
25) How is aluminium extracted from its ore? Give four operational details and draw a diagram.
26) Write down the redox equations for how aluminium is obtained from its ore.
27) Explain why the electrolysis of aluminium is so expensive.
28) How is copper extracted from its ore?
29) How is copper then purified, and why does it need to be?
30) Draw a diagram for the purifying process.
31) Where is the pure copper obtained?
32) Describe fully the colour of universal indicator for every pH value from 1 to 14.
33) What type of ions are always present in a) acids and b) alkalis? What is neutralisation?
34) What is the equation for reacting acid with metal? Which metal(s) don't react with acid?
35) Give three real-life examples of the practical benefits of neutralising acids and alkalis.
36) To what extent do Cu, Al, Mg, Fe and Zn react with dilute acid? What would you see?
37) When a burning splint is held over the test tubes, how loud would the different squeaky pops be?
38) What type of salts do hydrochloric acid and sulphuric acid produce?
39) What type of reaction is "acid + metal oxide", or "acid + metal hydroxide"?

Useful Materials

Limestone is a sedimentary rock, formed mainly from sea shells. It is mostly calcium carbonate.

1) **Limestone** used as a **building material**

1) It's great for making into blocks for building with. Fine old buildings like cathedrals are often made purely from limestone blocks. Acid rain can be a problem though.
2) For statues and fancy carved bits on nice buildings. But acid rain is even more of a problem.
3) It can just be crushed up into chippings and used for road surfacing.

2) **Limestone** for **neutralising acid** in **lakes** and **soil**

1) Ordinary limestone ground into powder can be used to neutralise acidity in lakes caused by acid rain. It can also be used to neutralise acid soils in fields.
2) It works better and faster if it's turned into slaked lime first:

*Turning **limestone** into **slaked lime**: first **heat it up**, then **add water***

1) The limestone is heated and it turns into calcium oxide (CaO) and carbon dioxide.

$$\text{limestone} \xrightarrow{\text{HEAT}} \text{quicklime} \quad \text{or} \quad CaCO_3 \xrightarrow{\text{HEAT}} CaO + CO_2$$

2) This reaction is a thermal decomposition.
3) Calcium oxide reacts violently with water to produce calcium hydroxide (or slaked lime):

$$\text{quicklime + water} \rightarrow \text{slaked lime} \quad \text{or} \quad CaO + HO_2 \rightarrow Ca(OH)_2$$

4) Slaked lime is a white powder and can be applied to fields just like powdered limestone.
5) The advantage is that slaked lime acts much faster at reducing the acidity.

3) **Limestone** and **clay** are **heated** to make **cement**

1) Clay contains aluminium and silicates and is dug out of the ground.
2) Powdered clay and powdered limestone are roasted in a rotating kiln to produce a complex mixture of calcium and aluminium silicates, called cement.
3) When cement is mixed with water a slow chemical reaction takes place.
4) This causes the cement to gradually set hard.
5) Cement is usually mixed with sand and chippings to make concrete.
6) Concrete is a very quick and cheap way of constructing buildings.

4) **Glass** is made by melting **limestone, sand** and **soda**

1) Just heat up limestone (calcium carbonate) with sand (silicon dioxide) and soda (sodium carbonate) until it melts.
2) When the mixture cools it comes out as glass. It's as easy as that.

Useful Materials

Fossil fuels were formed from **dead plants and animals**

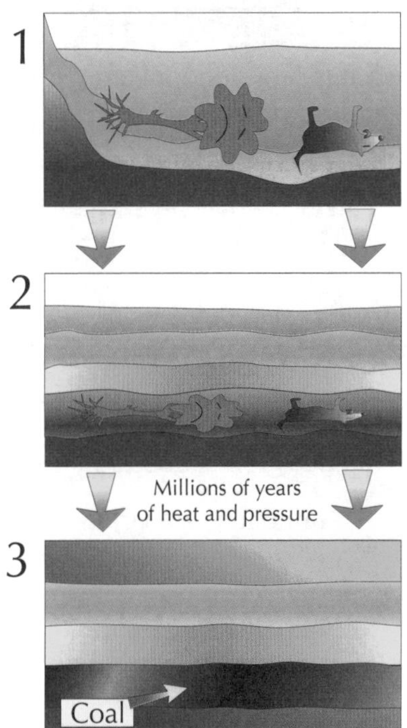

1) Fossil fuels have formed over millions of years.
2) Plants and animals died and were immediately covered by sediment in seas or swamps.
3) This stopped them decaying.
4) Further layers of sediment buried the plant and animal remains deeper and deeper.
5) After millions of years of pressure and heat (90°C to 120°C), in an environment with no air, these remains turned into coal, oil and natural gas.
6) When we burn fossil fuels we're using the Sun's energy that has been stored as chemical energy underground for millions of years.

Crude oil is a very big part of **modern life**

1) It provides the fuel for most modern transport.
2) It also provides the raw material for making various chemicals including plastics. The world without plastics? Why, it would be the end of civilisation as we know it...

Crude oil has to be split up to make it useful

1) Crude oil is a mixture of different sized hydrocarbon molecules.
2) Hydrocarbons are basically fuels such as petrol and diesel.
3) The bigger and longer the molecules, the less runny the hydrocarbon (fuel) is.
4) Fractional distillation splits crude oil up into its separate fractions.
5) The shorter the molecules, the lower the temperature at which that fraction condenses.

Dead things + time and pressure = useful fuels

When those little sea creatures died all those millions of years ago, they had no idea they would one day become the cornerstones of 21st century civilisation. Anyway, learn the whole page.

Warm-Up and Exam Questions

This stuff isn't particularly hard, so make the most of it.
Quickly run through this warm-up then have a look at the exam questions below.

Warm-up Questions

1) What is limestone mixed with to make cement?
2) Why is slaked lime used on fields and lakes?
3) How are fossil fuels formed?

Exam Questions

1 This question is about the uses of limestone.

a) Name the two compounds which are mixed with limestone and heated to make glass.

....

....

(1 mark)

b) Limestone is mostly calcium carbonate.

Complete this equation to show the reaction which takes place when limestone is heated.

$CaCO_3 \rightarrow$ .... + ...

(2 marks)

2 Fossil fuels were formed over a period of millions of years.

a) Describe how fossil fuels were formed.

....

....

....

....

(4 marks)

b) Fractional distillation separates crude oil into different products, which are more useful than crude oil itself. Name two uses for the products of crude oil.

....

....

(2 marks)

Refining Oil

Crude oil is **split** into **separate hydrocarbons** (fuels)

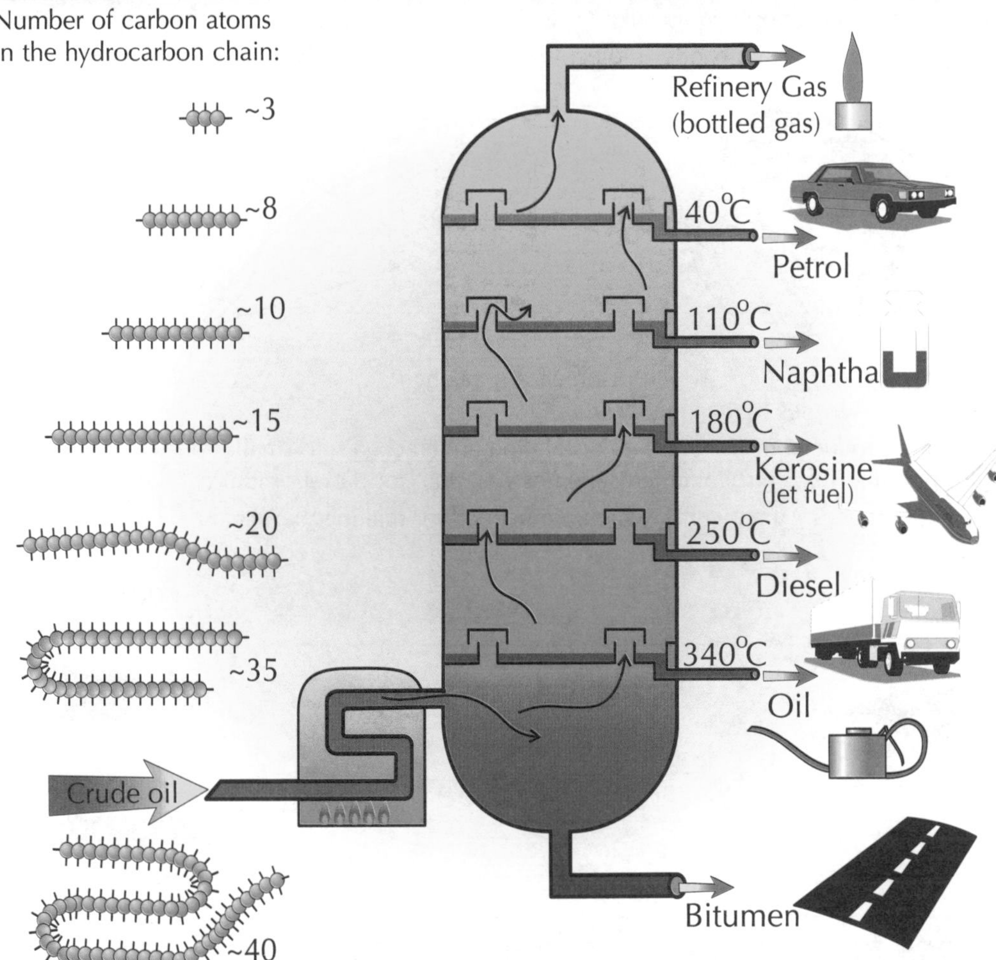

The fractionating column works continuously, with heated crude oil piped in at the bottom and the various fractions being constantly tapped off at the different levels where they condense.

Hydrocarbons range from **short** to **long chain molecules**

As the size of the hydrocarbon molecule increases:

1) The **boiling point** increases

2) It gets **less flammable**

(doesn't set fire so easily)

3) It gets **more viscous**

(doesn't flow so easily)

4) It gets **less volatile**

(ie: doesn't evaporate so easily)

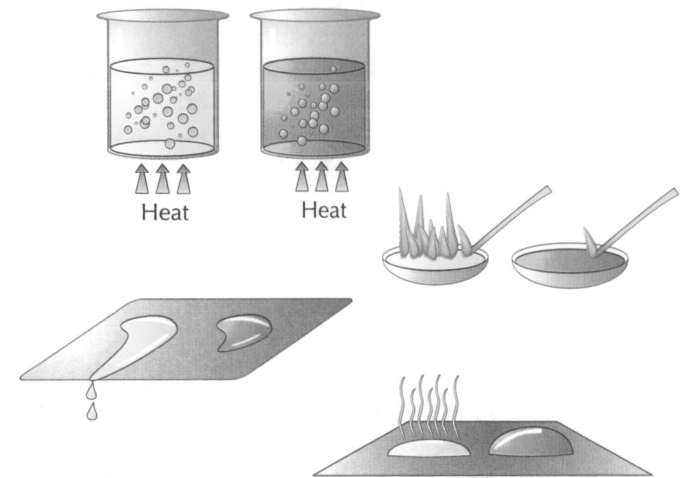

The vapours of the more volatile hydrocarbons are very flammable and pose a serious fire risk.
So don't smoke at the petrol station.

Refining Oil

Cracking — **splitting up** long chain hydrocarbons

1) Long chain hydrocarbons form thick gloopy liquids like tar which aren't all that useful.
2) The process called cracking turns them into shorter molecules which are much more useful.

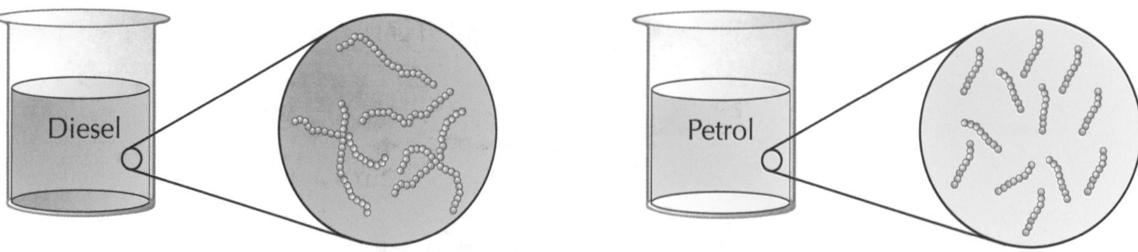

3) Cracking is a form of thermal decomposition, which just means breaking molecules down into simpler molecules by heating them.
4) A lot of the longer molecules produced from fractional distillation are cracked into smaller ones because there's more demand for products like petrol and kerosene (jet fuel) than for diesel or lubricating oil.
5) More importantly, cracking produces extra alkenes which are needed for making plastics.

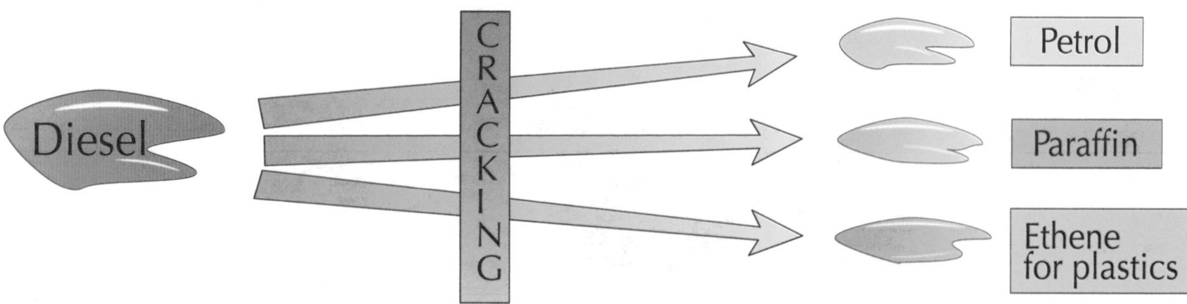

Industrial conditions for cracking: **hot, plus a catalyst**

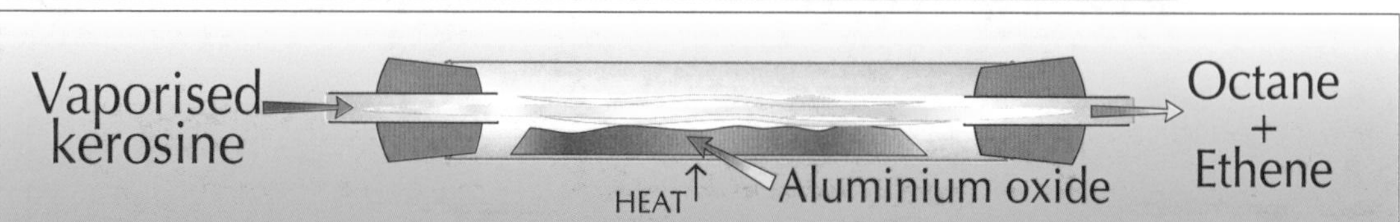

1) Vaporised hydrocarbons are passed over a powdered catalyst at about 400°C – 700°C.
2) Aluminium oxide is the catalyst used.
The long chain molecules split apart or "crack" on the surface of the bits of catalyst.
This is another of those thermal decomposition reactions.

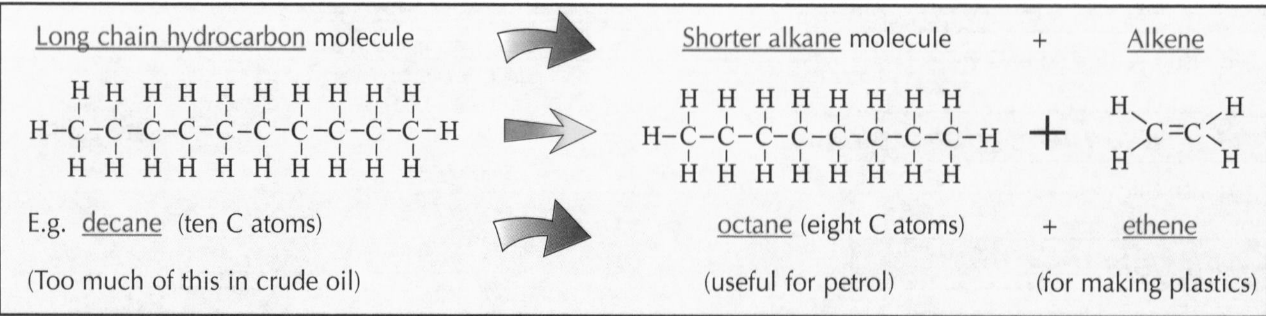

The one burning question is... have you learnt it all...

You need to learn the four features of hydrocarbons which change with increasing chain length, and the five details about cracking, two details on industrial conditions and a specific example showing typical products: a shorter chain alkane and an alkene. LEARN IT ALL.

Warm-Up and Exam Question

Without a good warm-up you're likely to strain a brain cell or two. So take the time to run through these simple questions and get the basic facts straight before plunging into the exam question.

Warm-up Questions

1) What elements are hydrocarbons made from?
2) What happens to the boiling point, flammability, viscosity and volatility of hydrocarbons as the size of molecule increases?
3) What is the name of the process used to turn long chain hydrocarbons into shorter molecules?

Exam Question

1 Crude oil is separated into fuels such as petrol, kerosine and diesel by fractional distillation.

a) Look at this diagram of a fractionating column.

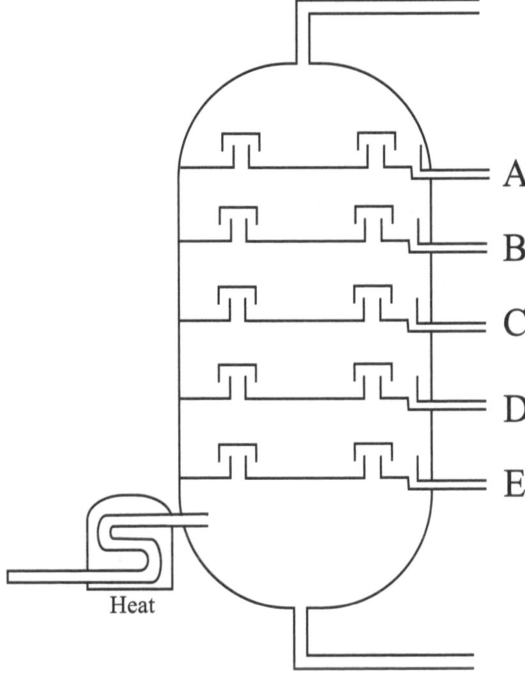

i) Petrol has a boiling range of 40-100°C. Write down the letter from the diagram that shows where petrol would be piped off.

(1 mark)

ii) Petrol has a lower boiling point than kerosene. Write down which of the two fuels has more carbon atoms in its molecules. Explain your answer by stating the relationship between the boiling range and the number of carbon atoms in the molecule.

(2 marks)

b) The products of the fractional distillation of crude oil are often used as fuels. Name another use of one of these products.

(1 mark)

Polymers and Plastics

Crude oil contains both alkanes and alkenes. Know the differences between them.

Alkanes have all C-C single bonds

1) They're made up of chains of carbon atoms with single covalent bonds between them.
2) They're called saturated hydrocarbons because they have no spare bonds left.
3) This is also why they don't decolourise bromine water — no spare bonds.
4) They won't form polymers — same reason again, no spare bonds.
5) The first four alkanes are methane (natural gas), ethane, propane and butane.
6) They burn cleanly producing carbon dioxide and water.

1) Methane

Formula: CH_4

```
   H
   |
H–C–H
   |
   H
```

(natural gas)

2) Ethane

Formula: C_2H_6

```
  H H
  | |
H–C–C–H
  | |
  H H
```

3) Propane

Formula: C_3H_8

```
  H H H
  | | |
H–C–C–C–H
  | | |
  H H H
```

4) Butane

Formula: C_4H_{10}

```
  H H H H
  | | | |
H–C–C–C–C–H
  | | | |
  H H H H
```

Alkenes have a C=C double bond

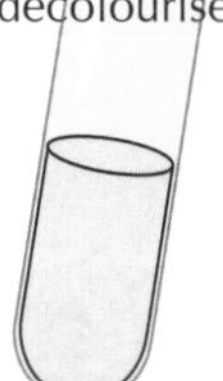

1) They're chains of carbon atoms with a double bond.
2) They are called unsaturated hydrocarbons because they have some spare bonds left.
3) This is why they will decolourise bromine water. They form bonds with bromide ions.
4) They form polymers by opening up their double bonds to "hold hands" in a long chain.
5) The first three alkenes are ethene, propene and butene.
6) They tend to burn with a smoky flame, producing soot (carbon).

1) Ethene

Formula: C_2H_4

```
H       H
 \     /
  C = C
 /     \
H       H
```

2) Propene

Formula: C_3H_6

```
  H H     H
  | |    /
H–C–C=C
  |      \
  H       H
```

3) Butene

Formula: C_4H_8

```
  H H   H
  | |   |
H–C–C=C–C–H
  |   | |
  H   H H
```

Important points to be noted:

1) Bromine water is the standard test to distinguish between alkanes and alkenes.
2) Alkenes are more reactive due to the double bond all poised and ready to just pop open.
3) Notice the names: "Meth-" means "one carbon atom", "eth-" means "two C atoms", "prop-" means "three C atoms", "but-" means "four C atoms", etc.
The only difference then between the names of alkanes and alkenes is just the "-ane" or "-ene" on the end.
4) All alkanes have the formula: C_nH_{2n+2} All alkenes have the formula: C_nH_{2n}

Polymers and Plastics

Polymers and plastics were first discovered in about 1933. By 1970 it was all too late. Leather seats and lovely wooden dashboards, were replaced by cheap, wipe-clean plastic.

Alkenes open their **double bonds** to form **polymers**

Under a bit of pressure and with a bit of a catalyst to help it along, many small alkenes will open up their double bonds and "join hands" to form very long chains called polymers. There's a couple of important points worth knowing here:

1) The process of joining up lots of individual alkenes to form a plastic is called polymerisation.
2) If no other products are formed during the polymerisation reaction, the process is called addition polymerisation.
3) The individual units which "hold hands" to form the polymer are called monomers.

Ethene becoming polyethene or "polythene" is the easiest example of polymerisation:

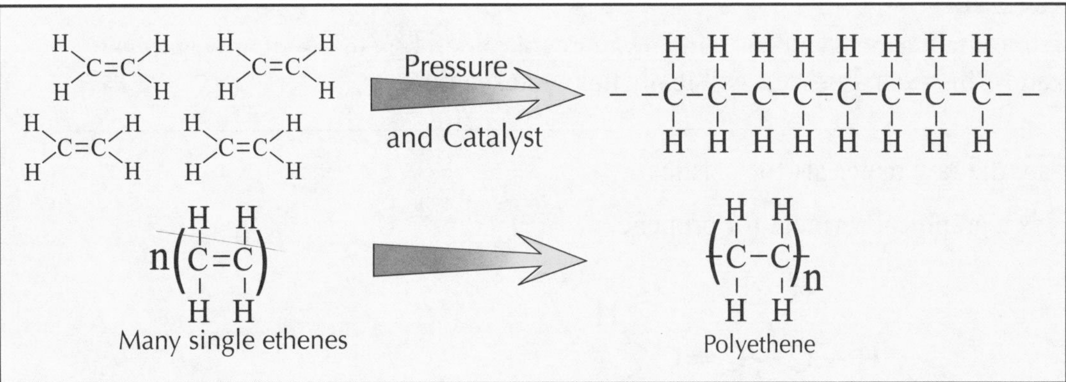

There are **loads of plastics** with **loads** of different **uses**

1) Polythene

1) Made from ethene.
2) Very cheap and strong.
3) Easily moulded.

2) Polypropene

1) Made from propene.
2) Forms strong fibres.
3) Has high elasticity.

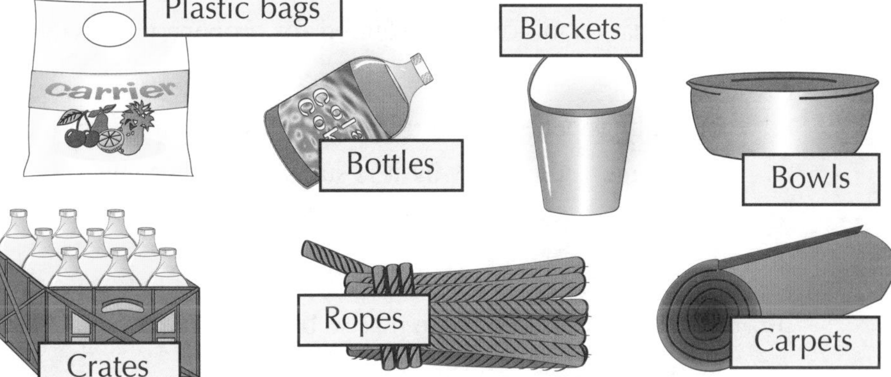

Most plastics **don't rot**, so they're hard to get rid of

1) Most plastics aren't 'biodegradable' — they're not broken down by microorganisms, so they don't rot.
2) It's difficult to get rid of them — if you bury them in a landfill site, they'll still be there years later. The best thing is to recycle them if you can.

Breaking the double bond lets alkenes join together

Learn what alkanes and alkenes are and what polymerisation is and practise the set of diagrams for ethene. Also learn all the examples given for the different types of plastics.

Warm-Up and Exam Question

It's easy to think you've learnt everything in the section until you try the warm-up questions.
Don't panic if there's a bit you've forgotten. Just go back over that bit until it's firmly fixed in your brain.

Warm-up Questions

1) What kind of bonds do alkanes have?
2) What are hydrocarbons with one C=C double bond called?
3) Can alkanes form polymers?
4) Can alkenes form polymers?

Exam Question

There's a knack to using the facts you've stored away in your brain box in the right way to get marks in the exam. This exam question will really help you see how...

1 Alkenes are the raw materials for plastics.

a) This is a graphical formula for propene.

```
    H
    |         H
H — C — C = C ⟨
    |   |         H
    H   H
```

(i) Draw a graphical formula of the repeating unit in polypropene.

(2 marks)

(ii) What conditions are required for propene to polymerise?

(2 marks)

(iii) Polypropene is used to make crates and fibres for carpets.
Suggest a reason why it is suitable for these uses.

(2 marks)

b) Polythene is used to make plastic bags and bottles. It does not biodegrade.

(i) Polythene can be disposed of by being buried. Suggest a disadvantage of disposing of polythene products in this way.

(1 mark)

(ii) Polythene can be recycled. Suggest one reason for recycling more polythene (other than the difficulties of disposing of it).

(1 mark)

(iii) Suggest a reason why recycling or reusing polythene products might be unpopular.

(1 mark)

Earth's Atmosphere

All we need is the oxygen, but there's a lot of stuff in the air that we're breathing in anyhow. Never mind what it's doing to your lungs, you've just got to learn what there is and how it got there.

Burning fuels releases CO_2, water and sulphur dioxide

1) When fossil fuels are burned they release mostly CO_2.
2) Water vapour is released too — it's an oxide of the hydrogen in the fuel.
3) But they also release two other harmful gases, sulphur dioxide and various nitrogen oxides.
4) The sulphur dioxide, SO_2, comes from sulphur impurities in the fossil fuels.

The oceans hold a lot of carbon

1) The oceans were formed by condensation of the steam in the early atmosphere.
2) The sea water then started absorbing the CO_2 from the atmosphere.
3) They now contain a large amount of carbon in three main forms:
   a) Carbon dioxide dissolved in the water
   b) Insoluble carbonates like calcium carbonate (shells, which form sediment and then limestone)
   c) Soluble compounds like hydrogen carbonates (of Ca, Mg)

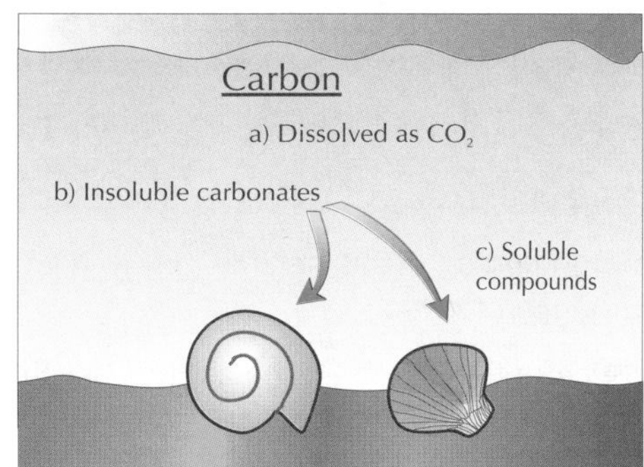

The level of CO_2 is increasing rapidly

1) The level of CO_2 in the atmosphere has risen due to the burning of massive amounts of fossil fuels in the last two hundred years or so.
2) This increased Greenhouse Effect is causing the Earth to warm up very slowly — all the extra CO_2 is adding to Global Warming. See also page 64-65.

Composition of today's atmosphere

Present composition of the atmosphere:

(That comes to over 100% because the first three are rounded up very slightly.)

78%	Nitrogen	(Often written as 79% Nitrogen for simplicity.)
1%	Argon	
21%	Oxygen	
0.04%	Carbon dioxide	

Also :

1) Varying amounts of WATER VAPOUR.
2) And other noble gases in very small amounts.

Earth's Atmosphere

The Earth's atmosphere wasn't always as it is today. Here's how the first 4.5 billion years have gone:

Phase 1 — **Volcanoes** gave out **steam, CO_2, NH_3 and CH_4**

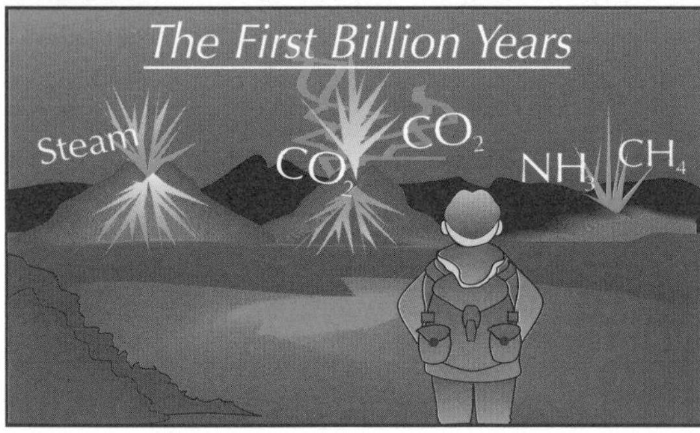

1) The Earth's surface was originally molten for many millions of years. Any atmosphere boiled away.
2) Eventually it cooled and a thin crust formed but volcanoes kept erupting, releasing mainly carbon dioxide.
3) But also some steam, ammonia and methane.
4) The early atmosphere was mostly CO_2 (virtually no oxygen).
5) The water vapour condensed to form the oceans.

Phase 2 — **Green plants evolved** and produced **oxygen**

1) Green plants evolved over most of the Earth.
2) A lot of the early CO_2 dissolved into the oceans.
3) But the green plants steadily removed CO_2 and produced O_2.
4) Much of the CO_2 from the air thus became locked up in fossil fuels and sedimentary rocks.
5) Methane and ammonia reacted with the oxygen, releasing nitrogen gas.
6) Nitrogen gas was also released by living organisms like denitrifying bacteria.

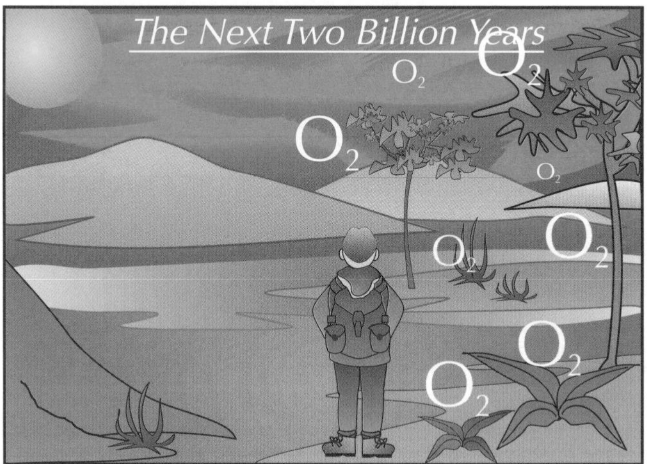

Phase 3 — **Ozone layer** allows **evolution** of **complex** animals

1) The build-up of oxygen in the atmosphere killed off early organisms that couldn't tolerate it.
2) It also enabled the evolution of more complex organisms that made use of the oxygen.
3) The oxygen also created the ozone layer (O_3) which blocked harmful rays from the sun and enabled even more complex organisms to evolve.
4) There is virtually no CO_2 left now.

4 million years ago was a whole other world

It's surprising just how much stuff there is on carbon dioxide and the atmosphere, but I'm afraid there are plenty of past exam questions which ask precisely these details. If you want those marks, you've got to learn these facts, and that's that. You know the drill: learn, cover, scribble, check... learn...

Warm-Up and Exam Questions

By the time the big day comes you need to know all the facts in these warm-up questions and all the exam questions like the back of your hand. It's not fun, but it's the only way to get good marks.

Warm-up Questions

1) Write down three of the main gases that were present in the Earth's original atmosphere.
2) Describe two processes that caused nitrogen to appear in the atmosphere.
3) Write down the name of the main noble gas in the air today.
4) Name two processes that remove carbon dioxide from the atmosphere.
5) Write down the formula for ozone.

Exam Questions

1 Describe how the following processes affect levels of carbon dioxide and oxygen in the atmosphere.

a) Photosynthesis

(1 mark)

b) Respiration

(1 mark)

c) Combustion

(1 mark)

2 The ozone layer is very important. Describe and explain its importance.

(2 marks)

3 The amounts of oxygen and carbon dioxide in the atmosphere have changed over the last 4.5 billion years.

a) Describe what happened to the amount of oxygen and explain how the change came about.

(2 marks)

b) Describe what happened to the amount of carbon dioxide and explain how the change came about.

(2 marks)

Rock Types

There are three different types: sedimentary, metamorphic and igneous.
Over millions of years they change from one into another. This is called the Rock Cycle.

The *Rock Cycle*

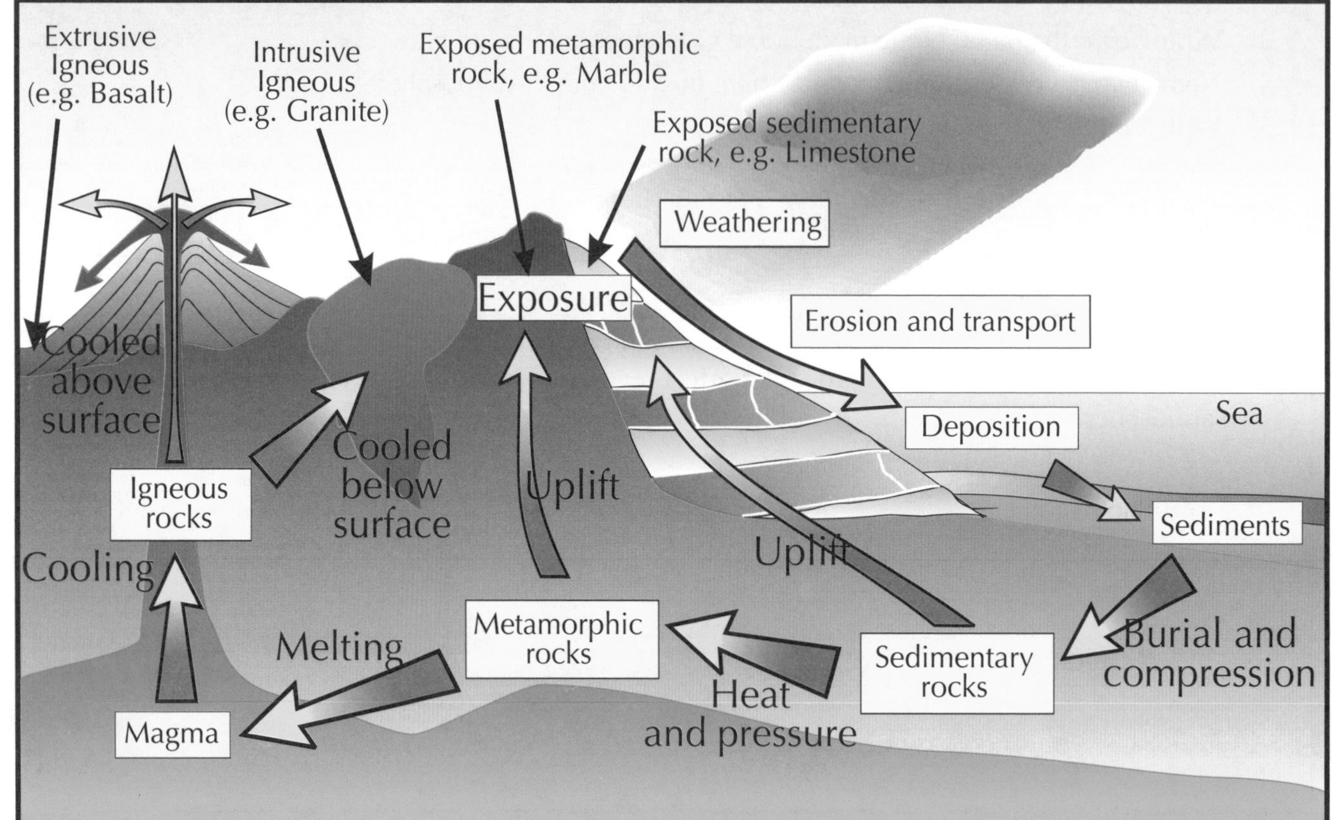

The rocks **change** from **one to another** in a **slow cycle**

1) Particles get washed to the sea and settle as sediment.

2) Over millions of years these sediments get crushed into sedimentary rocks (hence the name).

3) At first they get buried, but they can either rise to the surface again to be discovered, or they can descend into the heat and pressure below.

4) If they do, the heat and pressure completely alter the structure of the rock and they then become metamorphic rocks (as in "metamorphosis" or "change").

5) These metamorphic rocks can either rise to the surface to be discovered by someone or else descend still further into the fiery abyss of the Earth's raging inferno where they will melt and become magma.

6) When magma reaches the surface it cools and sets and is then called igneous rock. ("igneous" as in "ignite" or "fire")

7) When any of these rocks reach the surface, then weathering begins and they gradually get worn down and carried off to the sea and the whole cycle starts over again.

Rock Types

Layers one on top of the other = sedimentary

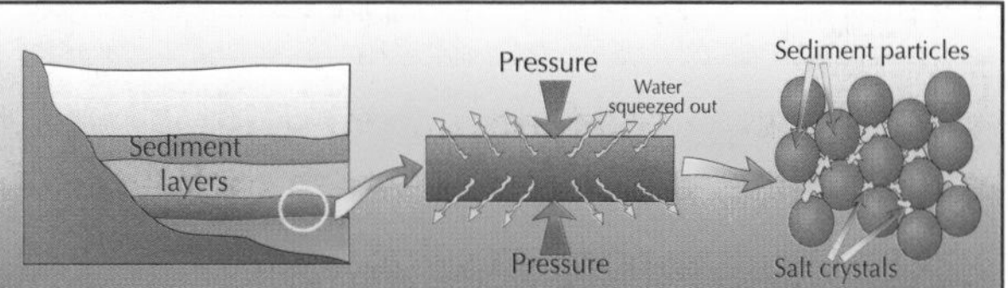

1) Sedimentary rocks are formed from layers of sediment deposited in lakes or seas.
2) Sandstone and limestone are sedimentary rocks.
3) Over millions of years the layers get buried under more layers and the weight pressing down squeezes out the water. As the water disappears, salts crystallize out and cement the particles together.

Fossils are only found in sedimentary rocks

1) Only sedimentary rocks contain fossils.
2) Fossils are a very useful way of identifying rocks as being of the same age.
3) This is because fossilised remains that are found change (due to evolution) as the ages pass.
4) This means that if two rocks have the same fossils in they must be from the same age.

Sediments contain evidence of how they were laid down

Sedimentary rocks contain evidence which tells geologists how the sediment was laid down. This could be:

1) RIPPLE MARKS — formed by currents or waves, like you see in sand when the tide's out.
2) DISCONTINUOUS DEPOSITION — this is when there's a gap in the fossil record (see page 83). A layer can be eroded (eg: if the water level drops) so when the next layer turns to rock, there's a layer missing.
3) SIZE OF PARTICLES — smaller particles take longer to settle to the bottom of the lake or sea so mud, clay or slate tells you the water was slow flowing. Bigger stuff like pebbles embedded in the sandstone was dumped by fast flowing water (eg: a river) when it got to the sea or lake.

The rock layers are often found all lining up nicely but just as often, they're found:
1) TILTED 2) FOLDED UP 3) FRACTURED ('FAULTED') 4) Turned completely UPSIDE DOWN.
The layers show that the Earth's crust is unstable and there have been very large forces acting on it.

Action of heat and pressure = metamorphic

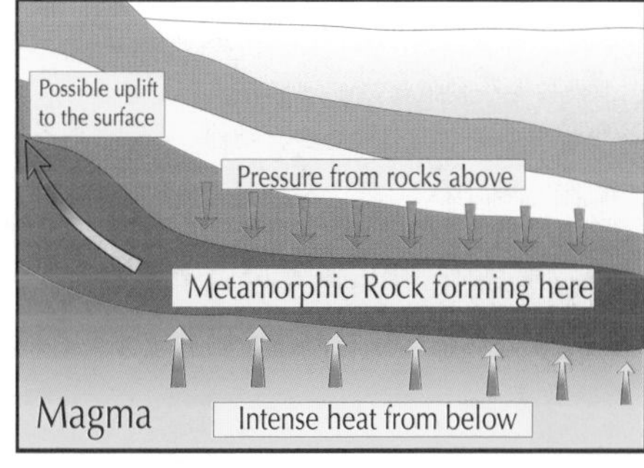

1) Earth movements can push all types of rocks deep underground.
2) Here they are compressed and heated and the mineral structure and texture may change over thousands of years.
3) As long as they don't actually melt, these changed rocks are classed as *metamorphic*.
4) The Earth shifting itself about creates mountain belts. Metamorphic rocks are the evidence of the high temperatures and pressures created when mountains were made.
5) New mountain ranges are created over millions of years. They replace ancient mountain ranges which are eventually worn down by weathering and erosion.

Mountain ranges form when the crust moves

1) Large scale movements of the Earth's crust push the rocks up to form mountains.
2) It's incredibly slow — it takes millions of years.
3) As new mountain ranges form, they are replacing older ranges which are worn down by erosion and weathering.

Rocks are a mystery — no, no, it's sedimentary my Dear Watson...

Pretty soon you won't be able to go to the beach without playing a fun game of 'Spot the Rock Types'. Lots to learn but it's straightforward stuff. Use the titles of the sections to do mini-essays.

Warm-Up and Exam Questions

Learning facts and practising exam questions is the only recipe for success. That's what the questions on this page are all about. All you have to do — is do them.

Warm-up Questions

1) A rock has been formed from seashells squashed together for millions of years. Name the rock and state which rock type it belongs to.
2) Describe the processes that affect clay as it changes into slate (a metamorphic rock).
3) Write down the name for the molten rock from which igneous rocks are formed.
4) Name one use for sandstone and one for marble.
5) Compare the processes by which intrusive and extrusive igneous rocks are formed.

Exam Questions

1 The diagram below shows part of the rock cycle.
Fill in the missing boxes.

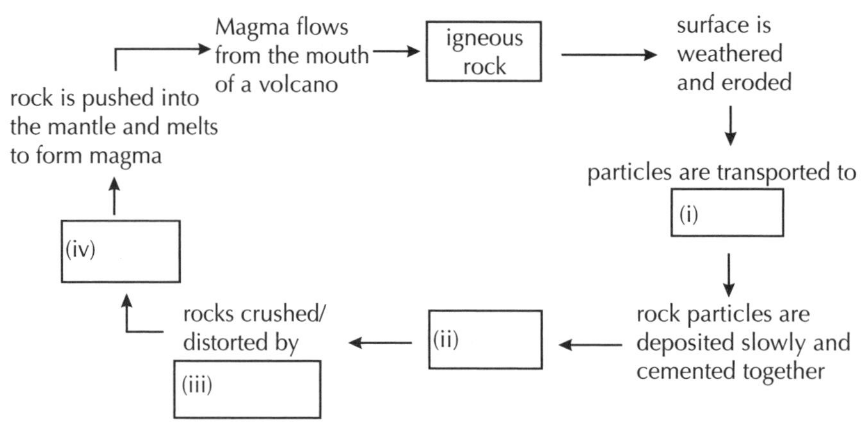

(4 marks)

2 The diagram below shows a typical rock micrograph slide of a type of rock.

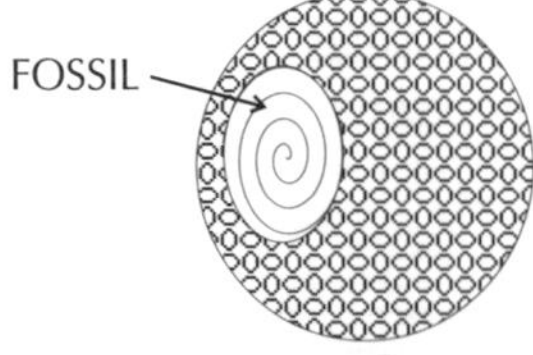

a) What type of rock does the micrograph show?

(1 mark)

b) Describe how rocks like this are formed.

(3 marks)

Tectonics

Crust, mantle, outer and inner core

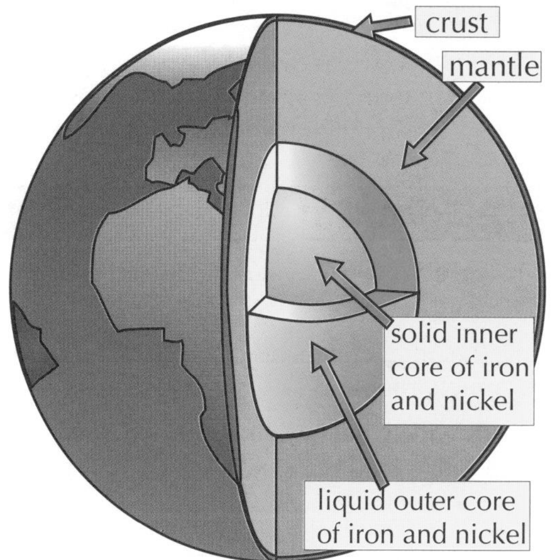

1) The crust is very thin (about 20km or so).
2) The mantle has the properties of a solid but it can flow very slowly.
3) The core is just over half the Earth's radius.
4) The core is made from iron and nickel. This is where the Earth's magnetic field originates.
5) The iron and nickel sank to the "bottom" long ago (i.e. the centre of the Earth) because they're denser.
6) The core has a solid inner bit and a liquid outer bit.
7) Radioactive decay creates all the heat inside the Earth.
8) This heat causes the convection currents which cause the plates of the crust to move.

Big clues: **Seismic waves, magnetism** and **meteorites**

1) We can tell how dense the Earth is by measuring seismic waves and the Earth's motion. We find that the inner core is much too dense to be made out of rock.
2) Meteorites which crash to Earth are often made of iron and nickel.
3) Iron and nickel are both magnetic and very dense.
4) If the core of the Earth was made of iron and nickel it would explain a lot: iron and nickel are about the right density, and being metals, this would explain the Earth's magnetic field (it's like a giant electromagnet).
5) Also, by following the paths of seismic waves as they travel through the Earth, we can tell that there is a change to liquid about halfway through the Earth.
6) There must be a liquid outer core of iron and nickel. The seismic waves also indicate a solid inner core.

The earth's surface is made up of **large plates of rock**

1) The Earth's lithosphere is the crust and the upper part of the mantle. It's cracked into pieces called plates.
2) These plates are like big rafts that float across the liquid mantle.
3) The map shows the edges of these plates. As they move, the continents move too.
4) The plates are moving at a speed of about 1cm or 2cm per year.

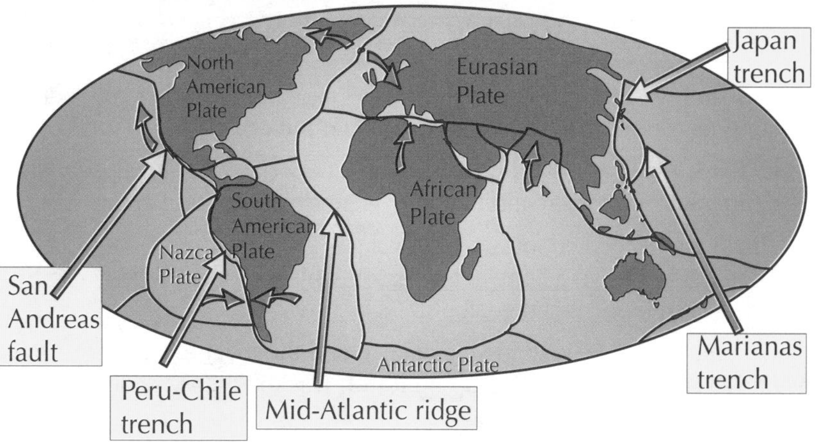

Tectonics

Plate Tectonics *explains things better than the* **cooling** *theory did*

The old theory was that all the features of the Earth's surface, e.g. mountains, were due to shrinkage of the crust as it cooled. In the Exam they may well ask you about that, and then they'll ask you for evidence in favour of plate tectonics as a better theory. Learn these pieces of evidence:

1) ***Jigsaw fit*** *— the supercontinent "Pangaea"*

a) There's a very obvious jigsaw fit between Africa and South America.

b) The other continents can also be fitted in without too much trouble.

c) It's widely believed that they once all formed a single land mass, now called Pangaea.

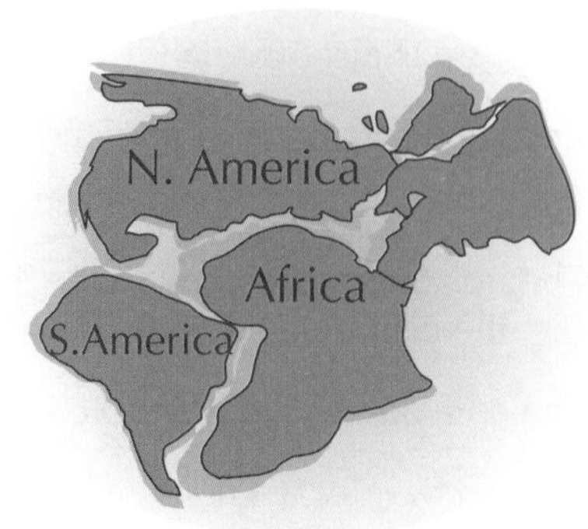

2) ***Matching fossils*** *in Africa and South America*

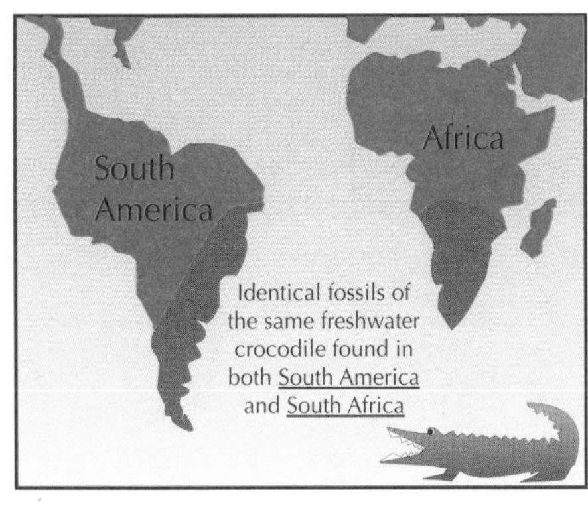

a) Identical plant fossils of the same age have been found in rocks in South Africa, Australia, Antarctica, India and South America, which strongly suggests they were all joined once upon a time.

b) Animal fossils support the theory too. There are identical fossils of a freshwater crocodile found in both Brazil and South Africa. It certainly didn't swim across.

3) ***Identical*** *rock sequences*

a) When rock strata of similar ages are studied in various countries they show remarkable similarity.

b) This is strong evidence that these countries were joined together when the rocks formed.

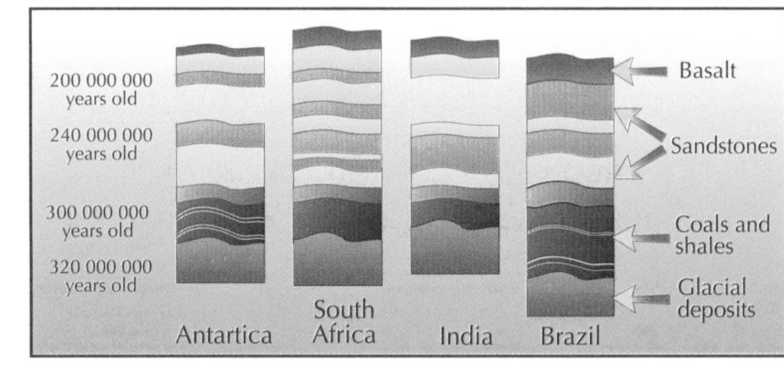

Wegener's theory *of crustal movement*

This stuff was noticed hundreds of years ago, but nobody really believed that the continents could once have actually been joined.

In 1915, Alfred Wegener proposed his theory of "continental drift" saying that they had definitely been joined and that they were slowly drifting apart.

This wasn't accepted for two reasons:
a) he couldn't give a convincing reason why it happened
b) he wasn't a qualified geologist

Only in the 1960s with fossil evidence and the magnetic pattern from the mid-Atlantic ridge (coming up on P.134) was the theory widely accepted.

Tectonics

At the boundaries between tectonic plates there's usually trouble like volcanoes or earthquakes. There are three different ways that plates interact: colliding, separating or sliding past each other.

Plates **sliding past** each other: **San Francisco**

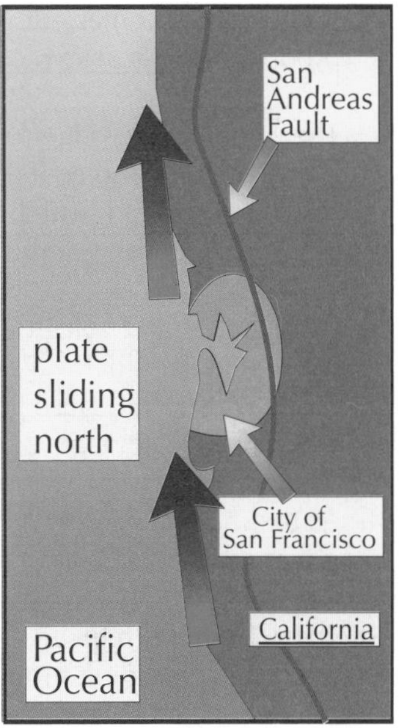

1) Sometimes the plates are just sliding past each other.
2) The best known example of this is the San Andreas Fault in California.
3) A narrow strip of the coastline is sliding north at about 7cm a year.
4) Big plates of rock don't glide smoothly past each other.
5) They catch on each other and as the forces build up they suddenly lurch.
6) This sudden lurching only lasts a few seconds — but it'll bring buildings down, no problem.
7) The city of San Francisco sits astride this fault line. (They didn't know that when they built it.)
8) The city was destroyed by an earthquake in 1906 and hit by another quite serious one in 1989. They could have another one any time.
9) In earthquake zones they try to build earthquake-proof buildings which are designed to withstand a bit of shaking.
10) Earthquakes usually cause much greater devastation in poorer countries where they may have overcrowded cities, poorly constructed buildings, and inadequate rescue services.

Oceanic and **continental** plates colliding: **The Andes**

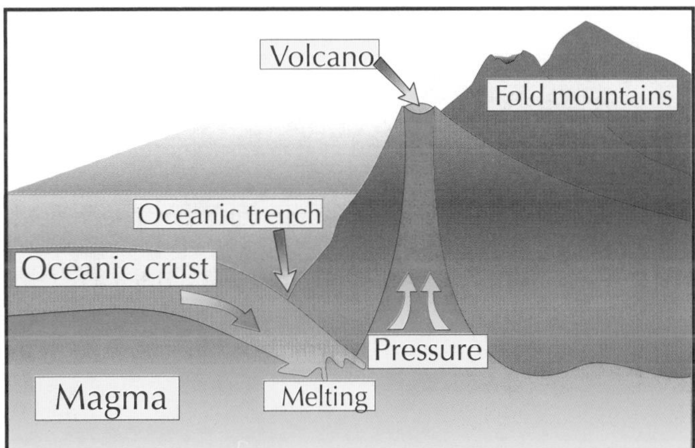

1) The oceanic plate is always forced underneath the continental plate.
2) This is called a subduction zone.
3) As the oceanic crust is pushed down it melts and pressure builds up due to all the melting rock.
4) This molten rock finds its way to the surface and volcanoes form.
5) There are also earthquakes as the two plates slowly grind past each other.
6) A deep trench forms on the ocean floor where the oceanic plate is being forced down.
7) The continental crust crumples and folds forming mountains at the coast.
8) The classic example of all this is the west coast of South America where the Andes mountains are. That region has all the features:

Volcanoes, earthquakes, an oceanic trench and mountains.

Tectonics

Sea floor spreading 1: The mid-Atlantic ridge

1) When tectonic plates move apart, magma rises up to fill the gap and produces new crust made of basalt (of course).
   Sometimes it comes out with great force producing undersea volcanoes.

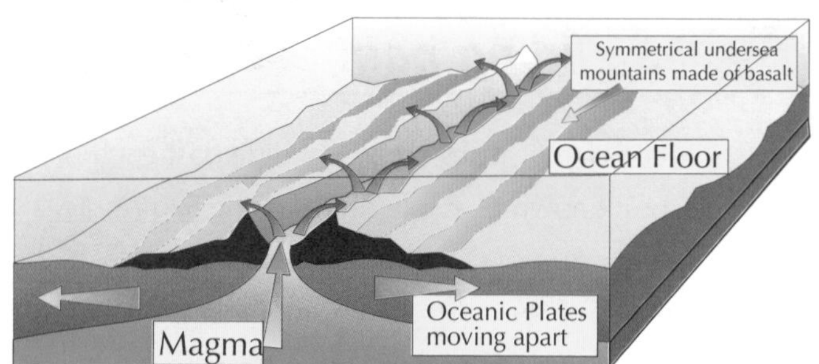

2) The Mid-Atlantic ridge runs the whole length of the Atlantic and actually cuts through the middle of Iceland, which is why they have hot underground water.

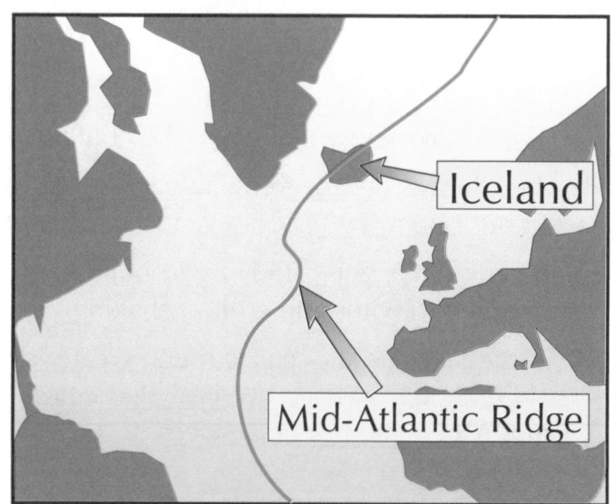

3) Earthquakes and volcanoes under the sea can cause massive tidal waves (tsunami).
   These waves can cause great destruction when they reach land.

4) As the magma rises up through the gap it forms ridges and underwater mountains.

5) These form a symmetrical pattern either side of the ridge, providing strong evidence for the theory of continental drift.

Sea floor spreading 2: Magnetic reversal patterns

1) However the most compelling evidence in favour of continental drift comes from the magnetic orientation of the rocks.

2) As the liquid magma erupts out of the gap, the iron particles in the rocks tend to align themselves with the Earth's magnetic field and as it cools they set in position.

3) Every half million years or so the Earth's magnetic field tends to swap direction.

4) This means the rock on either side of the ridge has bands of alternate magnetic polarity.

5) This pattern is found to be symmetrical either side of the ridge.

6) These magnetic stripes were only discovered in the 1960s.

7) These stripes spread out at a rate of about 2 cm per year, which is pretty slow.
   In fact, continents move at pretty much the same speed your fingernails grow at. It's sad, but you probably won't observe any continental drift in your lifetime.

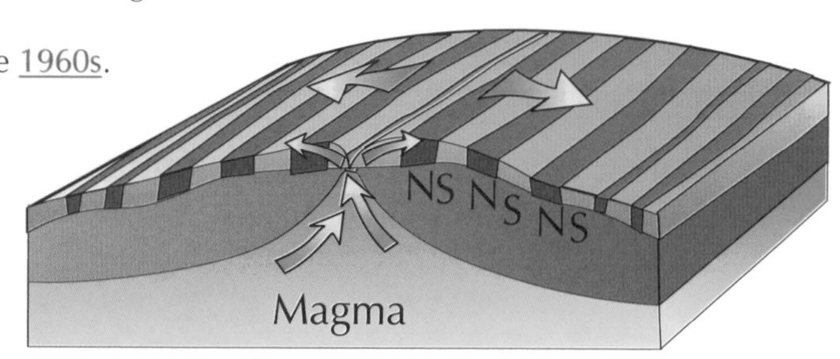

Learn Wegener's Theory and all the evidence

Another couple of bits of evidence which support Wegener's Theory. Along with the three bits on P.132, that makes five in total. Learn all five well enough to be able to answer a question like this: "Describe evidence which supports the theory of Plate Tectonics" (5 marks). Mini-essay time.

Warm-Up and Exam Questions

Warm-up Questions

1) How do the shapes of South America and Africa provide evidence for plate tectonics?
2) Give two reasons, other than shape, why scientists think South America and Africa were once joined together.
3) What were the two main reasons Wegener's theory of 'continental drift' was not accepted in the early part of the 20th century?
4) Write down one of the geological features often seen at a plate boundary.
5) Describe how the Andes Mountains were formed.

Exam Questions

1 The diagram below shows the movement of two pieces of the Earth's crust.

a) What is the name for these large pieces of rock?

(1 mark)

b) i) Rock pieces X and Y are moving towards one another.
Suggest a reason why X is pushed over and above Y.

(1 mark)

ii) Describe what might happen to rock piece Y as it is slowly pushed beneath X.

(1 mark)

2 The city of San Francisco sits on a fault line.

a) Explain what is meant by a fault line.

(1 mark)

b) At San Francisco, the Pacific plate is rubbing against the North American plate.
Explain how this causes frequent earthquakes in this area.

(2 marks)

3 In the middle of the Atlantic Ocean, the South American plate and the African plate are moving apart.

Explain how this movement has resulted in the formation of the Mid-Atlantic Ridge.

(2 marks)

Revision Summary for Section Six

Well let's face it, this section on Earth Materials is definitely the easy interlude in the Double Science syllabus. However, easy or not, there's still a lot of stuff to learn. Try these questions and see how much you know:

1) Write down the four uses of limestone. What's slaked lime?
2) What are fossil fuels? Describe how they were formed.
3) Why is crude oil so important?
4) Draw the full diagram of fractional distillation of crude oil.
5) What are the seven main fractions obtained from crude oil, and what are they used for?
6) What are hydrocarbons? Describe four properties and how they vary with molecular size.
7) Give a typical example of a substance which is cracked and the products that you get.
8) What are the industrial conditions used for cracking?
9) Draw the structures of the first four alkanes and the first three alkenes and give their names.
10) List four differences in the chemical properties of alkanes and alkenes.
11) Draw diagrams to show how ethene and propene form polymers.
12) Name two types of plastic, give their physical properties and say what they're used for.
13) What does biodegradable mean?
14) Which gases are produced when fossil fuels are burned?
15) Explain the three ways in which the oceans contain carbon.
16) What are the percentages of gases in today's atmosphere?
17) How old is the Earth? What was it like for the first billion years or so?
18) What gases did the early atmosphere consist of? Where did these gases come from?
19) What was the main thing which caused phase two of the atmosphere's evolution?
20) Which gas allowed phase three to take place?
21) What are the three types of rock? Draw a fully labelled diagram of the rock cycle.
22) Explain how the three types of rock change from one to another. How long does this take?
23) Draw diagrams to show how sedimentary rocks form.
24) What type of rock contains fossils?
25) How can fossils be used to identify rocks as being the same age?
26) What three things tell geologists how sediments were laid down?
27) As well as lining up neatly, what other four ways might you find sedimentary rock layers? What is this evidence of?
28) Draw a diagram to show how metamorphic rocks are formed. What does the name mean?
29) How are new mountain ranges formed? What happens to older mountain ranges?
30) Draw a diagram of the internal structure of the Earth, with labels.
31) What was the old theory about the Earth's surface? What is the theory of Plate Tectonics?
32) Give details of the three bits of evidence which support the theory of plate tectonics.
33) What are the three different ways that tectonic plates interact at boundaries?
34) Where is the San Andreas fault? What are the tectonic plates doing along this fault line?
35) Why does it cause earthquakes — and why did they build a city right on top of it?
36) What happens when an oceanic plate collides with a continental plate? Draw a fully labelled diagram.
37) What four features does this produce? Which part of the world is the classic case of this?
38) What is the mid-Atlantic ridge? What happens there?
39) Which country lies on top of it? Do they suffer Earthquakes? What *do* they get?
40) Why do magnetic reversal patterns provide us with good evidence of continental drift?

Tests and Symbols

You need to know these five easy lab tests:

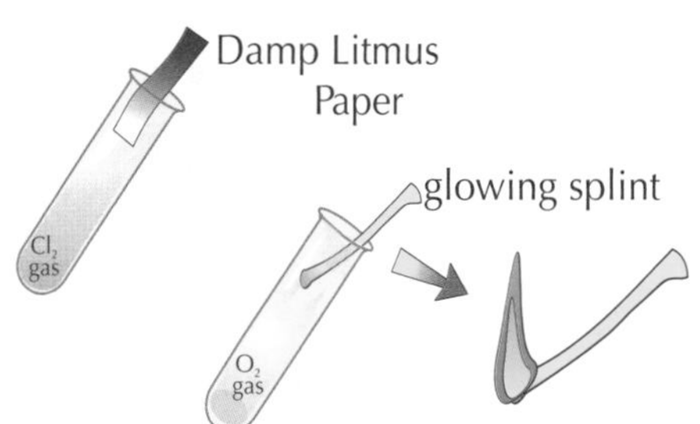

1) Chlorine **bleaches damp litmus paper**

(i.e. it turns it white).

2) Oxygen **relights a glowing splint**

The standard test for oxygen is that it relights a glowing splint.

3) Carbon dioxide **turns limewater milky**

Carbon dioxide can be detected by the way it turns limewater from colourless to cloudy when it's bubbled through it.

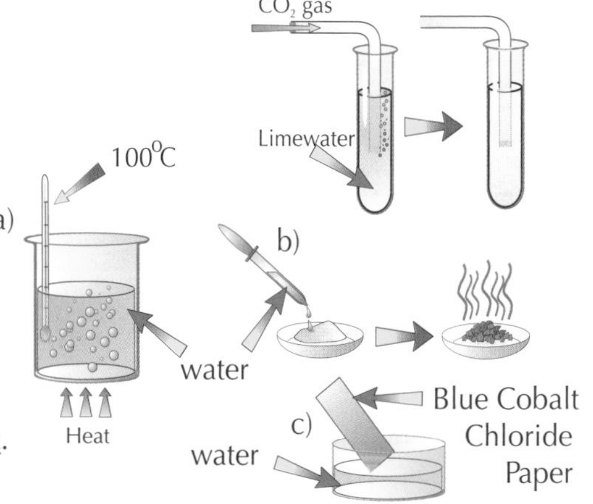

4) The **three lab tests for water**

Water can be detected in three ways:

a) by its boiling point of 100°C (this is a physical test)
b) by turning white anhydrous copper sulphate to blue hydrated copper sulphate (and getting hot)
c) by turning anhydrous cobalt chloride paper from blue to pink.

5) Lab test for hydrogen — **the notorious "Squeaky pop"**

Just bring a lighted splint near the gas with air around. If it's hydrogen it'll make a 'squeaky pop' as it burns with the oxygen in the air to form H_2O.

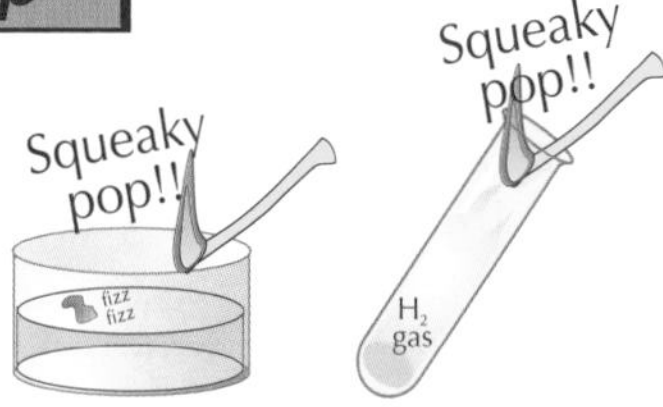

Hazard symbols

Oxidising

Provides oxygen which allows other materials to burn more fiercely.
Example: Liquid Oxygen.

Harmful

Similar to toxic but not quite as dangerous.
Example: meths.

Highly Flammable

Catches fire easily.
Example: Petrol.

Corrosive

Attacks and destroys living tissues, including eyes and skin.
Example: Sulphuric acid.

Toxic

Can cause death either by swallowing, breathing in, or absorption through the skin.
Example: Potassium Cyanide.

Irritant

Not corrosive but can cause reddening or blistering of the skin.
Example: Bleach

This is basic stuff — you need to know it all

This is pretty easy, but people still lose marks in the Exam because they don't make sure they've learnt all the little details really thoroughly. That's true for just about everything in this book.

Warm-Up and Exam Questions

These warm-up questions are here to make sure you know the basics.
If there's anything you've forgotten, check up on the facts before you go any further.

Warm-up Questions

1) An unknown gas will relight a glowing splint. What does this fact suggest the gas is?
2) Describe a test for carbon dioxide.
3) What does the hazard symbol showing a 'skull and crossbones' on a container tell us about its contents?
4) Draw the symbol meaning 'oxidising'.

Exam Questions

Tests are really important — you need to know how to work out what a substance is.
Have a go at these exam questions and see how you're getting on.

1 Name a gas that:

a) bleaches damp litmus paper

....

(1 mark)

b) relights a glowing splint

....

(1 mark)

c) turns limewater milky

....

(1 mark)

d) is a compound made of simple molecules

....

(1 mark)

2 A chemist finds a beaker in the lab containing a clear liquid.
She believes it is water, but is not sure.

Suggest two safe methods of confirming that the liquid is water.

1..

....

2..

....

(2 marks)

Speed of Reactions

The **rate of a reaction** depends on **four things:**

1) Temperature
2) CONCENTRATION — (or *PRESSURE* for gases)
3) Catalyst
4) SIZE OF PARTICLES — (or *SURFACE AREA*)

Typical graphs for rate of reaction

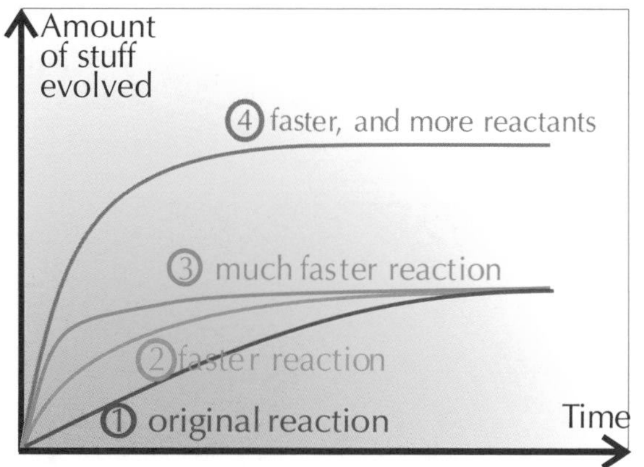

1) Graph 1 represents the original fairly slow reaction.
2) Graphs 2 and 3 represent the reaction taking place quicker but with the same initial amounts.
3) The increased rate could be due to any of these:
   a) increase in temperature
   b) increase in concentration (or pressure)
   c) catalyst added
   d) solid reactant crushed up into smaller bits.
4) Graph 4 produces more product as well as going faster. This can only happen if more reactant(s) are added at the start.

Reactions can go at all sorts of different **rates**

1) One of the slowest is the rusting of iron (it's not that slow though).
2) A moderate speed reaction is a metal (like magnesium) reacting with acid to produce a gentle stream of bubbles.
3) A really fast reaction is an explosion, where it's all over in a fraction of a second.

Three ways to measure the **speed** of a reaction

The speed of reaction can be observed either by how quickly the reactants are used up or how quickly the products are forming. It's usually a lot easier to measure products forming.
There are three different ways that the speed of a reaction can be measured:

1) **Precipitation**

This is when the product of the reaction is a precipitate which clouds the solution. Observe a marker through the solution and measure how long it takes for it to disappear.

CLOUDY

2) **Change in mass** (usually gas given off)

Any reaction that produces a gas can be carried out on a mass balance and as the gas is released the mass disappearing is easily measured.

3) The **volume** of gas given off

This involves the use of a gas syringe to measure the volume of gas given off. But that's about all there is to it.

Increasing the Speed of Reactions

Reaction rates are explained perfectly by Collision Theory. It's really simple.
It just says that the rate of a reaction simply depends on how often and how hard the reacting particles collide with each other. The basic idea is that particles have to collide in order to react, and they have to collide with enough energy as well.

More collisions *increase the* ***rate of reaction***

All four methods of increasing the rate of reactions can be explained in terms of increasing the number of collisions between the reacting particles;

1) ***Temperature*** *increases the number of* ***collisions***

When the temperature is increased the particles all move quicker.
If they're moving quicker, they're going to have more collisions.

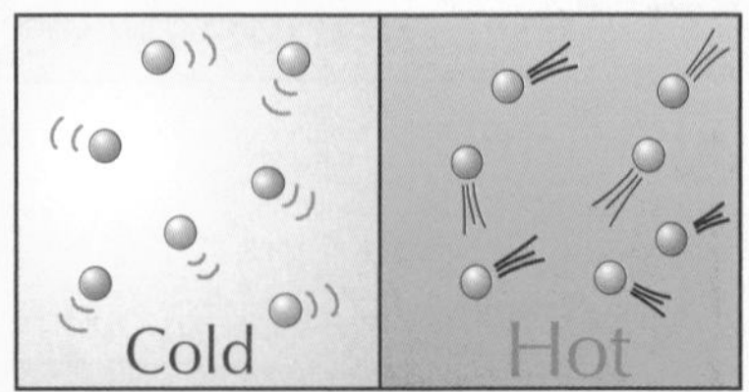

2) ***Concentration*** *(or pressure) increases the number of* ***collisions***

If the solution is made more concentrated it means there are more particles of reactant knocking about between the water molecules which makes collisions between the important particles more likely.
In a gas, increasing the pressure means the molecules are more squashed up together so there are going to be more collisions.

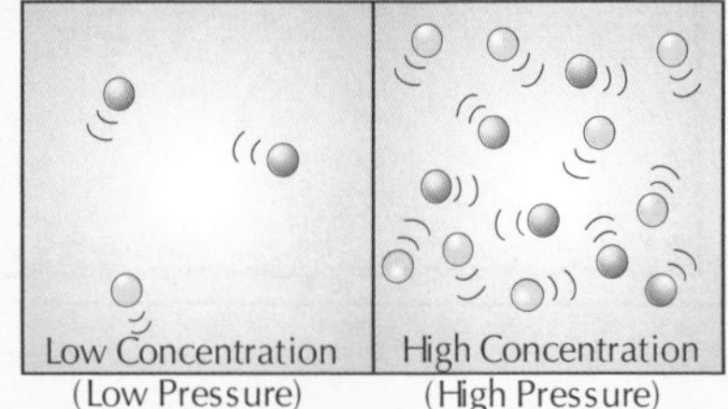

3) ***Size of solid particles*** *(or surface area) increases* ***collisions***

If one of the reactants is a solid then breaking it up into smaller pieces will increase its surface area. This means the particles around it in the solution will have more area to work on so there'll be more useful collisions.

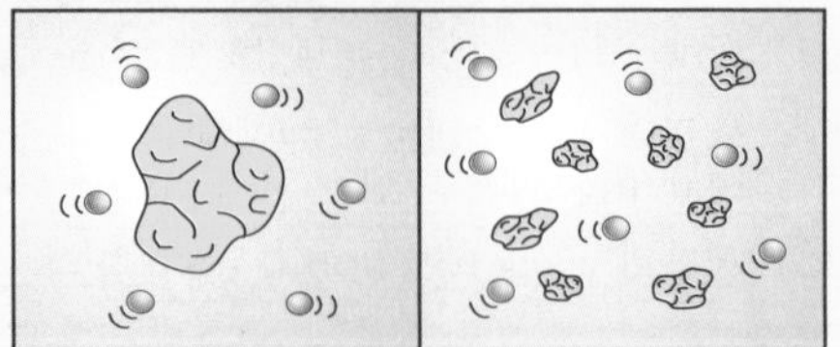

4) A ***catalyst*** *increases the number of successful* ***collisions***

A solid catalyst works by giving the reacting particles a surface to stick to where they can bump into each other.
This increases the number of successful collisions.

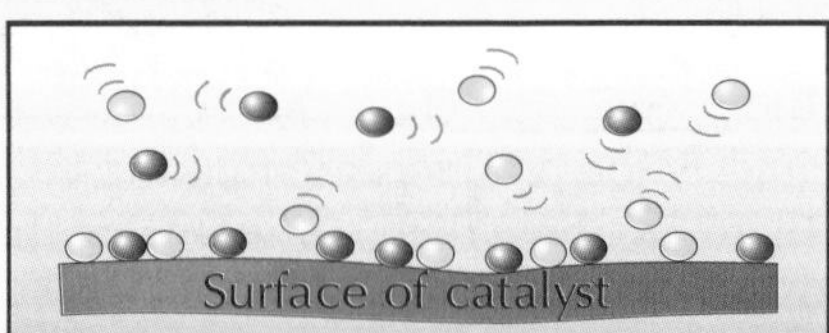

Faster collisions *increase the rate of reaction*

Higher temperature also increases the energy of the collisions, because it makes all the particles move faster.

Faster collisions are ONLY caused by increasing the temperature

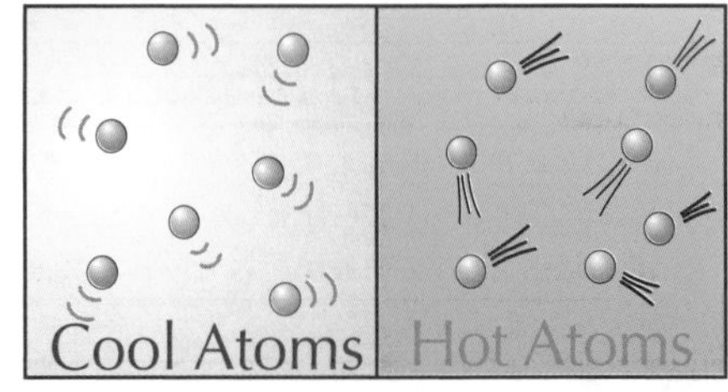

Reactions only happen if the particles collide with enough energy. At a higher temperature there will be more particles colliding with enough energy to make the reaction happen. This minimum energy is known as the *ACTIVATION ENERGY*, and it's needed to break the initial bonds.

Catalysts

Many reactions can be speeded up by adding a catalyst.

1) Catalysts **increase the speed** of the reaction

A CATALYST is a substance which INCREASES the speed of a reaction, without being CHANGED or USED UP in the reaction.

2) Solid catalysts **work best** when they have a **big surface area**

1) Catalysts are usually used as a powder or pellets or a fine gauze.
2) This gives them maximum surface area to enable the reacting particles to meet up and do the business.

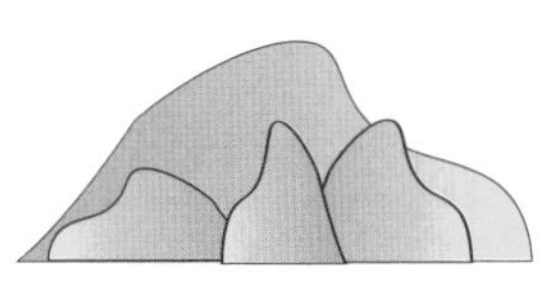
Catalyst Powder

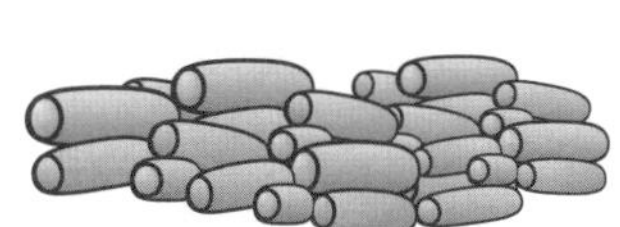
Catalyst Pellets

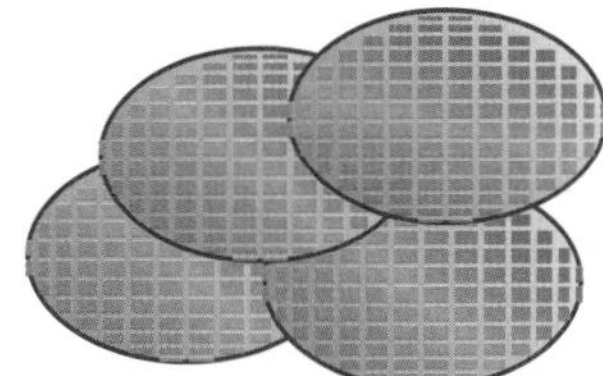
Catalyst Gauzes

3) Catalysts help **reduce costs** in industrial reactions

1) Catalysts increase the rate of many industrial reactions, which saves a lot of money simply because the plant doesn't need to operate for as long to produce the same amount of stuff.
2) Alternatively, a catalyst will allow the reaction to work at a much lower temperature and that can save a lot of money too. Catalysts are therefore very important for commercial reasons.
3) Catalysts are used over and over again. They may need cleaning but they don't get used up.
4) Different reactions use different catalysts.
5) Transition metals are common catalysts in many industrial reactions. Know these two:

a) An **iron catalyst** is used in the **Haber Process**

$$N_{2\,(g)} + 3H_{2\,(g)} \xrightleftharpoons{\text{Iron Catalyst}} 2NH_{3\,(g)}$$

(See P.150)

b) A **platinum catalyst** is used in the production of **nitric acid**

$$\text{Ammonia} + \text{Oxygen} \xrightarrow{\text{Platinum Catalyst}} \text{Nitrogen monoxide} + \text{Water}$$

(See P.151)

There's always a question on reaction rates

Make sure you learn the definition in the top box word for word. The fact is they can easily ask you: *"What is a catalyst?" (2 Marks).* This is much easier to answer if you have a "word for word" definition at the ready. If you don't, you're likely to lose half the marks on it. That's a fact.

Warm-Up and Exam Questions

Warm-up Questions

1) Write down four things that the rate of a reaction depends on.
2) How can liquid particles be made to move faster?
3) Particles can only react if they collide. Write down three ways of decreasing the number of collisions in one minute.
4) A piece of zinc is dropped into a beaker of dilute acid. In the reaction, hydrogen gas is given off. Give two methods of measuring the reaction rate.
5) Describe how a solid catalyst works.

Exam Questions

1 Marble chips (calcium carbonate) react with hydrochloric acid like this:

calcium carbonate + hydrochloric acid → calcium chloride + water + carbon dioxide

Sarah investigated the rate of the reaction using this apparatus:

a) What would you expect to happen to the mass reading during the experiment?

(1 mark)

b) Sarah plotted a graph of her results:

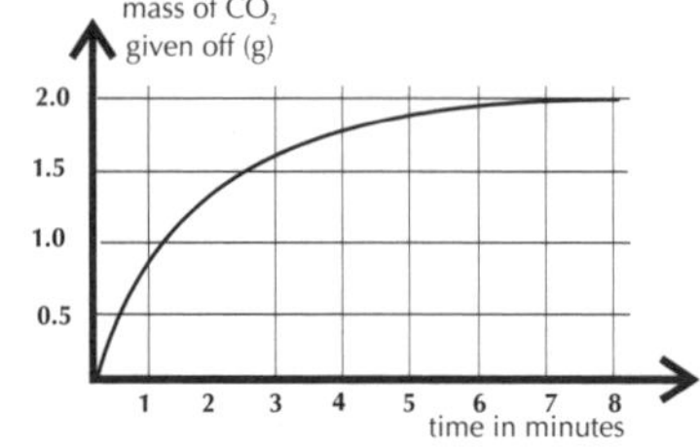

Approximately how many minutes did the reaction take to finish completely?

(1 mark)

c) Sarah repeated the experiment with larger marble chips. She used the same mass of marble chips and the same amount of hydrochloric acid as in the first experiment.

i) Add a curve to the graph to show the progress of the reaction with the larger marble chips.

(2 marks)

ii) Explain in terms of particles why the rate of this reaction depends on the size of the marble chips.

(3 marks)

2 a) What catalyst is used in the Haber Process?

(1 mark)

b) What catalyst is used when making nitrogen monoxide (as part of nitric acid synthesis)?

(1 mark)

Enzymes

Enzymes are biological catalysts

1) Living things have thousands of different chemical processes going on inside them.
2) The quicker these happen the better, and raising the temperature of the body is an important way to speed them up.
3) However, there's a limit to how far you can raise the temperature before cells start getting damaged, so living things also produce enzymes which act as catalysts to speed up all these chemical reactions without the need for high temperatures.

Enzymes are produced by living things and are great

1) Every different biological process has its own enzyme designed especially for it.
2) Enzymes have two main advantages over traditional non-organic catalysts:

   a) They're not scarce like many metal catalysts e.g. platinum.

   b) They work best at low temperatures, which keeps costs down.

Enzymes like it warm but not too hot

The chemical reactions in living cells are quite fast in conditions that are warm rather than hot.

This is because the cells use enzyme catalysts, which are protein molecules.

Enzymes are usually damaged by temperatures above about 45°C, and as the graph shows, their activity drops off sharply when the temperature gets a little too high.

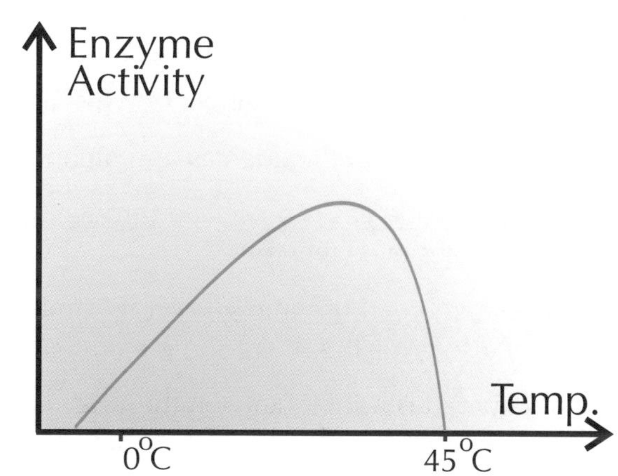

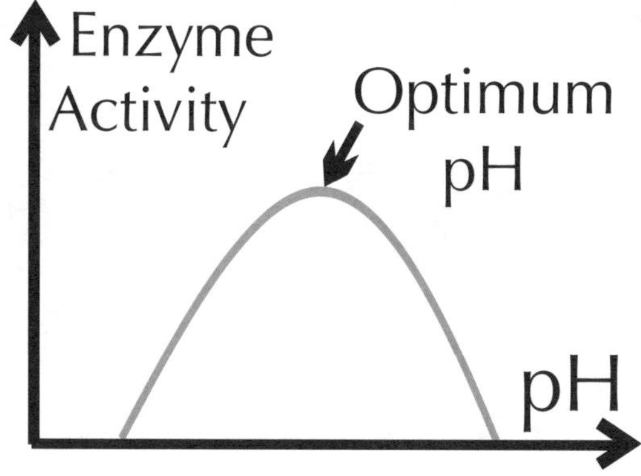

Enzymes like it the right pH too

The pH affects the activity of enzymes, in a similar way to temperature.

Uses of Enzymes

Living cells use chemical reactions to produce new materials. Many of these reactions provide products which are useful to us. Here are three important examples:

Yeast** in brewing of beer and wine: **Fermentation

1) Yeast cells convert sugar into carbon dioxide and alcohol.
2) The main thing is to keep the temperature just right.
3) If it's too cold the enzyme won't work very quickly.
4) If it's too hot it will destroy the enzyme.
5) This biological process is called fermentation and is used for making alcoholic drinks like beer and wine.

FERMENTATION is the process of yeast converting sugar into carbon dioxide and alcohol.

$$\text{Glucose} \xrightarrow{\text{Enzyme}} \text{Carbon dioxide} + \text{Ethanol} \quad (+\text{ Energy})$$

Yeast** in bread-making: **Fermentation again

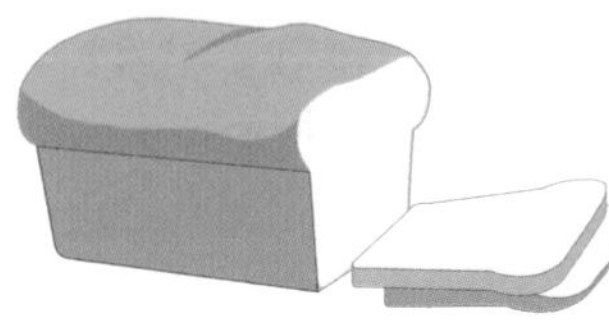

1) The reaction in bread-making is exactly the same as that in brewing.
2) Yeast cells use an enzyme to break down sugar and this gives them energy.
3) It also releases carbon dioxide gas and alcohol as waste products.
4) The carbon dioxide gas is produced throughout the bread mixture and forms in bubbles everywhere.
5) This makes the bread rise and gives it its familiar texture. The small amount of alcohol also gives the bread some extra flavour, no doubt.
6) When the bread is put in the oven the yeast is killed and the reaction stops.

*Enzymes are used to do **weird things to foods***

1) The proteins in some baby foods are 'pre-digested' using proteases (protein-digesting enzymes).
2) The centres of chocolates can be softened using enzymes.
3) Carbohydrases can turn starch syrup (yuk) into sugar syrup (yum) by breaking the starch (carbohydrate) down into sugar.
4) Glucose syrup can be turned into fructose syrup using isomerase. Fructose is sweeter, so you can use less of it — good for slimming foods and drinks.

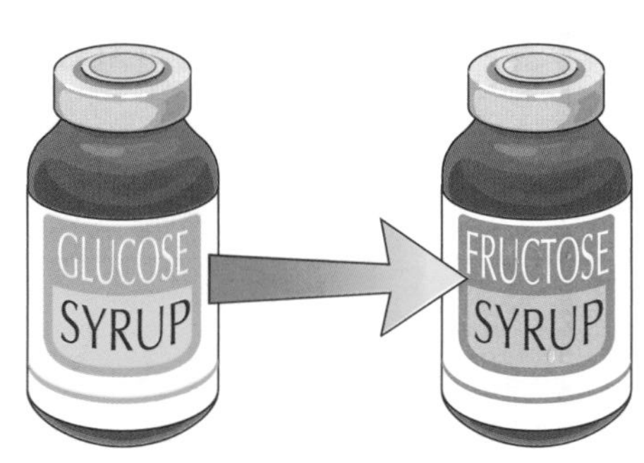

Uses of Enzymes

Yoghurt *and* ***cheese*** *making — only* ***pasteurised milk***

1) Pasteurised milk is usually used for making cheese and yoghurt, because fresh unpasteurised milk contains many unwanted bacteria.
2) Instead the pasteurised milk is mixed with specially grown cultures of bacteria.
3) This mixture is kept at the ideal temperature for the bacteria and their enzymes to work.
4) For yoghurt this is pretty warm at about 45°C.
5) The yoghurt-making bacteria convert lactose, (the natural sugar found in milk), into lactic acid. This gives yoghurts their slightly bitter taste.

6) Cheese on the other hand matures better in cooler conditions.
7) Various bacterial enzymes can be used in cheese making to produce different textures and tastes.

Enzymes are used in ***biological detergents***

1) Enzymes are the 'biological' ingredients in biological detergents and washing powders.
2) They're mainly proteases (protein-digesting enzymes) and lipases (fat-digesting enzymes).
3) Because the enzymes attack animal and plant matter, they're ideal for removing stains like food or blood.

Using *enzymes in* ***industry*** *takes careful monitoring*

1) In an industrial process, the temperature and pH have to be right so the enzymes aren't damaged, and keep working for a long time.
2) The enzymes have to be kept from washing away. They can be mixed into plastic beads, or trapped in an alginate bed (seaweed mush). Both these methods make sure the enzymes are immobile.
3) Because enzymes work for a long time, you can continually pass chemicals to react over them, and tap off the product at the other end. You don't need to do separate batches with new enzymes each time.

Enzymes are mighty useful things

You're expected to know all these details of making bread, wine, cheese, yoghurt, weird sugars and baby food, detergents, and the industrial bit. Mini-essays again, I'd say. Enjoy.

Warm-Up and Exam Questions

Warm-up Questions

1) What is an enzyme?
2) What is the maximum operating temperature of most enzymes?
3) Describe two methods used in industry to prevent enzymes washing away during processing.
4) Biological washing powders contain proteases and lipases. What kind of stains do these enzymes digest?

Exam Questions

1 a) Beer is brewed from sugary barley malt. Alcohol is produced by fermentation.

i) Write down a definition of fermentation.

(2 marks)

ii) Write down a word equation for fermentation.

(2 marks)

iii) Fermentation does not happen if the barley malt is too hot or too cold. Explain why.

(2 marks)

b) Advertisements for biological detergents claim that they can digest stains in a 40°C wash.

i) Would you expect a biological detergent to function as well at 60°C? Explain why.

(2 marks)

ii) What kind of enzyme would be able to digest stains like egg and blood?

(1 mark)

2 This question is about enzymes in food preparation.

a) Corn contains a lot of starch. Briefly describe how syrup containing a lot of glucose is made from corn.

(1 mark)

b) Fructose is sweeter than sucrose. Explain why fructose is used in some "diet" or "healthy option" foods in place of sucrose.

(1 mark)

3 This graph shows enzyme activity against temperature.

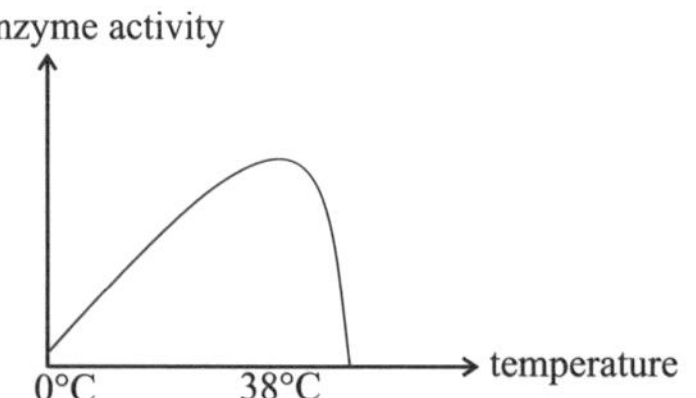

a) Explain why the enzyme activity drops off sharply over about 38°C.

(1 mark)

b) i) Explain in terms of bacterial enzyme activity why freezing food stops it going off.

(2 marks)

ii) Will frozen food go off once it is thawed? Explain your answer.

(2 marks)

Energy in Reactions

Whenever chemical reactions occur energy is transferred to or from the surroundings.

*In an **exothermic reaction**, heat is **given out***

An EXOTHERMIC reaction is one which gives out energy to the surroundings, usually in the form of heat and usually shown by a rise in temperature

1) The best example of an exothermic reaction is burning fuels. This obviously gives out a lot of heat — it's very exothermic.
2) Neutralisation reactions (acid + alkali) are also exothermic.
3) Addition of water to anhydrous copper(II) sulphate to turn it into blue crystals produces heat, so it must be exothermic.

*In an **endothermic reaction**, heat is **taken in***

An ENDOTHERMIC reaction is one which takes in energy from the surroundings, usually in the form of heat and usually shown by a fall in temperature

Endothermic reactions are less common and less easy to spot.
So LEARN these three examples, in case they ask for one:

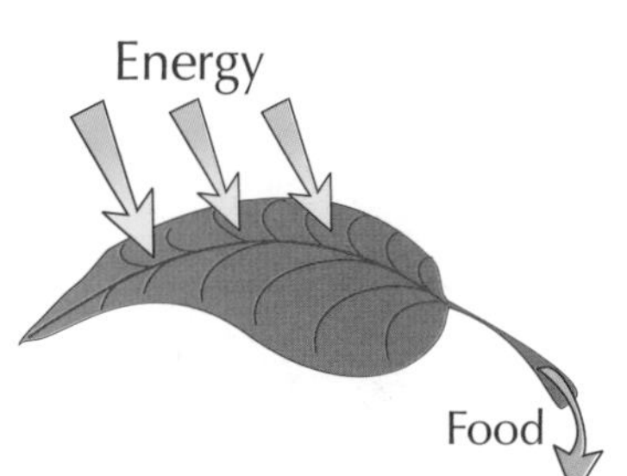

*1) **Photosynthesis** is endothermic*

— it takes in energy from the sun.

*2) **Dissolving certain salts in water***

e.g. 1) potassium chloride 2) ammonium nitrate

*3) **Thermal decomposition***

Heat must be supplied to cause the compound to decompose.
The best example is converting calcium carbonate into quicklime (calcium oxide):

$$CaCO_3 \rightarrow CaO + CO_2$$

A lot of heat energy is needed to make this happen. In fact the calcium carbonate has to be heated in a kiln and kept at about 800°C. It takes almost 30,000kJ of heat to make 10kg of calcium carbonate decompose. That's pretty endothermic.

*Energy must always be **supplied** to **break bonds**...*

*...and energy is always **released** when **bonds form***

1) During a chemical reaction, old bonds are broken and new bonds are formed.
2) Energy must be supplied to break existing bonds — so bond breaking is an endothermic process.
3) Energy is released when new bonds are formed — so bond formation is an exothermic process.

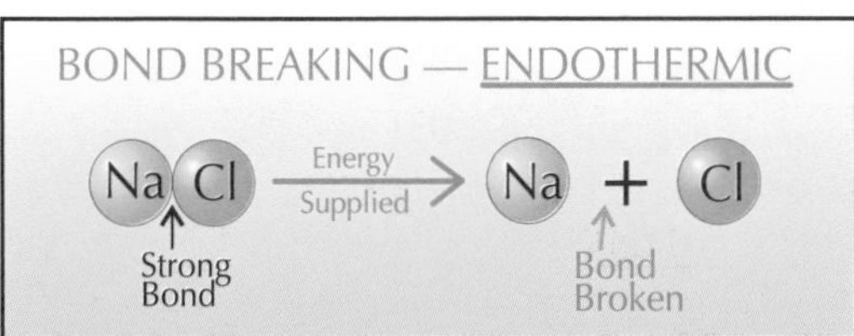

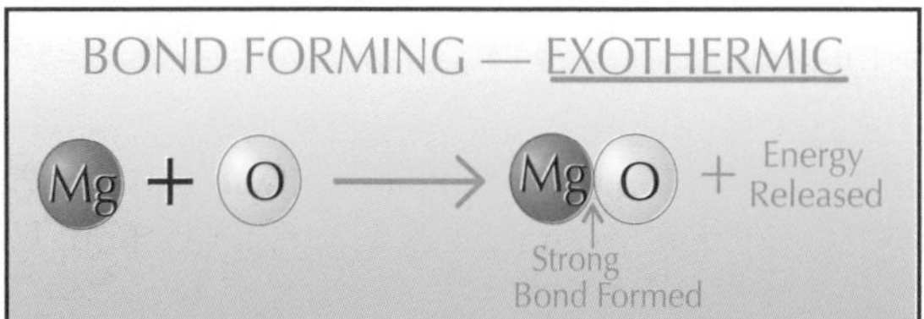

4) In an exothermic reaction, the energy released in bond formation is greater than the energy used in breaking old bonds.
5) In an endothermic reaction, the energy required to break old bonds is greater than the energy released when new bonds are formed.

Energy in Reactions

Energy level diagrams *show if it's exo- or endo- thermic*

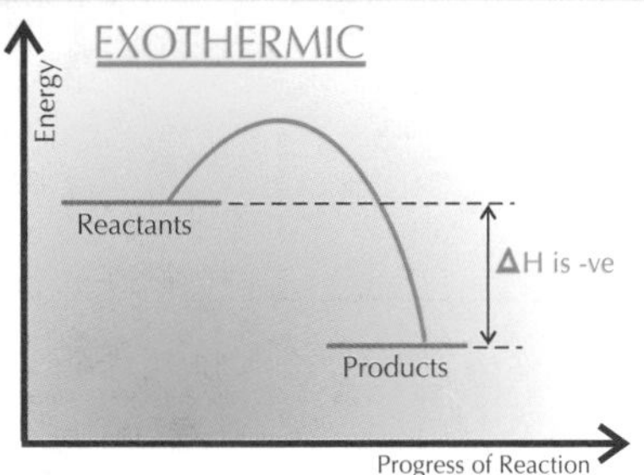

In ***exothermic*** *reactions* ***ΔH is -ve***

1) This shows an exothermic reaction because the products are at a lower energy than the reactants.
2) The difference in height represents the energy given out in the reaction (per mole). ΔH is -ve in this case.
3) The initial rise in the line represents the energy needed to break the old bonds. This is the activation energy.

ENDOTHERMIC

Energy

Products

ΔH is +ve

Reactants

Progress of Reaction

In ***endothermic*** *reactions* ***ΔH is +ve***

1) This shows an endothermic reaction because the products are at a higher energy than the reactants. ΔH is +ve.
2) The difference in height represents the energy taken in during the reaction.

The activation energy is ***lowered*** *by* ***catalysts***

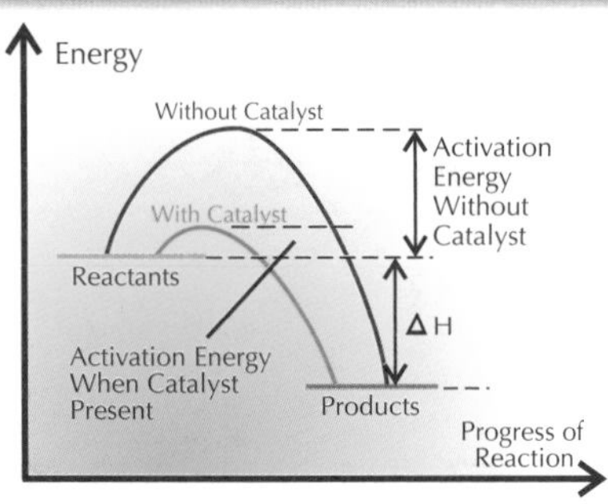

1) The activation energy represents the minimum energy needed by reacting particles for the reaction to occur.
2) A catalyst makes reactions happen easier (and therefore quicker) by reducing the initial energy needed.
3) This is represented by the lower curve on the diagram showing a lower activation energy.
4) The overall energy change for the reaction, ΔH, remains the same though.

Bond energy calculations — need to be ***practised***

1) Every chemical bond has a particular bond energy associated with it.
2) This bond energy is always the same no matter what compound the bond occurs in.
3) We can use these known bond energies to calculate the overall energy change for a reaction.
4) You need to practise a few of these, but the basic idea is really very simple.

Example: ***The formation of HCl***

The bond energies we need: H—H 436kJ/mole; Cl—Cl 242kJ/mole; H—Cl 431kJ/mole.

Using these known bond energies we can calculate the energy change for this reaction:

1) Breaking one mole of H—H and one mole of Cl—Cl bonds requires 436 + 242 = +678kJ
2) Forming two moles of H—Cl bonds releases 2×431 = 862kJ
3) Overall there is more energy released than used: 862 – 678 = 184kJ/mol released.
4) Since this is energy released, then if we wanted to show ΔH we'd need to put a –ve in front of it to indicate that it's an exothermic reaction, like this: ΔH = -184kJ/mol

Remember — breaking bonds requires energy

Exothermic and endothermic reactions are really quite simple. You've just got to get used to the big words. Bond energy calculations though, need quite a bit of practice, as do any calculation questions. You can't just do a couple and think that'll be OK. You've got to do loads of them.

Warm-Up and Exam Questions

Endothermic and exothermic are simply big words for straightforward ideas. Seeing them in terms of bond energy is a bit trickier. Calculations relating to bond breaking and making need lots of attention.

Warm-up Questions

1) What's the name for a reaction which gives out heat?
2) What's the name for a reaction which takes in heat?
3) When ammonium nitrate is dissolved in water, the temperature of the water decreases. Is this an exothermic or an endothermic reaction?
4) In a chemical reaction, bonds are broken. Does bond breaking take in energy, or give out energy?

Exam Questions

You could get questions just like these in the exam. Notice how you could be asked to calculate the energy released in a reaction. 5 marks up for grabs if you can do it.

1 a) Give an example of an exothermic reaction.

(1 mark)

b) Look at this diagram of the energy change during a reaction.

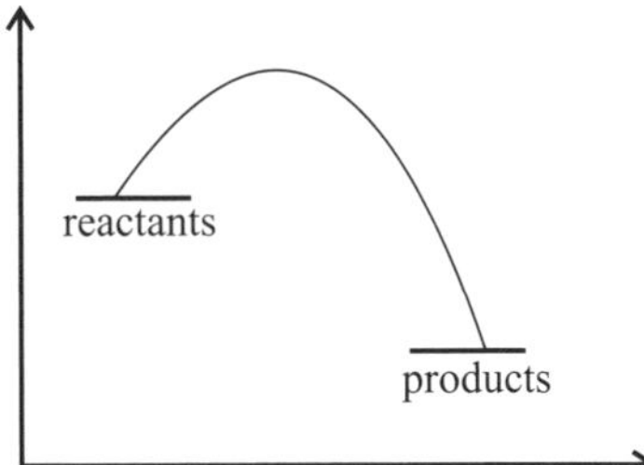

i) Is ΔH positive or negative in this case?

(1 mark)

ii) Mark and label the activation energy on the diagram.

(1 mark)

c) When a reaction takes place, old bonds are broken and new bonds are formed. Which process is exothermic?

(1 mark)

2 Ethene is burnt in oxygen, producing heat. The equation for this reaction is as follows:

$$C_2H_4 + 3O_2 \rightarrow 2CO_2 + 2H_2O$$

The structure of ethene is shown on the right.

$$\begin{matrix} H & & & & H \\ & \searrow & C=C & \swarrow & \\ H & \nearrow & & \nwarrow & H \end{matrix}$$

Bond energies required: C – H +414 kJ/mole; C = C +615 kJ/mole;
O = O +498 kJ/mole; C = O +749 kJ/mole;
H – O +463 kJ/mole.

Calculate the energy released when one mole of ethene is burnt in air.

(5 marks)

The Haber Process

This is an important industrial process. It produces ammonia which is needed for making fertilisers.

Nitrogen and hydrogen are needed to make ammonia

1) The nitrogen is obtained easily from the air, which is 78% nitrogen (and 21% oxygen).
2) The hydrogen is obtained from water (steam) and natural gas (methane, CH_4).
   The methane and steam are reacted together like this:

$$CH_{4\,(g)} + H_2O_{(g)} \rightarrow CO_{(g)} + 3H_{2\,(g)}$$

3) Hydrogen can also be obtained from crude oil, by cracking.

The Haber Process is a reversible reaction

A reversible reaction is one where the products can react with each other and convert back to the original chemicals. In other words, it can go both ways. See pages 153-155.

The equation for the Haber Process is:

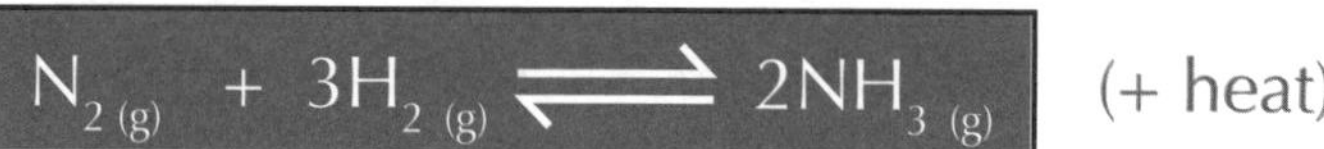

$$N_{2\,(g)} + 3H_{2\,(g)} \rightleftharpoons 2NH_{3\,(g)}$$

(+ heat)

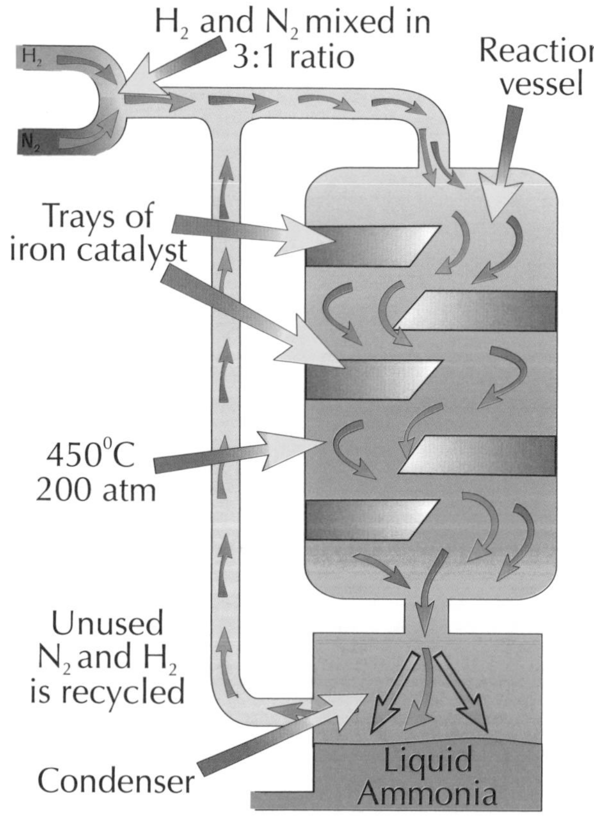

Industrial conditions:

PRESSURE:	200 atmospheres (at least)
TEMPERATURE:	450°C
CATALYST:	Iron

Because the Reaction is Reversible, there's a compromise to be made:

1) Higher pressures favour the forward reaction, hence the 200 atmospheres operating pressure.
2) However, it turns out that lower temperatures improve the forward reaction. At least it does in terms of the proportion of hydrogen and nitrogen converting to ammonia. This is called the yield.
3) The trouble is, lower temperatures mean a slower rate of reaction. (This is different from yield.)
4) So the 450°C is a compromise between maximum yield and speed of reaction.
5) The pressure used is also a compromise. Even higher pressures would increase the yield further, but the plant would be more expensive to build. In the end it all comes down to minimising costs.

Extra Notes:

1) The hydrogen and nitrogen are mixed together in a 3:1 ratio.
2) Because the reaction is reversible, not all of the nitrogen and hydrogen will convert to ammonia.
3) The ammonia is formed as a gas but as it cools in the condenser it liquefies and is removed.
4) The N_2 and H_2 which didn't react are recycled and passed through again so none is wasted.

Fertiliser from Ammonia

On this page are two reactions involving ammonia that you need to be familiar with.

1) Ammonia can be **oxidised** to form **nitric acid**

There are two stages to this reaction:

a) Ammonia gas reacts with **oxygen** over a **hot platinum catalyst**:

$$4NH_{3\,(g)} + 5O_{2\,(g)} \rightarrow 4NO_{(g)} + 6H_2O_{(g)}$$

This first stage is very exothermic and produces its own heat to keep it going.
The nitrogen monoxide must be cooled before the next stage, which happens easily:

b) The **nitrogen monoxide** reacts with **water and oxygen**...

$$6NO_{(g)} + 3O_{2\,(g)} + 2H_2O_{(g)} \rightarrow 4HNO_{3\,(g)} + 2NO_{(g)}$$

...to form nitric acid, HNO_3

Gripping stuff. Anyway, the nitric acid produced is very useful for other chemical processes. One such use is to make ammonium nitrate fertiliser.

2) Ammonia can be **neutralised** with **nitric acid**...

... to make **ammonium nitrate** fertiliser

This is a straightforward and spectacularly unexciting neutralisation reaction between an alkali (ammonia) and an acid. The result is of course a neutral salt:

$$NH_{3\,(g)} + HNO_{3\,(aq)} \rightarrow NH_4NO_{3\,(aq)}$$

Ammonia + Nitric acid → Ammonium nitrate

Ammonium nitrate is an especially good fertiliser because it has nitrogen from two sources, the ammonia and the nitric acid. Kind of a double dose. Plants need nitrogen to make proteins.

Excessive nitrate fertiliser causes **eutrophication** and **health problems**

1) If nitrate fertilisers wash into streams they set off a cycle of mega-growth, mega-death and mega-decay. Plants and green algae grow out of control, then start to die off because there's too many of them, then bacteria take over, feeding off the dying plants and using up all the oxygen in the water. Then the fish all die because they can't get enough oxygen. It's called eutrophication (see page 66).
2) If too many nitrates get into drinking water it can cause health problems, especially for young babies. Nitrates prevent the blood from carrying oxygen properly and children can turn blue and even die.
3) To avoid these problems it's important that artificial nitrate fertilisers are applied carefully by all farmers — they must take care not to apply too much, and not if it's going to rain soon.

The Haber process and NH_4NO_3 fertilisers — it's important stuff

In the Exams they're pretty keen on the Haber process and how ammonia is turned into ammonium nitrate fertiliser — so you'd be well advised to learn all this. They could easily ask you on any of it.

Warm-Up and Exam Question

Questions about ammonia and fertilisers will either ask you to write down the equations for making ammonia and ammonium nitrate, or they'll ask you to describe the Haber Process.

Warm-up Questions

1) Is ammonia a base or an acid?
2) What is used as a catalyst in the Haber Process?
3) Name the environmental problem caused by nitrate fertilisers washing into streams.

Exam Question

This exam question is about the Haber Process.
Work through it, and make sure you know exactly what to write.

1 Ammonia is made from nitrogen and hydrogen using the Haber Process.

a) i) Describe the industrial conditions used in the Haber Process.

....

....

(3 marks)

ii) Lower temperatures produce higher yields of ammonia. Why is the temperature used in the Haber Process so high?

....

....

(2 marks)

b) Ammonia is reacted with acid to make fertiliser.

i) Write a balanced equation for the reaction between nitric acid and ammonia.

....

(2 marks)

ii) Describe what happens when excess nitrate fertiliser washes into streams and rivers.

....

....

....

(3 marks)

Simple Reversible Reactions

A reversible reaction is one which can go in both directions. In other words the products of the reaction can be turned back into the original reactants. Here are some examples you should know about in case you get one in the Exam.

The thermal decomposition of **ammonium chloride**

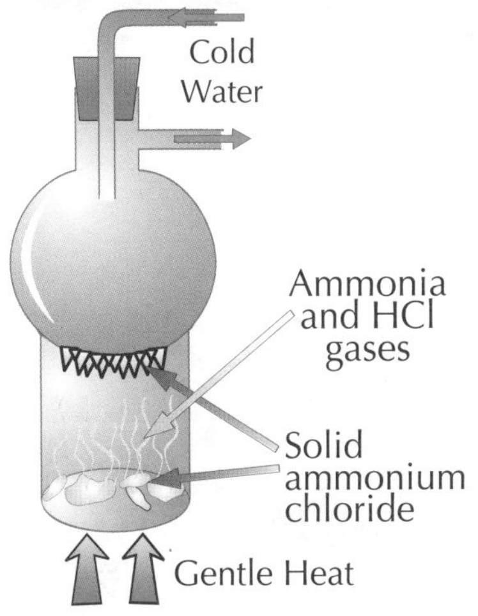

1) When ammonium chloride is heated it splits up into ammonia gas and HCl gas.
2) When these gases cool they recombine to form solid ammonium chloride.
3) This is a typical reversible reaction because the products recombine to form the original substance very easily.

The thermal decomposition of **hydrated copper sulphate**

1) It's those blue copper(II) sulphate crystals again.
2) Here they're displaying their usual trick, but under the guise of a reversible reaction.
3) If you heat them it drives the water off and leaves white anhydrous copper(II) sulphate powder.

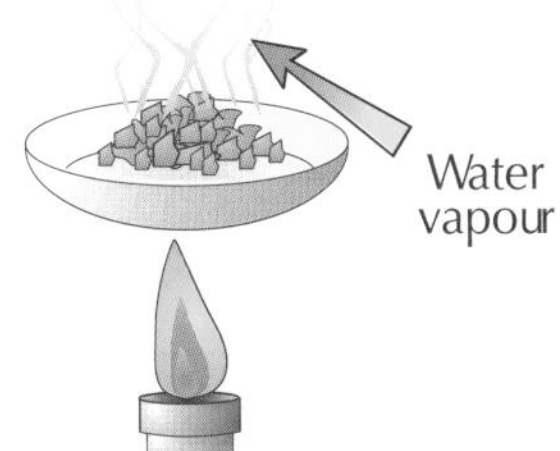

4) If you then add a couple of drops of water to the white powder you get the blue crystals back again. This can be used as a test for water.

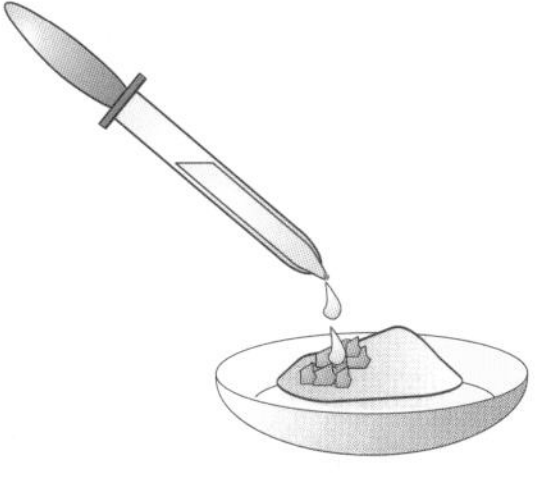

The proper name for the *blue crystals* is *hydrated copper(II) sulphate*. "*Hydrated*" means "*with water*". When you drive the water off they become a white powder, *anhydrous copper(II) sulphate*. "*Anhydrous*" means "*without water*".

Reacting iodine with chlorine to get **iodine trichloride**

There's a reversible reaction between the mucky brown liquid of iodine monochloride (ICl), and nasty green chlorine gas to form nice clean yellow crystals of iodine trichloride (ICl_3).

$$ICl + Cl_2 \rightleftharpoons ICl_3$$

1) Which way the reaction goes depends on the concentration of chlorine gas in the air around.
2) A lot of chlorine will favour formation of the yellow crystals.
3) A lack of chlorine will encourage the crystals to decompose back to the horrid brown liquid.

Reversible Reactions in Equilibrium

A reversible reaction is one where the products can react with each other and convert back to the original chemicals. In other words, it can go both ways.

A *REVERSIBLE REACTION* IS ONE WHERE THE *PRODUCTS* OF THE REACTION CAN *THEMSELVES REACT* TO PRODUCE THE *ORIGINAL REACTANTS*

$$A + B \rightleftharpoons C + D$$

Reversible reactions will reach **dynamic equilibrium**

1) If a reversible reaction takes place in a closed system then a state of equilibrium will always be reached.

2) Equilibrium means that the relative (%) quantities of reactants and products will reach a certain balance and stay there. A 'closed system' just means that none of the reactants or products can escape.

3) It is in fact a dynamic equilibrium, which means that the reactions are still taking place in both directions but the overall effect is nil because the forward and reverse reactions cancel each other out. The reactions are taking place at exactly the same rate in both directions.

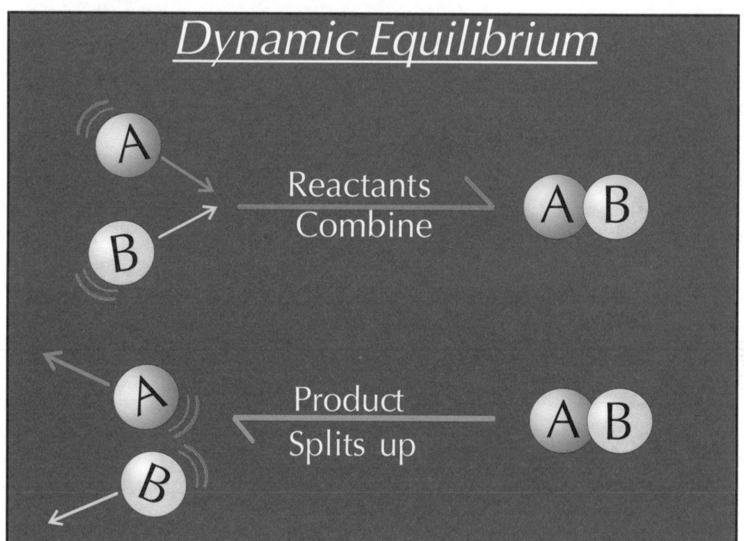

Changing temperature and pressure to get **more product**

1) In a reversible reaction the 'position of equilibrium' (the relative amounts of reactants and products) depends very strongly on the temperature and pressure surrounding the reaction.

2) If we deliberately alter the temperature and pressure we can move the "position of equilibrium" to give more product and less reactants.

Two **very simple rules** for which way the equilibrium will **move**

1) All reactions are exothermic in one direction and endothermic in the other.
If we raise the temperature, the endothermic reaction will increase to use up the extra heat.
If we reduce the temperature the exothermic reaction will increase to give out more heat.

2) Many reactions have a greater volume on one side, either of products or reactants.
If we raise the pressure it will encourage the reaction which produces less volume.
If we lower the pressure it will encourage the reaction which produces more volume.

The Haber Process — A Reversible Reaction

Other details of the Haber Process are given on P.150.

The **Haber Process** is a controlled **reversible reaction**

The Equation is:

$$N_{2\,(g)} + 3H_{2\,(g)} \rightleftharpoons 2NH_{3\,(g)}$$

ΔH is -ve, (see P.148)
i.e. the forward reaction is exothermic

Higher pressure will favour the **forward** reaction **so build it strong...**

1) On the left side of the equation there are four moles of gas ($N_2 + 3H_2$), whilst on the right side there are just two moles (of NH_3).
2) So any increase in pressure will favour the forward reaction to produce more ammonia. Hence the decision on pressure is simple. It's just set as high as possible to give the best % yield without making the plant too expensive to build. 200 to 350 atmospheres are typical pressures used.

Lower temperature would favour the forward reaction **but...**

The reaction is exothermic in the forward direction which means that increasing the temperature will actually move the equilibrium the wrong way, away from ammonia and more towards H_2 and N_2. But they increase the temperature anyway... this is the tricky bit:

Learn this really well:

1) The proportion of ammonia at equilibrium can only be increased by lowering the temperature.
2) But instead they raise the temperature and accept a reduced proportion (or yield) of ammonia.
3) The reason is that the higher temperature gives a much higher rate of reaction.
4) It's better to wait just 20 seconds for a 10% yield than to have to wait 60 seconds for a 20% yield.
5) Remember, the unused hydrogen, H_2, and nitrogen, N_2, are recycled so nothing is wasted.

The iron catalyst **speeds up** the reaction and keeps **costs down**

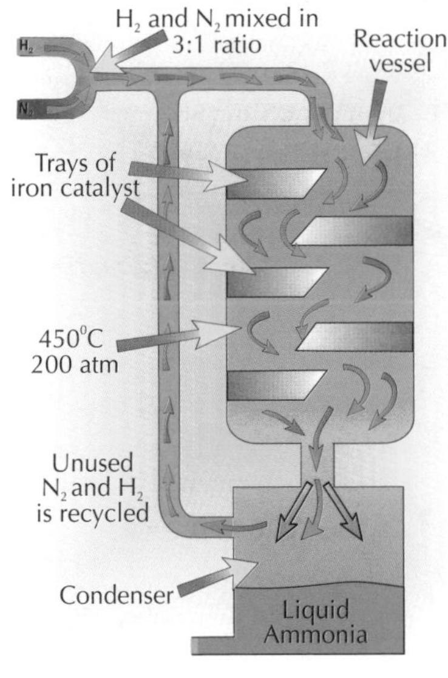

1) The iron catalyst makes the reaction go quicker which gets it to the equilibrium proportions more quickly. But remember, the catalyst doesn't affect the position of equilibrium (i.e. the % yield).
2) Without the catalyst the temperature would have to be raised even further to get a quick enough reaction and that would reduce the % yield even further. So the catalyst is very important.
3) Removing product would be an effective way to improve yield because the reaction keeps chasing equilibrium while the product keeps disappearing. Eventually the whole lot is converted.
4) This can't be done in the Haber Process because the ammonia can't be removed until afterwards when the mixture is cooled to condense out the ammonia.

The Haber process is the favourite example of a reversible reaction

If they're going to use any reversible reaction for an Exam question, it'll probably be this one.
The trickiest bit is that the temperature is raised not for a better equilibrium, but for speed.
Try the mini-essay method to scribble down all you know about equilibrium and the Haber process.

Warm-Up and Exam Questions

Warm-up Questions

1) Ammonia reacts with hydrogen chloride to make ammonium chloride. Is this a reversible reaction?
2) What happens to blue hydrated copper(II) sulphate crystals when they are heated?
3) What is a closed system?
4) If a reaction is endothermic in the forward direction, can it be endothermic in the backward direction as well?

Exam Questions

1 This question is about reversible reactions and equilibrium.

a) A reversible reaction in a closed system reaches dynamic equilibrium.
Describe what is meant by dynamic equilibrium.

(2 marks)

b) The reaction between reactant A and reactant B to produce product AB is reversible.

i) The reaction between reactant A and reactant B to produce product AB is exothermic. Is the decomposition of AB into A and B endothermic or exothermic?

(1 mark)

ii) If the temperature in the reaction vessel is raised, which reaction will speed up, and which reaction will slow down?

(2 marks)

iii) If the temperature is raised, how will the concentration of AB change?

(1 mark)

2 Ammonia is made using the Haber Process.
This question is about the industrial conditions chosen for the Haber Process.

a) The Haber Process involves a reversible reaction.
It takes place at 200-350 atmospheres pressure and 450°C with an iron catalyst.
The equation for the reaction in the Haber Process is $\mathbf{N_{2\,(g)} + 3H_{2\,(g)} \rightleftharpoons 2NH_{3\,(g)}}$

i) Explain why the Haber Process is carried out at high pressure.

(2 marks)

ii) Lower temperatures than 450°C would give higher yields.
Why is the reaction carried out at 450°C?

(3 marks)

iii) How would the yield be affected if ammonia was removed as the reaction took place? Explain your answer.

(3 marks)

b) i) What effect does the iron catalyst have on the yield?

(1 mark)

ii) The iron catalyst speeds up the reaction without increasing the temperature.
Why is this particularly useful in the Haber Process?

(2 marks)

Relative Formula Mass

The biggest trouble with relative atomic mass and relative formula mass is that they sound intimidating. In fact, they're not that complicated at all. Just read this carefully...

Relative atomic mass, A_r

1) This is just a way of saying how heavy different atoms are compared to each other.
2) The relative atomic mass A_r is nothing more than the mass number of the element.
3) On the periodic table, the elements all have two numbers. The smaller one is the atomic number (how many protons it has). But the bigger one is the mass number (how many protons and neutrons it has) which, kind of obviously, is also the relative atomic mass.

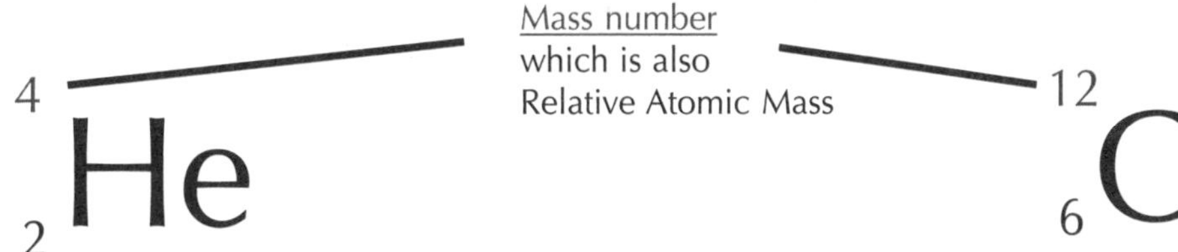

Helium has $A_r = 4$. Carbon has $A_r = 12$. (So carbon atoms are 3 times heavier than helium atoms)

Relative formula mass, M_r

If you have a compound like $MgCl_2$ then it has a relative formula mass, M_r, which is just all the relative atomic masses added together.

For $MgCl_2$ it would be:

$$MgCl_2$$

$$24 + (35.5 \times 2) = 95$$

So the M_r for $MgCl_2$ is simply 95

You can easily get the A_r for any element from the Periodic Table (see inside front cover), but in a lot of questions they give you them anyway. Here's another example for you:

Question: *Find the relative formula mass for calcium carbonate, $CaCO_3$ using the given data:*
A_r for Ca = 40 A_r for C = 12 A_r for O = 16

ANSWER:

So the Relative Formula Mass for $CaCO_3$ is 100

And that's all there is to it.

Mass and Volume Calculations I

Although Relative Atomic Mass and Relative Formula Mass are easy enough, it can get just a little bit trickier when you start getting into other calculations which use them. It depends on how good your maths is basically, because it's all to do with ratios and percentages.

Calculating % mass of an element in a compound

This is really easy — so long as you've learnt this formula:

$$\text{PERCENTAGE MASS OF AN ELEMENT IN A COMPOUND} = \frac{A_r \times \text{No. of atoms in the formula (of that element)}}{M_r \text{ (of whole compound)}} \times 100$$

If you don't learn the formula then you'd better be pretty smart — or you'll struggle.

EXAMPLE: *Find the percentage mass of sodium in sodium carbonate, Na_2CO_3*

ANSWER:

A_r of sodium = 23, A_r of carbon = 12, A_r of oxygen = 16

M_r of Na_2CO_3 = (2×23)+12+(3×16)=106

Now use the formula: Percentage mass = $\frac{A_r \times n}{M_r} \times 100 = \frac{23 \times 2}{106} \times 100 = 43.4\%$

And there you have it. Sodium represents 43.4% of the mass of sodium carbonate.

Finding the empirical formula (from masses or percentages)

This also sounds a lot worse than it really is. Try this for an easy step by step method:

1) LIST ALL THE ELEMENTS in the compound (there are usually only two or three).
2) Underneath them, write their EXPERIMENTAL MASSES OR PERCENTAGES.
3) DIVIDE each mass or percentage BY THE A_r for that particular element.
4) Turn the numbers you get into A NICE SIMPLE RATIO by multiplying and/or dividing them by well-chosen numbers.
5) Get the ratio in its SIMPLEST FORM, and that tells you the formula of the compound.

Example: *Find the empirical formula of the iron oxide produced when 44.8g of iron react with 19.2g of oxygen. (A_r for iron = 56, A_r for oxygen =16)*

Method:

1) *List the two elements:*	Fe	O
2) Write in the *experimental masses*:	44.8	19.2
3) *Divide by the A_r* for each element:	$44.8/56 = 0.8$	$19.2/16 = 1.2$
4) Multiply by 10...	8	12
...then divide by 4:	2	3

5) So the *simplest formula* is 2 atoms of Fe to 3 atoms of O, i.e. Fe_2O_3. And that's it done.

You need to realise (for the Exam) that this empirical method (i.e. based on experiment) is the only way of finding out the formula of a compound. Rust is iron oxide, sure, but is it FeO, or Fe_2O_3? Only an experiment to determine the empirical formula will tell you for certain.

Mass and Volume Calculations I

These can be kind of scary too, but you'll soon get used to it.

*Finding the **mass** of **product** of a reaction — three important steps:*

(Miss one out and it'll all go horribly wrong, believe me)

1) WRITE OUT the balanced EQUATION
2) Work out M_r — just for the TWO BITS YOU WANT
3) Apply the rule: DIVIDE TO GET ONE, THEN MULTIPLY TO GET ALL
   (But you have to apply this first to the substance they give information about, and then the other one.)

EXAMPLE: *What mass of magnesium oxide is produced when 60g of magnesium is burned in air?*

ANSWER:

1) *Write out the BALANCED EQUATION*:

$$2Mg + O_2 \rightarrow 2MgO$$

2) *Work out the RELATIVE FORMULA MASSES:*
   (don't do the oxygen — we don't need it)

$$2 \times 24 \rightarrow 2 \times (24+16)$$
$$48 \rightarrow 80$$

3) Apply the rule: Divide to get one, then multiply to get all
   The two numbers, 48 and 80, tell us that *48g of Mg react to give 80g of MgO.*
   You've now got to be able to write this down:

48g of Mg ...... reacts to give ..... 80g of MgO
1g of Mg ...... reacts to give .....
60g of Mg ..... reacts to give ......

The big clue is that in the question they've said we want to burn "60g of magnesium"
i.e. they've told us how much magnesium to have, and that's how you know to write down the left hand side of it first, because:

We'll first need to ÷ by 48 to get 1g of Mg
and then need to × by 60 to get 60g of Mg.

Then you can work out the numbers on the other side (shown in blue below) by realising that you must divide both sides by 48 and then multiply both sides by 60. It's tricky.

÷48 ↓ 48g of Mg .... 80g of MgO ↓ ÷48
×60 ↓ 1g of Mg .... 1.67g of MgO ↓ ×60
60g of Mg .... 100g of MgO

You should realise that in practise 100% yield may not be obtained in some reactions, so the amount of product might be slightly less than calculated.

This finally tells us that 60g of magnesium will produce 100g of magnesium oxide.

If the question had said "Find how much magnesium gives 500g of magnesium oxide.", you'd fill in the MgO side first instead, because that's the one you'd have the information about.

Get plenty of practice at these

Learn all three examples on these two pages till you can do them fluently.

Warm-Up and Exam Questions

You know the drill — check you can do the straightforward stuff first with this warm-up, then have a go at the exam questions below.

Warm-up Questions

1) How many times heavier is one atom of oxygen than one atom of helium?
2) Write down the relative formula mass of Na_2CO_3, $(NH_4)_2SO_4$, $Ca(OH)_2$.
3) Find the percentage mass of nitrogen in NH_3, NH_4Cl, NH_4NO_3.
4) If 16g of CH_4 react to give 44g of CO_2, how much CO_2 would be produced from 50g of CH_4?

Exam Questions

1 Ribose is another sugar used by living cells to produce energy.
Ribose contains 40.0% carbon, 6.67% hydrogen and 53.33% oxygen by mass.

(a) How many grams of carbon, hydrogen and oxygen are in 100g of ribose?

(1 mark)

(b) Use this information to calculate the empirical formula of ribose.

(2 marks)

2 The empirical formula for copper(II) sulphate is $CuSO_4$.

(a) Calculate the percentage composition of each element in copper(II) sulphate.

(3 marks)

(b) Calculate the mass of copper in 180g of copper(II) sulphate.

(2 marks)

3 Aspirin has the chemical formula $C_9H_8O_4$.
Calculate the percentage mass of carbon in aspirin.

(2 marks)

Mass and Volume Calculations II

These are OK as long as you LEARN the formula in the dark blue box and know how to use it.

1) Calculating the volume when you know the masses

For this type of question there are two stages:

1) Find the reacting mass, exactly like in the examples on the last page.
2) Then convert the mass into a volume using this formula:

$$\frac{\text{VOL. OF GAS (in cm}^3\text{)}}{24{,}000} = \frac{\text{MASS OF GAS}}{M_r \text{ of gas}}$$

This formula comes from the well known fact that:

A MASS OF M_r IN GRAMS, of any gas, will always occupy 24 LITRES (at room temperature and pressure) — and it's the same for ANY GAS.

I reckon it's easier to learn and use the formula, but it's certainly worth knowing that fact too.

EXAMPLE: *Find the volume of carbon dioxide produced (at room T and P) when 2.7g of carbon is completely burned in oxygen. (A_r of carbon = 12, A_r of oxygen = 16)*

ANSWER:

1) Balanced equation: $C + O_2 \rightarrow CO_2$
2) Fill in M_r for each: 12, 32, 44
3) Divide for one, times for all: ÷12: 1 .... 3.6666667 (÷12); ×2.7: 2.7 .... 9.8999999 (×2.7) = 9.9
4) So 2.7g of C gives 9.9g of CO_2.

Now the new bit:

5) Using the above formula:

$$\frac{\text{Volume}}{24{,}000} = \frac{\text{MASS}}{M_r} \qquad \text{Volume} = \frac{\text{MASS}}{M_r} \times 24{,}000$$

so Volume = (MASS/M_r) × 24,000 = (9.9/44) × 24000 = 5400. = 5400cm^3 or 5.40 litres

2) Calculating the mass when you're given the volume

For this type of question the two stages are in the reverse order:

1) First find the mass from the volume using the same formula as before:

$$\frac{\text{VOL. OF GAS (in cm}^3\text{)}}{24{,}000} = \frac{\text{MASS OF GAS}}{M_r \text{ of gas}}$$

2) Then find the reacting mass, exactly like in the examples on the last page.

Example: Find the mass of 6.2 litres of oxygen gas. (A_r of oxygen = 16)

Answer: Using the above formula: $\frac{6{,}200}{24{,}000} = \frac{\text{Mass of Gas}}{32}$ (Look out, it's 32 because it's O_2)

Hence, Mass of Gas = (6,200/24,000) × 32 = 8.2666667 = 8.27g

The question would likely go on to ask what mass of CO_2 would be produced if this much oxygen reacted with carbon. In that case you would now just apply the same old method from page 159 (as used above).

Mass and Volume Calculations II

The important bit here is to get the balanced half equations, because they determine the relative amounts of the two substances produced at the two electrodes. After that it's all the same as before, working out masses using M_r values, and volumes using the "M_r(g) = 24 litres" rule.

***The three steps** for electrolysis calculations*

1) Write down the TWO BALANCED HALF EQUATIONS (i.e. match the number of electrons)
2) Write down the BALANCED FORMULAE for the two products obtained from the two electrodes.
3) WRITE IN THE M_r VALUES underneath each and carry on as for previous calculations.

Example: In the electrolysis of sodium chloride, sodium is deposited at the cathode and chlorine gas is released at the anode. If 2.5 g of sodium are collected at the cathode, find the volume of chlorine released.

Answer:

1) Balanced half equations: $2Na^+ + 2e^- \rightarrow 2Na$
$2Cl^- - 2e^- \rightarrow Cl_2$

2) Balanced formulae of products: (as obtained from the balanced half equations) 2Na Cl_2

3) Write in M_r values: ...and carry on as usual

	2Na	Cl_2	
	46	71	
÷46	1	3.8586956	÷46
×2.5	2.5...............	3.8586956	×2.5
		= 3.86	

(2×23 because it's 2Na not just Na)

(2×35.5 because it's Cl_2 not just Cl)

So 2.5g of sodium will yield 3.86g of chlorine gas. Now we need this as a volume, so we use the old 'mass to volume converting formula':

$$\frac{VOLUME}{24,000} = \frac{\text{MASS OF GAS}}{M_r} \Rightarrow VOLUME = \frac{\text{MASS} \times 24,000}{M_r} = \frac{3.86 \times 24,000}{71} = 1304.3478$$

$= 1304\ cm^3$

And there it is done. Just the same old stuff every time isn't it — balanced formulae, fill in M_r values, "divide and times" on both sides, and then use the "24,000 rule" to find the volume. Simple.

*Calculation of A_r from **% abundances of isotopes***

Some elements, like chlorine, have A_r values which are not whole numbers. This is because there are two stable isotopes of chlorine, ^{35}Cl and ^{37}Cl, and the mixture of the two gives an average A_r of 35.5. There is a simple formula for working out the overall A_r from the percentage abundances of two different isotopes:

$$\text{Overall } A_r = [(A_1 \times \%_{(1)}) + (A_2 \times \%_{(2)})] \div 100$$

For example if chlorine consists of 76% ^{35}Cl and 24% ^{37}Cl, then the overall value for A_r is:
Overall A_r = [(35 × 76) + (37 × 24)] ÷ 100 = 35.48 = 35.5 to 1 d.p.

Learn all the examples

With electrolysis calculations the main tricky bit is getting the balanced half equations right and then using the balanced symbol amounts for both products (e.g. 2Na and Cl_2).

Warm-Up and Exam Questions

Warm-up Questions

1) Calculate the volume of 3.5g of $O_{2(g)}$ (at room temperature/pressure).
2) The balanced equation for the reaction between sodium and chlorine is $2Na + Cl_2 \rightarrow 2NaCl$.
   a) Calculate the mass of sodium chloride that will be produced when 50g of sodium reacts with chlorine gas.
   b) Calculate the mass of chlorine that is needed to react with the 50g of sodium.
   c) Find the volume of chlorine gas that reacts (at room temperature/pressure).
3) Find the mass of 7.5 dm^3 of oxygen gas (at room temperature/pressure).

Exam Questions

1 One of the main ores of copper contains copper sulphide.
Copper can be extracted easily from it:

$$\mathbf{CuS \rightarrow Cu + S}$$

a) Calculate the mass of copper that will be produced from 192g of copper sulphide.
(2 marks)

b) The sulphur produced in the reaction in part a) went on to react with oxygen to form sulphur dioxide:

$$\mathbf{S + O_2 \rightarrow SO_2}$$

i) Calculate the mass of sulphur produced in part a).
(2 marks)

ii) Calculate the volume of sulphur dioxide produced at room temperature/pressure.
(3 marks)

2 When calcium carbonate decomposes, it forms calcium oxide and carbon dioxide.

a) Write the balanced equation for this reaction.
(1 mark)

b) What mass of calcium carbonate would produce 168g of calcium oxide?
(2 marks)

c) Calculate the volume of carbon dioxide that will be formed in the reaction.
(3 marks)

3 Aluminium is extracted from aluminium oxide by electrolysis.

a) Write balanced half equations for the reactions happening at the cathode and anode.
(2 marks)

b) Find the mass of aluminium produced if 24g of oxygen is liberated in the reaction.
(2 marks)

Revision Summary for Section Seven

Here are some more straightforward questions to check you know your stuff. Remember, if you can't answer one, look at the appropriate page and learn it. Then go back and try them again.

1) Describe lab tests for: a) chlorine b) oxygen c) CO_2 d) water e) hydrogen.
2) What are the four factors which the rate of a reaction depends on?
3) What are the three different ways of measuring the speed of a reaction? Describe each method as fully as possible, using a diagram.
4) Explain how each of the four factors that increase the rate of a reaction increase the *number of collisions* between particles.
5) What is the other aspect of collision theory which determines the rate of reaction?
6) What is the definition of a catalyst?
7) Why is it best to maximise the surface area of a catalyst? How is this done?
8) Why are catalysts important in industry? What do iron and platinum catalyse?
9) What are enzymes? How are they affected by temperature and pH?
10) Give the word-equation for fermentation. Which organism is involved?
11) Explain what happens in brewing and bread-making. What is the difference between them?
12) List four weird things that food manufacturers use enzymes for.
13) Describe how enzymes are used in cheese and yoghurt making.
14) How can you make enzymes *immobile*? What other factors do industries have to consider?
15) What are endothermic and exothermic reactions? Give three examples of each type.
16) How do bond breaking and bond forming relate to these types of reaction?
17) Draw energy level diagrams for these two types of reaction.
18) What are bond energies and what can you calculate from them?
19) What is the Haber process? What are the raw materials for it and how are they obtained?
20) Draw a full diagram for the Haber process and explain the temperature and pressure used.
21) Give full details of how ammonia is turned into nitric acid, including equations.
22) Give two problems resulting from the use of nitrate fertilisers.
23) What is a reversible reaction? Describe three simple reversible reactions involving solids.
24) Explain what is meant by dynamic equilibrium in a reversible reaction.
25) How does changing the temperature and pressure of a reaction alter the equilibrium?
26) How does this influence the choice of pressure for the Haber Process?
27) What determines the choice of operating temperature for the Haber process?
28) Find A_r or M_r for these (use the periodic table at the front of the book):
    a) Ca b) Ag c) CO_2 d) $MgCO_3$ e) Na_2CO_3 f) ZnO g) butane h) sodium chloride
29) What is the formula for calculating the percentage mass of an element in a compound?
    a) Calculate the percentage mass of oxygen in magnesium oxide, MgO
    b) Calculate the percentage mass of carbon in i) $CaCO_3$ ii) CO_2 iii) Methane
    c) Calculate the percentage mass of metal in these oxides: i) Na_2O ii) Fe_2O_3 iii) Al_2O_3
30) What is meant by an empirical formula (EF)? Work these out (using the periodic table):
    a) Find the EF for the iron oxide formed when 45.1g of iron reacts with 19.3g of oxygen.
    b) Find the EF for the compound formed when 227g of calcium reacts with 216g of fluorine.
31) Write down the three steps of the method for calculating reacting masses.
    a) What mass of magnesium oxide is produced when 112.1g of magnesium burns in air?
    b) What mass of sodium is needed to produce 108.2g of sodium oxide?
32) Write down the formula for calculating the volume of a known mass of gas (at room T & P).
    a) What is the volume of 56.0g of nitrogen at room T & P?
    b) What mass of carbon dioxide is produced when 4.7 litres of oxygen reacts with carbon?
33) a) In the electrolysis of NaCl, find the mass of Cl_2 released if 3.4g of sodium are collected.
    b) In the electrolysis of copper(II) chloride, what volume of chlorine gas would be produced for every 100g of copper obtained?

Changes of State

Changes of state always involve heat energy going either in or out.

Melting — the rigid lattice breaks down

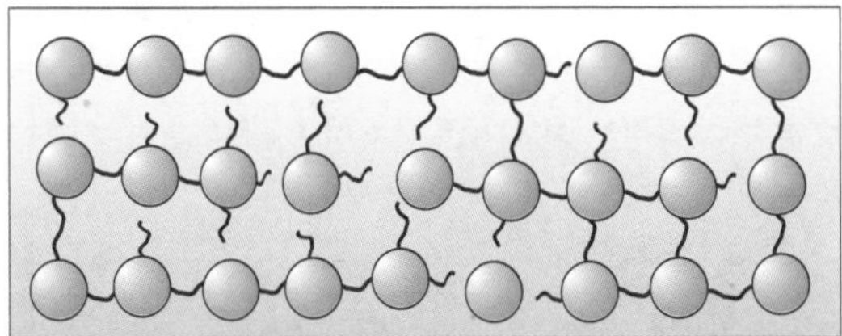

1) When a solid is heated, the heat energy goes to the molecules.
2) It makes them vibrate more and more.
3) Eventually the strong forces between the molecules (that hold them in the rigid lattice) are overcome, and the molecules start to move around. The solid has now melted.

Evaporation — the fastest molecules escape

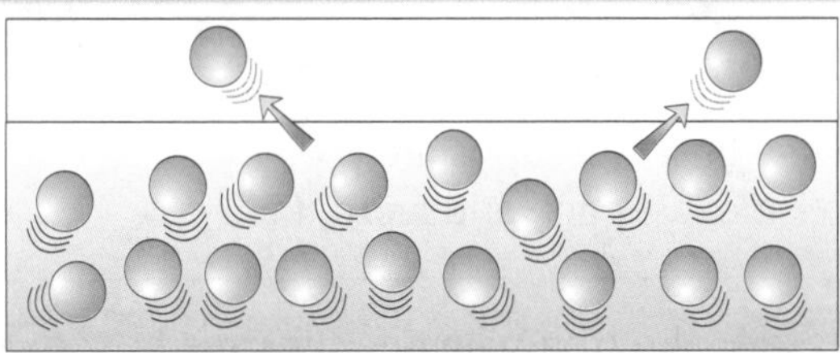

1) When a liquid is heated, the heat energy goes to the molecules, which makes them move faster.
2) Some molecules move faster than others.
3) Fast-moving molecules at the surface will overcome the forces of attraction from the other molecules and escape. This is evaporation.

Boiling — all molecules are fast enough to escape

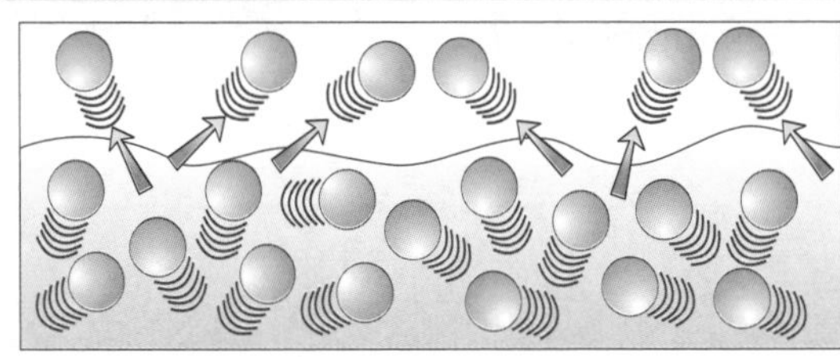

1) When the liquid gets hot enough, virtually all the molecules have enough speed and energy to overcome the forces and escape each other.
2) At this point big bubbles of gas form inside the liquid as the molecules break away from each other. This is boiling.

Heating and cooling graphs have important flat spots

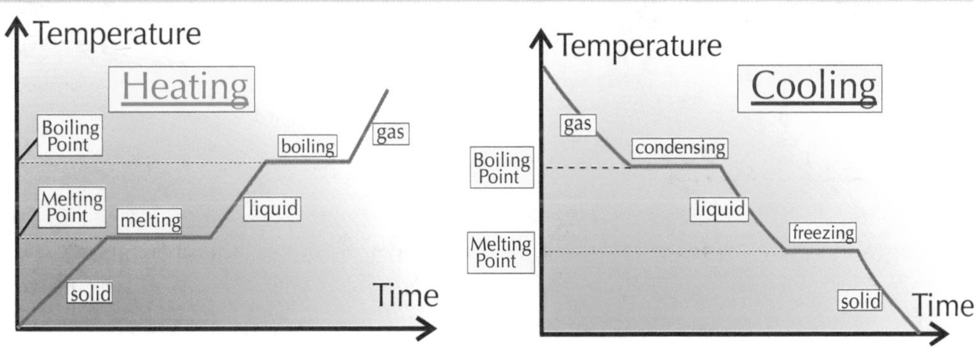

1) When a substance is melting or boiling, all the heat energy supplied is used for breaking bonds rather than raising the temperature, hence the flat spots in the heating graph.
2) When a liquid is cooled, the graph for temperature will show a flat spot at the freezing point.
3) As the molecules fuse into a solid, heat is given out as the bonds form, so the temperature won't go down until all the substance has turned to solid.

It's all about energy

There are five diagrams and a total of 11 numbered points on this page. They wouldn't be there if you didn't need to learn them. So learn them. Then cover the page and scribble them all down. You have to realise this is the only way to really learn stuff properly. And learn it you must.

Warm-Up and Exam Questions

By the time the big day comes you need to know all the facts in these warm-up questions and all the exam questions like the back of your hand. It's the only way to get good marks.

Warm-up Questions

1) What are the three states of matter?
2) With reference to the spacing of molecules, explain why gases can be compressed and solids cannot be compressed.
3) Describe how water particles evaporate from the surface of a beaker of water.
4) Explain what happens to water particles when ice melts.

Exam Questions

There's nearly always a question about movement of molecules. These questions are pretty straightforward — if you're struggling, you need to go back over the last page and learn it all.

1 a) Describe the movement of the molecules in a piece of solid iron when it is warmed.

(1 mark)

b) What effect does heating have on the movement of gas molecules?

(1 mark)

2

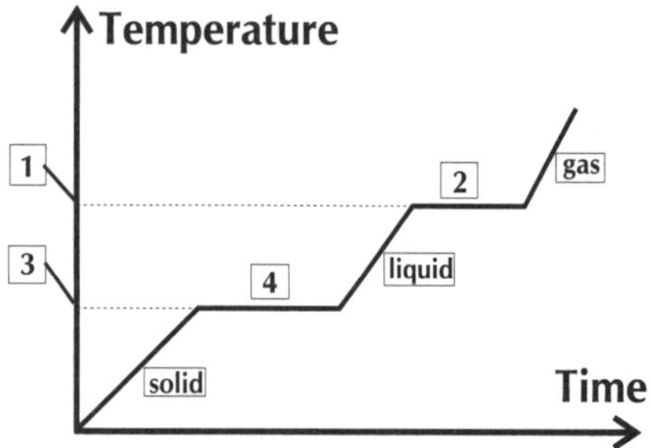

a) On the above graph, which number represents the melting point of the substance?

(1 mark)

b) Which number represents the time when the substance is melting?

(1 mark)

c) During the transition from solid to liquid the temperature remains the same even though the substance is being heated. Explain this in terms of bonds between the molecules.

(3 marks)

Atoms

Dalton reintroduced the idea of atoms

The Greeks had the right idea — they knew about atoms. After that, all kinds of different ideas went around until, in 1804, John Dalton reintroduced the idea of atoms. But it was Ernest Rutherford who really sorted it all out. See page 280 for more info.

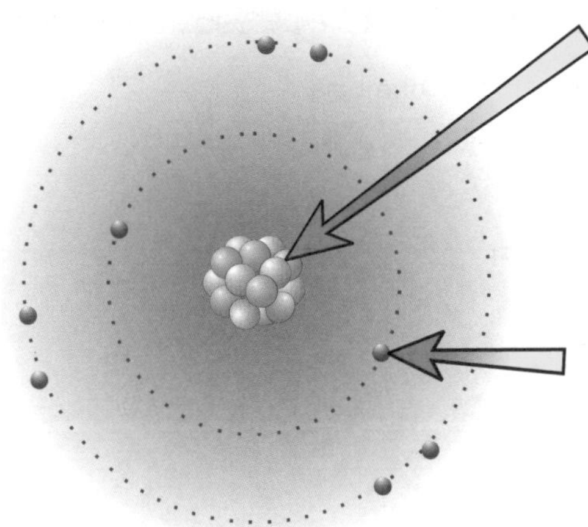

Atoms are really tiny, don't forget. They're too small to see with an ordinary microscope.

The nucleus

1) It's in the middle of the atom.
2) It contains protons and neutrons.
3) It has a positive charge because of the protons (which are positive).
4) Almost the whole mass of the atom is concentrated in the nucleus.
5) But size-wise it's tiny compared to the rest of the atom.

The electrons

1) Move around the nucleus.
2) They're negatively charged.
3) They're tiny, but they cover a lot of space.
4) The volume their orbits occupy determines how big the atom is.
5) They have virtually no mass.
6) They occupy shells around the nucleus.
7) These shells explain the whole of Chemistry.

Number of protons equals number of electrons

1) Atoms are neutral — they have no charge overall.
2) The charge on the electrons is the same size as the charge on the protons but opposite. (See below.)
3) This means the number of protons always equals the number of electrons in a neutral atom.
4) If some electrons are added or removed, the atom becomes charged and is then an ion.
5) The number of neutrons isn't fixed but is usually just a bit higher than the number of protons.

Know your particles

Protons are Heavy and Positively Charged
Neutrons are Heavy and Neutral
Electrons are Tiny and Negatively Charged

PARTICLE	MASS	CHARGE
Proton	1	+1
Neutron	1	0
Electron	1/2000	- 1

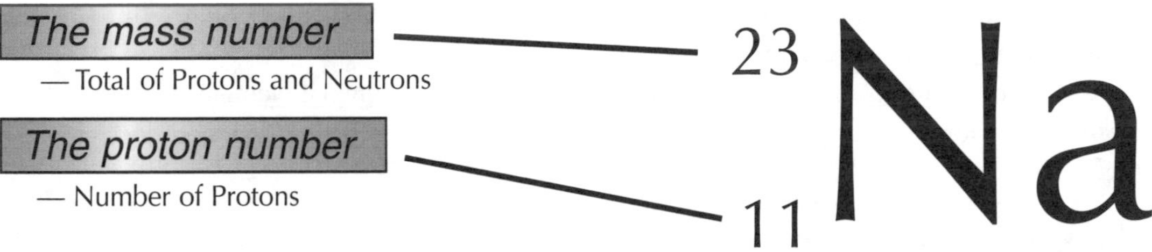

Points to note

1) The proton number (or atomic number) tells you how many protons there are (oddly enough).
2) This also tells you how many electrons there are in an atom.
3) The proton number is what distinguishes one particular element from another.
4) To get the number of neutrons — just subtract the proton number from the mass number.
5) The mass number is always the biggest number. It tells you the relative mass of the atom.
6) The mass number is always roughly double the proton number.
7) Which means there's about the same number of protons as neutrons in any nucleus.

Atoms

*Isotopes are the **same** except for an extra **neutron** or two*

ISOTOPES ARE: different atomic forms of the same element, which have the SAME number of PROTONS but a DIFFERENT number of NEUTRONS.

1) The upshot is: isotopes must have the same proton number but different mass numbers.
2) If they had different proton numbers, they'd be different elements altogether.
3) A very popular pair of isotopes are carbon-12 and carbon-14.

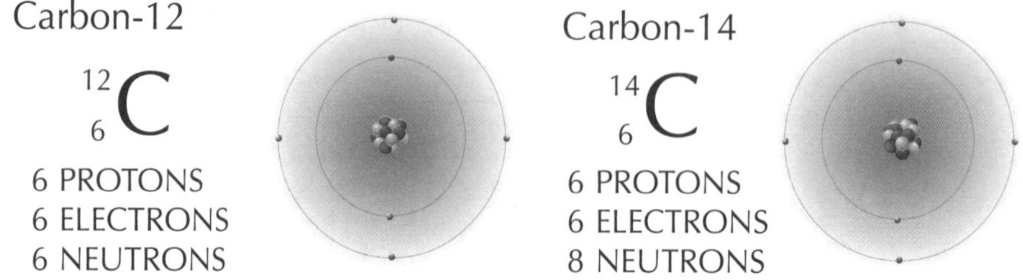

Elements and compounds

You'd better be sure you know the subtle difference between these.

Elements consist of one type of atom only

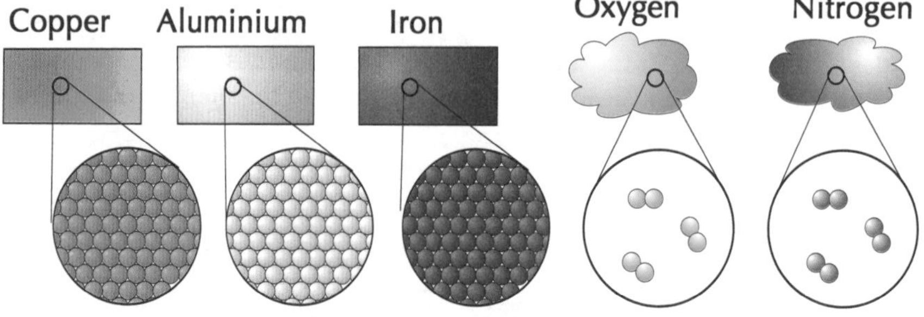

Compounds are chemically bonded

1) Carbon dioxide is a compound formed from a chemical reaction between carbon and oxygen.
2) It's very difficult to separate the two original elements out again.
3) The properties of a compound are totally different from the properties of the original elements.
4) If iron and sulphur react to form iron sulphide, the compound formed is a grey solid lump, and doesn't behave anything like either iron or sulphur.

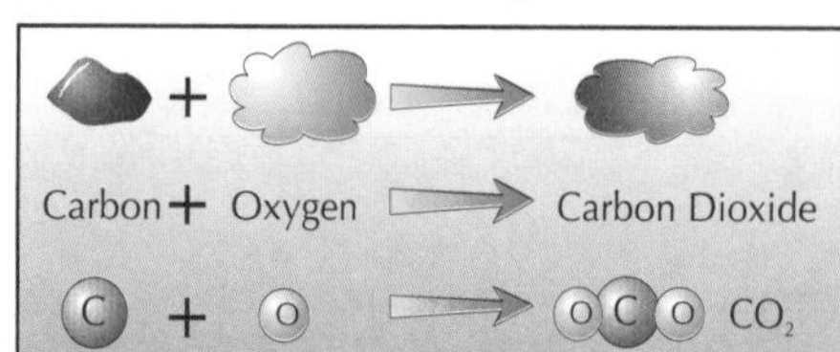

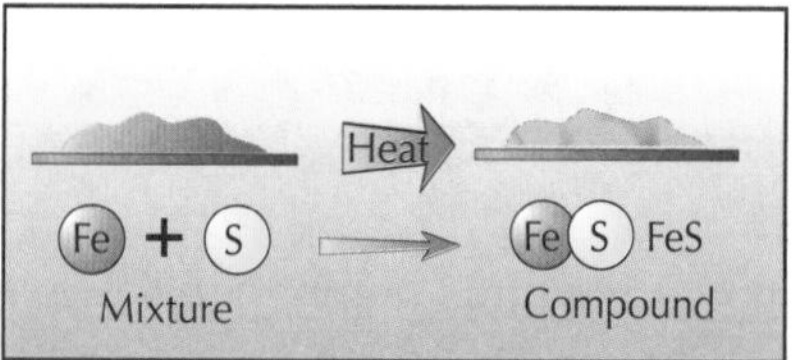

5) Don't confuse compounds with mixtures.
   A mixture consists of two or more elements or compounds not chemically combined together.
   The chemical properties of each substance in the mixture are unchanged.
6) Air is a mixture of gases.
   The oxygen, nitrogen, argon and carbon dioxide can all be separated out quite easily.

Atoms

The fact that electrons occupy "shells" around the nucleus is what causes the whole of Chemistry. Remember that, and watch how it applies to each bit of it.

Electron shell rules:

1) Electrons always occupy shells (sometimes called energy levels).
2) The lowest energy levels are always filled first.
3) Only a certain number of electrons are allowed in each shell:
   1st shell: 2 2nd Shell: 8 3rd Shell: 8
4) Atoms are much happier when they have full electron shells.
5) In most atoms the outer shell is not full and this makes the atom want to react.

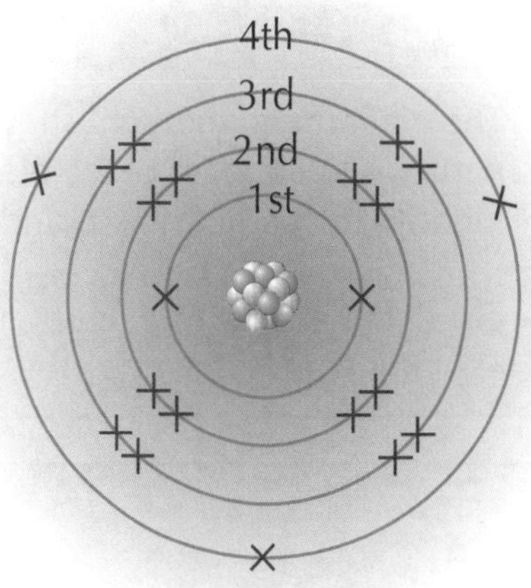

4th shell still filling

Working out electron configurations

You need to know the electron configurations for the first 20 elements. But they're not hard to work out. For a quick example, take Nitrogen. Follow the steps...

1) The periodic table (see below) tells us Nitrogen has seven protons... so it must have seven electrons.
2) Follow the 'Electron Shell Rules' above. The first shell can only take 2 electrons and the second shell can take a maximum of 8 electrons.
3) So the electron configuration for Nitrogen must be 2,5.
4) Now you try it for Argon.

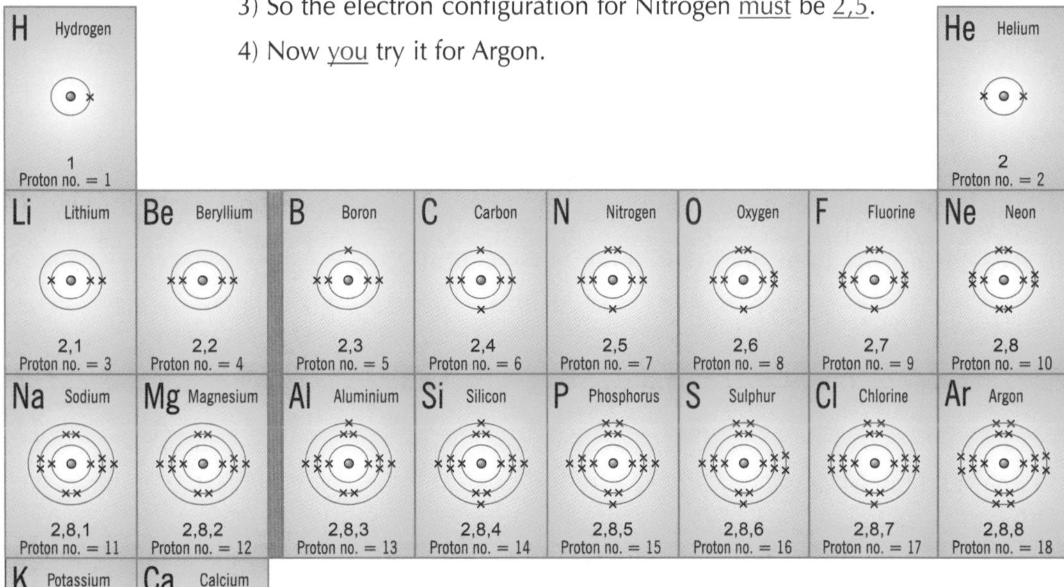

Answer... To calculate the electron configuration of argon, *follow the rules*. It's got 18 protons, so it *must* have 18 electrons. The first shell must have *2* electrons, the second shell must have *8*, and so the third shell must have *8* as well. It's as easy as *2,8,8*.

Electrons rule...

There's some really important stuff on this page and you really do need to learn all of it. Once you have, it'll make all of the rest of the stuff in this section an awful lot easier. Practise calculating electron configurations and drawing electron shell diagrams.

Warm-Up and Exam Questions

Warm-up questions first, then an exam question or two to practise.
So make the most of this page by working through everything carefully — it's all useful stuff.

Warm-up Questions

1) The diagram on the right shows the arrangement of particles in an atom of the element lithium. Identify the particles A, B and C.

2) Using the examples of carbon-12 and carbon-14, explain what is meant by the term 'isotope'.

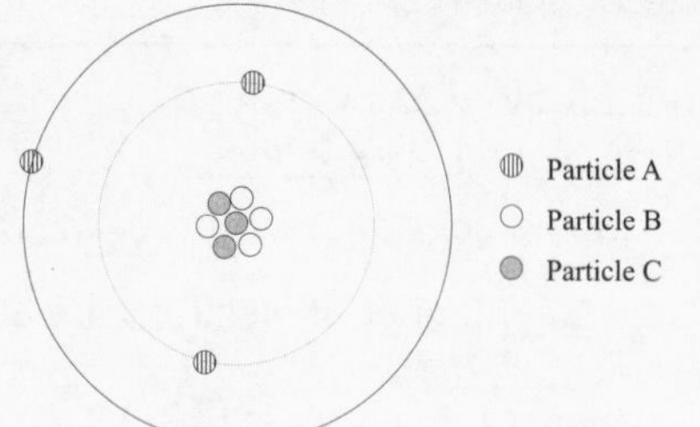

Exam Questions

1 Write the electron arrangement for:

a) sodium, Na (atomic number 11).

....

(1 mark)

b) phosphorous, P (atomic number 15).

....

(1 mark)

2 Carbon-12 has atomic number 6 and mass number 12. Carbon-14 has mass number 14.

a) How many neutrons are there in the nucleus of a:

(i) carbon-12 atom?

....

(1 mark)

(ii) carbon-14 atom?

....

(1 mark)

b) Explain how carbon-12 and carbon-14 are isotopes of carbon.

....

....

(2 marks)

Bonding

Simple ions — groups **1 & 2** and **6 & 7**

1) Remember, atoms that have lost or gained an electron (or electrons) are ions.
2) The elements that most readily form ions are those in Groups 1, 2, 6, and 7.
3) Group 1 and 2 elements are metals and they lose electrons to form +ve ions or cations.
4) Group 6 and 7 elements are non-metals. They gain electrons to form –ve ions or anions.
5) Make sure you know these easy ones:

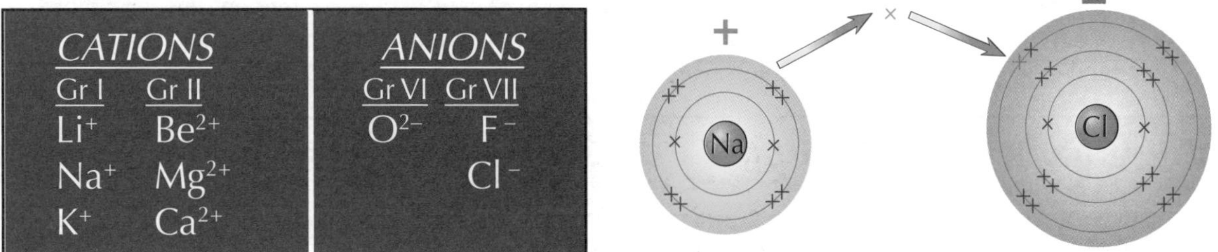

CATIONS		ANIONS	
Gr I	Gr II	Gr VI	Gr VII
Li^+	Be^{2+}	O^{2-}	F^-
Na^+	Mg^{2+}		Cl^-
K^+	Ca^{2+}		

6) When any of the above elements react together, they form ionic bonds.
7) Only elements at opposite sides of the periodic table will form ionic bonds, e.g. Na and Cl, where one of them becomes a cation (+ve) and one becomes an anion (–ve).

Remember, the + and – charges we talk about, e.g. Na^+ for sodium, just tell you what type of ion the atom WILL FORM in a chemical reaction. In sodium metal there are only neutral sodium atoms, Na. The Na^+ ions will only appear if the sodium metal reacts with something like water or chlorine.

Electronic structure of some **simple** ions

A useful way of representing ions is by specifying the ion's name, followed by its electron configuration and the charge on the ion. For example, the electronic structure of the sodium ion Na^+ can be represented by $[2,8]^+$. That's the electron configuration followed by the charge on the ion. Simple enough. A few ions and the ionic compounds they form are shown below.

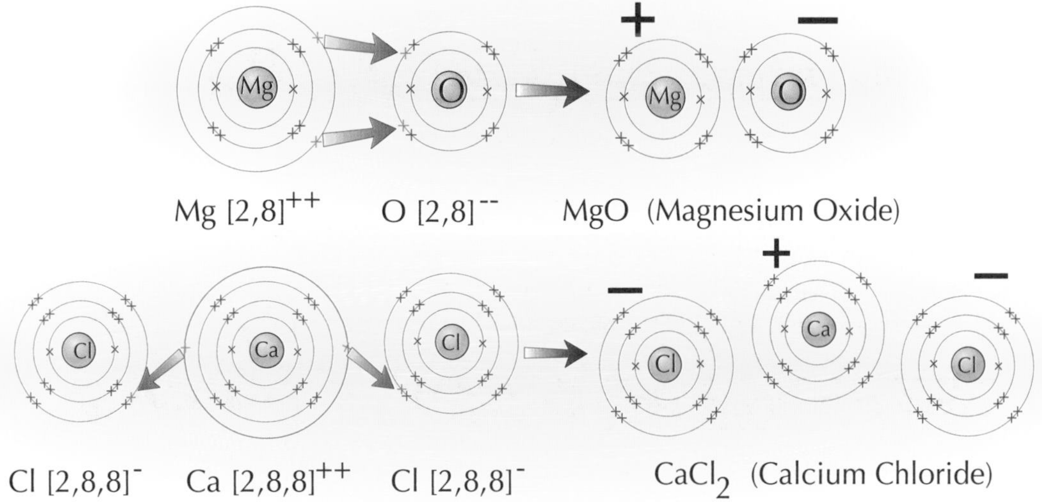

Bonding

Ionic bonding — *transferring* electrons

In ionic bonding, atoms lose or gain electrons to form charged particles (ions) which are then strongly attracted to one another, (the attraction of opposite charges, + and –).

A shell with just **one** electron is **keen to get rid...**

All the atoms over at the left hand side of the periodic table, such as sodium, potassium, calcium etc. have just one or two electrons in their outer shell. Basically they're keen to get rid of their outer electrons, because then they'll only have full shells left, which is how they like it. So when they get the chance, these atoms get rid of an electron or two, and become ions instead. Because these ions have lost electrons, they have a + charge. This means they tend to leap at the first passing ion with an opposite charge and stick to it like glue.

A **nearly full** shell is **keen** to get that **extra electron...**

On the other side of the periodic table, the elements in Group Six and Group Seven, such as oxygen and chlorine, have outer shells which are nearly full. They're obviously keen to gain that extra one or two electrons to fill the shell up. When they do of course they become ions, with a negative charge as they have more electrons than protons. They're attracted to positive ions, and so latch on to the ion they've just taken electrons from, which is now positively charged. The reaction of sodium and chlorine is a classic case:

The sodium atom gives up its outer electron and becomes an Na^+ ion.

The chlorine atom picks up the spare electron and becomes a Cl^- ion.

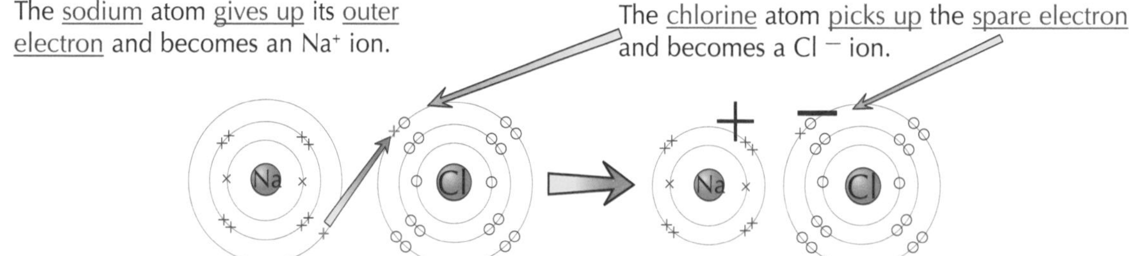

Giant ionic structures don't melt easily, but when they do...

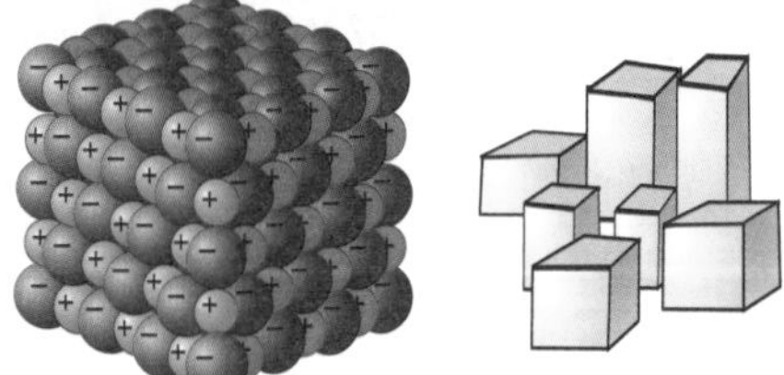

1) Ionic bonds always produce giant ionic structures.
2) The ions form a closely packed regular lattice arrangement.
3) There are very strong chemical bonds between all the ions.
4) A single crystal of salt is one giant ionic lattice, which is why salt crystals tend to be cuboid in shape.

1) They have **high melting points and boiling points**

due to the very strong bonds between all the ions in the giant structure.

2) They **dissolve** to form solutions that **conduct electricity**

When dissolved the ions separate and are all free to move in the solution, so obviously they'll carry electric current.

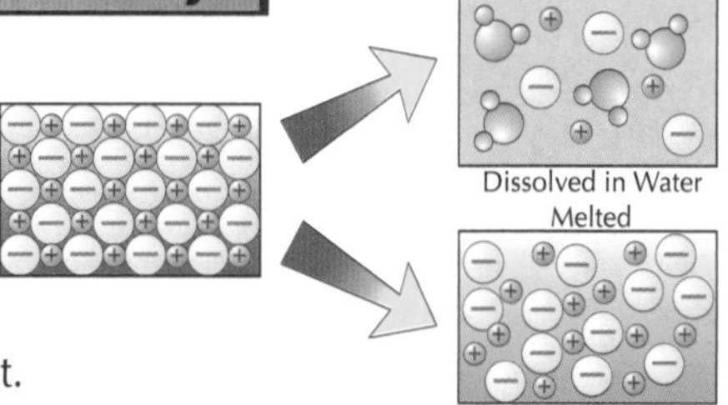

3) They **conduct** electricity when **molten**

When it melts, the ions are free to move and they'll carry electric current.

Bonding

Covalent bonds — sharing electrons

1) Sometimes atoms prefer to make covalent bonds by sharing electrons with other atoms.
2) This way both atoms feel that they have a full outer shell, and that makes them happy.
3) Each covalent bond provides one extra shared electron for each atom.
4) Each atom involved has to make enough covalent bonds to fill up its outer shell.
5) Learn these five important examples:

1) Hydrogen gas, H_2

Hydrogen atoms have just one electron. They only need one more to complete the first shell...

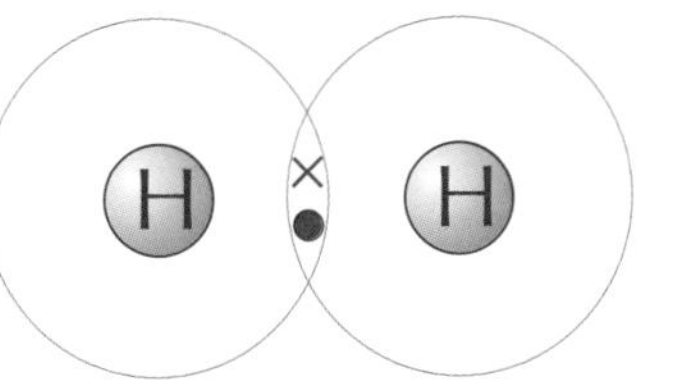

or
H-H

...so they form single covalent bonds to achieve this.

2) Hydrogen Chloride, HCl

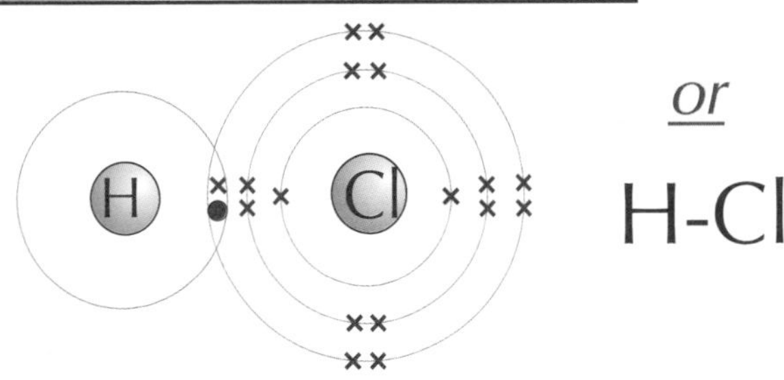

or
H-Cl

This is very similar to H_2. Again, both atoms need one more electron to complete their outer shells.

3) Ammonia, NH_3

Nitrogen has five outer electrons...

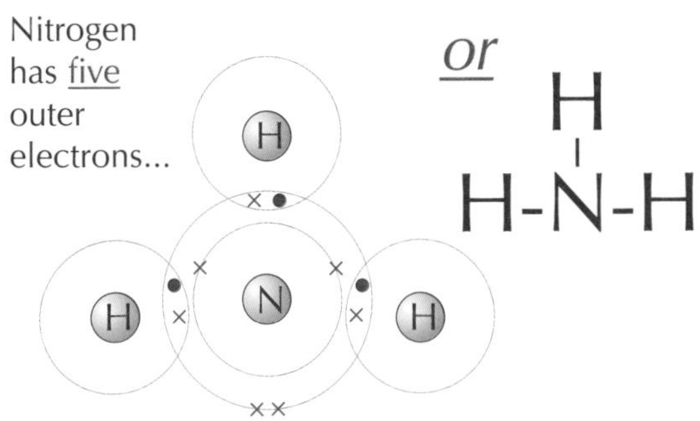

or

H
|
H-N-H

...so it needs to form three covalent bonds to make up the extra three electrons needed.

4) Methane, CH_4

Carbon has four outer electrons, which is a half full shell.

or

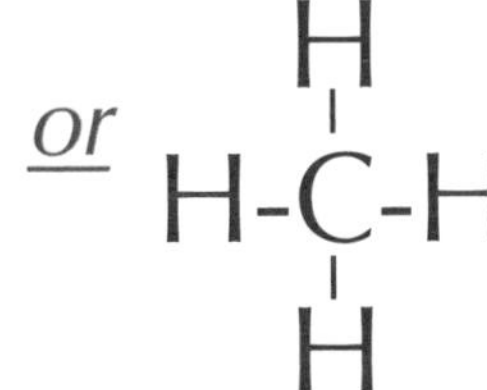

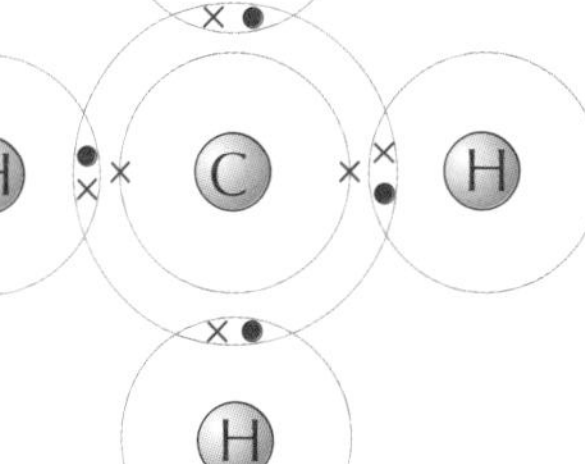

To become a 4+ or a 4– ion is hard work so it forms four covalent bonds to make up its outer shell.

5) Oxygen gas O_2 and water H_2O

The oxygen atom has six outer electrons. Sometimes it forms ionic bonds by taking two electrons to complete the outer shell. However it will also cheerfully form covalent bonds and share two electrons instead, as in the case of oxygen gas, and of water molecules, where it shares electrons with the H atoms.

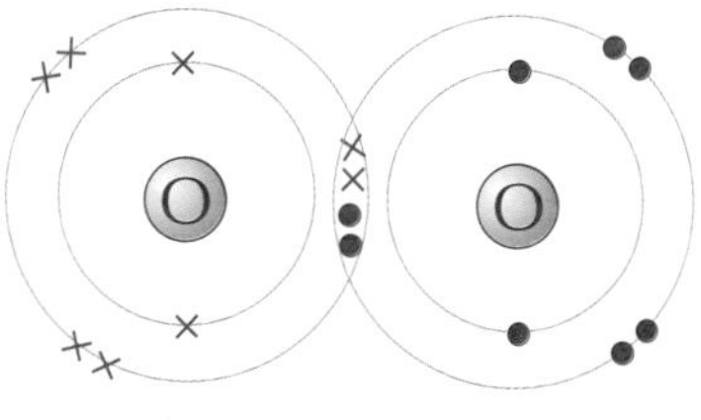

OXYGEN GAS

or

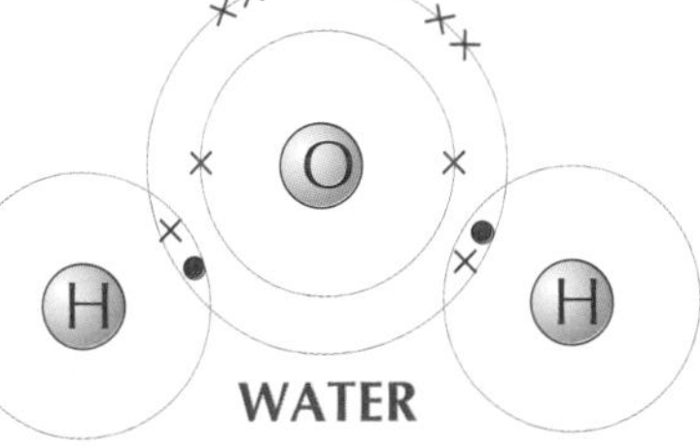

WATER

or

O
H H

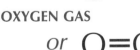

Learn the difference between ionic and covalent bonding

LEARN which atoms form 1+, 1-, 2+ and 2- ions, and why. Make sure you know exactly how and why ionic bonds are formed. Then learn the four numbered points about covalent bonds and the five examples. Make sure you can draw all five molecules and explain exactly why they form the bonds that they do. All from memory of course.

Warm-Up and Exam Question

You must be getting used to the routine by now — the warm-up questions run over the basic facts, the exam question shows you the kind of thing you'll get on the day.

Warm-up Questions

Using 'dot and cross' diagrams show the bonding in molecules of:

1) chlorine gas (Cl_2)
2) oxygen gas (O_2)
3) methane (CH_4).

Exam Question

1 Sodium has the electron arrangement 2,8,1.
Chlorine has the electron arrangement 2,8,7.

a) Write the electron arrangement of:

(i) a sodium ion Na^+

....

(1 mark)

(ii) a chloride ion Cl^-

....

(1 mark)

b) What type of bonding is found in sodium chloride?

....

(1 mark)

c) Using a 'dot and cross' diagram, show the bonding between sodium and chlorine in sodium chloride.

(2 marks)

d) Using a 'dot and cross' diagram show the bonding between hydrogen and oxygen in water.

(2 marks)

Properties

Substances formed from covalent bonds can either be simple molecules or giant structures.

Properties of simple molecular substances:

1) The atoms form very strong covalent bonds to form small molecules of several atoms.
2) By contrast, the forces of attraction between these molecules are very weak.
3) The result of these feeble intermolecular forces is that the melting- and boiling-points are very low, because the molecules are easily parted from each other.
4) Most molecular substances are gases or liquids at room temperature.
5) Molecular substances don't conduct electricity, simply because there are no ions.
6) They don't dissolve in water, usually.
7) You can usually tell a molecular substance just from its physical state, which is always kind of "mushy" — i.e. liquid or gas or an easily-melted solid.

Very weak inter-molecular forces

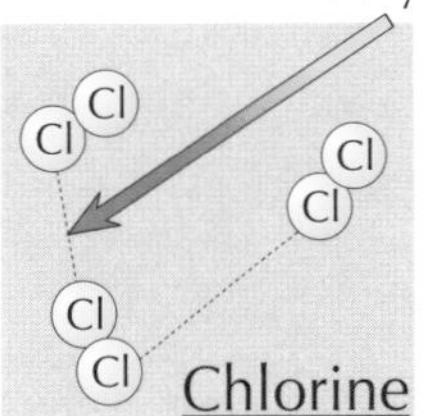

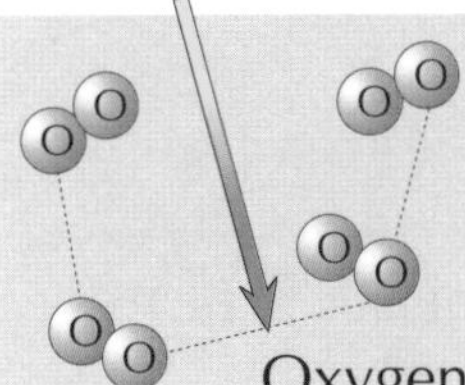

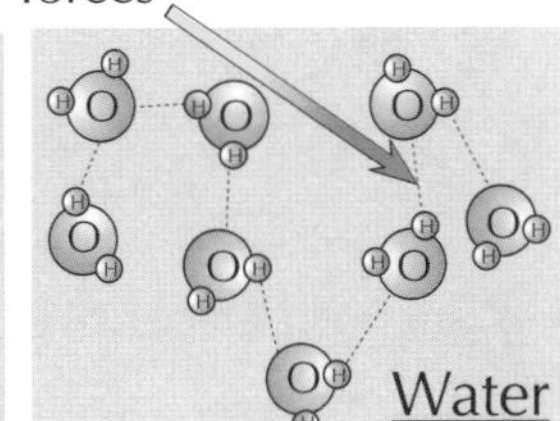

Buckminster Fullerene

1) 60 carbon atoms joined in a big ball.
2) Each carbon atom forms three covalent bonds.

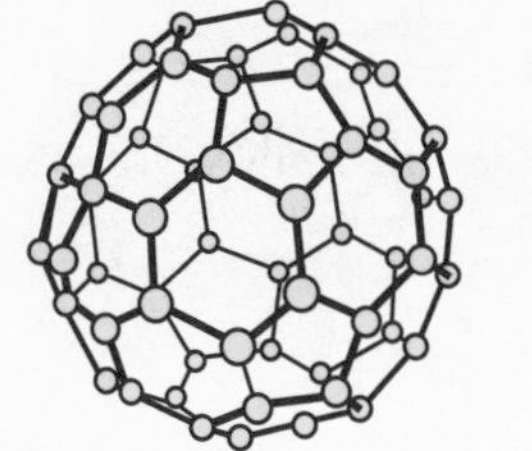

Properties of Giant covalent structures:

1) These are similar to giant ionic structures except that there are no charged ions.
2) All the atoms are bonded to each other by strong covalent bonds.
3) They have very high melting and boiling points.
4) They don't conduct electricity — not even when molten.
5) They're usually insoluble in water.
6) The main examples are diamond and graphite which are both made only from carbon atoms.

Diamond

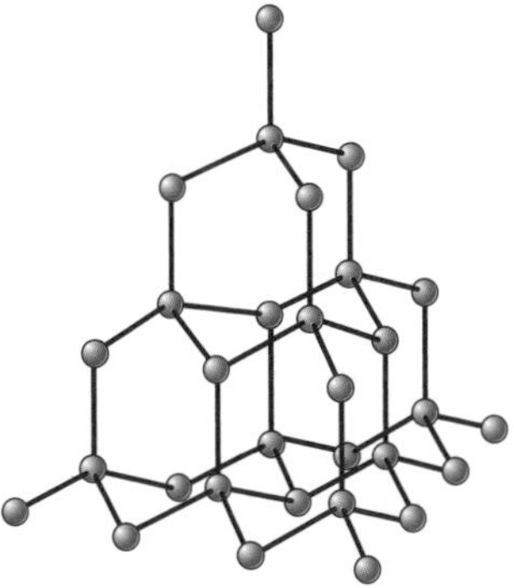

Each carbon atom forms four covalent bonds in a very rigid giant covalent structure.

Graphite

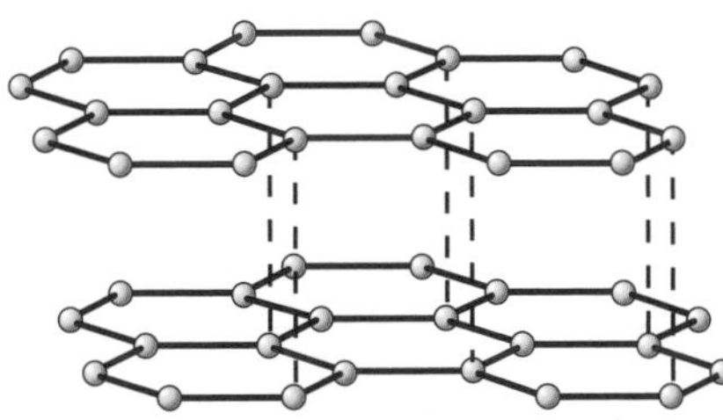

Each carbon atom only forms three covalent bonds, creating layers which are free to slide over each other, and leaving free electrons, so graphite is the only non-metal which conducts electricity.

Silicon Dioxide

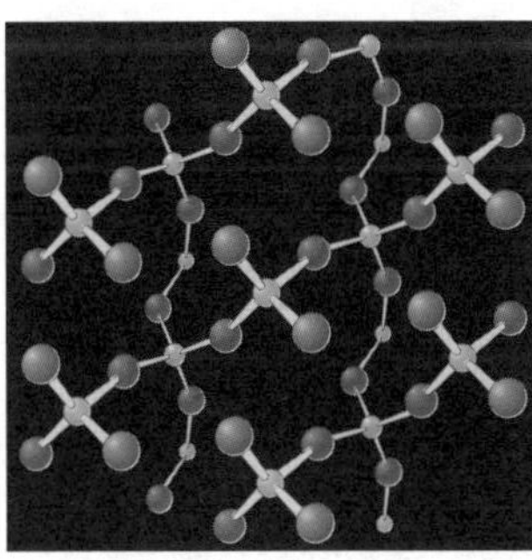

Sometimes called silica, this is what sand is made of.
Each grain of sand is one giant structure of silicon and oxygen.

Properties

Metal properties are all due to the *sea of free electrons*

1) Metals also consist of a giant structure.

2) Metallic bonds involve the all-important "free electrons", which produce all the properties of metals. These free electrons come from the outer shell of every metal atom in the structure.

3) These electrons are free to move and so metals conduct heat and electricity.

4) These electrons also hold the atoms together in a regular structure.

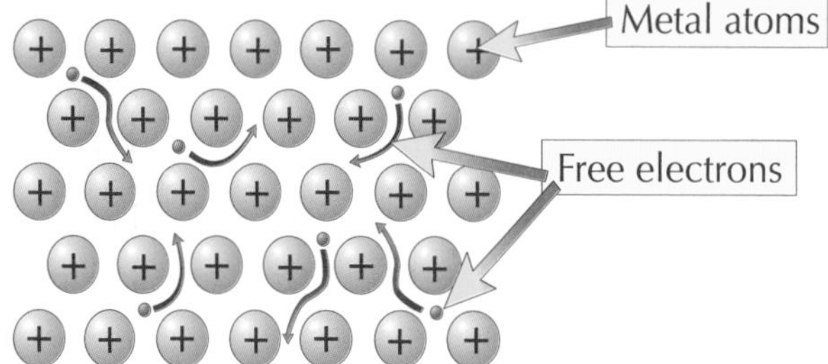

5) They also allow the atoms to slide over each other causing metals to be malleable.

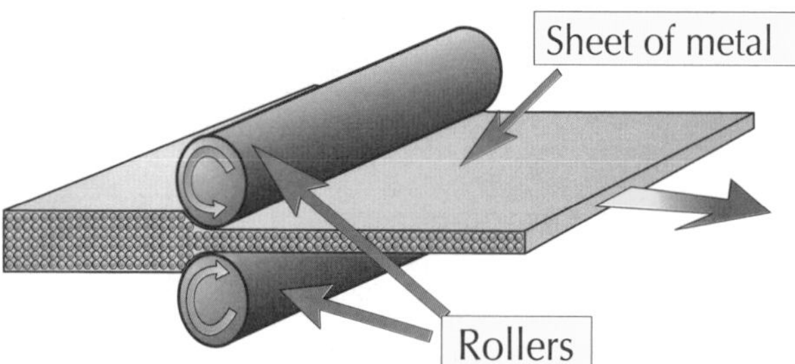

Identifying the bonding in a substance *by its properties*

If you've learnt the properties of the four types of substance properly, together with their names of course, then you should be able to easily identify most substances just by the way they behave as either:

IONIC,

GIANT-COVALENT,

MOLECULAR or

METALLIC.

The way they're likely to test you in the Exam is by describing the physical properties of a substance and asking you to decide which type of bonding it has and therefore what type of material it is. If you know your stuff you'll have no trouble at all. If not, you're going to struggle.

The type of bonding affects the properties

A good approach for learning these two pages is the mini-essay method.

Warm-Up and Exam Questions

Warm-up Questions

1) Water and diamond are both covalent compounds. Explain why water melts at 0°C and diamond at more than 3000°C.
2) Common salt (sodium chloride) and aluminium both have giant structures. Explain why aluminium conducts electricity and solid salt does not.

Exam Questions

1 Magnesium and oxygen react to form magnesium oxide. The symbol equation is shown below.

$$2Mg_{(s)} + O_{2(g)} \rightarrow 2MgO_{(s)}$$

a) Explain why magnesium is solid at room temperature.

(3 marks)

b) Explain why oxygen is a gas at room temperature.

(3 marks)

2 Four unknown substances are labelled A, B, C and D.

	Boiling point	Conducts electricity?	Solubility in water
A	High	Yes when molten or in solution	Dissolves readily
B	High	Yes	Does not dissolve
C	Very High	No	Does not dissolve
D	Low	No	Does not dissolve

Study the table above showing the properties of each substance.

a) Which substance is a metal?

(1 mark)

b) Explain why metals are good conductors of electricity.

(3 marks)

The History of the Periodic Table

The early Chemists were keen to try and find patterns in the elements.

They had two obvious ways to categorise elements:

1) Their physical and chemical properties

2) Their Relative Atomic Mass

Remember, they had no idea of atomic structure or of protons or electrons, so there was no such thing as proton number to them.

It was only in the 20th Century after protons and electrons were discovered, that it was realised the elements should be arranged in order of proton number.

Newlands' Octaves were the first good effort

A scientist called Newlands had the first good stab at it in 1863. He noticed that every eighth element had similar properties and so he listed some of the known elements in rows of seven:

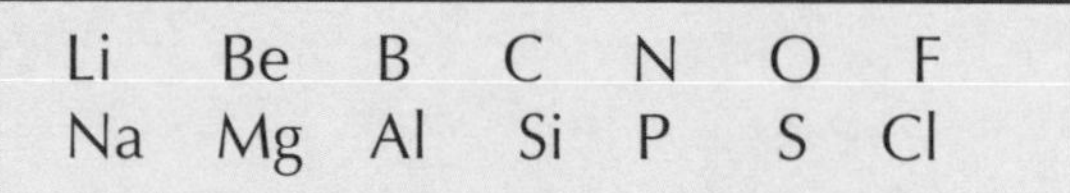

Li	Be	B	C	N	O	F
Na	Mg	Al	Si	P	S	Cl

These sets of eight were called Newlands' Octaves, but unfortunately the pattern broke down on the third row with many transition metals like Fe and Cu and Zn not fitting in.

Dmitri Mendeleev **left gaps** *and* **predicted new elements**

1) In 1869, Dmitri Mendeleev in Russia, armed with about 50 known elements, arranged them into his Table of Elements with various gaps.

2) Mendeleev ordered the elements in order of atomic mass (like Newlands did).

3) But Mendeleev found he had to leave gaps in order to keep elements with similar properties in the same vertical groups — and he was prepared to leave some very big gaps in the first two rows before the transition metals come in on the third row.

4) The gaps were really clever because they predicted the properties of undiscovered elements.

Electron Arrangements

This diagram shows the electron arrangements of the first twenty elements. Learn it really well.

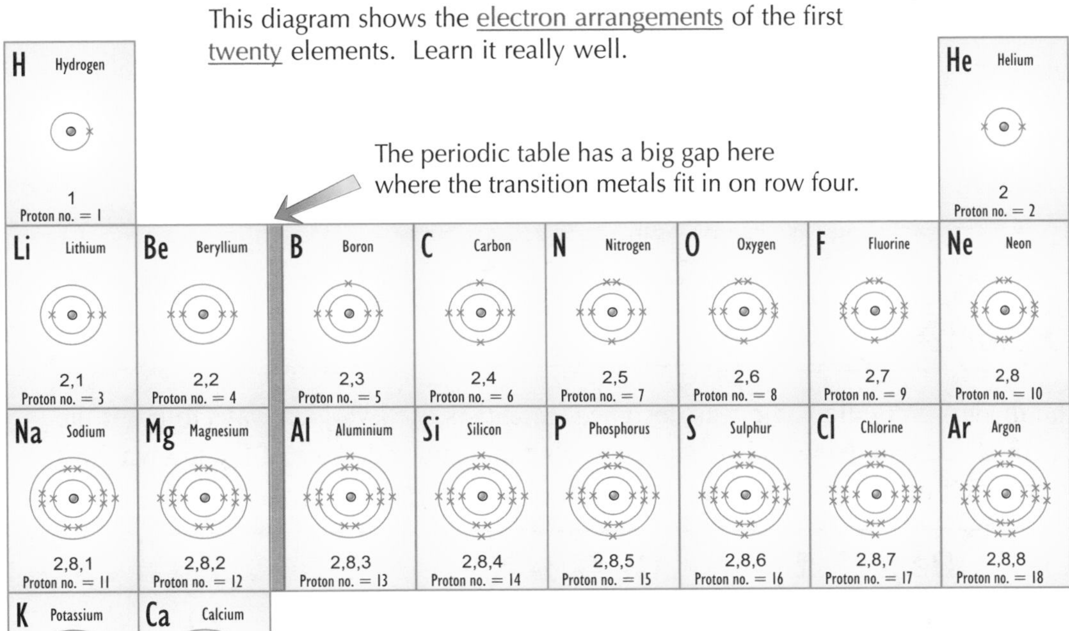

Reactivity changes *down the groups due to* ***shielding***

1) As atoms get bigger, they have more full shells of electrons.
2) As you go down any Group, each new row has one more full shell.
3) The number of outer electrons is the same for each element in a Group.
4) However, the outer shell of electrons is increasingly far from the nucleus.
5) You have to learn to say that the inner shells provide 'shielding'.
6) This means that the outer shell electrons get shielded from the attraction of the +ve nucleus. The upshot of all this is:

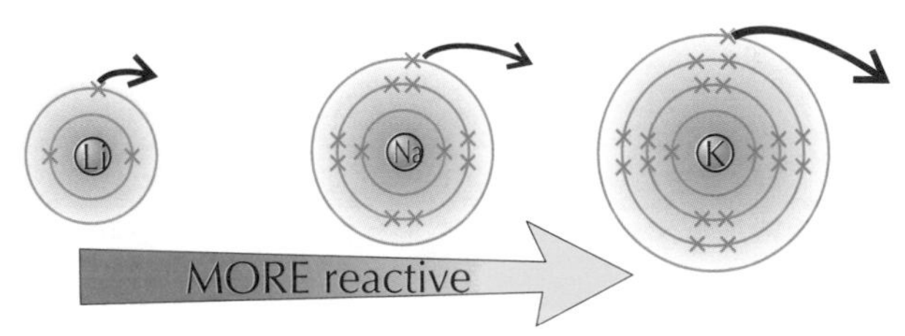

As metal atoms get bigger, the outer electron is more easily lost.

This makes *METALS MORE REACTIVE* as you go *DOWN* Group I and Group II

As non-metal atoms get bigger, the extra electrons are harder to gain.

This makes *NON-METALS LESS REACTIVE* as you go *DOWN* Group VI and Group VII

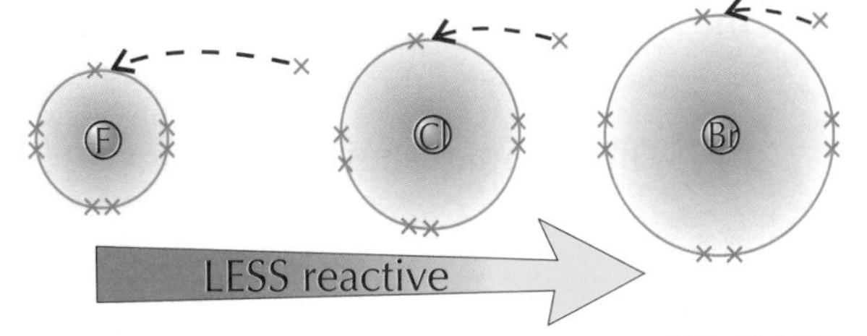

Learn the six points about shielding

The last page has a bit of history of the periodic table for you. Learn who discovered what, and when, then concentrate on learning about the reactivity trends stuff on this page.

Warm-Up and Exam Questions

Warm-up Questions

1) True or false? — "Elements in the same row of the Periodic Table have similar chemical properties."
2) How many electrons are there in the innermost shells of carbon, nitrogen and calcium?
3) How many electrons are there in the outer shell of a Group 1 atom?

Exam Questions

1 Before the modern Periodic Table was designed, scientists tried various ways to order the elements. In 1863, John Newlands designed a table that showed some of the known elements arranged in groups of seven.

Li	**Be**	**B**	**C**	**N**	**O**	**F**
Na	**Mg**	**Al**	**Si**	**P**	**S**	**Cl**

a) Which element in the table has similar chemical properties to oxygen?

(1 mark)

b) Did Newlands have any idea of atomic structure or electron arrangement when he made his table of elements?

(1 mark)

2 This diagram shows the electron arrangement of an atom.

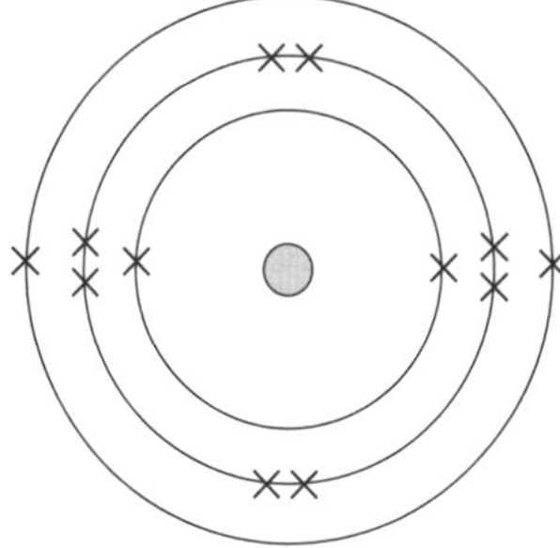

a) What element does this diagram show?

(1 mark)

b) Use the diagram to explain why this element is in Group II of the Periodic Table.

(1 mark)

c) This diagram shows beryllium.

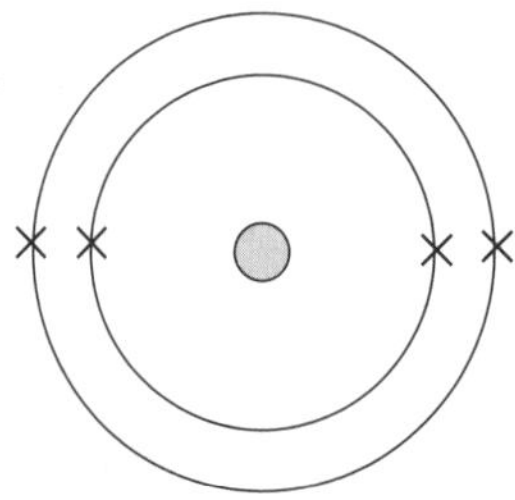

Explain why beryllium is less reactive than the element shown in the first diagram.

(3 marks)

Group 0 — The Noble Gases

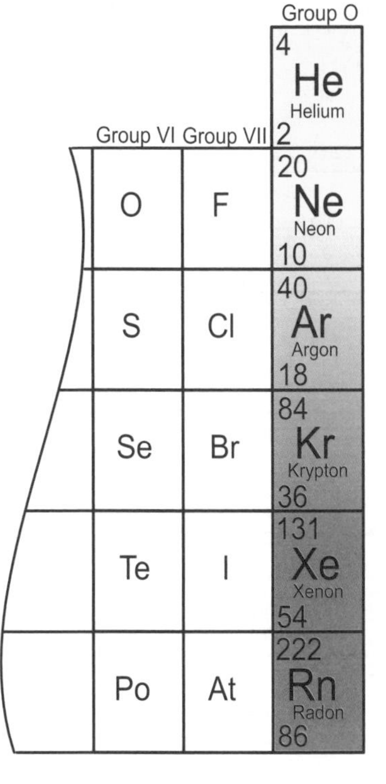

Group O
Group VI Group VII
4 He Helium 2
O F
20 Ne Neon 10
S Cl
40 Ar Argon 18
Se Br
84 Kr Krypton 36
Te I
131 Xe Xenon 54
Po At
222 Rn Radon 86

*As you go **down** the Group:*

1) The density increases
because the atomic mass increases.

2) The boiling point increases
Helium boils at –269°C (that's cold)
Xenon boils at –108°C (that's still cold)

They all have full outer shells
— That's why they're so inert

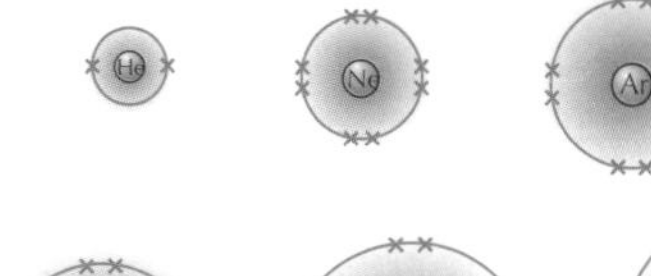

Inert means "doesn't react". This group is also sometimes called the Inert gases.

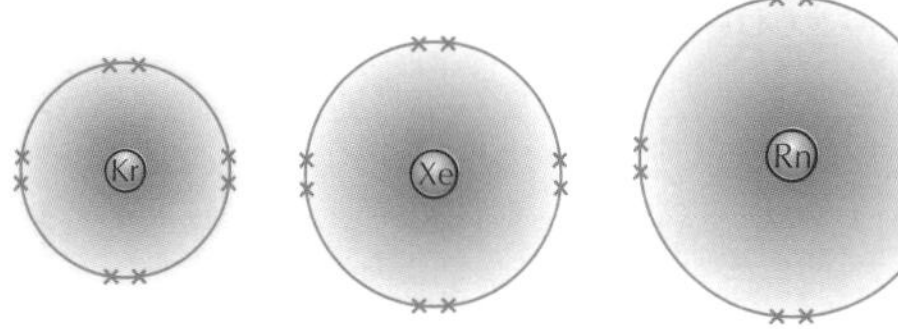

***Helium, neon** and **argon** are noble gases*

There's also Krypton, Xenon and Radon, which you may be asked about.

*They're all **colourless, monatomic** gases*

Most gases are made up of molecules, but the noble gases are monatomic — which means they only exist as individual atoms (and won't form bonds with anything — see below).

*The noble gases **don't react** at all*

Helium, Neon and Argon don't form any kind of chemical bonds with anything — so they can't react. They always exist as separate atoms. They won't even join up in pairs.

Helium** is used in **airships** and **party balloons

Helium is ideal: it has very low density and won't set on fire, (like hydrogen does).

Neon** is used in **electrical discharge tubes

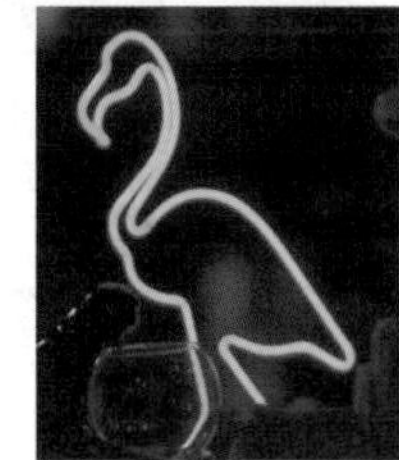

When a current is passed through neon it gives out a bright light.

***Argon** is used in **filament lamps** (light bulbs)*

It provides an inert atmosphere which stops the very hot filament from burning away (i.e. being oxidised).

*All three are used in **lasers** too*

There's the famous little red Helium-Neon laser and the more powerful Argon laser.

Group I — The Alkali Metals

There's more on the alkali metals on p.96. This page concentrates on the trends in Group I.

Learn these trends:

As you go *DOWN* Group I, the Alkali Metals become:

1) Bigger atoms
...because there's one extra full shell of electrons for each row you go down.
2) More reactive
...because the outer electron is more easily lost, because it's further from the nucleus.
3) Higher density
because the atoms have more mass.
4) Even softer to cut
5) Lower melting point
6) Lower boiling point

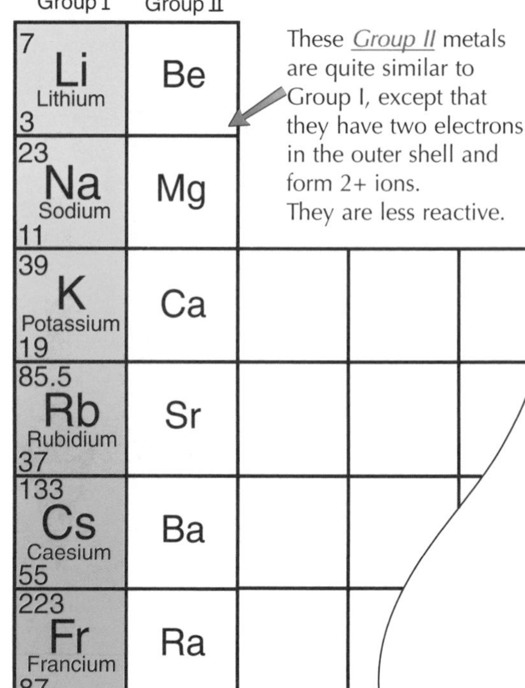

1) The alkali metals are very **reactive**

They have to be stored carefully (see p.96).

2) They are:

Lithium, Sodium, Potassium, Rubidium, Caesium and Francium.

3) The alkali metals all have **one outer electron**

This makes them very reactive and gives them all similar properties.

4) The alkali metals all form **1^+ ions**

They are keen to lose their one outer electron to form a 1^+ ion:

5) The alkali metals always form **ionic compounds**

They are so keen to lose the outer electron that there's no way they'd consider sharing so covalent bonding is out of the question.

6) Reaction with cold water produces **hydrogen gas**

E.g.

$$2Na_{(s)} + 2H_2O_{(l)} \rightarrow 2NaOH_{(aq)} + H_{2\,(g)}$$

$$2K_{(s)} + 2H_2O_{(l)} \rightarrow 2KOH_{(aq)} + H_{2\,(g)}$$

(See p.96 for more on these reactions.)

Group VII — The Halogens

Learn these trends:

As you go DOWN Group VII, the HALOGENS have the following properties:

1) Less reactive
2) Higher melting point
3) Higher boiling point

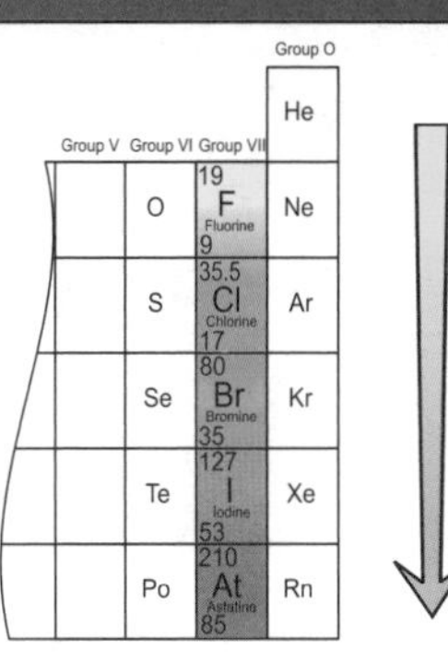

1) The halogens are all **non-metals** with **coloured vapours**

Fluorine is a very reactive, poisonous yellow gas.
Chlorine is a fairly reactive, poisonous dense green gas.
Bromine is a dense, poisonous, red-brown volatile liquid.
Iodine is a dark grey crystalline solid or a purple vapour.

2) They all form molecules which are **pairs of atoms**:

F_2 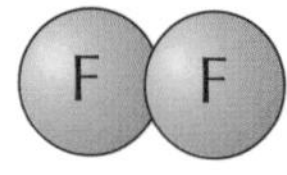

Cl_2 

Br_2 

I_2 

3) The halogens do **both ionic** and **covalent bonding**

The Halogens all form ions with a 1⁻ charge: F^- Cl^- Br^- I^- as in Na^+Cl^- or $Fe^{3+}3Br^-$
They form covalent bonds with themselves and in various molecular compounds like these:

Carbon tetrachloride: (CCl_4)

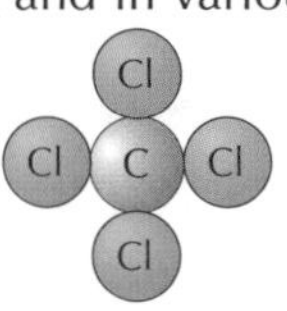

Hydrogen chloride: (HCl)

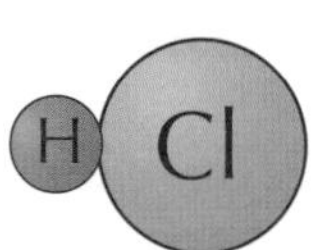

4) The halogens react with **metals** to form **salts**

They react with most metals including iron and aluminium, to form salts (or 'metal halides').

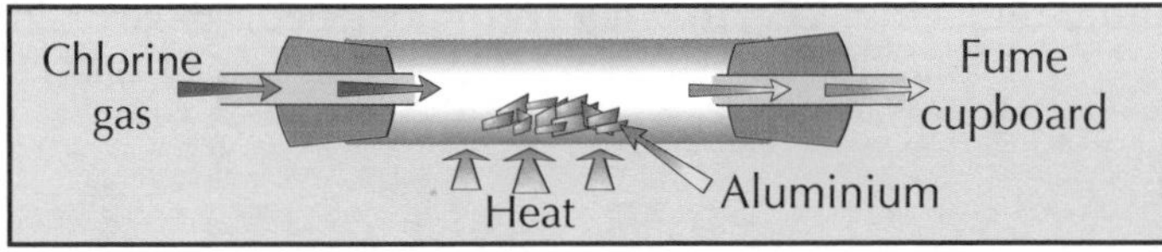

$$2Al_{(s)} + 3Cl_{2\,(g)} \rightarrow 2AlCl_{3\,(s)}$$
(Aluminium chloride)

$$2Fe_{(s)} + 3Br_{2\,(g)} \rightarrow 2FeBr_{3\,(s)}$$
(Iron(III) bromide)

5) More reactive halogens will **displace** less reactive ones

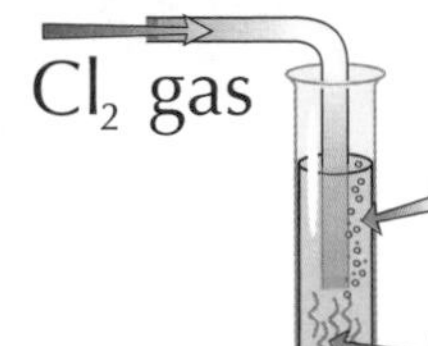

Chlorine can displace bromine and iodine from a solution of bromide or iodide.
Bromine will also displace iodine because of the trend in reactivity.

$$Cl_{2\,(g)} + 2KI_{(aq)} \rightarrow I_{2\,(aq)} + 2KCl_{(aq)}$$
$$Cl_{2\,(g)} + 2KBr_{(aq)} \rightarrow Br_{2\,(aq)} + 2KCl_{(aq)}$$

Warm-Up and Exam Questions

Doing these warm-up questions will soon find out if you've got the basic facts straight.
If not, you'll really struggle, so take the time to go back over the bits you don't know.

Warm-up Questions

1) What ion is formed by lithium?
2) Does helium form any compounds?
3) Why does neon exist as a monatomic gas, while fluorine and oxygen are diatomic gases?
4) Is the boiling point of potassium lower or higher than that of lithium?
5) What colour is fluorine gas?
6) In what physical state is bromine at room temperature and pressure?

Exam Questions

It's no good learning all the facts in the world if you go to pieces or just write nonsense in the exam.
Get this stuff practised.

1 a) Sodium is stored carefully under oil. Why must sodium be stored carefully?

(1 mark)

b) All alkali metals are soft enough to be cut with a knife.

Which of the alkali metals is the hardest?

(1 mark)

c) The elements in Group I get more reactive the further down the group you go.
Explain this trend in terms of electron arrangement and ease of ion formation.

(3 marks)

2 This question is about the noble gases.

a) The noble gases are also called the inert gases, because they do not react.

(i) Explain why the noble gases do not form compounds.

(1 mark)

(ii) Oxygen gas is found as a diatomic molecule, O_2. In what form does neon exist?

(1 mark)

b) The noble gases are used in lighting.

(i) Which noble gas is used in fluorescent tube lighting?

(1 mark)

(ii) Argon is used in filament light bulbs. Explain why.

(1 mark)

c) The *Hindenburg* was a hydrogen-filled airship which exploded disastrously in 1935.
After the disaster, helium was used to fill airships instead of hydrogen. Why was this?

(2 marks)

Alkali Metals and Halogen Compounds

*Some **uses** of **halogens** you really should know*

Fluorine**, (or rather **fluoride**) reduces **dental decay

1) Fluorides can be added to drinking water and toothpastes to help prevent tooth decay.
2) In its natural state fluorine appears as a pale yellow gas.

Chlorine** is used in **bleach** and for **sterilising water

1) Chlorine dissolved in sodium hydroxide solution is called bleach.
2) Chlorine compounds are also used to kill germs in swimming pools and drinking water.
3) It's used to make insecticides and in the manufacture of HCl.
4) It's also used in the manufacture of the plastic PVC (polyvinyl chloride)

***Iodine** is used as an **antiseptic**...*

...but it stings like nobody's business and stains the skin brown. Nice.

Silver halides** are used on black and white **photographic film

1) Silver is very unreactive. It does form halides but they're very easily split up.
2) In fact, ordinary visible light has enough energy to do so.
3) Photographic film is coated with colourless silver bromide.
4) When light hits parts of it, the silver bromide splits up into silver and bromine:

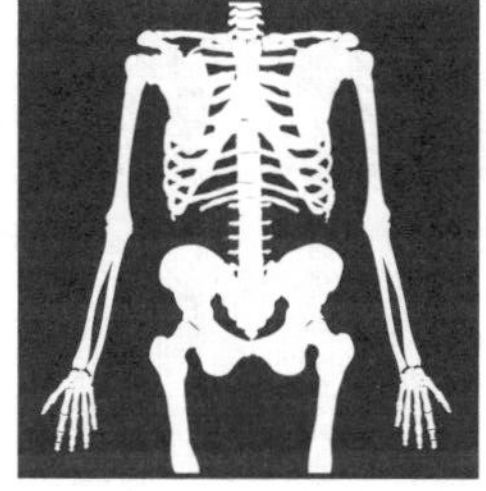

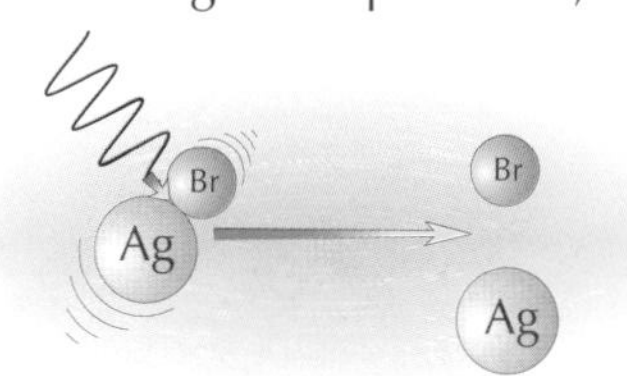

$$2AgBr \rightarrow Br_2 + 2Ag \text{ (silver metal)}$$

5) The silver metal appears black. The brighter the light, the darker it goes.
6) This produces a black and white negative, like an X-ray picture for example.

Hydrogen halides** dissolve to form **acidic solutions

1) Hydrogen halides are gases.
2) They dissolve easily in water forming strong acids.
3) Halide gases react with water to produce halide ions and H^+ ions, which is what makes it acidic.
4) The proper method for dissolving hydrogen halides in water is to use an inverted funnel as shown:

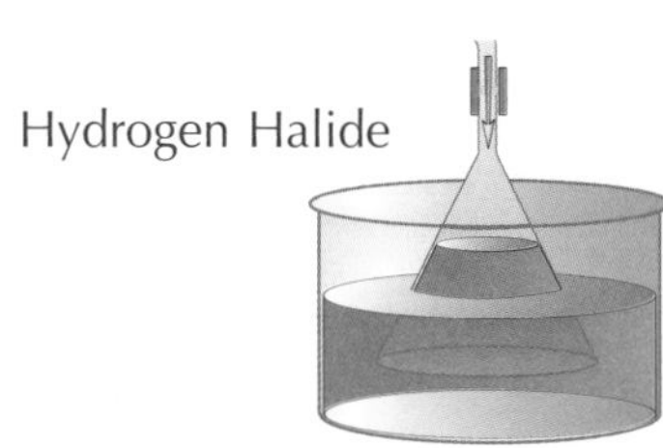

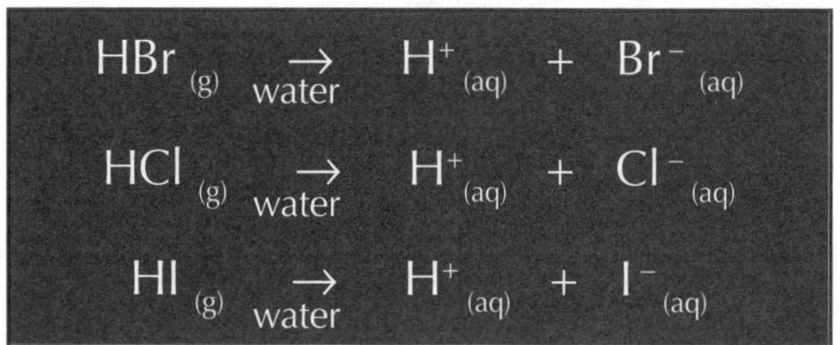

$$HBr_{(g)} \xrightarrow{water} H^+_{(aq)} + Br^-_{(aq)}$$

$$HCl_{(g)} \xrightarrow{water} H^+_{(aq)} + Cl^-_{(aq)}$$

$$HI_{(g)} \xrightarrow{water} H^+_{(aq)} + I^-_{(aq)}$$

Alkali Metals and Halogen Compounds

Salt is taken from **the sea** — and from **underneath Cheshire**

1) Common salt is a compound of sodium (an alkali metal) and chlorine (a halogen).
2) It is found in large quantities in the sea and in underground deposits.
3) In hot countries they just pour sea water into big flat open tanks and let the sun evaporate the water to leave salt. This is no good in cold countries because there isn't enough sunshine.
4) In Britain (a cold country — as if you need reminding), salt is extracted from underground deposits left millions of years ago when ancient seas evaporated. There are massive deposits of this rock salt in Cheshire.

Electrolysis of salt gives **hydrogen, chlorine** and **NaOH**

Salt dissolved in water is called brine.
When concentrated brine is electrolysed there are three useful products:

a) Hydrogen gas is given off at the cathode.
b) Chlorine gas is given off at the anode.
c) Sodium hydroxide is left in solution.

These are collected, and then used in all sorts of industries to make various products as detailed below.

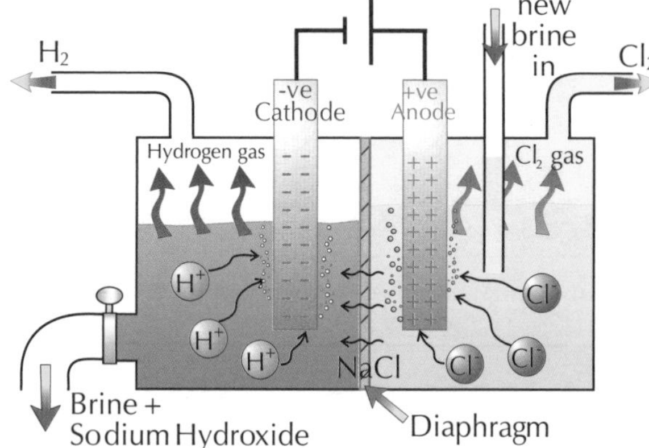

Useful products from the **electrolysis of brine**

With all that effort and expense going into the electrolysis of brine, there'd better be some pretty useful stuff coming out of it — and so there is... and you have to learn it all too. Ace.

1) Chlorine

1) Used in disinfectants 2) killing bacteria (e.g. in swimming pools)
3) plastics 4) HCl 5) insecticides. (As you just read on page 185.)
Don't forget the simple lab test for chlorine — it bleaches damp litmus paper.

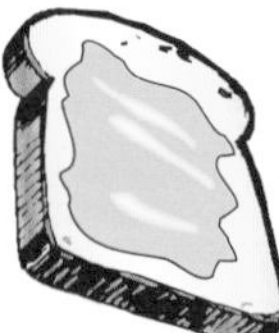

2) Hydrogen

1) Used in the Haber Process to make ammonia.
2) Used to change oils into fats for making margarine ("hydrogenated vegetable oil"). Think about that when you spread it on your toast in the morning.

3) Sodium hydroxide

Sodium Hydroxide is a very strong alkali and is used widely in the chemical industry,
e.g. 1) soap 2) ceramics 3) organic chemicals 4) paper pulp 5) oven cleaner.

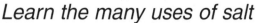

Learn the many uses of salt

There's not much to learn on this couple of pages so you've got no excuse for not learning it all. Write down where salt is found and the products from the electrolysis of brine, giving a few uses for each.

Warm-Up and Exam Questions

You could read through this page in a few minutes, but there's no point unless you check over any bits you don't know and make sure you understand everything. It's not quick — but it's the only way.

Warm-up Questions

1) Which common halide is added to food to enhance flavour?
2) Why is chlorine added to swimming pools?
3) Why is fluorine added to tap water?

Exam Questions

Take your time to go through these exam questions and make sure you can do all the parts. If any of the questions are baffling you, it's not too late to take another peek over the section.

1 This question is about the extraction and uses of sodium chloride and other halides.

a) Describe how salt is extracted from sea water in hot countries.

(1 mark)

b) Silver halides are used in photographic film.

i) Write a balanced equation for what happens when silver bromide is exposed to light.

(1 mark)

ii) What colour does the photographic film appear where the light has hit it?

(1 mark)

2 This question is about making hydrochloric acid.
Hydrogen gas and chlorine gas react together to make hydrogen chloride.

$$Cl_{2(g)} + H_{2(g)} \rightarrow 2HCl_{(g)}$$

a) How is hydrogen chloride gas bonded?

(1 mark)

b) Hydrogen chloride gas dissolves very readily in water.

i) Write an equation to show this.

(2 marks)

ii) Which product of this reaction makes the solution acidic?

(1 mark)

Symbols, Formulas and Equations

Equations need a lot of practice if you're going to get them right. They can get really tricky, unless you know your stuff. Every time you do an equation you need to practise getting it right rather than skating over it.

Chemical formulas tell you how many atoms there are

1) Hydrogen chloride has the chemical formula HCl. This means that in any molecule of hydrogen chloride there will be: one atom of hydrogen bonded to one atom of chlorine.
2) Ammonia has the formula NH_3. This means that in any molecule of ammonia there will be: three atoms of hydrogen bonded to one atom of nitrogen. Simple.
3) A chemical reaction can be described by the process reactants → products.
   e.g. methane reacts with oxygen to produce carbon dioxide and water
   e.g. magnesium reacts with oxygen to produce magnesium oxide.
   You have to know how to write these reactions in both words and symbols, as shown below:

The symbol equation shows the atoms on both sides:

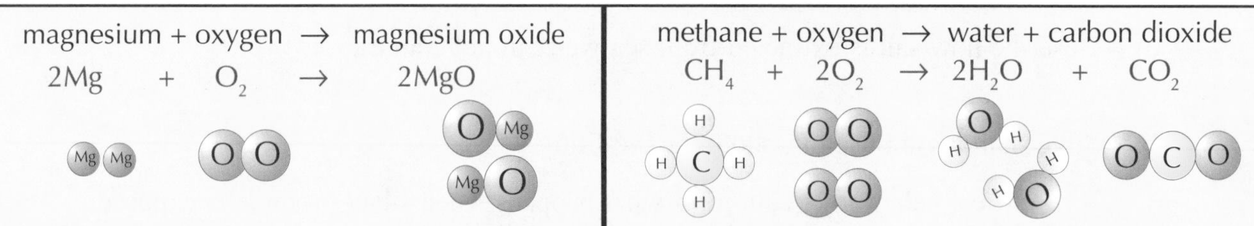

You need to know how to write out any equation...

You really do need to know how to write out chemical equations.

In fact you need to know how to write out equations for pretty well all the reactions in this book. That might sound like an awful lot, but there aren't nearly as many as you think. Have a look.

You also need to know the formulae for all the common ionic and covalent compounds in here too.

State symbols tell you what physical state it's in

These are easy enough, just make sure you know them, especially aq (aqueous).

(s) — Solid (l) — Liquid (g) — Gas (aq) — Dissolved in water

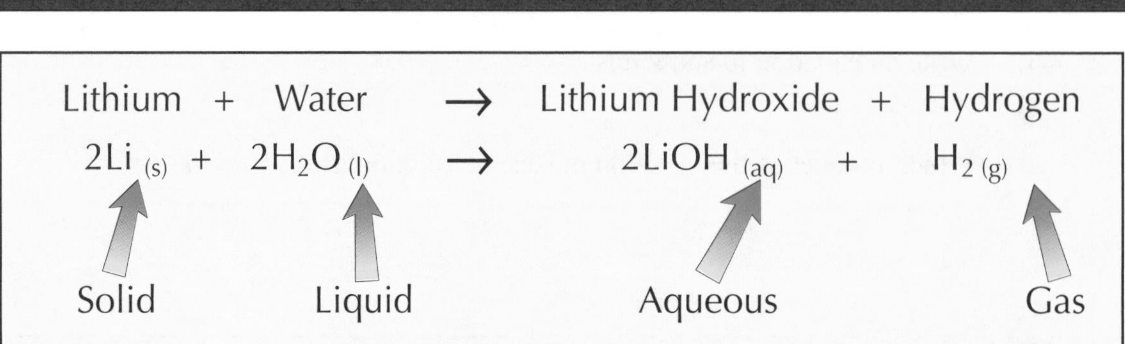

Symbols, Formulas and Equations

Things start to get a bit tricky now. Remember... practice makes perfect.

Balancing the equation — match them up one by one

1) There must always be the same number of atoms on both sides, they can't just disappear.
2) You balance the equation by putting numbers in front of the formulas where needed. Here's an example equation for reacting sulphuric acid with sodium hydroxide:

$$H_2SO_4 + NaOH \rightarrow Na_2SO_4 + H_2O$$

The formulas are all correct but the numbers of some atoms don't match up on both sides. You can't change formulas like H_2SO_4 to H_2SO_5. You can only put numbers in front of them:

Method: Balance just one type of atom at a time

The more you practise, the quicker you get, but all you do is this:

1) Find an element that doesn't balance and pencil in a number to try and sort it out.
2) See where it gets you. It may create another imbalance but pencil in another number and see where that gets you.
3) Carry on chasing unbalanced elements and it'll sort itself out pretty quickly.

I'll show you. In the equation above you soon notice we're short of H atoms on the RHS.

1) The only thing you can do about that is make it $2H_2O$ instead of just H_2O:

$$H_2SO_4 + NaOH \rightarrow Na_2SO_4 + 2H_2O$$

2) But that now causes too many H atoms and O atoms on the RHS, so to balance that up you could try putting 2NaOH on the LHS (Left Hand Side):

$$H_2SO_4 + 2NaOH \rightarrow Na_2SO_4 + 2H_2O$$

3) And suddenly there it is — everything balances. And you'll notice the Na just sorted itself out.

Electrolysis equations — make sure the electrons balance

The main thing is to make sure the number of electrons is the same for both half-equations. For the cell shown the basic half equations are:

Cathode: $H^+_{(aq)} + e^- \rightarrow H$

Anode: $Cl^-_{(aq)} \rightarrow Cl + e^-$

These equations aren't finished because both the hydrogen and the chlorine come off as gases. They must be rewritten with H_2 and Cl_2, like this:

Cathode: $2H^+ + 2e^- \rightarrow H_{2\,(g)}$

Anode: $2Cl^-_{(aq)} \rightarrow Cl_{2\,(g)} + 2e^-$

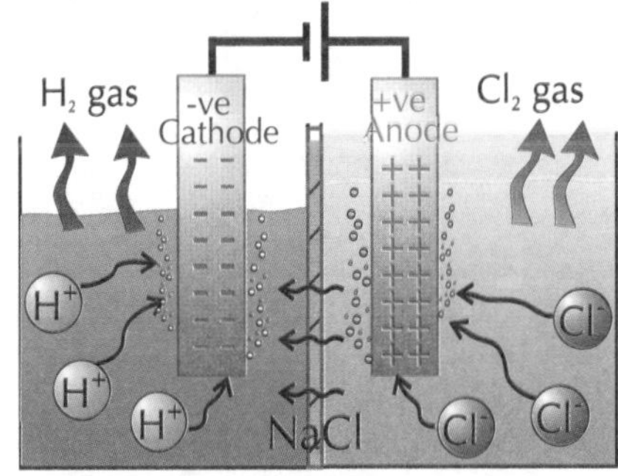

Note that there are two electrons in both half equations, which means they're nice and balanced. This gives the overall equation:

$$2HCl_{(aq)} \rightarrow H_{2\,(g)} + Cl_{2\,(g)}$$

Check how much of this stuff you know...

Practise scribbling down all these details, mini-essay style. Electrolysis can be a bit confusing. I think you have to make an effort to learn all the details. The confusing bit is that the two half equations are really just one equation which kind of happens in two places, joined by a battery.

Warm-Up and Exam Questions

Balancing equations is incredibly important. The best way to learn how to do it is to practise.

Warm-up Questions

1) Is this equation balanced? $HNO_{3(aq)} + NaOH_{(aq)} \rightarrow NaNO_{3(aq)} + H_2O$
2) How many atoms are there in each of these molecules?
   O_2 NaCl H_2O
3) Write a balanced symbol equation (including state symbols) for the reaction of solid sodium (Na) with water (H_2O) to produce sodium hydroxide (NaOH) in solution and hydrogen (H_2) gas.
4) Hydrogen chloride solution can be electrolysed. Write down the ionic half equation showing what happens at the cathode.

Exam Questions

1 Equations are used to represent chemical reactions.

a) This is a word equation for the decomposition of hydrogen peroxide (H_2O_2):

hydrogen peroxide → oxygen + water

Write a balanced symbol equation for this reaction.

....

(2 marks)

b) Potassium hydroxide reacts with sulphuric acid to produce a salt and water. Write a balanced symbol equation to show this.

....

(2 marks)

c) Ammonia gas reacts with oxygen over a hot platinum catalyst to produce nitrogen monoxide and water. Write a balanced equation to show this.

....

(3 marks)

2 A solution of copper sulphate is electrolysed using graphite electrodes.

Balance the following ionic half equations to show what happens at the electrodes.

At the positive electrode: ....$H_2O_{(l)} \rightarrow O_{2(g)} +$ ....$H^+_{(aq)} + 4e^-$

At the negative electrode: ....$Cu^{2+}_{(aq)} + 4e^- \rightarrow$ ....$Cu_{(s)}$

(2 marks)

Revision Summary for Section Eight

These certainly aren't the easiest questions you're going to come across. That's because they test what you know without giving you any clues. At first you might think they're impossibly difficult. Eventually you'll realise that they simply test whether you've learnt the stuff or not.
If you're struggling to answer these then you need to do some serious learning.

1) Explain, in terms of bonds and heat energy, what happens in melting, boiling and evaporation.
2) Sketch and label a heating graph and a cooling graph. Explain why the graphs have flat spots.
3) Sketch an atom. Give five details about the nucleus and five details about the electrons.
4) What are the three particles found in an atom? What are their relative masses and charges?
5) What do the mass number and proton number represent?
6) Explain what an isotope is. Give a well-known example.
7) What's the difference between elements, mixtures and compounds?
8) List five facts (or "Rules") about electron shells.
9) Calculate the electron configuration for each of the following elements: $^{4}_{2}He$, $^{12}_{6}C$, $^{31}_{15}P$, $^{39}_{19}K$.
10) What is ionic bonding? Which kind of atoms like to do ionic bonding? Why is this?
11) Draw a diagram of a giant ionic lattice and give three features of giant ionic structures.
12) List the three main properties of ionic compounds.
13) Which atoms form 1+, 1-, 2+ and 2- ions?
14) What is covalent bonding? Which kind of atoms tend to do covalent bonding? Why is this?
15) Why do some atoms do covalent bonding instead of ionic bonding?
16) Draw diagrams and use symbols to illustrate the bonding in: H_2, HCl, NH_3, CH_4, O_2 and H_2O.
17) What are the two types of covalent substance? Give three examples of each type.
18) What is buckminster fullerene?
19) Give three physical properties for each of the two types of covalent substance.
20) Why can graphite sometimes be used as a lubricant? Why is it used for pencil 'leads'?
21) Diamond and sand are both very hard. Why is this?
22) What is special about the bonding in metals?
23) What enables metals to conduct heat and electricity?
24) What two properties were early periodic tables based on?
25) Who had the best attempt at it and why was his table so clever?
26) What feature of atoms determines the order of the modern Periodic Table?
27) Draw diagrams to show the electron arrangements for the first twenty elements.
28) Explain the trend in reactivity of metals and non-metals using the notion of "shielding".
29) What are the electron arrangements of the noble gases? What are the properties of them?
30) List two chemical properties of the alkali metals.
31) Describe the trends in appearance and reactivity of the halogens as you go down the Group.
32) List four properties common to all the halogens. Write down four uses of halogens.
33) Give details, with equations, of the reaction of the halogens with metals, including silver.
34) Is hydrogen chloride covalent or ionic in its *natural* state? What about in acidic form?
35) What are the two sources of common salt and what are the three main uses of it?
36) Draw a *detailed* diagram showing *clearly* how brine is electrolysed.
37) Write down the three products of this electrolysis and write down uses for each of them.

Energy Transfer

Learn these **ten types** of **energy**

You should know all of these well enough to list them from memory, including the examples:

1) Electrical energy.. — whenever a current flows.
2) Light Energy.. — from the Sun, light bulbs etc.
3) Sound Energy... — from loudspeakers or anything noisy.
4) Kinetic Energy, or Movement Energy.................. — anything that's moving has it.
5) Nuclear Energy.. — released only from nuclear reactions.
6) Thermal Energy or Heat Energy........................... — flows from hot objects to colder ones.
7) Radiant Heat Energy, or Infra Red Heat............... — given out as EM radiation by hot objects.
8) Gravitational Potential Energy.............................. — possessed by anything which can fall.
9) Elastic Potential Energy.. — stretched springs, elastic, rubber bands, etc.
10) Chemical Energy.. — possessed by foods, fuels and batteries.

Potential- and **chemical-** are forms of **stored energy**

The last three above are forms of stored energy because the energy is not obviously doing anything, it's kind of waiting to happen, i.e. waiting to be turned into one of the other forms.

They like giving **exam questions** on **energy transfers**

These are very important examples. You must learn them till you can repeat them all easily.

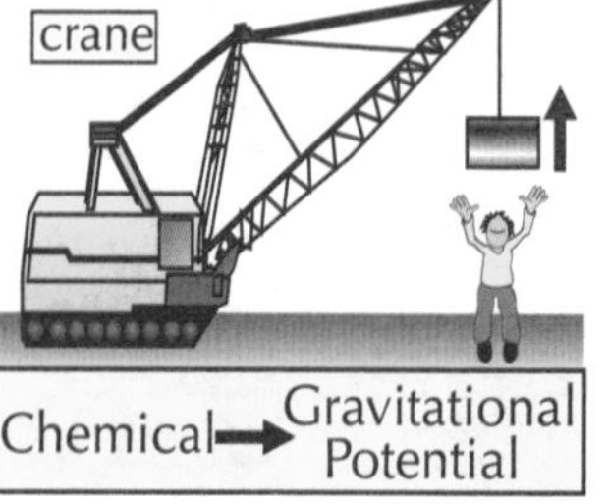

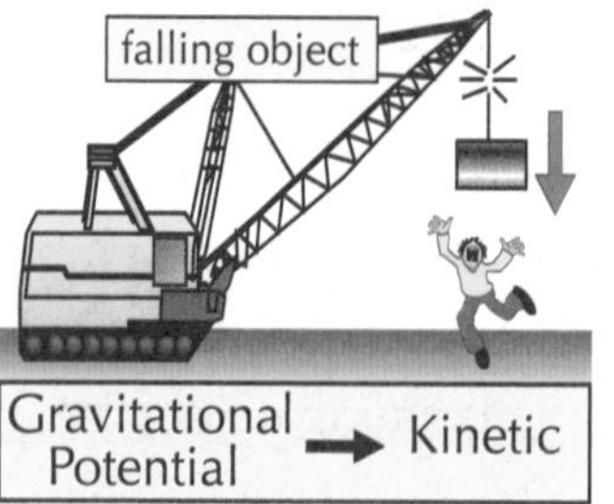

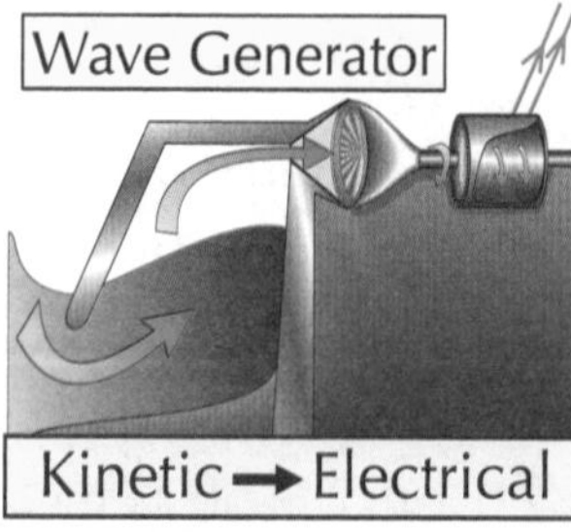

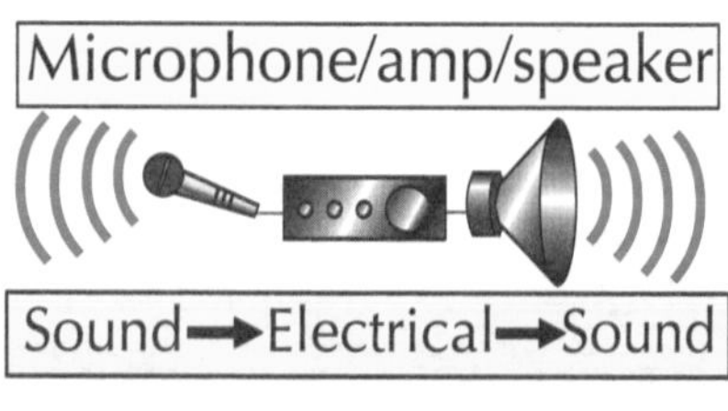

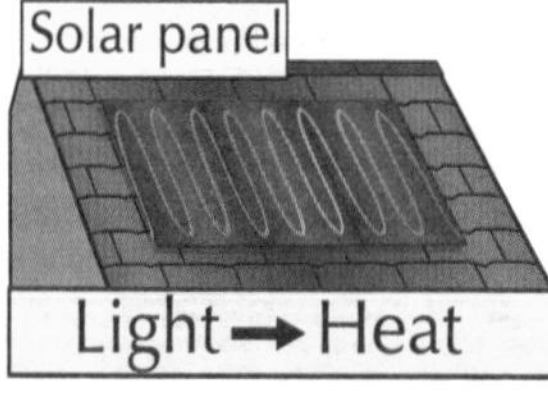

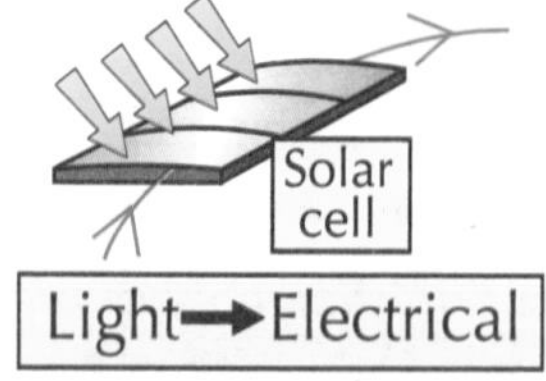

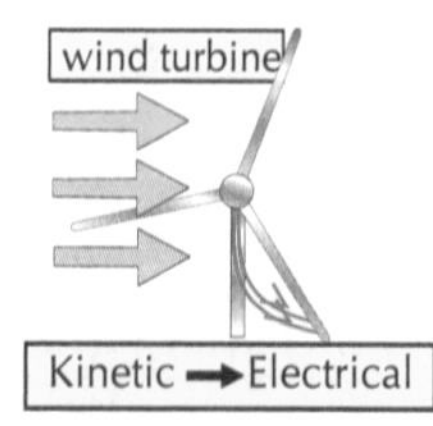

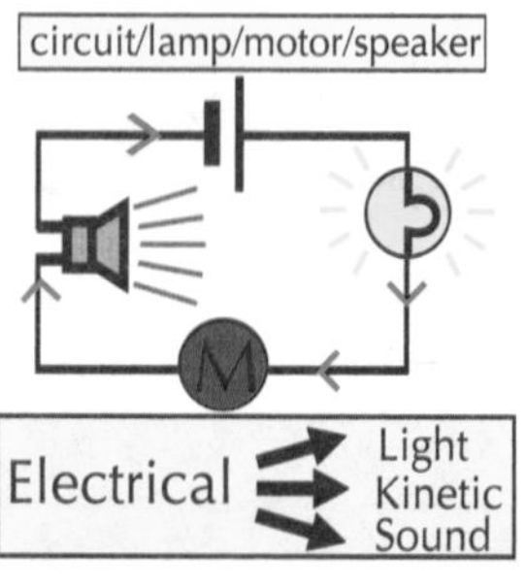

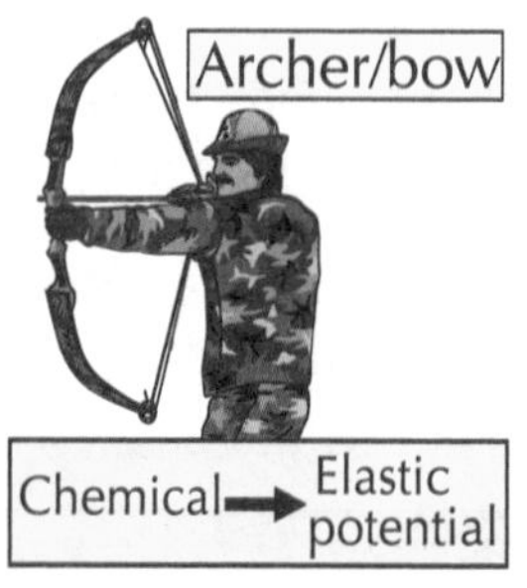

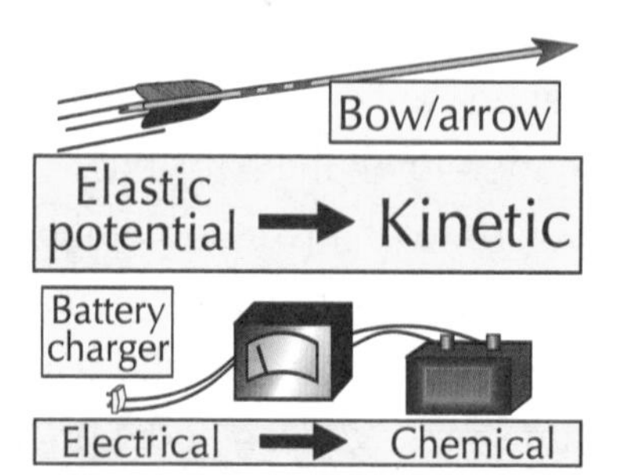

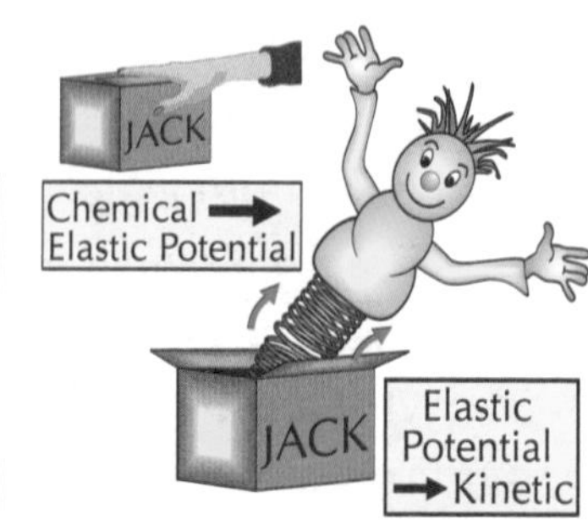

And DON'T FORGET — ALL types of ENERGY are measured in JOULES

Energy Transfer

*The **Principle of the Conservation of Energy** can be stated thus:*

These few pages are about how energy is transferred.
But before you tackle any of that you must learn this basic principle:

ENERGY CAN NEVER BE CREATED NOR DESTROYED — IT'S ONLY EVER TRANSFERRED FROM ONE FORM TO ANOTHER.

Heat energy** causes **molecules** to **move faster

1) Heat energy causes gas and liquid molecules to move around faster, and causes particles in solids to vibrate more rapidly.
2) When particles move faster it shows up as a rise in temperature.
3) This extra kinetic energy in the particles tends to get dissipated to the surroundings.
4) In other words the heat energy tends to flow away from a hotter object to its cooler surroundings. But then you knew that already.

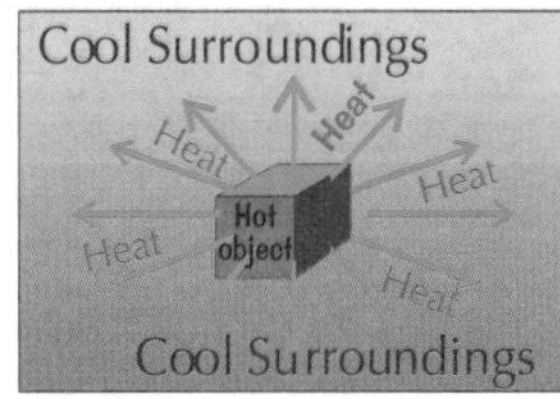

If there's a DIFFERENCE IN TEMPERATURE between two places then HEAT WILL FLOW between them.

***Conduction, convection** and **radiation** compared*

There are three distinct methods of heat transfer: conduction, convection *and* radiation.
To answer Exam questions you must use those three key words in just the right places.
And that means you need to know exactly what they are, and all the differences between them.

1) Conduction occurs mainly in solids. (See page 195.)
2) Convection occurs mainly in gases and liquids. (See page 196.)
3) Gases and liquids are very poor conductors — convection is usually the dominant process. Where convection can't occur, the heat transfer by conduction is very slow indeed.
4) Radiation travels through anything see-through (transparent), including a vacuum. (See page 197.)
5) Heat radiation is given out by anything which is warm or hot (compared with its surroundings).
6) The amount of heat radiation which is absorbed or emitted depends on the colour and texture of the surface. But don't forget, convection and conduction are totally unaffected by surface colour or texture. A shiny white surface conducts just as well as a matt black one.

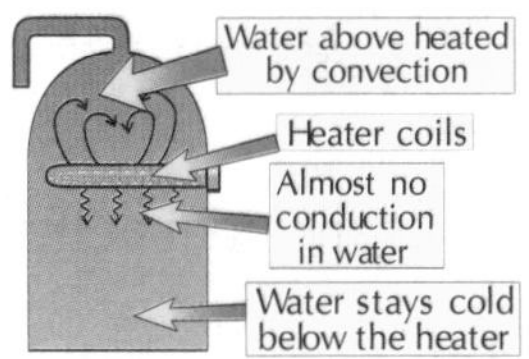

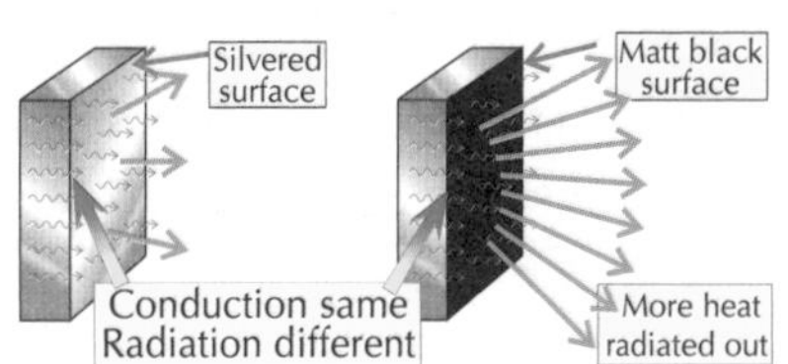

Learn the facts on energy transfer

They're pretty keen on the conservation of energy and also energy transfers. You'll definitely get an Exam question on it, and if you learn all the stuff on these pages, you should have it pretty well covered. Learn, cover, scribble, check, learn, cover, scribble, etc. etc.

Warm-Up and Exam Questions

The warm-up questions run quickly over the basic facts you'll need in the exam. The exam questions come later — but unless you've learnt the facts first you'll find the exams tougher than leather sandwiches.

Warm-up Questions

1) Gavin fires a stone from his new catapult into the air and it lands on the roof of a nearby building. State the main energy transfers in the following situations:
   a) Gavin's arm stretches the catapult.
   b) Gavin releases the stone and it flies out.
   c) The stone flies upwards and lands on the roof.

Exam Questions

1 The diagram shows the energy transfers in a car accelerating along a motorway.

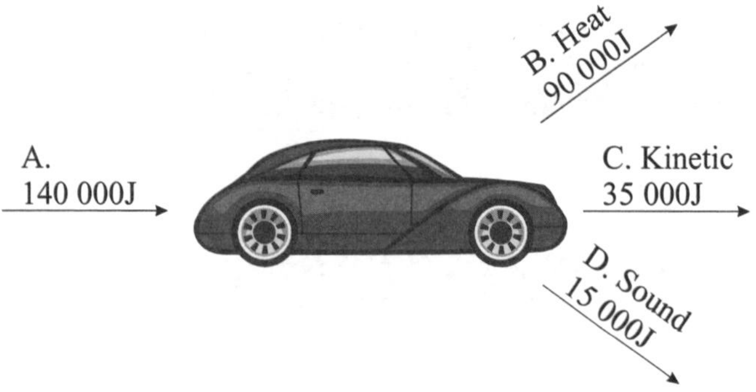

What energy type is represented by arrow A?

....

(1 mark)

2 At the top of a waterfall, a river has both gravitational potential energy and kinetic energy. As the water falls, it loses gravitational potential energy.

a) What is the main energy transfer that the water undergoes as it falls?

....

(1 mark)

b) In what two ways is this energy dissipated as the water hits the pool at the bottom?

....

(2 marks)

Conduction

Conduction of heat — occurs mainly in solids

CONDUCTION OF HEAT is the process where VIBRATING PARTICLES pass on their EXTRA VIBRATION ENERGY to NEIGHBOURING PARTICLES.

This process continues throughout the solid and gradually the extra vibrational energy (or heat) is passed all the way through the solid, causing a rise in temperature at the other side.

Non-metals are good insulators

1) This normal process of conduction as illustrated above is always very slow.
2) But in most non-metal solids it's the only way that heat can pass through.
3) So non-metals, such as plastic, wood, rubber etc. are very good insulators.
4) Non-metal gases and liquids are even worse conductors.
   Metals, on the other hand, are a totally different thing altogether...

All metals are good conductors due to their free electrons

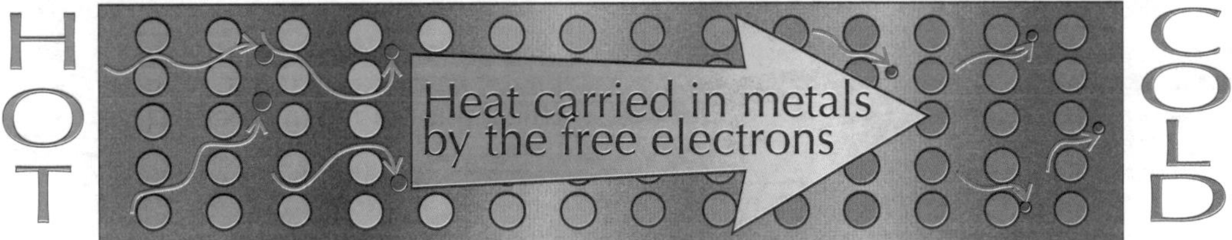

1) Metals 'conduct' so well because the electrons are free to move inside the metal.
2) At the hot end the electrons move faster and diffuse more quickly through the metal.
3) So the electrons carry their energy quite a long way before giving it up in a collision.
4) This is obviously a much faster way of transferring the energy through the metal than slowly passing it between jostling neighbouring atoms. This is why heat travels so fast through metals.

Metals always feel hotter or colder because they conduct so well

You'll notice if a spade is left out in the sun that the metal part will always feel much hotter than the wooden handle. But it isn't hotter — it just conducts the heat into your hand much quicker than the wood, so your hand heats up much quicker.

In cold weather, the metal bits of a spade, or anything else, always feel colder because they take the heat away from your hand quicker. But they're not colder... Remember that.

Convection

Gases and liquids are usually free to move about — and that allows them to transfer heat by convection, which is a much more effective process than conduction.

Convection of heat — liquids and gases only

Convection simply can't happen in solids because the particles can't move.

> *CONVECTION* occurs when the more energetic particles MOVE from the hotter region to the cooler region — AND TAKE THEIR HEAT ENERGY WITH THEM.

When the more energetic (i.e. hotter) particles get somewhere cooler they then transfer their energy by the usual process of collisions which warm up the surroundings.

Natural convection currents are caused by changes in density

The diagram shows a typical convection current. Make sure you learn all the bits about expansion and density changes which cause the convection current. It's all worth marks in the Exam.

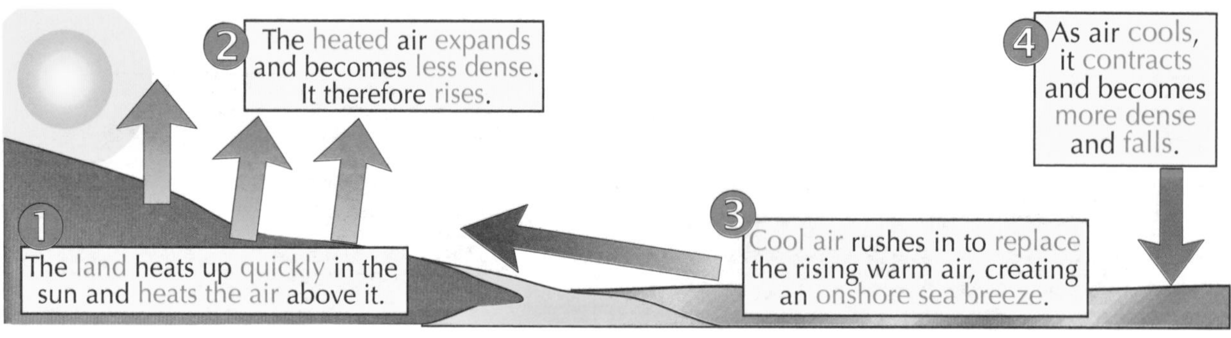

2 The heated air expands and becomes less dense. It therefore rises.
4 As air cools, it contracts and becomes more dense and falls.
1 The land heats up quickly in the sun and heats the air above it.
3 Cool air rushes in to replace the rising warm air, creating an onshore sea breeze.

Forced convection is used to cool machinery

1) Forced convection is simply where you have a fan or pump making the gas or liquid move around much faster.
2) In a car engine the water pump pushes the water around quickly to transfer heat away from the engine and get rid of it at the radiator. That's forced convection.
3) Inside, we use cooling fans to blow air over us to cool us down, or alternatively fan heaters blow warm air around the room much quicker than the natural convection currents would.

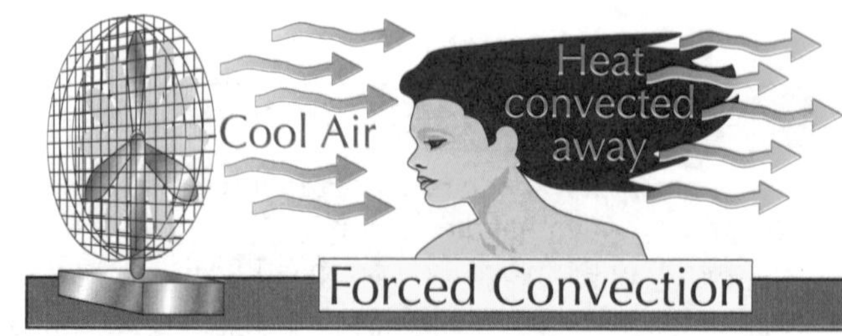

Radiation

Heat radiation can also be called infrared radiation, and it consists purely of electromagnetic waves of a certain frequency. It's just below visible light in the electromagnetic spectrum.

Heat radiation can travel through a vacuum

Heat radiation is different from the other two methods of heat transfer in quite a few ways:

1) It travels in straight lines at the speed of light.
2) It travels through a vacuum. This is the only way that heat can reach us from the Sun.
3) It can be very effectively reflected away again by a silver surface.
4) It only travels through transparent media, like air, glass and water.
5) Its behaviour is strongly dependent on surface colour and texture. This definitely isn't so for conduction and convection.
6) No particles are involved. It's transfer of heat energy purely by waves.

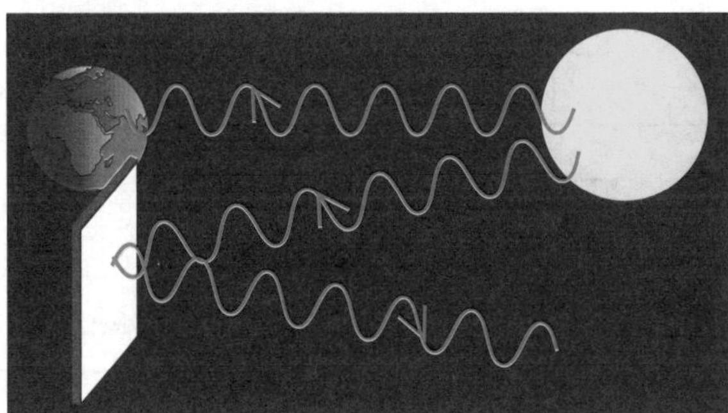

Emission and absorption of heat radiation

1) All objects are continually emitting and absorbing heat radiation.
2) The hotter they are, the more heat radiation they emit.
3) Cooler ones around them will absorb this heat radiation. You can feel this heat radiation if you stand near something hot like a fire.

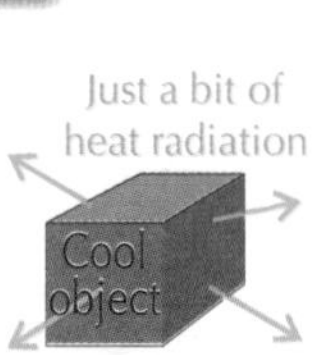

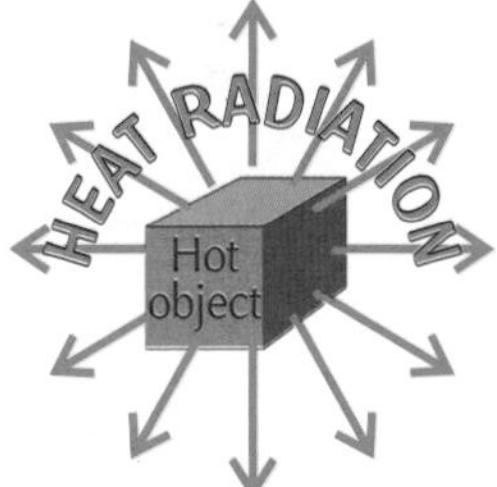

It depends a lot on surface colour and texture

1) Dark matt surfaces absorb heat radiation falling on them much more strongly than bright glossy surfaces, such as gloss white or silver. They also emit heat radiation much more too.
2) Silvered surfaces reflect nearly all heat radiation falling on them.
3) In the lab there are several fairly dull experiments to demonstrate the effects of surface on emission and absorption of heat radiation. Here are two of the most common:

Leslie's cube

The matt black side emits most heat so it's that thermometer which gets hottest.

The melting wax trick

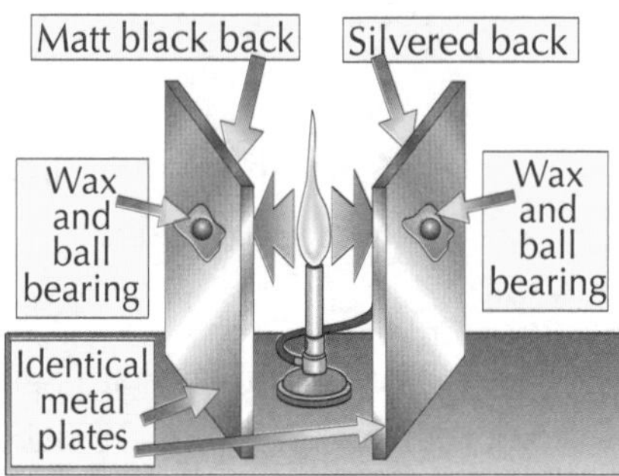

The matt black surface absorbs most heat so its wax melts first and the ball bearing drops.

If radiation couldn't travel through a vacuum, we'd all be very cold

Conduction and convection rely completely on transferring energy from one molecule to another.
Heat radiation is totally different — it can move quite happily without involving any molecules at all.

Warm-Up and Exam Question

Warm-up Questions

1) Anna visits Spain and notices that many of the houses are painted white on the outside. Explain why this is likely to help the houses remain cool.
2) Choose the correct name for each of the methods of heat transfer described below.
   a) Heat energy travelling through space as electromagnetic waves.
   b) Heat travelling through a solid due to energetic atoms colliding with their neighbours and passing on energy.
   c) Heat moving upwards through a gas due to the expansion of warm areas of gas.

Exam Question

1 The inside of a fridge is kept cool by the continual transfer of heat energy from inside the fridge to the outside. A cooling element at the back of the fridge is designed to quickly release this heat into the air.

An example of such a cooling element is shown here:

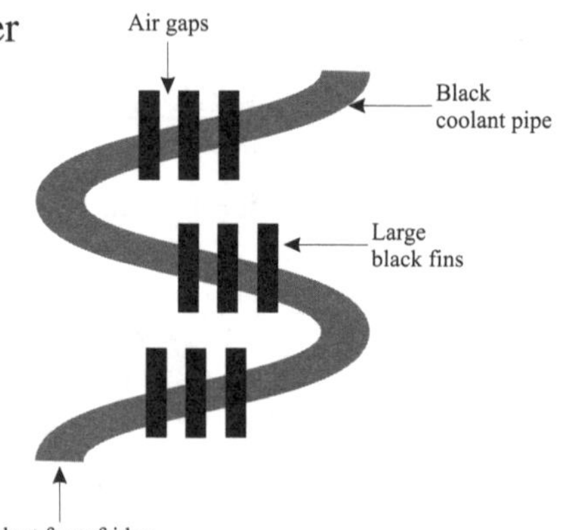

a) Identify two features of the element that help to increase heat loss by radiation.

(2 marks)

b) Suggest a suitable material to make the element from. Explain your choice.

(2 marks)

Fridges are surrounded by thick layers of insulation to keep heat energy out. A cross-section of one design for such insulation is shown here:

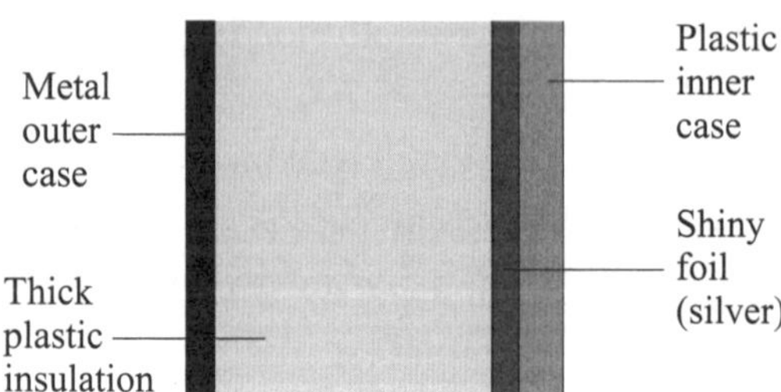

c) Describe what is meant by heat radiation.

(1 mark)

d) What feature of the insulation is designed to reduce the amount of heat radiation entering the fridge?

(1 mark)

e) The plastic shown is an insulator. Despite this, heat energy is still conducted through the solid plastic in the fridge. Give an explanation, in terms of the plastic particles, of how this happens.

(2 marks)

f) Suggest a modification to the insulation which would reduce the amount of heat energy conducted through the plastic.

(1 mark)

Domestic Energy

Loft insulation
Initial Cost: £200
Annual Saving: £50
Payback time: 4 years

Hot water tank jacket
Initial Cost: £10
Annual Saving: £15
Payback time: 1 year

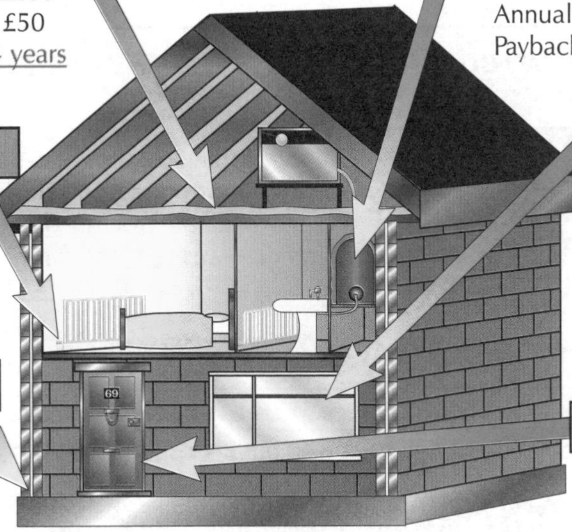

Thermostatic controls
Initial Cost: £100
Annual Saving: £20
Payback time: 5 years

Double glazing
Initial Cost: £3,000
Annual Saving: £60
Payback time: 50 years

Cavity wall insulation
Initial Cost: £500
Annual Saving: £70
Payback time: 7 years

Draught-proofing
Initial Cost: £50
Annual Saving: £50
Payback time: 1 year

Effectiveness and cost-effectiveness are not the same...

1) The figures above are all in the right area, but of course it'll vary from house to house.
2) The cheaper methods of insulation tend to be a lot more cost-effective than the pricier ones.
3) The ones that save the most money each year could be considered the most 'effective', i.e. cavity wall insulation. How cost-effective it is depends on what time-scale you're looking at.
4) If you subtract the annual saving from the initial cost repeatedly then eventually the one with the biggest annual saving must always come out as the winner, if you think about it.
5) But you might sell the house (or die) before that happens. If instead you look at it over say, a five year period, then the cheap and cheerful draught-proofing wins.
6) But double glazing is always by far the least cost-effective, strangely.

Know which types of heat transfer are involved:

1) Cavity Wall Insulation — foam squirted into the gap between the bricks reduces convection and radiation across the gap.
2) Loft insulation — a thick layer of fibre glass wool laid out across the whole loft floor reduces conduction and radiation into the roof space from the ceiling.
3) Draught proofing — strips of foam and plastic around doors and windows stop draughts of cold air blowing in, i.e. they reduce heat loss due to convection.
4) Double Glazing — two layers of glass with an air gap reduce conduction and radiation.
5) Thermostatic Radiator valves — these simply prevent the house being over-warmed.
6) Hot water tank jacket — lagging (e.g. fibre-glass wool) reduces conduction and radiation from hot water tanks.
7) Thick Curtains — big bits of cloth you pull across the window to stop people looking in at you, but also to reduce heat loss by conduction and radiation.

Domestic Energy

Electricity is by far the most useful form of energy.
Compared to gas or oil or coal etc. it's much easier to turn it into the four main types of useful energy: heat, light, sound and motion.

Reading your **electricity meter** and working out the **bill**

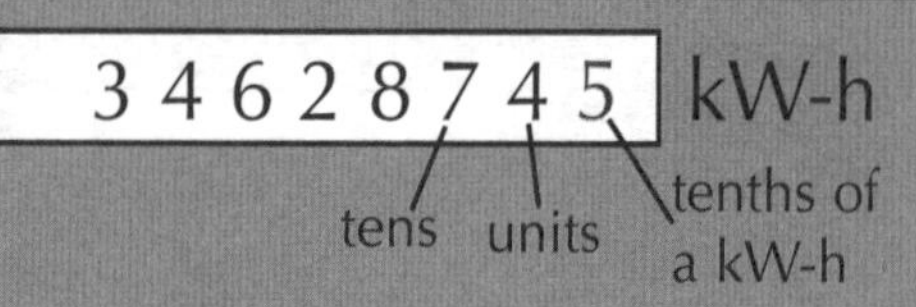

The reading on your meter shows the total number of units (kW-h) used since the meter was fitted. Each bill is worked out from the increase in the meter reading since it was last read for the previous bill.

Kilowatt-hours (kW-h) are **'units'** of **energy**

1) Your electricity meter counts the number of 'UNITS' used. A 'UNIT' is otherwise known as a kilowatt-hour, or kW-h. A 'kW-h' might sound like a unit of power, but it's not — it's an amount of energy.

A KILOWATT-HOUR is the amount of electrical energy used by a 1 KW APPLIANCE left on for 1 HOUR.

2) Make sure you can turn 1 kW-h into 3,600,000 joules like this:
"E=P×t" =1kW × 1 hour =1000W × 3,600 secs = 3,600,000 J (=3.6 MJ)
(The formula is "Energy = Power × time", and the units must be converted to SI first).

The **two easy formulae** for calculating the **cost of electricity**

These must surely be the two most trivial and obvious formulae you'll ever see:

No. of units (kW-h) used = Power (in kW) × Time (in hours) — **Units = kW × hours**

Cost = No. of UNITS × price per UNIT — **Cost = Units × Price**

N.B. Always turn the power into kW (not watts) and the time into hours (not minutes)

Power ratings of appliances

A light bulb converts electrical energy into light and has a power rating of 100W which means it transfers 100 joules/second.

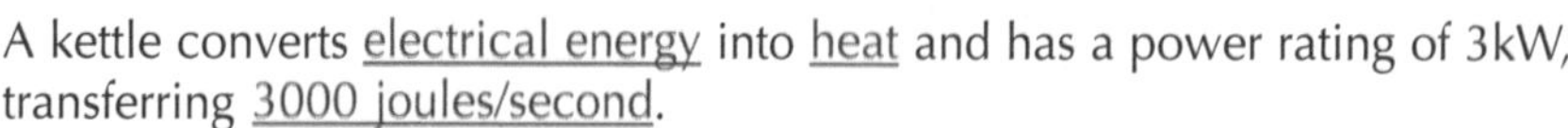

A kettle converts electrical energy into heat and has a power rating of 3kW, transferring 3000 joules/second.

The total amount of energy transferred by an appliance therefore depends on how long the appliance is on and its power rating (E = P × t). For example the kettle is on for an hour — the energy transferred by the kettle in this time is 3600×3000 = 10800 kJ (3600s = 1 hour).

Practise these calculations

Remember, the most effective insulation measure is the one which keeps the most heat in, (biggest annual saving). But cost-effectiveness depends very much on the time-scale involved. You also need to practise the calculations on this page — they're all the same so if you can do one you can do them all.

Warm-Up and Exam Questions

Warm-up Questions

1) Double glazing can be an effective way of reducing energy loss from a house. Why is it unlikely to be a cost-effective way of saving energy?
2) This picture shows an electricity meter on May 1st. 03788·1 kWh

   This picture shows the same meter on June 1st. 04814·5 kWh

   a) How many units of electricity have been used?
   b) If the cost of electricity is 5p per unit, how much did the electricity used in this period cost?

Exam Questions

1 The new owner of a house buys a jacket for the hot water tank. The jacket costs £12 and is expected to save £15 per year. The diagram shows a close-up of the structure of the jacket.

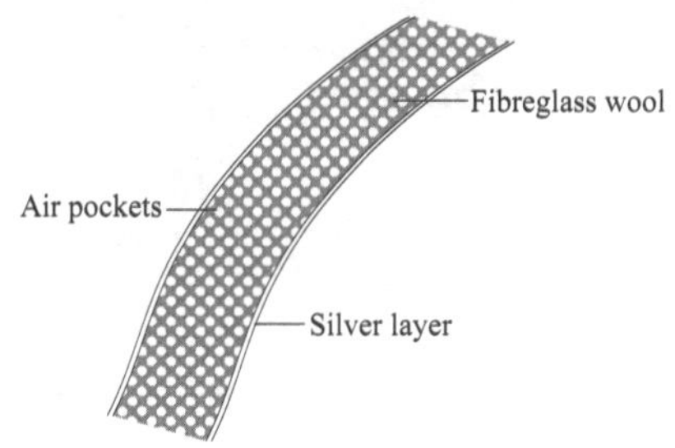

a) Explain how the air in the hot water jacket now reduces heat loss from the tank.

(2 marks)

A salesman suggests to the owner that it would be a good idea to invest in cavity wall insulation, as this could save £65 per year.

b) Suggest reasons why cavity wall insulation may not be a good investment.

(2 marks)

2 The Meadowes family's electricity bill for the last quarter looks like this:

Present Reading	Previous Reading	Units Used	p per Unit	Amount
16969	14303	A	4.680	B

Service charge	£8.64
Total charges excluding VAT	C
Plus VAT at 17.5%	D
Total payment due	E

Calculate A, B, C, D and E.

(5 marks)

Potential Energy

Gravitational potential energy is energy *due to height*

Gravitational potential energy is the energy stored in an object because it has been raised to a specific height against the force of gravity.

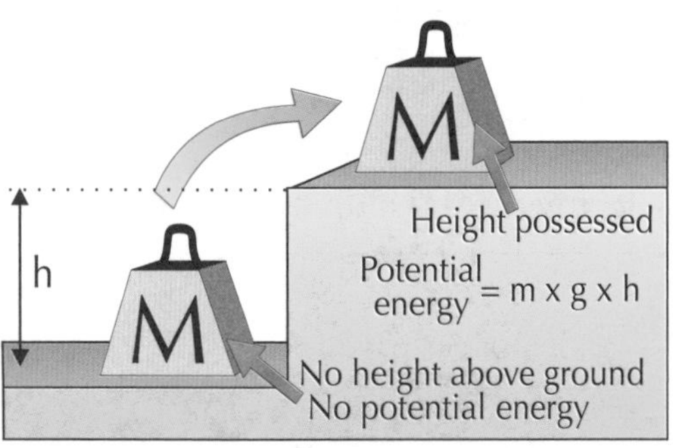

Potential Energy = mass × g × height

Quite often gravitational potential energy is just called 'potential energy', but you should use its full name really. The proper name for g is 'gravitational field strength'. On Earth this has the value of g ≈ 10 N/kg, which results in a gravitational acceleration of $10 m/s^2$.

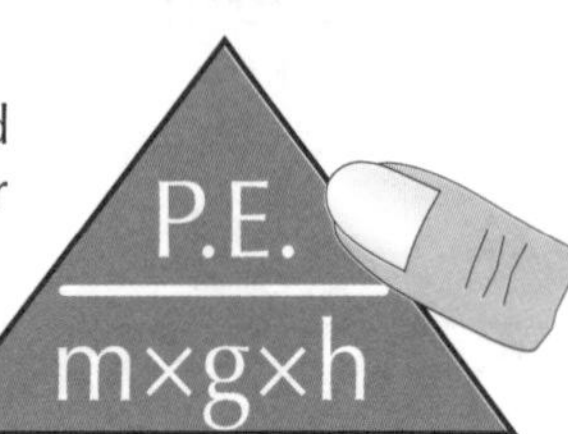

*1) Working out **potential energy***

Example: A box of mass 47 kg is slowly raised through 6.3 m. Find the gain in potential energy.

Answer: *This is pretty easy.*
You just plug the numbers into the formula:
PE = mgh = 47 × 10 × 6.3 = 2 961 J
(Joules again because it's energy again.)

*2) Calculating the **kinetic energy** of **falling objects***

When something falls, its potential energy is converted into kinetic energy. There's more about kinetic energy on p.249.

In practice, some of the PE will be dissipated as heat due to air resistance, but in Exam questions they'll probably say you can ignore air resistance. In which case you'll just need to remember this simple and really quite obvious formula:

Kinetic energy GAINED = Potential Energy LOST

Example: A beanbag of mass 140 g is dropped from a height of 1.7 m. Calculate its kinetic energy at 1 m above the floor.

Answer: There are three key steps to this method — and you've got to learn them:

Step 1) Find the initial PE: = mgh = 0.14×10×1.7 = 2.38 J

Step 2) Find the PE at 1 m: = mgh = 0.14×10×1.0 = 1.4 J

Step 3) KE gained = PE lost: = 2.38 – 1.4 = 0.98J

Ignore air resistance for these questions

A couple of straightforward formulas for you here. There's more on kinetic energy calculations in Section 11 — when you get there I'd advise you to have a look back at this page.

Warm-Up and Exam Question

There's no point in skimming through the section and glancing over the questions. Do the warm-up questions and go back over any bits you don't know. Then practise and practise the exam question.

Warm-up Questions

1) Write down the formula for calculating gravitational potential energy, including what each letter stands for.
2) What is potential energy measured in?
3) What is the main energy change of an object when it falls off Blackpool Tower?
4) A stone has a mass of 50g. Richard lifts it to a height of 1.6 m.
   How much gravitational potential energy does the stone have? *(Use g = 10 m/s²)*

Exam Question

Have a go at this exam question.
Come on, it's only *'waffer-thin'*...

1 Marcel is working on the Eiffel Tower. He is 50 metres up, carrying his bag of tools, when he drops a spanner. The spanner has a mass of 500g.

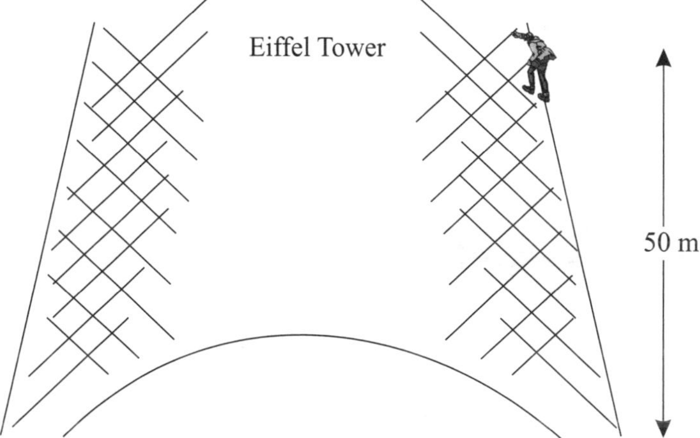

(a) Calculate the potential energy lost by the spanner as it falls to the ground.

....

(2 marks)

(b) How much kinetic energy does the spanner have just before it hits the ground (ignoring air resistance)?

....

(1 mark)

Efficiency

*Most **energy transfers** involve some **losses**, as **heat***

Energy is ONLY USEFUL when it's CONVERTED from one form to another.

1) Useful devices are only useful because they convert energy from one form to another.
2) In doing so, some of the useful input energy is always lost or wasted as heat.
3) The less energy that is wasted, the more efficient the device is said to be.
4) The energy flow diagram is pretty much the same for all devices. You must learn this basic energy flow diagram:

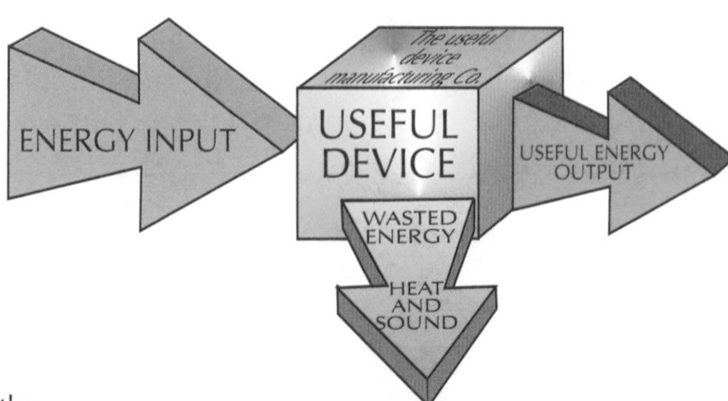

For any specific example you can give more detail about the types of energy being input and output, but remember this:

NO device is 100% efficient and the WASTED ENERGY is always dissipated as HEAT and SOUND.

Electric heaters are the exception to this. They're 100% efficient because all the electricity is converted to 'useful' heat. What else could it become? Ultimately, all energy ends up as heat energy. If you use an electric drill, it gives out various types of energy but they all quickly end up as heat. The wasted energy and the useful energy both end up just warming the air around us. This energy very quickly spreads out into the surroundings and then it becomes harder and harder to make use of it for further energy transfers. That's an important thing to realise.

*Learn all these ways **energy** is **wasted***

Make sure you know all these easy examples — one of them is bound to come up in your Exams.

Device	Energy input	Useful output	Wasted energy
1) Television	Electrical	Light and Sound	Heat
2) Light Bulb	Electrical	Light	Heat
3) Electric Drill	Electrical	Movement	Heat and Sound
4) Hairdrier	Electrical	Heat	Heat and Sound
5) Car Engine	Chemical	Movement	Heat and Sound
6) Horse	Chemical	Movement and ...	Heat and Sound

Efficiency

A machine is a device which turns one type of energy into another.
The efficiency of any device is defined as:

$$\text{Efficiency} = \frac{\text{USEFUL energy OUTPUT}}{\text{TOTAL energy INPUT}}$$

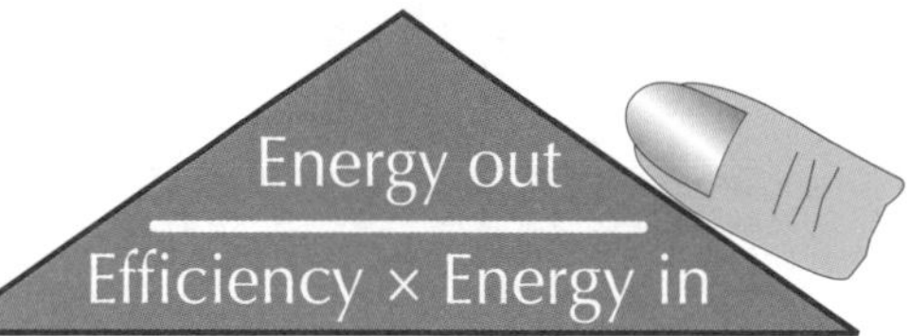

You can give efficiency as a fraction, decimal or percentage. i.e. ¾ or 0.75 or 75%

Efficiency is really simple

1) You find how much energy is supplied to a machine (The Total Energy INPUT).
2) You find how much useful energy the machine delivers (The Useful Energy OUTPUT). They either tell you this directly or they tell you how much it wastes as heat/sound.
3) Either way, you get those two important numbers and then just divide the smaller one by the bigger one to get a value for efficiency somewhere between 0 and 1 (or 0 and 100%). Easy.
4) The other way they might ask it is to tell you the efficiency and the input energy and ask for the energy output. The best way to tackle that is to learn this other version of the formula:

$$\text{USEFUL ENERGY OUTPUT} = \text{Efficiency} \times \text{TOTAL energy INPUT}$$

*Five **important examples** on efficiency for you to **learn***

1

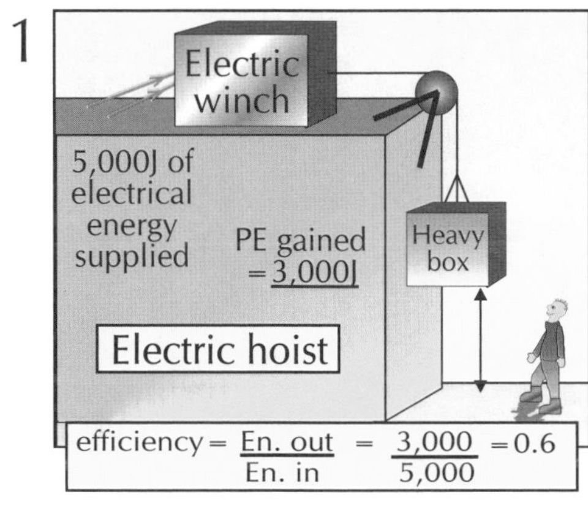

2

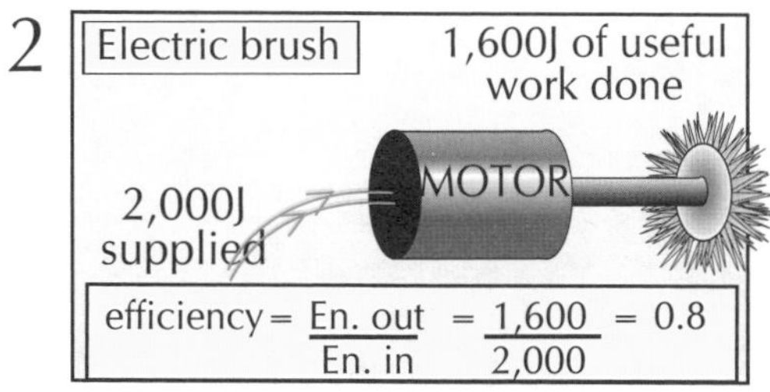

3

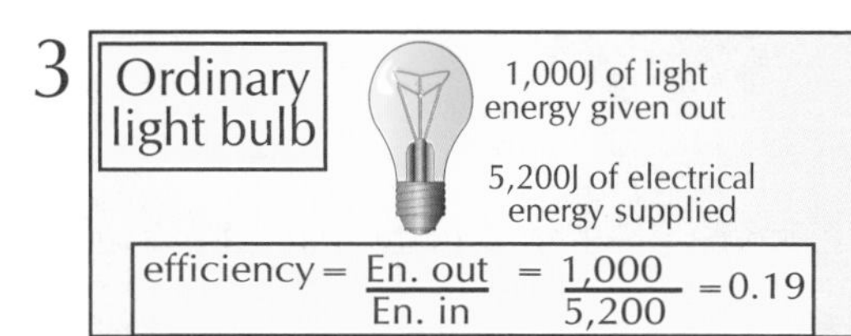

Ordinary light bulb
1,000J of light energy given out
5,200J of electrical energy supplied
efficiency = En. out / En. in = 1,000 / 5,200 = 0.19

4

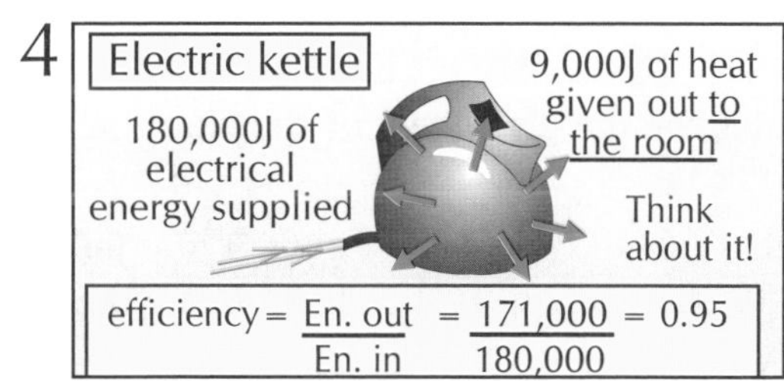

5

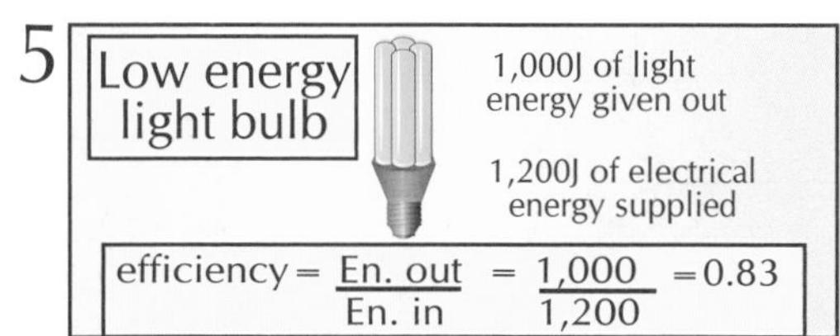

Low energy light bulb
1,000J of light energy given out
1,200J of electrical energy supplied
efficiency = En. out / En. in = 1,000 / 1,200 = 0.83

*Energy is usually lost as **heat***

Efficiency is a very simple concept — divide En. out by En. in and there it is, done.

Warm-Up and Exam Question

Warm-up Questions

1) For each of the energy transfer devices shown below state the useful energy output.

a)  b)  c) 

2) The diagram on the right shows the energy output of an electric drill.
How much energy was put into the drill?

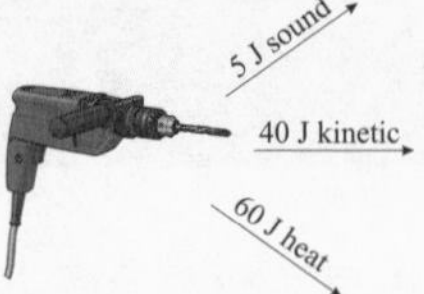

Exam Question

1 An energy transfer diagram for a battery charger is shown below.

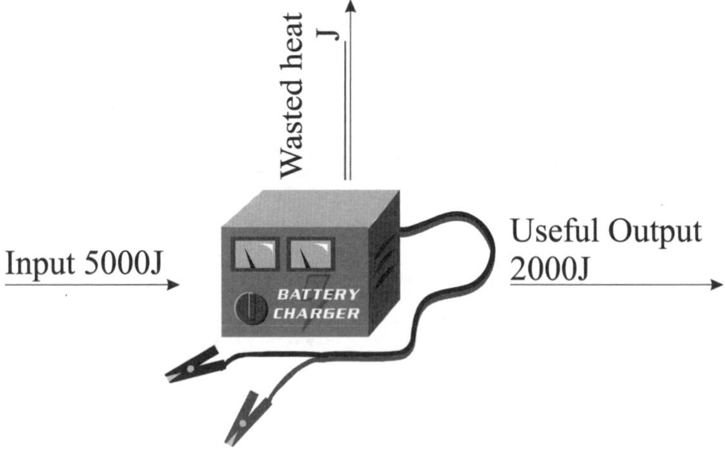

(a) What type of energy is the useful energy output?

(1 mark)

(b) How much energy is wasted as heat?

(1 mark)

(c) Calculate the efficiency of the charging process.

(2 marks)

The battery charger is used to recharge a nickel-cadmium cell.
The fully charged cell is then used in a MiniDisc player.

(d) Complete the energy transfer diagram for the MiniDisc player.

(2 marks)

(e) The MiniDisc player is 12% efficient. Calculate the useful energy output for the MiniDisc player if 2000 J of energy is supplied by the cell.

(2 marks)

Energy Resources

There are twelve different types of energy resource.
They fit into two broad types: renewable and non-renewable.

Non-renewable** energy resources will **run out one day

The non-renewables are the three fossil fuels and nuclear:

1) Coal
2) Oil
3) Natural gas
4) Nuclear fuels (uranium and plutonium)

a) They will all run out one day.
b) They all do damage to the environment.
c) But they provide most of our energy.

Renewable** energy resources will **never run out

The renewables include:

1) Wind
2) Waves
3) Tides
4) Hydroelectric
5) Solar
6) Geothermal
7) Food
8) Biomass (wood)

a) These will never run out.
b) They do not damage the environment (except visually).
c) The trouble is they don't provide much energy and many of them are unreliable because they depend on the weather.

Comparison** of **renewables** and **non-renewables

1) They're quite likely to give you an Exam question asking you to "evaluate" or "discuss" the relative merits of generating power by renewable and non-renewable resources.
2) The way to get the marks is to simply list the pros and cons of each method.
3) Full details are given on the next few pages. However there are some clear generalisations you should definitely learn to help you answer such questions. Make sure you can list these easily from memory:

***Non-renewable** resources (**coal, oil, gas** and **nuclear**):*

Advantages:

1) High output.
2) Reliable output.
3) They don't take up much land.
4) They can match demand for power.

Disadvantages:

1) Very polluting.
2) They involve mining or drilling, and transportation of fuels.
3) They are running out quite quickly.
4) High cost of building & de-commissioning of power stations.

***Renewable** resources (**wind, waves, solar**, etc.):*

Advantages:

1) No pollution.
2) No fuel costs.
(although the initial costs are high).

Disadvantages:

1) Require large areas of land or water and often spoil the landscape ('visual pollution').
2) They don't always deliver when needed — if the weather isn't right, for example.

Energy Resources

Most of the electricity we use is generated from the four NON-RENEWABLE sources of energy (coal, oil, gas and nuclear) in big power stations, which are all pretty much the same apart from the boiler. Learn the basic features of the typical power station shown here and also the nuclear reactor.

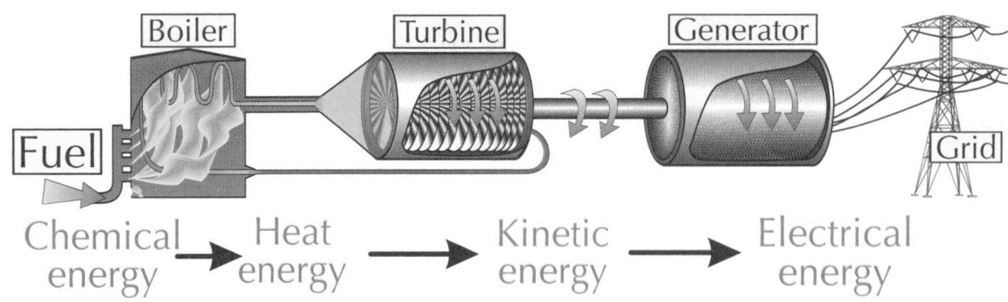

Nuclear reactors are just elaborate boilers

1) A nuclear power station is mostly the same as the one shown above, where heat is produced in a boiler to make steam to drive turbines etc. The difference is in the boiler, as shown here:
2) They take the longest time of all the non-renewables to start up. Natural gas takes the shortest time.

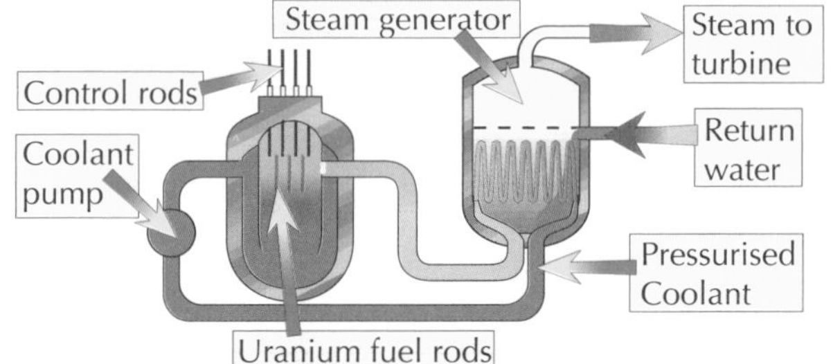

Environmental problems with the use of non-renewables

1) All three fossil fuels, (coal, oil and gas) release CO_2. For the same amount of energy produced, coal releases the most CO_2, followed by oil then gas. All this CO_2 adds to the Greenhouse Effect, causing global warming. Unfortunately there's no feasible way to stop it being released either.
2) Burning coal and oil releases sulphur dioxide which causes acid rain. This is reduced by taking the sulphur out before it's burned or cleaning up the emissions (though you can't do this with coal).
3) Coal mining makes a mess of the landscape, especially 'open-cast mining'.
4) Oil spillages cause serious environmental problems. We try to avoid them, but they'll always happen.
5) Nuclear power is clean but the nuclear waste is very dangerous and difficult to dispose of.
6) Nuclear fuel (i.e. uranium) is cheap but the overall cost of nuclear power is high due to the cost of the power plant and final de-commissioning.
7) Nuclear power always carries the risk of major catastrophe like the Chernobyl disaster.

The non-renewables need to be conserved

1) When the fossil fuels eventually run out we will have to use other forms of energy.
2) More importantly however, fossil fuels (especially crude oil) are also a very useful source of chemicals, which will be hard to replace when they are all gone.
3) To stop the fossil fuels running out so quickly there are two things we can do:

1) Use less energy by being more efficient with it:

(i) Better insulation of buildings,
(ii) Turning lights and other things off when not needed,
(iii) Making everyone drive cars with small engines.

2) Use more of the renewable sources of energy

as detailed on the following pages.

Energy Resources

Wind power — lots of wind turbines

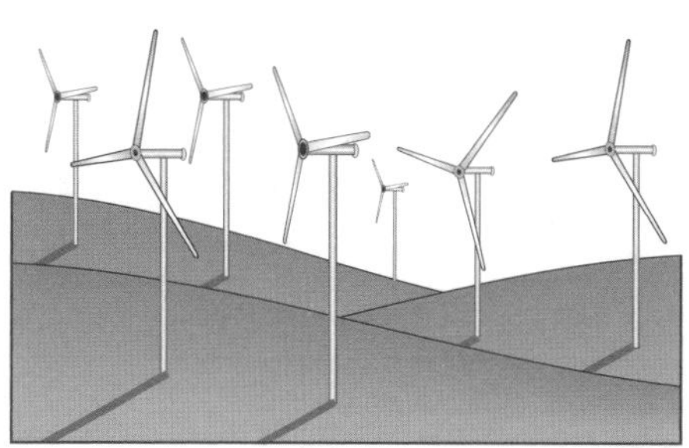

1) This involves putting lots of windmills (wind turbines) up in exposed places like on moors or round coasts.
2) Each wind turbine has its own generator inside it so the electricity is generated directly from the wind turning the blades, which turn the generator. There's no pollution.
3) But they do spoil the view. You need about 5000 wind turbines to replace one coal-fired power station and 5000 of them cover a lot of ground — that wouldn't look very nice at all.
4) There's also the problem of no power when the wind stops, and it's impossible to increase supply when there's extra demand.

Hydroelectricity — flooding valleys

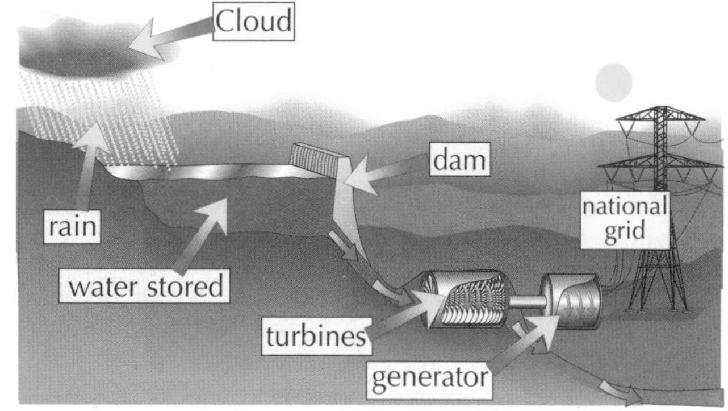

1) Hydroelectric power usually requires the flooding of a valley by building a big dam.
2) Rainwater flows into the reservoir, and is then allowed out through turbines. There is no pollution.
3) There is quite a big impact on the environment due to the flooding of the valley and possible loss of habitat for some species.
4) A big advantage is immediate response to increased demand and there's no problem with reliability except in times of drought — but remember this is *Britain* we're talking about.

Wood burning — environmentally OK

1) It involves the cultivation of fast-growing trees which are then harvested, chopped up and burnt in a power station furnace to produce electricity.

2) The trees are grown as quickly as they are burnt, so they will never run out. This does not apply to the burning of rainforests where the trees take much longer to grow.

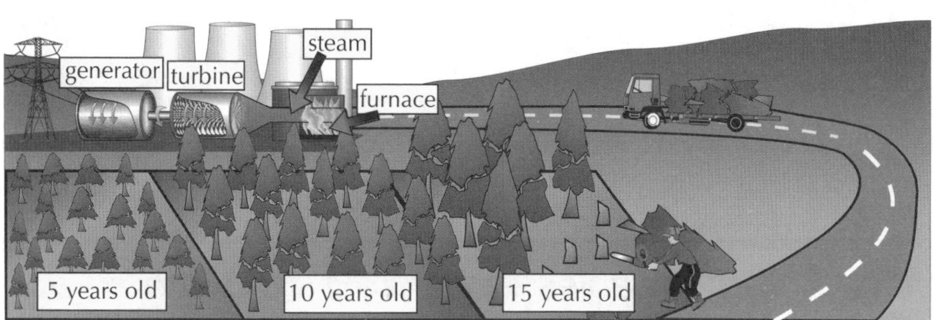

Energy Resources

Wave power — lots of wave converters

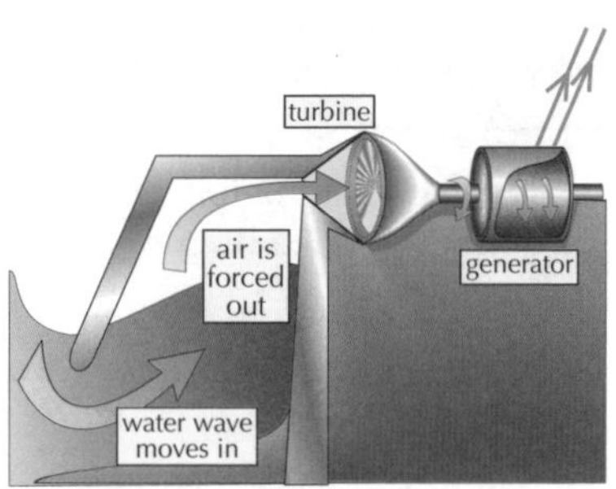

1) You need lots of small wave generators located around the coast.
2) As waves come in to the shore they provide an up and down motion which can be used to drive a generator.
3) They are fairly unreliable, since waves tend to die out when the wind drops.
4) The main environmental problem is spoiling the view.

Tidal barrages — using the sun and moon's gravity

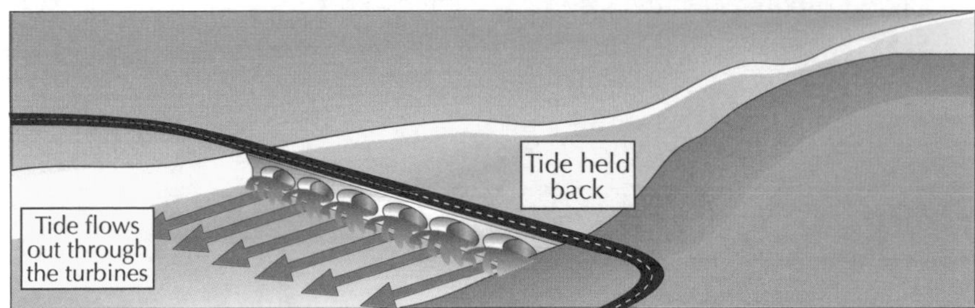

1) Tidal barrages are big dams built across river estuaries with turbines in them.
2) As the tide comes in it fills up the estuary to a height of several metres. This water can then be allowed out through turbines at a controlled speed. It also drives the turbines on the way in.
3) The main problems are preventing free access by boats, spoiling the view and altering the habitat of the wildlife eg: wading birds, sea creatures and beasties who live in the sand.
4) Tides are pretty reliable in the sense that they happen twice a day without fail, and always to the predicted height. The only drawback is that the height of the tide is variable so lower (neap) tides will provide significantly less energy than the bigger spring tides. But tidal barrages are excellent for storing energy ready for periods of peak demand.

Solar energy — solar cells

Sunlight | Electric current | Solar cell | Electrical components

1) SOLAR CELLS generate electric currents directly from sunlight. Initial costs are high but after that the energy is free and running costs almost nil.
2) Despite the cost, solar cells are the best source of energy for calculators and watches which don't use much electricity. Solar power is the only choice for remote places like Antarctica and satellites.
3) Solar cells are the most expensive energy resource per Unit of electricity they produce — except for non–rechargeable batteries, of course.
4) There's absolutely no pollution — and in sunny countries solar power is a very reliable source of energy — but only in the daytime.

Geothermal energy — heat from underground

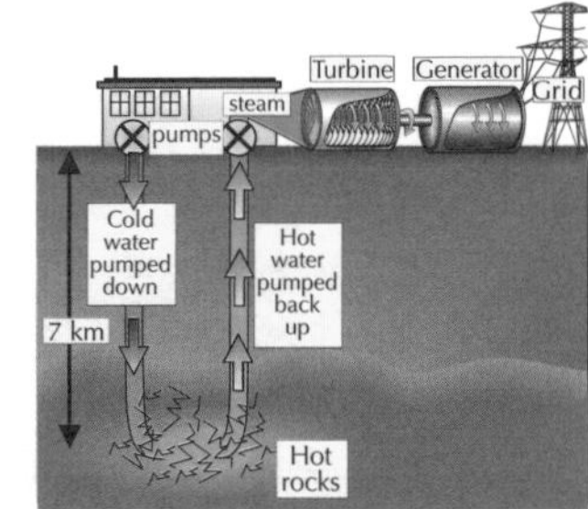

1) This is only possible in places where hot rocks lie quite near the surface. The source of much of the heat is the slow decay of various radioactive elements including uranium deep inside the Earth.
2) Water is pumped down to hot rocks and returns as steam to drive a generator.
3) This is actually free energy with no real environmental problems. The main drawback is the cost of drilling down several km to the hot rocks.

Learn about the non-renewables — before it's too late

There are a lot of details here on sources of energy — an awful lot of details.
Trouble is, in the Exam they could test you on any of them, so I guess you've just got to learn them.

Warm-Up and Exam Questions

Warm-up Questions

1) What is meant by renewable and non-renewable energy sources?
   Give four examples of each type of energy resource.
2) Describe the basic features of a typical power station.
3) Describe briefly how wind power is used to generate electricity.
4) Draw an annotated diagram to show how hydroelectricity works.
5) What is the difference between wave power and tidal power?
6) Describe briefly how electricity is generated from geothermal energy.

Exam Questions

1 Medina is an island in the north Atlantic, which has a cool climate. It does not have any reserves of fossil fuels. The residents are concerned that pipelines and storage terminals would spoil their environment. They have also decided not to use nuclear power.

a) Give three other energy sources the islanders could use.

(3 marks)

b) The islanders should be encouraged to conserve energy.
Suggest two ways in which they could do this.

(2 marks)

c) Nuclear power stations produce very little pollution when they are working properly. Despite this, many people are opposed to them. Explain the main arguments against using nuclear power.

(3 marks)

2 Much has been said in the media about the use of alternative sources of energy. However, most of the electricity in the UK is generated from fossil fuels or nuclear fuel.

a) Why are these fuels used much more than other sources of energy?

(2 marks)

b) Describe the environmental problems associated with the use of fossil fuels.

(4 marks)

3 a) Geothermal energy is used in Iceland to provide energy without badly damaging the environment.

(i) What is the original source of geothermal energy?

(1 mark)

(ii) Geothermal energy is not widely used across the world.
Briefly explain why.

(1 mark)

b) A family living in the north of Scotland is considering having a solar cell put onto their roof to provide part of their household energy requirements.

Other than cost, give one advantage and one disadvantage of using solar power in Scotland.

(2 marks)

Revision Summary for Section Nine

There are three distinct parts to Section Nine. First there's heat transfer, which is trickier to fully understand than most people realise. Then there's a section involving formulae and calculations which covers domestic electricity, gravitational potential and efficiency. Finally, there's the stuff on generating power, which is basically easy but there are lots of details to learn. Make sure you realise the different approach needed for all three bits and structure your revision accordingly.

1) List ten different types of energy, and give twelve different examples of energy transfers.
2) What causes heat to flow from one place to another? What do molecules do as they heat up?
3) Explain briefly the difference between conduction, convection and radiation.
4) Give a strict definition of conduction of heat and say which materials are good conductors.
5) Give a strict definition of convection. Give two examples of natural and forced convection.
6) List five properties of heat radiation. Which kind of objects emit and absorb heat radiation?
7) Which surfaces absorb heat radiation best? Which surfaces emit it best?
8) Describe two experiments to demonstrate the effect of different surfaces on radiant heat.
9) Describe insulation measures which reduce a) conduction b) convection c) radiation.
10) Name some materials that are good insulators and describe some uses for them in the home.
11) List the seven main ways of insulating houses and say which are the most effective and which are the most cost-effective measures. How do you decide on cost-effectiveness?
12) Which types of heat transfer are insulated against in: a) double glazing; b) draught proofing.
13) What is a kilowatt-hour? Calculate how many joules of energy a kilowatt-hour is equivalent to.
14) How many units of electricity (in kWh) would a kettle of power 3000W use in 2 minutes?
15) Write down the formula for gravitational potential energy.
16) Calculate the gain in potential energy of a log of mass 23 kg raised through a height of 8.2 m.
17) A 450 g potato is dropped from a height of 2.4 m. Calculate the speed at which it hits the ground.
18) Sketch the basic energy flow diagram for a typical 'useful device'.
19) What forms does the wasted energy nearly always take?
20) What's the formula for efficiency? What are the three numerical forms suitable for efficiency?
21) Is efficiency really easy or really complicated? Give three worked examples on efficiency.
22) List the four non-renewable sources of energy and say why they are non-renewable.
23) List eight kinds of renewable energy.
24) List the broad advantages and disadvantages of using renewable or non-renewable sources of energy. What does it mean when a question says "Discuss..."?
25) Which kind of resources do we get most of our energy from? Sketch a typical power station.
26) List seven environmental hazards with non-renewables and four ways that we can use less.
27) Give full details of how we can use wind power, including the advantages and disadvantages.
28) Give full details of how a hydroelectric scheme works.
29) Explain the principles of wood-burning for generating electricity. Give the pros and cons.
30) Sketch a wave generator and explain the pros and cons of this as a source of energy.
31) Explain how tidal power can be harnessed. What are the pros and cons of this idea?
32) Explain where geothermal energy comes from. Describe how we can make use of it.
33) Describe how solar cells work. What's the drawback of solar cells? Where are they used?

Electric Circuits

Electricity is pretty bad news if the words don't mean anything to you.
Learn these now:

1) *ELECTRIC CURRENT* — is caused by the flow of electrons round the circuit. Current will only flow through a component if there is a voltage across that component.
(The electrons flow from negative to positive, but conventionally we think of current flowing from positive to negative.)
2) *VOLTAGE* — is the driving force that pushes the current round. Kind of like 'electrical pressure'.
3) *RESISTANCE* — is anything in the circuit which slows the flow down.
4) There's a *BALANCE* — the voltage is trying to push the current round the circuit, and the resistance is opposing it — the relative sizes of the voltage and resistance decide how big the current will be:

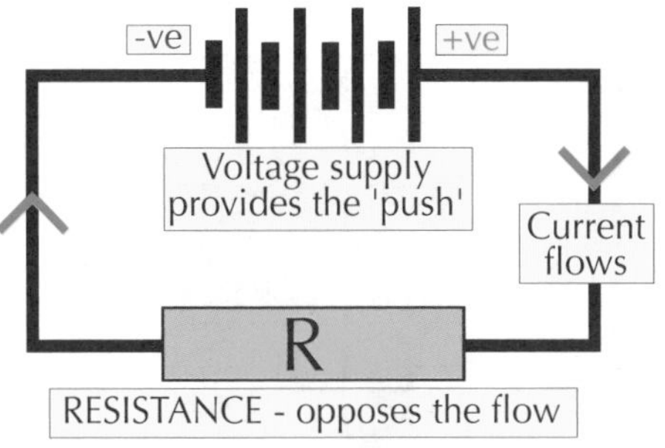

If you increase the VOLTAGE — then MORE CURRENT will flow.
If you increase the RESISTANCE — then LESS CURRENT will flow
(or more voltage will be needed to keep the same current flowing).

The standard test circuit

This is the most basic circuit — so learn it.

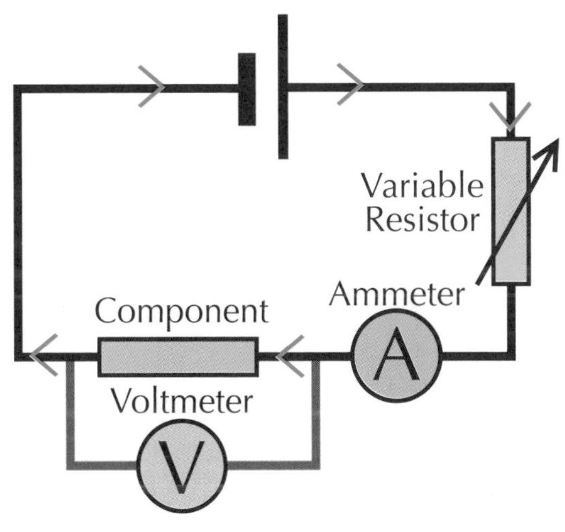

The ammeter

1) Measures the current (in amps) flowing through the component.
2) Must be placed in series.
3) Can be put anywhere in series in the main circuit, but never in parallel like the voltmeter.

The voltmeter

1) Measures the voltage (in volts) across the component.
2) Must be placed in parallel around the component under test — NOT around the variable resistor or the battery.
3) The proper name for 'voltage' is 'potential difference' or 'p.d.'

Five important points

1) This very basic circuit is used for testing components, and for getting V-I graphs (voltage-current graphs) for them.
2) The component, the ammeter and the variable resistor are all in series, which means they can be put in any order in the main circuit. The voltmeter, on the other hand, can only be placed in parallel around the component under test, as shown. Anywhere else is a definite no-no.
3) As you vary the variable resistor it alters the current flowing through the circuit.
4) This allows you to take several pairs of readings from the ammeter and voltmeter.
5) You can then plot these values for current and voltage on a V-I graph (see P.215).

Circuit Symbols

Circuit symbols you should know:

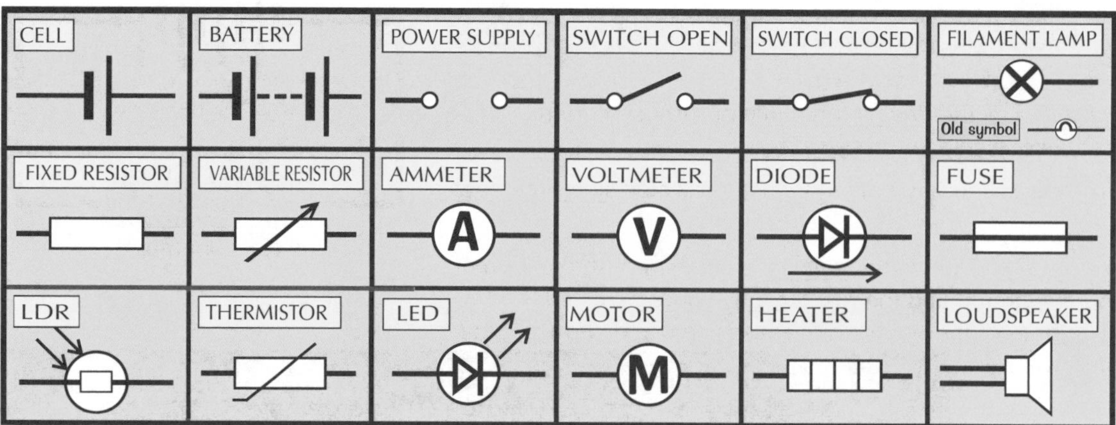

1) Variable resistor

1) A resistor whose resistance can be changed by twiddling a knob or something.
2) The old-fashioned ones are huge coils of wire with a slider on them.
3) They're great for altering the current flowing through a circuit.
   Turn the resistance up, the current drops. Turn the resistance down, the current goes up.

2) 'Semiconductor diode' or just 'diode'

A special device made from semiconductor material such as silicon.
It lets current flow freely through it in one direction, but not in the other (i.e. there's a very high resistance in the reverse direction).
This turns out to be really useful in various electronic circuits.

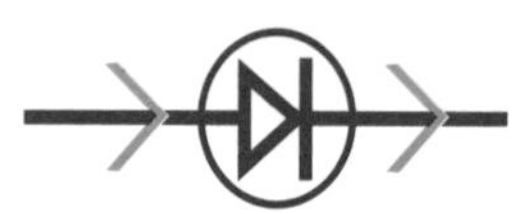

3) Light dependent resistor or 'LDR'

1) In bright light, the resistance falls.
2) In darkness, the resistance is highest.
3) This makes it a useful device for various electronic circuits eg: automatic night lights; burglar detectors.

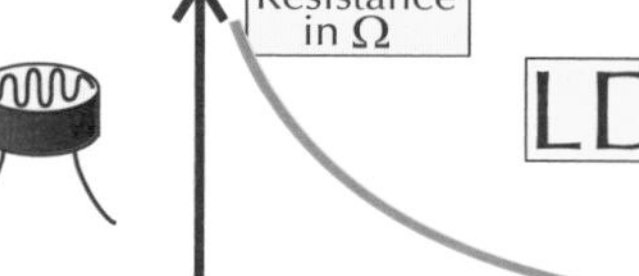

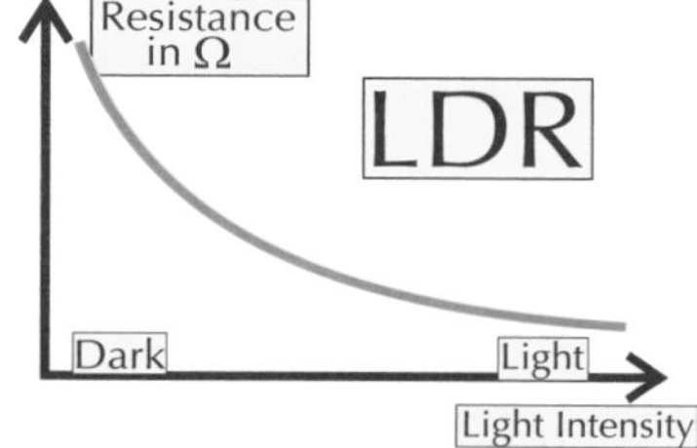

4) Thermistor (temperature-dependent resistor)

1) In hot conditions, the resistance drops.
2) In cool conditions, the resistance goes up.
3) Thermistors make useful temperature detectors, eg: car engine temperature sensors and electronic thermostats.

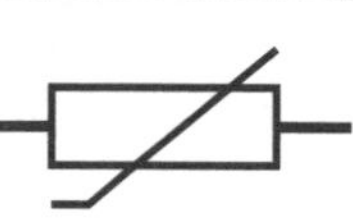

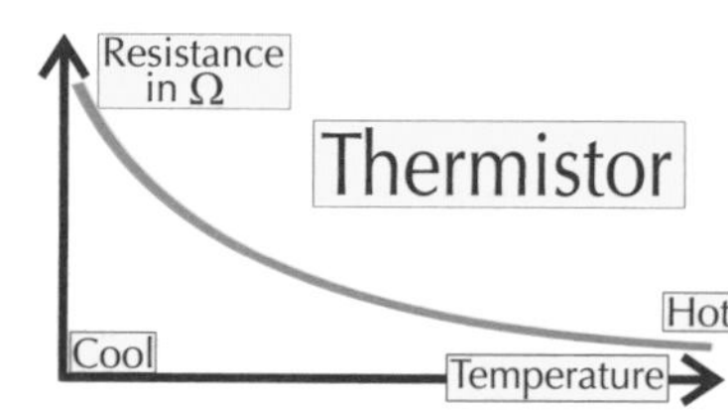

Resistance

Four important voltage-current graphs

V-I graphs show how the current varies as you change the voltage. Learn these four well:

Resistor	Different Wires	Filament Lamp	Diode

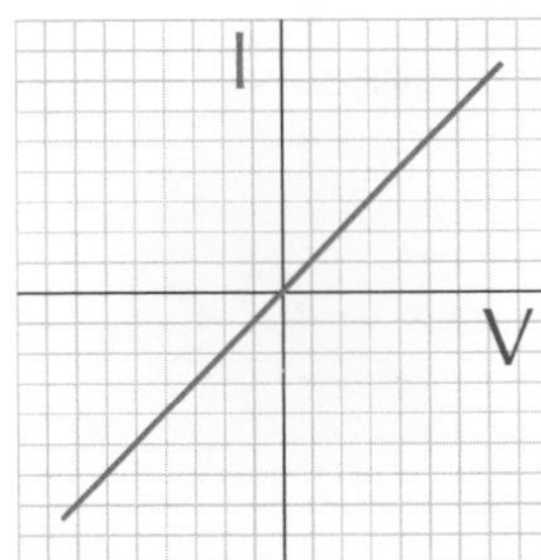

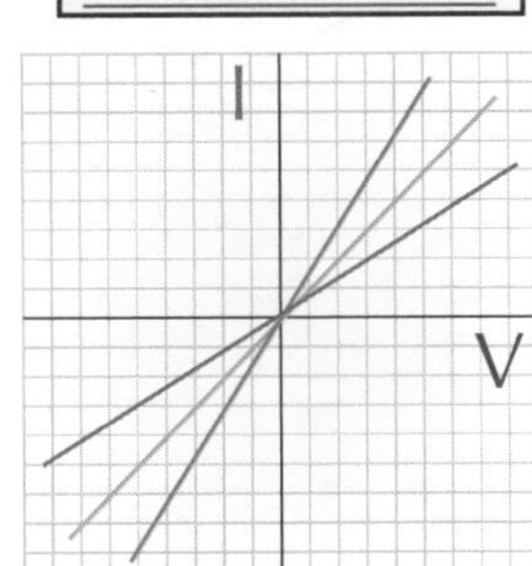

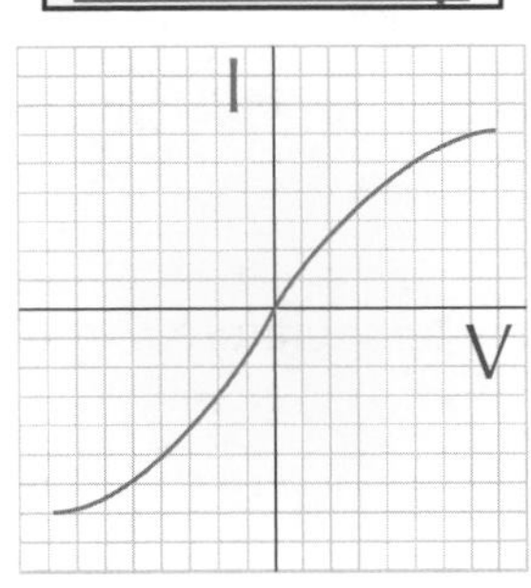

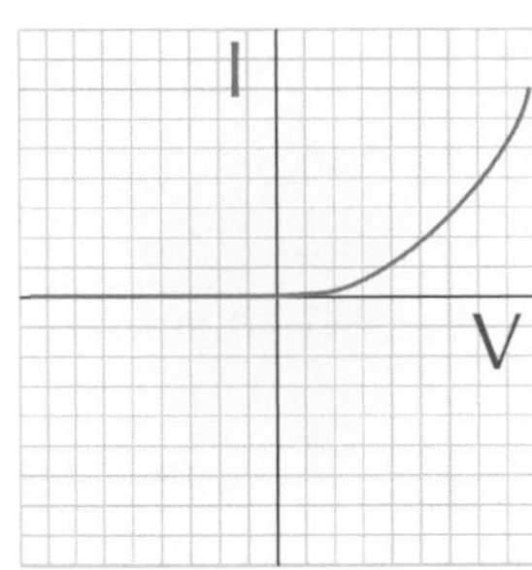

Explaining the graphs above:

Resistor

The current through a resistor (at constant temperature) is proportional to voltage.

Different Wires

Different wires have different resistances, hence the different slopes.

Filament Lamp

As the temperature of the filament increases, the resistance increases, hence the curve.

Diode

Current will only flow through a diode in one direction, as shown.

Calculating resistance: R = V/I, (or R = '1/gradient')

For the straight-line graphs the resistance of the component is steady and is equal to the inverse of the gradient of the line, or '1/gradient'. In other words, the steeper the graph the lower the resistance.

If the graph curves, it means the resistance is changing. In that case R can be found for any point by taking the pair of values (V,I) from the graph and sticking them in the formula R =V/I. Easy.

$$\text{Resistance} = \frac{\text{Potential Difference}}{\text{Current}}$$

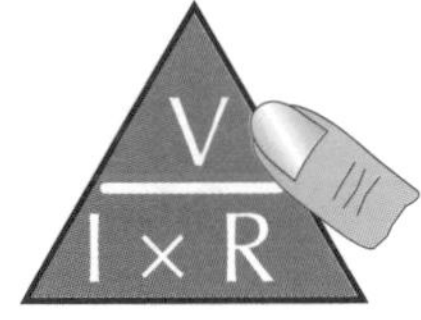

Calculating resistance — an example

EXAMPLE. Voltmeter V reads 6V and resistor R is 4Ω, what is the current through Ammeter A ?

ANSWER. Taking the formula V = I × R, we need to find I so the version we need is I = V/R.
The answer is then: 6/4 which is 1½ A.

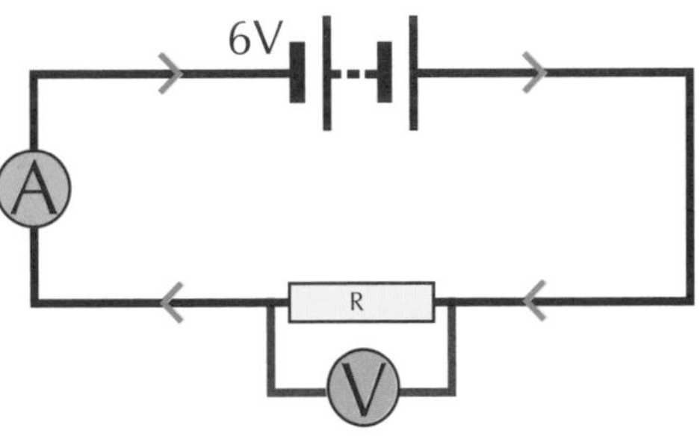

In the end, you'll have to learn this — resistance is futile

Three pages of basic but important details about electrical circuits. You need to know all those circuit symbols as well as the extra details for the special devices and the resistance graphs and calculations. When you think you know it all try covering the page and scribbling it all down.

Warm-Up and Exam Question

Warm-up Questions

1) Complete the blanks in this passage: An electric current is a flow of ________ round a circuit. These particles carry a _______ electric charge. They are pushed out of the ________ pole of the cell and round to the _______ pole, the opposite direction to ________ current. No current will flow through a circuit unless the circuit is ________.
2) Draw the following circuit symbols: a) fuse b) filament lamp c) motor d) thermistor
3) When you increase the resistance of a variable resistor, what happens to the current flowing through it?
4) When you increase the temperature of a filament lamp in a circuit, what happens to its resistance?
5) Give one practical use for each of the following: LED, Light Dependent Resistor, thermistor.

Exam Question

1 Look at the circuit diagram below.

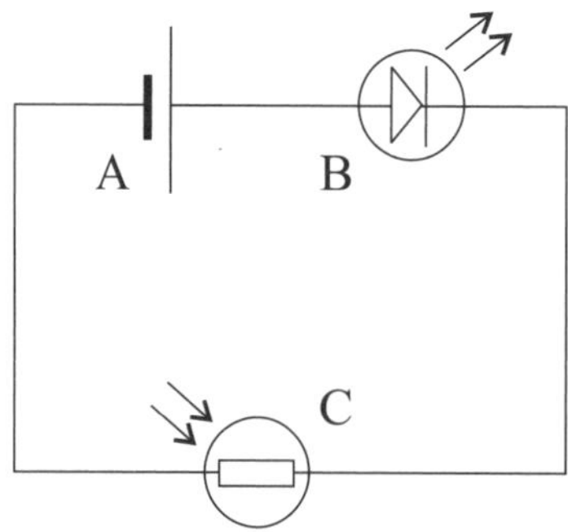

a) (i) Which component (A, B or C) is a Light Dependent Resistor (LDR)?

(ii) Which component is the cell?

(iii) Which component is the Light Emitting Diode (LED)?

(3 marks)

b) A bright light is shone on the circuit.
On the axes below, sketch how the resistance of the LDR will vary as the amount of light falling on it increases.

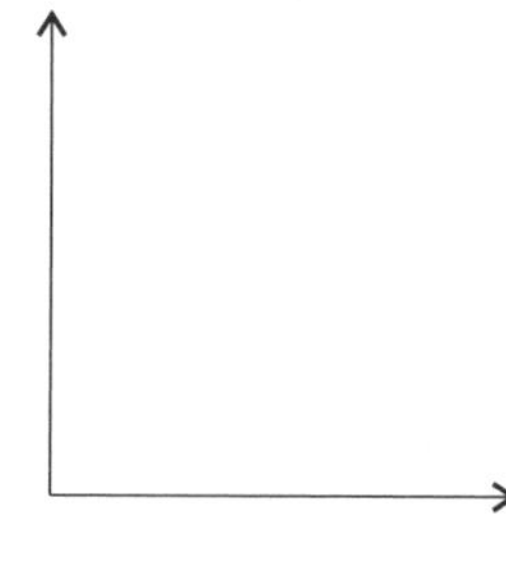

(1 mark)

c) What will the LED do when the light shines?

(1 mark)

d) What would happen to the current in the circuit if the cell were reversed, and why?

(2 marks)

Series Circuits

You need to be able to tell the difference between series and parallel circuits just by looking at them. You also need to know the rules about what happens with both types. Read on.

Series circuits — all or nothing

1) In series circuits, the different components are connected in a line, end to end, between the +ve and –ve of the power supply (except voltmeters, which are always connected in parallel, but don't count as part of the circuit).
2) If you remove or disconnect one component, the circuit is broken and they all stop.
3) This is generally not very handy, and in practice, very few things are connected in series.

1) Potential difference is **shared**:

1) In series circuits the total p.d. of the supply is shared between the various components.
2) The voltages round a series circuit always add up to equal the source voltage:

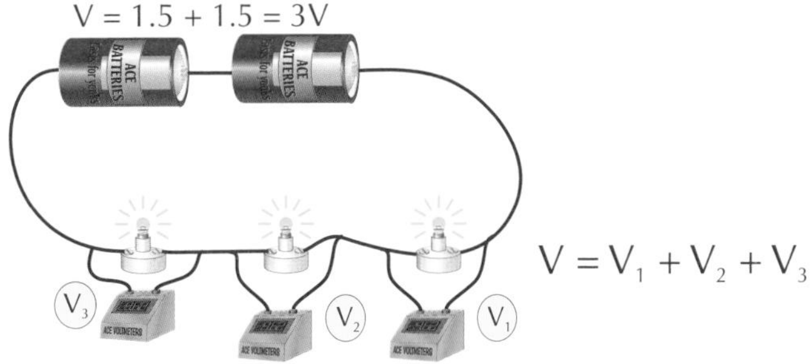

2) Current is the **same** everywhere:

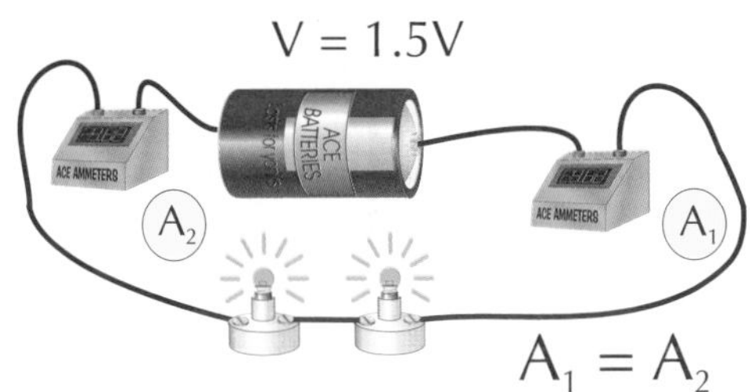

1) In series circuits the same current flows through all parts of the circuit.
i.e. The reading on ammeter A_1 is the same as the reading on ammeter A_2:

$$A_1 = A_2$$

2) The size of the current is determined by the total p.d. of the cells and the total resistance of the circuit: i.e. $I = V/R$

3) Resistance **adds up**:

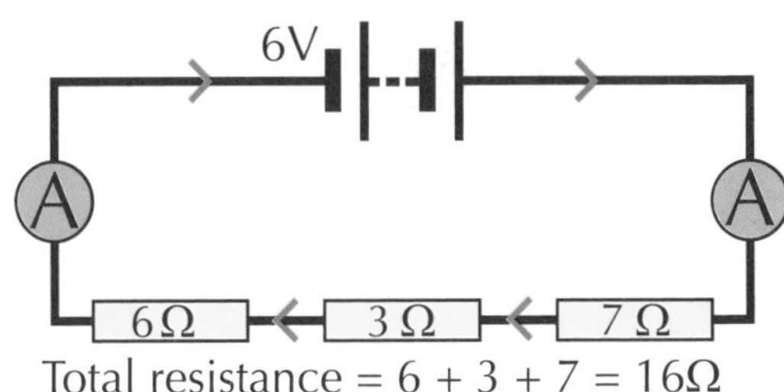

1) In series circuits the total resistance is just the sum of all the resistances:

$$R = R_1 + R_2 + R_3$$

2) The bigger the resistance of a component, the bigger its share of the total potential difference.

Series Circuits

Cell voltages add up:

1) There is a bigger potential difference with more cells in series, provided the cells are all connected the same way.
2) For example when two batteries of voltage 1.5V are connected in series they supply 3V between them.

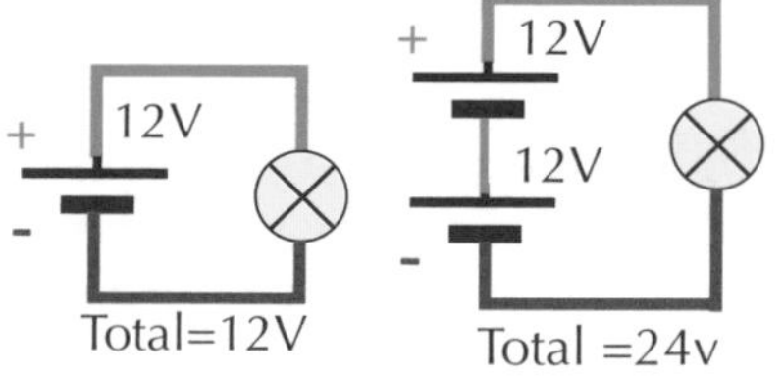

More lamps in series means dimmer lamps:

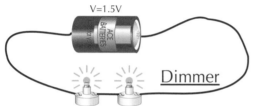

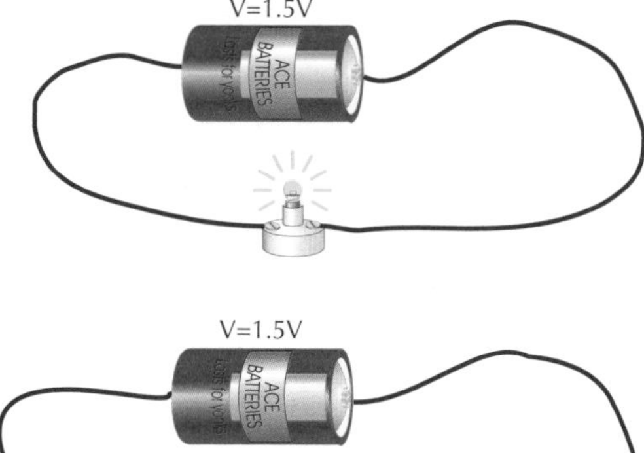

1) If a lamp is connected in series with a battery then it lights up with a certain brightness.
2) However with more lamps (of the same resistance) connected in series then all the lamps will light up at a reduced brightness.
3) This is because in a series circuit the voltage is shared out between the components in the circuit.
4) When a second cell is connected in series with the first then the brightness of the lamps will increase because there is a bigger source p.d.

Example on series circuits

With the circuit opposite the rules on these two pages apply:
Voltages add to equal the source voltage:
1.5 + 2 + 2.5 = 6V
Total resistance is the sum of the resistances in the circuit: 3 + 4 + 5 = 12 ohms
Current flowing through all parts of the circuit
= V/R = 6/12 = 0.5A
(If an extra cell was added of voltage 3V then the voltage across each resistor would increase).

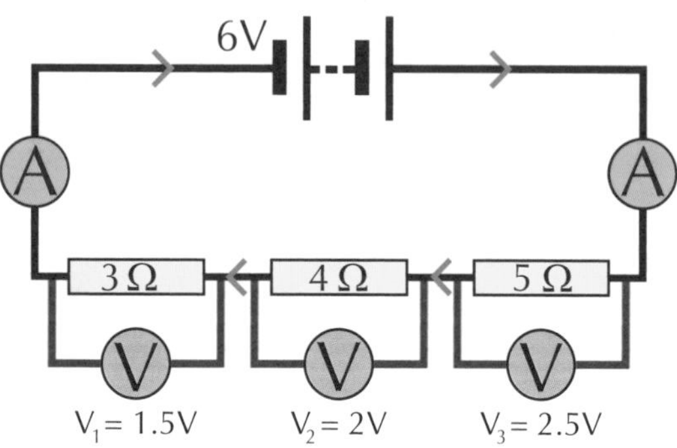

Christmas fairy lights are wired in series

Christmas fairy lights are about the only real-life example of things connected in series, and we all know what a pain they are when the whole lot go out just because one of the bulbs fails.

The only advantage is that the bulbs can be very small because the total 230V is shared out between them, so each bulb only has a small voltage across it.

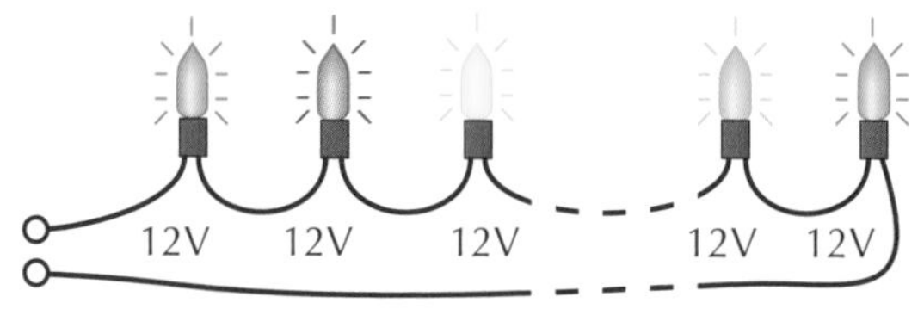

Parallel Circuits

Parallel circuits are much more sensible than series circuits and so they're much more common in real life.

Parallel circuits — *independence* and *isolation*

1) In parallel circuits, each component is separately connected to the +ve and –ve of the supply.
2) If you remove or disconnect one of them, it will hardly affect the others at all.
3) This is obviously how most things must be connected, for example in cars and in household electrics. You have to be able to switch everything on and off separately.

Potential Difference is the *same* across *all* components:

1) In parallel circuits all components get the full source p.d., so the voltage is the same across all components:

$$V_1 = V_2 = V_3$$

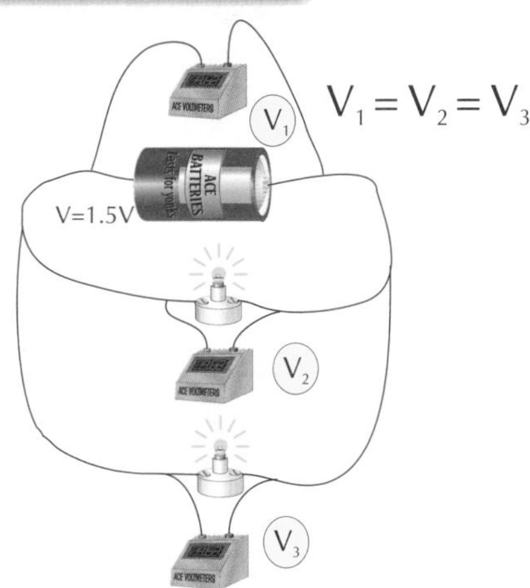

2) This means that identical bulbs connected in parallel will all be at the same brightness. This is totally different from bulbs connected in series.

Current is *shared* between branches:

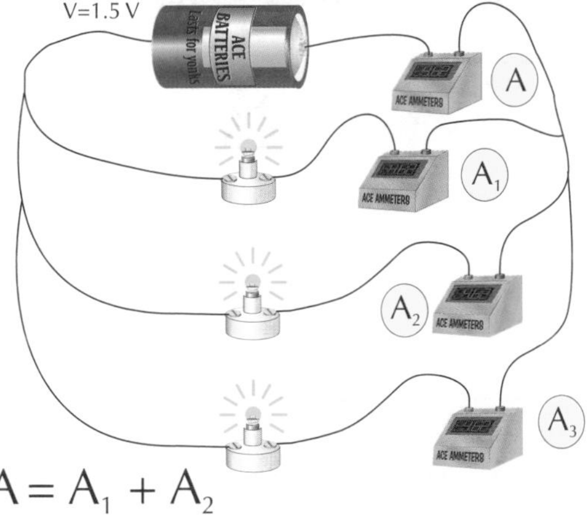

$A = A_1 + A_2$

1) In parallel circuits the total current flowing around the circuit is equal to the total of all the currents in the separate branches.

$$A = A_1 + A_2 + A_3$$

2) In a parallel circuit, there are junctions where the current either splits or rejoins. The total current going into a junction always equals the total currents leaving — fairly obviously.

3) If two identical components are connected in parallel then the same current will flow through each component.

Resistance is *tricky*:

1) The current through each component depends on its resistance. The lower the resistance, the bigger the current that'll flow through it.
2) The total resistance of the circuit is tricky to work out, but it's always less than the branch with the smallest resistance.

Parallel Circuits

Parallel circuits **example**

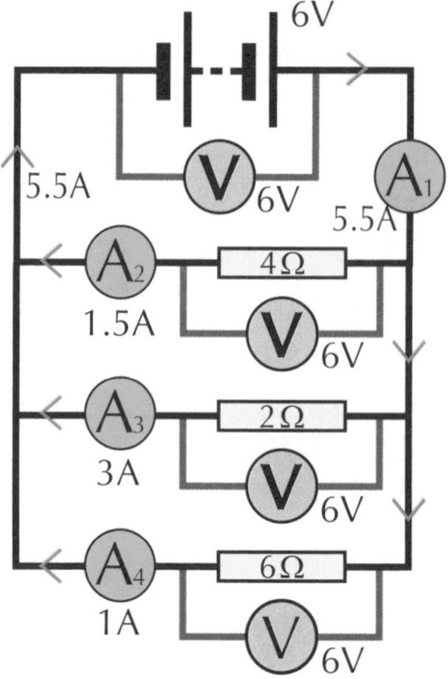

1) The voltage across each resistor in the circuit is the same as the supply voltage. Each voltmeter will read 6V.
2) The current through each resistor will be different because they have different values of resistance.
3) The current through the battery is the same as the sum of the other currents in the branches. ie: $A_1 = A_2 + A_3 + A_4$ $\qquad A_1 = 1.5 + 3 + 1 = 5.5\text{A}$
4) The total resistance in the whole circuit is less than the lowest branch, i.e. lower than 2Ω.
5) The biggest current flows through the middle branch because that branch has the lowest resistance.

Everything **electrical** in a **car** is connected in **parallel**

Parallel connection is essential in a car to give these two features:

1) Everything can be turned on and off separately.
2) Everything always gets the full voltage from the battery.

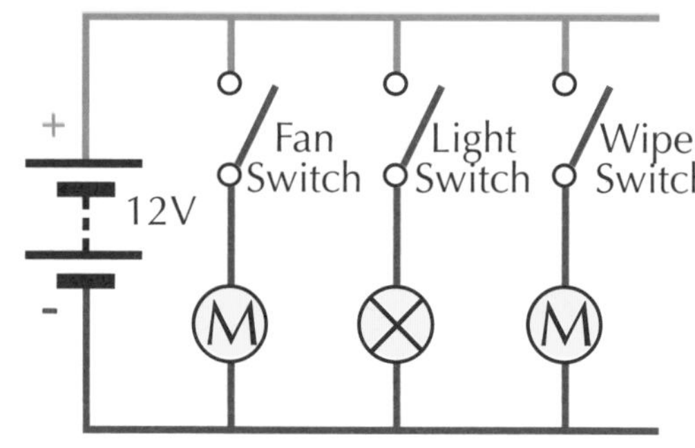

The only slight effect is that when you turn lots of things on the lights may go dim because the battery can't provide full voltage under heavy load. This is normally a very slight effect. You can spot the same thing at home when you turn a kettle on, if you watch very carefully.

Voltmeters and ammeters are exceptions to the rule:

1) Ammeters and voltmeters are exceptions to the series and parallel rules.
2) Ammeters are always connected in series even in a parallel circuit.
3) Voltmeters are always connected in parallel with a component even in a series circuit.

Learn all the details for both types of circuit

Make sure you can scribble down a series circuit and a parallel circuit and know what the advantage(s) and disadvantage(s) are of each. Learn the two examples and the details for connecting ammeters and voltmeters, and also what two features make parallel connection essential in a car.

Warm-Up and Exam Questions

Warm-up Questions

1) A circuit consists of a cell and two resistors connected in series. The potential difference (p.d.) across the cell is 6V. The p.d. across one of the resistors is 4V. What is the p.d. across the other resistor?
2) State whether the resistors or lamps in each of the circuits shown are in series or parallel.

(i) 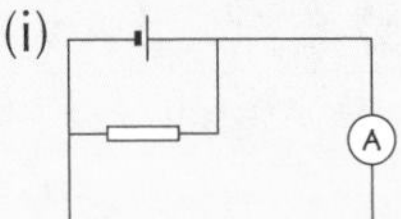

(ii) 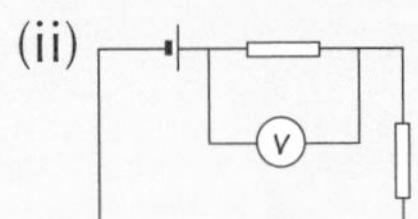

(iii) 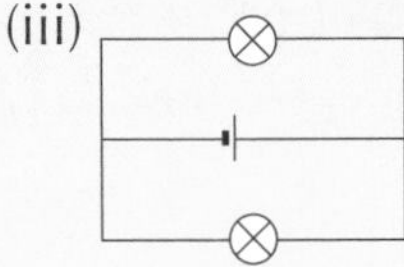

3) Why are series circuits not often used in real life?

Exam Questions

1

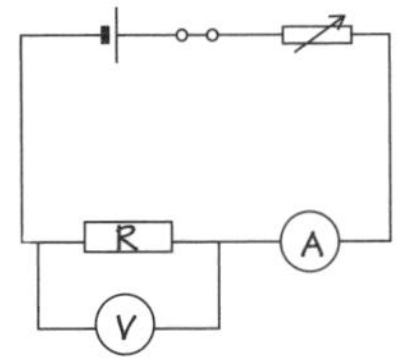

a) Is the ammeter connected in series or parallel?

(1 mark)

b) The potential difference (p.d.) across component R is measured as 4V and the current through it is measured as 2A. What is the resistance of component R?

(1 mark)

c) If the current through component R rose to 2.5A, what would the p.d. across it be?

(1 mark)

d) Would moving the ammeter to another position in the circuit change its reading? Explain your answer.

(1 mark)

e) If the switch were open, how much current would flow through the circuit?

(1 mark)

2 a) In the circuit on the right, if ammeter A_2 reads 2A and resistor R_2 is 6Ω, what is the p.d. across R_2?

(1 mark)

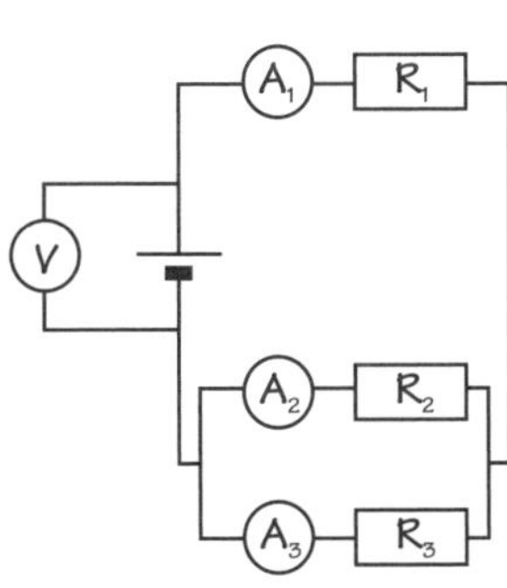

b) If A_3 reads 3A, what is the value of R_3?

(1 mark)

c) What is the current measured at A_1?

(1 mark)

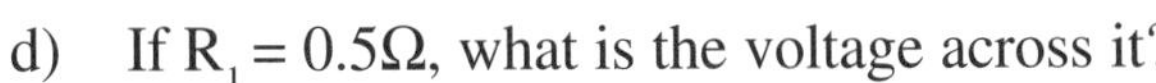

d) If $R_1 = 0.5\Omega$, what is the voltage across it?

(1 mark)

e) What is the voltage across the cell?

(2 marks)

Electric Charge

In the two examples below the charges are free to move in the substance in which they are formed.

In ***metals*** *the* ***current*** *is carried by* ***electrons***

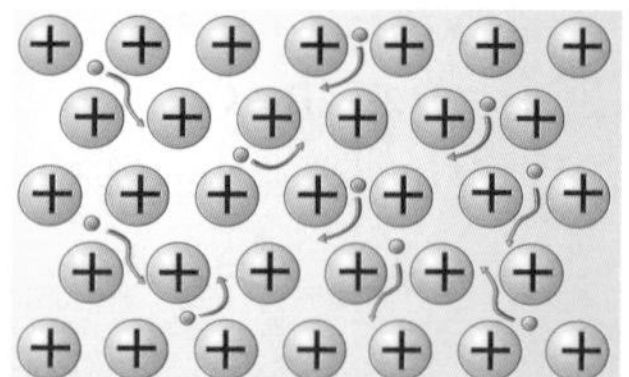

1) Electric current will only flow if there are charges which can move freely.
2) Metals contain a 'sea' of free electrons (which are negatively charged) and which flow throughout the metal.
3) This is what allows electric current to flow so well in all metals.

In ***electrolysis****, current is carried by both* ***+ve and -ve charges***

Copper chloride will not conduct electricity in its normal state as a solid because there are no free charges moving around. In order for copper chloride to conduct electricity then charges need to be able to flow freely in the substance, this is achieved by either dissolving the substance in water or heating it until it is molten. The substance then becomes an electrolyte:

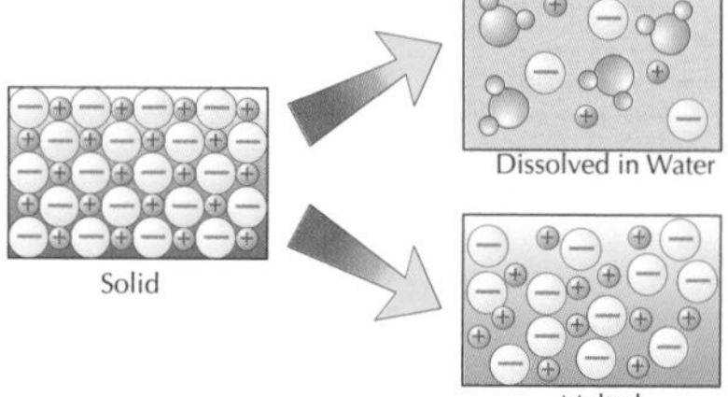

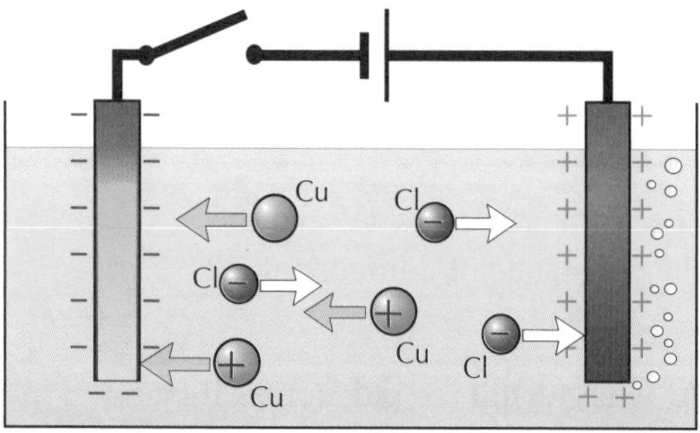

1) Electrolytes are liquids which contain charges which can move freely.
2) When a voltage is applied across the liquid the positive charges move towards the –ve electrode, and the negative charges move towards the +ve electrode. This is an electric current.
3) This process is called electrolysis. The substance is now conducting electricity.
4) Substances form at the electrodes during this process, for example in copper chloride solution, copper forms at the negative electrode.

This build up of matter increases when:

1) The current increases.
2) The current flows for a longer period.

Don't forget: *more current means more charge* — which gives us this important rule:

The amount of matter deposited is proportional to the amount of charge that has flowed.

EXAMPLE:
1200 coulombs of charge flowing through copper chloride solution produces 0.5g of copper at the negative electrode.

How much copper is produced by:

a) A 1 amp current flowing for 10 minutes?
b) A 4 amp current flowing for 5 minutes?

ANSWER:
a) First find the amount of charge that has flowed in 10 minutes:
Charge = Current × time (Q=I×t). Q = 1 × 600 = 600 coulombs.
This is half the original charge that flowed and so the matter deposited is half the original amount, i.e. 0.25g.
b) Q = 4 × 300 = 1200 coulombs.
This is the same amount of charge that originally flowed so 0.5g of copper forms at the negative electrode.

Static Electricity

Static electricity is all about charges which are not free to move. This causes them to build up in one place and it often ends with a spark or a shock when they do finally move.

1) Build up of **static** is caused by **friction**

1) When two insulating materials are rubbed together, electrons will be scraped off one and dumped on the other.
2) This'll leave a positive static charge on one and a negative static charge on the other.
3) Which way the electrons are transferred depends on the two materials involved.
4) Electrically charged objects attract small objects placed near them. (You must've tried rubbing a balloon on a woolly jumper then making someone's long hair stick to it.)
5) The classic examples are polythene and acetate rods being rubbed with a cloth duster, as shown in the diagrams on the right:

With the polythene rod, electrons move from the duster to the rod.

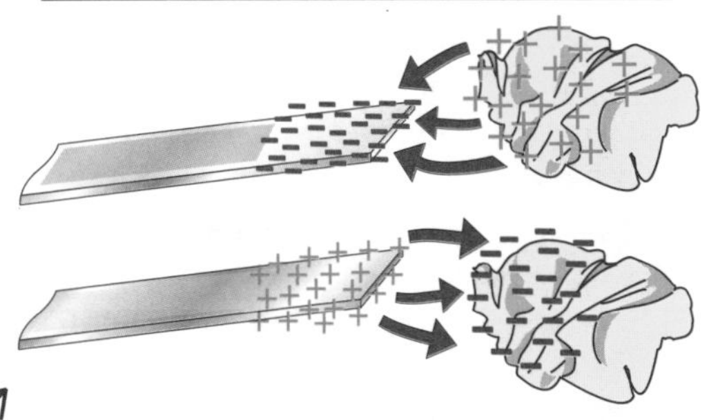

With the acetate rod, electrons move from the rod to the duster.

2) **Only electrons move** — never the positive charges

Watch out for this in Exams. Both +ve and –ve electrostatic charges are only ever produced by the movement of electrons (which are negative of course). The positive charges definitely do not move. A positive static charge is always caused by electrons moving away elsewhere — don't forget that.

A charged conductor can be discharged safely by connecting it to earth with a metal strap. The electrons flow down the strap to the ground if the charge is negative and flow up the strap from the ground if the charge is positive.

3) **Like** charges repel, **opposite** charges attract

This is easy and fairly obvious.
Two things with opposite electric charges are attracted to each other.
Two things with the same electric charge will repel each other.
These forces get weaker the further apart the two things are.

4) As **charge** builds up, so does the **voltage** — causing **sparks**

The greater the charge on an isolated object, the greater the voltage between it and the Earth. If the voltage gets big enough there's a spark which jumps across the gap. High voltage cables can be dangerous for this reason. Big sparks have been known to leap from overhead cables to earth. But not often.

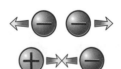

'ZAP!'

Static Electricity

They like asking you to give *quite detailed examples* in Exams. Make sure you *learn all these details*.

Uses *of* ***Static*** *electricity*

1) ***Inkjet printer****:*

1) Tiny droplets of ink are forced out of a *fine nozzle*, making them *electrically charged*.
2) The droplets are *deflected* as they pass between two metal plates. A *voltage* is applied to the plates — one is *negative* and the other is *positive*.
3) The droplets are *attracted* to the plate of the *opposite* charge and *repelled* from the plate with the *same* charge.
4) The *size* and *direction* of the voltage across each plate changes so each droplet is deflected to hit a *different place* on the paper.
5) Loads of tiny dots make up your printout.

+ve
jet of ink
-ve
printout

2) ***Photocopier****:*

1) The *metal plate* is electrically charged. An image of what you're copying is projected onto it.
2) Whiter bits of the thing you're copying make *light* fall on the plate and the charge *leaks away*.
3) The charged bits attract *black powder*, which is transferred onto paper.

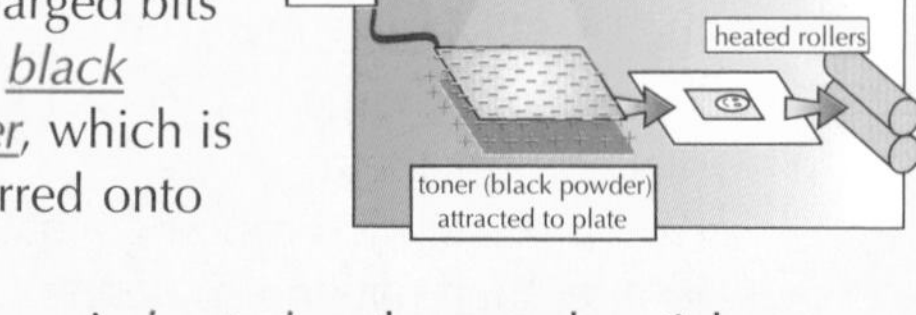

4) The paper is *heated* so the powder sticks.
5) Voilà, a photocopy of your piece of paper (or whatever else you've shoved in there).

3) There are a load of other uses...

...such as spray painting and dust removal in chimneys.

Minor Problems *with* ***Static*** *electricity*

1) ***Car shocks***

Air rushing past your car can give it a +ve charge.

When you get out and touch the door it gives you a real buzz — in the Exam make sure you say "electrons flow from earth, through you, to neutralise the +ve charge on the car".

Some cars have conducting rubber strips which hang down behind the car. This gives a safe discharge to earth.

2) ***Clothing crackles***

When synthetic clothes are dragged over each other (like in a tumble drier) or over your head, electrons get scraped off, leaving static charges on both parts.

That leads to the inevitable — attraction (they stick together) and little sparks / shocks as the charges rearrange themselves.

Major Problems *with* ***Static*** *electricity*

1) ***Lightning***

Rain droplets fall to Earth with positive charge. This creates a huge voltage and a big spark.

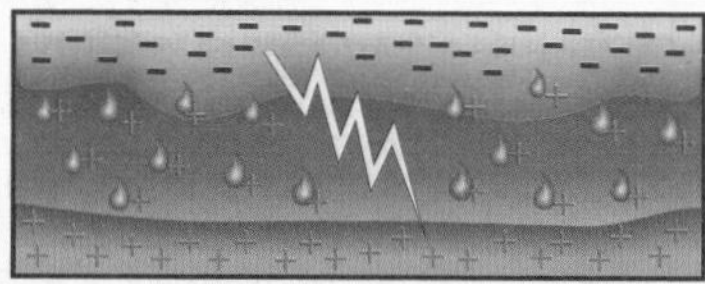

2) ***Grain shoots, paper rollers*** *and potential* ***fuel filling disasters****:*

1) As fuel flows out of a filler pipe, or paper drags over rollers, or grain shoots out of pipes, then static can build up.
2) This can easily lead to a spark — which in dusty or fumey places could cause an explosion.
3) The solution: make the nozzles or rollers out of metal so that the charge is conducted away, instead of building up.
4) It's also good to have earthing straps between the fuel tank and the fuel pipe.

Energy Transfer in Circuits

You can look at electrical circuits in two ways. The first is in terms of a voltage pushing the current round and the resistances opposing the flow, as on P.213. The other way of looking at circuits is in terms of energy transfer. Learn them both and be ready to tackle questions about either.

Energy is transferred from cells and other sources

Anything which supplies electricity is also supplying energy.
So cells, batteries, generators etc. all transfer energy to components in the circuit.
Learn these as examples:

MOTION: motors	*LIGHT*: light bulbs	*HEAT*: hairdriers/kettles	*SOUND*: speakers

Kinetic Energy — Light Energy — Cell provides the energy — Heat Energy — Sound Energy

All resistors produce heat when a current flows through them

1) This is important. Whenever a current flows through anything with electrical resistance (which is pretty well everything) then some electrical energy is converted into heat energy.
2) The more current that flows, the more heat is produced.

Calculating electrical power and fuse ratings

1) The standard formula for electrical power is: P=V×I
2) Most electrical goods indicate their power rating and voltage rating. To work out the fuse needed, you need to work out the current that the item will normally use. That means using 'P=VI', or rather, 'I=P/V'.
   Example: *A hairdrier is rated at 240V, 1.1kW. Find the fuse needed.*
   ANSWER: I = P/V =1100/240 = 4.6A. Normally, the fuse should be rated just a little higher than the normal current, so a 5 amp fuse is ideal for this one.

Charge, voltage and energy change

Q
I× t

1) Current is the flow of electrical charge around a circuit.
   When current (I) flows past a point in a circuit for a length of time (t) then charge (Q) has passed. This is given by the formula: Q = It
   More charge passes around the circuit when a bigger current flows.
2) When electrical charge (Q) goes through a change in voltage (V), then energy (E) is transferred.
   Energy is supplied to the charge at the power source to raise it through a voltage. The charge gives up this energy when it falls through any voltage drop in components elsewhere in the circuit.
   The formula is simply: E = QV
3) The bigger the change in voltage (or p.d.), the more energy is transferred for a given amount of charge passing through the circuit.
   That means that a battery with a bigger voltage will supply more energy to the circuit for every coulomb of charge which flows round it, because the charge is raised up 'higher' at the start (see above diagram) — and as the diagram shows, more energy will be dissipated in the circuit too.

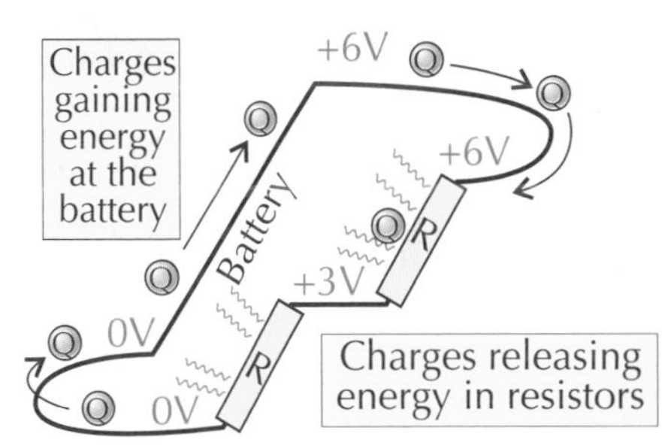

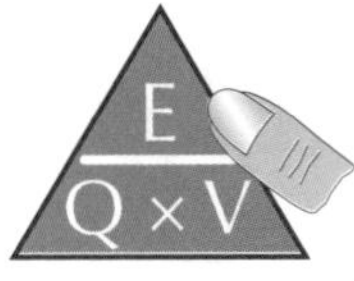

Loads of details to learn

That's quite a big section — packed with information. Write a mini-essay on electrolysis, including an example. Then write a mini-essay on static electricity, explaining the situations where it's useful and where it's a problem. And last but not least learn all the tricky details on this page. Cover and scribble.

Warm-Up and Exam Questions

Warm-up Questions

1) What usually causes a build-up of static electricity?
2) There are three types of particle found inside an atom — neutrons, electrons and protons.
   a) From the three types of particle above, name the one that has a positive electric charge.
   b) Which type of particle has to move in order to create a build up of static electricity?
3) Name two devices used in an office which rely on static electricity to work.
4) Describe two real-life situations in which a build-up of static electricity can be dangerous.
5) Which is the correct statement about the voltage of a circuit?
   a) Voltage = resistance per unit charge
   b) Voltage = resistance per second
   c) Voltage = energy transferred per second
   d) Voltage = energy transferred per unit charge

Exam Questions

1 a) (i) In a metal wire, what type of particles carry the electric current?

(1 mark)

(ii) Describe in terms of moving charged particles what is happening in a metal wire when the ends are connected to the positive and negative poles of an electric cell.

(2 marks)

(iii) If the voltage across the cell is increased, what happens to the current?

(1 mark)

b) Describe how the electric current flows in an electrolyte.

(2 marks)

2 Paul holds a polythene rod in his hand and rubs it with a duster.
It becomes negatively charged.

a) What has happened in terms of the movement of subatomic particles to make the rod negatively charged?

(2 marks)

b) State whether the electric charge on the duster is now positive, negative or zero.
Explain your answer.

(2 marks)

c) Janine now holds a metal rod in her hand and rubs it with the duster.
The rod does not become charged. Why not?

(2 marks)

3 a) The following electrical devices can all convert electrical energy into other forms of energy. Write down which type of energy is the main output of each of the devices below.
(i) Buzzer (ii) Kettle (iii) Resistor (iv) Motor (v) Lamp

(5 marks)

b) (i) Write down the formula that shows how much energy E is transferred when a charge Q undergoes a change of voltage V.

(1 mark)

(ii) Does the charge gain or lose electrical energy when it passes through a resistor?

(1 mark)

Mains Electricity

Hazards in the home — eliminate them before they eliminate you

A likely Exam question will show you a picture of a home but with various electrical hazards in the picture, and they'll ask you to list all the hazards.
This should be mostly common sense, but it will definitely help if you've already learnt this list:

1) Long cables or frayed cables.
2) Cables in contact with something hot or wet.
3) Pets or children.
4) Water near sockets, or shoving things into sockets.
5) Damaged plugs, or too many plugs into one socket.
6) Lighting sockets without bulbs in.
7) Appliances without their covers on.

Plugs and cables — learn the safety features

Get the wiring right:

1) The right coloured wire to each pin, and firmly screwed in.
2) No bare wires showing inside the plug.
3) Cable grip tightly fastened over the cable outer layer.

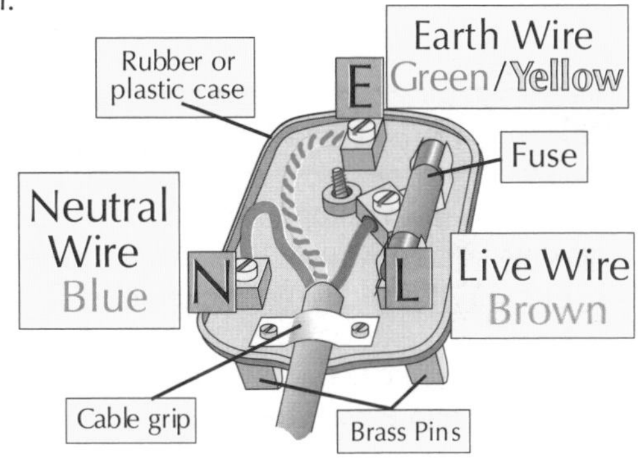

Plug features:

1) The metal parts are made of copper or brass because these are very good conductors.
2) The case, cable grip and cable insulation are all made of plastic because this is a really good insulator and is flexible too.
3) This all keeps the electricity flowing where it should.

Plug wiring errors

They're pretty keen on these diagrams in the Exam so make sure you know them.
The diagram above shows how to wire a plug properly.
Shown below are examples of how not to wire a plug.
A badly wired plug is very dangerous so learn these diagrams.

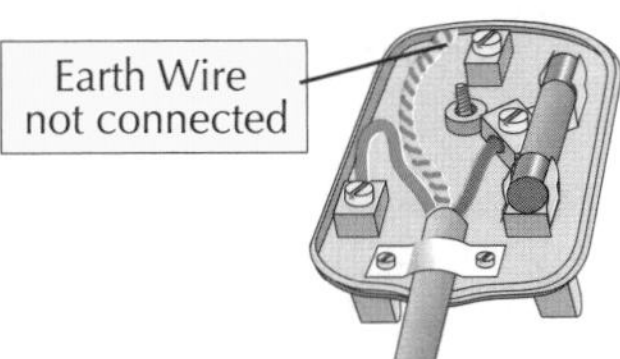

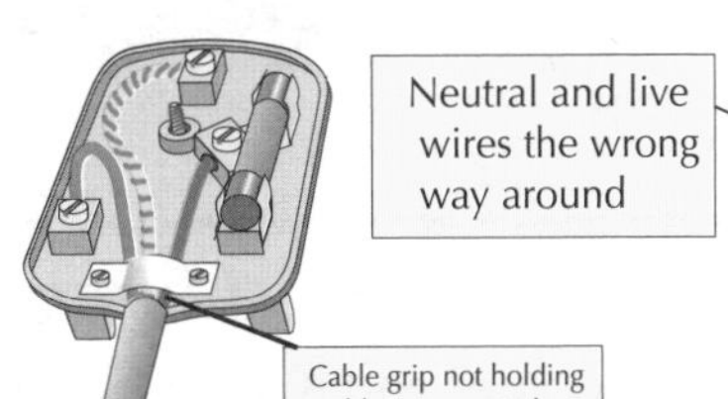

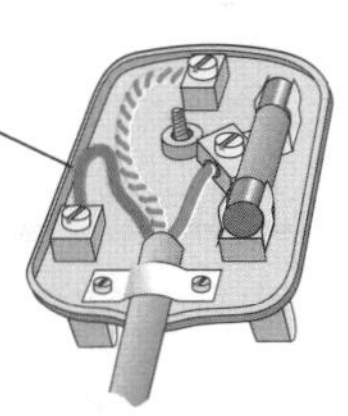

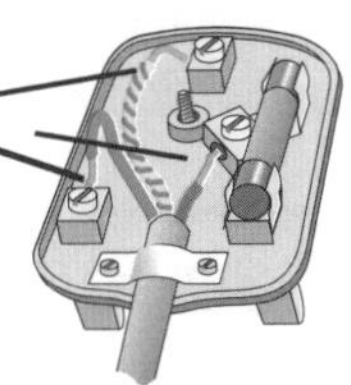

Mains Electricity

Mains supply is AC, battery supply is DC

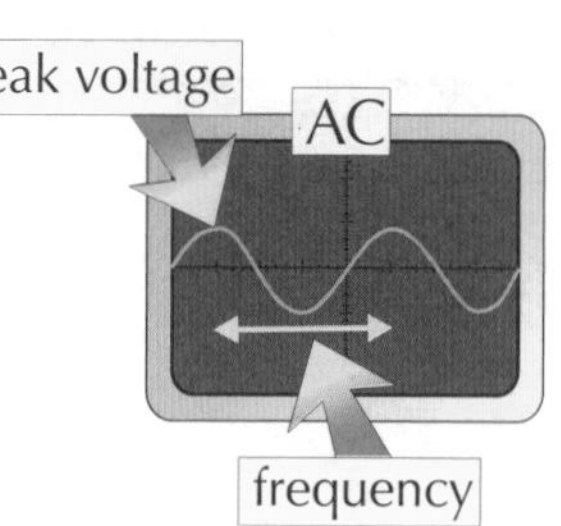
peak voltage
AC
frequency

1) The U.K. mains supply is 230 – 240 volts.
2) It is an AC supply (alternating current), which means the current is constantly changing direction. The CRO trace is always a wave.
3) The frequency of the AC mains supply is 50 cycles per second or 50Hz.

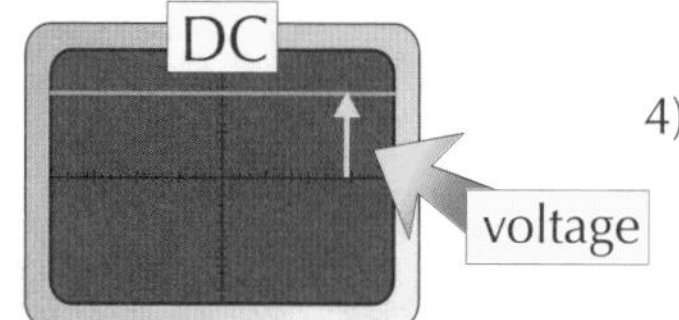
DC
voltage

4) By contrast, cells and batteries supply direct current (DC). This just means that the current keeps flowing in the same direction. The CRO trace is a horizontal line.

You need to learn these CRO traces.

Fuses prevent electric shocks

1) To prevent surges of current in electrical circuits and danger of electric shocks, a fuse is normally placed in the circuit.
2) If the current in the circuit gets too big (bigger than the fuse rating), the fuse wire heats up and breaks (the fuse blows), breaking the circuit, thus preventing any electric shocks.
3) Fuses should be rated as near as possible but just higher than the normal operating current of the appliance.
4) The fuse should always be the same value as the manufacturer recommends.

Earthing prevents fires and shocks

The LIVE WIRE in a mains supply alternates between a HIGH +VE AND –VE VOLTAGE.
The NEUTRAL WIRE is always at 0 V. Electricity normally flows in and out through the live and neutral wires only. The EARTH WIRE and fuse (or circuit breaker, see P.233) are just for safety and work together like this:

1) The earth pin is connected to the case via the earth wire (the yellow and green wire).
2) If a fault develops in which the live somehow touches the metal case, then because the case is earthed, a big current flows in through the live, through the case and out down the earth wire.
3) This surge in current blows the fuse (or trips the circuit breaker), which cuts off the live supply. This prevents electric shocks from the case.

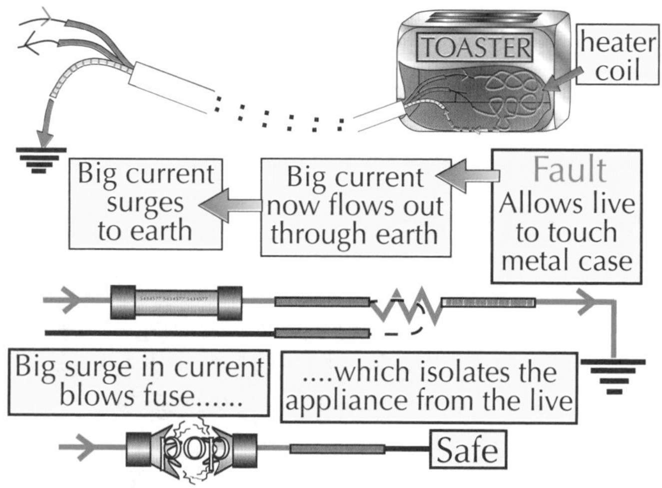
TOASTER
heater coil
Big current surges to earth
Big current now flows out through earth
Fault Allows live to touch metal case
Big surge in current blows fuse......
....which isolates the appliance from the live
POP
Safe

All appliances with metal cases must be 'earthed' to avoid the danger of electric shock. 'Earthing' just means the metal case must be attached to the earth wire in the cable.

230 volts is pretty dangerous — safety's a big issue

Make sure you can list all those hazards in the home, and that you know all the details for wiring a plug. You also need to be able to spot when a plug is not wired properly and how to fix it. Once you've learnt that, draw the CRO traces for AC and DC then write a mini-essay on earthing and fuses.

Warm-Up and Exam Question

Warm-up Questions

1) Describe three possible electrical hazards in the home that involve electrical cables.
2) State the correct colours for the following wires in a plug:
   a) neutral   b) earth   c) live
3) Does the National Grid use alternating or direct current?

Exam Question

1 a) A careless student is wiring a plug to operate a kettle rated at 2000W for a voltage of 240V. He connects the brown wire to the live terminal, the blue wire to the earth terminal and the green and yellow wire to the neutral terminal.

What was wrong with the way he wired the plug?

....

(2 marks)

b) Another student corrects the wiring, and fits a 5A fuse.

(i) Explain what happens when he tries to boil the kettle, and why.

....

(1 mark)

(ii) Which would have been a more suitable fuse to use, a 3A one or a 13A one?

....

(1 mark)

c) What is the most important reason for making the casing of the plug from plastic?

....

(1 mark)

d) What is the danger from a live wire within an appliance, such as a toaster, coming into contact with its metal case?

....

(1 mark)

e) Explain how this danger can be prevented using the earth wire in combination with a fuse. Start by saying what the earth wire must be connected to. Include an explanation of which wire must be fused, and why it is that one.

....

....

....

(3 marks)

Magnets

There's a proper definition of a magnetic field which you really ought to learn:

A magnetic field is a region where magnetic materials (like iron and steel) and also wires carrying currents experience a force acting on them.

*Learn all these **magnetic field diagrams**, arrow-perfect*

They're real likely to give you one of these diagrams to do in your Exam.
So make sure you know them, especially which way the arrows point — always from N to S.

***Bar** magnet*

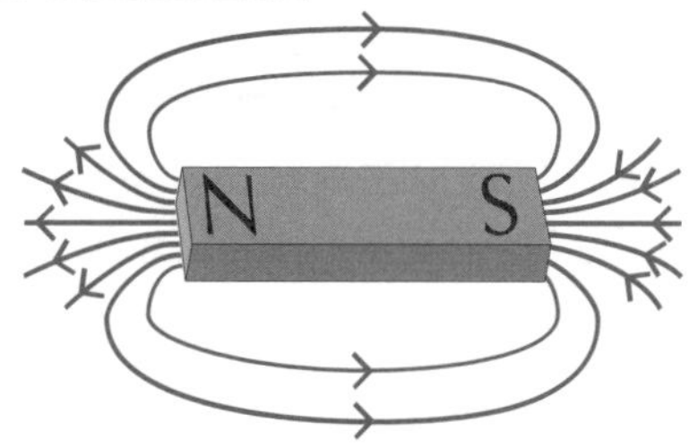

Solenoid

Same field as a bar magnet outside. Strong and uniform field on the inside.

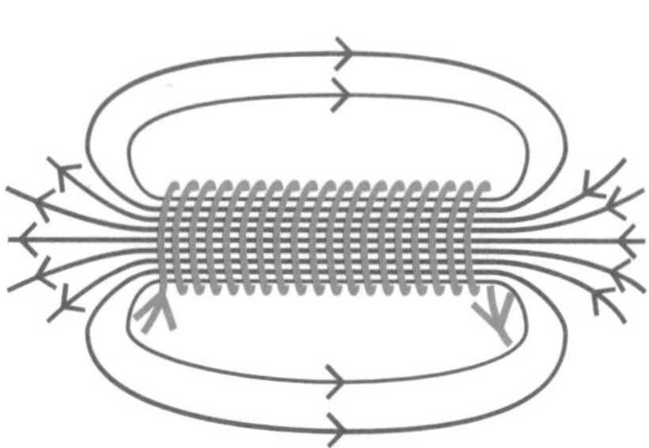

*Two bar magnets **attracting***

Opposite poles attract, as I'm sure you know.

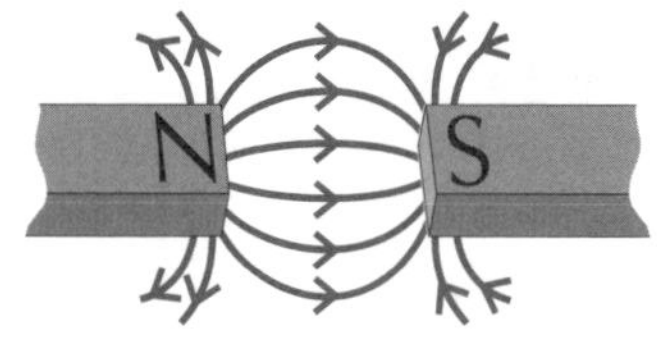

*Two bar magnets **repelling***

Like poles repel, as you must surely know.

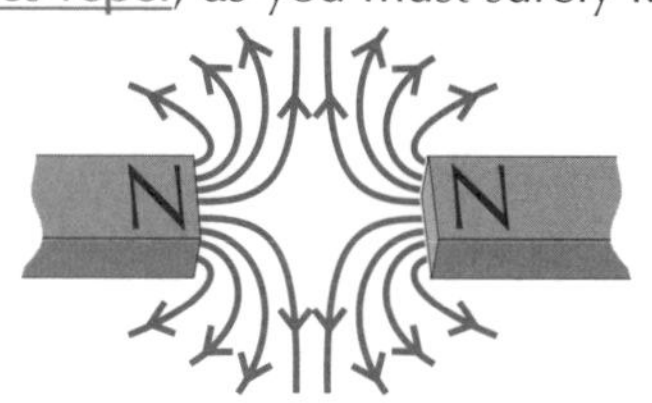

*The **Earth's** magnetic field*

Note that the magnetic poles are opposite to the Geographic Poles, i.e. the south pole is at the North Pole.

*The magnetic field round a **current-carrying wire***

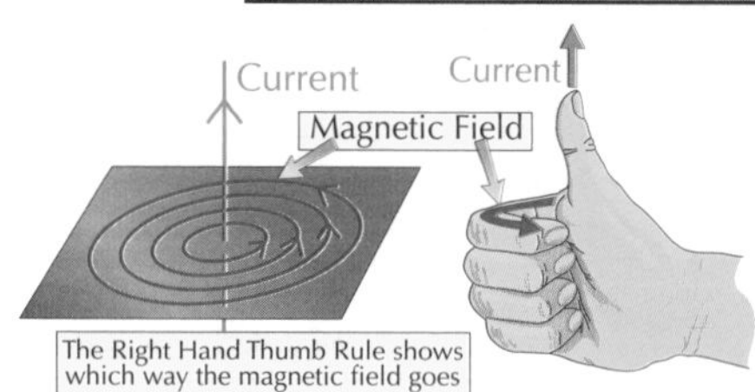

*A **plotting compass** is a **freely suspended magnet***

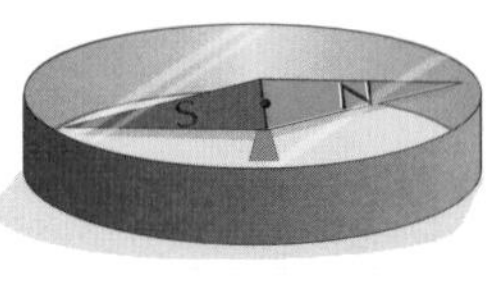

1) This means it always aligns itself with the magnetic field that it's in.
2) This is great for plotting magnetic field lines like around the bar magnets shown above.
3) Away from any magnets, it will align with the magnetic field of the Earth and point North.
4) Any magnet suspended so it can turn freely will also come to rest pointing North-South.
5) The end of the magnet which points North is called a 'North-seeking pole' or 'magnetic North'. The end pointing South will therefore be a 'magnetic South pole'. This is how they got their names.

Electromagnets

An **electromagnet** is just a **coil of wire** with an **iron core**

1) Electromagnets are really simple.
2) They're simply a solenoid (which is just a coil of wire) with a piece of 'soft' iron inside.
3) When current flows through the wires of the solenoid it creates a magnetic field around it.
4) The soft iron core has the effect of increasing the magnetic field strength.

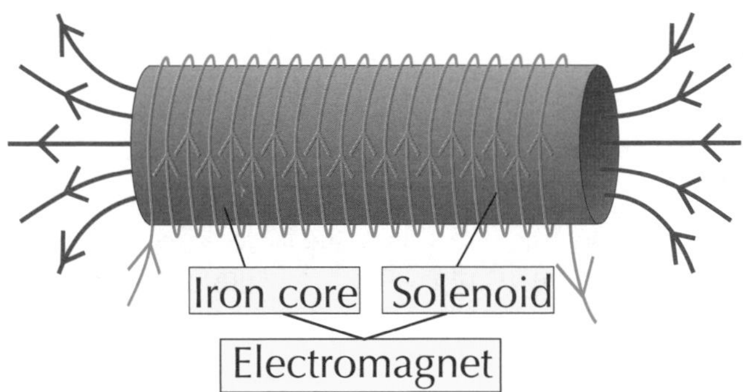

The **field** of an electromagnet is the same as an ordinary magnet, mostly

1) The magnetic field around an electromagnet is just like the one round a bar magnet, only it can be made much stronger.
2) This means that the ends of a solenoid act like the North Pole and South Pole of a bar magnet.
3) Pretty obviously, if the direction of the current is reversed, the N and S poles will swap ends.
4) If you imagine looking directly into one end of a solenoid, the direction of current flow tells you whether it's the N or S pole you're looking at, as shown by the two diagrams on the right: You need to remember those diagrams. They may show you a solenoid in the Exam and ask you which pole it is.

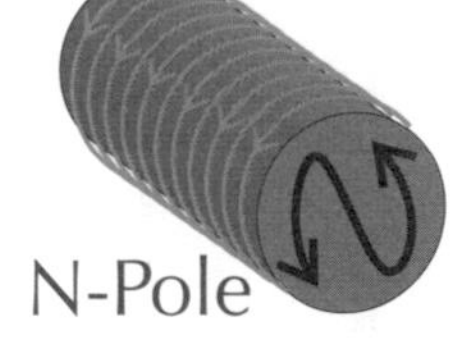

The **strength** of an electromagnet increases if you:

1) Increase the size of the *CURRENT*.
2) Increase the number of *TURNS* the coil has.
3) Replace the *CORE* with an iron core.

Iron is magnetically **'soft'** — ideal for **electromagnets**

In magnetic terms, 'soft' means it changes easily between being magnetised and demagnetised. Iron is 'soft' which makes it perfect for electromagnets which need to be turned on and off.

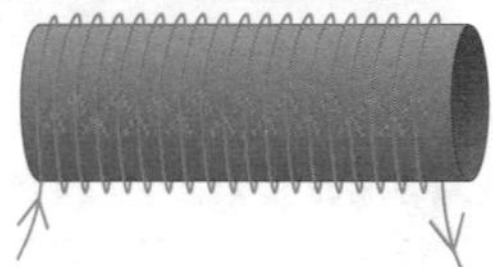

Steel is magnetically **'hard'** — ideal for **permanent** magnets

Magnetically 'hard' means that the material retains its magnetism. This would be hopeless in an electromagnet, but is exactly what's required for permanent magnets.

Electromagnetic Force

Anything carrying a current in a magnetic field will experience a force. There are three important cases:

A current in a magnetic field experiences a force

The two tests below demonstrate the force on a current-carrying wire placed in a magnetic field.
The force gets bigger if either the current or the magnetic field is made bigger.

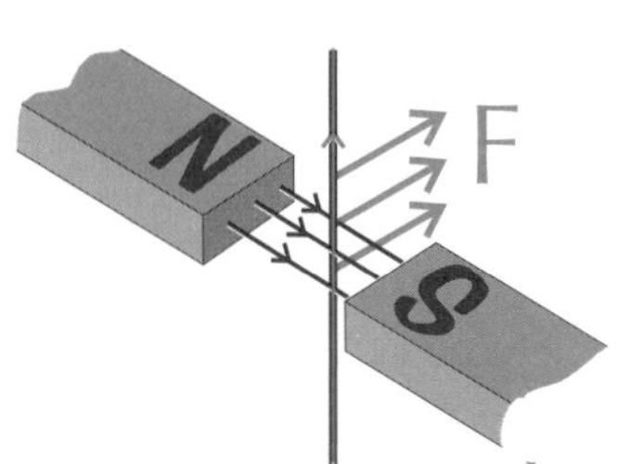

1) Note that in both cases the force on the wire is at 90° to both the wire and to the magnetic field.
2) You can always predict which way the force will act using Fleming's LHR as shown below.
3) To experience the full force, the wire has to be at 90° to the magnetic field.
4) The direction of the force is reversed if either:
   a) the direction of the current is reversed, or
   b) the direction of the magnetic field is reversed.

The **size** of the force increases if you:

1) Increase the strength of the *MAGNETIC FIELD*
2) Increase the size of the *CURRENT*

The simple electric motor

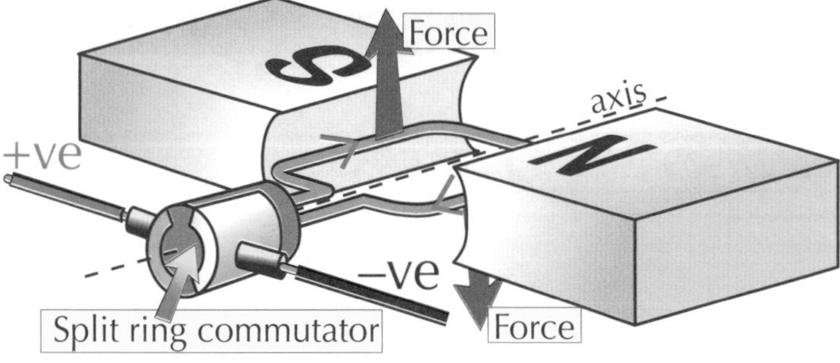

4 factors which speed it up

1) More *CURRENT*
2) More *TURNS* on the coil
3) *STRONGER MAGNETIC FIELD*
4) A *SOFT IRON CORE* in the coil

1) The diagram shows the forces acting on the two side arms of the coil.
2) These forces are just the usual forces which act on any current in a magnetic field.
3) Because the coil is on a spindle and the forces act one up and one down, it rotates.
4) The direction of the motor can be reversed either by swapping the polarity of the DC supply or swapping the magnetic poles over.

Fleming's left hand rule tells you which way the force acts

1) They could test if you can do this, so practise it.
2) Using your left hand, point your First finger in the direction of the Field and your seCond finger in the direction of the Current.
3) Your thumb will then point in the direction of the force *(motion)*.

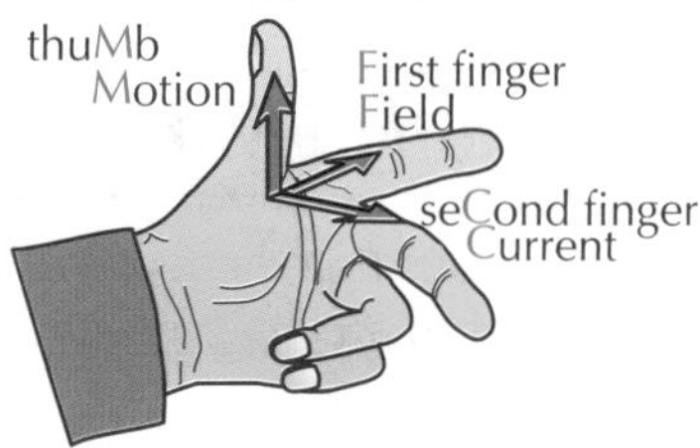

Uses of Electromagnets

Electromagnets always have a soft iron core, which increases the strength of the magnet. The core has to be soft (magnetically soft, that is), so that when the current is turned off, the magnetism disappears with it. The four applications below depend on that happening.

Loudspeakers

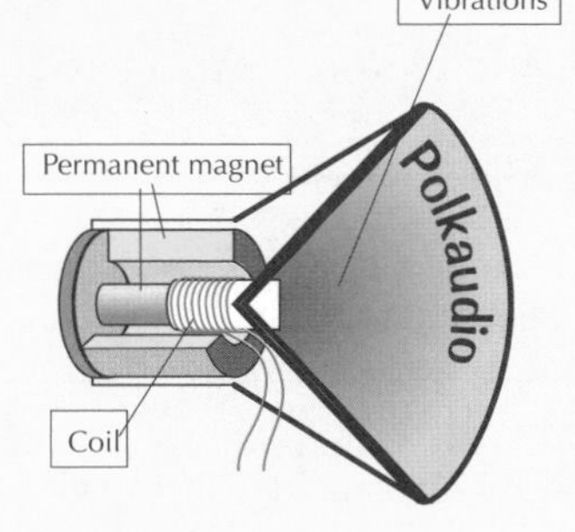

1) AC electrical signals from the amplifier are fed to the speaker coil (shown red).
2) These make the coil move back and forth over the North pole of the magnet.
3) These movements make the cardboard cone vibrate and this creates sounds.

Circuit breaker

or resettable fuse.

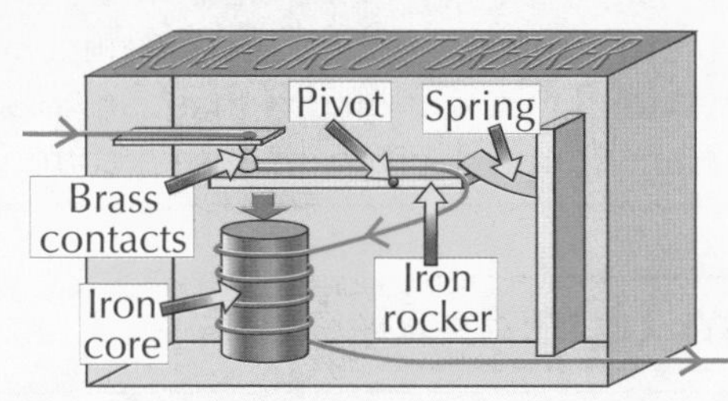

1) This is placed on the incoming live wire.
2) If the current gets too high, the magnetic field in the coil pulls the iron rocker which 'trips' the switch and breaks the circuit.
3) It can be reset manually, but will always flick itself off if the current is too high.

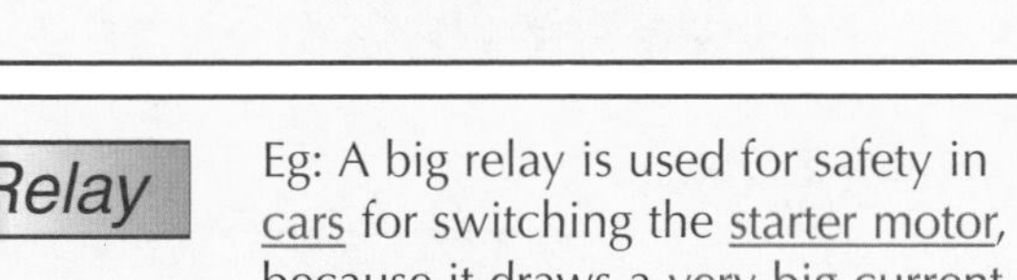

Relay

Eg: A big relay is used for safety in cars for switching the starter motor, because it draws a very big current.

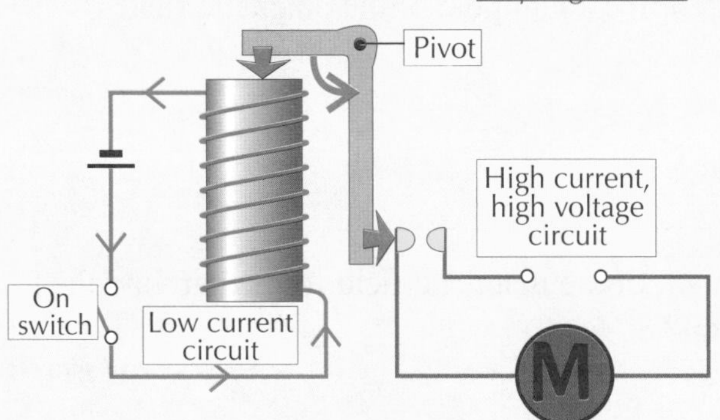

1) A relay is a device which uses a low current circuit to switch a high current circuit on/off.
2) When the switch in the low current circuit is closed it turns the electromagnet on which attracts the iron rocker.
3) The rocker pivots and closes the contacts in the high current circuit.
4) When the low current switch is opened, the electromagnet stops pulling, the rocker returns, and the high current circuit is broken again.

Electric bell

These are the ones they use in schools.

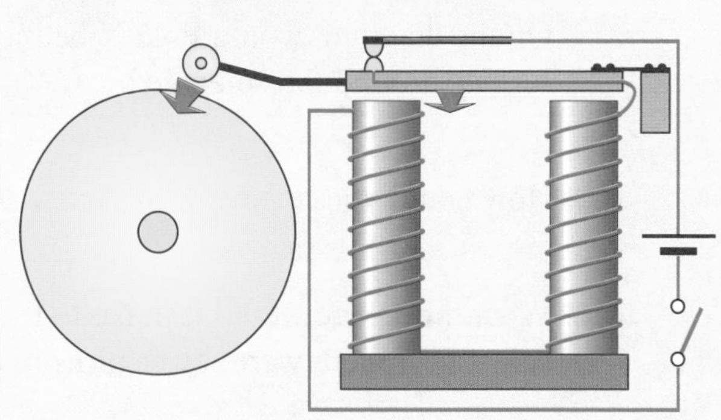

1) When the switch is closed, the electromagnets are turned on.
2) They pull the iron arm down which clangs the bell, but at the same time breaks the contact, which immediately turns off the electromagnets.
3) The arm then springs back, which closes the contact, and it starts again.
4) The whole sequence happens very quickly, maybe 10 times a second, so the bell sounds like a continuous "brrriiinnngg" sound.

Only *iron, steel* and *nickel* are *magnetic*

Don't forget that only iron, steel and nickel experience a force from a magnet. So a magnet won't stick to aluminium ladders or copper kettles or brass trumpets or gold rings or silver spoons.

Magnetism is an exam certainty

Make sure you know the definition of a magnetic field and the field diagrams, those five details about plotting compasses and which way the poles are compared to the Earth. Learn the details about electromagnets — they nearly always have one of the circuits in the Exam. Usually they'll give you a circuit diagram and ask you to explain exactly how it works. Make sure you learn all the tricky details.

Warm-Up and Exam Questions

Warm-up Questions

1) What is a solenoid?
2) State three factors that affect the strength of an electromagnet.
3) What does it mean to say that steel is "magnetically hard"?
4) In Fleming's Left Hand Rule, write down what quantities have their direction shown by the thumb, first finger and second finger.
5) Write down four factors that can speed up an electric motor.
6) Name three devices that use electromagnets.

Exam Questions

1 You are provided with a steel rod and a solenoid connected to a 12V power supply, as shown in the diagram.

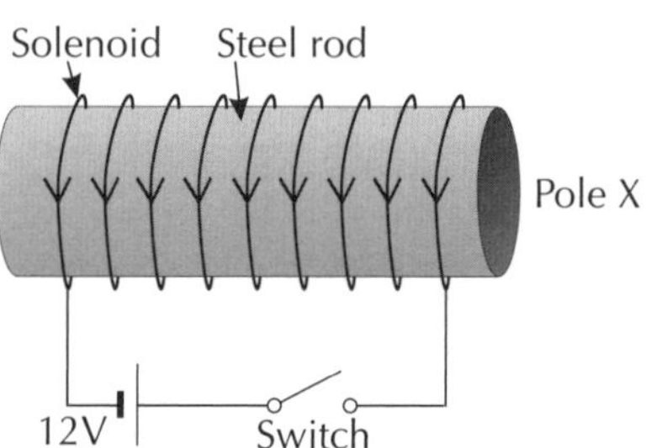

a) On the diagram, would Pole X be the north or the south pole of the magnetic field formed around the solenoid?

(1 mark)

b) How could you reverse the polarity of Pole X?

(1 mark)

c) What difference would it make to the strength of the magnetic field formed around the solenoid if there were fewer turns in the coil?

(1 mark)

2 The diagram on the right shows how an electric bell works. Study the diagram and put the six sentences A to F in the correct order to describe what happens when the switch is closed.

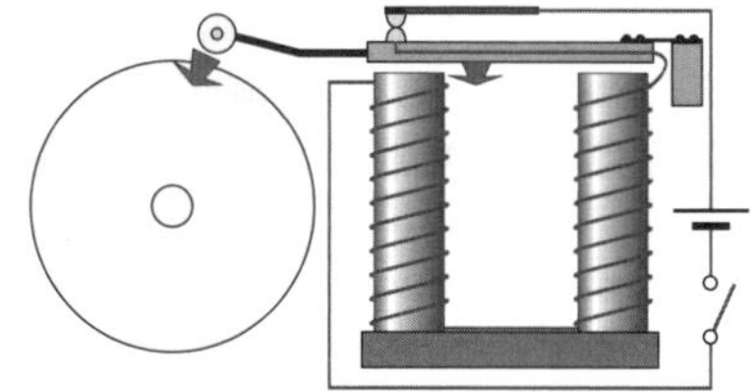

A - The contacts joining the iron arm to the circuit pull apart, breaking the circuit.

B - The iron arm is attracted to the electromagnet, causing the gong to strike the bell.

C - The iron arm, no longer attracted to the electromagnet, springs back.

D - The electromagnet is turned on.

E - The contacts close again, so current again runs in the circuit.

F - The electromagnet is turned off.

(5 marks)

Electromagnetic Induction and Generators

Sounds terrifying. Well sure it's quite mysterious, but it isn't that complicated:

ELECTROMAGNETIC INDUCTION: The creation of a VOLTAGE (and maybe current) in a wire which is experiencing a CHANGE IN MAGNETIC FIELD.

For some reason they use the word 'induction' rather than 'creation', but it amounts to the same thing.

EM induction — a) Field cutting b) Field through a coil

Electromagnetic induction is the induction of a voltage and/or current in a conductor.
There are two different situations where you get EM induction. You need to know about both of them:

a) The conductor moves across a magnetic field and 'cuts' through the field lines.
b) The magnetic field through a closed coil changes, i.e. gets bigger or smaller or reverses.

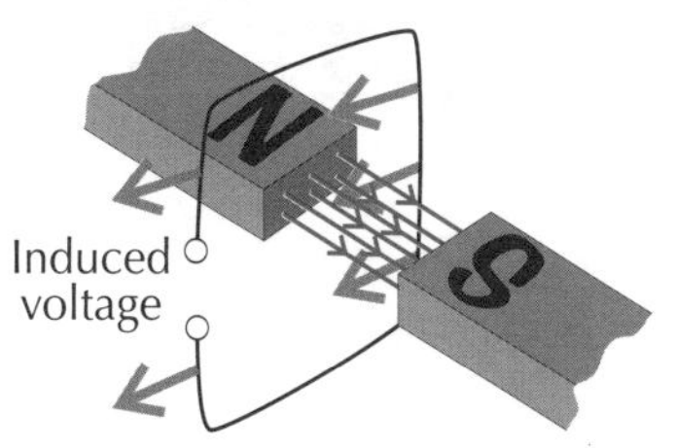

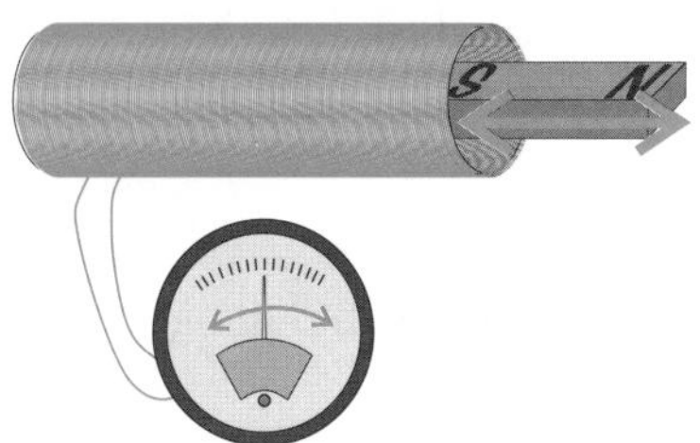

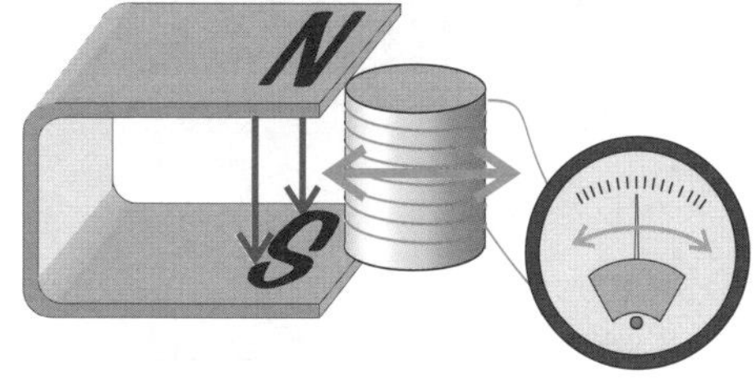

1) If the direction of movement is reversed, then the voltage/current will be reversed too.
2) The current will also be reversed if the opposite pole of the magnet is shoved into the coil.

Four factors affect the size of the induced voltage:

1) The STRENGTH of the MAGNET
2) The SPEED of movement
3) The number of TURNS on the COIL
4) The AREA of the COIL

Generators and dynamos

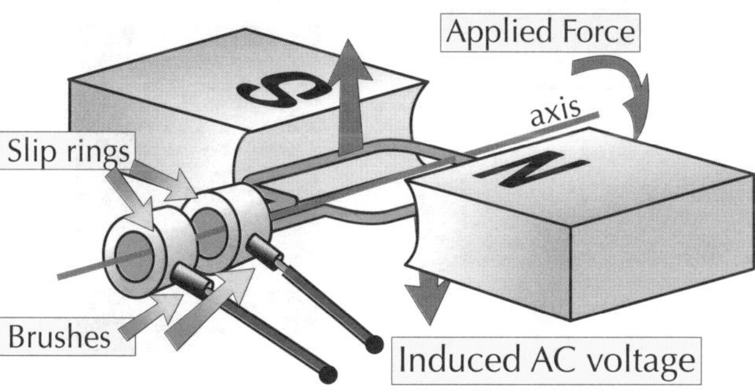

1) Generators rotate a coil in a magnetic field.
2) Their construction is pretty much like a motor.
3) The difference is the slip rings which are in constant contact with the brushes, so the contacts don't swap every ½ turn.
4) This means they produce AC voltage, as shown by the CRO displays. Note that faster revs produce not only more peaks but higher overall voltage too.

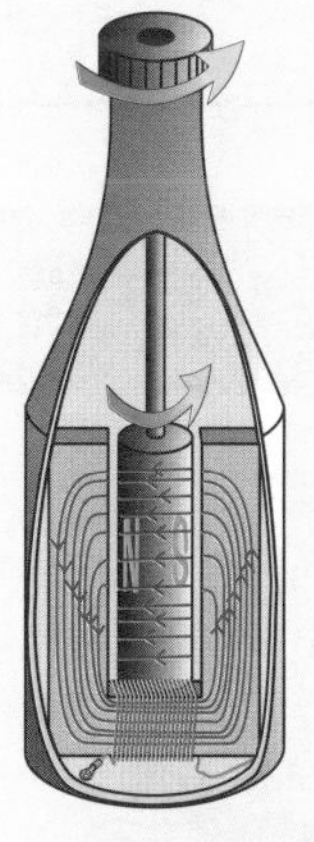

Dynamos are slightly different from generators because they rotate the magnet. This still causes the field through the coil to swap every half turn, so the output is just the same, as shown in the CRO displays below.

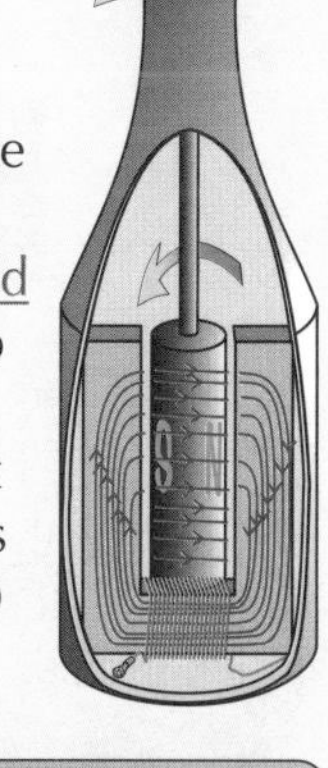

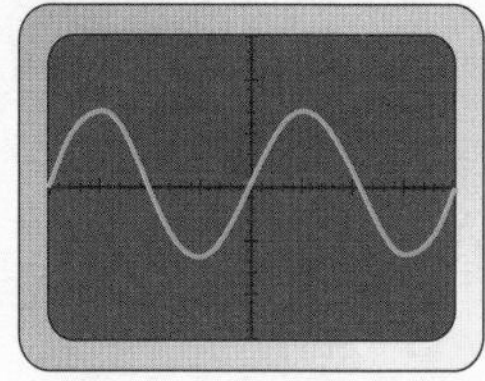

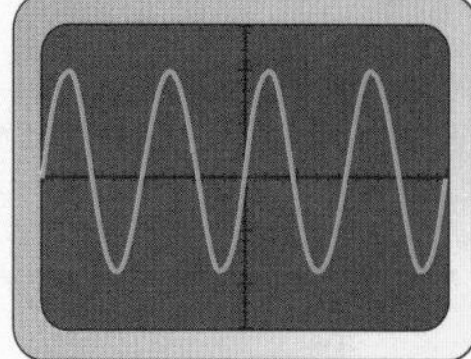

Transformers

Transformers use Electromagnetic Induction. So they will only work on AC.

Transformers change the **voltage** — but only **AC voltages**

1) Step-up transformers step the voltage up. They have more turns on the secondary coil.
2) Step-down transformers step the voltage down. They have fewer turns on the secondary. They drop the voltage from 400,000V to a 'safe' 230 V for our homes.

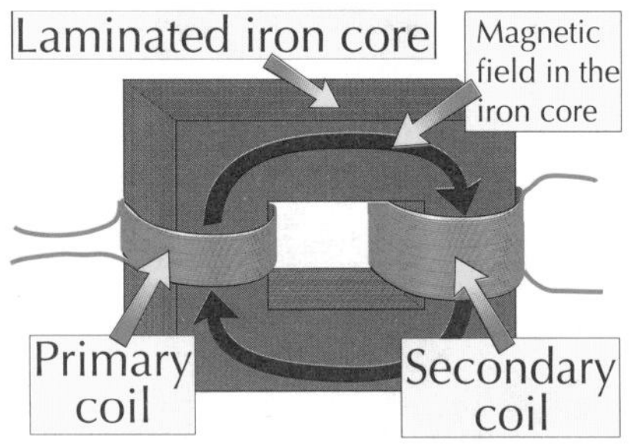

1) The laminated iron core is purely for transferring the magnetic field from the primary coil to the secondary.
2) The iron core is laminated with layers of insulation to reduce the eddy currents which heat it up, and therefore waste energy.

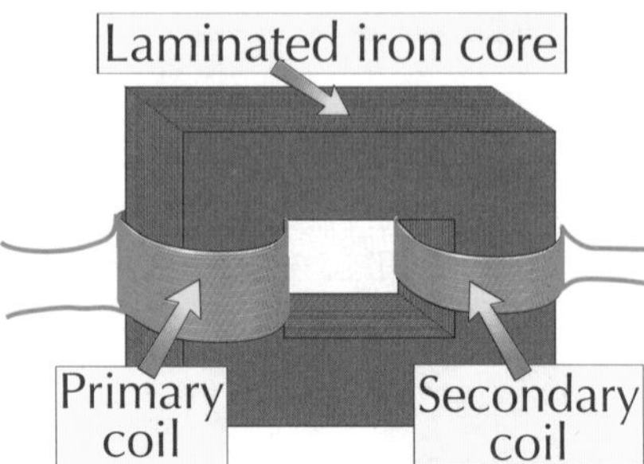

1) The primary coil produces a magnetic field which stays within the iron core and this means it all passes through the secondary coil.
2) Because there is alternating current (AC) in the primary coil, this means that the magnetic field in the iron core is reversing (50 times a second, usually) — i.e. it's a changing field.
3) This rapidly changing magnetic field is then experienced by the secondary coil and this induces an alternating voltage in it — electromagnetic induction of a voltage in fact.
4) The relative number of turns on the two coils determines whether the voltage created in the secondary is greater or less than the voltage in the primary.
5) If you supplied DC to the primary, you'd get nothing out of the secondary at all. There would still be a field in the iron core, but it wouldn't be constantly changing so there'd be no induction in the secondary because you need a changing field to induce a voltage.
   So don't forget it — transformers only work with AC. They won't work with DC at all.

The **transformer equation** — use it **either way up**

In words: The ratio of turns on the two coils equals the ratio of their voltages.

$$\frac{\text{Primary Voltage}}{\text{Secondary Voltage}} = \frac{\text{Number of turns on Primary}}{\text{Number of turns on Secondary}}$$

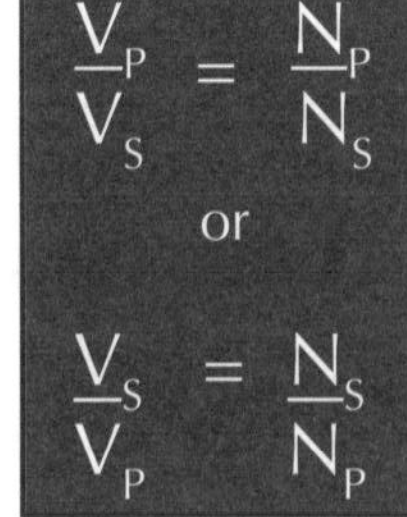

$$\frac{V_P}{V_S} = \frac{N_P}{N_S}$$

or

$$\frac{V_S}{V_P} = \frac{N_S}{N_P}$$

It's just another formula. You stick in the numbers you've got and work out the one that's left. It's real useful to remember you can write it either way up — this example's much trickier algebra-wise if you start with V_S on the bottom...

Example: *A transformer has 40 turns on the primary and 800 on the secondary. If the input voltage is 1000V find the output voltage.*

ANSWER: $V_S/V_P = N_S/N_P$ so $V_S/1000 = 800/40$ $V_S = 1000\times(800/40) = 20{,}000\text{V}$

The National Grid

1) The National Grid is the network of pylons and cables which covers the whole country.

2) It takes electricity from the power stations, to just where it's needed in homes and industry.

3) It enables power to be generated anywhere on the grid, and to then be supplied anywhere else on the grid.

*All **power stations** are pretty much the **same***

They all have a boiler of some sort, which makes steam which drives a turbine which drives a generator. The generator produces electricity (by induction) by rotating an electromagnet within coils of wire (see P. 235).

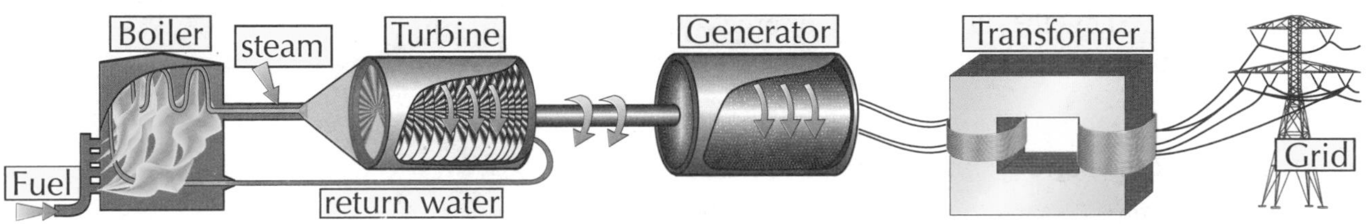

Learn all these features of the national grid -- power stations, transformers, pylons, etc.:

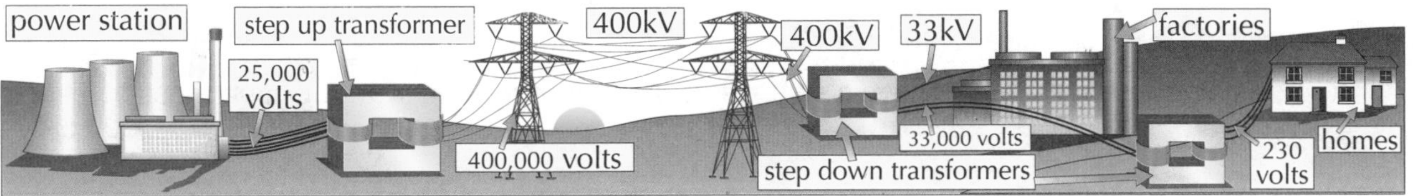

*Pylon cables are at **400,000 V** to keep the **current low***

You need to understand why the voltage is so high and why it's AC. Learn these points:

1) The formula for power supplied is: Power = Voltage × Current or: $P = V \times I$
2) So to transmit a lot of power, you either need high voltage or high current.
3) The problem with high current is the loss (as heat) due to the resistance of the cables.
4) The formula for power loss due to resistance in the cables is: $P = I^2 R$.
5) Because of the I^2 bit, if the current is 10 times bigger, the energy losses will be 100 times bigger.
6) It's much cheaper to boost the voltage up to 400,000V and keep the current very low.
7) This requires transformers as well as big pylons with huge insulators, but it's still cheaper.
8) The transformers have to step the voltage up at one end, for efficient transmission, and then bring it back down to safe useable levels at the other end.
9) This is why it has to be AC on the National Grid — so that the transformers will work.

Remember — transformers only work with AC

Quite a few tricky details here. The power station and National Grid are easy enough, but fully explaining why pylon cables are at 400,000 V is a bit trickier — but you need to learn it. When you boil the kettle, think of the route the electricity has to travel. Scribble it down.

Warm-Up and Exam Questions

Warm-up Questions

1) Explain what electromagnetic induction is.
2) A generator consists of a wire coil rotating in a magnetic field. Write down the factors which significantly affect the size of the induced voltage in the coil.
3) A transformer has 20 turns on the primary coil and 100 turns on the secondary coil. If 4V a.c. is supplied to the primary coil, what voltage would there be across the secondary coil, assuming the transformer was 100% efficient?

Exam Questions

1 a) On the diagram of a d.c. motor on the right:
   (i) Label the split ring commutator.
   (ii) Label the current direction in the coil.
   (iii) Show the direction of the forces on the two side arms of the coil.

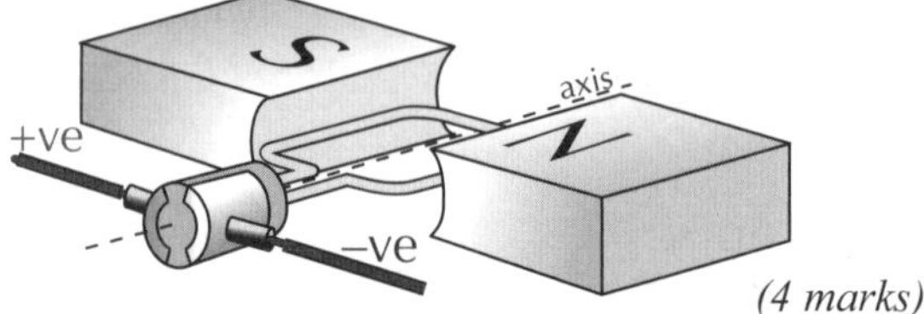

(4 marks)

b) Pick the correct ending for this sentence:
The split ring commutator in a d.c. motor...
   (i) *reverses the voltage across the cell twice in each revolution.*
   (ii) *reverses the direction of rotation of the coil twice in each revolution.*
   (iii) *reverses the direction of the current in the coil twice in each revolution.*
   (iv) *reverses the polarity of the magnet twice in each revolution.*

(1 mark)

c) Why must a d.c. motor have a split ring commutator to keep working continuously?

(2 marks)

d) What would be the effect of swapping both the direction of the magnetic field and the direction of the current?

(1 mark)

2 A power station transformer puts out a voltage of 20 000 V. Then a step-up transformer is used to step up this voltage to 400 000 V so that the power can be transmitted at a high voltage across the National Grid. Assume the transformer is perfectly efficient.

a) Is the ratio of the number of turns in the primary coil to the number of turns in the secondary coil: A) 1:20 B) 2000:1 C) 1:20 000 D) 40:1?

(1 mark)

b) If the current in the National Grid cables is 0.1A, what is the current going into the transformer? Assume the transformer is 100% efficient.

(2 marks)

c) What role do transformers play in the National Grid? (Write no more than 3 lines.)

(3 marks)

d) In real life no transformer is 100% efficient, although they often come close. Explain one way in which energy is wasted in a transformer and how it can be constructed to make this wastage as small as possible.

(2 marks)

Revision Summary for Section Ten

This is definitely tricky Physics. The big problem with Physics in general is that usually there's nothing to 'see'. You're told that there's a current flowing or a magnetic field round something, but there's nothing you can actually see with your eyes. That's what makes it so difficult.
To get to grips with Physics you have to get used to learning about things which you can't see.
Try these questions and see how well you're doing.

1) Describe what current, voltage and resistance are.
2) Sketch out the standard test circuit with all the details. Describe how it's used.
3) Draw 18 circuit symbols that you know, with their names.
4) Write down two facts about: a) variable resistor b) diode c) LDR d) thermistor.
5) Sketch a typical series circuit and say why it is a series circuit, not a parallel one.
6) State five rules about the current, voltage and resistance in a series circuit.
7) Give examples of lights wired in series and wired in parallel and explain the main differences.
8) Sketch a typical parallel circuit, showing voltmeter and ammeter positions.
9) State five rules about the current, voltage and resistance in a parallel circuit.
10) Draw a circuit diagram of part of a car's electrics, and explain why they are in parallel.
11) Sketch the four important V-I graphs and explain their shapes. How do you get R from them?
12) Find the voltage when a current of 0.5 A flows through a resistance of 10 Ω.
13) What carries current in metals?
14) Draw a diagram of electrolysis in action and explain how it works.
15) What two things cause the build up of matter at the electrodes to increase?
16) What is static electricity? What is nearly always the cause of it building up?
17) Which particles move when static builds up, and which ones don't?
18) Describe how these machines use static electricity: a) inkjet printer b) photocopier.
19) Give *one* example of static being: a) useful b) dangerous.
20) Write down six electrical hazards in the home.
21) Sketch a properly wired plug. Explain how fuses work.
22) Explain fully how earthing works.
23) What are the four types of energy that electricity can easily be converted into?
24) Calculate the fuse rating for a toaster rated at 240 V, 0.5 kW.
25) Sketch a view of a circuit to explain the formula E = QV. Which definitions go with it?
26) Sketch magnetic fields for: a) a bar magnet, b) a solenoid, c) two magnets attracting, d) two magnets repelling, e) the Earth's magnetic field, f) a current-carrying wire.
27) What's the Right Hand Rule for?
28) What is an electromagnet made of? Explain how to decide on the polarity of the ends?
29) What is meant by magnetically hard and soft?
30) Sketch 2 demos of the motor effect. Sketch a simple motor and list the 4 factors affecting speed.
31) Describe the three details of Fleming's left hand rule. What is it used for?
32) Sketch and give details of: a) Loudspeaker, b) Circuit breaker, c) Relay, d) Electric bell.
33) Give the definition of electromagnetic induction. Sketch three cases where it happens.
34) List the four factors which affect the size of the induced voltage.
35) Sketch a generator with all the details. Describe how it works, and how a dynamo works.
36) Sketch the two types of transformer, and highlight the main details. Explain how they work.
37) Write down the transformer equation. Do your own worked example — it's good practice.
38) Sketch a typical power station, and the National Grid and explain why it's at 400 kV.
39) Find: a) The current when a resistance of 96 Ω is connected to a battery of 12 V.
    b) The voltage when a current of 0.25 A passes through a resistance of 54 Ω.

Speed, Velocity and Acceleration

Speed and **velocity** are **both** just **how fast** you're going

Speed and velocity are both measured in m/s (or km/h or mph). They both simply say how fast you're going, but there's a subtle difference between them which you need to know:

> SPEED is just how fast you're going (e.g. 30mph or 20m/s) with no regard to the direction.
> VELOCITY however must also have the DIRECTION specified, e.g. 30mph North or 20m/s, 060°.

You need to remember that distinction.

Speed, distance and time — the **formula**:

$$\text{Speed} = \frac{\text{Distance}}{\text{Time}}$$

You really ought to get confident with this very easy formula.
As usual the formula triangle version makes it all much easier.
You just need to try and think up some interesting word for remembering the order of the letters in the triangle, s^{d}t. Sedit, perhaps... or you think up your own.

Example: *A cat walks 20m in 35s. Find a) its speed b) how long it takes to walk 75m.*
Answer: *Using the formula triangle:* a) *s = d/t = 20/35 =* 0.57 m/s
b) *t = d/s = 75/0.57 = 131s =* 2 min 11s

A lot of the time we tend to use the words "speed" and "velocity" interchangeably.
For example to calculate a velocity you'd just use the same formula as for speed, except that you'd need to specify a direction as well.

Acceleration is **how quickly** you're **speeding up**

Acceleration is definitely not the same as velocity or speed.
Every time you read or write the word acceleration, remind yourself: "acceleration is completely different from velocity. Acceleration is how quickly the velocity is changing."
Velocity is a simple idea. Acceleration is altogether more subtle, which is why it's confusing.

Acceleration — the **formula**:

$$\text{Acceleration} = \frac{\text{Change in Velocity}}{\text{Time Taken}}$$

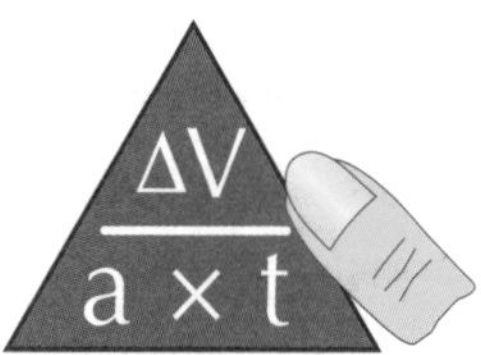

It's just another formula. Just like all the others. Three things in a formula triangle.
Mind you, there are two tricky things with this one. First there's the "ΔV", which means working out the "change in velocity", as shown in the example below, rather than just putting a simple value for speed or velocity in.
Secondly there's the units of acceleration which are m/s^2.
Not m/s, which is velocity, but m/s^2. Remember that: Not m/s, but m/s^2.

Example: *A cat accelerates in a straight line from 2 m/s to 6 m/s in 5.6s. Find its acceleration.*

Answer: *Using the formula triangle:* $a = \Delta V/t = (6 - 2) / 5.6 = 4 \div 5.6 =$ 0.71 m/s^2
All pretty basic stuff.

Distance-Time and Velocity-Time Graphs

Make sure you learn all these details. Make sure you can distinguish between them too.

Distance-time graphs

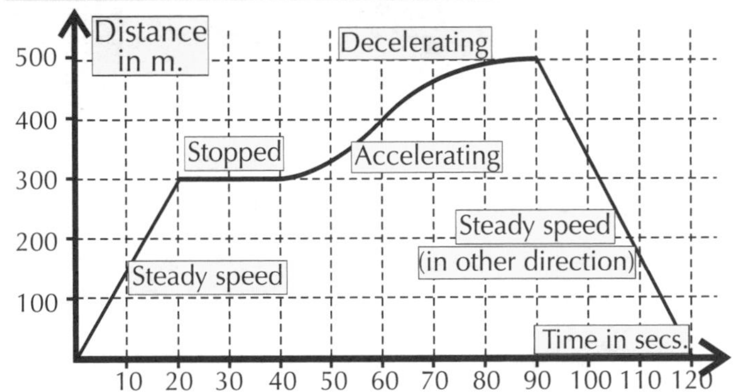

Very important notes:

1) Gradient = speed.
2) Flat sections are where it's stopped.
3) The steeper the graph, the faster it's going.
4) Downhill sections mean it's coming back toward its starting point.
5) Curves represent acceleration or deceleration.
6) A steepening curve means it's speeding up (increasing gradient).
7) A levelling off *curve* means it's slowing down (decreasing gradient).

Calculating speed from a distance-time graph — it's just the gradient

For example the speed of the return section of the graph is:

$$\text{Speed} = \text{gradient} = \frac{\text{vertical}}{\text{horizontal}} = \frac{500}{30} = 16.7 \text{ m/s}$$

Don't forget that you have to use the scales of the axes to work out the gradient. Don't measure in cm.

Velocity-time graphs

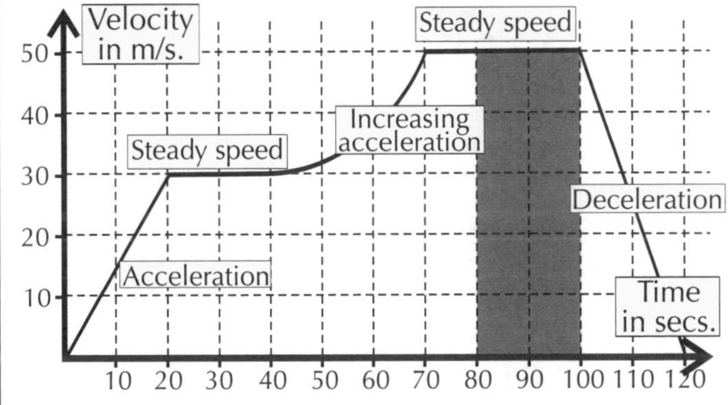

Very important notes:

1) Gradient = acceleration.
2) Flat sections represent steady speed.
3) The steeper the graph, the greater the acceleration or deceleration.
4) Uphill sections (/) are acceleration.
5) Downhill sections (\) — deceleration.
6) The area under any section of the graph (or all of it) is equal to the distance travelled in that time interval.
7) A curve means changing acceleration.

Calculating acceleration, speed and distance from a velocity-time graph

1) The acceleration represented by the first section of the graph is:

$$\text{Acceleration} = \text{gradient} = \frac{\text{vertical}}{\text{horizontal}} = \frac{30}{20} = 1.5 \text{ m/s}^2$$

2) The speed at any point is simply found by reading the value off the speed axis.
3) The distance travelled in any time interval is equal to the area. For example, the distance travelled between t=80 and t=100 is equal to the shaded area which is equal to 1000m.

Velocity and acceleration — learn the difference

Velocity and acceleration are totally different — make sure you learn the definitions and the formulae. The tricky thing about the graphs is that they look similar but represent totally different kinds of motion. If you want to be able to do them then there's no substitute for simply learning all the numbered points.

Warm-Up and Exam Questions

Warm-up Questions

1) A train travels 280m in 8s. Calculate its speed.
2) A motorbike starts from rest at traffic lights and reaches 15m/s after 3s. Find its acceleration.
3) A car is travelling at 16m/s. How far does it travel in 6s?

Exam Questions

1 This graph shows the motion of a car from the top of a hill to the bottom of the hill. After 12s the car reaches the bottom of the hill.

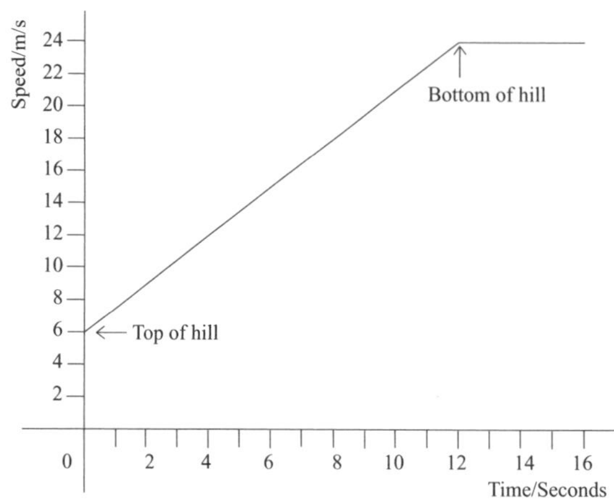

a) Calculate the acceleration of the car.

(3 marks)

b) Use the graph to find the distance travelled by the car down the hill.

(3 marks)

2 As part of an aerobatic display, a skydiver jumps out of an aeroplane and falls towards the ground. She does not open her parachute until she reaches her terminal velocity. The graph shows her motion as she falls.

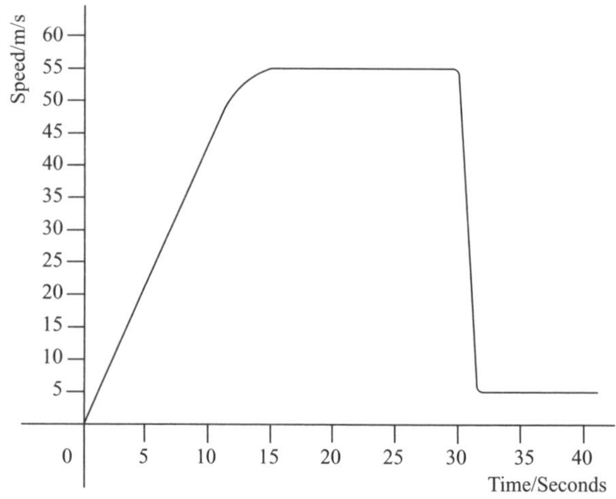

a) Calculate the distance travelled between 15s and 30s.

(3 marks)

b) Describe and explain what is happening between 30s and 35s.

(2 marks)

Laws of Motion

Around about the time of the Great Plague in the 1660s, a man called Isaac Newton worked out The Three Laws of Motion. At first they might seem obscure or irrelevant, but to be perfectly blunt, if you can't understand these three simple laws then you'll never fully understand forces and motion:

*First law — **Balanced forces** mean **no change** in **velocity***

So long as the forces on an object are all *BALANCED*, then it'll just *STAY STILL*, or else if it's already moving it'll just carry on at the *SAME VELOCITY* — so long as the forces are all *BALANCED*.

1) When a train or car or bus or anything else is moving at a constant velocity then the forces on it must all be balanced.
2) Never let yourself think that things need a constant overall force to keep them moving — that's wrong.
3) To keep going at a steady speed, there must be zero resultant force — and don't you forget it.

*Second law — A **resultant force** means **acceleration***

If there is an *UNBALANCED FORCE*, then the object will *ACCELERATE* in the direction of the overall force.

1) An unbalanced force will always produce acceleration (or deceleration).
2) This "acceleration" can take five different forms: Starting, stopping, speeding up, slowing down and changing direction.
3) On a force diagram (like on the right), the arrows will be unequal:

Don't ever say: "If something's moving there must be an overall resultant force acting on it".

Not so. If there's an overall force it will always accelerate.
You get steady speed from balanced forces.

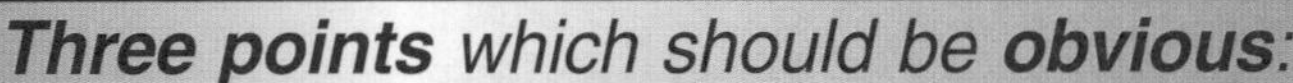

***Three points** which should be **obvious**:*

1) The bigger the force, the greater the acceleration or deceleration.
2) The bigger the mass, the smaller the acceleration.
3) To get a big mass to accelerate as fast as a small mass it needs a bigger force. Just think about pushing heavy trolleys and it should all seem fairly obvious.

*The overall **unbalanced force** is often called the **resultant force***

Any resultant force will produce acceleration and this is the formula for it:

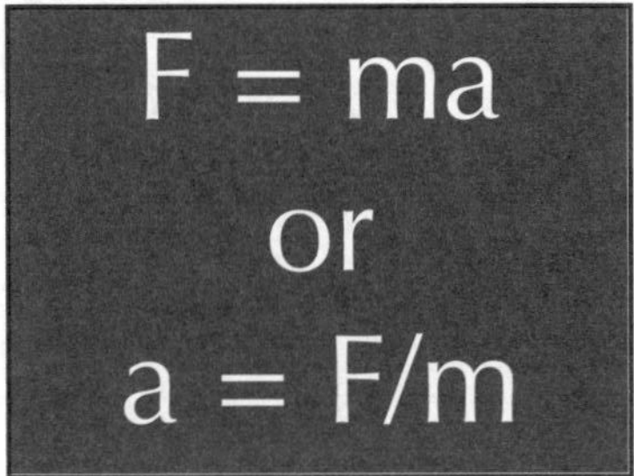

m = mass
a = acceleration
F is always the resultant force

Laws of Motion

Calculations using F = ma — an example

Q) What force is needed to accelerate a mass of 12kg at $5m/s^2$?

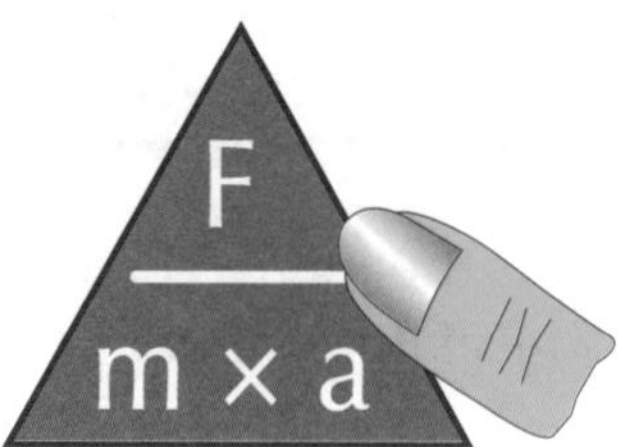

Ans. The question is asking for force
— so you need a formula with "F = something-or-other".

Since they also give you values for mass and acceleration, the formula "F = ma" really should be a pretty obvious choice.

So just stick in the numbers they give you where the letters are:
m = 12, a = 5, so "F = ma" gives $F = 12 \times 5 = 60N$
(It's newtons because force always is)

(Notice that you don't really need to fully understand what's going on — you just need to know how to use formulae.)

The third law — reaction forces

If object A *EXERTS A FORCE* on object B then object B exerts *THE EXACT OPPOSITE FORCE* on object A

1) That means if you push against a wall, the wall will push back against you, just as hard.
2) And as soon as you stop pushing, so does the wall. Quite clever really.
3) If you think about it, there must be an opposing force when you lean against a wall — otherwise you (and the wall) would fall over.

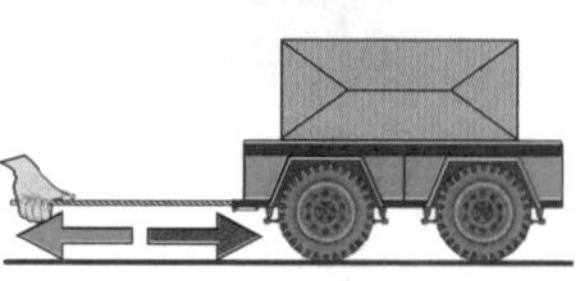

4) If you pull a cart, whatever force you exert on the rope, the rope exerts the exact opposite pull on you.

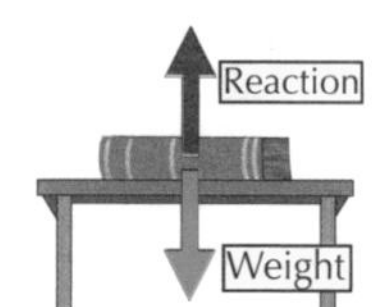

5) If you put a book on a table, the weight of the book acts downwards on the table — and the table exerts an equal and opposite force upwards on the book.

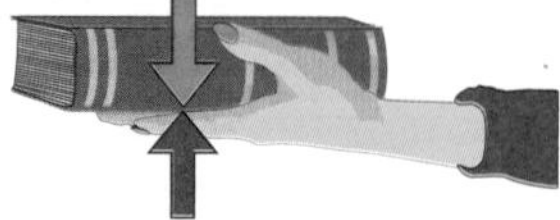

6) If you support a book on your hand, the book exerts its weight downwards on you, and you provide an upwards force on the book and it all stays nicely in balance.

In Exam questions they may well test this by getting you to fill in some extra arrow to represent the reaction force. Learn this very important fact:

Whenever an object is on a horizontal *SURFACE*, there'll always be a *REACTION FORCE* pushing *UPWARDS*, supporting the object. The total *REACTION FORCE* will be *EQUAL AND OPPOSITE* to the weight.

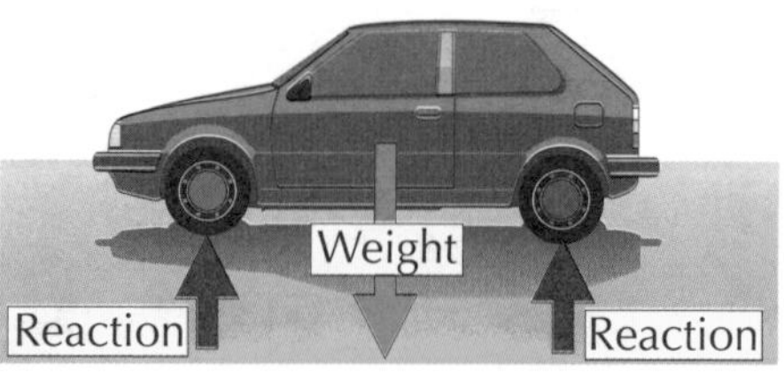

Just three laws — learn them all

Those three laws of motion are pretty important — you could do with learning them. Unfortunately in this topic there are hardly any nice easy facts that'll help — in the end there's no substitute for fully understanding The Three Laws.

Warm-Up and Exam Questions

Warm-up Questions

1) In each of the following situations, say whether the forces are balanced or unbalanced:
a) a car travelling in a straight line at a constant speed of 15 m/s; b) the Moon orbiting the Earth; c) a ballet dancer standing on the points of her toes; d) a coin dropping from a building
2) a) A car has a mass of 900kg. If it accelerates at 3 m/s^2, what is the resultant force on it?
b) A force of 18N acts on a mass of 3kg. What is the size of the acceleration?
3) A tractor is towing a trailer. If the tractor exerts a force of 100N on the trailer, how much force will the trailer exert on the tractor?

Exam Questions

1 The Saturn V rocket was used to launch the Apollo spacecraft.
On the launch pad, the total mass of the rocket and spacecraft was 2 700 000 kg (2.7×10^6 kg).
The rocket had five engines, each producing a thrust of 7 000 000N (7.0×10^6N).

a) If the gravitational field strength at the Earth's surface, g = 10N/kg, calculate the weight of the combined Saturn V rocket and Apollo spacecraft.

(1 mark)

b) Calculate the resultant force on the rocket at take-off, when each engine was producing its maximum thrust.

(2 marks)

c) What would the acceleration of the rocket have been as it left the Earth's surface?

(2 marks)

d) Assuming that the thrust of the engines remained constant, describe and explain what would have happened to the acceleration in the first few minutes of the flight.

(2 marks)

e) Once out of the Earth's atmosphere, the rocket continued to accelerate.
By considering the forces involved, explain how this was possible.

(2 marks)

2

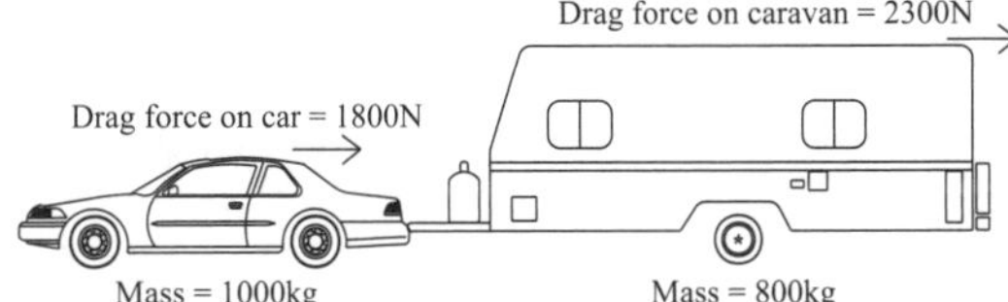

The car in the diagram is towing a caravan at a constant speed on a level road.
The car has a mass of 1000kg and the caravan has a mass of 800kg.

a) Draw a diagram of the caravan, marking on the two vertical forces.
What can you say about the size of these vertical forces?

(3 marks)

b) Calculate the force exerted by the car on the caravan.

(2 marks)

c) What will be the thrust exerted by the car's engine?

(2 marks)

d) The driver wishes to accelerate the car and caravan at 2 m/s^2. Assuming that the drag forces stay constant, what will be the new thrust force from the engine?

(2 marks)

Mass, Weight and Gravity

Gravity is the *force of attraction* between *all masses*

There's gravitational attraction between all masses, but you only notice it when one of the masses is really really big, e.g. a planet. Anything near a planet or star is attracted to it very strongly. This has two important effects:

1) It makes all things accelerate towards the ground (all with the same acceleration, g, which ≈ $10 m/s^2$ on Earth).
2) It gives everything a weight.

Weight and *mass* are *not the same*

To understand this you must learn all these facts about mass and weight.

1) Mass is the amount of matter in an object. For any given object this is the same anywhere in the Universe.
2) Weight is caused by the pull of gravity. In most questions the weight of an object is just the force of gravity pulling it towards the centre of the Earth.
3) This is the definition of a newton — you need to know it.

ONE NEWTON is the force needed to give a MASS OF 1 kg an ACCELERATION OF $1 m/s^2$

The *very important formula* relating *mass, weight and gravity*

$$W = m \times g$$ (Weight = mass × g)

1) Remember, weight and mass are not the same. Mass is in kg, weight is in newtons.
2) The letter "g" represents the strength of the gravity and its value is different for different planets. On Earth g ≈ 10 N/kg. On the moon, where the gravity is weaker, g is just 1.6 N/kg.

Force Diagrams

There are basically only a few different force diagrams you can get:

Stationary object — *All forces in balance*

1) The force of gravity (or weight) is acting downwards.
2) This causes a reaction force from the surface pushing the object back up.
3) This is the only way it can be in balance.
4) Without a reaction force, it would accelerate downwards due to the pull of gravity.
5) The two horizontal forces must be equal and opposite otherwise the object will accelerate sideways.

Reaction

Weight

Steady velocity — *All forces in balance*

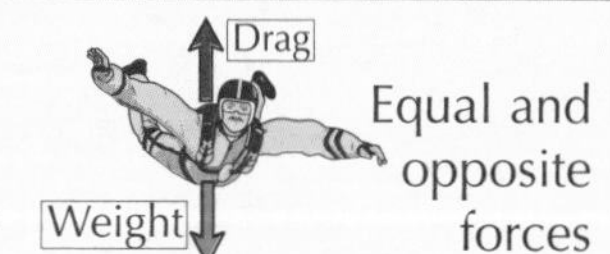

Take note. To move with a steady speed the forces must be in balance. If there is an unbalanced force then you get acceleration, not steady speed. That's very important.

Acceleration — *Un*balanced forces

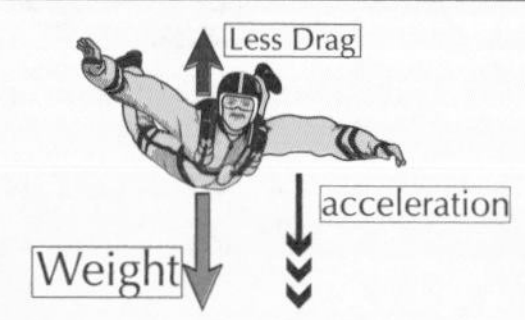

1) You only get acceleration with an overall resultant (unbalanced) force.
2) The bigger this unbalanced force, the greater the acceleration.
3) Note that the forces in the other direction are still balanced.

Resultant force is important — especially for *"F = ma"*

In most real situations there are at least two forces acting on an object along any direction. The overall effect of these forces will decide the motion of the object — whether it will accelerate, decelerate or stay at a steady speed. The "overall effect" is found by just adding or subtracting the forces which point along the same direction. The overall force you get is called the RESULTANT FORCE.

And when you use the formula "F = ma", F must always be the RESULTANT FORCE.

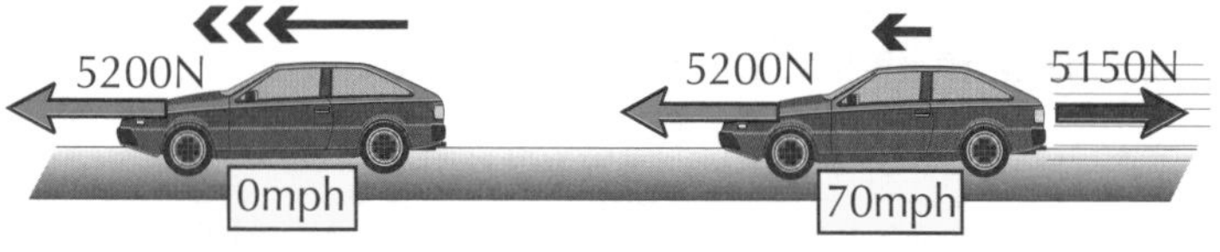

Car at 0 mph:
Resultant force = 5,200 N
Car at 70 mph:
Resultant force = 5,200 – 5150 = 50 N

Friction and Terminal Velocity

1) Friction is always there to slow things down

1) If an object has no force propelling it along, it will always slow down and stop because of friction.
2) Friction always acts in the opposite direction to movement.
3) To travel at a steady speed, the driving force needs to balance the frictional forces.
4) Friction occurs in two main ways:

a) Friction between solid surfaces which are sliding past each other

For example between brake pads and brake discs. There's just as much force of friction here as between the tyres and the road. In fact in the end, if you brake hard enough the friction here becomes greater than at the tyres, and then the wheel skids.

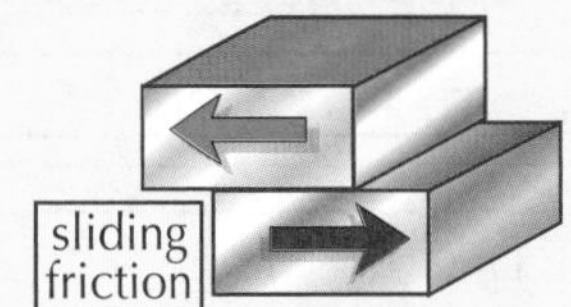

b) Resistance or "drag" from fluids (air or liquid)

The most important factor by far in reducing drag in fluids is keeping the shape of the object streamlined, like fish bodies or boat hulls or bird wings/bodies. The opposite extreme is a parachute which is about as high drag as you can get — which is, of course, the whole idea.

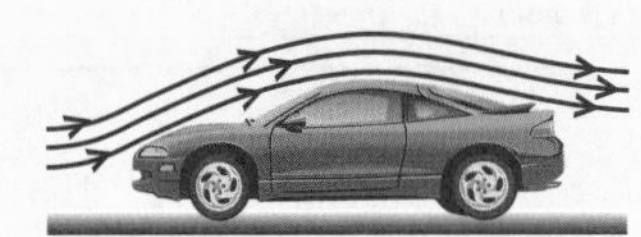

2) But we also need friction to move and to stop

It's easy to think of friction as generally a nuisance because we always seem to be working against it, but don't forget that without it we wouldn't be able to walk or run or go sky-diving etc. It also holds nuts and bolts together.

3) Friction causes wear and heating

1) Friction acts between surfaces that are sliding past each other. Machinery has lots of surfaces doing that.
2) Friction always produces heat and wearing of the surfaces.
3) Lubricants keep the friction low and thus reduce wear.

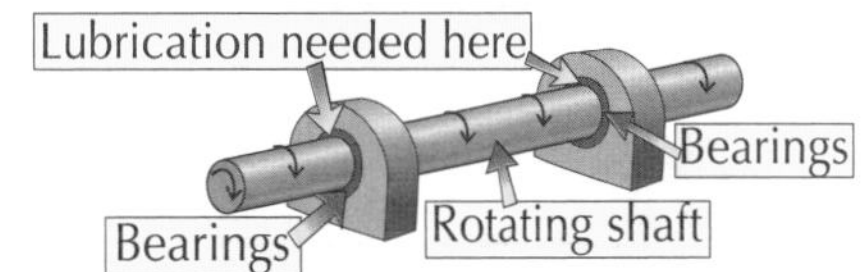

Cars and free-fallers all reach a terminal velocity

When cars and free-falling objects first set off they have much more force accelerating them than resistance slowing them down. As the speed increases, the resistance builds up. This gradually reduces the acceleration until eventually the resistance force is equal to the accelerating force and then it won't be able to accelerate any more.
It will have reached its maximum speed or TERMINAL VELOCITY.

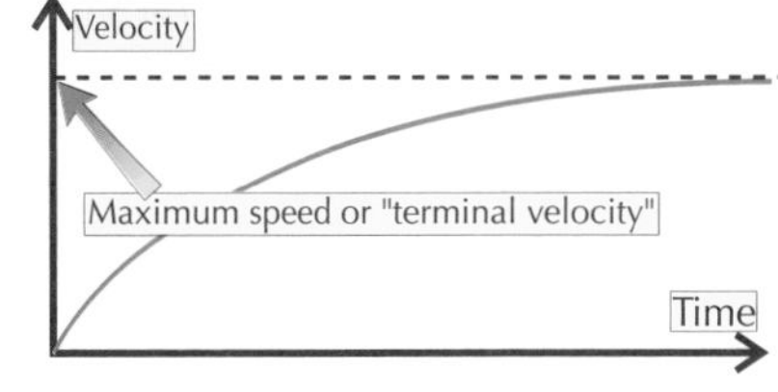

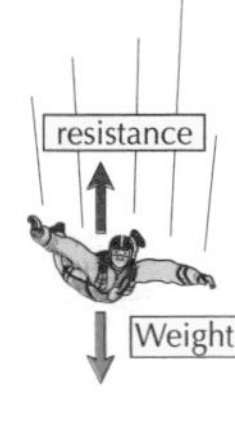

The most important example is the human skydiver. Without his parachute open he has quite a small area and a force of "W=mg" pulling him down. He reaches a terminal velocity of about 120mph.
But with the parachute open, there's much more air resistance (at any given speed) and still only the same force "W=mg" pulling him down.
This means his terminal velocity comes right down to about 15mph, which is a safe speed to hit the ground at.

Stopping Distances for Cars

They're pretty keen on this for Exam questions, so make sure you learn it properly.

The *many factors* which affect your total *stopping distance*

The distance it takes to stop a car is divided into the thinking distance and the braking distance.

1) Thinking distance

"The distance the car travels in the split-second between a hazard appearing and the driver applying the brakes."

It's affected by three main factors:

a) How FAST you're going — obviously. Whatever your reaction time, the faster you're going, the further you'll go.

b) How ALERT (OR NOT) you are — This is affected by tiredness, drugs, alcohol, old-age, and a careless blasé attitude.

c) How BAD the VISIBILITY is — lashing rain and oncoming lights, etc. make hazards harder to spot.

2) Braking distance

"The distance the car travels during its deceleration whilst the brakes are being applied."

It's affected by four main factors:

a) How FAST you're going — obviously. The faster you're going, the further it takes to stop.

b) How HEAVILY LOADED the vehicle is — with the same brakes, a heavily-laden vehicle takes longer to stop. A car won't stop as quickly when it's full of people and luggage and towing a caravan.

c) How good your BRAKES are — all brakes must be checked and maintained regularly. Worn or faulty brakes will let you down catastrophically just when you need them the most, i.e. in an emergency.

d) How good the GRIP is — this depends on three things: 1) road surface, 2) weather conditions, 3) tyres.

Leaves and diesel spills and dirt on the road are serious hazards because they're unexpected. Wet or icy roads are always much more slippery than dry roads, but often you only discover this when you try to brake hard.

Tyres should have a minimum tread depth of 1.6mm. This is essential for getting rid of the water in wet conditions. Without tread, a tyre will simply ride on a layer of water and skid very easily. This is called "aquaplaning" and is very dangerous.

The figures on the right for typical stopping distances are taken from the Highway code. It's frightening to see just how far it takes to stop when you're going at 70mph.

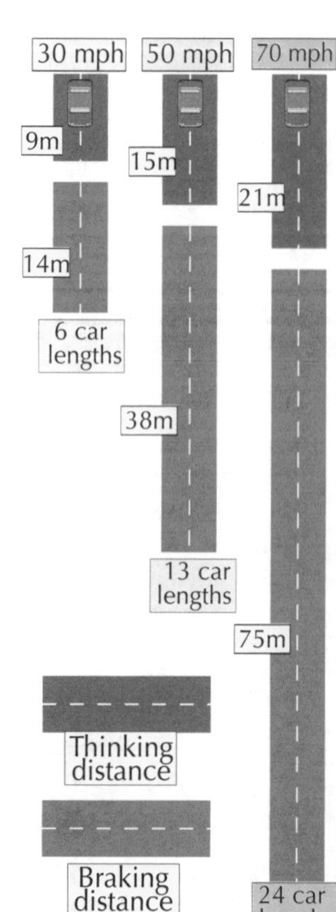

Work and Energy

Work is *Energy Transferred*

When a *force* moves an *object*, *ENERGY IS TRANSFERRED* and *WORK IS DONE*

That statement sounds far more complicated than it needs to. Try this:

1) Whenever something moves, something else is providing some sort of "effort" to move it.
2) The thing putting the effort in needs a supply of energy (like fuel, food or electricity, etc.).
3) It then does "work" by moving the object — and one way or another it transfers the energy it receives (as fuel) into other forms.
4) Whether this energy is transferred "usefully" (e.g. by lifting a load) or "wasted" (e.g. lost as friction), you can still say that "work is done". "Work done" and "energy transferred" are "one and the same" (& they're both in *joules*).

It's a simple Formula:

Work Done = Force × Distance

Whether the force is friction or weight or tension in a rope, it's always the same. To find how much energy has been transferred (in joules), you just multiply the force in N by the distance moved in m. Easy as that.

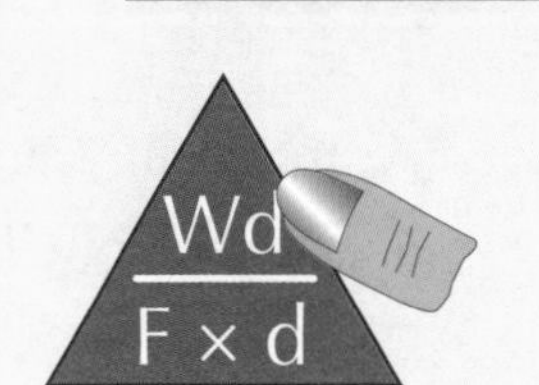

Example: Some children drag an old tractor tyre 5m over rough ground. They pull with a total force of 340N. Find the energy transferred.

Answer: *Wd = F×d = 340 × 5 = 1700J*.

Kinetic energy is energy of movement

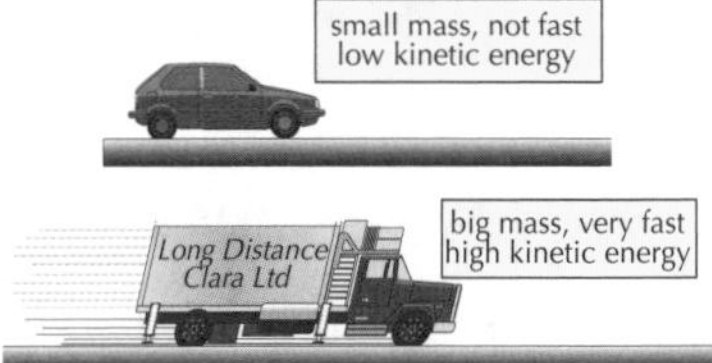

Anything which is moving has kinetic energy.
The kinetic energy of something depends both on mass and speed.
The more it weighs and the faster it's going, the bigger its kinetic energy will be.

There's a slightly tricky formula for it, so you have to concentrate a bit harder for this one.

Kinetic Energy = ½ × mass × velocity²

K.E. / ½×m×v²

Example: A car of mass 2450kg is travelling at 38m/s. Calculate its kinetic energy.

Answer: It's pretty easy. You just plug the numbers into the formula but watch the "V^2"
$KE = \frac{1}{2} m v^2 = \frac{1}{2} \times 2450 \times 38^2$ = 1 768 900J (Joules because it's energy)
(When the car stops suddenly, all this energy is dissipated as heat at the brakes — it's a lot of heat)

Tricky Example (see also p202 on potential energy)

Example: A beanbag of mass 140 g is dropped from a height of 1.7 m. Calculate its speed as it hits the floor.

Answer: There are four key steps to this method — and you've got to learn them:

Step 1) Find the PE lost: = mgh = 0.14 × 10 × 1.7 = 2.38 J This must also be the KE gained.

Step 2) Equate the number of joules of KE gained to the KE formula with v in, " $\frac{1}{2}mv^2$ ":

$$2.38 = \tfrac{1}{2}mv^2$$

Step 3) Stick the numbers in and find a value for v^2:

$2.38 = \frac{1}{2} \times 0.14 \times v^2$ or $2.38 = 0.07 \times v^2$ so $2.38 \div 0.07 = v^2$ or $v^2 = 34$

Step 4) Find the square root: $v = \sqrt{34}$ = 5.83 m/s

Practise learning the four steps and that won't be too bad.

If you learn these eight things you won't go far wrong:

1) Learn that weight and mass are not the same. 2) Learn the 3 force diagrams. 3) Learn the three main effects of friction. 4) Learn all the factors affecting total stopping distance. 5) Learn how to calculate the resultant force. 6) Learn that "Energy transferred" and "work done" are the same thing. 7) Learn the KE formula and the examples. 8) Learn that "work done divided by time taken" = power (i.e. power = energy/time, which you already know).

Warm-Up and Exam Questions

Warm-up Questions

1) Name the force that makes the Earth orbit the Sun.
2) When an astronaut travels from the Earth to the Moon, does the astronaut's mass increase, decrease or stay the same?
3) This car is accelerating to the left along a horizontal road.
   a) Copy the diagram and add the thrust and drag forces.
   b) Which pair of forces will be i) balanced; ii) unbalanced?

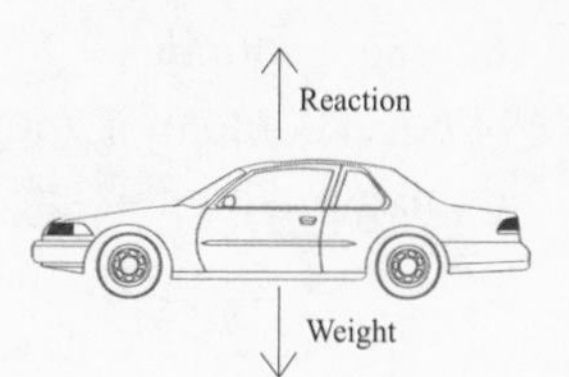

4) Name two situations where friction is a) a nuisance and b) useful.

Exam Questions

1 a) Why must a car driver use less braking force in icy conditions than in dry conditions?

(2 marks)

b) In recent years, most lorries have been fitted with aerofoils, as shown in the diagram. By thinking about the forces acting on the lorry, explain what the aerofoil does and why it is fitted.

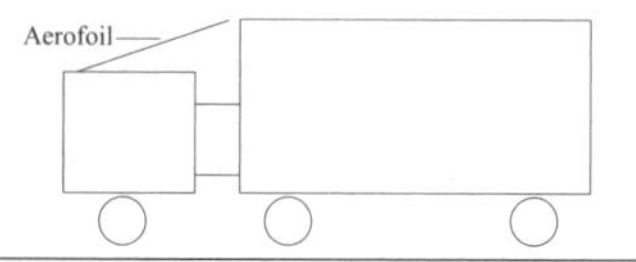

(3 marks)

c) A lorry driver receives extra pay if she can use less petrol on her journey. Explain why she decides to go no faster than 65 km/h, even on the motorway.

(2 marks)

2 A satellite has a mass of 85kg on the Earth's surface (gravitational field strength, g = 10N/kg).

a) What is the weight of the satellite when it is on the Earth's surface?

(1 mark)

b) This satellite is put into orbit around the Earth at a place where g = 6 N/kg. Find:
i) The mass of the satellite in orbit and ii) The weight of the satellite in orbit

(2 marks)

c) Explain why little money is generally spent on designing satellites that are aerodynamic.

(2 marks)

3 A car of mass 1200kg travels on a level road at a constant velocity of 24m/s.

a) What is the resultant force on the car? Explain your answer.

(2 marks)

b) Calculate the kinetic energy of the car.

(3 marks)

c) By considering the work done in stopping the car, find the average braking force exerted on the car to bring it to rest in a distance of 50m.

(3 marks)

d) The actual braking force will be less than your answer to part (c). Explain why.

(2 marks)

e) If three extra people sat in the car, how would its braking distance at this speed be affected, assuming that the same braking force was used? Explain your answer.

(2 marks)

Planets and Satellites

You need to revise the order of the planets, which is made easier by using the little mnemonic below:

Mercury,	Venus,	Earth,	Mars,	(Asteroids),	Jupiter,	Saturn,	Uranus,	Neptune,	Pluto
(My	Very	Energetic	Maiden	Aunt	Just	Swam	Under	North	Pier)

Mercury, Venus, Earth and Mars are known as the inner planets.

Jupiter, Saturn, Uranus, Neptune and Pluto are much further away and are the outer planets.

Planets **reflect sunlight** and orbit in **ellipses**

1) You can see some of the nearer planets with the naked eye at night, e.g. Mars and Venus.
2) They look just like stars, but they are of course totally different.
3) Stars are huge and very far away and give out lots of light. The planets are smaller and nearer and they just reflect sunlight falling on them.
4) The Sun, like other stars, produces heat from nuclear fusion reactions which turn hydrogen into helium. It gives out the full spectrum of EM radiation.
5) Planets always orbit around stars. In our Solar System the planets orbit the Sun of course.
6) These orbits are all slightly elliptical (elongated circles).
7) All the planets in our Solar System orbit in the same plane except Pluto (as shown in the picture above).
8) The further the planet is from the Sun, the longer its orbit takes (see below about Gravity).

Gravity decreases **quickly** as you get further away

1) With very large masses like stars and planets, gravity is very big and acts a long way out.
2) The closer you get to a star or a planet, the stronger the force of attraction.
3) To counteract the stronger gravity, planets nearer the Sun move faster and cover their orbit quicker.
4) Comets are also held in orbit by gravity, as are moons and satellites and space stations.
5) The size of the force of gravity follows the fairly famous "inverse square" relationship. The main effect of that is that the force decreases very quickly with increasing distance. The formula is $F \propto 1/d^2$, but it's easier just to remember the basic idea in words:

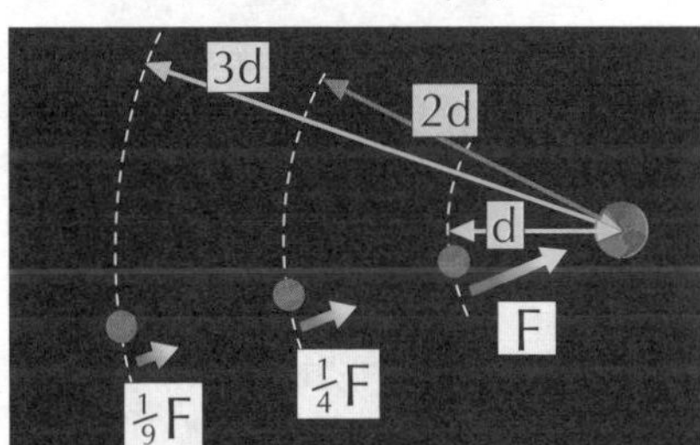

a) If you double the distance from a planet, the size of the force will decrease by a factor of four (2^2).
b) If you treble the distance, the force of gravity will decrease by a factor of nine (3^2), and so on.
c) On the other hand, if you get twice as close the gravity becomes four times stronger.

Planets in the **night sky** seem to **move** across the **constellations**

1) The planets look just like stars except that they wander across the constellations over periods of days or weeks, often going in the opposite direction to the stars.
2) Their position and movement depends on where they are in their orbit, compared to us.
3) This peculiar movement of the planets made the early astronomers such as Copernicus realise that the Earth was not the centre of the Universe after all, but was in fact just the third rock from the Sun. It's very strong evidence for the Sun-centred model of the Solar System.
4) Unfortunately, the Spanish Inquisition was less than keen on such heresy, and Copernicus had a pretty hard time of it for a while. In the end though, "the truth will out".

Planets and Satellites

Moons are sometimes called natural satellites.

Artificial satellites are sent up by humans for four main purposes:

1) Monitoring Weather.
2) Communications, e.g. phone and TV.
3) Space research such as the Hubble Telescope.
4) Spying.

There are two different orbits useful for satellites:

The *speed* of a satellite is *important*

All satellites in orbit about a body, be they artificial or natural, have to move at a certain speed to stay in orbit at a certain distance. The greater the distance away the longer it takes to complete a full orbit. This also means that the further away then the slower the satellite must travel to maintain its orbit.

Geostationary satellites are used for *communications*

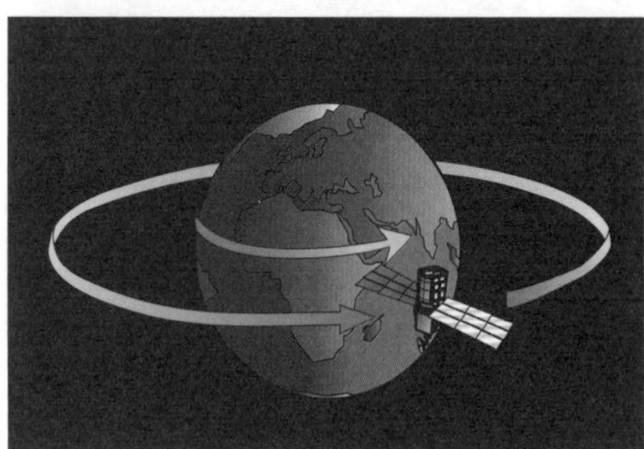

1) These can also be called *geosynchronous* satellites.
2) They are put in quite a high orbit over the Equator which takes exactly 24 hours to complete.
3) This means that they stay above the same point on the Earth's surface because the Earth rotates with them — hence the name Geo-(Earth)stationary.
4) This makes them ideal for telephone and TV because they're always in the same place and they can transfer signals from one side of the Earth to another in a fraction of a second.
5) There is room for about 400 geostationary satellites — any more and their orbits will interfere.

Low polar orbit satellites are for *weather* and *spying*

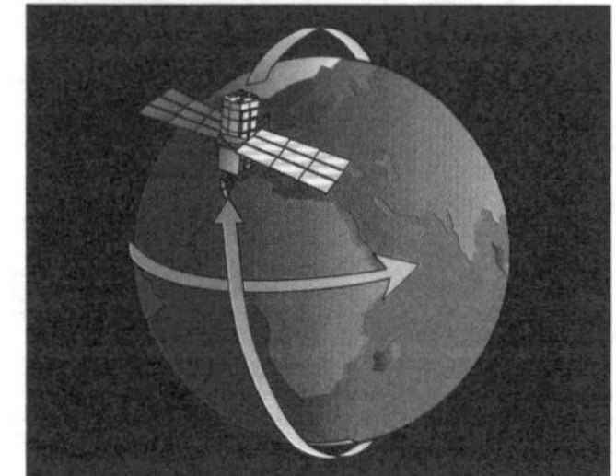

1) In a low polar orbit the satellite sweeps over both poles whilst the Earth rotates beneath it.
2) The time taken for each full orbit is just a few hours.
3) Each time the satellite comes round it can scan the next bit of the globe.
4) This allows the whole surface of the planet to be monitored each day.
5) Geostationary satellites are too high to take good weather or spying photos, but the satellites in polar orbits are nice and low.

Comets orbit the *Sun*, but have very *eccentric* (elongated) *orbits*

1) Comets only appear every few years because their orbits take them very far from the Sun and then back in close, which is when we see them.
2) The comet travels much faster when it's nearer the Sun than it does when it's in the more distant part of its orbit. This is because the pull of gravity makes it speed up as it gets closer, and then slows it down as it gets further away.

Orbits are all about gravity and speed

You can actually see the low polar orbit satellites on a nice dark clear night. They look like stars except they move quite fast in a dead straight line across the sky. You'll never spot the geostationary ones though. Learn all the details about planets, gravity and satellites, ready for seizing plenty of marks.

Warm-Up and Exam Questions

Warm-up Questions

1) Which planet takes the longest time to orbit the Sun?
2) Why are planets sometimes referred to as 'wanderers'?
3) Name two planets that can easily be seen at night using just your eyes.
4) Write a phrase to remember the order of the planets (including the Asteroid Belt), starting with Mercury.
5) Name a natural satellite of the Earth.
6) Give four uses for artificial satellites.

Exam Questions

1 This question is about objects which orbit the Sun.

a) Name the four inner planets.

(1 mark)

b) Explain why the Earth orbits the Sun.

(2 marks)

c) Describe the orbit of the Earth around the Sun.

(1 mark)

2 Geostationary satellites are used for communications.

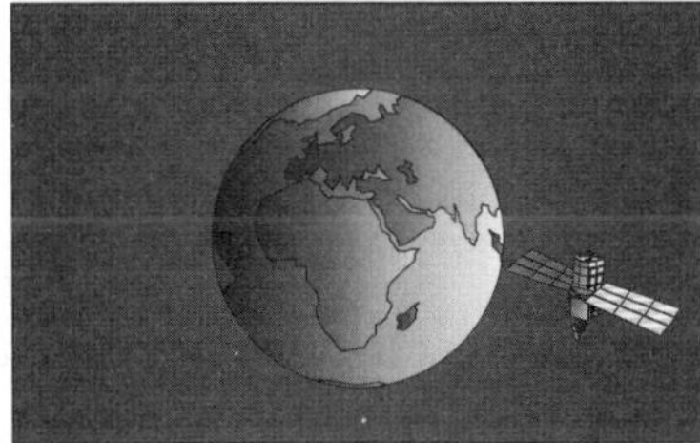

a) Describe the orbit of a geostationary satellite.

(3 marks)

b) Why is a satellite in a polar orbit better for spying than one in a geostationary orbit?

(2 marks)

Searching for Life on Other Planets

There's a good chance that life exists somewhere else in the Universe.
Scientists use three methods to search for anything from amoebas to little green men.

1) SETI looks for radio signals from other planets

1) Here on Earth we are constantly beaming radio, TV and radar into space for any passing aliens to detect. There might be life out there that's as clever as we are, or even more clever. They may have built transmitters to send out signals like ours.
2) SETI stands for "Search for Extra Terrestrial Intelligence". Scientists on the SETI project are looking for narrow bands of radio wavelengths coming to Earth from outer space. They're looking for meaningful signals in all the 'noise'.
3) Signals on a narrow band can only come from a transmitter. The 'noise' comes from giant stars and gas clouds.
4) It takes ages to analyse all the radio waves so the SETI people get help from the public — you can download a screen saver off the internet which analyses a chunk of radio waves.

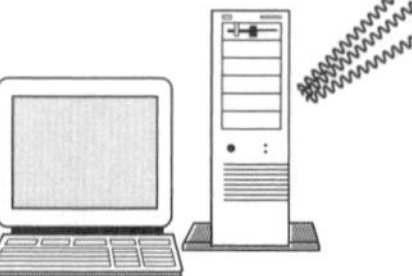

5) SETI has been going for the last 40 years but they've not found anything yet.

6) Scientists are now looking for possible laser signals from outer space. Watch this space.

2) Robots collect photos and samples

This could be a microscopic fossil of a bacteria-like organism from Mars.
500 nm

1) Scientists have sent robots in spacecraft to Mars and Europa (one of Jupiter's moons) to look for microorganisms.
2) The robots wander round the planet, sending photographs back to Earth or collecting samples for analysis.
3) Scientists can detect living things or evidence of them, such as fossils or remains, in the samples. This "fossil" is from Mars, though no one really seems sure *what* it is.

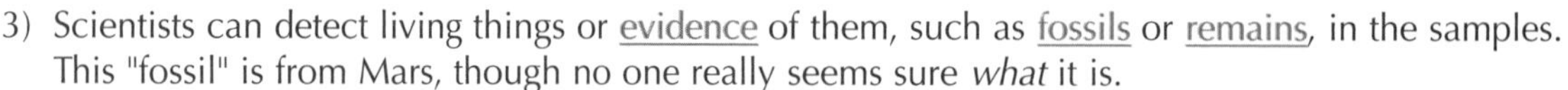

4) A couple of bacteria may not seem that interesting, but that's how we started out on Earth.

3) Chemical changes and reflected light are big clues

Changes show there's life

1) Scientists are looking for chemical changes in the atmospheres of other planets.
2) Some changes are just caused by things like volcanoes but others are a clue that there's life there.
3) The amounts of oxygen and carbon dioxide in Earth's atmosphere have changed over time — it's very different to what it'd be like if there was no life here. Plants have made oxygen levels go up but carbon dioxide levels go down.

Light gives away what's on the surface

4) They look at planet's atmospheres from Earth — no spacecraft required.
A planet's reflected light (from the Sun) is different depending on whether it's bounced off rock, trees, water or whatever. It's a good way to find out what's on the surface of a planet.
Scientists haven't found anything exciting but they are using these methods to search for planets with suitable conditions for life.

The Universe

Stars and planetary systems form from clouds of dust

1) Stars form from clouds of dust which spiral in together due to gravitational attraction.
2) The gravity compresses the matter so much that intense heat develops and sets off nuclear fusion reactions and the star then begins emitting light and other radiation.
3) At the same time that the star is forming, other lumps may develop in the spiralling dust clouds and these eventually gather together and form planets which orbit around the star.

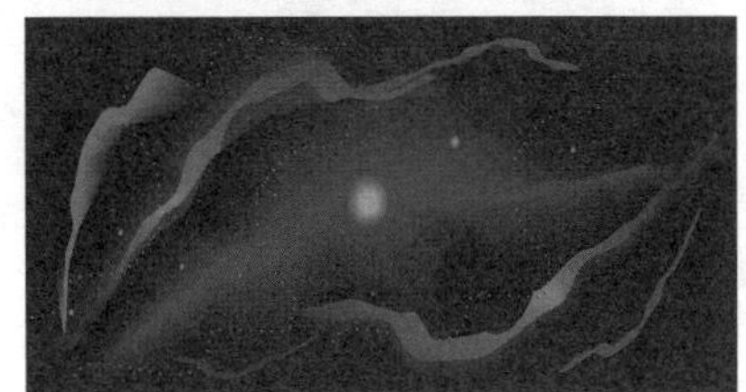

Our Sun is in the Milky Way Galaxy

1) The Sun is one of many millions of stars which form the Milky Way Galaxy.
2) The distance between neighbouring stars is usually millions of times greater than the distance between planets in our Solar System. The Milky Way is 100,000 light years across.
3) Gravity is of course the force which keeps the stars together in a galaxy and, like most things in the Universe, the galaxies all rotate, a bit like a catherine wheel only much slower.
4) Our Sun is out towards the end of one of the spiral arms of the Milky Way galaxy.

The whole universe has more than a billion galaxies

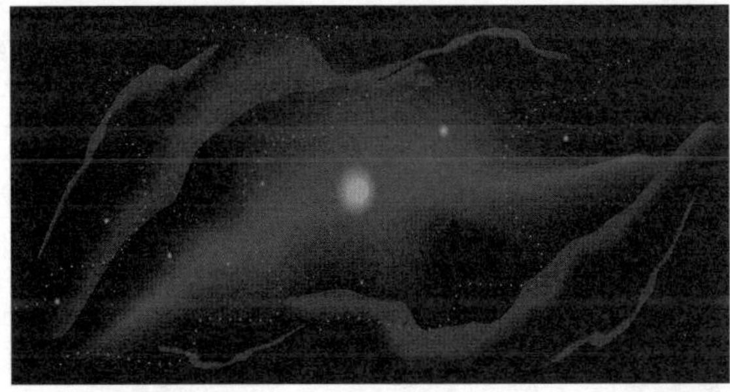

1) Galaxies themselves are often millions of times further apart than the stars are within a galaxy.
2) You should now realise that the Universe is mostly empty space and is really really big.

Black holes don't let anything escape

1) The gravity on neutron stars, white dwarfs and black dwarfs is so strong that it crushes atoms. The stuff in the stars gets squashed up so much that they're MILLIONS OF TIMES DENSER than anything on Earth.
2) If enough matter is left behind after a supernova explosion, it's so dense that nothing can escape the powerful gravitational field. Not even electromagnetic waves. The dead star is then called a black hole. Black holes aren't visible because any light being emitted is sucked right back in there (that's why it's called 'black', of course).
3) Astronomers can detect black holes in other ways — they can observe X-rays emitted by hot gases from other stars as they spiral into the black hole.

The Life Cycle of Stars

Stars go through many traumatic stages in their lives.

1) Stars initially form from clouds of dust and gas.

2) The force of gravity makes the dust particles come spiralling in together. As they do, gravitational energy is converted into heat energy and the temperature rises.

3) When the temperature gets high enough, hydrogen nuclei undergo nuclear fusion to form helium nuclei and give out massive amounts of heat and light. A star is born. It immediately enters a long stable period where the heat created by the nuclear fusion provides an outward pressure to balance the force of gravity pulling everything inwards. In this stable period it's called a main sequence star and it lasts about 10 billion years. (The Earth will already have been around for half its time before the Sun engulfs it.)

4) Eventually the hydrogen begins to run out and the star then swells into a Red Giant. It becomes red because the surface cools.

5) A small star like our Sun will then begin to cool and contract into a white dwarf and then finally, as the light fades completely, it becomes a black dwarf.

6) Big stars, however, start to glow brightly again as they undergo more fusion and expand and contract several times forming heavier elements in various nuclear reactions. Eventually they explode in a supernova.

7) The exploding supernova throws the outer layers of dust and gas into space leaving a very dense core called a neutron star. If the star is big enough this will become a black hole.

8) The dust and gas thrown off by the supernova will form into *SECOND GENERATION STARS* like our Sun. The heavier elements are only made in the final stages of a big star just before the final supernova, so the presence of heavier elements in the Sun and the inner planets is clear evidence that our world, with its warm sunsets and fresh morning dews, was formed out of the remains of a very old star.

9) The matter from which neutron stars and white dwarfs and black dwarfs are made is millions of times denser than any matter on Earth because the gravity is so strong it even crushes the atoms.

The Origin of the Universe

The Big Bang Theory of the Universe is the most convincing at the present time. There is also the steady state theory which is quite presentable but it doesn't explain some of the observed features too well.

Red-shift needs explaining

There are two important bits of evidence you need to know about:

1) Light from other galaxies is red-shifted

1) When we look at light from distant galaxies we find that all the frequencies are shifted towards the red end of the spectrum.
2) In other words, the frequencies are all slightly lower than they should be. It's the same effect as a car horn sounding lower-pitched when the car is travelling away from you. The sound drops in frequency.
3) This is called the *DOPPLER EFFECT*.
4) Measurements of the red-shift suggest that all the galaxies are moving away from us very quickly — and it's the same result whichever direction you look in.

2) The further away a galaxy is, the greater the red-shift

1) More distant galaxies have greater red-shifts than nearer ones.
2) This means that more distant galaxies are moving away faster than nearer ones.
3) The inescapable conclusion appears to be that the whole Universe is expanding.

The Big Bang Theory — the popular theory

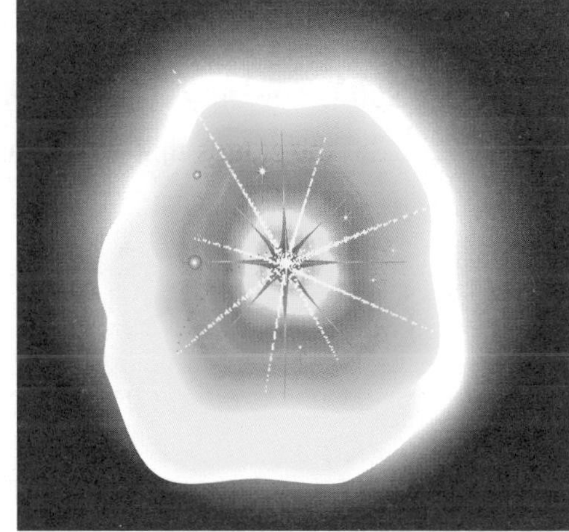

1) Since all the galaxies appear to be moving apart very rapidly, the obvious conclusion is that there was an initial explosion: the Big Bang.
2) All the matter in the Universe must have been compressed into a very small space and then it exploded — and the expansion is still going on.
3) The Big Bang is believed to have happened around 15 billion years ago.
4) The age of the Universe can be estimated from the current rate of expansion.
5) These estimates are not very accurate because it's hard to tell how much the expansion has slowed down since the Big Bang.
6) The rate at which the expansion is slowing down is an important factor in deciding the future of the Universe.
7) Without gravity the Universe would expand at the same rate forever.
8) However, the attraction between all the mass in the Universe tends to slow the expansion down.

We really are very very small

You need to learn the three different ways that scientists are looking for life on other planets. There are also some amazing numbers to ponder in this section: there are millions of stars in the Milky Way and it's 100,000 light years across, the Universe contains billions of galaxies, all millions of times further apart than 100,000 light years... how do they know all this stuff? They also seem to know the whole life cycle of stars, even though they're all billions and billions of km away. Amazing. Anyway, the other things to learn here are the seven points about red shift and the important bits about the big bang theory (and how it explains red shift).

Warm-Up and Exam Questions

Warm-up Questions

1) It is possible that TV signals from Earth could be picked up by aliens in the future. Explain how this could happen.
2) Place the following in order of increasing size: galaxy, moon, planet, solar system, sun, universe.
3) What is happening inside a star to produce energy?
4) a) What is a galaxy? b) What force keeps it together?
5) Why is the word 'black' used in the expression 'black hole'?
6) What was the Big Bang? How long ago is it believed to have happened?
7) What force may prevent the Universe from expanding forever?
8) How do scientists measure how fast a galaxy is moving away from us?

Exam Questions

1 Scientists are searching for other life in the Universe.

a) How could robots sent from Earth help in this task?

....

(1 mark)

b) Describe two different methods that scientists on Earth can use to search for life elsewhere.

....

....

(2 marks)

2 Our Sun is now in its stable period as a main sequence star.
Describe the stages that will happen to the Sun between now and it becoming a black dwarf.

....

....

....

....

(5 marks)

3 If a star is massive enough, it will eventually turn into a supernova.

a) What is left behind after a supernova?

....

(1 mark)

b) How is a supernova linked to the presence of heavier elements in our Sun and its inner planets?

....

....

(3 marks)

Revision Summary for Section Eleven

There are lots of facts about forces and motion that you definitely need to know. Some bits are tricky to understand, but there's also loads of straightforward stuff which just needs to be learnt, ready to reproduce in the Exam. You have to practise these questions over and over and over again, until you can answer them all really easily.

1) Write down the formula for working out speed. Find the speed of a ball that rolls 3.2 m in 35 s. Find how far it would get in 25 minutes at the same speed.
2) What's acceleration? Is it the same thing as speed or velocity? What are the units of it?
3) Write down the formula for acceleration. What's the acceleration of a beanbag, kicked from rest to a speed of 14 m/s in 0.4 s?
4) Sketch a typical distance-time graph and point out all the important parts of it.
5) Sketch a typical velocity-time graph and point out all the important parts of it.
6) Explain how to calculate velocity from a distance-time graph.
7) Explain how to find speed, distance and acceleration from a velocity-time graph.
8) Write down the First Law of Motion. Illustrate with a diagram.
9) Write down the Second Law of Motion. Illustrate with a diagram. What's the formula for it?
10) A force of 30 N pushes on a trolley of mass 4 kg. What will be its acceleration?
11) What's the mass of a cat which accelerates at 9.8 m/s^2 when acted on by a force of 56 N?
12) Write down the Third Law of Motion. Illustrate it with four diagrams.
13) Explain what reaction force is and where it occurs. Is it important to know about it?
14) What is gravity? List the three main effects that gravity produces.
15) Explain the difference between mass and weight. What are the units for mass?
16) What's the formula for weight? Illustrate it with a worked example of your own.
17) List the two main types of friction with a sketch to illustrate each one.
18) What 2 effects does friction have on machinery?
19) What is "terminal velocity"? Is it the same thing as maximum speed?
20) What are the two main factors affecting the terminal velocity of a falling object?
21) What are the two different parts of the overall stopping distance of a car?
22) List the three or four factors which affect each of the two sections of stopping distance.
23) What's the formula for work done? A truck pulls a trailer 12 m, pulling with a force of 535 N. How much energy is transferred?
24) What two things affect the kinetic energy of an object?
25) Calculate the kinetic energy of a 78 kg sheep running at a speed of 5 m/s.
26) List the eleven parts of the Solar System starting with the Sun, and get them in the right order.
27) How does the Sun produce all its heat? What does the Sun give out?
28) What are constellations? What do planets do in the constellations?
29) What is it that keeps the planets in their orbits? What other things are held in orbits?
30) What happens to the force of gravity as you move away from a planet?
31) Explain fully what a geostationary satellite does, and state what they're used for.
32) Explain fully what a low polar orbit satellite does, and state what they're used for.
33) Which of the two types of satellite takes longer to orbit the Earth? Explain why.
34) What's unusual about the orbit of comets?
35) What does SETI stand for? Why are they looking for narrow band signals?
36) What two things do robots on planets send back? Which places have they sent robots to?
37) Describe 2 ways that scientists look for life on a planet without sending a spacecraft there.
38) Has life been found on other planets?
39) What do stars and planetary systems form from? What force causes it all to happen?
40) What is the Milky Way? Sketch it and show our Sun in relation to it.
41) Describe the first stages of a star's formation. Where does the initial energy come from?
42) What process eventually starts inside the star to make it produce so much heat and light?
43) What are the final two stages of: a) a small star's life? b) a big star's life?
44) What is the main theory for the origin of the Universe? Give brief details of the theory.
45) Give two important bits of evidence which need explaining by this theory?

Waves — Basic Principles

Waves are different from anything else. They have various features which only waves have:

Amplitude, wavelength and frequency

Too many people get these wrong. Take careful note:

1) The amplitude goes from the middle line to the peak, NOT from a trough to a peak.
2) The wavelength covers a full cycle of the wave, e.g. from peak to peak, not just from *"two bits that are sort of separated a bit"*.
3) Frequency is how many complete waves there are per second (passing a certain point).

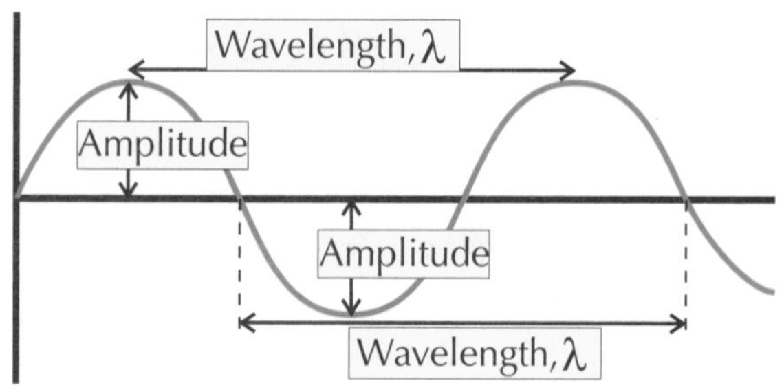

Transverse waves have sideways vibrations

Most waves are transverse:

1) Light and all other EM radiation.
2) Ripples on water.
3) Waves on strings.
4) A slinky spring wiggled up and down.

In transverse waves the vibrations are at 90° to the direction of travel of the wave.

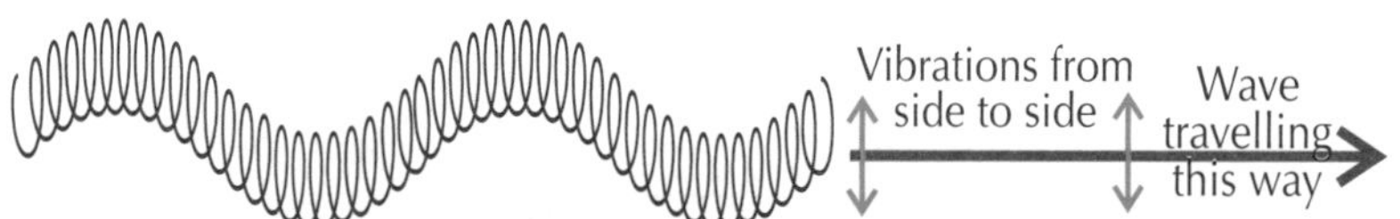

Longitudinal waves have vibrations along the same line

The only longitudinal waves are:

1) Sound. It travels as a longitudinal wave through solids, liquids and gases.
2) Shock waves e.g. seismic P-waves.
3) A slinky spring when plucked.

In longitudinal waves the vibrations are along the same direction as the wave is travelling.

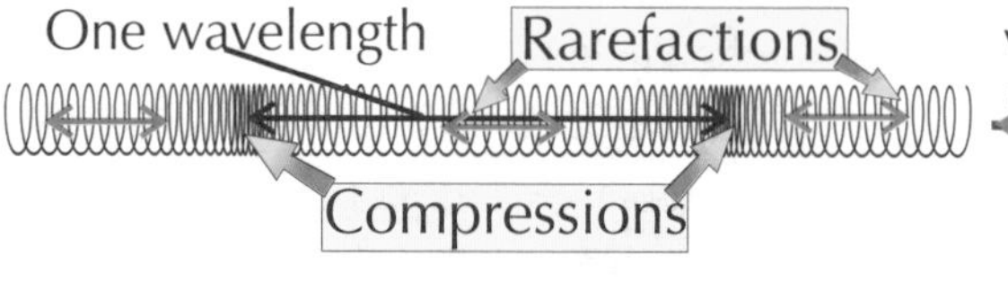

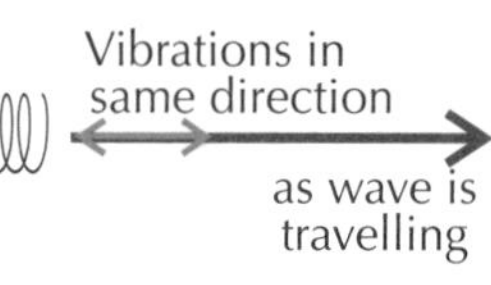

4) Don't get confused by CRO displays which show a transverse wave when displaying sounds. The real wave is longitudinal — the display shows a transverse wave just so you can see what's going on.

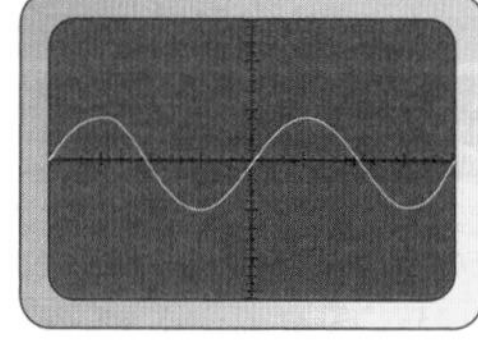

All waves carry energy — without transferring matter

1) Light, infrared, and microwaves all make things warm up. X-rays and gamma rays can cause ionisation and damage to cells, which also shows that they carry energy.
2) Loud sounds make things vibrate or move. Even the quietest sound moves your ear drum.
3) Waves on the sea can toss big boats around and can generate electricity.

Waves can be reflected and refracted and diffracted

1) They might test whether or not you realise these are properties of waves, so learn them.
2) The three words are confusingly similar but you must learn the differences between them.
3) Light and sound are reflected, refracted and diffracted and this shows they travel as waves.

Wave Formulas and Reflection

These are just formulas, just like all the other formulas, and the same rules apply.
There are a few extra details that go with these wave formulas though. Learn them now:

The first rule: Try and choose the right formula

1) People have too much difficulty deciding which formula to use.
2) All too often the question starts with "*A wave is travelling...*", and in they leap with "$v = f\lambda$".
3) To choose the right formula you have to look for the three quantities mentioned in the question.
4) If the question mentions speed, frequency and wavelength then sure, "$v = f\lambda$" is the one to use.
5) But if it has speed, time and distance then "$s = d/t$" is more like it.

Example — water ripples

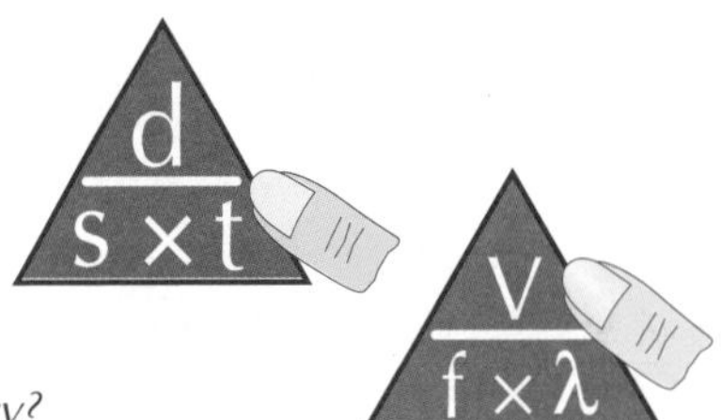

a) *Some ripples travel 55cm in 5 seconds. Find their speed in cm/s.*
Answer: Speed, distance and time are mentioned in the question, so we must use "s=d/t": $s = d/t = 55/5 = 11$ cm/s

b) *The wavelength of these waves is found to be 2.2cm. What is their frequency?*
Answer: This time we have f and λ mentioned, so we use "$v = f\lambda$", and we'll need this: which tells us that $f = v/\lambda = 11\text{cm/s} \div 2.2\text{cm} = 5\text{Hz}$ (It's fine to use cm/s with cm, s and Hz)

The ripple tank is really good for displaying waves

Learn all these diagrams showing reflection of waves. They could ask you to complete any one of them in the Exam. It can be quite a bit trickier than you think unless you've practised them well beforehand.

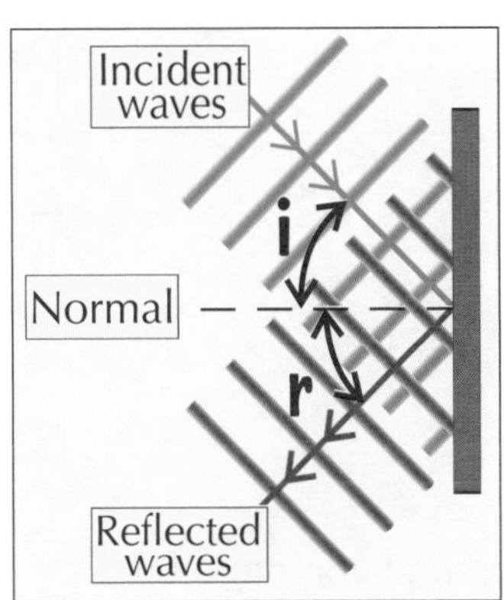

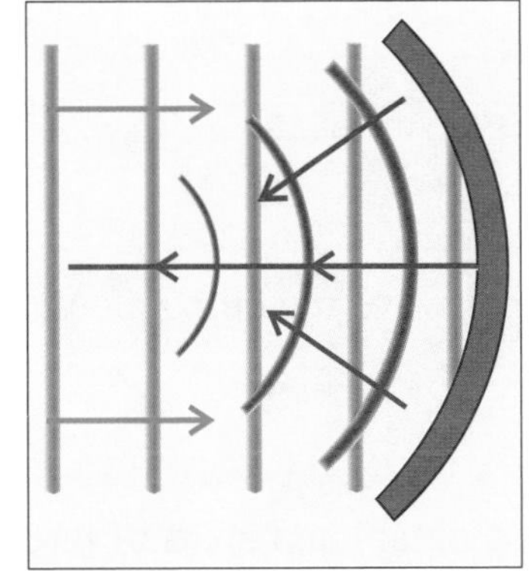

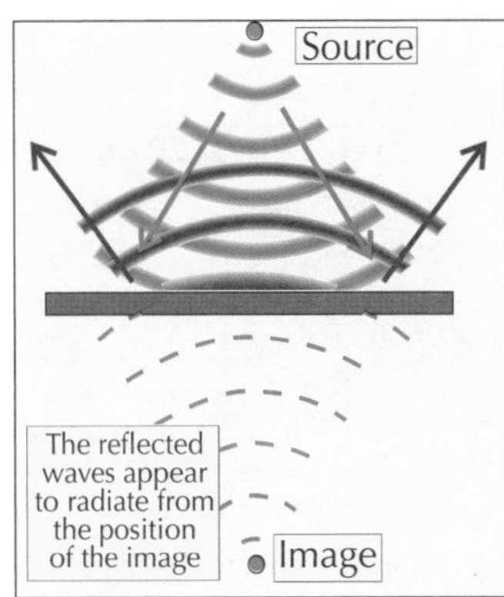

Reflection of light

Reflection of light is what allows us to see objects.
When light reflects from an even surface (smooth and shiny like a mirror) then it's all reflected at the same angle and you get a clear reflection.
Sound also reflects off hard surfaces in the form of echoes.
Reflection of light and of sound gives evidence that light and sound travel as waves.
And don't forget, the law of reflection applies to every reflected ray:

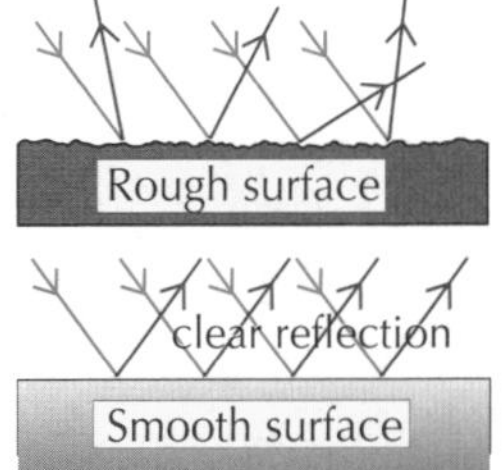

Angle of INCIDENCE = Angle of REFLECTION

Learn reflection thoroughly — try to look at it from all sides

First learn the five sections on the basics. Then make sure you can draw all those diagrams from memory and that you've learned the rest well enough to answer typical exam questions like: "Explain why you can see a piece of paper." "Explain why your voice echoes in a tunnel."

Warm-Up and Exam Questions

Warm-up Questions

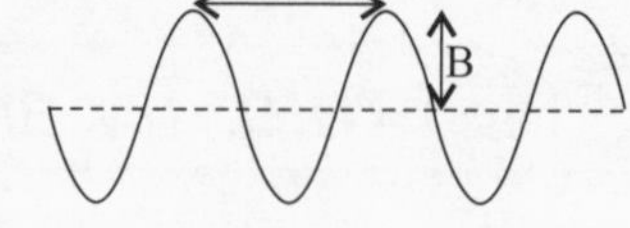

1) Name the features A and B shown on the diagram on the right.
2) Name the two types of wave and give one example of each type.
3) Explain how we can tell that gamma rays carry energy.
4) Calculate the speed of a sound wave which has frequency 2500 Hz and wavelength 13.2 cm.
5) a) The radio waves for Radio 4 have a wavelength of 1.5 km in air. Find their frequency.
   b) A cricketer hits a ball and a man hears the knock 0.8 s later. How far away is the man? (Take the speed of sound in air to be 330 m/s.)
6) A ship sends a sonar signal to the sea bed and detects the echo 0.7 s later. How deep is the sea at that point? (The speed of sound in water is 1400 m/s.)

Exam Questions

1 Here is a diagram of a transverse wave.

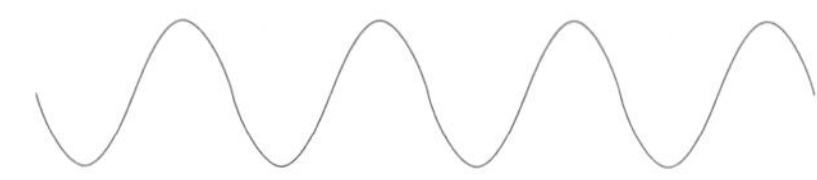

a) The wave has a frequency of 20 Hz. Explain what this means.

(1 mark)

b) The period is the time for one complete wave. Calculate the period of this wave.

(2 marks)

c) Give two examples of transverse waves.

(2 marks)

2 The diagram shows a longitudinal wave travelling along a slinky spring.

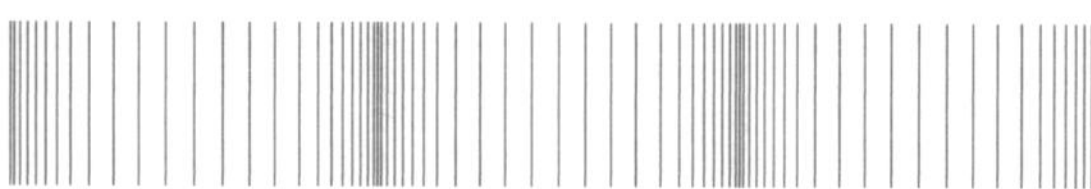

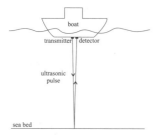

a) Label a wavelength on the diagram and areas of rarefaction and compression.

(3 marks)

b) Give another example of a longitudinal wave.

(1 mark)

3 The speed of sound in water is 1400 m/s.

a) An ultrasonic wave has a frequency of 28 000 Hz. Calculate its wavelength in water.

(2 marks)

b) A boat uses ultrasonic waves to calculate the depth of the sea, as shown in the diagram.

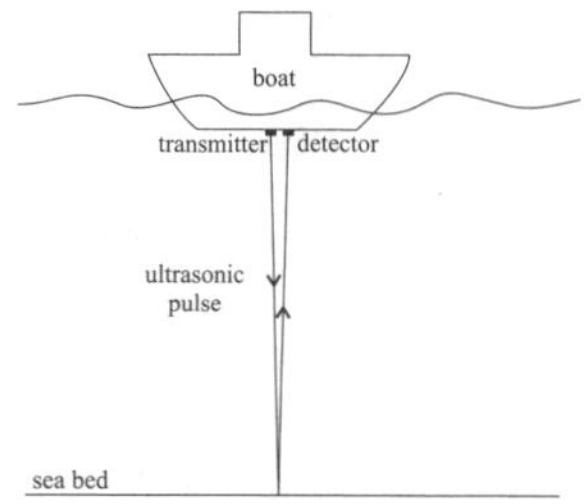

The pulse takes 0.2s to travel from the transmitter to the seabed and back to the detector.
Calculate the distance to the seabed.

(3 marks)

Refraction and Dispersion

1) Refraction is when waves change direction as they enter a different medium.
2) This is caused entirely by the change in speed of the waves.
3) It also causes the wavelength to change, but remember that the frequency does not change.

1) Refraction is shown by waves in a ripple tank slowing down

1) The waves travel slower in shallower water, causing refraction as shown.
2) There's a change in direction, and a change in wavelength but NO change in frequency.

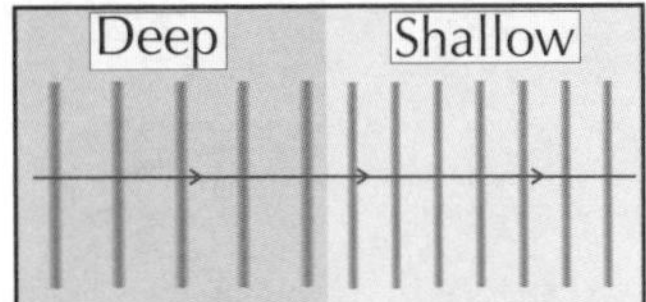

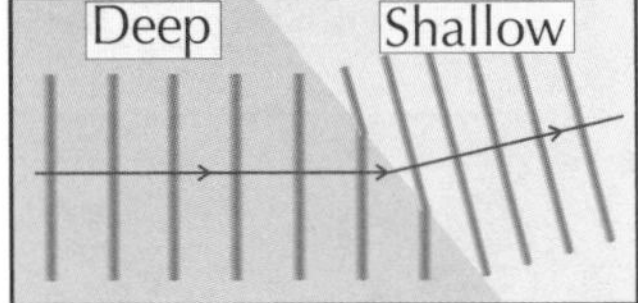

2) Refraction of light — the glass block demo

You can't fail to remember the "ray of light through a rectangular glass block" trick.
Make sure you can draw this diagram from memory, with every detail perfect.

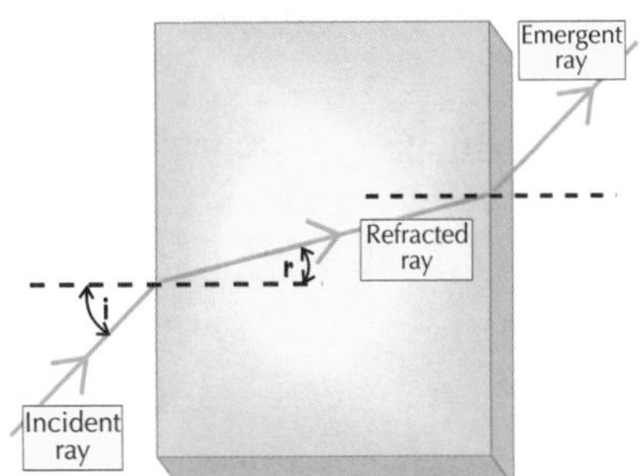

1) Take careful note of the positions of the normals and the exact positions of the angles of incidence and refraction (and note it's the angle of refraction — not reflection).
2) Most important of all remember which way the ray bends — towards the normal as it enters the denser medium, away from the normal as it emerges into the less dense medium.
3) Try to visualise the shape of the wiggle in the diagram — that can be easier than remembering the rule in words.

3) Refraction is always caused by the waves changing speed

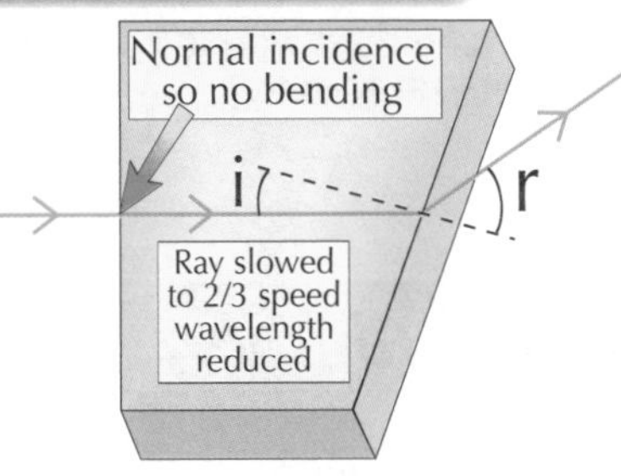

1) When waves slow down they bend towards the normal.
2) When light enters glass it slows down to about 2/3 of its speed in air.
3) When waves hit the boundary along a normal, i.e. at exactly 90°, then there will be no change in direction — this is important. There'll still be a change in speed and wavelength, though.
4) Some light is also reflected when light hits a different medium such as glass.
5) Sound refracts too...

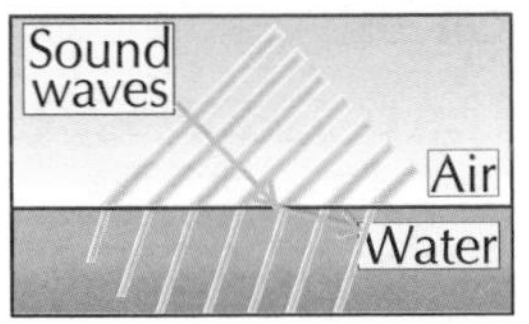

Sound will also refract (change direction) as it enters different media. However, since sound is always spreading out so much, the change in direction is hard to spot. Just remember, sound does refract. The fact that sound and light are both refracted gives further evidence that they travel as waves.

4) Dispersion produces rainbows

1) Different colours of light are refracted by different amounts. This is because they travel at slightly different speeds in any given medium.
2) If white light enters a prism, each different colour in it emerges at a different angle, producing a spectrum of the rainbow colours. This effect is known as DISPERSION. 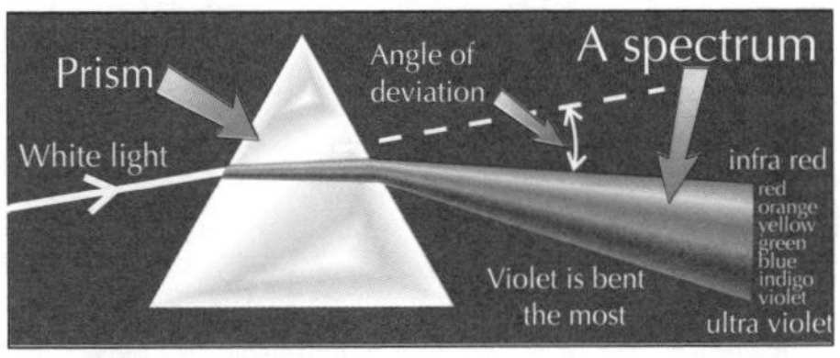
3) You will need to remember the order of the colours and this can be done by learning the following....
   Red Orange Yellow Green Blue Indigo Violet
   Richard Of York Gave Battle In Vain
4) You need to know that red light is refracted the least — and violet is refracted the most. Also learn where infrared and ultraviolet light would appear if you could detect them.

Prism
White light
Angle of deviation
A spectrum
infra red
red
orange
yellow
green
blue
indigo
violet
ultra violet
Violet is bent the most

Total Internal Reflection

Total internal reflection and the critical angle

1) This only happens when light is coming out of something dense like glass or water or perspex.
2) If the angle is shallow enough the ray won't come out at all, but it reflects back into the glass (or whatever). This is called total internal reflection because all of the light reflects back in.
3) You definitely need to learn this set of three diagrams which show the three conditions:

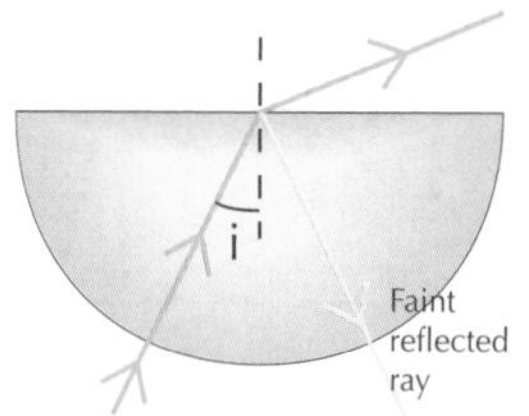

Angle of Incidence LESS than the Critical Angle.
Most of the light passes through into the air but a little bit of it is internally reflected.

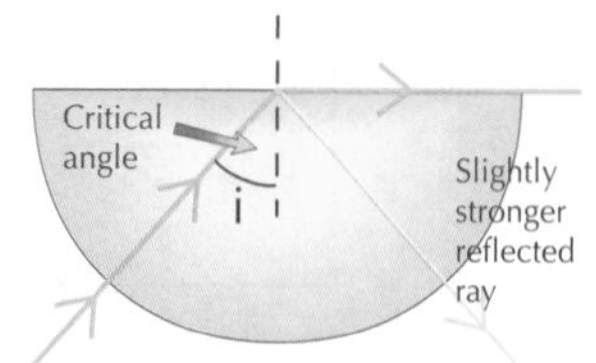

Angle of Incidence EQUAL TO the Critical Angle.
The emerging ray comes out along the surface. There's quite a bit of internal reflection.

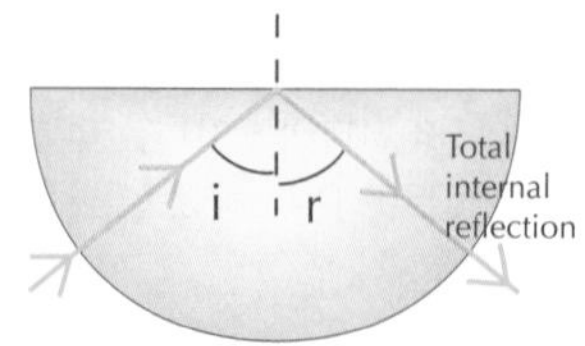

Angle of Incidence GREATER than the Critical Angle.
No light comes out. It's all internally reflected, ie: *total internal reflection*.

1) The Critical Angle for glass is about 42°. This is very handy because it means 45° angles can be used to get total internal reflection as in the prisms in the periscope shown below.
2) In diamond the Critical Angle is much lower, about 24°. This is the reason why diamonds sparkle so much, because there are lots of internal reflections.

Periscope

Periscopes use Total Internal Reflection of light in 45° prisms.
Prisms are used because they give a slightly better reflection than a mirror would and they're also easier to hold accurately in place.
They could ask you to complete a diagram of a periscope and unless you've practised beforehand you'll find it pretty tricky to draw the prisms in properly.

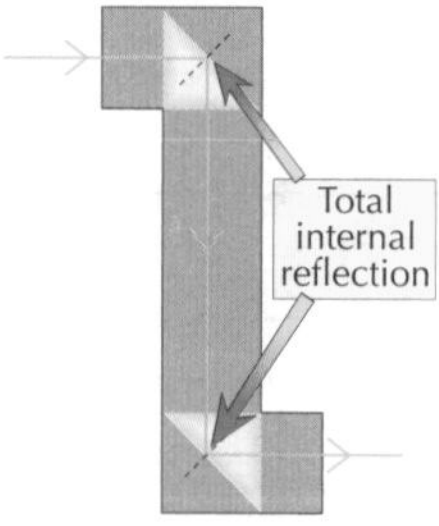

Optical fibres — communications and endoscopes

1) Optical fibres can carry information over long distances by repeated total internal reflections.
2) Optical communications have several advantages over electrical signals in wires:
   a) a cable of the same diameter can carry a lot more information.
   b) the signals cannot be tapped into, or suffer interference from electrical sources.
   c) the signal doesn't need boosting as often.
3) The fibre must be narrow enough to keep the angles below the critical angle, as shown, so the fibre mustn't be bent too sharply anywhere.

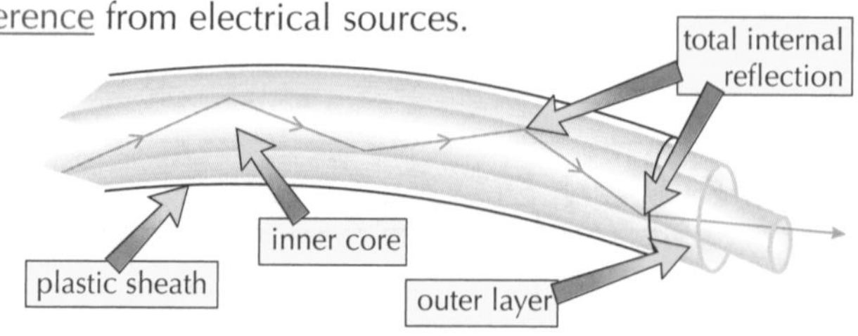

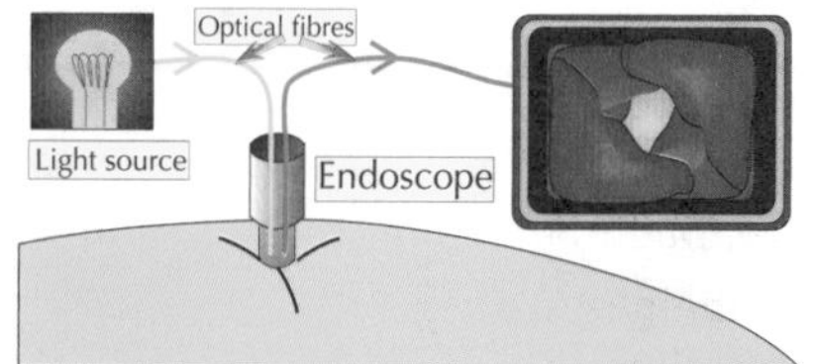

An endoscope is a narrow bunch of optical fibres with a lens system at each end. Another bunch of fibres carries light down inside to see with. The image is displayed as a full colour moving image on a TV screen. This means they can do operations without cutting big holes in people.

Diffraction

This word sounds a lot more technical than it really is.

Diffraction is just the "spreading out" of waves

All waves tend to spread out at the edges when they pass through a gap or past an object. Instead of saying that the wave "spreads out" or "bends" round a corner you should say that it diffracts around the corner. It's as easy as that. That's all diffraction means.

A wave spreads more if it passes through a narrow gap

The ripple tank shows this effect quite nicely. The same effect applies to light and sound too.

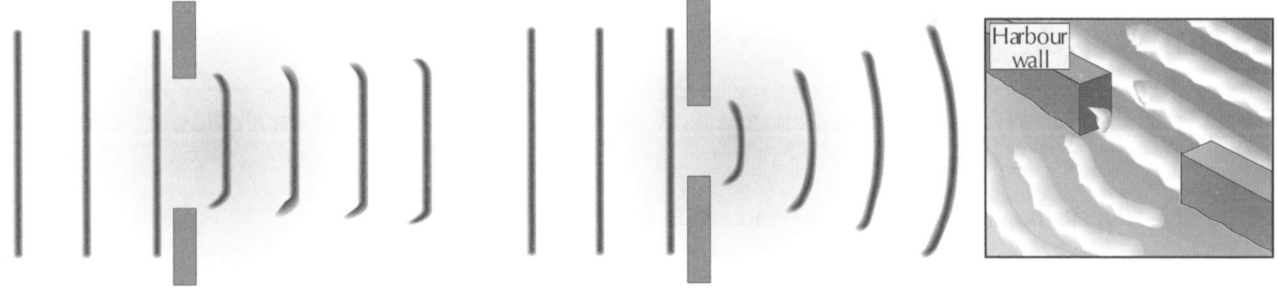

1) A "narrow" gap is one which is about the same size as the wavelength or less.
2) Obviously then, the question of whether a gap is "narrow" or not depends on the wave in question. What may be a narrow gap for a water wave will be a huge gap for a light wave.
3) It should be obvious then, that the longer the wavelength of a wave the more it will diffract.

Sounds always diffract quite a lot, because λ is quite big

1) Most sounds have wavelengths in air of around 0.1m, which is quite long.
2) This means they spread out round corners so you can still hear people even when you can't see them directly (the sound usually reflects off walls too which also helps).
3) Higher frequency sounds will have shorter wavelengths and so they won't diffract as much, which is why things sound more "muffled" when you hear them from round corners.

Long wavelength radio waves diffract easily over hills and into buildings

Visible light on the other hand...

has a very short wavelength, and it'll only diffract with a very narrow slit:

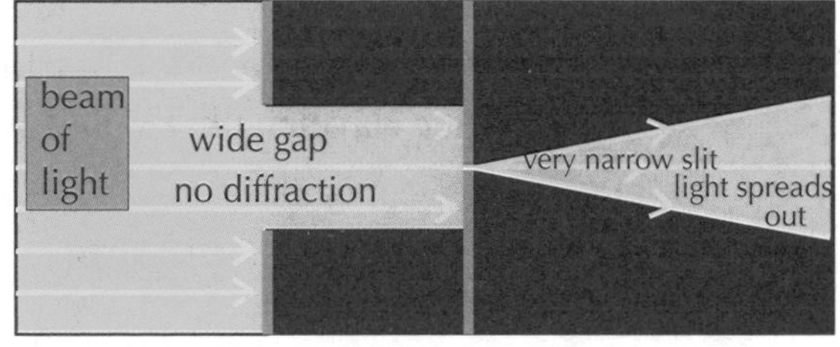

This spreading or diffraction of light is strong evidence for the wave nature of light.

The radio waves example often comes up in Exams

Make sure you know the difference between the words refraction, reflection and diffraction. You need to learn all the stuff — so you know exactly what they are. Make sure you know all those diagrams inside out. You also need to know all about total internal reflection too — it's a classic choice for exam questions.

Warm-Up and Exam Questions

Warm-up Questions

1) Describe the property of light waves being demonstrated in each of these pictures:

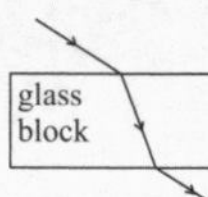

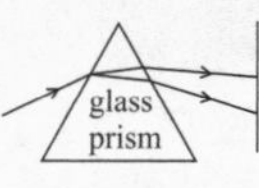

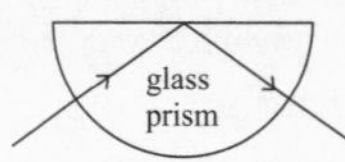

2) Which colour of light is refracted most by a prism?
3) What is meant by the term 'critical angle'?
4) Why are prisms used in binoculars and periscopes instead of ordinary mirrors?
5) In communications, what are the main advantages of using optical signals over using electrical signals?

Exam Questions

1 a) Name two properties that change as water waves travel from deep to shallower water.

(2 marks)

b) Describe how light waves bend when they travel from:

(i) air into glass; (ii) glass into air.

(2 marks)

c) What happens to the frequency of these waves as they cross the boundary?

(1 mark)

2 In a science lesson, the teacher shows the students a ripple tank with water in it. She makes straight water waves move towards the gap in a straight barrier as shown:

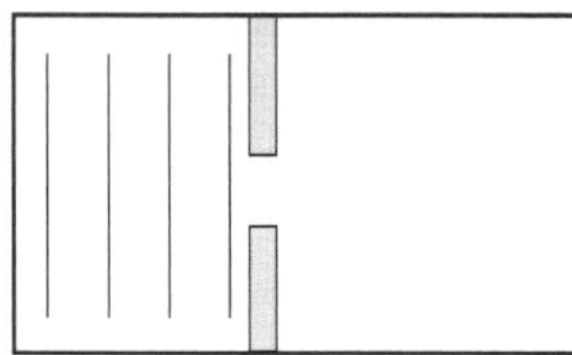

a) Complete the diagram to show what happens to the waves that have passed through the gap.

(1 mark)

b) What is this effect called?

(1 mark)

The teacher moves the barrier to widen the gap as shown below.

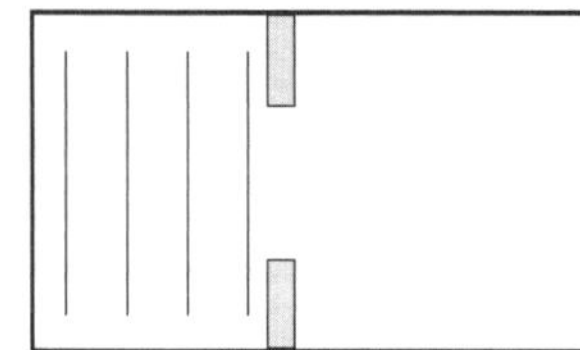

c) Sketch how the waves on the other side of the gap would look now.

(1 mark)

d) If the waves were made to have a higher frequency, in what way would the effect differ?

(1 mark)

This same effect is experienced by radio waves as they travel over hills.

e) Which are diffracted more — long wavelength radio waves, or shorter wavelength TV and FM radio waves?

(1 mark)

3 The diagram shows an optic fibre as used in an endoscope.

a) Complete the diagram to show how light travels along the fibre.

(2 marks)

b) Describe what endoscopes are used for in medicine.

(1 mark)

The Electromagnetic Spectrum

There are seven basic types of electromagnetic wave

We group electromagnetic waves (EM waves) into seven basic types as shown below.
These EM waves form a continuous spectrum so the different regions do actually merge into each other.

RADIO WAVES	MICRO WAVES	INFRA RED	VISIBLE LIGHT	ULTRA VIOLET	X-RAYS	GAMMA RAYS
1m-10^4m	10^{-2}m (3cm)	10^{-5}m (0.01mm)	10^{-7}m	10^{-8}m	10^{-10}m	10^{-12}m

Our eyes can only detect a very narrow range of EM waves which are the ones we call (visible) light.
All EM waves travel at exactly the same speed as light in a vacuum, and pretty much the same speed as light in other media like glass or water — though this is always slower than their speed in vacuum.

As the wavelength changes, so do the properties

1) As the wavelength of EM radiation changes, its interaction with matter changes. In particular the way any EM wave is absorbed, reflected or transmitted by any given substance depends entirely on its wavelength — that's the whole point of these three pages.
2) When any EM radiation is absorbed it can cause two effects:
   a) Heating b) Creation of a tiny alternating current with the same frequency as the radiation.
3) You need to know all the details that follow about all the different parts of the EM spectrum:

Radio waves are used mainly for communications

1) Radio waves are used mainly for communication.
2) Both TV and FM radio use short wavelength radio waves of about 1m wavelength.
3) To receive these wavelengths you need to be more or less in direct sight of the transmitter, because they will not bend (diffract) over hills or travel very far through buildings.
4) The longer wavelengths can travel further because they are reflected from an electrically charged layer in the Earth's upper atmosphere (the ionosphere). This means they can be sent further around the Earth.

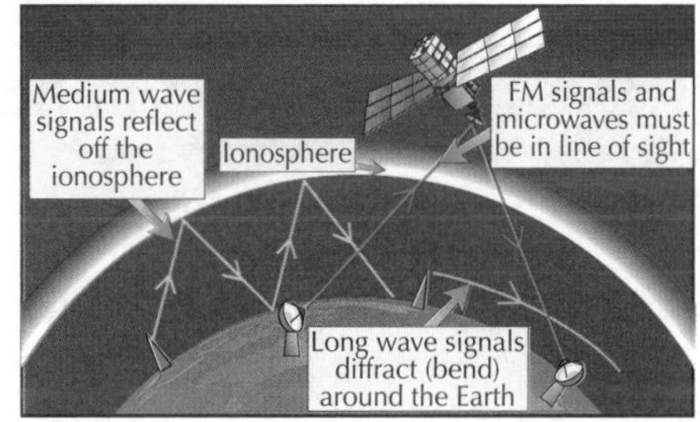

Microwaves are used for cooking and satellite signals

1) Microwaves have two main uses: cooking food and satellite transmissions.
2) Satellite transmissions use a frequency of microwaves which passes easily through the Earth's atmosphere, including clouds, which seems pretty sensible.
3) The frequency used for cooking, on the other hand is one which is readily absorbed by water molecules. The microwaves pass easily into the food and are then absorbed by the water molecules and turn into heat inside the food.
4) Microwaves can therefore be dangerous because they can be absorbed by living tissue and the heat will damage or kill the cells causing a sort of "cold burn".

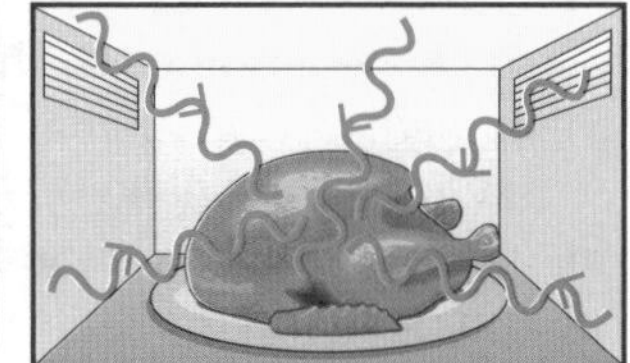

The Electromagnetic Spectrum

Visible light is used to see with and in optical fibres

Visible light is pretty useful. It's used in Optical Fibre Digital Communications and endoscopes which are the best ones for your answer in the Exam (see P.264).

Infrared radiation — toasters and remote controls

1) Infrared (or IR) is otherwise known as heat radiation. This is given out by all hot objects and you feel it on your skin as radiant heat. Infrared is readily absorbed by all materials and causes heating.
2) Radiant heaters (i.e. those that glow red) emit infrared radiation, including toasters and grills.
3) Over-exposure to infrared causes damage to cells. This is what causes sunburn.
4) Infrared is also used for all the remote controls of TVs and videos.

Ultraviolet light causes skin cancer

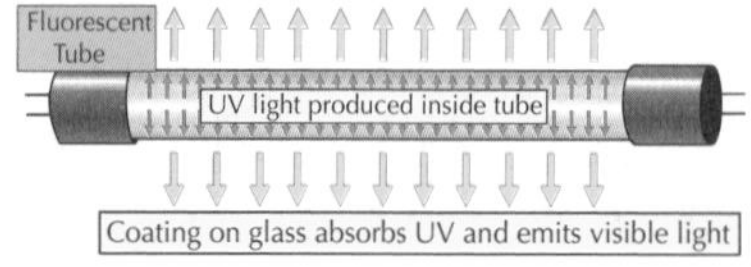

1) This is what causes skin cancer if you spend too much time in the sun.
2) It also causes your skin to tan. Sunbeds give out UV rays but less harmful ones than the Sun does.
3) Darker skin protects against UV rays by preventing them from reaching more vulnerable skin tissues deeper down.
4) There are special coatings which absorb UV light and then give out visible light instead. These are used to coat the inside of fluorescent tubes and lamps.
5) Ultra violet is also useful for hidden security marks which are written in special ink that can only be seen with an ultraviolet light.

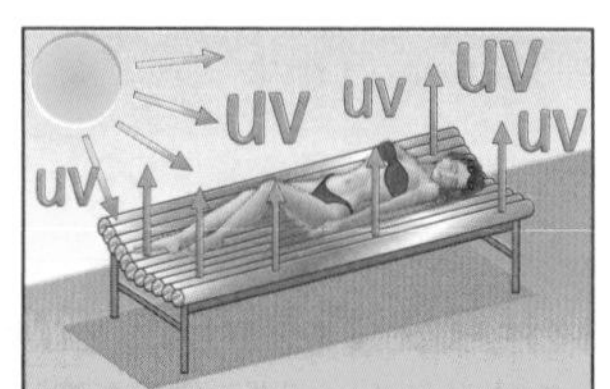

X-Rays are used in hospitals, but are pretty dangerous

1) These are used in hospitals to take X-ray photographs of people to see whether they have any broken bones.
2) X-rays pass easily through flesh but not through denser material such as bones or metal.
3) X-rays can cause cancer, so radiographers, who take X-ray pictures all day long wear lead aprons and stand behind a lead screen to keep their exposure to X-rays to a minimum.

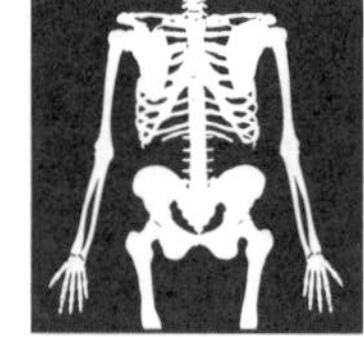

Gamma rays cause cancer but are used to treat it too

1) Gamma rays are used to kill harmful bacteria in food to keep it fresher for longer.
2) They are also used to sterilise medical instruments, again by killing the bacteria.
3) They can also be used in the treatment of cancer because they kill cancer cells.
4) Gamma rays tend to pass through soft tissue but some are absorbed by the cells.
5) In high doses, Gamma rays (along with X-rays and UV rays) can kill normal cells.
6) In lower doses all these three types of EM Waves can cause normal cells to become cancerous.

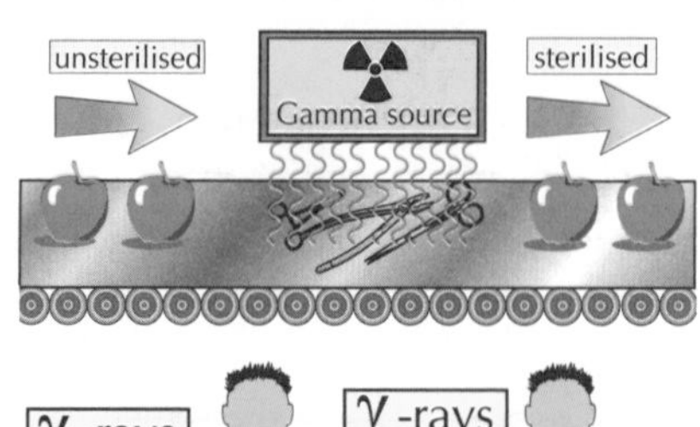

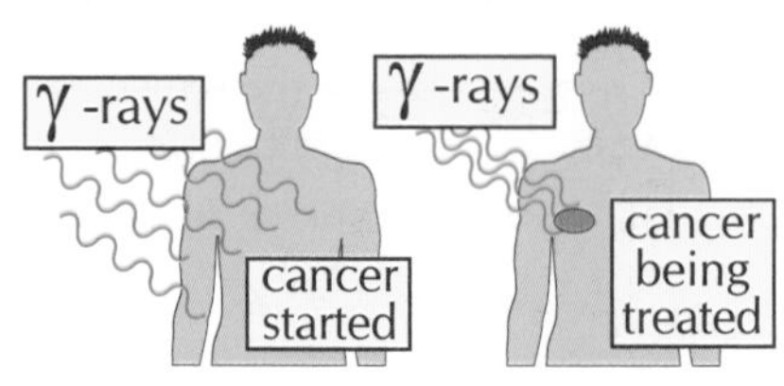

Digital and Analogue Signals

You've got to learn the two different ways of transmitting information.
Life would be pretty dull without signals — no phones, no computers, even digital watches wouldn't exist.

Information is converted into *signals*

1) Information (eg: sound, speech, pictures) is converted into electrical signals before it's transmitted.
2) It's then sent long distances down cables, like telephone calls or internet, or carried on EM waves, like radio or TV.
3) Information can also be sent down optical fibres by converting it into visible light or infrared signals.

Analogue varies but *digital's* either *on or off*

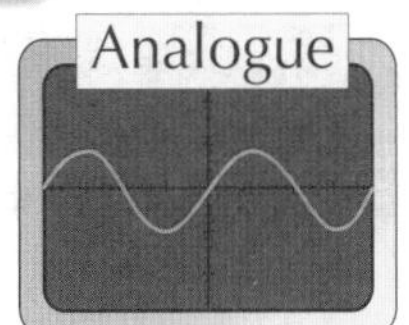

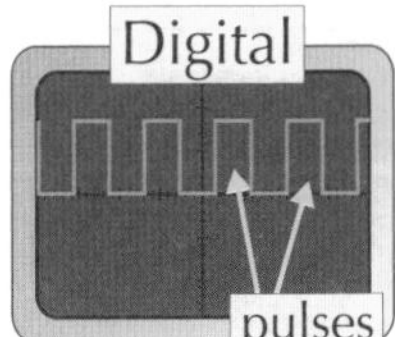

1) The amplitude and frequency of analogue signals vary continuously like in sound waves. Parts of an analogue signal have any value in a range.
2) Dimmer switches, thermometers, speedometers and old fashioned watches are all analogue devices.
3) Digital signals are coded pulses — they have one of only two values: on or off, true or false, 0 or 1...
4) On/off switches, digital clocks and digital meters are digital devices.

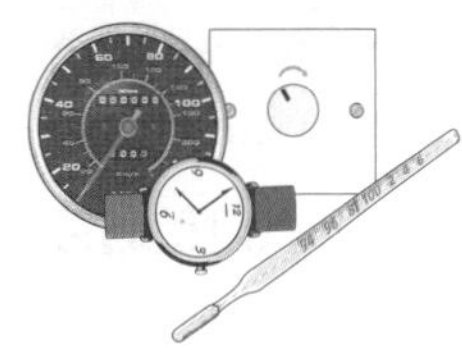

Signals have to be *amplified*

Both digital and analogue signals weaken as they travel so they need to be amplified along their route. They also pick up random disturbances, called noise.

Analogue signals *lose* quality

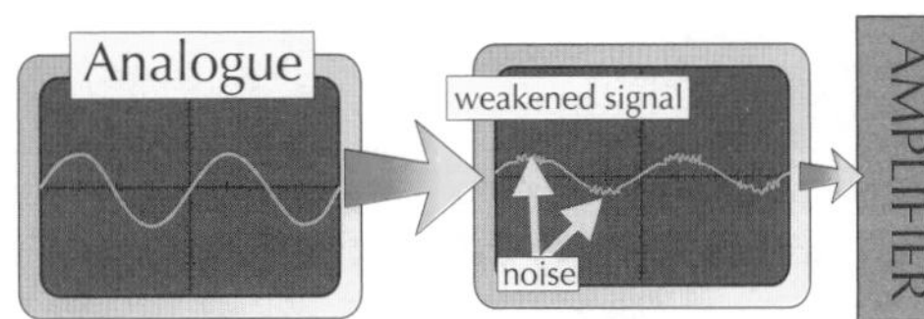

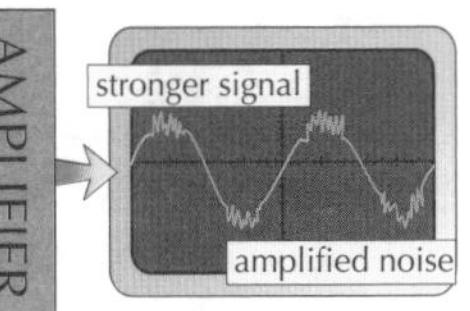

Each time it's amplified, the analogue signal gets less and less like the original. The different frequencies in it weaken differently at different times — when the signal is amplified, the differences and noise are amplified too.

Digital signals stay the *same*

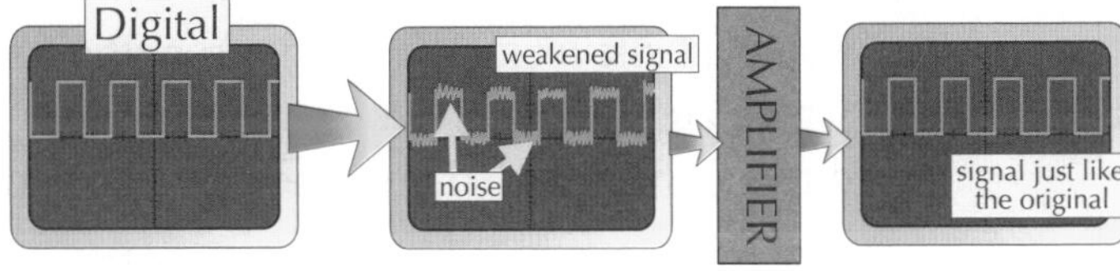

Noise is usually low amplitude so it's just ignored — it's amplified as OFF. Even a weak signal will still be picked up as an ON pulse so it's amplified as ON. The signal stays exactly the same as the original.

Digital signals are *far better quality*

1) Digital signals don't change while they're being transmitted. This makes them higher quality — the information transmitted is the same as the original.
2) Loads more information can be sent as digital signals compared to analogue (in a certain time). Many digital signals can be transmitted at once by a clever way of overlapping them on the same cable or EM wave — but you don't need to learn *how* they do it.

There are loads of little details to learn

This section contains all the parts of the EM spectrum for you to learn. Do a mini-essay for each kind of EM wave, including example uses, then check, re-learn, re-scribble, re-check, etc. Then make sure you know the differences between digital and analogue signals and why digital ones are better.

Warm-Up and Exam Questions

Warm-up Questions

1) What type of radiation lies between visible light and X-rays in the electromagnetic spectrum?
2) Give one use for each of the following types of radiation:
   a) microwaves b) infrared c) gamma rays.
3) Which type of radiation has the longer wavelength — gamma rays or radio waves?
4) List three examples of analogue devices and three examples of digital devices.
5) Draw an analogue signal and a digital signal, then draw them both again after they've been amplified several times.

Exam Questions

Imagine if you opened up your exam paper and all the answers were already written in for you. Hmm, well I'm afraid that's not going to happen, the only way you'll do well is hard work now.

1 Microwaves are used for sending communications between satellite dishes. These signals cannot be detected by an ordinary radio.

a) Name one difference between radio and microwave signals.

(1 mark)

b) How do the microwaves used in communications differ from those used for cooking?

(1 mark)

c) How does this difference make those used for cooking more dangerous to people?

(1 mark)

2 Signals can be classed as either analogue or digital.

a) What is meant by a digital signal?

(1 mark)

b) Make a table using the words from the following list, to show which are analogue and which are digital devices.
dimmer switch; thermometer; electronic scales; speedometer; light switch

(2 marks)

c) The diagram shows an analogue signal.

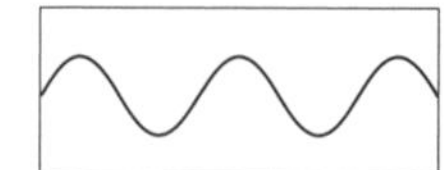

Describe what happens to the analogue signal as it is amplified repeatedly.

(2 marks)

d) The diagram shows a digital signal.

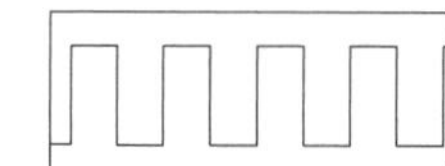

Draw a diagram to show the signal after it has been amplified several times.

(2 marks)

e) Suggest a situation where digital signals are used in preference to analogue signals.

(1 mark)

Sound Waves

1) Sound travels as a *wave*:

Sound can be reflected off walls (echoes), it can be refracted as it passes into different media and it can diffract around doors. These are all standard properties of waves so we deduce that sound travels as a wave. This "sound" reasoning can also be applied to deduce the wave nature of light.

2) The *frequency* of a sound wave determines its *pitch*

1) High frequency sound waves sound high pitched like a squeaking mouse.
2) Low frequency sound waves sound low pitched like a mooing cow.
3) Frequency is the number of complete vibrations each second. It's measured in hertz, Hz.
4) Other common units are kHz (1000 Hz) and MHz (1,000,000 Hz).
5) High frequency (or high pitch) also means shorter wavelength.
6) The range of frequencies heard by humans is from 20Hz to 20kHz.
7) These CRO screens are very important so make sure you know all about them:

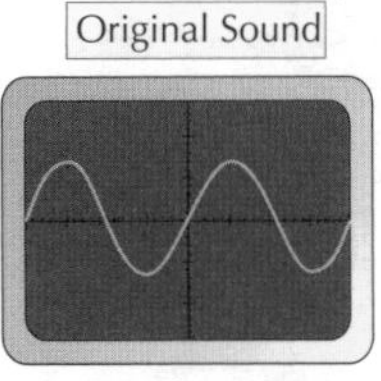

The CRO screens tell us about the pitch and loudness of the sound:

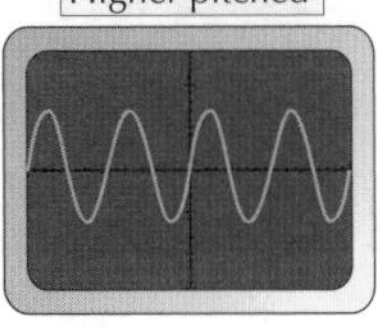

1) The closer the peaks are together, the higher pitched the sound (and the higher the frequency).

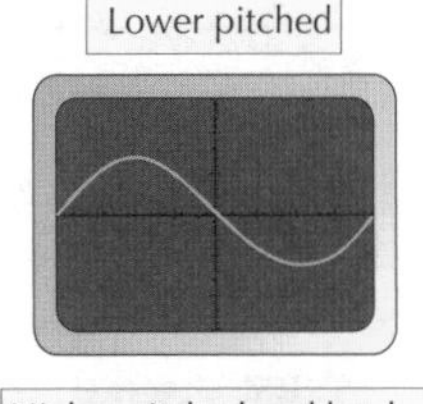

2) When the peaks are further apart then the sound is at a lower pitch (a lower frequency).

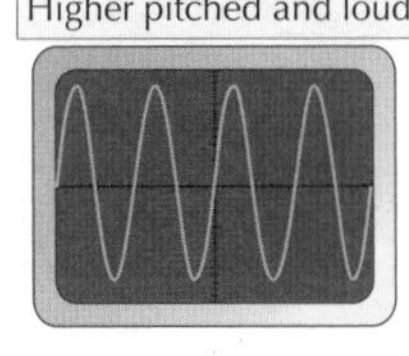

3) The CRO screen will show large peaks for a loud noise (sound waves with a big amplitude).

3) *Amplitude* is a measure of the *energy* carried by any wave

1) The greater the amplitude, the more energy the wave carries.
2) In sound this means it'll be louder.
3) Bigger amplitude means a louder sound.
4) With light, a bigger amplitude means it'll be brighter.

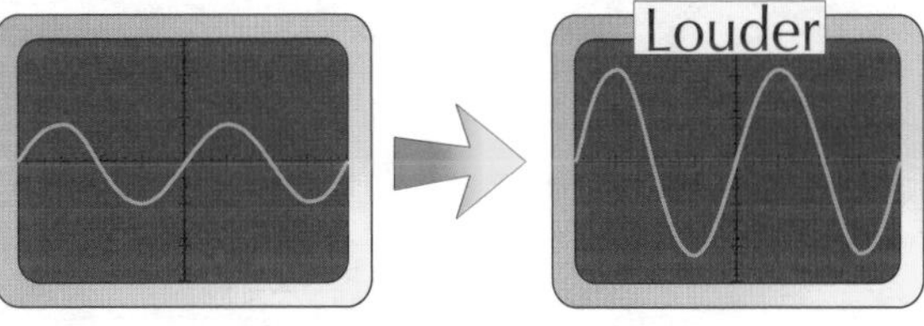

4) *Echoes* and *reverberation* are due to *reflected* sound

1) Sound will only be reflected from hard flat surfaces. Things like carpets and curtains act as absorbing surfaces which will absorb sounds rather than reflect them.
2) This is very noticeable in the reverberation in an empty room. A big empty room sounds completely different once you've put carpet and curtains in, and a bit of furniture, because these things absorb the sound quickly and stop it echoing (reverberating) around the room.

Ultrasound

Ultrasound is sound with *a higher frequency* than we can *hear*

Electrical devices can be made which produce electrical oscillations of any frequency. These can easily be converted into mechanical vibrations to produce sound waves beyond the range of human hearing (ie: frequencies above 20kHz). This is called ultrasound and it has loads of uses:

1) Industrial cleaning

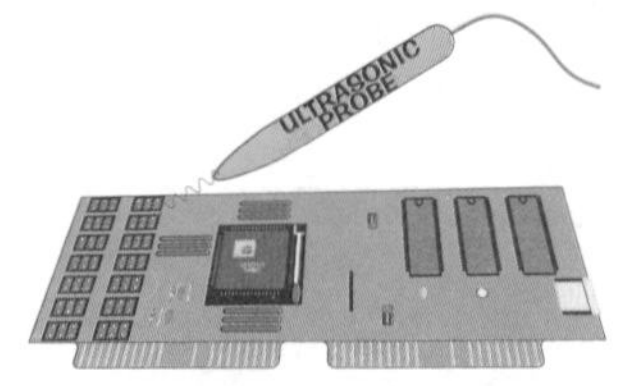

Ultrasound can be used to CLEAN DELICATE MECHANISMS without them having to be dismantled. The ultrasound waves can be directed on very precise areas and are extremely effective at removing dirt and other deposits which form on delicate equipment. The alternatives would either damage the equipment or else would require it to be dismantled first.
The same technique is used for CLEANING TEETH.
Dentists use ultrasonic tools to easily and painlessly remove hard deposits of tartar which build up on teeth and which would lead to gum disease.

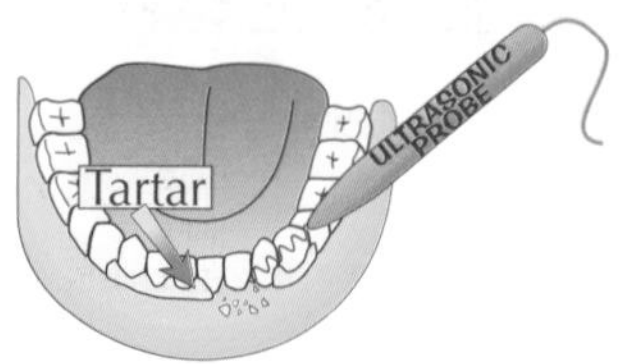

2) Industrial quality control

Ultrasound waves can pass through something like a metal casting and whenever they reach a boundary between two different media (like metal and air) some of the wave is reflected back and detected.

The exact timing and distribution of these echoes give detailed information about the internal structure. The echoes are usually processed by computer to produce

a visual display of what the object must be like inside.
If there are cracks where there shouldn't be they'll show up.

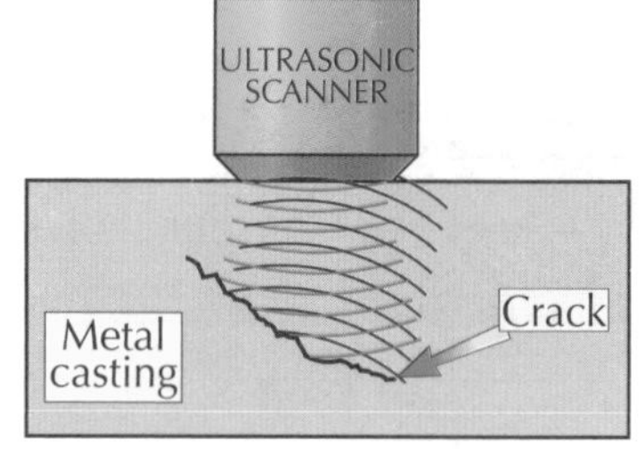

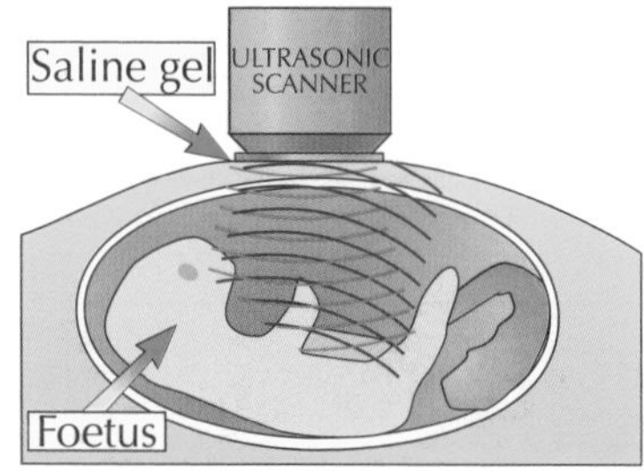

3) For *pre-natal scanning* of a foetus

This follows the same principle as the industrial quality control. As the ultrasound hits different media some of the sound wave is reflected and these reflected waves are processed by computer to produce a video image of the foetus. No one knows for sure whether ultrasound is safe in all cases but X-rays would definitely be dangerous to the foetus.

4) Range and direction finding — *sonar*

Bats send out high-pitched squeaks (ultrasound) and pick up the reflections with their big ears. Their brains are able to process the reflected signal and turn it into a picture of what's around.

So the bats basically "see" with sound waves, well enough in fact to catch moths in mid-flight in complete darkness — it's a nice trick if you can do it.

The same technique is used for SONAR which uses sound waves underwater to detect features on the sea-bed. The pattern of the reflections indicates the depth and basic features.

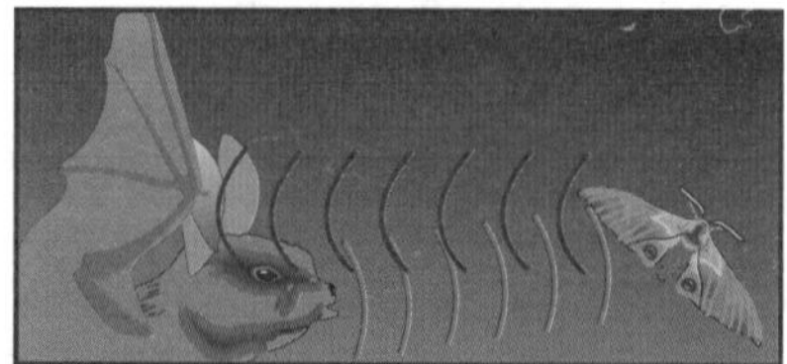

Ultrasound is exactly like normal sound — just higher frequency

That's two pages on sound with eight sections in total. No numbered points this time though. That means the mini-essay method is going to be a better idea. Learn the eight headings, then cover the pages and scribble a mini-essay for each, with diagrams.

Warm-Up and Exam Questions

Warm-up Questions

1) Finish the sentences by picking the right word from each pair.
Sound is caused by a vibrating/stationary object. Sound is a transverse/longitudinal wave.
Sound travels faster in a solid/gas than a solid/gas. Sound cannot travel through a vacuum/pipe.
2) A dog whistle produces a sound with a frequency of 35kHz. a) What does "frequency of 35kHz" mean? b) Give two reasons why 35kHz is an ideal frequency for a dog whistle.
3) Match these sounds to their frequencies:

deep bass drum	8000 Hz
high-pitched squeak	100 Hz
ultrasound scan	40 000 Hz

Exam Questions

1 Diagrams A, B, C and D show oscilloscope traces for four different sounds.

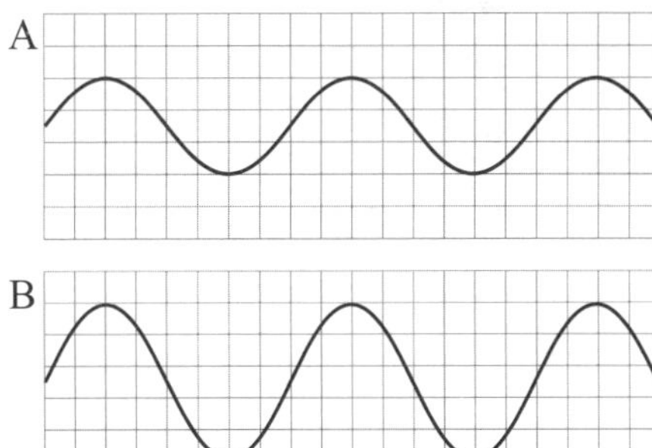

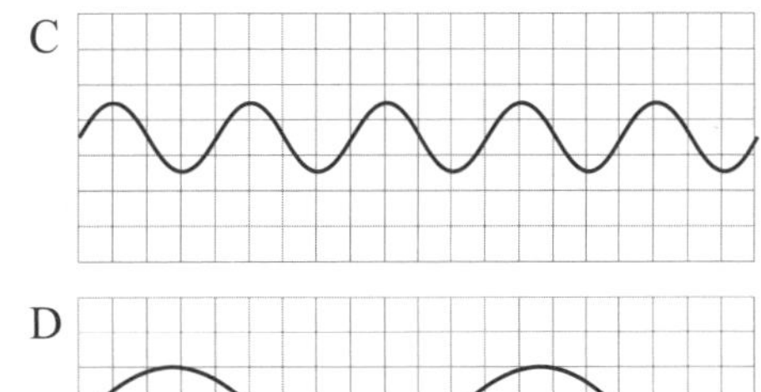

D

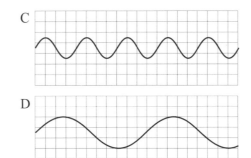

The oscilloscope settings are the same for each trace.

a) Which trace shows the loudest sound?

(1 mark)

b) Which trace shows the lowest pitched sound?

(1 mark)

c) Which sound has the shortest wavelength?

(1 mark)

d) Which two sounds have the same amplitude?

(1 mark)

2 Ultrasonic waves are used to examine the foetus inside the mother's womb.

a) What are ultrasonic waves?

(2 marks)

b) Why are ultrasonic waves used instead of X-rays?

(1 mark)

c) Describe how ultrasound is used to produce an image of the foetus.

(2 marks)

d) Name two other uses of ultrasonic waves.

(2 marks)

Seismic Waves

Seismic waves are caused by earthquakes

1) We can only drill about 10km or so into the crust of the Earth, which is not very far, so seismic waves are really the only way of investigating the inner structure.
2) When there's an Earthquake somewhere the shock waves travel out from it and we detect them all over the surface of the planet using seismographs.
3) We measure the time it takes for the two different types of shock wave to reach each seismograph.
4) We also note the parts of the Earth which don't receive the shock waves at all.
5) From this information you can work out all sorts of stuff about the inside of the Earth as shown below:

S-waves and P-waves take different paths

P-Waves are Longitudinal

P-Waves travel through both solids and liquids. They travel faster than S-waves.

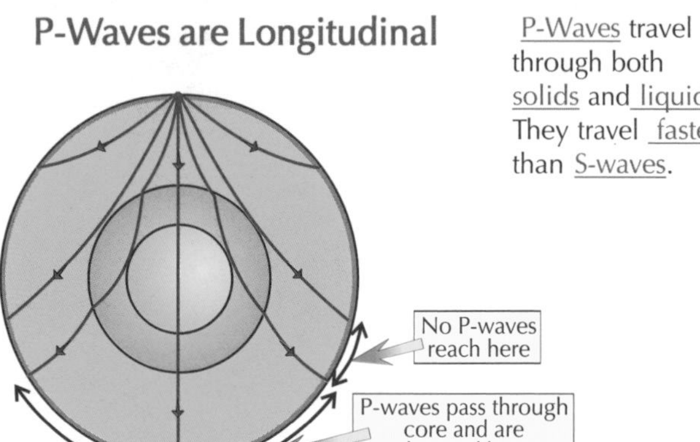

S-Waves are TranSverSe

S-Waves will only travel through solids. They are slower than P-waves.

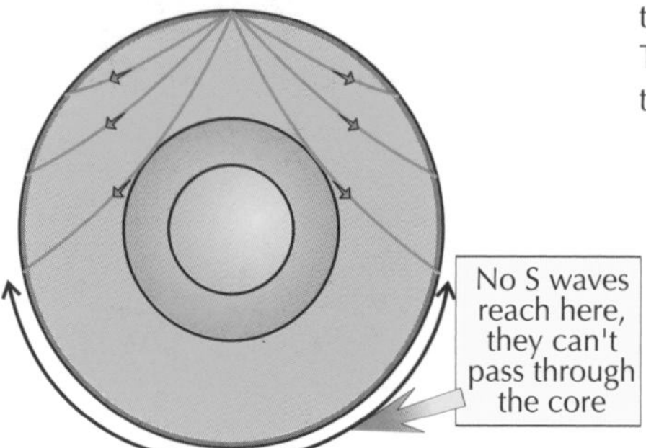

The seismograph results tell us what's down there

1) About halfway through the Earth, there's an abrupt change in direction of both types of wave. This indicates that there's a sudden increase in density at that point — the core.
2) The fact that S-waves are not detected in the shadow of this core tells us that it's very liquid.
3) It's also found that P-waves travel slightly faster through the middle of the core, which strongly suggests that there's a solid inner core.
4) Note that S-waves do travel through the mantle which suggests that it's sort of solid, though I always thought it was made of molten lava which looks pretty liquid to me when it comes rushing out of volcanoes. Just another one of life's mysteries, I suppose.

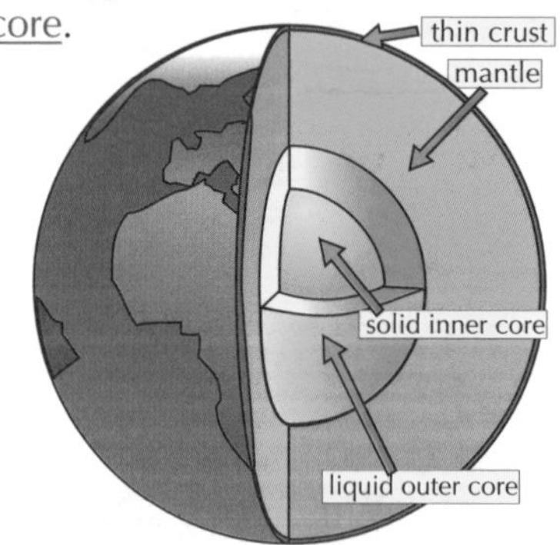

The paths curve due to increasing density (causing refraction)

1) Both S-waves and P-waves travel faster in more dense material.
2) The curvature of their paths is due to the increasing density of the mantle and core with depth.
3) When the density changes suddenly, the waves change direction abruptly, as shown above.
4) The paths curve because the density of both the mantle and the core increases steadily with increasing depth. The waves gradually change direction because their speed is gradually changing, due to gradual changes in the density of the medium. This is refraction, of course.

Learn those diagrams

Four sections to learn. Learn the headings first, then try scribbling down all the details for each heading, including the diagrams. Remember that S-waves are tranSverSe — so P-waves must be the longitudinal ones.

Warm-Up and Exam Question

Warm-up Questions

1) All waves are either longitudinal or transverse. What types of wave are S-waves and P-waves?
2) Complete the following sentences:
   The Earth is made up of________ layers. These layers are the _________,
   the __________, the ___________ core and the ________ core.

Exam Question

1 The diagram shows the inside of the earth.

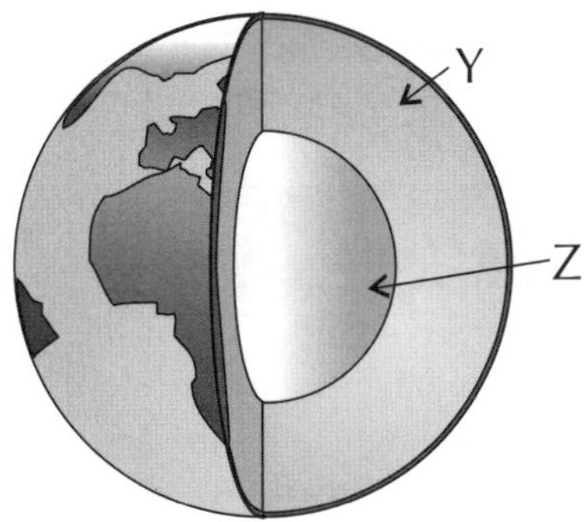

a) Name the layers marked Y and Z.

(2 marks)

b) Two types of seismic wave produced during an earthquake are P-waves and S-waves.
What type of wave are P-waves — longitudinal or transverse?

(1 mark)

c) The diagram shows S-waves travelling through the earth after an earthquake.

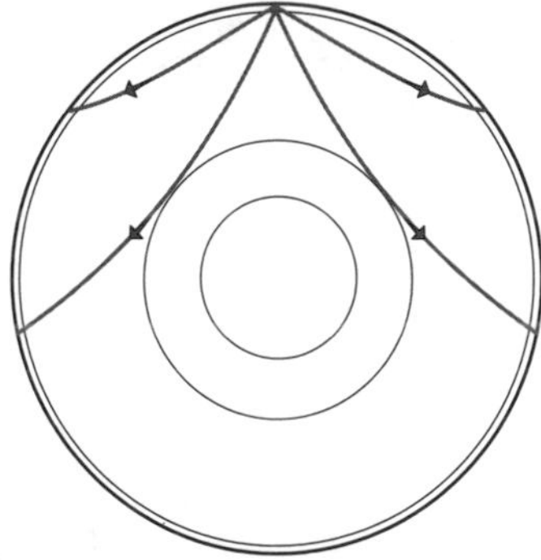

None of the S-waves travel through the Earth's core.
What does this tell us about the structure of the Earth's core?

(1 mark)

d) Scientists believe that the Earth's inner core is solid. Why do they believe this?

(1 mark)

e) Explain why the paths of the waves curve as shown in the diagram above.

(1 mark)

Types of Radiation

Don't get mixed up between nuclear radiation (which is dangerous) — and electromagnetic radiation (which generally isn't). Gamma radiation is included in both, of course.

A substance which gives out nuclear radiation all the time is called radioactive.

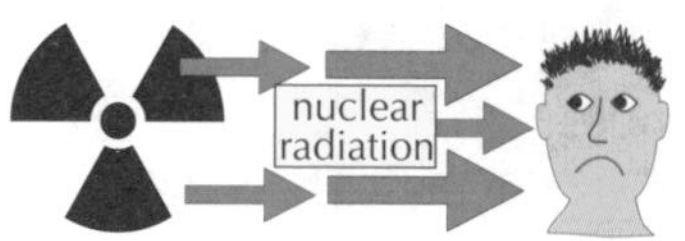

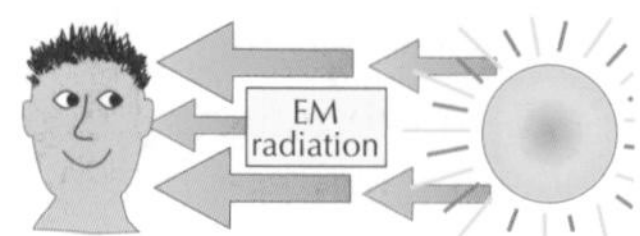

Nuclear radiation: Alpha, Beta and Gamma (α, β and γ)

You need to remember three things about each type of radiation:

1) What they actually are.
2) How well they penetrate materials.
3) How strongly they ionise that material (i.e. bash into atoms and knock electrons off).
   There's a pattern — the further the radiation can penetrate before hitting an atom and getting stopped, the less damage it will do along the way and so the less ionising it is.

Alpha particles are helium nuclei

$^{4}_{2}\text{He}$

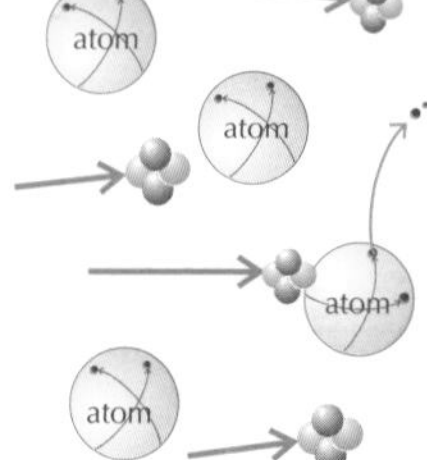

1) They're made of two protons and two neutrons so they're relatively big, heavy and slow moving. They therefore don't penetrate into materials but are stopped quickly.
2) Because of their size they are strongly ionising, which just means they bash into a lot of atoms and knock electrons off them before they slow down, which creates lots of ions — hence the term "ionising".

Beta particles are high energy electrons

$^{0}_{-1}\text{e}$

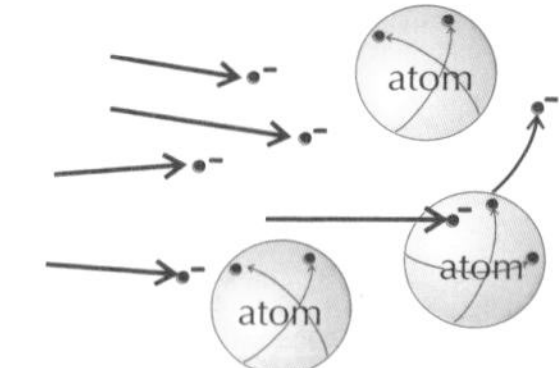

1) These are in between alpha and gamma in terms of their properties.
2) For every β-particle emitted, a neutron turns to a proton in the nucleus.
3) They move quite fast and they are quite small (they're electrons).
4) They penetrate moderately before colliding and are moderately ionising too.

Gamma rays are very short wavelength EM waves

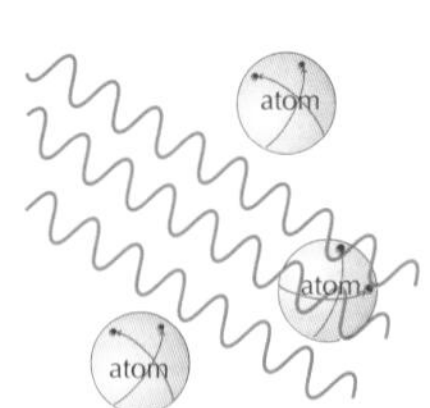

1) They are the opposite of alpha particles in a way.
2) They penetrate a long way into materials without being stopped.
3) This means they are weakly ionising because they tend to pass through rather than colliding with atoms. Eventually they hit something and do damage.

Remember what blocks the three types of radiation...

As radiation passes through materials some of the radiation is absorbed.
The greater the thickness of material, the more absorption occurs.

They really like this for Exam questions, so make sure you know what it takes to block each of the three:

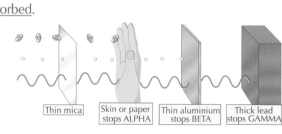

Alpha particles are blocked by paper.
Beta particles are blocked by thin aluminium.
Gamma rays are blocked by thick lead.

Thin mica

Skin or paper stops ALPHA

Thin aluminium stops BETA

Thick lead stops GAMMA

Of course anything equivalent will also block them, e.g. skin will stop alpha, but not the others; a thin sheet of any metal will stop beta; and very thick concrete will stop gamma just like lead does.

Background Radiation

Background radiation comes from many sources

Natural background radiation comes from:

1) Radioactivity of naturally occurring unstable isotopes which are all around us — in air, in food, in building materials and in rocks.
2) Radiation from space — cosmic rays. These come mostly from the Sun.
3) Radiation due to human activity. ie: fallout from nuclear explosions or dumped nuclear waste. But this represents a tiny proportion of the total background radiation.

The relative proportions of background radiation:

- 51% Radon and Thoron gas
- 10% Cosmic rays
- 12% Food
- 12% Medical X-rays
- 14% Rocks and Building materials
- Just 1% from the Nuclear Industry

The level of background radiation changes, depending on where you are:

1) At high altitudes (eg: in jet planes) it increases because of more exposure to cosmic rays.

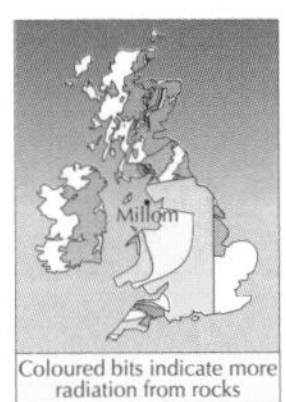

Coloured bits indicate more radiation from rocks

2) Underground in mines, etc. it increases because of the rocks all around. Rocks like granite have a high background count.
3) Certain underground rocks can cause higher levels at the surface, especially if they release radioactive radon gas, which tends to get trapped inside people's houses. This varies widely across the UK depending on the rock type, as shown.

Radiation harms living cells

1) Alpha, beta and gamma radiation enter living cells and collide with molecules.
2) These collisions cause ionisation, which damages or destroys the molecules.
3) Lower doses tend to cause minor damage without killing the cell.
4) This can give rise to mutant cells which divide uncontrollably. This is cancer.
5) Higher doses tend to kill cells completely, which causes radiation sickness if a lot of your body cells all get exposed to it at once.
6) The extent of the harmful effects depends on two things:
   a) How much exposure you have to the radiation.
   b) The energy and penetration of the radiation emitted, since some types are more hazardous than others, of course.

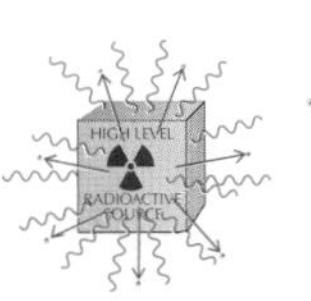

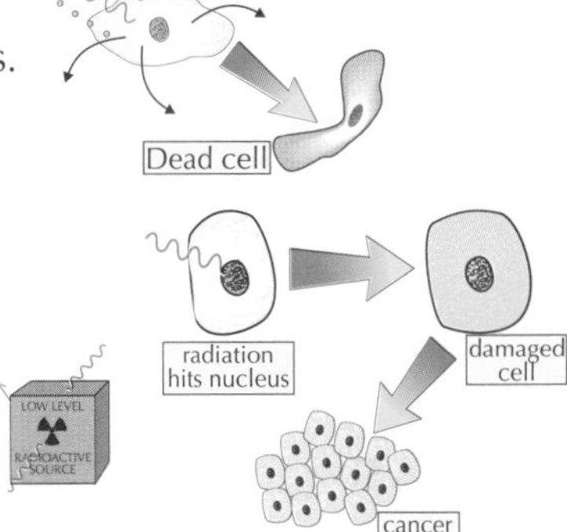

Radiotherapy — the treatment of cancer using γ-rays

Since high doses of gamma rays kill all living cells they are used to treat cancers. The rays are directed carefully at just the right dosage so they kill the cancer cells without damaging too many normal cells.

Outside the body, β- and γ-sources are the most dangerous

This is because beta and gamma can get inside to the delicate organs, whereas alpha is much less dangerous because it can't penetrate the skin.

Inside the body, an α-source is the most dangerous

Inside the body alpha-sources do all their damage in a very localised area. Beta and gamma sources on the other hand are less dangerous inside the body because they mostly pass straight out without doing much damage.

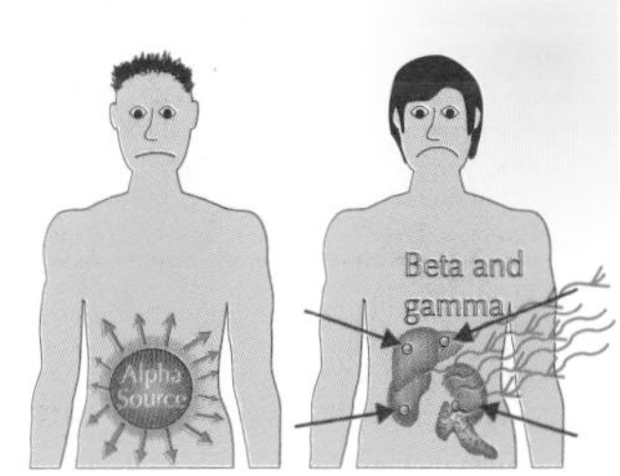

Photographic film also detects radiation

1) Radiation was discovered by accident when uranium was left on photographic plates which became "fogged" by it. These days, photographic film is a useful way of detecting radiation.
2) Workers in the nuclear industry or those using X-ray equipment such as dentists and radiographers wear little badges which have a bit of photographic film in them.
3) The film is checked every now and then to see if it's got fogged too quickly, which would mean the person was getting too much exposure to radiation.

Uses of Radioactive Materials

This is a nice easy bit of straightforward learning. Below are three uses for radioactive isotopes. Make sure you learn all the details. In particular, make sure you get the grip of why each application uses a particular radio-isotope according to its half-life and the type of radiation it gives out.

1) Tracers in medicine — always short half-life γ-emitters

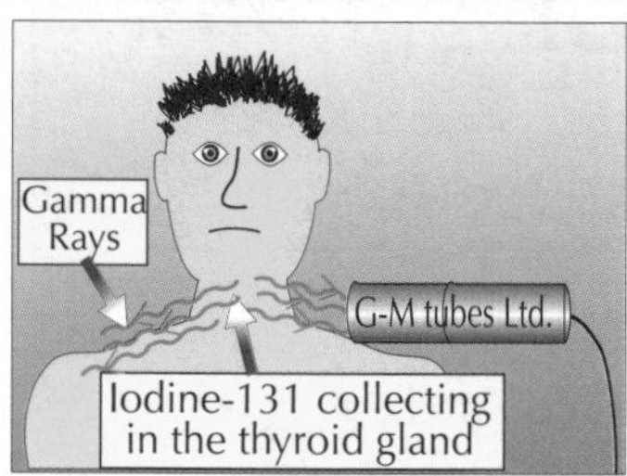

1) Certain radioactive isotopes can be injected into or swallowed by people, and their progress around the body can be monitored using a detector, whose signal can be converted to a TV display showing where the strongest reading is coming from. A well known example is the use of Iodine-131 which is absorbed by the thyroid gland, just like normal Iodine-127, but it gives out radiation which can be detected to indicate whether or not the thyroid gland is taking in the iodine as it should.
2) All isotopes which are taken into the body must always be gamma sources, (never alpha or beta), so that the radiation passes out of the body and they must also have a short half-life of just a few hours, so that the radioactivity inside the patient quickly disappears.

2) Tracers in industry — for finding leaks

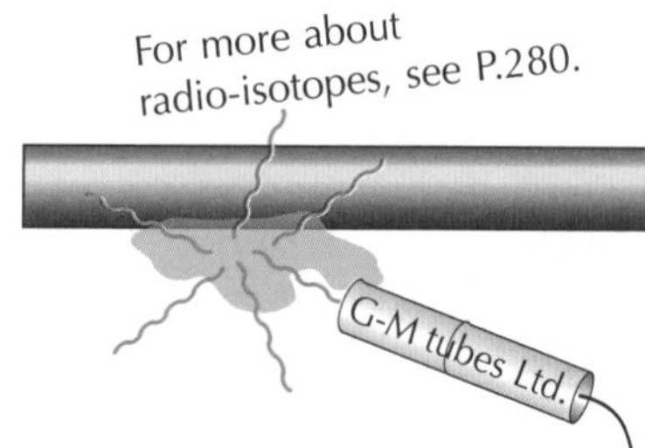

This is much the same technique as the medical tracers.

1) Radio-isotopes can be used to detect leaks in pipes. Just add the radio-isotope to the liquid and use a detector to find the areas along the pipe where radioactivity is high, which is where the leaks are.
2) This is really useful for concealed or underground pipes, to save you digging up half the road trying to find the leak.
3) A gamma emitter must be used so that the radiation can be detected even through metal or earth which may be surrounding the pipe. Metal or earth would easily block alpha and beta rays.
4) It should also have a short half-life so as not to cause a hazard if it collects somewhere.

3) Thickness control in industry and manufacturing

1) You have a radioactive source and you direct it through the stuff being made, usually a continuous sheet of paper or cardboard or metal etc.
2) The detector is on the other side and is connected to a control unit.
3) When the amount of radiation detected goes down, it means the stuff is coming out too thick and so the control unit pinches the rollers up a bit to make it thinner again.

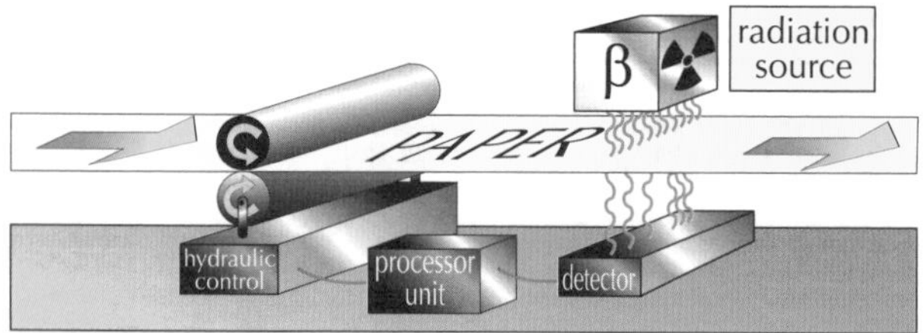

4) If the reading goes up, it means it's too thin, so the control unit opens the rollers out a bit.
5) The most important thing is the choice of isotope. First and foremost it must have a nice long half-life (of several years at least!), otherwise the strength would gradually decline and the control unit would keep pinching up the rollers trying to compensate.
6) Secondly, the source must be a beta source for paper and cardboard, or a gamma source for metal sheets. This is because the stuff being made must partly block the radiation. If it all goes through, (or none of it does), then the reading won't change at all as the thickness changes. Alpha particles are no use for this since they would all be stopped.

One other use of radioactivity is sterilising food and surgical instruments by exposing them to gamma rays (see p268)

What isotope you use depends on half life and whether it's α, β or γ

Alpha, beta and gamma. Those are just the first three letters of the Greek alphabet: α, β, γ — just like a, b, c. They might sound like complex names to you but they were just easy labels at the time. Anyway, learn all the facts about them, then tackle the two pages on uses. As usual, the best way to check what you know is to do a mini-essay for each section. Then check back and see what details you missed.

Warm-Up and Exam Questions

Warm-up Questions

1) Why do certain parts of the UK have a higher level of natural background radiation than others?
2) What type of radiation source (alpha, beta or gamma) must be stored in a lead-lined container?
3) State whether each of the following uses of radiation should use a source of alpha, beta or gamma radiation:
   a) sterilisation of medical instruments; b) controlling the thickness of paper;
   c) killing cancer cells deep within the body.

Exam Questions

1 This question is about radioactive isotopes.

a) How can you determine whether an unstable isotope is present in a sample?

(1 mark)

b) This diagram shows how uranium-238 decays, emitting alpha and gamma radiation.

Which of the these two types of nuclear radiation is the more strongly ionising, and what quality of this radiation makes it so?

(2 marks)

2 The diagram shows a device used to control the thickness of paper in a factory. A radiation detector is used to detect how much radiation from the source penetrates the paper. The output of the detector can then be used to change the position of the rollers to alter the thickness of the paper.

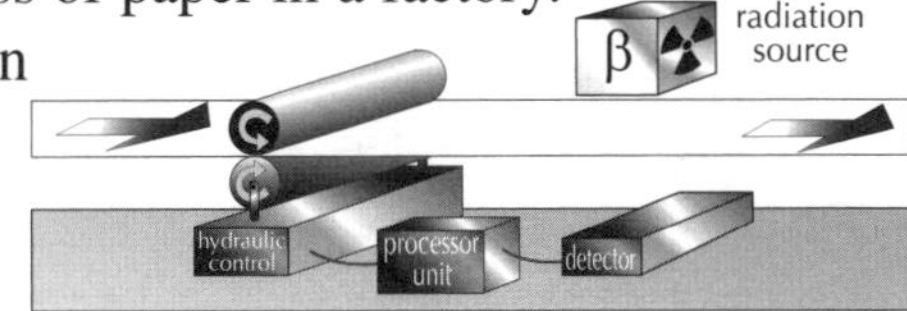

a) The designer decides to use a source of beta particles in the device. Explain why this is a good choice of source.

(2 marks)

b) What would happen to the amount of radiation reaching the detector if the paper became thicker?

(1 mark)

A beta source of half-life 8 days is used in the device. A test run carried out over several days shows that the device gradually produces thinner and thinner paper, despite being left on the same setting.

c) Why does this happen, and what should be done to solve the problem?

(3 marks)

It is suggested that the device could be modified to roll metal sheets to the correct thickness.

d) Explain why a source of beta particles will not work for this application, and suggest a type of source that would be more suitable.

(2 marks)

Atomic Structure

This is also covered in Section 8 — but it's important that you fully understand it for this section, so here's a reminder of the basics:

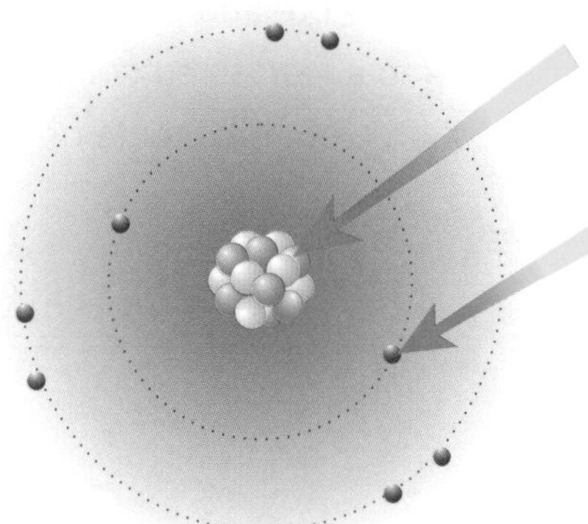

The nucleus contains protons and neutrons. Most of the mass of the atom is contained in the nucleus, but it takes up virtually no space — it's tiny.

The electrons fly around the outside. They're negatively charged and really really small. They occupy a lot of space and this gives the atom its overall size, even though it's mostly empty space. The number of electrons is equal to the number of protons. This means that the whole atom has no overall charge.

Make sure you learn this table:

PARTICLE	MASS	CHARGE
Proton	1	+1
Neutron	1	0
Electron	1/2000	- 1

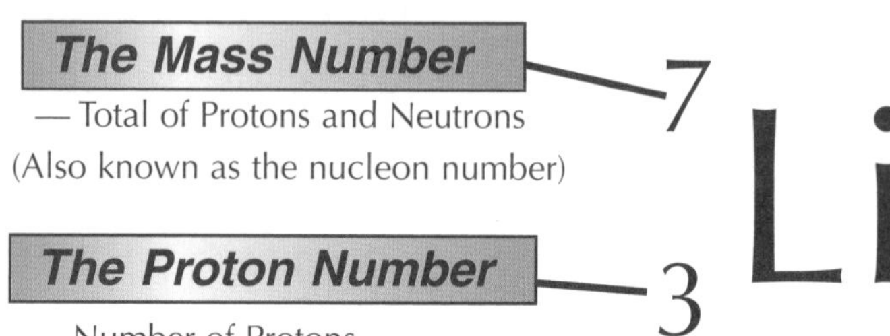

Isotopes are different forms of the same element

1) All atoms of a particular element have the same number of protons.
2) Isotopes are atoms with the same number of protons but a different number of neutrons.
3) Hence they have the same proton number, but different mass number.
4) Carbon-12 and Carbon-14 are good examples:
5) Most elements have different isotopes but there's usually only one or two stable ones.
6) Radioisotopes are radioactive isotopes, which means they decay into other elements and give out radiation. This is where all radioactivity comes from — unstable radioactive isotopes undergoing nuclear decay and spitting out high energy particles.

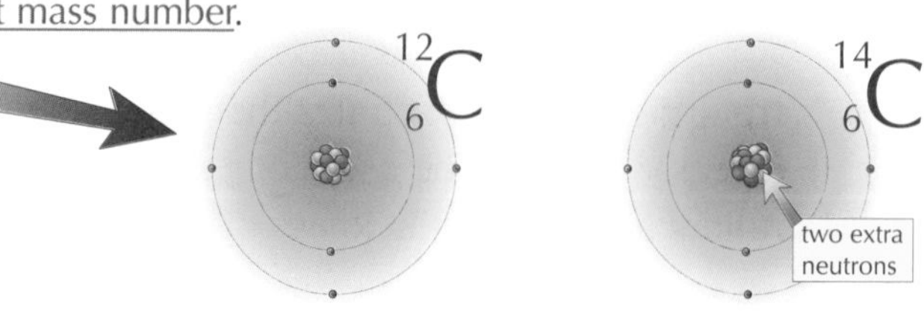

Rutherford's Scattering put an end to the Plum Pudding Theory

1) In 1804 John Dalton said matter was made up of tiny solid spheres which he called atoms.
2) Later they discovered electrons could be removed from atoms. They then saw atoms as spheres of positive charge with tiny negative electrons stuck in it like plums in a plum pudding.
3) Then Ernest Rutherford and his colleagues tried firing alpha particles at a thin gold foil. Most of them just went straight through, but the odd one came straight back at them, which was rather surprising.
4) However, they realised this meant that most of the mass of the atom was concentrated at the centre in a tiny nucleus, with a positive charge.
5) This means that most of an atom is just made up of empty space, which is also pretty surprising when you think about it.

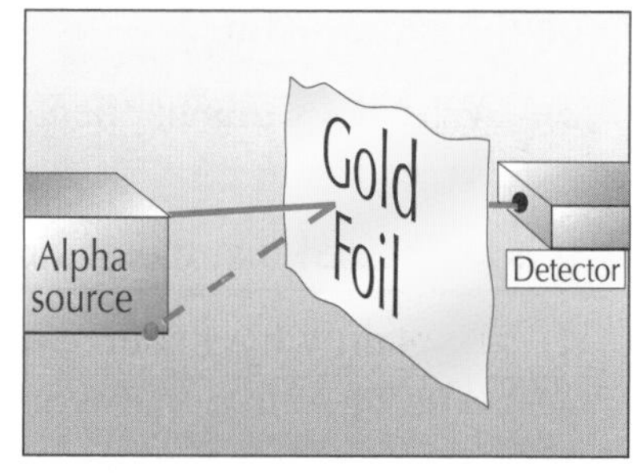

Nuclear Fission

Nuclear fission — the splitting up of atoms

Nuclear power stations and nuclear submarines are both powered by nuclear reactors.

In a nuclear reactor, a controlled chain reaction takes place in which uranium atoms split up and release energy in the form of heat. This heat is then simply used to heat water to drive a steam turbine. (See also page 208.)

So nuclear reactors are really just basically steam engines.

The chain reaction:

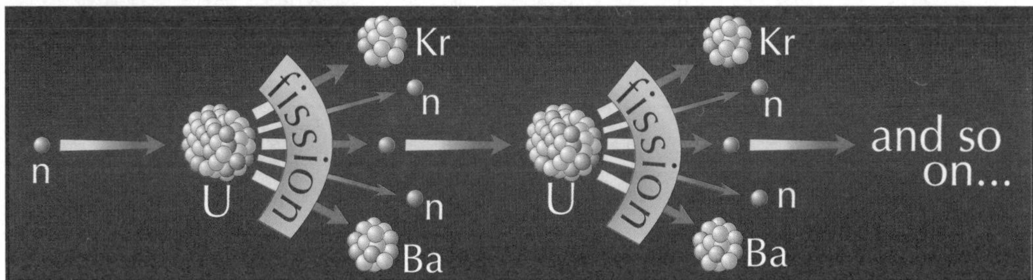

1) Each time a uranium atom splits up, it spits out two or three neutrons, any of which may hit another uranium nucleus, causing it to split also, and thus keeping the chain reaction going.
2) When a uranium atom splits in two it will form two new lighter elements. These new nuclei are unstable because they have the "wrong" number of neutrons in them — they're usually radioactive. This is the big problem with nuclear power — it produces huge amounts of radioactive material which is very difficult and expensive to dispose of safely.
3) Each nucleus splitting (called a fission) gives out a lot of energy — a lot more energy than you get with a chemical bond between two atoms. Make sure you remember that. Nuclear processes release much more energy than chemical processes do. That's why nuclear bombs are so much more powerful than ordinary bombs (which rely on chemical reactions).

Decay processes of α, β and γ emission

1) Alpha emission:

A typical alpha-emission:

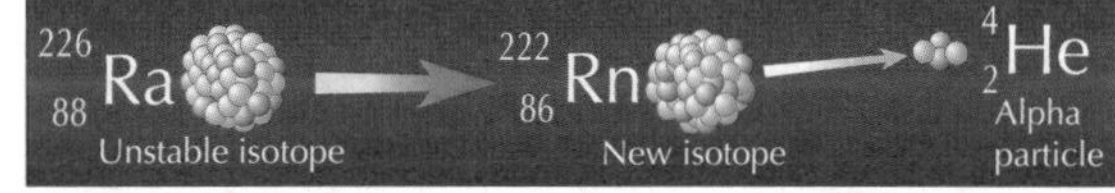

An α-particle is simply a helium nucleus, mass 4 and charge of +2 made up of 2 protons and 2 neutrons.

2) Beta emission:

A typical beta-emission:

A β-particle is simply an electron, with virtually no mass and a charge of -1.
Every time a beta particle is emitted from the nucleus, a neutron in the nucleus is converted to a proton.

3) Gamma emission:

A typical combined α- and γ-emission:

A γ-ray is a very short wavelength radiation with no mass and no charge.
After an alpha or beta emission the nucleus sometimes has extra energy to get rid of. It does this by emitting a gamma ray. Gamma emission never changes the proton or mass numbers of the nucleus.

Half-Life

The **radioactivity** of a sample always **decreases** over time

1) This is pretty obvious when you think about it. Each time a decay happens and an alpha, beta or gamma is given out, it means one more radioactive nucleus has disappeared.
2) Obviously, as the unstable nuclei all steadily disappear, the activity as a whole will also decrease. So the older a sample becomes, the less radiation it will emit.
3) How quickly the activity drops off varies a lot from one radio-isotope to another. For some it can take just a few hours before nearly all the unstable nuclei have decayed, whilst others can last for millions of years.
4) The problem with trying to measure this is that the activity never reaches zero, which is why we have to use the idea of half-life to measure how quickly the activity drops off.
5) Learn either of these important definitions of half-life:

one half-life → one half-life

HALF-LIFE is the TIME TAKEN for THE NUMBER OF PARENT atoms in a sample to HALVE	HALF-LIFE is the TIME TAKEN for the ACTIVITY (or count rate) of the original substance to fall to HALF its ORIGINAL LEVEL

(The number of parent atoms is the number of radioactive atoms in the source that haven't decayed yet.)

6) A short half-life means the activity falls quickly, because lots of the nuclei decay quickly.
7) A long half-life means the activity falls more slowly because most of the nuclei don't decay for a long time — they just sit there, basically unstable, but kind of biding their time.

Half-life *calculations*

Carbon-14 makes up a fairly constant 1/10 000 000 (One ten-millionth) of the carbon in the air, and the same proportion is also found in living things. However, when they die, the C-14 trapped inside the wood or wool or whatever, gradually decays with a half-life of 5,600 years. By simply measuring the proportion of C-14 found in something you can easily calculate how long ago the item was living material.

The basic idea of half-life is maybe a little confusing, but Exam calculations are pretty straightforward so long as you do them slowly, STEP BY STEP. Like this one:

EXAMPLE: An axe handle was found to contain 1 part in 40 000 000 C-14. Calculate the age of the axe.

ANSWER: ORIGINAL proportion of C-14 was 1/10 000 000 → After ONE HALF LIFE... Proportion of C-14 is 1/20 000 000 → After TWO HALF-LIVES... Proportion of C-14 is 1/40 000 000

Hence the axe handle is two C-14 half-lives old, ie: 2 × 5,600 = 11,200 years old.

Uranium isotopes have a very long half-life and decay via a series of short-lived particles to produce stable isotopes of lead. The relative proportions of uranium and lead isotopes in a sample of igneous rock can therefore be used to date the rock, using the known half-life of the Uranium (= 4.5 billion years). It's as simple as this:

INITIALLY:	*After one half-life:*	*After two half-lives:*	*After three half-lives:*
100% Uranium	50% Uranium	25% Uranium	12.5% Uranium
0% lead	50% lead	75% lead	87.5% lead

Ratio of Uranium to lead:

Initially	After *one half-life*	After *two half-lives*	After *three half-lives*
1:0	1:1	1:3	1:7

Similarly, the proportions of potassium-40 and its stable decay product argon-40 can be used to date igneous rocks, so long as the argon gas hasn't been able to escape. The relative proportions are exactly the same as for the uranium and lead example above.

And that's it — it's tricky but it's the last page on radiation

Learn all the details about nuclear fission in one easy mini-essay. Next up: half life. People can get very confused by the idea of half-life. Think — a radioactive sample never completely decays away because the amount left just keeps halving. The only way to measure how long it "lasts", is to time how long it takes to drop by half.

Warm-Up and Exam Questions

Warm-up Questions

1) What is the name for a negatively charged particle that orbits a nucleus?
A – a proton, B – an element, C – an electron, D – a neutron, E – a molecule, F – an ion
2) When an electron is knocked off an atom, what is the atom then called?
A – a proton, B – an element, C – an electron, D – a neutron, E – a molecule, F – an ion
3) Carbon-14 and uranium-238 are radioactive isotopes which can be used to determine the approximate age of substances. Decide which isotope would be best used for the following:
a) to determine the age of a sample of granite; b) to determine the age of a sample of wood from a shipwreck; c) to determine the age of an Egyptian mummy.
4) State which types of radiation each of the following statements refer to:
a) This is a fast moving electron. b) This radiation has a positive charge.
c) Emission of this type of radiation reduces the mass number of the nucleus.
d) This is a high energy photon. e) This radiation has no charge.
f) Emission of this type of radiation increases the atomic number of the nucleus.

Exam Questions

1 In a famous Physics experiment Ernest Rutherford and his team fired alpha particles at very thin sheets of gold foil. He observed the following results:

A – Most of the alpha particles went straight through the foil.
B – A very few (about 1 in 20,000) alpha particles were deflected a lot (90° or more).
C – Some alpha particles were deflected a little, by one or two degrees.

a) Explain each of these results.

(3 marks)

b) Rutherford's layer of foil was very thin indeed — only a few hundred atoms thick.

Would he still have been able to carry out the experiment if he had made the foil any thicker, e.g. as thick as a sheet of paper? Briefly explain your answer.

(2 marks)

c) A strontium-90 radiation source is separated from a radiation detector by a panel of aluminium and a sheet of paper. No radiation is detected. When the aluminium is taken away, radiation is detected.
Is this alpha, beta or gamma radiation?

(1 mark)

2 A university student uses a Geiger counter to measure the average radiation level in a laboratory before she carries out an experiment. She finds this to be 90 counts per minute.

a) What is the name given to this radiation?

(1 mark)

The student then brings a radioactive sample into the laboratory and measures the count rate from the sample, as shown in the table:

Time in Minutes	Count Rate in Counts per Minute	Corrected Count Rate
0	490	
5	373	
10	290	
15	232	
20	190	

b) Work out the corrected count rate values for the final column of the table.

(2 marks)

c) Plot a graph of your corrected values, with Corrected Count Rate on the vertical axis and Time in minutes on the horizontal axis.

(2 marks)

d) Use the graph to work out the half-life of the sample. Explain clearly how you arrived at your answer.

(2 marks)

e) How long after the start of the experiment will the sample's count rate reduce to 25?

(2 marks)

Revision Summary for Section Twelve

One thing's for sure — there are loads of fairly easy facts to learn about waves and radioactivity. Of course there are still some bits which need thinking about, but really, most of it is fairly easy stuff which just needs learning. Don't forget, this book contains all the important information which they've specifically mentioned in the syllabus, and this is precisely the stuff they're going to test you on in the Exams. You must practise these questions over and over again until they're easy.

1) Sketch a) a transverse wave, b) a longitudinal wave. Give a definition and four examples of each.
2) Define frequency, amplitude and wavelength for a wave and label the amplitude and wavelength on your sketches above.
3) Sketch the patterns when plane ripples reflect at a) a plane surface, b) a curved surface.
4) Sketch the reflection of curved ripples at a plane surface.
5) What is the law of reflection? Are sound and light reflected?
6) Find the speed of a wave with frequency 50kHz and wavelength 0.3cm.
7) What is refraction? What causes it? How does it affect wavelength and frequency?
8) Sketch a ray of light going through a rectangular glass block, showing the angles i and r. What if i=90°?
9) What is dispersion? Sketch the diagram which illustrates it with all the labels.
10) Sketch the three diagrams to illustrate Total Internal Reflection and the Critical Angle.
11) Sketch an application of total internal reflection which uses 45° prisms, and explain it.
12) Give details of the two main uses of optical fibres. How do optical fibres work?
13) What is diffraction? Sketch the diffraction of a) water waves b) sound waves c) light.
14) What aspect of EM waves determines their differing properties?
15) Sketch the EM spectrum with all its details. What happens when EM waves are absorbed?
16) Give full details of the uses of radio waves, microwaves and infrared.
17) Detail two uses of UV light, X-rays and gamma rays and say how harmful different dosages are.
18) Describe the differences between analogue and digital signals.
19) Why do signals have to be amplified? Why are digital signals better quality?
20) What's the connection between amplitude and the energy carried by a wave?
21) What's the relationship between frequency and pitch for a sound wave?
22) What is ultrasound? Give details of two applications of ultrasound.
23) What causes seismic waves? Sketch diagrams showing the paths of both types, and explain.
24) What do seismographs tell us about the structure of the Earth? Describe the Earth's inner structure.
25) Describe in detail the nature and properties of the three types of radiation: α, β, and γ.
26) How do the three types compare in penetrating power and ionising power? What blocks them?
27) List three places where the level of background radiation is increased and explain why.
28) What damage does a low dose of ionising radiation cause to body cells? What effects do higher doses have?
29) Which kind of radioactive sources are most dangerous a) inside the body b) outside the body?
30) Describe in detail how radioactive isotopes are used in each of the following: a) treating cancer b) tracers in medicine c) tracers in industry d) thickness control
31) Write down the number of electrons, protons and neutrons there are in an atom of $^{226}_{88}Ra$.
32) Explain what isotopes are. Give an example. Are most isotopes stable or unstable?
33) Describe Rutherford's Scattering Experiment with a diagram. What was concluded about the atom?
34) Draw a diagram to illustrate the fission of uranium and explain how the chain reaction works.
35) Describe the decay processes of: a) alpha particles b) beta particles c) gamma rays.
36) Give a proper definition of half-life. How long and how short can half-lives be?
37) A rock contains Uranium-238 atoms and stable lead atoms in the ratio 1:3. If the half-life of Uranium-238 is 4.5×10^9 years, how old is the rock?

ge 4

arm-Up Questions

a) vacuole b) cell wall c) chloroplast d) nucleus e) cell membrane

Contains a huge food reserve to provide nutrition for the developing embryo; membrane changes instantly once a sperm has penetrated it to prevent any more sperm getting in.

Liver.

Villi.

Anus.

To kill bacteria and give the correct pH for protease to work.

Fatty acids and glycerol.

am Question

a) A — Liver; B — Anus; C — Stomach; D — Pancreas
(1 mark for each correct answer; maximum 4 marks.)

b) To reabsorb water. ***(1 mark)***

c) Any two from: long and folded to increase surface area; villi to increase surface area further; good blood supply for absorption of food molecules; villi just have a single layer of cells to assist quick absorption.
(1 mark for each correct feature; maximum 2 marks.)

d)

Food substance	Digestive Enzyme	Product(s) of digestion
Starch	AMYLASE	SIMPLE SUGARS, e.g. maltose
PROTEIN	Protease	AMINO ACIDS
FAT	LIPASE	Fatty acids and glycerol

(Answers are in capitals. ***1 mark for each correct answer; maximum 6 marks***.)
The 'products of digestion' are the small molecules that the food substances are broken down into — they are absorbed into the bloodstream, to be used by your body.

ge 8

arm-Up Questions

Intercostal (rib) muscles and diaphragm.

Respiration is the process of converting glucose to energy, which goes on in every cell.

glucose + oxygen → carbon dioxide + water + energy

They increase.

am Questions

a) A – trachea; B – ribs; C – alveoli; D – diaphragm; E – bronchiole
(5 marks available; 1 mark for each correct answer)

b) Oxygen ***(1 mark)*** and carbon dioxide ***(1 mark)***.

c) The intercostal (rib) muscles and diaphragm contract. This increases the volume of the thorax, so the pressure inside the thorax decreases and air rushes in through the mouth or nose. ***(4 marks)***

d) Answers include: large surface area; a layer of moisture for gases to dissolve in; very thin walls; good blood supply.
(4 marks available; 1 mark for each correct answer)

a)

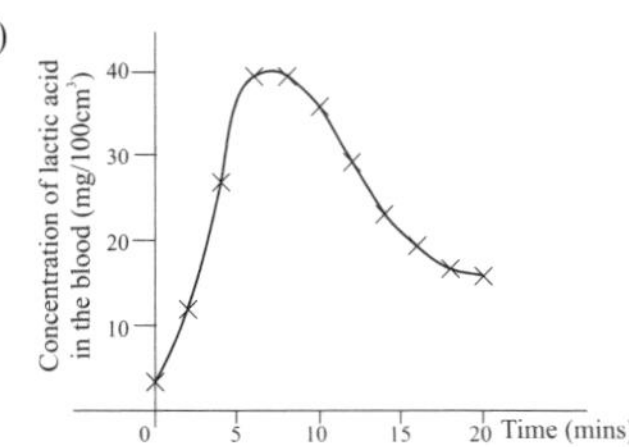

(4 marks available — 1 mark each for correctly labelled axis; 1 mark for points correctly plotted; 1 mark for a smooth curve joining the points.)

b) Approximately 2.5 minutes. ***(1 mark)***
Always include the units in number questions — e.g. here, you wouldn't get a mark if you just wrote 2.5 without including the word 'minutes'.

c) The muscles get tired/muscle fatigue and can be painful. ***(1 mark)***

d) The oxygen you have to repay your muscles because they did not get enough earlier on ***(1 mark)***. This oxygen is used to oxidise the lactic acid produced during anaerobic respiration ***(1 mark)***.

e) Human muscle cells: glucose → energy + lactic acid ***(1 mark)***
Make sure you know this equation for anaerobic respiration off by heart — it often crops up in the exam.

Page 13

Warm-Up Questions

1) A system where the blood goes through the heart twice for every complete cycle of the body.
2) One cell thick.
3) The right side.
4) They prevent the backflow of blood.
5) They carry oxygen to all cells in the body.
6) Haemoglobin.

Exam Questions

1 a) A – pulmonary artery; B – pulmonary vein; C – left atrium; D – left ventricle; E – heart valve (pulmonary valve)
(5 marks available; 1 mark for each)

b)

Vein	Artery
Carries blood **towards** heart	Carries blood **away from** heart
Carries blood at **low** pressure	Carries blood at **high** pressure
Carries **deoxygenated** blood (except pulmonary vein)	Carries **oxygenated** blood (except pulmonary artery)
Size of lumen is **large** compared to thickness of walls	Size of lumen is **small** compared to thickness of walls

(4 marks)

2) a) i) White blood cells — defend the body against disease. ***(1 mark)***

ii) Plasma — carries substances around the body (e.g. nutrients, carbon dioxide, urea, hormones, antibodies, blood cells, platelets). ***(1 mark)***
You need to learn <u>all</u> the different substances that plasma carries around the body.

iii) Platelets — help the blood to clot. ***(1 mark)***

b) Any two out of: squashed disc shaped to increase surface area for absorbing oxygen; contain haemoglobin to bind to the oxygen; no nucleus, so more room for haemoglobin.
(1 mark for each correct answer; maximum 2 marks.)

Page 16

Warm-Up Questions

1) Nucleus
2) Bacteria
3) It has an outer protein coat, which surrounds a strand of genetic material.
4) E.g. Skin and Eyes — Skin acts as a barrier to stop the entry of microbes. If the skin is broken the blood clots to form a scab. Eyes produce a chemical that kills microbes.
   The Digestive System — Stomach produces hydrochloric acid, which kills most microbes present in food.
   The Respiratory System — The respiratory tract is lined with cilia and mucus, which traps microbes before they enter the lungs.
5) Drugs that kill bacteria (not viruses) without harming the body cells.

Exam Questions

1 a) They damage cells ***(1 mark)*** and produce harmful toxins ***(1 mark)***.

b) If you are naturally immune to a microbe, you cannot become ill as a result of being infected by that microbe ***(1 mark)***. You become naturally immune by being infected by the microbe ***(1 mark)***. The white blood cells produce antibodies against that specific microbe ***(1 mark)***. The antibodies and the cells that produce them stick around in the body and if they come across the microbe again they kill it before it makes you ill ***(1 mark)***.

c) The cilia may stop working ***(1 mark)***. This means the mucus, with the trapped dust and bacteria ***(1 mark)***, is not removed from the respiratory tract so it can lead to infection ***(1 mark)***.

2 a) Antibiotic C is the most effective at killing the bacteria ***(1 mark)*** as the clear zone around the disc, where the bacteria have been killed, is larger than in the case of the other two antibiotics ***(1 mark)***.
This is a simple matter of looking carefully at the experimental results and interpreting them — it's common sense more than anything else.

b) He could repeat the experiment to check that his results were the same. ***(1 mark)***
Fair test questions are very common in exams — the most obvious ways of making an experiment fair are by having as big a sample size as possible (e.g. by doing an experiment lots of times), and by keeping all variables constant, except for the one you're investigating.

c) Viruses cannot grow on the agar plate as they need cells in order to reproduce. ***(1 mark)*** Antibiotics cannot be used to kill viruses. ***(1 mark)***

Page 19

Warm-Up Questions

1) The net movement of particles from a region of high concentration to a region of low concentration.
2) The rate of diffusion increases.
3) Starch molecules are too big to pass through a cell membrane.
4) They increase the surface area through which diffusion can happen, and they have a very good blood supply and thin walls to assist quick absorption.

Exam Question

1 a) The net movement of particles ***(1 mark)*** from an area of high concentration to an area of low concentration ***(1 mark)***.

b) Any reasonable answer with matching reason,
e.g. gut; ***(1 mark)*** Diffusion needed here for food molecules, e.g. glycerol and amino acids, to get into the blood. ***(1 mark)***

lungs; ***(1 mark)*** Diffusion needed here so that oxygen can pass into the blood and carbon dioxide can pass out of the blood. ***(1 mark)***

Page 23

Warm-Up Questions

1) Packed with chloroplasts; tall shape so a large surface area is exposed down the side for absorbing carbon dioxide and there is a good chance of light hitting a chloroplast before it reaches the bottom of the cell.
2) Photosynthesis.
3) To attract insects or birds to pollinate the plant / to release pollen to the wind. Also to receive pollen.
4) Xylem tubes.

Exam Question

1 a) A - cell wall; B - cell membrane; C - cytoplasm; D - nucleus; E - chloroplast; F - vacuole ***(1 mark for each; maximum 6 marks.)***

b)

STRUCTURE	Mitochondrion	Cell membrane	Chloroplast	Cell wall	Nucleus
JOB	To release energy from food	Controls what goes in and out of cell / holds cell together	Makes food by photosynthesis	supports cell	Controls what the cell does

(1 mark for each correctly filled in box in the table; maximum 4 marks.)

c) Organ - a group of different tissues
Organism - a living thing
Tissue - a group of similar cells
Organ system - a group of organs working together.

(1 mark for each correct answer; maximum 4 marks.)

d) (i) To open and close the stomata, which allows gases into and out of the leaves. ***(1 mark)***

(ii) Possible features include:
Thin outer walls and thicker inner walls to make the opening and closing function work properly.
Special kidney shaped cells to open and close stomata.

(1 mark for each correct feature; maximum 2 marks.)

Page 28

Warm-Up Questions

1) CARBON DIOXIDE + WATER $\xrightarrow[\text{chlorophyll}]{\text{sunlight}}$ GLUCOSE + OXYGEN
2) They control the opening and closing of the stomata and hence control gaseous exchange.
3) Chlorophyll.
4) The rate drops because the high temperature denatures the chlorophyll enzymes.
5) Starch.
6) Yellow leaves with dead spots.

Exam Questions

1 a)

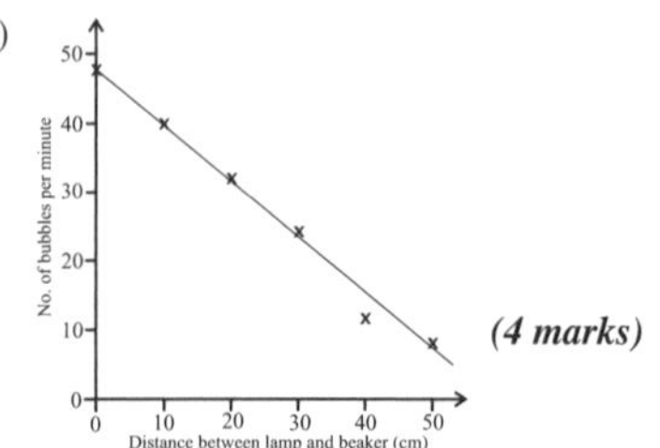

(4 marks)

Don't let technical names like 'Elodea' put you off — the rules are the same, whatever the plant.

b) To allow the Elodea to adjust to the new light intensity. ***(1 mark)***

c) To provide the Elodea with carbon dioxide for photosynthesis. ***(1 mark***

d) As light intensity increases, rate of photosynthesis increases. ***(1 mark)***

e) Carbon dioxide level, temperature ***(2 marks)***

2 a)

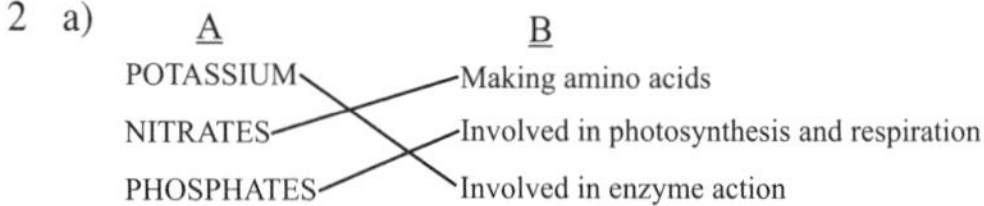

(3 marks available; 1 mark for each correct answer)

b) Stunted growth and yellow older leaves. ***(2 marks)***
2 marks are available, so make sure you put down at least 2 symptoms.

Page 32

Warm-Up Questions

1) The loss of water, by evaporation, from the leaves.
2) Amount of light, temperature, amount of air movement, humidity of the surrounding air.
3) They allow diffusion of gases in and out of the leaf.
4) It is full of water, and so is rigid/swollen.

Exam Question

1 a) $\frac{2.3 - 1.6}{2.3} \times 100\%$

$= 30\%$

(2 marks for correct answer, otherwise 1 mark for the correct workin
It's important to show your method when you have to work something out — you could still get marks, even if your final answer is wrong.

b) To make a fairer comparison between the leaves, as they all started at a different mass. ***(1 mark)***

c) Leaf A — lost least water through transpiration, as all stomata were covered by waterproof petroleum jelly. ***(1 mark)***

Leaf B — lost more water through transpiration than leaf A, but less the leaves C and D, as the large number of stomata on the bottom of the lea were covered in petroleum jelly. ***(1 mark)***

Leaf C — lost more water through transpiration than leaves A and B, bu less than D. Petroleum jelly covered the smaller number of stomata on top of the leaf, leaving the larger number of stomata on the bottom of th leaf exposed to the air. ***(1 mark)***

Leaf D — lost the most water through transpiration, as all stomata were open to the air. ***(1 mark)***
Remember that water and carbon dioxide move in and out of plants through stomata in the leaves, and that stomata are mainly found on the bottom surface of leaves.

d) Any three from: light; temperature; wind; humidity. ***(1 mark for each correct factor, maximum 3 marks.)***

e) Xylem ***(1 mark)***

ge 36

arm-Up Questions

Food — sugars, fats and proteins.

Xylem

A membrane that allows some particles through, but not all particles.

The movement of water molecules across a partially permeable membrane from a region of high water concentration to a region of lower water concentration.

Active uptake (or active transport)

am Question

a) Water moved into the Visking tubing ***(1 mark)*** by osmosis ***(1 mark)***.

b) 250mm ***(1 mark for answer between 230 and 270 mm)***

c) 9½ – 5 = 4½ minutes ***(1 mark)***

ge 39

arm-Up Questions

Plant growth hormones.

More auxin is produced on the shaded side of the shoot, causing it to grow faster on this shaded side and so bend towards the light.

Plant growth hormones that only affect broad-leaved plants.

There is less chance of the fruit being damaged.

It means they can grow cuttings from really good plants very quickly, producing clones.

am Question

a)

	LIGHT	GRAVITY
SHOOT	Towards	Away from
ROOT	Away from	Towards

(1 mark for filling in the 'shoot' row correctly; 1 mark for filling in the 'root' row correctly.)

Remember that roots and shoots act in opposite directions to each other (i.e. they grow away from each other).

b) Auxin. ***(1 mark)***

c) (i) SHOOT ROOT

(1 mark for drawing the shoot horizontal; 1 mark for drawing the root horizontal.)

(ii) The clinostat removes the effect of gravity and there is no light available ***(1 mark)***, therefore no stimuli for the root and shoot to respond to ***(1 mark)***.

(iii) The shoot would be growing up, away from gravity ***(1 mark)***; the root would be growing down, towards gravity ***(1 mark)***.

d) Any two from: producing seedless fruits; controlling ripening of fruit; growing cuttings in rooting compound; killing weeds. ***(1 mark for each correct use; maximum 2 marks.)***

ge 43

arm-Up Questions

Detect changes (stimuli). (Could also say they turn energy into electrical impulses.)

Eyes, ears, nose, tongue, skin.

The circular muscles in the iris contract, closing up the pupil. Less light gets into the eye.

Sensory, relay (or connector) and motor.

An automatic response to a stimulus.

Exam Questions

1 a) A – receptor; B – sensory neuron; C – synapse; D – relay neuron; E – motor neuron; F – effector (or 'muscle' in this case) ***(6 marks available; 1 mark for each correct answer)***

b) Stimulus – a change that can be detected
Receptor – this detects the change
Effector – this brings about the response to the change
(3 marks available; one for each correct answer)
When you're asked to explain terms, it means you need to give a definition of the words — you don't need to explain how they work.

c)

Sense Organ	Receptor(s)
Eyes	Light
Ears	Sound and balance.
Nose	Smell.
Tongue	Taste.
Skin	Pressure and temperature

(6 marks available; 1 for each correct answer)

2 a) Synapse ***(1 mark)***

b)

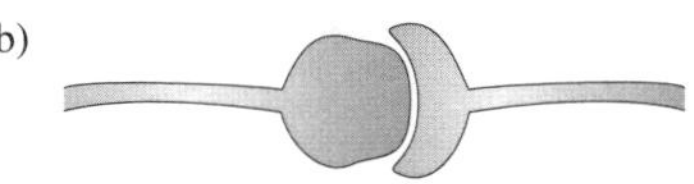

(1 mark)
Sensory neurons always connect to relay neurons.

c) Chemicals/neurotransmitters are released into the gap ***(1 mark)*** and diffuse across to the next neuron, setting off a new electrical impulse ***(1 mark)***.

d) Stimulus → **Receptor** → Neurons → **Effector** → Response

(Answers are underlined. ***1 mark for each correct answer; maximum 2 marks***.)
Make sure you know this block diagram of a reflex arc — it's an examiner favourite. It's easier to learn if you apply it to a real life situation, e.g. touching a hot kettle.

e) Help protect the body from injury. ***(1 mark)***

Page 48

Warm-Up Questions

1) Homeostasis is the maintenance of a constant internal environment.
2) The lungs.
3) Urea.
4) The kidneys.
5) The liver and the pancreas.
6) Anti Diuretic Hormone or ADH.

Exam Questions

1 a) The pituitary gland. ***(1 mark)***

b) When the pituitary gland receives the message from the brain that there is too little water in the blood, it releases more ADH than usual. ***(1 mark)***

This causes the nephrons/kidneys to reabsorb more water than usual into the blood ***(1 mark)*** and so less water is lost in urine. ***(1 mark)***

c) The pituitary releases less ADH than usual. ***(1 mark)***

This causes the nephrons to reabsorb less water than usual into the blood ***(1 mark)*** and so more water is lost in the urine. ***(1 mark)***
Question 1c) is easy — you just write the opposite of what you put for 1b).

d) Excess ions ***(1 mark)*** and urea ***(1 mark)***.

2 a) Answers include:
Ultrafiltration ***(1 mark)***, reabsorption ***(1 mark)***, release of wastes ***(1 mark)***

b) Water ***(1 mark)***, ions ***(1 mark)***, urea ***(1 mark)***.

Page 52

Warm-Up Questions

1) Chemical messengers, which travel in the blood to activate target cells.
2) When glucose levels in the blood are too high.

3) A disease in which the pancreas does not produce enough insulin.

4) The adrenal gland.

Exam Questions

1 a)

	Nerves	Hormones
Speed of message	**fast** slow	fast **slow**
How long the effect lasts	long **short**	**long** short
Precision of area affected	**very precise** more general	very precise **more general**

(3 marks available; 1 mark for each correctly filled in row.)

b) A — pituitary gland; B — adrenal gland; C — pancreas;
D — ovary; E — testis.

(1 mark for each correctly named gland; maximum 5 marks available)
Remember that A, B and C are found in males and females, but ovaries are only found in females and testes are only found in males.

c) Adrenaline. ***(1 mark)***

d) Any 3 from: increases blood sugar levels; increases heart rate; increases breathing rate; diverts blood away from the skin to the muscle.
(1 mark for each correct answer; maximum 3 marks available.)

2 a) 09:00 hours, 15:00 hours and 22:00 hours (roughly)
(1 mark for each correct time; maximum 3 marks available.)
Questions about reading answers off graphs are easy marks — just make sure you study the graph carefully, so you don't make a careless mistake and lose marks.

b) Eating. ***(1 mark)***

c) Insulin is released.
This converts blood glucose to glycogen to be stored.
Glucose is also used up in the normal metabolism of cells
(2 marks available for any two of the above points)

d) The blood sugar levels out and does not fall below a certain amount (approximately 98mg/100cm^3). ***(1 mark)***

Page 56

Warm-Up Questions

1) Animals compete for space, food and water.
Plants compete for space, water, nutrients and light.

2) Any five of the following:
Can store a lot of water.
Loses very little water in urine and sweat.
Tolerates big fluctuations in temperature.
Large feet so that it doesn't sink into the soft sand.
Does not have a layer of fat insulating its body – therefore loses heat easily.
Large surface area also means it loses heat easily.
Sandy colour for camouflage.

3) Any five of the following:
Large size and compact shape to keep surface area to a minimum.
Thick layer of blubber for insulation and also a fat resource to survive hard times when food is scarce.
Thick hairy coat for keeping the body heat in.
Greasy fur which sheds water after swimming to prevent cooling due to evaporation.
White fur to match the surroundings for camouflage.
Strong swimmer to catch food in the water and strong runner to run down prey on land.
Big, wide feet to spread the weight on snow and ice.

Exam Questions

1 a) Food, predators, competition and disease are all factors which can limit the size of a population. ***(2 marks available; 1 mark for each factor)***

b) Foxes would have more food, so their population would increase.
(1 mark)

c) The fox population would fall because they would have less food ***(1 mark)***. The grass population would rise because fewer rabbits feed off it ***(1 mark)***.

2) a) The adaptive features of cacti include – they have no leaves, a thick ste
spines, small surface area and shallow but extensive roots.
(1 mark each for any 4 answers.)

b) Having no leaves reduces water loss. A thick stem allows it to store a lo
of water. Spines protect them from being eaten by herbivores. A small surface area reduces water loss. The shallow roots are designed to allo
lots of water to quickly be absorbed from a large area.
(1 mark each for four explanations matching answers to part a.)

Page 59

Warm-Up Questions

1) The number of organisms decreases as you move up the trophic levels.

2)

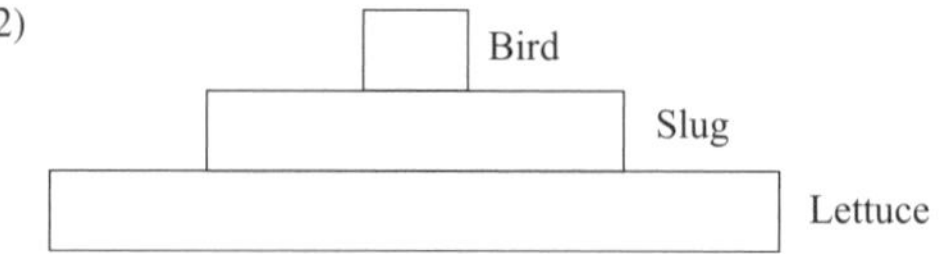

3) The energy is lost through respiration, heat loss and in animal waste.

Exam Question

1 a) A trophic level is a particular stage in a food chain. ***(1 mark)***

b) There are four trophic levels in the food chain. ***(1 mark)***

c) Any two of the following:
Reducing the number of stages in the food web, e.g. by growing crops rather than having grazing animals; limiting the movement of animals; keeping the animals warm. ***(2 marks available; 1 mark for each correc answer)***
The wording of this question is a bit cryptic.
Don't let it put you off — it's just factual recall from page 58.

d) The farmers will not need to give them as much food. ***(1 mark)***

Page 62

Warm-Up Questions

1) It decomposes — it is broken down by microorganisms and its nutrients are returned to the soil.

2) Burning, decay and respiration all return CO_2 to the environment.

3) Nitrates.

4) Decay of dead animals, plants and faeces all produce ammonium compoun

5) All living organisms need nitrogen to be able to make proteins.

Exam Questions

1 a) Proteins. ***(1 mark)***

b) Nitrifying bacteria. ***(1 mark)***

c) A = decay by microbes ***(1 mark)***
B = conversion by nitrifying bacteria ***(1 mark)***
C = eating ***(1 mark)***

d) Detritus is organic debris from decomposing plants and animals. ***(1 ma***

2 a) The breakdown of dead organic matter ***(1 mark)*** by microbes ***(1 mark)***.

b) Bacteria ***(1 mark)*** and fungi ***(1 mark)***.

c) If decay is to occur, then all these conditions are needed:
warmth ***(1 mark)***, moisture ***(1 mark)*** and oxygen ***(1 mark)***.

3 a) photosynthesis

b) respiration, decay, burning

c) nitrifying bacteria

d) fungi
(6 marks — 1 for each correct word picked.)
The key to all questions on the Carbon or Nitrogen Cycle is to know the diagrams. You've got to practise drawing them till it's as routine as sleepin

ge 67

arm-Up Questions

Methane and carbon dioxide

Any two consequences, e.g.
There will be an increase in average global temperature;
Polar ice caps may melt, raising sea-levels and flooding coastal cities;
Weather patterns and climate may be affected, causing droughts/floods.

Burning fossil fuels produces carbon dioxide, sulphur dioxide and nitrogen oxides; these mix with clouds and fall as acid rain.

Use less fossil fuels; use catalytic converters in cars to clean up exhaust fumes; use acid gas scrubbers in factories to remove harmful gases before they are released.

Use of CFCs in aerosols, fridges, air-conditioning units and polystyrene foam; use of leaded petrol in cars; methane from rice growing and cattle rearing.

xam Questions

a) Any three correct answers, e.g. farming; building more houses; dumping waste; quarrying.
(1 mark for each correct answer; maximum 3 marks available.)

b) To provide wood for construction and fuel ***(1 mark)*** and to clear land for agriculture ***(1 mark)***.

c) Trees unsuitable for use as timber are burned. ***(1 mark)***
Burning releases carbon dioxide directly into the air. ***(1 mark)***
Decay of felled trees by microorganisms also releases more CO_2 into the air. ***(1 mark)***
Trees remove carbon dioxide from the environment for use in photosynthesis. ***(1 mark)***
Fewer trees means that less CO_2 is removed. ***(1 mark)***
Remember the photosynthesis equation here: plants use up carbon dioxide + water (using chlorophyll and sunlight) in order to produce oxygen and glucose.

a) When fossil fuels burn, they release mostly $\underline{CO_2}$. ***(1 mark)***
When oxides of sulphur and nitrogen mix with clouds, they form acids. ***(1 mark)***
Acid causes aluminium salts from the soil to dissolve into the water. ***(1 mark)***
When aluminium salts are in the soil they are safe, but as soon as they dissolve in water, the resulting aluminium ions are poisonous to many plant and animal species, and can kill them.

b) Use less fossil fuels. ***(1 mark)***
Use acid gas scrubbers at power stations to remove harmful gases before being released. ***(1 mark)***
Use catalytic converters in engines to clean up exhaust fumes. ***(1 mark)***

a) Crops remove nitrates from the soil, which are essential for crop growth ***(1 mark)***. Fertilisers contain nitrates and replace the lost nutrients ***(1 mark)***.

b) When too many nutrients in the soil have been washed into a lake, swamp, etc., leading to excess growth and decay. ***(1 mark)***

c) Fertilisers washed into river → Rapid growth of plants and algae → Some plants die due to competition for light and oxygen → More decay microbes using up O_2 → Fish and more plants die (→ back to More decay microbes using up O_2)
(4 marks)

age 72

arm-Up Questions

Genetic and environmental.

Temperature, sunlight, moisture level and soil composition.

Eye colour, hair colour at birth, inherited diseases, blood group.

Characteristics in plants are determined by 'hereditary units'. Hereditary units are passed on from both parents, one unit from each parent. Hereditary units can be dominant or recessive — if an individual has both the dominant and recessive unit for a characteristic, the dominant characteristic will be expressed.

A short length of chromosome / a length of DNA that codes for a particular protein.

23

Exam Questions

1 a)

Genetic	Genetic and Environmental
Eye colour	Height
Blood group	Hair length
	Weight
	Middle finger length

(Answers don't have to be in a table.)
(3 marks available — 1 mark for every two correct answers.)

2 a) Genes ***(1 mark)***

b) 3 smooth : 1 wrinkled

	B	b
B	BB	Bb
b	Bb	bb

(3 marks available — 2 marks for correct diagram or similar working, 1 mark for correct answer.)

Page 77

Warm-Up Questions

1) Mitosis and meiosis.
2) To produce cells with half the normal number of chromosomes (to allow sexual reproduction).
3) The fusion of haploid male and female gametes, restoring the diploid number of chromosomes in a zygote.

Exam Questions

1 a) D, A, E, C, B ***(5 marks available; 1 mark for each correct box)***

b) Growth ***(1 mark)***, repair ***(1 mark)***, asexual reproduction ***(1 mark)***

c) Any two of:
Meiosis produces haploid cells, mitosis produces diploid cells.
Meiosis produces four cells at the end of division, mitosis produces two.
Meiosis leads to variation, cells produced in mitosis are genetically identical.
In meiosis there are two cell divisions, in mitosis there is just one.
(1 mark each for up to 2 correct answers.)
Mitosis and meiosis are pretty nasty — the basics are simple enough, but you've really got to understand them in detail to do questions like part c).

2 a) There should be one long chromosome and one short chromosome in each circle, and there should be two of each original chromosome overall, e.g.

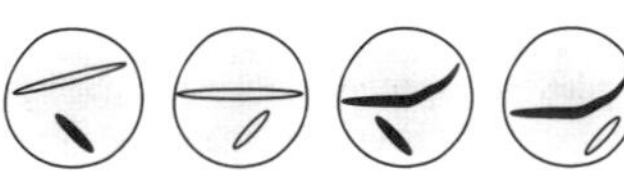

(2 marks for correct answer or 1 mark for 2 chromosomes in each cell)
This is a particularly tricky bit — remember, cell meiosis produces "gametes" with half the original number of chromosomes. In the original cell, the chromosomes are in pairs — a long pair and a short pair. The gametes end up with 1 chromosome from each pair.

b) So that when the male and female gametes fuse, the normal number of chromosomes is restored. If the numbers of chromosomes were not halved in meiosis then the number of chromosomes would double each time fertilisation occurred. It also produces variation — the offspring are genetically different from the parents.
(2 marks)

c) The sex organs (testes and ovaries). ***(1 mark)***

d) Gametes. ***(1 mark)***

Page 82

Warm-Up Questions

1) Humans artificially select the organisms that they are going to breed according to what they want from them.
2) Reduction in the gene pool.
3) Genetically identical organisms.
4) The modification of the genetics of an organism to the benefit of man.
5) Issues include:
People are worried about the possible option of 'designer babies'.
Changing the genetic make-up of organisms could unbalance their ecosystems.
Large seed companies are producing seeds that develop into plants that do not produce fertile seeds, or plants that only respond to their fertilisers.

Exam Questions

1 a) Cut out by enzymes. ***(1 mark)***

b) (i) Clones are genetically identical organisms ***(1 mark)*** or cells produced from a single parental cell by asexual reproduction.

(ii) They reproduce asexually, therefore making identical copies of themselves; reproduce rapidly; can be cultured on waste materials from the food industry which are low cost.
(1 mark each for any 2 answers.)
Make sure you remember why bacteria are so useful — you could easily get asked this kind of thing...

c) Does not cause side effects in patient; large amounts can be produced, therefore no shortage; better for pigs. ***(1 mark each for any 2 answers.)***
The answer is out there (and it's not hard to find if you think a bit...)

2 a) They are genetically identical. ***(1 mark)***

b) Any three out of:
very fast — thousands of plantlets can be produced in a few weeks;
very little space required;
can grow all year (no weather problems);
new plants are disease free;
new plants can be developed very quickly by splicing new genes into plantlets.
(1 mark for each up to maximum of 3 marks)

c) Sexual reproduction. ***(1 mark)***

d) It leads to genetic variation, and it's easier. ***(1 mark for either reason)***
Remember — one of the main problems with genetic engineering is the reduction of the "gene pool"...

Page 87

Warm-Up Questions

1) The remains of long-dead organisms that are preserved in some way.
2) That all the organisms on Earth gradually evolved over millions of years.
3) Fossils and similarities between living organisms
4) Each finch had a beak and body suited to the food on its particular island. He proposed that seed-eating finches had flown over from the mainland and, over millions of years, they had become adapted to the foods on their particular islands.
5) Extinction is where an entire species completely dies out.
It can happen:
when the environment changes too quickly,
as a result of a new predator or disease,
when the species can't compete with another (new) species for food, etc.
6) Charles Darwin
7) Predators, disease, competition.
8) A change in a gene, DNA or the number of chromosomes in a cell, which leads to genetic variation.
9) A mutation in body cells where the mutant cells multiply out of control, often invading other parts of the body.

Exam Questions

1 a) Palaeozoic ***(1 mark)***

b) Silurian ***(1 mark)***

c) Devonian ***(1 mark)***

d) They are the remains of long-dead animals and plants preserved in various ways. ***(1 mark)***

e) Answers include:
The fins slowly evolved into limbs for movement on land.
The gills evolved into lungs to get oxygen from the air.
(2 marks available — 1 mark for each correct answer)

2) a) Mutation ***(1 mark)***

b) Natural selection (survival of the fittest) ***(1 mark)***

c) Black peppered moths seen more clearly as amount of soot on trees decreased; chance of being eaten by birds increased ***(1 mark)***; frequency of their genes in the population decreased ***(1 mark)***.
Light coloured moths now better camouflaged / less likely to be eaten / better suited to lower pollution levels ***(1 mark)***; number of their genes in the population increased ***(1 mark)***.
So it's basically what happened to the white moths now happening to th black moths. If you've understood the passage, it's all quite simple.

d) Any three observations, such as: variation within the population means some organisms are better adapted to their environment than others; organisms produce more offspring than could possibly survive; struggle for existence — most populations do not rapidly increase in size, therefo there must be considerable competition; only organisms well adapted to the environment survive; these advantageous characteristics are then passed onto offspring.
(1 mark for each point up to a maximum of 3 marks)

Page 91

Warm-Up Questions

1) Physical characteristics resulting from a particular gene or combination of genes.
2) Both alleles are the same.
3) Shaking, erratic body movements and severe mental deterioration.
4) Recessive.
5) It is dominant.

Exam Question

1 a) (i) The allele for short pea plants. ***(1 mark)***

(ii) They are heterozygous, the parents are homozygous. ***(1 mark)***

b) (i) A sticky, thick mucus is produced in the lungs and pancreas ***(1 mark)*** causing chest infections and digestive problems ***(1 mark)***.

(ii)

	F	f
F	FF	Ff
f	Ff	ff

(4 marks for correct answer, lose a mark for each mistake.)

(iii) They do not show signs of the disease ***(1 mark)***, but one of their alleles is the recessive allele for cystic fibrosis and this can be passed on to their children ***(1 mark)***.

(iv) The one with the genotype ff (homozygous recessive). ***(1 mark)***

Page 93

Warm-Up Questions

1) Either oestrogen or progesterone (only oestrogen covered in this book).
2) Follicle Stimulating Hormone (FSH) and Luteinising Hormone (LH).
3) Oestrogen causes pituitary gland to produce LH (which in turn stimulates release of an egg), and inhibits further release of FSH.

Exam Question

1 a) Any two of: Follicle Stimulating Hormone (FSH), oestrogen, progesteror
(2 marks available; 1 mark for each correct answer)

b) Pituitary gland ***(1 mark)***, ovaries ***(1 mark)***

c) Stimulates release of egg (ovulation). ***(1 mark)***

d) (i) Oestrogen levels kept high ***(1 mark)***, which inhibits production of FS ***(1 mark)***, which eventually stops egg production ***(1 mark)***.

(ii) Any reasonable answer, e.g. can produce side-effects such as nausea and headaches; not 100% effective, doesn't protect against STDs. ***(1 mark)***

ge 98

arm-Up Questions

Roughly ¾

Fizzes violently, producing hydrogen gas and a hydroxide solution.
lithium + water → lithium hydroxide + hydrogen

Lithium, sodium or potassium

e.g. iron in Haber Process, Manganese(IV) oxide in decomposing hydrogen peroxide.

xam Questions

a) Potassium hydroxide and hydrogen ***(1 mark)***

b) $2K + 2H_2O \rightarrow 2KOH + H_2$ ***(1 mark)***

c) Sodium has fewer electron shells than potassium ***(1 mark)*** so the outer electron is closer to and less shielded from the nucleus ***(1 mark)***. This means sodium gives up its outer electron less readily ***(1 mark)***.
I can't stress how vitally important it is that you learn about shielding. It's really, really important for understanding why reactivity changes down the groups.

a) Yes, as they are typical metals. ***(1 mark)***

b) Nickel ***(1 mark)***

c) Purple ***(1 mark)*** *See, you really do need all those fiddly details.*

age 101

arm-Up Questions

aluminium

yes

aluminium

It's cheap and strong.

xam Question

a) Gold, silver, copper ***(1 mark)***

b) Potassium, sodium, calcium, magnesium, aluminium ***(1 mark)***

c) Silver is lower down the series than hydrogen. Only metals above hydrogen in the reactivity series react with water. ***(2 marks)***

age 104

arm-Up Questions

yes

no — it will react with steam

You would see bubbles as the zinc reacts with the acid
(there would be a small squeaky pop if you stuck a lit splint in the test tube).

You would see the same thing but much more vigorous — lots of bubbles (and a big squeaky pop if you put a lighted splint in).

The iron nail will become coated with copper, and the blue copper sulphate solution will turn colourless (as it becomes iron sulphate).

Iron is more reactive than copper, so it displaces the copper from the copper sulphate solution. (iron + copper sulphate → copper + iron sulphate)

xam Questions

a) Sodium hydroxide and hydrogen ***(2 marks)***
You should know this from work on Group I metals.

b) Aluminium oxide and hydrogen ***(2 marks)***

c) Nothing ***(1 mark)***

a) sulphuric acid ***(1 mark)***

b) (i) Hydrogen. A burning splint makes hydrogen ignite with a squeaky pop. ***(2 marks)***

(ii) $2HCl + Mg \rightarrow MgCl_2 + H_2$ ***(2 marks)***
Make sure it's balanced.

(iii) Zinc is less reactive than magnesium, so it reacts more slowly. ***(1 mark)***

(iv) No. ***(1 mark)*** Copper is less reactive than hydrogen. ***(1 mark)***

Page 107

Warm-Up Questions

1) A mineral containing enough metal to make the metal worth extracting.
2) Reduction with carbon in a blast furnace.
3) Aluminium.
4) As the metal.

Exam Questions

1 a) carbon ***(1 mark)***

b) (i) $C + O_2 \rightarrow CO_2$ ***(2 marks)***

(ii) 2CO ***(1 mark)***

c) (i) $3CO + Fe_2O_3 \rightarrow 2Fe + 3CO_2$ ***(2 marks)***

(ii) It collects at the bottom of the furnace and is tapped off. ***(1 mark)***

Page 110

Warm-Up Questions

1) Aluminium
2) Bauxite
3) Cathode: $Al^{3+}_{(aq)} + 3e^- \rightarrow Al_{(s)}$ Anode: $2O^{2-}_{(aq)} \rightarrow O_{2(g)} + 4e^-$
4) Cathode: $Cu^{2+}_{(aq)} + 2e^- \rightarrow Cu_{(s)}$ Anode: $Cu_{(s)} \rightarrow Cu^{2+}_{(aq)} + 2e^-$

Exam Questions

1 a) For electrolysis to work, the Al^{3+} ions must be free to move ***(1 mark)***. This is not possible in a solid ***(1 mark)***.

b) The melting point of aluminium oxide is over 2000°C ***(1 mark)***. It would be very expensive to heat it to this temperature. Aluminium oxide dissolved in molten cryolite is liquid at a lower temperature which makes things cheaper ***(1 mark)***.
When you're answering a question about an industrial process, remember that manufacturers are obsessed with cost. They want things done quickly using cheaper materials and cheaper processes. Well, they need to pay for their new Ferraris somehow.

c) about 900°C ***(1 mark)***

d) (i) $Al^{3+} + 3e^- \rightarrow Al$ ***(1 mark for correct equation, 1 mark for balancing)***

(ii) $2O^{2-} \rightarrow O_2 + 4e^-$ ***(1 mark for correct equation, 1 mark for balancing)***

(iii) The graphite anode reacts with oxygen produced at the anode ***(1 mark)*** to form CO_2 ***(1 mark)***.

2 a) It would get bigger. ***(1 mark)***

b) They would fall to the bottom as sludge. ***(1 mark)***

c) $Cu^{2+}_{(aq)}$; $2e^-$ ***(1 mark)***

d) It allows Cu^{2+} ions to flow between the electrodes without having to use molten copper which is expensive to heat. ***(2 marks)***

Page 114

Warm-Up Questions

1) red
2) alkali
3) alkali
4) H^+
5) water
6) hydrogen

Exam Questions

1 a) (i) H^+ ***(1 mark)***

(ii) OH^- ***(1 mark)***

(iii) H^+; OH^- ***(2 marks)***

b) (i) substance B ***(1 mark)***

(ii) substance D ***(1 mark)***

(iii) stomach acid / hydrochloric acid ***(1 mark)***

c) slaked lime / calcium hydroxide: $Ca(OH)_2$ / limestone: $CaCO_3$ ***(1 mark)***

Page 118

Warm-Up Questions

1) Clay
2) To neutralise unwanted acidity
3) Plants and animals die and are covered by sediment in seas or swamps. The heat and pressure over millions of years turn the remains into fossil fuels (coal, oil and natural gas).

Exam Questions

1 a) sand (silicon dioxide) and soda (sodium carbonate) ***(1 mark)***

b) $CaCO_3 \rightarrow CaO$ ***(1 mark)*** + CO_2 ***(1 mark)***

2 a) Plants and animals die and are covered by sediment ***(1 mark)***. The sediment stops them from decaying ***(1 mark)***. Further layers of sediment bury the remains deep underground ***(1 mark)***. No oxygen, high pressures and heat ***(1 mark)*** over millions of years changes the remains into coal, oil and gas.

b) E.g. fuels, plastics, petrochemicals ***(1 mark for each, up to 2 marks)***

Page 121

Warm-Up Questions

1) hydrogen and carbon
2) boiling point increases, flammability decreases, viscosity increases, volatility decreases
3) cracking

Exam Questions

1 a) (i) A ***(1 mark)***

(ii) Kerosene. ***(1 mark)*** The more carbon atoms in the molecule, the higher the boiling range. ***(1 mark)***

b) Making plastics, surfacing roads, lubrication etc. ***(1 mark)***

Page 124

Warm-Up Questions

1) Single covalent bonds
2) Alkenes
3) No
4) Yes

Exam Questions

1 a) (i)

$$\left(\begin{array}{cc} H & H \\ | & | \\ -C- & C- \\ | & | \\ H & CH_3 \end{array} \right)_n$$

(2 marks)

(ii) Pressure ***(1 mark)*** and a catalyst ***(1 mark)***

(iii) Polypropene is tough/not brittle ***(1 mark)*** and forms durable fibres ***(1 mark)***

b) (i) Polythene is not biodegradable, so it takes up space in landfill sites for a very long time. ***(1 mark)***

(ii) Save crude oil resources which are needed to make plastics. ***(1 mark)***

(iii) Consumers need to sort their rubbish or wash and reuse polythene products. Consumers might not want the hassle. ***(1 mark)***

Page 127

Warm-Up Questions

1) Main gases: carbon dioxide, carbon monoxide — also ammonia and methane. Also accept steam or water vapour (though that's not actually a gas).
2) Methane and ammonia reacted with oxygen to release nitrogen. Nitrogen was released by denitrifying bacteria during the decay of organic matter.
3) Argon
4) Photosynthesis. Dissolving in sea/rain water.
5) O_3

Exam Questions

1 a) Photosynthesis by plants removes CO_2 from the atmosphere, and release oxygen. ***(1 mark)***

b) Respiration by plants and animals releases CO_2 into the atmosphere, and removes oxygen. ***(1 mark)***

c) Combustion of fossil fuels releases CO_2 into the atmosphere and remove oxygen. ***(1 mark)***

2 The ozone layer is important because it absorbs harmful UV rays ***(1 mark)*** from the sun. This has meant that more complex organisms were able to evolve. ***(1 mark)***.

3 a) Oxygen increased ***(1 mark)*** as green plants photosynthesised ***(1 mark)***.

b) Carbon dioxide decreased ***(1 mark)*** as water vapour condensed to form oceans and rain, which dissolved it ***(1 mark)***.

Page 130

Warm-Up Questions

1) Limestone, sedimentary
2) The clay gets heated and compressed
3) Magma
4) e.g. sandstone – buildings; marble – headstones, statues
5) Both formed from molten magma that cools and solidifies. Intrusive cool slowly underground and extrusive cool quickly on the surface.

Exam Questions

1 i) the sea, lakes, etc. ***(1 mark)***

ii) sedimentary rocks ***(1 mark)***

iii) heat and pressure ***(1 mark)***

iv) metamorphic rocks ***(1 mark)***

2 a) sedimentary ***(1 mark)***

b) Sedimentary rocks are formed from layers of sediment deposited in lak or seas ***(1 mark)***. Over millions of years layers get buried under more layers, and the weight squeezes out the water ***(1 mark)***. Salts crystallize out and cement the particles together ***(1 mark)***.

Page 135

Warm-Up Questions

1) They look like they can fit together like a jigsaw, suggesting they were once joined together but have moved apart.
2) E.g. matching fossils, identical rock sequences
3) He couldn't give a convincing reason why it happened, and he wasn't a qualified geologist.
4) Any one from: volcano, large cracks, mountains, ocean trench
5) The collision between an oceanic plate and a continental plate forced the oceanic plate underneath. It melted, leading to magma at pressure below. The magma pushed up through the crust to form volcanoes. The continental crust crumpled to form mountains.

Exam Questions

1 a) (tectonic) plates ***(1 mark)***

b) i) X may be a continental plate, while Y is an oceanic plate, or: rock X is less dense than rock Y ***(1 mark)***

ii) It will start to melt and turn into magma ***(1 mark)***

2 a) The line along which two or more tectonic plates (or parts of tectonic plates) meet. ***(1 mark)***

b) When tectonic plates rub together, there is a lot of friction. The plates often get stuck, which results in a build up of force and then a sudden movement of one or both of the plates. ***(2 marks)***
You always need to make two points to get the two marks.

3 As the plates move apart, magma keeps rising up to fill the gap. The water cools this magma, leaving a ridge of new crust under the Atlantic Ocean. ***(2 marks — 1 mark for each of the main points)***

ge 138

arm-Up Questions

oxygen

It turns limewater milky.

The contents are toxic.

:am Questions

a) chlorine *(1 mark)*

b) oxygen *(1 mark)*

c) carbon dioxide *(1 mark)*

d) e.g. carbon dioxide, methane *(1 mark)*

Two from:
Heat it to check that it has a boiling point of 100°C.
Add it to anhydrous copper sulphate. If this turns blue, the liquid is water.
Check if it turns anhydrous cobalt chloride paper from blue to pink.
(2 marks)

ge 142

arm-Up Questions

temperature, concentration (or pressure), catalyst, surface area

Increase the temperature

Three from: decrease the temperature, decrease the concentration, decrease the pressure (for a gas), decrease the surface area (or use bigger pieces of solid)

Place the beaker on some scales. Record the fall in mass at regular intervals. Attach a gas syringe to the beaker with an air-tight seal. Record the volume of gas given off at regular intervals.

A solid catalyst works by giving the reacting particles a surface to stick to where they can bump into each other. This increases the number of successful collisions.

:am Questions

a) The mass will decrease. *(1 mark)*

b) about 7 minutes *(1 mark)*

c) i)

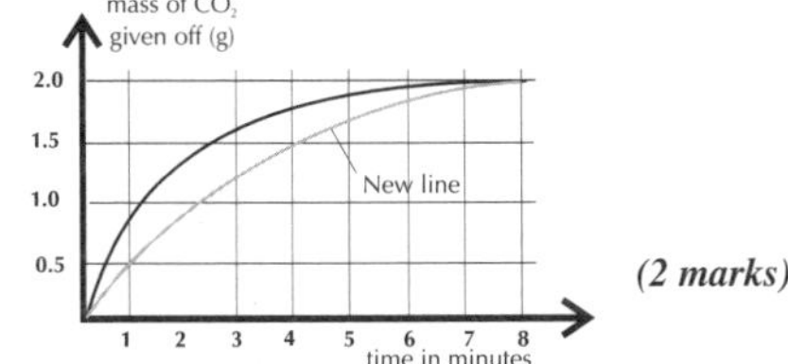

(2 marks)

ii) For a certain mass of marble chips, the total surface area of bigger pieces is less than the total surface area of smaller pieces *(1 mark)*. The smaller the surface area, the smaller the number of exposed particles *(1 mark)* and the fewer successful collisions *(1 mark)*.

a) Iron *(1 mark)*

b) Platinum *(1 mark)*

ıge 146

'arm-Up Questions

A biological catalyst — it speeds up reactions in living things without the need for high temperatures and is not used up.

about 45°C

They can be mixed into plastic beads, or trapped in an alginate bed.

Proteases digest proteins. Lipases digest fats.

xam Questions

a) i) Fermentation is the process of yeast converting sugar *(1 mark)* to carbon dioxide and alcohol *(1 mark)*.

ii) Glucose $\xrightarrow{\text{enzyme}}$ carbon dioxide + ethanol
(1 mark for reactants, 1 mark for products)

iii) Too hot and the enzyme is destroyed *(1 mark)*.
Too cold and the enzyme will work very slowly *(1 mark)*.

b) i) No — the enzymes in the detergent work best at 40°C and would be destroyed at high temperatures. *(2 marks)*

ii) Protease *(1 mark)*

Enzymes = biological catalysts. They're pretty fussy and work best at a certain temperature and pH.

2 a) Enzymes are used to turn the starch in corn into sugar. *(1 mark)*

b) You need less fructose to give the same sweetness as sucrose. *(1 mark)*

3 a) The enzyme becomes destroyed (denatured) above 38°C. *(1 mark)*

b) i) Bacterial enzymes make food go off *(1 mark)*. Freezing virtually stops enzyme activity *(1 mark)*, so the bacterial enzymes can't make the food go off.

ii) Yes. *(1 mark)* Once the food is thawed, the bacterial enzymes will work again. *(1 mark)*

Page 149

Warm-Up Questions

1) exothermic

2) endothermic

3) endothermic

4) takes in energy

Exam Questions

1 a) ***1 mark for any example*** from:
burning fuels, neutralisation reactions (or any specific reaction between an acid and an alkali), addition of water to anhydrous copper(II) sulphate, etc.

b) i) ΔH is negative *(1 mark)*

ii)

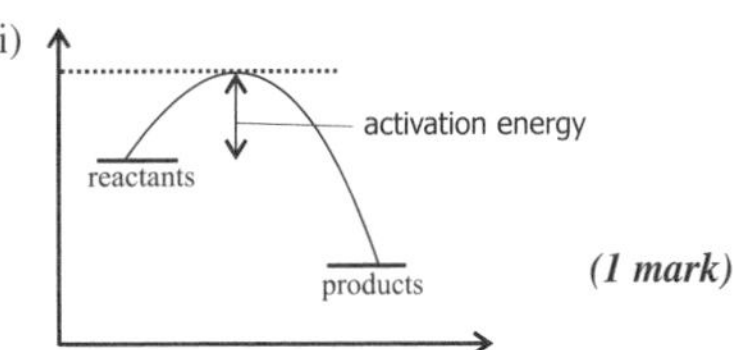

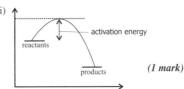

(1 mark)

c) Making new bonds is exothermic *(1 mark)*

2 $C_2H_4 + 3O_2 \rightarrow 2CO_2 + 2H_2O_{(g)}$

Bonds broken: three O=O bonds in oxygen, four C-H single bonds and one C=C double bond in ethene *(1 mark)*. (OR ***1 mark*** for writing down (3×498) + (4×414) + 615)

(3×498) + (4×414) + 615 = 3765 kJ/mole *(1 mark)*

Bonds formed: four C=O double bonds and four H-O single bonds. *(1 mark)*. (OR ***1 mark*** for writing down (4×749) + (4×463))

(4×749) + (4×463) = 4848 kJ/mole *(1 mark)*

Difference = 1083 kJ/mole *(1 mark for final answer)*

Bond energy calculations are simple — you just need to practise them. Remember, it's vitally important to check how many moles of each thing there are.

Page 152

Warm-Up Questions

1) A base

2) Iron

3) Eutrophication

Exam Question

1 a) (i) High pressure (200-350 atmospheres) *(1 mark)* and moderately high temperature (450°C) *(1 mark)*. Presence of an iron catalyst *(1 mark)*.

(ii) At a lower temperature the reaction rate would be slower *(1 mark)*. Reducing the speed would make production less profitable *(1 mark)*.

b) (i) $NH_{3(g)} + HNO_{3(aq)} \rightarrow NH_4NO_{3(aq)}$ *(2 marks)*

(ii) The fertilisers promote excessive growth of plants and algae *(1 mark)*. Then the plants die off and bacteria feed off them, using up all the oxygen in the water *(1 mark)*. Fish and more plants die because there isn't enough oxygen in the water *(1 mark)*.

Page 156

Warm-Up Questions

1) Yes
2) The water is driven off to leave white anhydrous copper(II) sulphate.
3) A system from which no reactants or products can escape or enter.
4) No

Exam Questions

1 a) In a dynamic equilibrium, the forward and reverse reactions are going at exactly the same rate, with no net change in % of products or reactants. ***(2 marks)***

b) i) endothermic ***(1 mark)***

ii) The reaction AB $\rightarrow$ A + B will speed up ***(1 mark)*** and the reaction A + B $\rightarrow$ AB will slow down ***(1 mark)***.

iii) It will decrease. ***(1 mark)***

2 a) i) Higher pressure favours the forward reaction ***(1 mark)*** because there are four volumes of gas on the reactant side and only two volumes of gas on the product side ***(1 mark)***. Increasing pressure will favour the side with least volume.

ii) At lower temperatures the rate of reaction would be too slow ***(1 mark)***. It's not worth waiting a lot longer for a slightly better yield ***(1 mark)***. 450°C is a compromise between rate of reaction and yield ***(1 mark)***.
There's no perfect solution that'll give the maximum amount of ammonia really quickly. Manufacturers just have to compromise.

iii) The yield would increase ***(1 mark)***. The concentration of ammonia would be reduced ***(1 mark)***, and so the rate of the forward reaction would increase to give more ammonia ***(1 mark)***.

b) i) It has no effect on the yield ***(1 mark)***

ii) High temperatures favour the backward reaction, and reduce the yield ***(1 mark)***. The catalyst speeds up the reaction without the temperature being raised and the yield dropping ***(1 mark)***.

Page 160

Warm-Up Questions

1) 4
2) Na_2CO_3 = 106, $(NH_4)_2SO_4$ = 132, $Ca(OH)_2$ = 74
3) NH_3 = 82.4%, NH_4Cl =26.2%, NH_4NO_3 = 35%
4) 137.5g

Exam Questions

1 a) carbon = 40g, hydrogen = 6.7g, oxygen = 53.3g ***(1 mark)***

b) C:H:O = 1:2:1 Empirical formula : CH_2O
(1 mark for ratios, 1 for formula)

2 a) Cu = 40%, S = 20%, O = 40% ***(3 marks)***

b) 40% of 180 g = 72g ***(2 marks)***

3 60% ***(2 marks)***

Page 163

Warm-Up Questions

1) 2,625 cm^3 or 2.63 litres
2) a) 127g
b) 77g
c) about 26,100 cm^3 or 26.1 litres (dm^3)
3) 10g

Exam Questions

1 a) M_r of CuS = 96 M_r of Cu = 64
1g CuS reacts to give $\frac{64}{96}$ = 0.67g Cu
0.67 × 192 = 128g of Cu ***(2 marks)***

b) (i) M_r of CuS = 96 M_r of S = 32
1g CuS gives $\frac{32}{96}$ = 0.33g sulphur
0.33 × 192 = 64g sulphur
OR
192 – 128 = 64 g
(2 marks)

(ii) M_r of S = 32 M_r of SO_2 = 64
1g S gives $\frac{64}{32}$ = 2g of SO_2 so mass of SO_2 = 2 × 64 = 128g
$\frac{128}{64}$ × 24,000 = 48,000 cm^3 or 48 litres of SO_2 ***(3 marks)***

2 a) $CaCO_3 \rightarrow CaO + CO_2$ ***(1 mark)***

b) M_r of $CaCO_3$... 40 + 12 + (16 × 3) = 100 M_r of CaO... 40 + 16 = 56
$\frac{100}{56}$ = 1.79g of $CaCO_3$ to produce 1g of CaO
1.79 ×168 = 300g of $CaCO_3$ ***(2 marks)***

c) CaO = 56 CO_2 = 12 + (16 × 2) = 44
1g CaO produces $\frac{44}{56}$ = 0.79g so 0.79 × 168 = 132g of CO_2
OR
300 – 168 = 132 g
Then apply the formula for finding the volume:
Vol CO_2 = $\frac{132}{44}$ × 24,000 = 72,000 cm^3 or 72 litres ***(3 marks)***

3 a) At the cathode: $4Al^{3+} + 12e^- \rightarrow 4Al$ ***(1 mark)***
At the anode: $6O^{2-} \rightarrow 3O_2 + 12e^-$ ***(1 mark)***

b) 4Al : $3O_2$
Work out the M_r of each... 4 × 27 = 108 and 3 × (2 × 16) = 96
...then carry on as usual:
$\frac{108}{96}$ = 1.125g : 1g
1.125 × 24 = 27g of Al ***(2 marks)***

Page 166

Warm-Up Questions

1) Solid, liquid, gas.
2) Gases have a lot of free space between their molecules. Molecules in solids are already packed very closely together.
3) Heat energy makes some molecules move faster than others. Faster moving molecules at the surface overcome the forces of attraction between them and other molecules and escape.
4) As the water molecules in the ice warm up they vibrate more and more and eventually overcome the strong forces that hold them in a rigid lattice.

Exam Questions

1 a) Molecules vibrate more. ***(1 mark)***

b) It makes them move quicker. ***(1 mark)***.

2 a) 3 ***(1 mark)***

b) 4 ***(1 mark)***

c) The heat energy supplied (put into the substance) ***(1 mark)*** is used up in breaking bonds (the strong bonds between the particles in the solid) ***(1 mark)*** rather than in raising the temperature ***(1 mark)***.

Page 170

Warm-Up Questions

1) Particle A = electron, Particle B = neutron, Particle C = proton
2) Atoms with the same atomic number but different mass numbers. *Or*, Atoms with the same number of protons but different numbers of neutrons.
Carbon-14 has the same number of protons and electrons as Carbon-12, but has two more neutrons.

Exam Questions

1 a) 2, 8, 1 ***(1 mark)***

b) 2, 8, 5 ***(1 mark)***

2 a) (i) 12 – 6 = 6 ***(1 mark)***

(ii) 14 – 6 = 8 ***(1 mark)***

b) They both have the same number of protons (atomic number 6) but different numbers of neutrons (6 & 8). ***(2 marks)***

ge 174

arm-Up Questions

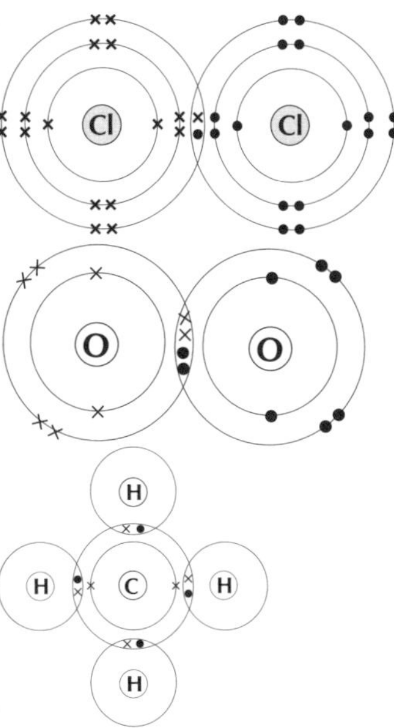

xam Questions

a) (i) 2, 8 ***(1 mark)***

(ii) 2, 8, 8 ***(1 mark)***

b) ionic bonding ***(1 mark)***

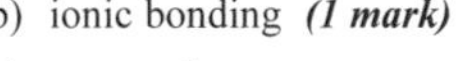

c)

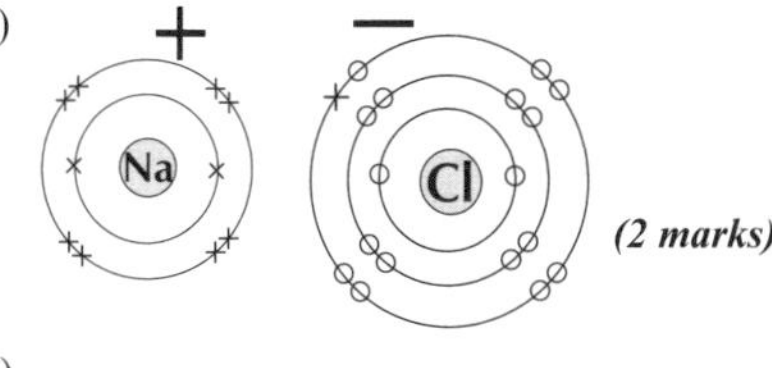

(2 marks)

d)

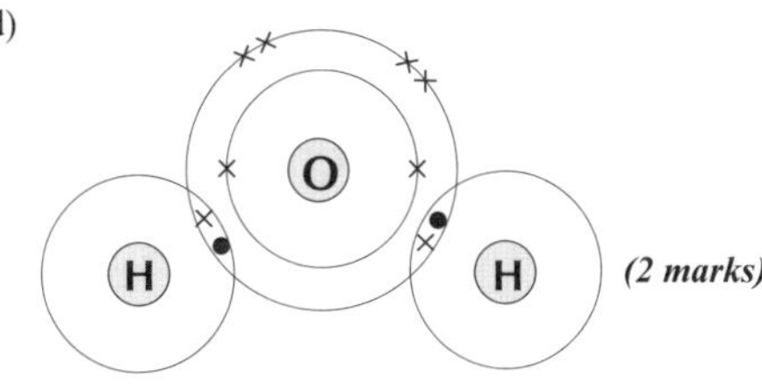

(2 marks)

ge 177

arm-Up Questions

Water has a simple molecular structure with weak intermolecular forces. Diamond has a giant molecular structure with strong bonds holding all the atoms together.

Aluminium atoms are held together by metallic bonds (involving a sea of electrons) so some electrons are free to move and conduct electric current.

When solid, the ions in salt can't move and so can't conduct electricity.

xam Questions

a) The 'free electrons' produce strong metallic bonds which hold the atoms in a giant structure. The bonds are hard to break, so the melting point is high. ***(3 marks)***

b) Oxygen atoms form small covalent molecules, and there are only very weak intermolecular forces between the oxygen molecules. These bonds are very easily broken, so the boiling point is low. ***(3 marks)***

a) B ***(1 mark)***

b) Metals have a giant structure with metallic bonding ***(1 mark)***. This means that the outer electrons of each atom are free to move ***(1 mark)*** through the metal, and can therefore carry an electric current ***(1 mark)***.

Page 180

Warm-Up Questions

1) False
2) 2
3) 1

Exam Questions

1 a) S, sulphur ***(1 mark)***

b) no ***(1 mark)***

2 a) magnesium ***(1 mark)***

b) Because it has two electrons in its outer shell. ***(1 mark)***

c) Beryllium has fewer electron shells than magnesium. Its outer electrons are less shielded from the attraction of the positive nucleus. Beryllium therefore gives up its outer electrons less readily. ***(3 marks)***

Page 184

Warm-Up Questions

1) Li^+
2) no
3) Noble gases have full outer electron shells — they do not form any bonds. Oxygen and fluorine have incomplete outer shells and do form bonds.
4) lower
5) yellow
6) liquid

Exam Questions

1 a) Because it's very reactive. ***(1 mark)***

b) Lithium ***(1 mark)***

c) As you go down the group, the outer electron is more easily lost to form an ion because it's further from the nucleus and it's better shielded from the attraction of the +ve nucleus by the other electron shells. ***(3 marks)***

2 a) i) They have complete outer electron shells ***(1 mark)***

ii) A monatomic gas ***(1 mark)***

b) i) Neon ***(1 mark)***

ii) It gives an inert atmosphere which stops the filament from burning away ***(1 mark)***

c) Helium is inert (it won't react).
This means it won't burn or explode
It's very light.
(1 mark for each of two correct answers,)

Page 187

Warm-Up Questions

1) sodium chloride
2) because chlorine kills germs — makes the swimming pool safer.
3) because it helps prevent tooth decay.

Exam Questions

1 a) Sea water is placed in big open tanks. The sun evaporates off the water, leaving the salt behind. ***(1 mark)***
The reference to 'hot countries' is a dead give away — it's got to be to do with the sun and evaporation.

b) i) $2AgBr \rightarrow Br_2 + 2Ag$ ***(1 mark)***

ii) black ***(1 mark)***

2 a) It is bonded covalently ***(1 mark)***

b) i) $HCl_{(g)} \xrightarrow{water} H^+_{(aq)} + Cl^-_{(aq)}$ ***(2 marks)***

ii) The H^+ ions. ***(1 mark)***

Page 190

Warm-Up Questions

1) yes
2) 2; 2; 3

3) $2Na_{(s)} + 2H_2O_{(l)} \rightarrow 2NaOH_{(aq)} + H_{2(g)}$
4) $2H^+ + 2e^- \rightarrow H_2$

Exam Questions

1 a) $2H_2O_2 \rightarrow O_2 + 2H_2O$ ***(2 marks)***
b) $2KOH_{(aq)} + H_2SO_{4(aq)} \rightarrow K_2SO_{4(aq)} + 2H_2O_{(l)}$ ***(2 marks)***
c) $4NH_3 + 5O_2 \xrightarrow{\text{platinum catalyst}} 4NO + 6H_2O$ ***(3 marks)***
Start by pencilling in a number in front of the NH_3 and then try to make it work...

2 At the positive electrode: $2H_2O_{(l)} \rightarrow O_{2(g)} + 4H^+_{(aq)} + 4e^-$
At the negative electrode: $2Cu^{2+}_{(aq)} + 4e^- \rightarrow 2Cu_{(s)}$
(2 marks)

Page 194

Warm-Up Questions

1) a) Chemical to Elastic Potential.
b) Elastic Potential to Kinetic.
c) Kinetic to Gravitational Potential.

Exam Questions

1 Chemical ***(1 mark)***
2 a) Gravitational Potential to Kinetic ***(1 mark)***
b) Sound and heat ***(2 marks total — 1 mark each)***

Page 198

Warm-Up Questions

1) White is a poor absorber of heat, so less heat from the Sun will enter the houses.
2) a) radiation, b) conduction, c) convection.

Exam Questions

1 a) Element is black, which is a good radiator of heat ***(1 mark)***. Fins create a large surface area ***(1 mark)***.
b) A metal ***(1 mark)***. Because it will quickly conduct the heat away (from the coolant to the air/into the fins) ***(1 mark)***.
c) Heat transferred by electromagnetic waves or infrared waves. ***(1 mark)***
d) The silver lining. ***(1 mark)***
e) The outer particles gain heat energy from the surroundings, giving them extra kinetic energy/making them vibrate more ***(1 mark)***. Some of the energy is passed on when they collide with neighbouring particles ***(1 mark)***.
f) Any sensible answer, e.g. trapping air bubbles in the plastic or replacing with foam containing air bubbles. ***(1 mark)***

Page 201

Warm-Up Questions

1) The high initial cost means that it will take a long time for the energy savings to pay back the money spent installing it.
2) a) 1026.4 units b) £51.32

Exam Questions

1 a) Air is a very poor conductor of heat. ***(1 mark)*** It cannot transfer heat by convection because the air is trapped in pockets and cannot move ***(1 mark)***.
b) The cost of installing cavity wall insulation is high ***(1 mark)*** so the payback period is likely to be high, even with the saving of £65 per year ***(1 mark)***.

2 A = no. of units used = 16969 – 14303 = 2666
B = 2666 × 4.68 = 12476.88p = £124.77
C = 124.77 + 8.64 = £133.41
D = £133.41 × 0.175 = £23.35
E = £133.41 + £23.35 = £156.76
(5 marks — 1 for each)

Page 203

Warm-Up Questions

1) PE = mgh (PE - gravitational potential energy, m - mass, g - gravitational field strength, h - height)
2) joules (J)
3) Gravitational Potential to Kinetic
4) PE = mgh = 0.05 × 10 × 1.6 = 0.8J

Exam Questions

1 a) Potential Energy = Mass × g × Height
= 0.5 × 10 × 50 = 250J ***(2 marks)***
b) 250J (because the potential energy lost is changed into kinetic energy). ***(1 mark)***

Page 206

Warm-Up Questions

1) a) sound
b) kinetic
c) thermal / heat
2) 105J

Exam Questions

1 a) electrical ***(1 mark)***
b) 3000 J ***(1 mark)***
c) Efficiency = Useful Energy Output ÷ Total Energy Input
= 2000 ÷ 5000 = 0.4 or 40%. ***(2 marks)***
d) **Chemical** → Electrical → Kinetic / Sound / **Heat**
(2 marks)
e) 12% efficient, so useful output is 12% of 2000 J = 240 J ***(2 marks)***

Page 211

Warm-Up Questions

1) Renewable — will never run out.
Non-renewable — will run out.
Renewable — any four of: wind, waves, tides, hydroelectric, solar, geothermal, food, biomass (wood).
Non-renewable — coal, oil, natural gas, nuclear fuels (uranium and plutonium).
2) It has a boiler containing water which is heated to produce steam, the steam used to drive a turbine, the turbine is attached to a generator. The generator turns to produce the electricity.
3) This involves putting wind turbines in exposed places. Each wind turbine has its own generator inside it so the electricity is generated directly from the wind turning the blades.
4) A dam is built to capture rainwater and flood a valley. Water is allowed out through turbines, which drive a generator. Diagram should include all features on the diagram in the middle of page 209.
5) Wave power uses energy from waves, which are caused by the wind. Wave converters around the coast rock up and down, pushing air through a turbine. Tidal power uses the energy from the tides, which are caused by the gravitational attraction of the Moon. A dam is built over an estuary, which fills up when the tide comes in, turning the turbines as it goes. The water is then allowed back through turbines at a controlled speed.
6) Water is pumped in pipes down to hot rocks and returns as steam to drive a generator.

Exam Questions

1 a) Any three of: wind, waves, tides, biomass. ***(3 marks)***
b) Any sensible answers, e.g. improve the insulation of their buildings (double glazing, roof insulation, draught excluders, cavity wall insulation) ***(1 mark)***; turn off lights and other electrical items when they are not needed ***(1 mark)***.

c) They produce solid waste which stays dangerously radioactive for thousands of years ***(1 mark)***. The power stations contain a lot of radioactive materials so dismantling them is dangerous and expensive ***(1 mark)***. There is the risk of a major accident or catastrophe ***(1 mark)***.

a) They match demand for energy ***(1 mark)***, and they are reliable (don't depend on weather) ***(1 mark)***.

b) • carbon dioxide is released, adding to the Greenhouse Effect which is causing global warming;
• burning coal and oil releases sulphur dioxide which causes acid rain;
• coal mining makes a mess of the landscape;
• oil spillages cause serious environmental problems. ***(4 marks)***

a) (i) mostly nuclear energy (radioactive decay) ***(1 mark)***

(ii) It is extremely expensive to drill down far enough to heat the water sufficiently. ***(1 mark)***

b) Advantages include: quite far north so high number of daylight hours in summer
Disadvantages include: it's often cloudy in Scotland, so at certain times of the year there will be little energy produced. Also fewer daylight hours in winter.
(2 marks for a reasonable advantage and disadvantage)
Whatever your views on alternative sources of energy, you need to learn both sides of the argument. Your marks will seriously suffer if you can only give a one-sided view.

ıge 216

arm-Up Questions

An electric current is a flow of ELECTRONS round a circuit. These particles carry a NEGATIVE electric charge. They are pushed out of the NEGATIVE pole of the cell and round to the POSITIVE pole, the opposite direction to CONVENTIONAL current. No current will flow through a circuit unless the circuit is COMPLETE.

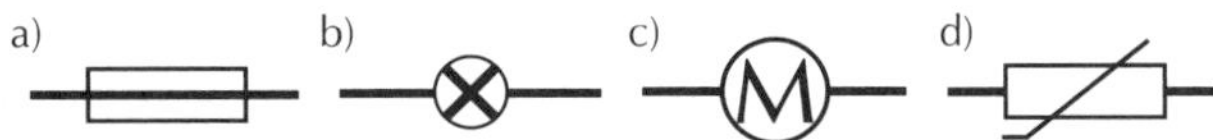

The current decreases.

The resistance increases.

Any sensible answers, e.g.
LED – used in a stereo system; the light that flashes red when the volume goes above a certain level.
Light Dependent Resistor – used in an alarm set to go off when a drawer is opened.
Thermistor – used in a temperature sensor in a car engine.

xam Questions

a) (i) Component C is the Light Dependent Resistor ***(1 mark)***

(ii) Component A is the cell. ***(1 mark)***

(iii) Component B is the Light Emitting Diode ***(1 mark)***

b) Resistance in Ω

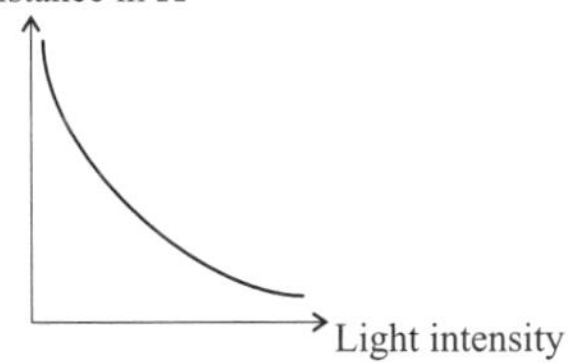

(1 mark)

You need to remember the shape of these graphs...

c) It will emit light. ***(1 mark)***

d) No current would flow because the diode (LED) lets current flow through it in one direction only. ***(2 marks)***

ıge 221

/arm-Up Questions

2V

i) Parallel

ii) Series

iii) Parallel

3) "Series circuits are not much used in real life because if one component does not work the whole circuit does not work." Or "Series circuits are not much used in real life because the components cannot be switched off independently." (or similar)

Exam Questions

1 a) Series ***(1 mark)***

b) 2 ohms ***(1 mark)***

c) 5 V ***(1 mark)***

d) No, because the same current flows through all points of a series circuit (unless it was connected in voltmeter branch of circuit). ***(1 mark)***

e) Zero ***(1 mark)***

2 a) 12V ***(1 mark)***

b) 4 ohms ***(1 mark)***

c) 5A ***(1 mark)***

d) 2.5V ***(1 mark)***

e) 14.5V (Hint: add the voltage across R_1 to the voltage across the parallel components.) ***(2 marks)***

Page 226

Warm-Up Questions

1) Friction

2) a) Proton

b) Electron

3) Inkjet printer and photocopier.

4) Any two of lightning, and/or a spark causing an explosion in any of the following situations: near a fuel tank or pipe, near paper rollers, near a grain chute, or near dusty or fume-filled places generally.

5) (d)

Exam Questions

1 a) i) electrons ***(1 mark)***

ii) Negatively charged electrons are repelled from the negative pole of the cell and pushed along the wire towards the positive pole. ***(2 marks)***

iii) The current increases. ***(1 mark)***

b) When a voltage is applied, the positively charged ions move towards the negative electrode, and the negatively charged ions move towards the positive electrode, producing an electric current. ***(2 marks)***

2 a) Electrons have been scraped off the duster onto the rod. ***(2 marks)***

b) The charge on the duster is now positive due to the negative electrons having left it for the polythene rod. ***(2 marks)***

c) Unlike the polythene rod, metal is a conductor. ***(1 mark)***
That means that any charge transferred to it will be conducted away easily. ***(1 mark)***

3 a) i) Sound ***(1 mark)***

ii) Heat ***(1 mark)***

iii) Heat ***(1 mark)***

iv) Kinetic ***(1 mark)***

v) Light ***(1 mark)***

b) i) E = QV ***(1 mark)***

ii) The charge loses electrical energy ***(1 mark)***

Page 229

Warm-Up Questions

1) Any three of frayed cables, too-long cables, cables in contact with something hot or wet, pets chewing cables, cables within reach of children.

2) a) Blue

b) Green and yellow

c) Brown

3) Alternating current.

Exam Questions

1 a) The blue wire should be connected to the neutral terminal, not the earth. The green and yellow wire should be connected to the earth terminal, not the neutral. ***(2 marks —1 mark for each wire)***

b) (i) The 5A fuse is too low. It would blow every time the kettle was used. The current through the kettle is given by I = P/V = 2000/240 = 8.33A, which is greater than 5A. ***(1 mark)***

(ii) A 13A fuse would be suitable. ***(1 mark)***
Don't forget — you always need a fuse that's just a little bit bigger than the operating current. If it's too small, it would blow straight away, like in (i). But likewise there's no point in it being too big, or it could allow a dangerous amount of current through before blowing.

c) Plastic is an insulator. ***(1 mark)***

d) If the live wire touches the case, then the case itself becomes live and anyone touching it could get an electric shock. ***(1 mark)***

e) The earth wire must be connected to the case. ***(1 mark)***
This provides a low resistance path to earth, meaning that if the case becomes accidentally connected to the live terminal, a big current will surge from the live wire, through the case, and out down the earth wire. ***(1 mark)***
The surge in the current will blow the fuse and isolate the live supply. The fuse must be placed in the live wire because that is the one we need to isolate from the appliance. ***(1 mark)***

Page 234

Warm-Up Questions

1) A solenoid is a coil of wire.
2) Strength of electric current; what the core is made of; number of turns in the solenoid.
3) It means that once magnetised, steel retains its magnetism.
4) Thumb: Motion (or Force); First finger: Field (i.e. magnetic field); Second finger: Current (i.e. electric current).
5) More current, more turns on the coil, stronger magnetic field, a soft iron core in the coil.
6) Any three of scrap yard/car breaker's yard electromagnet, circuit breaker, relay switch ("reed relay" or just "relay" is also acceptable), electric bell, loudspeaker.

Exam Questions

1 a) The north pole. ***(1 mark)***

b) By changing the direction of the current. ***(1 mark)***

c) The field would be weaker. ***(1 mark)***

2 The correct order is D, B, A, F, C, E. ***(5 marks)***

Page 238

Warm-Up Questions

1) Electromagnetic induction is the creation of a voltage (and maybe a current) in a wire which is experiencing a change in magnetic field.
2) speed of movement of coil, number of turns on coil, area of coil, strength of magnetic field.
3) 20V

Exam Questions

1 a)

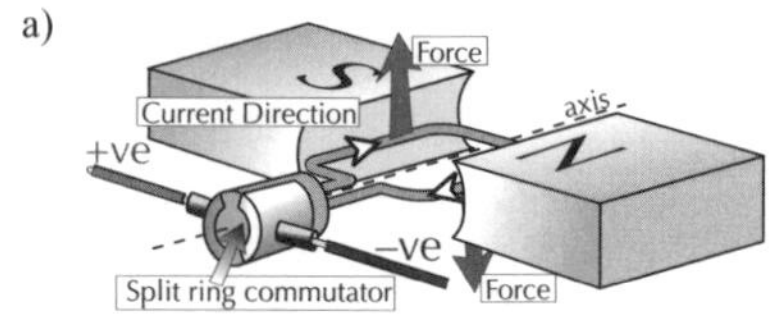

(4 marks)

b) (iii) ***(1 mark)***

c) Without the split ring commutator the forces acting on the side arms of the coil would only act so as to make the coil rotate for half a cycle. Because the current direction is changed as the coil reaches the vertical position, however, the coil continues to rotate. ***(2 marks)***

d) There would be no effect — the two changes would cancel each other out. ***(1 mark)***

2 a) A ***(1 mark)***

b) Power in = Power out, so $P = V_PI_P = V_SI_S$
Rearranging: $I_P = V_SI_S/V_P$ = 400,000 × 0.1/20,000 = 2A ***(2 marks)***

c) Efficient power transmission requires high voltages and low currents. Transformers are used to step up the voltages produced by the power stations to a very high value for efficient transmission, and also to step down the voltages to safe useable levels at the other end. ***(3 marks)***

d) Energy is wasted when eddy currents form in the iron core of the transformer and heat it up. To minimize eddy currents the core is laminated with layers of insulation. ***(2 marks)***
Questions about electricity transmission through the National Grid are a rea exam favourite. Make sure you fully understand this stuff — if this question was hard, you don't know it well enough.

Page 242

Warm-Up Questions

1) s = d/t = 280/8 = 35m/s
2) a = Δv/t = 15/3 = 5m/s²
3) d = s × t = 16 × 6 = 96m

Exam Questions

1 a) Either: a = Δv/t ***(1 mark)*** = (24 – 6)/12 ***(1 mark)*** = 1.5m/s² ***(1 mark)***
or a = gradient = vertical/horizontal ***(1 mark)*** = (24 – 6)/12 ***(1 mark)***
= 1.5m/s² ***(1 mark)***

b)

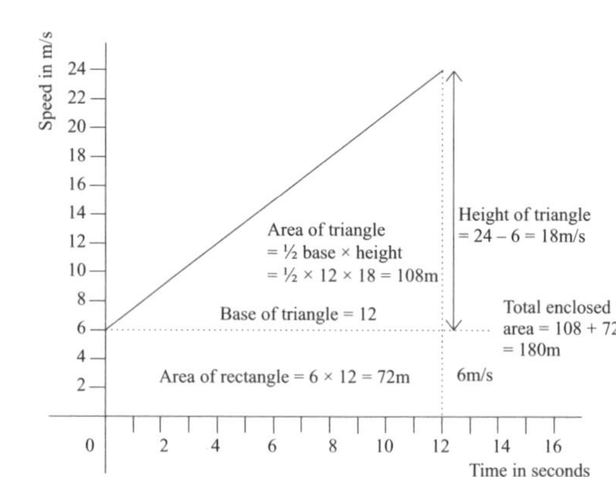

Total enclosed area = distance travelled = 180 m ***(3 marks)***

2 a) distance = the area under the graph between 15s and 30s ***(1 mark)***
= (30s – 15s) × 55m/s
= 15s × 55m/s ***(1 mark)***
= 825m ***(1 mark)***

b) She opens her parachute, which unbalances the forces so she slows right down, then reaches a new terminal velocity when the forces balance aga ***(2 marks)***

Page 245

Warm-Up Questions

1) a) balanced

b) unbalanced (the Moon is travelling in a circle and, therefore, has a constantly changing velocity)

c) balanced

d) unbalanced (the coin will accelerate towards the ground)

2) a) F = ma = 900kg × 3m/s² = 2700N

b) a = F/m = 18N/3kg = 6m/s²

3) From Newton's Third Law the trailer will exert a force of 100N on the tractor.

Exam Questions

1 a) Weight = mass × g = 2 700 000kg × 10N/kg = 27 000 000N (=2.7 × 10⁷ ***(1 mark)***

b) Each engine produces 7 000 000N of thrust, therefore the total thrust

$= 5 \times 7\ 000\ 000N = 35\ 000\ 000\ N\ (=3.5 \times 10^7N)$ ***(1 mark)***

The resultant force = thrust – weight = 35 000 000 – 27 000 000N

$= 8\ 000\ 000N\ (= 8.0 \times 10^6N)$ ***(1 mark)***

c) Acceleration = resultant force/mass of rocket = 8 000 000N/2 700 000kg ***(1 mark)*** $= 2.96m/s^2 \approx 3.0m/s^2$ ***(1 mark)***

d) The acceleration of the rocket will increase ***(1 mark)*** because the mass of the rocket will decrease as fuel is burnt ***(1 mark)***. (Another possible, but less good, explanation is that the weight of the rocket decreases since the gravitational field strength decreases as the rocket rises above the Earth.)

e) The rocket exerts a force on its exhaust gases backwards ***(1 mark)***. From Newton's Third Law, the exhaust gases exert an equal force on the rocket forwards, causing it to accelerate ***(1 mark)***.

a)

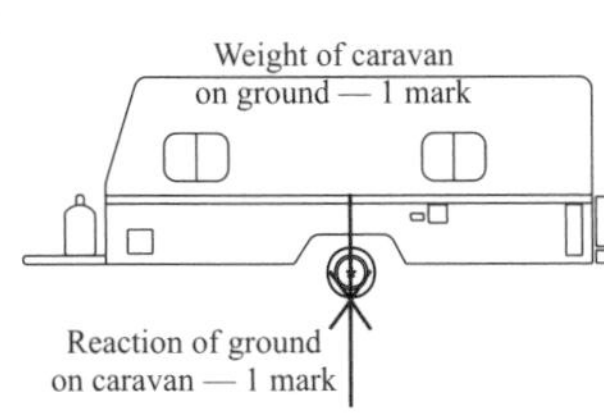

(1 mark for each correct force)

The two forces are equal in size ***(1 mark)***

b) If the car and caravan are travelling at a constant velocity, the resultant force on the caravan must be zero ***(1 mark)*** from Newton's First Law. Therefore the force of the car on the caravan is equal and opposite to the drag force on the caravan = 2300N ***(1 mark)***.

c) The resultant force on the car and caravan is zero ***(1 mark)***. Therefore the engine force = drag force on car + drag force on caravan.

= 1800N + 2300N = 4100N ***(1 mark)***

d) The extra force needed to accelerate the car and caravan $= \text{total mass} \times \text{acceleration} = (1000kg + 800kg) \times 2m/s^2 = 3\ 600N$ ***(1 mark)***

Therefore, the new thrust force = total drag force + acceleration force = 4100N + 3600N = 7700N ***(1 mark)***

It's all about unbalanced forces...

age 250

arm-Up Questions

Gravity (or gravitational attraction).

The astronaut's mass stays the same.

a)

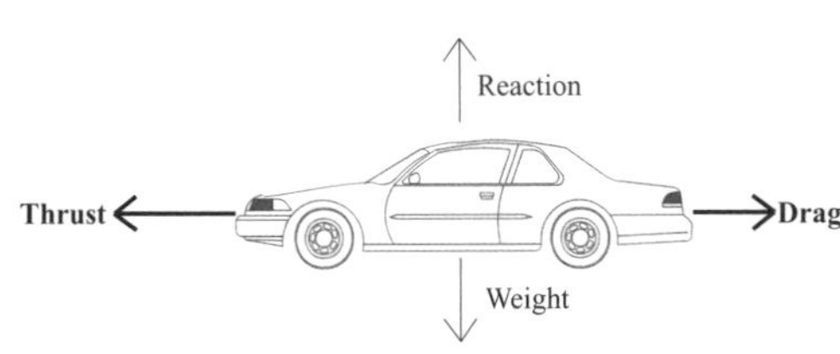

b) i) The reaction and weight forces will be balanced.

ii) The thrust force and drag force are unbalanced (thrust greater than drag, thus allowing acceleration).

a) Any examples where useful energy is lost due to friction, e.g. in machinery where surfaces are sliding over each other, such as inside a car's engine, in the wheel hub of a bicycle, on the hinge of a door, etc.

b) Any examples where friction helps something to work, e.g. in the brakes of a vehicle, when we strike matches, when we walk, to hold knots in string, to hold nails and screws in wood, etc.

xam Questions

a) In icy conditions, the maximum force of friction between the tyres and the road is less than it is in dry conditions ***(1 mark)***, therefore the braking force must be reduced so that it does not exceed the maximum force of friction ***(1 mark)***.

b) The aerofoil makes the lorry's shape more streamlined ***(1 mark)*** reducing the drag force on the lorry ***(1 mark)*** and therefore saving fuel ***(1 mark)***.

c) The lorry has to do more work against friction as it goes faster ***(1 mark)*** so the lorry's engine works less hard and uses less fuel if it is driven at a lower speed ***(1 mark)***.
This may seem like common sense, but to get the marks in a science exam you need to think about the forces involved.

2 a) Weight = mass × g = 85 kg × 10 N/kg = 850N ***(1 mark)***

b) i) The mass of the satellite is the same everywhere = 85kg. ***(1 mark)***
ii) Weight = mass × g = 85kg × 6N/kg = 510N ***(1 mark)***

c) At the height of the satellite's orbit there will be little or no air ***(1 mark)***, so the drag force on the satellite will be very small or non-existent. ***(1 mark)***.

3 a) Resultant force must be zero ***(1 mark)*** because the car is not accelerating, and hence the forces must be balanced ***(1 mark)***.

b) The kinetic energy $= \frac{1}{2}mv^2$ ***(1 mark)*** $= \frac{1}{2} \times 1200 \times 24^2$ ***(1 mark)***

= 345 600J ***(1 mark)***

c) The work done by the brakes in stopping the car = the kinetic energy transferred ***(1 mark)***.
Therefore forces of brakes × braking distance = 345 600J;
therefore force = 345 600 / 50 ***(1 mark)*** = 6912 N ***(1 mark)***

d) The force calculated above = the total opposing force ***(1 mark)*** which will include the drag force as well as the braking force ***(1 mark)***.

e) The car's braking distance would be greater ***(1 mark)*** because the car's extra mass would mean that it would have more kinetic energy and, therefore, would require more work to be done in order to stop it ***(1 mark)***.

Page 253

Warm-Up Questions

1) Pluto.
2) Their orbits look strange compared with the constellations, which makes it look like they just 'wander' randomly amongst the stars seen at night.
3) Venus, Mars, Jupiter or Saturn (any two).
4) Any phrase giving the correct order, e.g. My Very Energetic Maiden Aunt Just Swam Under North Pier.
5) The moon.
6) e.g. monitoring weather, communications, space research, spying.

Exam Questions

1 a) Mercury, Venus, Earth and Mars (in any order). ***(1 mark)***

b) Gravity attracts the Earth towards the Sun. The Earth is travelling fast enough not to get pulled towards the Sun, but isn't fast enough to escape the pull of gravity altogether, so instead it stays in a steady orbit around the Sun. ***(2 marks)***

c) Slightly elliptical or oval shaped. ***(1 mark)***

2 a) Has an orbit of 24 hours, is situated over the equator and travels eastwards. ***(3 marks)***

b) Nearer to the Earth to see detail, travels over the whole of the Earth. ***(2 marks)***

Page 258

Warm-Up Questions

1) Some of the signal is lost into space so could in theory be picked up by aliens, if they had the correct equipment.
2) moon, planet, sun, solar system, galaxy, universe.
3) Nuclear fusion (usually of hydrogen to produce helium).
4) a) An independent group or collection of stars (held together by gravity).
   b) gravity
5) It has such large gravity, that even light cannot escape (so it looks black).
6) Explosion that started the Universe. For age, accept answer between 12 and 16 billion years.
7) Gravity
8) By looking at the amount of red shift in the light from the galaxy.

Exam Questions

1 a) Go to other places, land and analyse samples or send back pictures. *(1 mark)*

b) Any two from: Look for intelligent signals coming from space. Look for chemical changes in the atmospheres of other planets. Study the light coming from planets in space to find out what the surface is like. *(2 marks)*

2 Points to include: hydrogen in core will run out; it will expand and form a red giant; it will cool and contract to become a white dwarf ***(1 mark for each underlined point)***.

3 a) Either a neutron star or a black hole. *(1 mark)*

b) Heavier elements are made in the final stages of a massive star, and during the supernova explosion. The supernova pushes these into space. They are brought together again when a new star system is made. ***(3 marks — 1 mark for each point)***

Page 262

Warm-Up Questions

1) A = Wavelength, B = Amplitude.
2) transverse, e.g. light, radio waves, water waves, microwaves longitudinal, e.g. sound, shock waves
3) They can cause ionisation/damage to cells.
4) $v = f\lambda = 2500 \times 13.2 / 100 = 330$ m/s
5) a) $f = v/\lambda = 3 \times 10^8 \div 1500 = 200\,000$ Hz = 200 kHz
   b) Speed of sound = 330 m/s: distance = speed × time = 330 × 0.8 = 264 m
6) s = vt = 1400 × 0.7 = 980m, so sea is 980/2 = 490m deep

Exam Questions

1 a) 20 waves pass a given point each second. *(1 mark)*

b) T = 1/f = 1/20 s = 0.05 s *(2 marks)*

c) Two from: light waves, radio waves, microwaves, X-rays, gamma rays, waves on strings, water waves, etc. *(2 marks)*.

2 a)

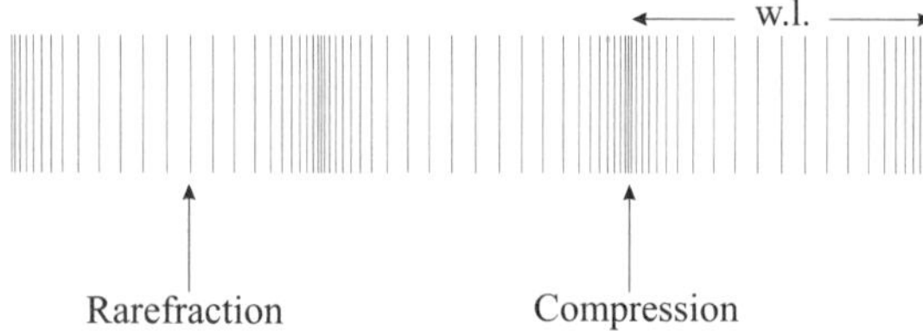

(3 marks — 1 mark for each correct label)

b) Any reasonable answer, e.g. shock waves, sound waves. *(1 mark)*

3 a) wavelength = speed/frequency
= 1400/28000 *(1 mark)*
= 0.05m *(1 mark)*

b) distance = speed × time
= 1400 × 0.2 *(1 mark)*
= 280m *(1 mark)* this is distance there and back
So, distance to seabed is 280/2 = 140m *(1 mark)*

Don't get these two formulas mixed up — think about which one you need before you plough in with your calculator.

Page 266

Warm-Up Questions

1) refraction, dispersion, total internal reflection.
2) violet
3) The largest angle of incidence at which light will still be refracted.
4) They give better quality reflection than a mirror, they're easier to hold in place and they're more robust.
5) signal doesn't need boosting as often, can carry more information, more secure, less interference

Exam Questions

1 a) Any two of: direction, wavelength and speed *(2 marks)*

b) air into glass: the ray bends towards the normal *(1 mark)*
glass into air: the ray bends away from the normal *(1 mark)*

c) Frequency stays the same. *(1 mark)*

2 a) 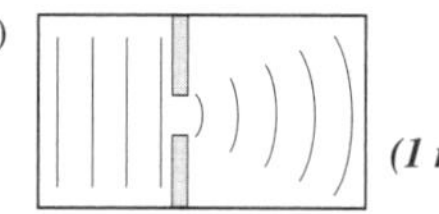 *(1 mark)*

b) Diffraction *(1 mark)*

c) 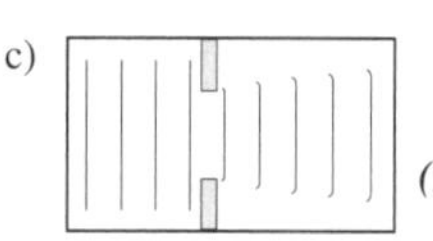 *(1 mark)*

d) The waves would diffract less — they would be less curved. *(1 mark)*

e) Long wavelength radio waves. *(1 mark)*

3 a)

(***2 marks*** — 1 for showing internal reflections, 1 for angles of incidence and reflection approximately equal.)

b) For looking inside patients without having to make a big hole. *(1 mark)*

Page 270

Warm-Up Questions

1) Ultraviolet.
2) a) Cooking, satellite signals. b) Night vision, remote controls, toasters
   c) Kill cancer cells, kill bacteria.
3) Radio waves.
4) Analogue examples include: clock with hands, thermometer, speedometer, dimmer switch
   Digital examples include: ordinary light switch, any other on/off switch, digital clocks, electronic scales
5) Analogue | Digital

After amplification

Exam Questions

1 a) Radio waves have a longer wavelength / lower frequency. *(1 mark)*

b) They have different frequencies (shorter for cooking). *(1 mark)*

c) The microwaves are absorbed by living tissue and the heat will damage/ kill the cells. *(1 mark)*

2 a) Signal can take only two different values ('on' and 'off') *(1 mark)*

b) Analogue: dimmer switch, thermometer, speedometer *(1 mark)*
Digital: electronic scales, light switch *(1 mark)*

c) It gets less and less like the original and there will be more noise *(2 marks)*

d) 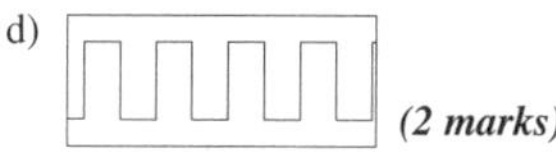 *(2 marks)*

e) E.g. mobile phones, cable TV, digital radio *(1 mark)*

age 273

arm-Up Questions

vibrating, longitudinal, solid, gas, vacuum.

a) 35000 vibrations (waves) each second.

b) Too high for people to hear. Not too high for dogs to hear.

Drum — 100Hz; Squeak — 8000Hz; Ultrasound — 40000Hz

xam Questions

a) B (biggest amplitude, therefore loudest).

b) D (longest wavelength).

c) C

d) A & D (same "height").

(4 marks available — 1 mark for each correct answer)

a) Sound waves ***(1 mark)***, with frequency too high for humans to hear ***(1 mark)***.

b) X-rays might damage foetus — ultrasound is much safer. ***(1 mark)***

c) Waves reflected from boundaries between different media. Reflected waves used to produce an image. ***(2 marks)***

d) Two of: cleaning, breaking kidney stones, quality control, sonar ***(2 marks)***

age 275

arm-Up Questions

S-waves are transverse, P-waves are longitudinal.

The Earth is made up of four layers. These layers are the crust, the mantle, the outer core and the inner core.

xam Questions

a) Y is the mantle, Z is the core. ***(2 marks)***

b) P-waves are longitudinal. ***(1 mark)***

c) The outer core is not solid (hence it must be liquid). ***(1 mark)***

d) P-waves travel faster through the middle of the core. ***(1 mark)***

e) The paths curve due to increasing density of the mantle (the waves are refracted). ***(1 mark)***

age 279

arm-Up Questions

Because certain rocks, which aren't distributed equally across the UK, are naturally more radioactive.

A gamma source.

a) gamma b) beta c) gamma

xam Questions

a) When unstable nuclei decay they give out radiation which can be detected. ***(1 mark)***

b) Alpha radiation is more strongly ionising, because of the size of its particles. Being relatively large they are more likely to hit atoms and knock electrons off than a gamma ray is. ***(2 marks)***

a) Some beta particles will pass through the paper. ***(1 mark)*** But the amount passing through will be affected by the thickness of the paper. ***(1 mark)***

b) The amount of radiation detected will decrease. ***(1 mark)***

c) The amount of beta particles emitted by the source is decreasing. ***(1 mark)***
The device makes the paper thinner to keep the amount of beta particles reaching the detector constant. ***(1 mark)***
A source with a much longer half-life should be used instead. ***(1 mark)***

d) Because the metal sheet will absorb almost all of the beta particles ***(1 mark)***. A gamma source would be better ***(1 mark)***.

Page 283

Warm-Up Questions

1) C

2) F

3) a) Uranium-238 b) Carbon-14 c) Carbon-14

4) a) Beta b) Alpha c) Alpha d) Gamma e) Gamma f) Beta

Exam Questions

1 a) A — Because most particles went straight through, most of the gold atom must have been empty space. ***(1 mark)***

B — Some particles were deflected a lot, implying they collided with something. This suggests most of the mass is concentrated in a small part of the whole volume (the 'nucleus'). ***(1 mark)***

C — Some of the (positively charged) α-particles were repelled slightly, implying that the nucleus must also be positively charged. ***(1 mark)***

b) No. Alpha radiation does not penetrate very far into metals, so all of it would have been blocked by a sheet of gold as thick as a sheet of paper, making the experiment impossible. ***(2 marks)***

c) beta radiation ***(1 mark)***

2 a) background radiation ***(1 mark)***

b)

Corrected Count Rate
400
283
200
142
100

(2 marks for all values correct, 1 mark for 3 or 4 values correct)

c)

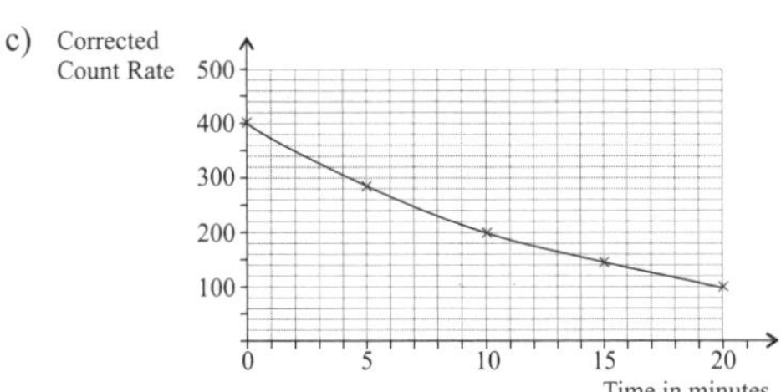

(2 marks for all points correct, 1 mark for 3 or 4 points correct)

d) half-life is 10 minutes ***(1 mark)***
This is the time it takes for the activity of the sample to halve. ***(1 mark)***

e) 40 minutes ***(1 mark)***
Because the sample must go through another two half-lives, making a total of four since the beginning of the experiment. ***(1 mark)***
And there you go — the end. Wasn't too painful, was it.

Index

Index

Index

Index

Index

Index